John Milton, And others

Britain under Trojan, Roman, Saxon rule...

John Milton, And others

Britain under Trojan, Roman, Saxon rule...

ISBN/EAN: 9783337021955

Printed in Europe, USA, Canada, Australia, Japan

Cover: Foto ©ninafisch / pixelio.de

More available books at **www.hansebooks.com**

BRITAIN

UNDER

TROJAN, ROMAN, SAXON RULE.

BY

JOHN MILTON.

ENGLAND UNDER RICHARD III.

BY

SIR THOMAS MORE.

THE REIGN OF HENRY VII.

BY

FRANCIS BACON, LORD VERULAM.

VERBATIM REPRINT FROM KENNET'S ENGLAND, ED. 1719.

LONDON:
WARD, LOCK & CO., WARWICK HOUSE, DORSET BUILDINGS,
SALISBURY SQUARE, E.C.

BIOGRAPHICAL NOTICES.

ALTHOUGH the fame of JOHN MILTON rests chiefly upon his poetry, yet his intellect was of so high an order, that no work of his but will be found well worth perusal. In the history now reprinted, will be found many passages characteristic of the writer, the materials being copious, curious, carefully arranged, written with great truthfulness, abounding energy, and sometimes with surpassing grandeur in sentiment and expression. The poet became a historian in 1639, soon after the blight of blindness had fallen upon him; the book was published in 1670, but mutilated by the censor of the press; many remarks of the gifted writer being distasteful to the cavalier interest. The suppressed passages appeared in the edition of 1681, and of the prose writings of Milton, published in 1738, his history of England forms a part—the copy whence were formed these pages will be found in Kennet's England, vol. i. fol. edition, 1719.

JOHN MILTON was born in Bread Street, London, December 9, 1608, his father being a scrivener there. From St. Paul's school, where, he received the rudiments of his education, he was sent to Christ's College, Cambridge, taking his B.A. there in 1628, and in 1632 his M.A. degree.

On the death of his mother, in 1638, his father permitted him to visit the continent, where he spent some fifteen months being received into the *elite* of literary circles in France and Italy.

The gathering troubles of civil war recalled Milton to England, where espousing the puritan side, soon after Cromwell became firm in power, he became Latin secretary to government, a place he was eminently qualified to fill. John Milton married in 1643 the daughter of Captain Powell, a cavalier; the choice was unhappy, as, on going to visit her parents the lady chose to remain with them, and her husband was on eve of remarrying when his repenting wife returned, her father and mother with her, who, in their then distressed circumstances, were cherished by Milton. The lady died in child-bed, as did also a second wife, but the third survived the poet, whose state of blindness did need a helpmate at home. After the restoration of monarchy, the republican writer fell into poverty and narrowly escaped penal persecution for opinions which he had warmly advocated.

Paradise Lost appeared in 1665, Simmons the publisher giving the author *five pounds* for the copyright or first edition of 1,300, a like sum for the second issue, but before a third was out the writer was dead. The latter years of the life of Milton were spent in Bunhill Row. He died Nov. 10, 1674, lies buried in the chancel of St. Giles, Cripplegate, and it was 1737 before the monument was erected to his memory in the Abbey of Westminster.

SIR THOMAS MORE may be best known as the writer of *Utopia*, but his History of England under Richard III. is a work of no ordinary merit, and few men could be more competent to produce it, as he lived near the time, and had been brought up as a page in the household of Cardinal Moreton, Archbishop of Canterbury, the main mover in the destruction of Richard and the elevation of Richmond his rival.

Sir Thomas More, a man of unparalleled virtue, according to the report of his friend Erasmus, was born in Milk Street, London April 13, 1480, educated at St. Anthony's, Threadneedle Street; he became a page to Cardinal Moreton in his fifteenth year, and was even then so advanced in wit and learning, that his patron declared to his friends that "this child here waiting at the table, whosoever shall live to see it, will prove a remarkable man!" More was a fellow student with Wolsey at Oxford; moved to New Inn Chancery; thence to Lincoln's Inn; was three years reader at Furnivals, and so devout that he narrowly escaped the cloister.

He married a Miss Colt of Newhall, Essex, lived in Bucklersbury;

and in his twenty-second year became a burgess of parliament, opposing court measures so keenly, that Henry VII., to punish the son, sent the father, a justice of the king's bench, to the Tower, whence he got out on paying a fine of £100. At the age of 31 he became under sheriff of London, a lucrative appointment, and soon after distinguished himself as an advocate in a case of the Pope v. the Crown, for seizure of a ship at Southampton. He became Speaker of Parliament in 1523, and so noted for wit and wisdom, that his society was sought for by his king, Henry VIII. He represented England at the league and peace of Cambray; was made Lord Chancellor in 1529, but declining to abet the divorce designs of his imperious master, and, as a good Catholic, refusing to acknowledge Henry's claim to be the supreme head of the church, Sir Thomas resigned office, became a poor man, (he had ever been an honest one), was sent to the Tower, confined for fourteen months, attainted, tried, condemned, and beheaded July 6, 1535. He was the greatest lawyer of the age, and one of the best of the men of the troublous times he lived in.

The History of England under Henry VII., was written in 1621 by Bacon, at request of James I., and the faults laid against it may have sprung from the desire of a displaced courtier seeking to regain favour. The faults of Henry VII. are many, but may have seemed venial in the eyes of a man more famed for strength of intellect than for purity of principle, yet no work from the pen of Sir Francis Bacon, Lord Verulam, but will reward the labour of perusal, and this, like the previous sections of this book, is a verbatim reprint from Kennet's England, ed. 1719.

FRANCIS BACON, youngest son of Sir Nicholas, Lord Keeper to Queen Elizabeth, was born at York House, Jan. 22, 1561. As a child he was delicate, but so grave in manner and advanced in mind that Elizabeth called the boy "her young Lord Keeper." At thirteen he entered Trinity College, Cambridge, then presided over by Whitgift, afterwards Archbishop of Canterbury. At sixteen he was sent to Paris to the house of Sir Amias Paulet, ambassador for England, and thence he wrote his "Notes on the State of Europe." His father dying in 1580, recalled him to England, where he looked for patronage from Lord Burleigh, his uncle, but in vain, the father being jealous of his abilities when brought to compete with those of his son Robert, also a candidate for place and power.

Bacon settled in Gray's Inn, and rose rapidly in his profession, becoming Queen's Counsel in 1590, obtaining reversion of the registrarship of the Star Chamber court, and became M.P. for Middlesex in 1593. A speech of his in the House gave offence to his Queen, but he won the patronage of the Earl of Essex, who presented him with an estate near Twickenham worth £2,000 a year. Kind as Essex had been to him, Bacon deserted him when he lost the favour of Elizabeth, and was counsel against him in the attainder which resulted in his execution. In 1597 he published a small volume of Essays. He was suitor for the hand of Lady Hatton, who preferred Sir E. Coke. Bacon married a daughter of an alderman of London.

When James VI. of Scotland became I. of England, he soon noticed the talents of Bacon, they securing him from contempt, while his manner and cool temperament saved him from hatred. In 1604 he rose to be King's Counsel ; in 1607 Solicitor General ; in 1612 Attorney General ; in 1612 Privy Counsellor ; in 1617 Lord Keeper ; and Lord Chancellor in 1620. In 1621 he became Baron Verulam, Viscount St. Albans. He early won the favour of Villiers, Duke of Buckingham ; but feeling too sure in his seat, he gained his enmity, lost his position, was impeached for "selling justice," fined £40,000, and imprisoned. He soon regained liberty, but not power, receiving a pension of £1,200 per annum, and dying 9th April, 1626.

THE
HISTORY OF ENGLAND,

CONTINU'D TO THE NORMAN CONQUEST.

By Mr. JOHN MILTON.

Author of Paradise Lost, &c.

BOOK I.

THE beginning of nations, those excepted of whom sacred books have spoken, is to this day unknown. Nor only the beginning, but the deeds also of many succeeding ages, yea, periods of ages, either wholly unknown, or obscur'd and blemish'd with fables. Whether it were that the use of letters came in long after, or were it the violence of barbarous inundations, or they themselves, at certain revolutions of time, fatally decaying, and degenerating into sloth and ignorance; whereby the monuments of more ancient civility have been some destroyed, some lost. Perhaps dis-esteem and contempt of the publick affairs then present, as not worth recording, might partly be in cause. Certainly oft-times we see that wise men, and of best ability, have forborn to write the acts of their own days, while they beheld with a just loathing and disdain, not only how unworthy, how perverse, how corrupt, but often how ignoble, how petty, how below all history the persons and their actions were; who either by fortune, or some rude election, had attain'd as a sore judgment, and ignominy upon the land, to have chief sway in managing the commonwealth. But that any law, or superstition of our old philosophers the Druids, forbade the Britains to write their memorable deeds, I know not why any out of Cæsar should (lib. 6.) alledge: he indeed saith, that their doctrine they thought not lawful to commit to letters; but in most matters else, both private and publick, among which well may history be reckon'd,[1]

[1] There are some objections, and those not inconsiderable, against this assertion. Græcis Literis utuntur, saith Cæsar: which does not necessarily imply that they used the Greek tongue, but only their Letters: for if he had meant the language, he would have rather said, Græcosermone, or Græcalingua. But this does not take off the difficulty neither: for if they made use of the Greek letters, it had been but a poor contrivance of Cæsar's, to write to Cicero (in Gaul) in the Greek character, for fear the letter should be intercepted, and their designs discovered. Hanc Græcis conscriptum literis mittit, ne intercepta epistola, nostra ab hostibus consilia cognoscantur, saith Cæsar, lib. 5. Now if the Druids (the great ministers of state) us'd the Greek character in their common business, why should Cæsar think, that this character would conceal his designs? The learned Selden believes, Græcis to have been foisted into that place of Cæsar, where he speaks of the Druids, (lib. 6.) and will have him mean no more, than that religious matters were never writ down, but in all secular affairs they made use of writing: a conjecture natural enough, and very probably true.

they us'd the Greek tongue: and that the British Druids, who taught those in Gaul, would be ignorant of any language known and us'd by their disciples, or so frequently writing other things, and so inquisitive into the highest, would for want of recording be ever children in the knowledge of times and ages, is not likely. Whatever might be the reason, this we find, that of British affairs, from the first peopling of the island, to the coming of Julius Cæsar, nothing certain, either by tradition, history, or ancient fame, hath hitherto been left us. That which we have of oldest seeming, hath by the greater part of judicious antiquaries been long rejected for a modern fable.

Nevertheless, there being others besides the first suppos'd author, men not unread, nor unlearned in antiquity, who admit that for approved story, which the former explode for fiction; and seeing that oft-times relations heretofore accounted fabulous, have been after found to contain in them many footsteps, and relics of something true, as what we read in poets of the flood, and giants little believed, till undoubted witnesses taught us, that all was not feign'd; I have therefore determin'd to bestow the telling over of these reputed tales; be it for nothing else but in favour of our English poets, and rhetoricians, who by their art will know how to use them judiciously.

I might also produce examples, as Diodorus among the Greeks, Livy and others of the Latines, Polydore and Virunnius among our own writers. But I intend not with controversies and quotations to delay or interrupt the smooth course of history; much less to argue and debate long who were the first inhabitants, with what probabilities, what authorities each opinion hath been upheld, but shall endeavour that which hitherto hath been needed most, with plain and lightsome brevity, to relate well and orderly things worth the noting, so as may best instruct and benefit them that read. Which imploring divine assistance, that it may redound to his glory, and the good of the British nation, I now begin.

THAT the whole earth was inhabited before the flood, and to the utmost point of habitable ground, from those effectual words of God in the creation, may be more than conjectur'd. Hence that this island also had her dwellers, her affairs, and perhaps her stories, even in that old world those many hundred years, with much reason we may infer.[1] After the flood, and the dispersing of nations, as they journey'd leisurely from the east, Gomer, the eldest son of Japhet, and his offspring, as by authorities, arguments, and affinity of divers names is generally believed, were the first that peopl'd all these west and northern climes. But they of our own writers, who thought they had done nothing, unless with all circumstance they tell us when, and who first

---

[1] Concerning the first peopling of Britain, Mr. Cambden has given us as distinct an account as can be drawn from probable conjectures, and as the great distance of time and want of records will allow. See his Brittannia, the English edit. p. 10.

set foot upon this island, presume to name out of fabulous and counterfeit authors a certain Samothes or Dis, a fourth or sixth son of Japhet, whom they make about two hundred years after the flood, to have planted with colonies, first the continent of Celtica, or Gaul, and next this island : Thence to have nam'd it Samothea, to have reign'd here, and after him lineally four kings, Magus, Saron, Druis, and Bardus. But the forg'd Berosus, whom only they have to cite, no where mentions that either he, or any of those, whom they bring did ever pass into Britain, or send their people hither. So that this out-landish figment may easily excuse our not allowing it the room here so much as of a British fable.

That which follows, perhaps as wide from truth, though seeming less impertinent, is, that these Samotheans, under the reign of Bardus, were subdu'd by Albian a giant, son of Neptune, who call'd the island after his own name, and ruled it forty-four years : till at length passing over into Gaul, in aid of his brother Lestrygon, against whom Hercules was hasting out of Spain into Italy, he was there slain in fight, and Bergion also his brother.

Sure enough we are that Britain hath been anciently term'd Albion, both by the Greeks and Romans. And Mela the geographer makes mention of a stony shoar in Languedoc, where by report such a battle was fought. The rest,[1] as his giving name to the isle, or ever landing here, depends altogether upon late surmises. But too absurd, and too unconscionably gross is that fond invention that wafted hither the fifty daughters of a strange Dioclesian king of Syria ; brought in doubtless by some illiterate pretender to something mistaken in the common poetical story of Danaus king of Argos, while his vanity, not pleas'd with the obscure beginning which truest antiquity affords the nation, labour'd to contrive us a pedigree, as he thought, more noble. These daughters, by appointment of Danaus on the marriage-night, having murder'd all their husbands, except Linceus, whom his wife's loyalty sav'd, were by him, at the suit of his wife their sister, not put to death, but turn'd out to sea in a ship unmann'd ; of which whole sex they had incurr'd the hate ; and as the tale goes, were driven on this island : where the inhabitants, none but devils, as some write, or as others, a lawless crew left here by Albion without head or governor, both entertained them, and had issue by them a second breed of giants, who tyranniz'd the isle till Brutus came.

The eldest of those dames in their legend they call Albina ; and from thence, for which cause the whole scene was fram'd, will have the same Albion deriv'd. Incredible it may seem, so sluggish a con-

---

[1] 'Tis possible enough he might give name to the isle, though he never landed here. Pliny tells us, it was call'd Albion, to distinguish it from the islands round Britain, which went under the general name of Britannicæ : and this likely enough was done by the Greeks, who delighted so much in fabulous names.

ceit should prove so ancient, as to be authoris'd by the elder Ninnius, reputed to have lived above a thousand years ago. This I find not in him, but that Histion sprung of Japhet, had four sons, Francus, Romanus (Holinshed), Alemannus, and Britto, of whom the Britains; as true, I believe, as that those other nations whose names are resembled, came of the other three; if these dreams give not just occasion to call in doubt the book itself, which bears that title.

Hitherto the things themselves have given us as a warrantable dispatch to run them soon over. But now (A.N. 2855.) of [1] Brutus and his line, with the whole progeny of kings, to the entrance of Julius Cæsar, we cannot so easily be discharg'd; descents of ancestry, long-continu'd laws and exploits, not plainly seeming to be borrow'd, or devis'd, which on the common belief have wrought no small impression; [2] defended by many, denyed utterly by few. For what though Brutus, and the whole Trojan pretence were yielded up, seeing they who first devis'd to bring us from some[3] noble ancestor, were content at first with Brutus the consul, till better invention, although not willing to forgo the name, taught them to remove it higher, into a more fabulous age, and by the same remove lighting on the Trojan tales, in affectation to make the Britain of one original with the Roman, pitch'd there, yet those old and inborn names of successive kings, never any to have been real persons, or done in their lives, at least some part of what so long hath been remember'd, cannot be thought without too strict an incredulity.

For these, and those causes above-mention'd, that which hath receiv'd approbation from so many, I have chosen not to omit. Certain or uncertain, be that upon the credit of those whom I must follow; so far as keeps aloof from impossible and absurd, attested by ancient writers from books more ancient, I refuse not, as the due and proper subject of story. The principal author is well known to be Geoffry of Monmouth;[4] what he was, and whence his authority, who in his age, or before him have deliver'd the same matter, and such like general discourses, will better stand in a treatise by themselves. All of them agree in this, that Brutus was the son of Silvius, he of

---

[1] That romantick story of Brutus and his posterity, is fairly confuted by Mr. Cambden, English Edit. p. 6.

[2] Leland has published a vindication of the story; and the Welsh are generally very unwilling to give it up for fabulous.

[3] If the Britains are so fond of a Trojan original, Mr. Cambden has pointed out a much better claim to it, than the story of Brutus can give them: For the Romans (descended from the Trojans) by their long continuance in this island, could not but have many inter-marriages with the Britains; whereby a great many Britains at this day must be of Roman, and, by consequence, of Trojan extraction.

[4] Nennius, who lived in the 7th century, makes the island to be first inhabited by Brito, son of Ascanius and grandson to Æneas; who, as he supposes, reign'd in Britain at the time when Eli judged Israel, about the year of the world, 2830. Sigebertus Gemblacensis, a French monk, who liv'd 20 years before Geoffry of Monmouth, writes, that Brute past from Gaul into Britain: and Henry Huntington, contemporary with Geoffry, is of opinion that Britain was peopled by Brute.

Ascanius, whose father was Æneas a Trojan prince, who at the burning of that city, with his son Ascanius, and a collected number that escap'd, after a long wandring on the sea, arriv'd in Italy : where at length by the assistance of Latinus king of Latium, who had given him his daughter Lavinia, he obtain'd to succeed in that kingdom, and left it to Ascanius, whose son Silvius (though Roman Histories deny Silvius to be the son of Ascanius) had married secretly a niece of Lavinia.

She being with child, the matter became known to Ascanius : who commanding his magicians to enquire by art, what sex the maid had conceiv'd ? had answer, that it was one who should be the death of both his parents : and banish'd for the fact, should after all in a far country attain to highest honour. The prediction fail'd not, for in travail the mother dy'd : and Brutus (the child was so call'd) at fifteen years of age, attending his father to the chace, with an arrow unfortunately kill'd him.

Banish'd therefore by his kindred, he retires into Greece : where meeting with the race of Helenus, king Priam's son, held there in servile condition by Pandrasus, then king ; with them he abides : for Pyrrhus, in revenge of his father slain at Troy, had brought thither with him Helenus, and many others, into servitude. There Brutus, among his own stock so thrives in vertue, and in arms, as renders him belov'd by kings, and great captains, above all the youth of that land. Whereby the Trojans not only began to hope, but secretly to move him, that he would lead them the way to liberty. They alledge their numbers, and the promis'd help of Assaracus, a noble Greekish youth, by the mother's side a Trojan ; whom for that cause his brother went about to dispossess of certain castles bequeath'd him by his father. Brutus considering both the forces offer'd him, and the strength of those holds, not unwillingly consents.

First, therefore, having fortify'd those castles, he, with Assaracus, and the whole multitude, betake them to the woods and hills, as the safest place from whence to expostulate ; and in the name of all sends to Pandrasus this message ; that the Trojans holding it unworthy their ancestors to serve in a Foreign Kingdom, had retreated to the woods ; chusing rather a savage life than a slavish ; if that displeas'd him, that then with his leave they might depart to some other soil.

As this may pass with good allowance, that the Trojans might be many in these parts ; for Helenus was by Pyrrhus made king of the Chaonians, and the sons of Pyrrhus by Andromache, Hector's wife, could not but be powerful through all Epirus : so much the more it may be doubted how these Trojans could be thus in bondage, where they had friends and countrymen so potent. But to examine these things with diligence, were but to confute the fables of Britain with the fables of Greece or Italy ; for of this age, what have we to say, as well concerning most other countries, as this island, is equally under question. Be't how it will, Pandrasus not expecting so bold a message from the sons of captives, gathers an army; and marching toward the woods, Brutus, who had notice of his approach nigh to a town call'd Sparantinum, (I know not what town, but certainly of no Greek name) over night planting himself there with good part of his men, suddenly sets upon him and with slaughter of the Greeks, pursues him to the passage of a river, which mine author names Akalon, meaning perhaps Achelous, or Acheron; where at the ford he overlays them afresh. This victory obtain'd, and a sufficient strength left in Sparantinum, Brutus with Antigonus, the king's brother, and his friend Anacletus, whom he had taken in the fight, returns to the residue of his friends in the thick woods: while Pandrasus with all speed re-collecting, besieges the town. Brutus to relieve his men besieg'd, who earnestly call'd him, distrusting the sufficiency of his force, bethinks himself of this policy: calls to him Anacletus, and threatening instant death else both to him and his Antigonus, enjoyns him, that he should go at the second hour of night to the Greekish league, and tell the guards he had brought Antigonus by stealth out of prison to a certain woody vale, unable through the weight of his fetters to move further; entreating them to come speedily and fetch him in. Anacletus, to save both himself and his friend Antigonus, swears this; and at a fit hour sets out alone for the camp: is met, examin'd, and at last unquestionably known. To whom, great profession of fidelity first made, he frames his tale, as had been taught him: and they now fully assur'd, with a credulous rashness leaving their stations, far'd accordingly by the ambush that there awaited them. Forthwith Brutus dividing his men into three parts, leads on in silence to the camp; commanding first each part at a several place to enter, and forbear execution, till he with his squadron possess'd of the king's tent, gave signal to them by trumpet. The sound whereof no sooner heard, but huge havock begins upon the sleeping and unguarded enemy; whom the besieged also now sallying forth, on the other side, assail. Brutus the while had special care to seize and secure the king's person; whose life still within his custody, he knew was the surest pledge to obtain what he should demand. Day appearing, he enters the town, there distributes the king's treasure, and leaving the place better fortify'd, returns with the king his prisoner to the woods. Strait the ancient and grave men he summons to counsel, what they should now demand of the king.

After long debate, Mempricius, one of the gravest, utterly dissuading them from thought of longer stay in Greece, unless they meant to be deluded with a subtle peace, and the awaited revenge of those whose friends they had slain, advises them to demand first the king's eldest daughter Innogen in marriage to their leader Brutus, with a rich dowry, next shipping, money, and fit provision for them all to depart the land.

This resolution pleasing best, the king now brought in, and placed in a high seat, is briefly told, that on these conditions granted, he might be free; not granted, he must prepare to die.

Press'd with fear of death, the king readily yields, especially to bestow his daughter on whom he confess'd so noble and so valiant: offers him also the third part of his kingdom, if they like to stay; if not, to be their hostage himself, till he had made good his word.

The marriage therefore solemniz'd and shipping from all parts got together, the Trojans in a fleet, no less written than three hundred four and twenty sail, betake them to the wide sea: where with a prosperous course, two days and a night bring them to a certain island, long before dispeopl'd and left waste by sea-rovers; the name whereof was then Leogecia, now unknown. They who were sent out to discover, came at length to a ruin'd city, where was a temple and image of Diana that gave oracles; but not meeting first or last save wild beasts, they return with this notice to their ships: wishing their general would enquire of that oracle what voyage to pursue.

Consultation had, Brutus taking with him Gerion his diviner, and twelve of the ancientest, with wonted ceremonies before the inward shrine of the goddess, in verse, as it seems the manner was, utters his request, *Diva potens nemorum;* &c.

> Goddess of shades, and huntress, who at will
> Walk'st on the rowling sphere, and thro' the deep,
> On thy third reign the earth look now and tell
> What land, what seat of rest thou bidst me seek,
> What certain seat, where I may worship thee
> For aye, with temples vow'd and virgin quires.

To whom sleeping before the altar, Diana in a vision that night thus answer'd, *Brute, sub occasum, Solis,* &c.

> Brutus, far to the west, in th' ocean wide
> Beyond the realm of Gaul, a land their lies:
> Sea-girt it lies, where giants dwelt or old,
> Now void, it fits thy people; thither bend
> Thy course, there shalt thou find a lasting seat,
> There to thy sons another Troy shall rise,
> And kings be born of thee, whose dreaded might
> Shall awe the world, and conquer nations bold.

These verses, originally Greek, were put in Latin, sait'. Virunnius, by Gildas, a British Poet, and him to have lived under C'.udius. Which granted true, adds much to the antiquity of this fable; and indeed the Latin verses are much better, than for the age of Geoffrey ap Arthur, unless perhaps Joseph of Exeter, the only smooth poet of those times, befriended him. In this Diana over-shot her oracle thus ending, *Ipsis totius terræ subditus orbis erit*, that to the race of Brute, kings of this island, the whole earth shall be subject.

But Brutus guided now, as he thought, by divine conduct, speeds him towards the west ; and after some encounters on the Afric side, arrives at a place on the Tyrrhene Sea, where he happens to find the race of those Trojans, who with Antenor, came into Italy; and Corineus, a man much fam'd, was their chief: though by surer authors it be reported, that those Trojans with Antenor, were seated on the other side of Italy on the Adriatic, not the Tyrrhene shoar. But these joyning company, and past the Herculean Pillars, at the mouth of Ligeris in Aquitania cast anchor. Where after some discovery made of the place, Corineus hunting nigh the shoar with his men, is by messengers of the king Gossarius Pictus met, and question'd about his errand there. Who not answering to their mind, Imbertus, one of them, lets fly an arrow at Corineus, which he avoiding, slays him : and the Pictavian himself hereupon levying his whole force, is overthrown by Brutus and Corineus ; who with the battle-ax, which he was wont to manage against the Tyrrhene Giants, is said to have done marvels. But Gossarius having drawn to his aid the whole country of Gaul, at that time govern'd by twelve kings, puts his fortune to a second trial, wherein the Trojans over-born by multitude, or driven back, and besieg'd in their own camp, which by good foresight was strongly situate. Whence Brutus unexpectedly issuing out, and Corineus in the mean while, whose device it was, assaulting them behind from a wood, where he had convey'd his men the night before, the Trojans are again victors, but with the loss of Turon a valiant nephew of Brutus ; whose ashes left in that place, gave name to the city of Tours, built there by the Trojans. Brutus finding now his powers much lessen'd, and this yet not the place foretold him, leaves Aquitain, and with an easie course,[1] arriving at Totness in Devonshire, quickly perceives here to be the promis'd end of his labours.

The Island not yet Britain, but Albion, was in a manner desart and inhospitable ; kept only by a remnant of giants : whose excessive force and tyranny had consum'd the rest. Them Brutus destroys, and to his people divides the land, which with some reference to his own name, he thenceforth calls Britain. To Corineus, Cornwall, as we now call it, fell by lot ; the rather by him lik'd, for that the hugest giants, in rocks and caves were said to lurk still there ; which kind of monsters to deal with was his old exercise.

And here, with leave bespoken, to recite a grand fable, though dignify'd by our best poets ; while Brutus on a certain festival day, solemnly kept on that shoar where he first landed, was with the people in great jollity and mirth, a crew of these savages breaking in upon them, began on the sudden another sort of game than at such a

---

[1] The time of his landing is suppos'd to be about 1200 years after the flood, A.M. 2830.

meeting was expected. But at length by many hands overcome, Goemagog the hugest, in height twelve cubits, is reserv'd alive ; that with him Corenius, who desir'd nothing more, might try his strength ; whom in a wrestle the giant catching aloft, with a terrible hugg broke three of his ribs : nevertheless Corenius enrag'd, heaving up by main force, and on his shoulders bearing him to the next high rock, threw him headlong all shattered into the sea, and left his name on the cliff, called ever since Langoemagog, which is to say the giant's leap.

After this, Brutus in a chosen place builds Troja Nova,[1] chang'd in time to Trinovantum, now London, and began to enact laws ; Heli being then high-priest in Judœa ; and having govern'd the whole isle 24 Years, dy'd, and was buried in his new Troy. His three sons, Locrine, Albanact and Camber, divide the land by consent. Locrine had the middle part Loegria ; Camber possessed Cambria or Wales ; Albanact, Albania, now Scotland. But he in the end by Humber, king of the Hunns, who with a fleet invaded that land, was slain in fight, and his people driven back into Loegria. Locrine and his brother go out against Humber; who now marching onward, was by them defeated, and in a river drown'd, which to this day retains his name. Among the spoils of his camp and navy were found certain young maids, and Estrildis, above the rest, passing fair, the daughter of a king in Germany, from whence Humber, as he went wasting the sea-coast, he led her captive: whom Locrine, though before contracted to the daughter of Corineus, resolves to marry. But being forc'd and threaten'd by Corineus, whose authority and power he fear'd; Guendolen the daughter he yields to marry, but in secret loves the other; and oft-times retiring as to some private sacrifice, through vaults and passages made under ground; and seven years thus enjoying her, had by her a daughter equally fair, whose name was Sabra. But when once his fears was off by the death of Corineus, not content with secret enjoyment, divorcing Guendolen, he made Estrildis now his queen. Guendolen all in rage departs into Cornwall, where Madan, the son she had by Locrine, was hitherto brought up by Corineus his grand-father. And gathering an army of her father's friends and subjects, gives battle to her husband by the river Sture; wherein Locrine shot with an arrow ends his life. But not so ends the fury of Guendolen, for Estrildis, and her daughter Sabra she throws into a river; and to leave a monument of revenge, proclaims, that the stream be thenceforth call'd after the damsel's name; which by length of time is chang'd now to Sabrina, or Severn.

Fifteen years she governs in behalf of her son, then resigning to him at age, retires to her father's dominion. This, saith my author, was (2909) in the days of Samuel. Madan hath the praise to have well and peaceably rul'd the space of 40 years; leaving (2949) behind

[1] He gives it a Latin name, tho' that language was not then us'd in Italy.

him two sons, Mempricius and Malim. Mempricius had first to do with the ambition of his brother, aspiring to share with him in the kingdom; whom therefore at a meeting to compose the matters, with a treachery which his cause needed not, he slew.

Nor was he better in the sole possession, whereof so ill he could endure a partner, killing his nobles, and those especially next to succeed him; till lastly given over to unnatural lust, in the twentieth of his reign, hunting in a forest, he was devour'd by wolves.

His son (2969), Ebranc, a man of mighty strength and stature, reign'd 40 years. He first after Brutus wasted Gaul; and returning rich and prosperous, builded Caerebranc, now York; in Albania, Alclud; Mount Agned, or the Castle of Maidens, now Edinburgh. He had 20 sons and 30 daughters by 20 wives. His daughters he sent to Silvius Alba into Italy, who bestow'd them on his peers of the Trojan line. His sons under the leading of Assaracus their brother, won them lands and signiories in Germany, thence call'd, from these brethren, Germania: a derivation too hastily suppos'd, perhaps before the word Germanus or the Latin tongue was in use. Some who have describ'd Henault, as Jacobus Bergomas, and Lessabeus, are cited to affirm, that Ebranc in his war there was by Brunchildis Lord of Henault put to the worse.

Brutus therefore, sirnamed Greenshield, succeeding to repair his father's losses, as the same Lessabeus reports, fought a second battle in Henault with Brunchild at the mouth of Scaldis, and (3000) encamp'd on the river Hania. Of which our Spencer also thus sings:

> Let Scaldis tell, and let tell Hania,
> And let the marsh of Esthambruges tell
> What colour were their waters that same day,
> And all the moor 'twixt Elversham and Dell,
> With blood of Henelois which therein fell;
> How oft that day did sad Brunchildis see
> The Greenshield dy'd in dolorous Vermeil, &c.

But Henault, and Brunchild, and Greenshield, seem newer names than for a story pretended thus ancient.

Him succeeded (3022) Leil, a maintainer of peace and equity; but slacken'd in his latter end, whence arose some civil discord. He built in the north Caerliel, in the days of Solomon.

Rudhuddibras, or Hudibras, appeasing (3040) the commotions which his father could not, founded Caerkeynt or Canterbury; Caerguent, or Winchester; and Mount Paladur, now Septonia or Shaftsbury: but this by others is contradicted.

Bladud his son built (3085) Caerbadus or Bath, and those medicinal waters he dedicated to Minerva, in whose temple there he kept fire continually burning. He was a man of great invention, and taught necromancy: till having made him wings to fly, he fell down upon the temple of Apollo in Trinovant, and so dy'd, after twenty years reign.

Hitherto from father to son the direct line (3105) hath run on: but Leir, who next reign'd, had only three daughters, and no male issue: govern'd laudably: and built Caer-Leir, now Leicester on the bank of Sora. But at last, failing through age, he determines to bestow his daughters, and so among them to divide his kingdom. Yet first to try which of them lov'd him best (a trial that might have made him, had he known as wise how to try, as he seem'd to know how much the trying behov'd him) he resolves a simple resolution, to ask them solemnly in order; and which of them should profess largest, her to believe. Gonoril, the eldest, apprehending too well her father's weakness, makes answer, invoking heaven, that she lov'd him above her soul, therefore, quoth the old man over-joy'd, since thou so honourest my declined age, to thee and the husband whom thou shalt chuse, I give the third part of my realm. So fair a speeding for a few words soon utter'd, was to Regan the second, ample instruction what to say. She on the same demand spares no protesting, and the gods must witness, that otherwise to express her thoughts she knew not, but that she lov'd him above all creatures; and so receives an equal reward with her sister. But Cordeilla the youngest, though hitherto best belov'd, and now before her eyes the rich and present hire of a little easie soothing, the danger also, and the loss likely to betide plain dealing, yet moves not from the solid purpose of a sincere and vertuous answer. 'Father, saith she, 'my love towards you is as my duty bids; what should a father seek? What can a child promise more? They who pretend beyond this, flatter.' When the old man, sorry to hear this, and wishing her to recall those words, persisted asking; with a loyal sadness at her father's infirmity, but something on the sudden harsh, and glancing rather at her sisters, than speaking her own mind, 'Two ways only,' sayth she, 'I have to answer what you require me; the former, your command is, I should recant; accept then this other which is left me; look how much you have, so much is your value, and so much I love you.' 'Then hear thou, quoth Leir, 'now all in a passion, what thy ingratitude hath gain'd thee; because thou hast not reverenc'd thy aged father equal to thy sisters, part in my kingdom, or what else is mine, reckon to have none.' And without delay gives in marriage his other daughters, Gonoril to Maglaunus duke of Albania, Regan to Henninus duke of Cornwall; with them in present, half his kingdom; the rest to follow at his death. In the mean while fame was not sparing to divulge the wisdom and other graces of Cordeilla, insomuch that Aganippus a great king in Gaul (however he came by his Greek name) seeks her to wife; and nothing alter'd at the loss of her dowry, receives her gladly in such manner as she was sent him. After this, king Leir, more and more drooping with years, became an easie prey to his daughters and their husbands who now by daily encroachment had seiz'd the whole kingdom into their hands, and the old king is put to sojourn with his eldest daughter, attended only by threescore knights. But they in a short while grudg'd at, as too numerous and disorderly for continual guests, are reduc'd to thirty. Not brooking that affront, the old king betakes him to his second daughter: but there also discord soon arising between the servants of differing masters in one family, five only are suffer'd to attend him. Then back again he returns to the other; hoping that she his eldest could not but have more pity on his grey hairs: but she now refuses to admit him unless he be content with one only of his followers. At last the remembrance of his youngest, Cordeilla, comes to his thoughts; and now acknowledging how true her words had been, though with little hope from one he had so injur'd, be it but to pay her the last recompence she can have from him, his confession of her wise fore-warning, that so perhaps his misery, the proof and experiment of her wisdom, might something soften her, he takes his journey into France. Now might be seen a difference between the silent and downright spoken affection of some children to their parents, and the talkative obsequiousness of others; while the hope of inheritance over-acts them, and on the tongues end enlarges their duty. Cordeilla out of mere love, without the suspicion of expected reward, at the message only of her father in distress pours forth true filial tears. And not enduring either that her own, or any other eye should see him in such forlorn condition as his messenger declar'd, discreetly appoints one of her most trusty servants, first to convey him privately toward some good sea town, there to array him, bath him, cherish him, furnish him with such attendants and state, as beseem'd his dignity. That then, as from his first landing, he might send word of his arrival to her husband Aganippus. Which done with all mature and requisite contrivance, Cordeilla with the king her husband, and all the barony of his realm, who then first had news of his passing the sea, go out to meet him; and after all honourable and joyful entertainment, Aganippus, as to his wife's father, and his royal guest, surrenders him, during his abode there, the power and disposal of his whole dominion: permitting his wife Cordeilla to go with an army, and set her father upon his throne. Wherein her piety so prosper'd, as that she vanquish'd her impious sisters with those dukes, and Leir again, as saith the story, three years obtain'd the crown. To whom dying, Cordeilla with all regal solemnities gave burial in the town of Leicester. And then as right heir succeeding, and her husband dead, rul'd the land five years in peace; until Marganus and Cunedagius, her two sisters' sons, not bearing that a kingdom should be govern'd by a woman, in the unseasonablest time to raise that quarrel against a woman so worthy, make war against her, depose her (3169) and imprison her; of which impatient, and now long unexercis'd to suffer, she there, as is related, kill'd herself. The victors between them part the land: but Marganus the eldest sister's son, who held by agreement from the north-side of

Humber to Cathness, incited by those about him, to invade all his own right, wars on Cunedagius, who soon met him, overcame, and overtook him in a town of Wales, where he left his life, and ever since, his name to the place.

Cunedagius was now sole king, and govern'd with much praise many years, about the time when Rome was built.[1] Him succeeded (3203) Rivallo his son, wise also and fortunate; save what they tell us of three days raining blood, and swarms of stinging flies, whereof men dy'd. In order then (3248) Gurgustius, Jago or Lago, his nephew;[2] Sisillus, Kinmarcus. Then (3287) Gorbogudo, whom others name Gorbodego, and Gorbodion, who had two sons, Ferrex and Porrex. They (3420) in the old age of their father falling to contend who should succeed, Porrex attempting (3477) by treachery his brother's life, drives him into France; and in his return, though aided with the force of that country, defeats and slays him. But by his mother Videna, who less lov'd him, is himself, with the assistance of her women, soon after slain in his bed: with whom ended, as is thought, the line of Brutus;[3] whereupon, the whole land with civil broils was rent into five kingdoms, long time waging war on each other; and some say 50 years. At length (3480) Dunwallo Molmutius, the son of Cloten king of Cornwall, one of the aforesaid five, excelling in valour and goodliness of person, after his father's decease found (3530) means to reduce again the whole island into a monarchy: subduing the rest at opportunities. First Ymner king of Loegria whom he slew; then Rudaucus of Cambria, Staterius of Albania, confederate together. In which fight Dunwallo is reported, while the victory hung doubtful, to have us'd this art. He takes with him 600 stout men, bids them put on the armour of their slain enemies, and so unexpectedly approaching the squadron, where those two kings had plac'd themselves in fight, from that part which they thought securest, assaults and dispatches them. Then displaying his own ensigns, which before he had conceal'd, and sending notice to the other part of his army what was done, adds to them new courage, and gains a final victory. This Donwallo was the first in Britain that wore a crown of gold; and therefore by some reputed the first king. He established the Molmutine laws, famous among the English to this day; written long after in Latin by Gildas, and in Saxon by king Alfred; so saith Geoffry; but Gildas denies to have known ought of the Britains before Cæsar, much less knew (3563) Alfred. These laws, whoever made them, bestow'd on temples the privilege of sanctuary; to cities also, and the ways thither leading, yea to plows

---

[1] Romulus built Rome, A.M. 3193.—*Tall. Tab.*
[2] Sisilius reign'd before Lago, who according to Mr. Tallent's chronological tables succeeded him, A.M. 3336, and was succeeded by Kimmachus or Kinmarchus, A.M. 3364.
[3] The line of Brutus reign'd in this island, according to Geoffry of Monmouth's account, six hundred and fifty years.

granted a kind of like refuge: and made such riddance of thieves and robbers, that all passages were safe. Forty years he govern'd alone, and was buried nigh to the Temple of Concord;[1] which he, to the memory of peace restor'd, had built in Trinovant.

His two sons, Belinus and Brennus, contending about the Crown, by decision of friends came at length to an accord; Brennus to have the north of Humber, Belinus the sovereignty of all. But the younger not long so contented, that he, as they whisper'd to him, whose valour had so oft repell'd the invasions of Ceulphus the Morine duke, should now be subject to his brother. upon new design sails into Norway; enters league and affinity with Elsing that king; which Belinus perceiving, in his absence dispossesses him of all the north. Brennus with a fleet of Norwegians makes towards Britain; but encounter'd by Guithlac the Danish king, who laying claim to his bride, pursu'd him on the sea, his haste was retarded, and he bereft of his spouse: who from the fight by sudden tempest, was by the Danish king driven on Northumberland, and brought to Belinus. Brennus nevertheless re-collecting his navy, lands in Albania, and gives battle to his brother in the wood Calaterium; but losing the day, escapes with one single ship into Gaul. Meanwhile the Dane, upon his own offer to become tributary, sent home with his new prize, Belinus returns his thoughts to the administring of justice, and the perfecting of his father's laws; and to explain what highways might enjoy the foresaid privileges, he caus'd to be drawn out and pav'd four main roads to the utmost length and breadth of the island, and two others athwart; which are since attributed to the Romans. Brennus on the other side solliciting to his aid the kings of Gaul, happens at last on Seginus duke of the Allobroges, where his worth and comeliness of person wan him the duke's daughter and heir. In whose right he shortly succeeding, and by obtain'd leave passing with a great host through the length of Gaul, gets footing once again in Britain. Nor was Belinus unprepar'd; and now the battle ready to joyn, Conuvena the mother of them both, all in a fright, throws herself between, and calling earnestly to Brennus her son, whose absence had so long depriv'd her of his sight, after embracements and tears, assails him with such a motherly power, and the mention of things so dear and reverend, as irresistably wrung from him all his enmity against Belinus.

Then all hands joyn'd, reconciliation made firm, and counsel held to turn their united preparations on foreign parts. Thence that by these two all Gallia was over-run, the story tells; and what did they in Italy, and at Rome, if these be they, and not Gauls, who took that city, the Roman authors can best relate. So far from home I undertake not for the Monmouth Chronicle; which here against the stream

---

[1] Said to be built on the ground where Blackwell-Hall now stands. Selden mentions Kinmarchus in his Janus Anglorum.

of history, carries up and down these brethren, now into Germany, then again to Rome, pursuing Gabius and Porsena, two unheard of consuls. Thus much is more generally believ'd, that both this Brennus, and another famous captain, Britomarus, whom the epitomist Florus and others mention, were not Gauls but Britains ; the name of the first in that tongue signifying a king, and of the other a great Britain. However, Belinus after a while returning home, the rest of his days rul'd in peace, wealth, and honour above all his predecessors ; building some cities, of which one was Caerose upon Osca, since Caerlegion ; beautifying others, as Trinovant with a gate, a haven, and a tower on the river Thames (Billingsgate), retaining yet his name ; on the top whereof his ashes are said to have been laid up in a golden urn.

After him Gurguntius Barbirus was (3596) king, mild and just, but yet inheriting his father's courage, he subdu'd the Dacian, or Dane, who refus'd to pay the tribute covenanted to Belinus for his enlargement. In his return finding about the Orkneys thirty ships of Spain, or Biscay, fraught with men and women for a plantation, whose captain also Bartholinus wrongfully banish'd, as he pleaded, besought him, that some part of his territory might be assign'd them to dwell in, he sent with them certain of his own men to Ireland, which then lay unpeopl'd, and gave them that island to hold of him as in homage.
[1] He was bury'd in Caerlegion, a city which he had wall'd about.

Guitheline his son, is (3615) also remember'd, as a just and good prince, and his wife Martia to have excell'd so much in wisdom, as to venture upon a new institution of laws : which king Alfred translating, call'd Marchen-League, but more truly thereby is meant the Mercian law ; not translated by Alfred, but digested or incorporated with the West-Saxon. In the minority of her son (3656) she had the rule, and then, as may be suppos'd, brought forth these laws, not herself, for laws are masculine births, but by the advice of her sagest counsellors ; and therein she might do virtuously, since it befel her to supply the nonage of her son: else nothing more away from the law of God and nature, than that a woman should give laws to men.

Her son Sisillius coming to years, receiv'd (3666) the rule ; then in order Kimarus ; then Danius or Elanius his brother ; then Morindus, his son by Tanguestula, a concubine, who is recorded a man of excessive strength, valiant, liberal, and fair of aspect, but immanely cruel ; not sparing in his anger, enemy or friend, if any weapon were in his hand. A certain king of the Morines, or Picards, invaded Northumberland ; whose army this king, though not wanting sufficient numbers, chiefly by his own prowess overcame ; but dishonour'd his victory by the cruel usage of his prisoners, whom his own hands, or

[1] He is said to have built Lancaster and Warwick. And Cambridge, as is pretended, was now built by Cantabar a Spaniard.

others in his presence, put all to several deaths. Well fitted to such a beastial cruelty was his end; for hearing of a huge monster that from the Irish sea infested the coast, and in the pride of his strength, foolishly attempting to set manly valour against a brute vastness, when his weapons were all in vain, by that horrible mouth he was catch'd up and devour'd.

Gorbonian the eldest of his five sons, than whom a juster man liv'd not in his age, was (3676) a great builder of temples, and gave to all what was their due; to his gods devout worship; to men of desert, honour and preferment; to the commons encouragement in their labours and trades, defence and protection from injuries and oppressions; so that the land flourish'd above her neighbours; violence and wrong seldom was heard of; his death was a general loss; he was buried in Trinovant. Archigallo the second brother follow'd (3686) not his example; but depress'd the ancient nobility; and by peeling the wealthier sort, stuff'd his treasury, and took the right way to be depos'd. Elidure the next brother, sirnam'd the pious, was set up in his place; a mind so noble and so moderate, as almost is incredible to have ever been found. For having held the sceptre five years, hunting one day in the forest of Calater, he chanc'd to meet his deposed brother wandring in mean condition; who had been long in vain beyond the seas, importuning foreign aids to his restorement; and was now in a poor habit, with only ten followers, privately return'd to find subsistence among his secret friends. At the unexpected sight of him, Elidure himself also then (3690) but thinly accompanied, runs to him with open arms; and after many dear and sincere welcomings, conveys him to the city Aleud, there hides him in his own bed-chamber. Afterwards faining himself sick, summons all his peers, as about greatest affairs: where admitting them one by one, as if his weakness endur'd not the disturbance of more at once, causes them, willingly or unwilling, once more to swear allegiance to Archigallo. Whom, after reconciliation made on all sides, he leads to York, and from his own head, places the crown on the head of his brother. Who thenceforth, vice itself dissolving in him, and forgetting her firmest hold with the admiration of a deed so heroick, became a true converted man, rul'd worthily ten years, dy'd and was bury'd in Caerlicur. Thus was a brother sav'd by a brother, to whom love of a crown, the thing that so often dazzles and vitiates mortal men, for which thousands of nearest blood have destroy'd each other, was, in respect of brotherly dearness, a contemptible thing. Elidure now (3700), in his own behalf, reassumes the government, and did as was worthy such a man to do. When providence, that so great virtue might want no sort of tryal to make it more illustrious, stirs up Virgenius and Peredure his younger brethren, against him who had deserv'd so nobly of that relation, as least of all by a brother to be injur'd: yet him they defeat, him they imprison in the tower of Trinovant, and divide his kingdom; the north to Peredure, the south to Vigenius. After whose death Peredure obtaining all, so much the better us'd his power, by how much the worse he got it. So that Elidure now is hardly miss'd. But yet in all right, owing to his elder the due place whereof he had depriv'd him, fate would that he should die first. And Elidure, after many years imprisonment, is (3715) now the third time seated on the throne; which at last he enjoyed long in peace; finishing the interrupted course of his mild and just reign, as full of vertuous deeds as days, to the end. After these five sons of Morindus, succeeded also their sons in order (3720): reign of Gorbonian, Marganus of Archigallo, both good kings. But Enniaunus his brother taking other courses, was after six years depos'd. Then Idwallo, taught by a near example, govern'd soberly. Then Runno, then Geruntius, he of Peredure, this last the son of Elidure. From whose loins (for that likely is the durable and surviving race that springs of just progenitors) issu'd a long descent of kings, whose names only for many successions, without other memory, stands thus register'd, Catellus, Coilbus, Porrex, Cherin, and his three sons; Fulgenius, Eldadus, and Andragius, his son Urianus; Eliud, Eledaucus, Clotenus, Gurguntius, Merianus, Bleduno, Capis, Oenus, Sisillius, twenty kings in a continu'd row, that either did nothing, or liv'd in ages that wrote nothing, at least a foul pretermission in the author of this, whether story or fable; himself weary, as seems, of his own tedious tale.

But to make amends for this silence, Blegabredus next succeeding (3800), is recorded to have excell'd all before him in the art of music; opportunely, had he but left us one song of his twenty predecessors doings. Yet after him nine more succeeded in name; his brother Archimailus, Eldol, Redion, Rederchius, Samulius, Penissel, Pir, Capoirus, but Cliguelius,[1] with the addition of modest, wise and just. His son Heli reign'd (3818) forty years, and had three sons, Lud Cassibelan and Nennius. This Heli seems to be the same whom Ninnius in his fragment calls Minocan; for him he writes to be the father of Cassibelan. Lud was he that enlarg'd and wall'd about Trinovant, there kept his court, made it the prime city, and call'd it from his own name Cear-Lud, or Lud's Town, now London. Which, as is alledg'd out of Gildas, became matter of great dissention betwixt him and his brother Nennius;[2] who (3878) took it hainously that the name of Troy, their ancient country, should be abolish'd for any new one. Lud was hardy and bold in war, in peace a jolly feaster. He conquer'd many islands in the sea, saith Huntingdon, (lib. i.), and was

---
[1] Cliguellus or Dinellius, the son of Capoire, about eight years after the death of Elidure, in which time there had reign'd thirty kings, came to the crown, and is the first of so many princes that Geoffrey could, or would say any thing of.
[2] 'Tis said, this Nennius wrote the history of Britain, which was turn'd into Latin by another Nennius.

bury'd by the gate which from thence we call Ludgate. His two sons, Androgeus and Tenuantius, were left to the tuition of Cassibelan; whose beauty and high demeanor so wrought with the common people, as got him easily the kingdom transferr'd upon himself. He nevertheless continuing to favour and support his nephews, confers (3880) freely upon Androgeus, London with Kent; upon Tenuanteus, Cornwall; reserving a superiority both over them, and all the other princes to himself; till the Romans for a while circumscrib'd his power. Thus far, though leaning only on the credit of Geoffrey Monmouth, and his assertors, I yet for the specify'd causes have thought it not beneath my purpose to relate what I found. Whereto I neither oblige the belief of other persons, nor overhastily subscribe mine own. Nor have I stood with others, computing or collating years and chronologies, lest I should be vainly curious about the time and circumstances of things whereof the substance is so much in doubt. By this time, like one who had set out on his way by night, and travell'd thro' a region of smooth or idle dreams, our history now arrives on the confines, where daylight and truth meets us with a clear dawn, representing to our view, though at a far distance, true colours and shapes. For albeit Cæsar, whose authority we are now first to follow, wanted not who tax'd him of misreporting in his commentaries, yea, in his civil wars against Pompey, much more may we think in the British affairs, of whose little skill in writing he did not easily hope to be contradicted, yet now in such variety of good authors, we hardly can miss from one hand or the other to be sufficiently inform'd, as of things past so long ago. But this will better be referr'd to a second discourse.

BOOK II.

I AM now to write of what befel the Britains from fifty and three years before the birth of our Saviour, when first the Romans came in, till the decay and ceasing of that empire; a story of much truth, and for the first hundred years and somewhat more, collected without much labour. So many and so prudent were the writers, which those two, the civilest, and wisest of European Nations, both Italy and Greece, afforded to the actions of that puissant city. For worthy deeds are not often destitute of worthy relators: as by a certain fate great acts and great eloquence have most commonly gone hand in hand, equalling and honouring each other in the same ages. 'Tis true, that in obscurest times, by shallow and unskilful writers, the indistinct noise of many battles, and devastations of many kingdoms over-run and lost, hath come to our ears. For what wonder, if in all ages, ambition and the love of rapine hath stirr'd up greedy and violent men to bold attempts in wasting and ruining wars, which to posterity have left the work of wild beasts and destroyers, rather than the deeds and monuments of men and conquerors? but he whose just and true valour uses the necessity of war and dominion, not to destroy but to prevent destruction, to bring in liberty against tyrants, law and civility among barbarous nations, knowing that when he conquers all things else, he cannot conquer Time or Detraction, wisely conscious of this his wants as well as of his worth not to be forgotten or conceal'd, honours and hath recourse to the aid of eloquence, his friendliest and best supply; by whose immortal record his noble deeds, which else were transitory, becoming fixt and durable against the force of years and generations, he fails not to continue through all posterity, over Envy, Death, and Time, also victorious. Therefore when the esteem of science and liberal study waxes low in the commonwealth, we may presume that also there all civil virtue and worthy action is grown as low to a decline: and then eloquence, as it were consorted in the same destiny, with the decrease and fall of virtue corrupts also and fades; at least resigns her office of relating, to illiterate and frivolous historians; such as the persons themselves both deserve, and are best pleas'd with; whilst they want either the understanding to chuse better, or the innocence to dare invite the examining and searching stile of an intelligent and faithful writer to the survey of their unfound exploits, better befriended by obscurity than fame. As for these, the only authors we have of British Matters, while the power of Rome, reach'd hither (for Gildas affirms, that of the Roman times no British writer was in his Days extant, or if any ever were, either burnt by enemies, or transported with such as fled the Pictish and Saxon invasions) these therefore only Roman authors there be, who in the English tongue have laid together, as much, and perhaps more than was requisite to a history of Britain. So that were it not for leaving an unsightly gap so near to the beginning, I should have judg'd this labour, wherein so little seems to be requir'd above transcription, almost superfluous. Notwithstanding, since I must through it, if ought by diligence may be added, or omitted, or by other disposing may be more explain'd, or more express'd, I shall assay.

Julius Cæsar (of whom, and of the Roman free state, more than what appertains, is not here to be discours'd) having subdu'd most part of Gallia, which by a potent faction he had obtain'd of the senate as his province for many years, stirr'd up with a desire of adding still more glory to his name, and the whole Roman empire to his ambition, some say, (Suetonius: Vit. Cæs.) with a far meaner and ignobler, the desire of British pearls, whose bigness he delighted to balance in his hand, determines, and that upon no unjust pretended occasion, to try his force in the conquest also of Britain. For he understood that the Britains in most of his Gallian wars had sent supplies against him, had receiv'd fugitives of the Bellovaci his enemies, and were call'd over to aid the cities of Armorica, which had the year before conspir'd all in a new rebellion. Therefore, Cæsar, A.C. 53, though now the summer well nigh ending, and the season unagreeable to transport a war, yet judg'd it would be great advantage, only to get entrance into the Isle, knowledge of the men, the places, the ports, the accesses, which then, it seems, were even to the Gauls their neighbours almost unknown. For except merchants and traders, it is not oft, saith he, that any use to travel thither; and to those that do, besides the sea-coast, and the ports next to Gallia, nothing else is known. But here I must require, as Pollio, (Suetonius: Cæs. Com. l. 1.) did, the diligence, at least the memory of Cæsar: for if it were true, as they of Rhemes told him, that Divitiacus, not long before, a puissant king of the Soisons, had Britain also under his command, besides the Belgian colonies, which he affirms to have nam'd and peopl'd many provinces there, if also the Britains had so frequently given them aid in all their wars; if lastly the Druid learning, honour'd so much among them, were at first taught them out of Britain, and they who soonest would attain that discipline, sent hither to learn, it appears not (Cæs. Com. l. 4.) how Britain at that time should be so utterly unknown in Gallia, or only known to merchants, yea to them so little, that being call'd together from all parts, none could be found to inform Cæsar of what bigness the isle, what nations, how great, what use of war they had, what laws, or so much as what commodious havens for bigger vessels. Of all which things, as it were then first to make discovery, he sends Caius Volusenus in a long galley, with command to return as soon as this could be effected. He in the meantime with his whole Power draws nigh to the Morine [1] coast, whence the shortest passage was into Britain. Hither his navy, which he us'd against the Armoricans, and what else of shipping can be provided, he draws together. This known in Britain, ambassadors are sent from many of the states there, who promise hostages, and obedience to the Roman Empire. Them, after audience given, Cæsar as largely promising, and exhorting to continue in that mind, sends home, and with them Comius of Arras, whom he had made king of that Country, and now secretly employ'd to gain a Roman Party among the Britains, in as many cities as he found inclineable, and to tell them, that he himself was speeding thither. Volusenus, with what discovery of the island he could make from aboard his ship, not daring to venture on the shoar, within five days

---

[1] The Morini inhabited the province of Picardy.

returns to Cæsar: who soon after, with two legions, ordinarily amounting, of Romans and their allies, to about 25000 foot, and 4500 horse; the foot in 80 ships of burthen, the horse in 18, besides what gallies were appointed for his chief commanders, sets off about the third watch of the night with a good gale to sea; leaving behind him Sulpitius Rufus to make good the port with a sufficient strength.[1] But the horse, whose appointed shipping lay wind-bound eight mile upward in another haven, had much trouble to imbark. Cæsar now within sight of Britain, beholds on every hill multitudes of armed men, ready to forbid his landing; and Cicero writes to his friend Atticus, (Lic. Alt. l. 4. Ep. 16.) that the accesses of the island were wondrously fortify'd with strong works or moles. Here from the fourth to the ninth hour of day he awaits at anchor the coming up of his whole fleet: mean while with his legates and tribunes consulting, and giving order to fit all things for what might happen in such a various and floating water fight as was to be expected. This place, which was a narrow bay, close environ'd with hills, appearing no way commodious, he removes to a plain and open shoar, eight mile distant, commonly suppos'd about Deal in Kent. Which when the Britains perceiv'd, their horse and chariots, as then they used in fight, scowring before, their main power speeding after, some thick upon the shoar, others not tarrying to be assail'd, ride in among the waves to encounter and assault the Romans, even under their ships, with such a bold and free hardihood, that Cæsar himself, between confessing and excusing that his soldiers were to come down from their ships, to stand in water heavy arm'd, and to fight at once, denies not but that the terror of such new and resolute opposition made them forget their wonted valour. To succour which he commands his gallies, a sight unusual to the Britains, and more apt for motion, drawn from the bigger vessels, to row against the open side of the enemy, and thence with slings, engines and darts, to beat them back. But neither yet, though amaz'd at the strangeness of those new sea-castles, bearing up so near and so swiftly, as almost to overwhelm them, the hurtling of oars, the battering of fierce engines against their bodies barely expos'd, did the Britains give much ground, or the Romans gain, till he who bore the eagle of the tenth legion, yet in the gallies, first beseeching his gods, said thus aloud: Leap down, soldiers, unless ye mean to betray your ensign; I, for my part, will perform what I owe to the common-wealth and my general. This utter'd, over-board he leaps, and with his eagle fiercely advanc'd, runs upon the enemy, the rest heartning one another not to admit the dishonour of so nigh losing their chief standard, follow him resolutely. Now was fought eagerly on both sides. Ours, who well knew their own advantages, and expertly us'd them, now in the shallows, now on

---

[1] Concerning the havens from whence Cæsar set sail for Britain, see Somner's Dissertation de Portu Iccio, publish'd at Oxford by Mr. Gibson.

the sand, still as the Romans went trooping to their ensigns, receiv'd them, dispatch'd them, and with the help of their horse, put them every where to great disorder. But Cæsar causing all his boats and shallops to be fill'd with soldiers, commanded to ply up and down continually with relief where they saw need ; whereby at length all the foot now disembark'd, and got together in some order on firm ground, with a more steady charge put the Britains to flight : but wanting all their horse, whom the winds yet withheld from sailing, they were not able to make pursuit. In this confused fight, (Valer. Max. Plutarch) Scæva a Roman soldier, having press'd too far among the Britains, and beset round, after incredible valour shown single against a multitude, swom back safe to his general ; and in the place that rung with his praises, earnestly besought pardon for his rash adventure against discipline : which modest confessing after no bad event, for such a deed wherein valour and ingenuity so much outweigh'd transgression, easily made amends, and preferr'd him to be a centurion.[1] Cæsar also, (Cæsarib) is brought in by Julian, attributing to himself the honour (if it were at all an honour to that person which he sustain'd) of being the first that left his ship, and took land : but this were to make Cæsar less understand what became him than Scæva. The Britains finding themselves master'd in fight, forthwith send ambassadors to treat of peace ; promising to give hostages, and to be at command. With them Comius of Arras also return'd ; whom hitherto, since his first coming from Cæsar, they had detain'd in prison as a spy ; the blame whereof they lay on the common people, for whose violence and their own imprudence they crave pardon. Cæsar complaining they had first sought peace, and then without cause had begun war, yet content to pardon them, commands hostages ; whereof part they bring in straight, others far up in the country to be sent for, they promise in a few days. Mean while the people disbanded and sent home, many princes and chief men from all parts of the isle submit themselves and their cities to the dispose of Cæsar, who lay then encamp'd, as is thought, on Barham Down. Thus had the Britains made their peace, when suddenly an accident unlook'd for put new counsels into their minds. Four days after the coming of Cæsar, those 18 ships of burthen, which from the upper haven had taken in all the Roman horse, born with a soft wind to the very coast, in sight of the Roman camp, where by a sudden tempest, scatter'd, and driven back, some to the port from whence they loos'd, others down into the west country; who finding there no safety either to land, or to cast anchor, chose rather to commit themselves again to the troubled sea; and as Orosius reports, were most of them cast away. The same night, it being full moon, the gallies left upon dry

---

[1] This Scæva afterwards became more famous for his bravery at the battle of Dyrrachium when he sided with Cæsar against Pompey.

land, were, unaware to the Romans, covered with a spring-tide, and the greater ships that lay off at anchor, torn and beaten with waves, to the great perplexity of Cæsar and his whole army; who now had neither shipping left to convey them back, nor any provision made to stay here, intending to have winter'd in Gallia. All this the Britains well perceiving, and by the compass of his camp, which without baggage appear'd the smaller, guessing at his numbers, consult together, and one by one slily withdrawing from the camp, where they were waiting the conclusion of a peace, resolve to stop all provisions, and to draw out the business till winter. Cæsar though ignorant of what they intended, yet from the condition wherein he was, and their other hostages not sent, suspected what was likely, begins to provide apace: all that might be, against what might happen: lays in corn, and with materials fetch'd from the continent, and what was left of those ships which were past help he repairs the rest. So that now by the incessant labour of his soldiers, all but twelve were again made serviceable. While these things are doing, one of the legions being sent out to forage, as was accustom'd, and no suspicion of war, while some of the Britains were remaining in the country about, others also going and coming freely to the Roman quarters, they who were in station at the camp gates sent speedy word to Cæsar, that from that part of the country, to which the legion went, a greater dust than usual was seen to rise. Cæsar guessing the matter, commands the cohorts of guard to follow him thither, two others to succeed in their stead, the rest all to arm and follow. They had not march'd long, when Cæsar discerns his legion sore over-charg'd: for the Britains not doubting but that their enemies on the morrow would be in that place which only they had left unreap'd of all their harvest, had plac'd an ambush; and while they were disperst and busiest at their labour, set upon them, kill'd some, and routed the rest. The manner of their fight was from a kind of chariots;[1] wherein riding about, and throwing darts, with the clatter of their horse, and of their wheels, they oft-times broke the rank of their enemies; then retreating among the horse, and quitting their chariots, they fought on foot. The charioteers (*Essedarii*) in the meanwhile somewhat aside from the battle, set themselves in such order, that their masters at any time oppress'd with odds, might retire safely thither, having perform'd with one person both the nimble service of a horse-man, and the stedfast duty of a foot soldier. So much they could with their chariots by use, and exercise, as riding on the speed down a steep hill, to stop suddenly, and with a short rein turn swiftly, now running on the beam (*temo*), now on the yoke (*jugum*), then in the seat. With this sort of new skirmishing, the Romans now overmatch'd, and terrify'd, Cæsar with opportune aid appears; for

[1] *Esseda*, a sort of open waggons.

then the Britains make a stand: but he considering that now was not fit time to offer battle, while his men were scarce recover'd of so late a fear, only keeps his ground, and soon after leads back his legions to the camp. Farther action for many days following was hinder'd on both sides by foul weather; in which time the Britains dispatching messengers round about, to how few the Romans were reduc'd, what hope of prize and booty, and now if ever of freeing themselves from the fear of like invasions hereafter, by making these an example, if they could but now uncamp their enemies; at this intimation, multitudes of horse and foot coming down from all parts make towards the Romans. Cæsar foreseeing that the Britains, tho' beaten and put to flight, would easily evade his foot, yet with no more than 30 horse, which Comius had brought over, draws out his men to battle, puts again the Britains to flight, pursues with slaughter; and returning, burns and lays waste all about. Whereupon ambassadors the same day being sent from the Britains to desire peace: Cæsar, as his affairs at present stood, for so great a breach of faith, only imposes on them double the former hostages to be sent after him into Gallia: and because September was nigh half spent, a season not fit to tempt the sea with his weather-beaten fleet, the same night with a fair wind he departs towards Belgia: whither two only of the Britain cities sent hostages, as they promis'd; the rest neglected. But at Rome, when the news came of Cæsar's acts here, whether it were esteem'd a conquest, or a fair escape, supplication of twenty days is decreed by the senate, as either for an exploit done, or a discovery made wherein both Cæsar and the Romans gloried not a little, though it brought no benefit either to him, or the commonwealth.

The winter following, Cæsar, as his custom (Dion) was, going into Italy, when as he saw that most of the Britains regarded not to send their hostages, appoints his legates (Cæs. com. 5.) whom he left in Belgia, to provide what possible shipping they could either build or repair. Low built they were to be, as thereby easier both to fraught, and to hale ashoar; nor needed to be higher, because the tide so often changing, was observ'd to make the billows less in our sea than those in the Mediterranean: broader likewise they were made, for the better transporting of horses, and all other fraughtage, being intended chiefly to that end. These all about 600 in a readiness, with 28 ships of burden, and what with adventurers, and other hulks above 200, Cotta, one of the legates wrote them, as Athenæus affirms, in all 1000, Cæsar from port Iccius,[1] a passage of some 30 mile over, leaving behind him Labienus to guard the haven, and for other supply at need, with five legions, though but 2000 horse, about sun set, hoisting

---

[1] This is the same with Geossoriacum, at this day Bolen, as is prov'd at large by Somner in his discourse de l'ortu Iccio, publish'd by Dr. Gibson, with a dissertation of Du Fresne the same subject.

sail with a slack south-west, at midnight was becalm'd. And finding when it was light, that the whole navy lying on the current, had fallen off from the isle, which now they could descry on their left hand, by the unwearied labour of his soldiers, who refus'd not to tug the oar, and kept course with ships under sail, he bore up (A. C. 52) as near as might be, to the same place where he had landed the year before; where about noon arriving, no enemy could be seen. For the Britains, which in great numbers, as was after known, had been there, at sight of so huge a fleet durst not abide. Cæsar forthwith landing his army, and encamping to his best advantage, some notice being given him by those he took, where to find the enemy, with his whole power, save only ten cohorts, and 300 horse, left to Quintus Atrius for the guard of his ships, about the third watch of the same night marches up to Chilham, twelve mile into the country. And at length by a river commonly thought the Stowre in Kent, espies embattel'd the British forces. They with their horses and chariots advancing to the higher banks, oppose the Romans in their march, and begin the fight; but repuls'd by the Roman cavalry, give back into the woods, to a place notably made strong both by art and nature; which, it seems, had been a fort, or hold of strength rais'd heretofore in times of wars among themselves. For entrance and access on all sides, by the felling of huge trees overthwart one another, was quite barr'd up; and within these Britains did their utmost to keep out the enemy. But the soldiers of the seventh legion locking all their shields together like a roof close over-head, and others raising a mount, without much loss of blood took the place, and drove them all to forsake the woods. Pursuit they made not long, as being through ways unknown; and now evening came on, which they more wisely spent, in chusing out where to pitch and fortifie their camp that night. The next morning Cæsar had but newly sent out his men in three bodies to pursue, and the last no further gone than yet in sight, when horsemen all in post from Quintius Atrius bring word to Cæsar, that almost all his ships in a tempest that night had suffer'd wreck, and lay broken upon the shoar. Cæsar at this news recals his legions, himself in all haste riding back to the sea-side, beheld with his own eyes the ruinous prospect. About forty vessels were sunk and lost, the residue so torn, and shaken, as not to be new rigg'd without much labour. Straight he assembles what number of ship-wrights, either in his own legions or from beyond sea, could be summon'd; appoints Labienus on the Belgian side to build more; and with a dreadful industry of ten days, not respiting his soldiers day or night, drew up all his ships, and entrench'd them round within the circuit of his camp. This done, and leaving to their defence the same strength as before, he returns with his whole forces to the same wood, where he had defeated the Britains: who preventing him with greater powers than before, had now repossess'd themselves of that place, under Cassibelan their chief leader: whose territory from the states bordering on the sea, was divided on the river Thames about 80 mile inward. With him formerly other cities had continual war; but now in the common danger had all made choice of him to be their general. Here the British horse and charioteers meeting with the Roman cavalry, fought stoutly; and at first, something over-match'd, they retreat to the near advantage of their woods and hills, but still follow'd by the Romans, made head again, cut off the forwardest among them, and after some pause, while Cæsar, who thought the day's work had been done, was busied about the entrenching of his camp, march out again, give fierce assault to the very stations of his guards and sentries; and while the main cohorts of two legions, that were sent to the alarm, stood within a small distance of each other, terrify'd at the newness and boldness of their fight, charged back again through the midst, without loss of a man. Of the Romans that day was slain Quintus Laberius Durus, a tribune: the Britains having fought their fill at the very entrance of Cæsar's camp, and sustain'd the resistance of his whole army entrench'd, gave over the assault. Cæsar here acknowledges that the Roman way both of arming and fighting, was not so well fitted against this kind of enemy; for that the foot in heavy armour could not follow their cunning flight, and durst not by ancient discipline stir from their ensign; and the horse alone disjoyn'd from the legions, against a foe that turn'd suddenly upon them, with a mixt encounter both of horse and foot, were in equal danger both following and retiring. Besides their fashion was, not in great bodies, and close order, but in small divisions, and open distances to make their onset; appointing others at certain spaces, now to relieve and bring off the weary, now to succeed and renew the conflict; which argu'd no small experience, and use of arms. Next day the Britains afar off upon the hills begin to shew themselves here and there, and though less boldly than before, to skirmish with the Roman horse. But at noon Cæsar having sent out three legions, and all his horse with Trebonius the legate, to seek fodder, suddenly on all sides they set upon the foragers, and charge up after them to the very legions, and their standards. The Romans with great courage beat them back, and in the chace, being well seconded by the legions, not giving them time either to rally, to stand or to descend from their chariots as they were wont, slew many. From this overthrow, the Britains that dwelt farther off, betook them home; and (Cambden) came no more after that time with so great a power against Cæsar. Whereof advertis'd, he marches onward to the frontiers of Cassibelan, which on this side were bounded by the Thames, not passable except in one place, and that uncouth, about Coway-stakes near Oatlands, as is conjectur'd. Hither coming, he descries on the other side great forces of the enemy plac'd in good array; the bank set all with sharp stakes, others in the bottom, cover'd with water; whereof the marks in Beda's time were to be seen, as he relates. This having learnt by such as were taken, or had run to him, he first commands his horse to pass over, then his foot, who wading up to the neck, went on so resolutely and so fast, that they on the further side not enduring the violence, retreated and fled. Cassibelan no more now in hope to contend for victory, dismissing all but 4000 of those charioteers, through woods and intricate ways attends their motion, where the Romans are to pass, drives all before him; and with continual sallies upon the horse, where they least expected, cutting off some and terrifying others, compels them so close together, as gave them no leave to fetch in prey or booty without ill success. Whereupon Cæsar strictly commanding all not to part from the legions, had nothing left him in his way but empty fields and houses, which he spoil'd and burnt. Meanwhile the Trinobantes,[1] a state or kingdom, and perhaps the greatest then among the Britains, less favouring Cassibelan, sent ambassadors, and yield to Cæsar upon this reason. Immanuentius had been their king: him Cassibelan had slain, and purpos'd the like to Mandubratius his son, wdom Orosius calls Androgorius, Beda, Androgius; but the youth escaping by flight into Gallia, put himself under the protection of Cæsar. These entreat that Mandubratius may be still defended, and sent home to succeed in his father's right. Cæsar sends him, demands forty hostages and provision for his army, which they immediately bring in, and have their confines protected from the soldier. By their example the Cenimagni,[2] Segontiaci,[3] Ancalites,[4] Bibroci,[5] Cassi[6] (so I write them, for the modern names are but guess'd) on like terms make their peace. By them he learns that the town of Cassibelan, suppos'd to be Verulam, was not far distant; fenc'd about with woods and marshes, well stuff'd with men and much cattle. For towns then in Britain were only woody places ditch'd round, and with a mud wall encompass'd against the inrodes of enemies. Thither goes Cæsar with his legions; and though a place of great strength both by art and nature, assaults it in two places. The Britains after some defence, fled out all at another end of the town; in the flight many were taken, many slain, and great store of cattle found there. Cassibelan, for all these losses, yet deserts not himself; nor was yet his authority so much impair'd, but that in Kent, though in a manner possess'd by the enemy, his messengers and

---

[1] They were the ancient inhabitants of Essex and Middlesex.
[2] Thought to be the same with the Iceni.
[3] On the north side of Hampshire, about Alton and Basingstoke.
[4] About Henly in Berks.
[5] About Bray in Berks. Libracte in France is now contracted into Bray. Cambd. Brit.
[6] The Hundred of Caishow in Hertfordshire.

commands find obedience enough to raise all the people. By his direction Cingetorix, Carvilius, Taximagulus, and Segonax, four kings[1] reigning in those countries which lie upon the sea, lead them on to assault that camp wherein the Romans had entrench'd their shipping: but they whom Cæsar left there, issuing out, slew many, and took prisoners Cingetorix a noted leader, without loss of their own. Cassibelan after so many defeats, mov'd especially by revolt of the cities from him, their inconstancy and falshood one to another, uses mediation by Comius of Arras to send ambassadors about treaty of yielding. Cæsar, who had determin'd to winter in the continent, by reason that Gallia was unsettl'd, and not much of the summer now behind, commands him only hostages, and what yearly tribute the island should pay to Rome, forbids him to molest the Trinobantes, or Mandubratius; and with his hostages, and great number of captives he puts to sea, having at twice embark'd his whole army. At his return to Rome, as from a glorious enterprize, he offers to Venus the patroness of his family, a corslet of British pearls. (Pliny.) Howbeit, other ancient writers have spoken more doubtfully of Cæsar's victories here; and that in plain terms he fled from hence; for which the common verse in Lucan, with divers passages here and there in Tacitus is alledg'd. Paulus Orosius, who took what he wrote from a history of Suetonius, now lost, writes, (Oros. lib. 6, cap. 7, and 9), that Cæsar in his first journey, entertain'd with a sharp fight, lost no small number of his foot, and by tempest nigh all his horse. Dion affirms, that once in the second expedition all his foot were routed; Orosius that another time all his horse. The British author, whom I use only then when others are all silent, hath many trivial discourses of Cæsar's being here, which are best omitted. Nor have we more of Cassibelan than what the same story tells, how he warr'd soon after with Androgeus, about his nephew slain by Evelinus, nephew to the other; which business at length compos'd, Cassibelan dies and was buried in York, if the Monmouth book fable not. But at Cæsar's coming hither, such likeliest were the Britains, as the writers of those times and their own actions represent them, in courage and warlike readiness to take advantage by ambush or sudden onset, not inferiour (Dion. Mela. Cæsar,) to the Romans, nor Cassibelan to Cæsar, in weapons, arms, and the skill of encamping. Embattleing, fortifying over-match'd; their weapons were a short spear and light target, a sword also by their side; their fight sometimes in chariots phang'd at the axle with iron sithes, their bodies most part naked, only painted with woad in sundry figures, to seem terrible (Herodian), as they thought, but pursu'd by enemies, not nice of their painting to run into bogs, worse than wild Irish, up to the neck, and there to stay many days, holding a certain (Dion) morsel in their mouths no bigger than a bean, to suffice

[1] Mr. Cambden writes that they were governors of Kent.

hunger; but that receit, and the temperance it taught, is long since unknown among us; their towns and strongholds (Cæsar) were spaces of ground fenc'd about with a ditch, and great trees fell'd overthwart each other; their buildings within were thatch'd houses for themselves and their cattle: in peace, (Strabo), the upland inhabitants, besides hunting, tended their flocks and herds, but with little skill (Dion) of country affairs; the making of cheese they commonly knew not; wool or flax they spun not (Strabo); gardening and planting many of them knew not; cloathing they had none, (Herodian), but what the skins of beasts afforded them, and that not always; yet gallantry they had, painting (Solinus) their own skins with several portraitures of beast, bird or flower, a vanity which hath not yet left us, remov'd only from the skin to the skirt, behung now with as many colour'd ribbons and gewgaws: toward the seaside they till'd the ground, and (Cæsar) liv'd much after the manner of the Gauls their neighbours, or first planters: their money was brazen pieces or iron rings, their best merchandize tin (Tacitus, Diodor. Strab.), the rest trifles of glass, ivory, and such like; yet gems and pearls they had, saith Mela, in some rivers: their ships of light timber wickered with osier between, and cover'd over with leather, serv'd not therefore to transport them far, and their commodities were fetch'd away by foreign merchants: their dealing, saith Diodorus, plain and simple without fraud; their civil government under many princes and states, not confederate (Tacitus) or consulting in common, but mistrustful, and oft-times warring one with the other, which (Mela) gave them up one by one an easie conquest to the Romans: their religion was govern'd by a sort of priests or magicians called Druides from the Greek name of an oak, which tree they had in great reverence, and the misletoe especially growing thereon: Pliny writes them skill'd in magick no less than those of Persia: by their abstaining from a hen, a hare, and a goose, from fish also, saith Dion, and their opinion of the soul's passing after death into other bodies, they may be (Cæsar) thought to have studied Pythagoras; yet philosophers I cannot call them, reported men factious and ambitious, contending sometimes about the arch-priesthood, not without (Cæsar) civil war and slaughter; nor restrain'd they the people under them from a lewd, adulterous and incestuous life, ten or twelve men absurdly against nature, possessing one woman as their common wife, though of nearest kin, mother, daughter, or sister; progenitors not to be glory'd in. But the gospel, not long after preach'd here, abolish'd such impurities, and of the Romans we have cause not to say much worse, than that they beat us into some civility; likely else to have continu'd longer in a barbarous and savage manner of life. After Julius (for Julius before his death tyrannously had made himself emperor of the Roman commonwealth, and was slain in the senate for so doing) he who next obtain'd the empire, Octavianus

Cæsar Augustus, either contemning the island, as Strabo (l. 2) would have us think, whose neither benefit was worth the having, nor enmity worth the fearing; or out of a wholesome state-maxim, as some say, to moderate and bound the empire from growing vast and unwieldy, made no attempt against the Britains: but the truer cause was partly civil war among the Romans, partly other affairs more urging. For about twenty years (A.C. 32, Dion, l. 49.) after, all which time the Britains had liv'd at their own dispose, Augustus in imitation of his uncle Julius, either intending, or seeming to intend an expedition hither, was come into Gallia, when the news of a revolt in Pannonia diverted him: about seven years (A. C. 25. Dion. l. 53. 3925.) after in the same resolution, what with the unsettl'dness of Gallia, and what with embassadors from Britain, which meet him there, he proceeded not. The next year, difference arising about covenants, he was again prevented by other new commotions in Spain. Nevertheless some of the British Potentates omitted not to seek his friendship by gifts offer'd in the capital, and other obsequious addresses; insomuch that the whole island became (Strabo l. 4) even in those days well known to the Romans; too well perhaps for them, who from the knowledge of us, were so like to prove enemies. But as for tribute, the Britains paid none to Augustus, except what easie customs were levy'd on the slight commodities wherewith they traded into Gallia. After Cassibelan, Tenantius the younger son of Lud, according to the Monmouth story was made king. For Androgeus the elder, conceiving himself generally hated, for siding with the Romans, forsook his claim here, and follow'd Cæsar's fortune. This king is recorded just and warlike. His son Kymbeline or Cunobeline succeeding, was brought up, as is said, in the court of Augustus, and with him held friendly correspondencies to the end; was a warlike prince; his chief seat Camalodunum, or Maldon,[1] as by certain of his coins yet to be seen, appears.[2] Tiberius the next emperor, adhering always to the advice of Augustus, and of himself, less caring to extend the bounds of his empire, fought not the Britains: and they as little to incite him, sent home courteously the soldiers of Germanicus, that by shipwreck had been cast on the Britain shore. But Caligula his successor, a wild and dissolute tyrant, having passed the Alps with intent to rob and spoil those provinces, and stirr'd up by Adminius the son of Cunobeline, who by his father banish'd, with a small number fled thither to him, made semblance of marching (Dion. Sueton. Cal. A.D. 40) toward Britain; but being come to the ocean, and there

---

[1] See the British coins publish'd in the late edition of Mr Camden. Tacit an. l. 2.
[2] Coin first stamp'd in Britain in this king's reign, in which time our Saviour Jesus Christ was born; and if we may believe Baronius, was preach'd here by Joseph of Arimathea three years after his crucifixion; which according to William of Malmsbury, in his antiquities of the church of Glastenbury, was in the 63rd year after Christ's passion. This legend is exploded by Archbishop Usher in his antiquities of the British churches, and Bishop Stillingfleet in his Origines Britanicæ.

behaving himself madly and ridiculously, went back the same way; yet sent before him boasting letters to the senate, as if all Britain had been yielded to him. Cunobeline now dead, Adminius the eldest by his father banish'd from his country, and by his own practice against it, from the crown, though by an old coin seeming to have also reign'd; Togodumnus, and Caractacus the two younger, uncertain whether equal or subordinate in power, were (Dion) advanc'd into his place. But through civil discord Bericus (what he was further is not known), with others of his party flying to Rome, persuaded Claudius the emperor to an invasion. Claudius now (A.D. 42) consul the third time, and desirous to do something, whence he might gain the honour of a triumph, at the perswasion of these fugitives, whom the Britains demanding, he had deny'd (Sueton) to render, and they for that cause had deny'd further amity with Rome, make choice of this island for his province: and sends before him Aulus Plautius the Prætor, with this command, if the business grew difficult to give him notice. Plautius with much ado perswaded the legions to move out of Gallia, murmuring that now they must be put to make war beyond the world's end; for so they counted Britain; and what welcome Julius the dictator found there, doubtless they had heard. At last prevail'd with, and hoisting sail from three several ports, lest their landing should in any one place be resisted, meeting cross winds, they were cast back and dishearten'd: till in the night a meteor shooting flames from the east, and, as they fansy'd, directing their course, they took heart again to try the sea, and without opposition landed. For the Britains having heard of their unwillingness to come, had been negligent to provide against them; and retiring to the woods and moors, intended to frustrate, and wear them out with delays, as they had serv'd Cæsar before. Plautius after much trouble to find them out, encountering first with Caractacus, then with Togodumnus, overthrew them; and receiving into conditions part of the Boduni, who then were subject to the Catuellani, and leaving there a garrison, went on toward a river; where the Britains not imagining that Plautius without a bridge could pass, lay on the further side careless and secure. But he sending first the Germans, whose custom was, arm'd as they were, to swim with ease the strongest current, commands them to strike especially at the horses, whereby the chariots, wherein consisted their chief art of fight, became unserviceable. To second them, he sent Vespasian, who in his latter days obtain'd the empire, and Sabinus his brother; who unexpectedly assailing those who were least aware, did much execution. Yet not for this were the Britains dismay'd; but re-uniting the next day fought with such a courage, as made it hard to decide which way hung the victory: till Caius Sidius Geta, at point to have been taken, recover'd himself so valiantly, as brought the day on his side; for which at Rome he received high honours. After this the Britains drew back toward the mouth of Thames, and acquainted with those places, cross'd over, where the Romans following them through bogs, and dangerous flats, hazarded the loss of all. Yet the Germans getting over, and others by a bridge at some place above, fell on them again with sundry alarms and great slaughter; but in the heat of pursuit running themselves again into bogs and mires, lost as many of their own. Upon which ill success, and seeing the Britains more enraged at the death of Togodumnus, who in one of these battles had been slain: Plautius fearing the worst, and glad that he could hold what he held, as was enjoyn'd him, sends to Claudius. He who waited ready with a huge preparation, as if not safe enough amidst the flower of all his Romans, like a great eastern king with arm'd elephants, marches through Gallia. So full of peril was this enterprize esteem'd, as not without all this equipage, and stranger terrors than Roman armies to meet the native and the naked British Valour defending their country. Join'd with Plautius, who encamping on the bank of Thames, attended him, he passes the river. The Britains, who had the courage, but not the wise conduct of old Cassibelan, laying all stratagem aside, in downright manhood scrupled not to affront in open field almost the whole power of the Roman Empire. But overcome and vanquish'd, part by force, others by treaty come in and yield. Claudius therefore, who took Camalonum, the royal seat of Cunobeline, was often by his army saluted Imperator; a military title, which usually they gave their general after any notable exploit; but to others not above once in the same war; as if Claudius by these acts had deserv'd more than the laws of Rome had provided honour to reward. Having therefore disarm'd the Britains, (Dion. l. 62) but remitted the confiscation of their goods, for which they worshipp'd him with (Tacit. an. 14) sacrifice and temple as a god; leaving Plautius to subdue what remain'd, he returns to Rome, from whence he had been absent only six months, and in Britain but sixteen days; sending the news before him of his victories, though in a small part of the island. To whom the senate, as for achievements of highest Merit, decreed excessive honours; Arches, Triumphs, Annual Solemnities, and the Sirname of Britannicus both to him and his son. Suetonius writes, that Claudius found here no resistance, and that all was done without stroke: but this seems not probable. The Monmouth Writer names these two sons of Cunobeline, Guiderius and Arviragus; that Guiderius being slain in fight, Arviragus to conceal it put on his brother's habilliments, and in his person held up the battle to a victory; the rest, as of Hamo the Roman captain, Genuissa the emperor's daughter and such like stuff, is too palpably untrue to be worth rehersing in the midst of truth. Plautius after this, (Suetonius. Claud. 5. 24) employing his fresh forces to conquer on, and quiet the rebelling countries, found work enough to deserve at his return a kind of triumphant riding into the capitol, side by side with the emperor. Vespasian[1] also under Plautius had thirty conflicts with the enemy (Sueton. Vesp. Dion. lib. 60.) in one of which encompass'd, and in great danger, he was valiantly and piously rescu'd by his son Titus : two powerful nations he subdu'd (47) here, above twenty towns and the isle of Wight, for which he received (49) at Rome triumphal ornaments, and other great dignities. For that city in reward of virtue, was ever magnificent ; and long after, when true merit was ceas'd among them, lest any thing resembling virtue should want honour, the same rewards were yet allow'd to the very shadow and ostentation of merit. (50.) Ostorius in the room of Plautius Vice-prætor, met with turbulent affairs: (Tacitus. an. 12.) the Britains not ceasing to vex with inrodes all those countries that were yielded to the Romans ; and now the more eagerly, supposing that the new general acquainted with his army, and on the edge of winter, would not hastily oppose them. But he weighing that first events were most available to breed fear or contempt, with such cohorts as were next at hand, sets out against them : whom having routed, so close he follows, as one who meant not to be every day molested with the cavils of a slight peace, or an embolden'd enemy. Lest they should make head again, he disarms whom he suspects ; and to surround them,[2] places many garrisons upon the rivers of[3] Antona and Sabrina. But the[4] Icenians, a stout people, untouch'd yet by these wars, as having before sought alliance with the Romans, were the first that brook'd not this. By their example others rise ; and in a chosen place, fenc'd with high banks of earth, and narrow lanes to prevent the horse, warily encamp. Ostorius, though yet not strengthen'd with his legions, causes the auxiliar bands, his troops also alighting, to assault the rampart. They within, tho' pester'd with their own number, stood to it like men resolv'd, and in a narrow compass did remarkable deeds. But over-power'd at last, and others by their success quieted, who till then wavered, Ostorius next (Tacit. An. lib. 12. c. 32.) bends his force upon the[5] Cangians, wasting all even to the sea of Ireland, without foe in his way, or them who durst ill handl'd : when the[6] Brigantes attempting new matters, drew him back to settle first what was unsecure behind him. They, of whom the chief were punish'd, the rest forgiven, soon gave over ; but the Silures, no way tractable, were not to be repress'd without a set war. To further this, Camalodunum was planted with a colony of veteran

[1] Afterwards Emperor. [2] See Cambden's Britannia, Eng. edit. p. 432 & 440.
[3] The rivers Severn and Avon.
[4] The Iceni inhabited the counties of Suffolk, Norfolk, Cambridge, and Huntingdon.
[5] The annotator on the Preface to the late Edition of Cambden's Britann. is of opinion, that Somersetshire and North Wiltshire were the country of the Cangi. 'Tis not well known who they were, but probably they inhabited Shropshire and Cheshire, bordering on Wales.
[6] Brigantes, suppos'd to have been the inhabitants of Lancashire, Yorkshire, and the other northern countries.   [7] They inhabited what we now call South Wales.

soldiers to be a firm and ready aid against revolts, and a means to teach the natives Roman law and civility. Cogidunus, also a British king, their fast friend, had (Tacit. Vit. Agric.) to the same intent certain cities given him : a haughty craft, which the Romans us'd, to make kings also the servile agents of enslaving others. But the Silures, hardy of themselves, rely'd more on the valour of Caractacus, whom many doubtful, many prosperous successes had made eminent above all that rul'd in Britain. He adding to his courage policy, and knowing himself to be of strength inferiour, in other advantages the better, makes the seat of his war among the⁷ (Tacit. An. lib. 12. c, 33.) Ordovices, a country wherein all the odds were to his own party, all the difficulties to his enemy. The hills and every access he fortify'd with heaps of stones, and guards of men ; to come at whom a river of unsafe passage must be first waded. The place, as Cambden conjectures, had thence the name of[3] Caer-Caradoc, on the west edge of Shropshire. He himself continually went up and down, animating his officers and leaders, that this was the day, this the field, either to defend their liberty, or to die free ; calling to mind the names of his glorious ancestors, who drove Cæsar the dictator out of Britain, whose valour hitherto had preserv'd them from bondage, their wives and children from dishonour. Inflam'd with these words, they all vow their utmost, with such undaunted resolution as amaz'd the Roman general ; but the soldiers less weighing, because less knowing, clamour'd to be led on against any danger. Ostorius. after wary circumspection, bids them pass the river : the Britains no sooner had them within reach of their arrows, darts and stones, but slew and wounded largely of the Romans. They on the other side closing their ranks, and over head closing their targets, threw down the loose rampiers of the Britains, and pursue them up the hills, both light arm'd, and legions : till what with gauling darts and heavy stroke, the Britains who wore neither helmet nor cuirass to defend them, were at last overcome. This the Romans thought a famous victory ; wherein the wife and daughter of[1] Caractacus were taken, his brothers also reduc'd to obedience ; himself escaping to Cartismandua queen of the Brigantes, against faith given, was to the victors deliver'd bound : having held out against the Romans nine years, saith Tacitus ; but by truer computation[2] seven. Whereby his name was up through all the adjoyning provinces, even to Italy and Rome : many desiring to see who he was that could withstand so many years the Romans puissance : and Cæsar, to extol his own victory, extoll'd the man whom he had

---

[1] The Ordovices possess'd the counties, which now make North Wales.
[2] Caradoc in the British tongue, is suppos'd to be the same with Caractacus in the Latin.
[3] Caractacus king of the Silures was routed by the Romans near Ludlow in Shropshire; Mr. Cambden says this battel was fought Anno 53. Camb. Tit Shrop.
[4] Tacitus in his Annals, lib. 12. cap. 36. writes, 'twas in the seventh year after this war began, that Caractacus was taken.

vanquish'd. Being brought to Rome, the people, as to a solemn spectacle, were call'd together, the emperor's guard stood in arms. In order came first the king's servants, bearing his trophies, won in other wars; next, his brothers, wife, and daughter; last, himself. The behaviour of others through fear was low and degenerate: he only, neither in countenance, word or action submissive, standing at the tribunal of Claudius, briefly spake to this purpose: 'If my mind, Cæsar, had been as moderate in the height of fortune, as my birth and dignity was eminent, I might have come a friend rather than a captive into this city. Nor could'st thou have dislik'd him for a confederate, so noble of descent, and ruling so many nations. My present estate, to me disgraceful, to thee is glorious; I had riches, horses, arms, and men; no wonder then if I contended, not to lose them. But if by fate, yours only must be empire, then of necessity ours among the rest must be subjection. If I sooner had been brought to yield, my misfortune had been less notorious, your conquest had been less renown'd, and in your severest determining of me, both will be soon forgotten. But if you grant that I shall live, by me will live to you for ever that praise which is so near divine, the clemency of a conqueror.' Cæsar mov'd at such a spectacle of fortune, but especially at the nobleness of his bearing it, gave him pardon, and to all the rest. They all unbound, submissively thank him, and did like reverence to Agrippina the emperor's wife, who sat by in state: a new and disdained sight to the manly eyes of Romans, a woman sitting publick in her female pride among ensigns and armed cohorts. To Ostorius, triumph is decreed; and his acts esteemed equal to theirs that brought in bonds to Rome famousest kings. But the same prosperity attended not his latter actions here: for the Silures, whether to revenge their loss of Caractacus, or that they saw Ostorius, as if now all were done, less earnest to restrain them, beset the præfect of his camp, left there with legionary bands to appoint garrisons: And had not speedy aid come in from the neighbouring holds and castles, had cut them all off; notwithstanding which, the Præfect with eight centurions, and many their stoutest men were slain: and upon the neck of this, meeting first with Roman foragers, then with other troops hasting to their relief, utterly foil'd and broke them also. Ostorius sending more after, could hardly stay their flight; till the weighty legions coming on, at first pois'd the battel, at length turn'd the scale, to the Britains without much loss, for by that time it grew night. Then was the war shivered as it were into small frays and bickerings, not unlike sometimes to so many robberies, in woods, at waters, as chance or valour, advice or rashness led them on, commanded or without command. That which most exasperated the Silures, was a report of certain words cast out by the emperor, that he would root them out to the very name. Therefore two cohorts more of auxiliars, by the avarice of their leaders too securely pillaging, they quite intercepted: and bestowing liberally the spoils and captives, whereof they took plenty, drew other countries to join with them. These losses falling so thick upon the Romans, Ostorius with the thought and anguish thereof ended his days: The Britains rejoicing, although no battle, that yet adverse war had worn out so great a soldier. Cæsar in his place ordains Aulus Didius: but ere his coming, tho' much hasten'd, that the province might not want a governor; the Silures had given an overthrow to Manlius Valens with his legion, rumour'd on both sides greater than was true; by the Silures to amate the new general: by him in a double respect, of the more praise if he quell'd them, or the more excuse if he fail'd. Mean time, the Silures forget not to infest the Roman pale with wide excursions; till Didius marching out, kept them somewhat more within bounds. Nor were they long to seek, who after Caractacus should lead them; for (Tac. An. 12.) next to him, in worth and skill of war, Venutius a prince of the Brigantines merited to be their chief. He at first faithful to the Romans, and by them protected, was the husband of Cratismandua queen of the Brigantes, himself perhaps reigning elsewhere. She who had betray'd Caractacus and her country to adorn the triumph of Claudius, thereby grown powerful and gracious with the Romans, presuming on the hire of her treason, deserted her husband; and marrying Vellocatus, one of his squires, confers on him the kingdom also. This deed, so odious and full of infamy, disturb'd the whole state: Venutius with other forces, and the help of her own subjects, who detested the example of so foul a fact, and with the uncomeliness of their subjection to the monarchy of a woman, a piece of manhood not every day to be found among Britains, though she had got by subtle train his brother with many of his kindred into her hands, brought her soon below the confidence of being able to resist longer. When imploring the Roman aid, with much ado, and after many a hard encounter, she escap'd the punishment which was ready to have seiz'd her. Venutius thus debarr'd the authority of ruling his own household, justly turns his anger against the Romans themselves; whose magnanimity, not wont to undertake dishonourable causes, had arrogantly intermeddled in his domestick affairs, to uphold the rebellion of an adultress against her husband. And the kingdom he retain'd against their utmost opposition; and of war gave them their fill; first in a sharp conflict of uncertain event, then against the legion of Cæsus Nasica. Insomuch that Didius growing old, and managing the war by deputies, had work enough to stand on his defence, with the gaining now and then of a small castle. And Nero (for in that part of the isle things continu'd in the same plight (Tacit. Vit. Agric.) to the reign of Vespasian) was minded but for shame to have withdrawn (55. Tac. Hist. 3. Sueton.) the

Roman forces out of Britain : in other parts whereof, about the same time, other things befel. Verannius, whom Nero sent hither to succeed Didius, dying in his first year, saw a few inrodes upon the Silures, left only a great boast behind him, that in two years, had he liv'd, he would have conquer'd all. But Suetonius Paulinus, who next was sent hither, esteem'd a soldier equal to the best in that age, for two years together went on prosperously : both confirming what was got, and subduing onward. At last, over-confident of his present actions, and emulating others, of whose deeds he heard from abroad, marches up as far as Mona, the isle of Anglesey, a populous place. For they, it seems, had both entertain'd fugitives, and given good assistance to the rest that withstood him. He makes him boats with flat bottoms, fitted to the shallows which he expected in that narrow frith : his foot so pass'd over, his horse waded or swam. Thick upon shoar stood several gross bands of men well weapon'd, many women like furies running to and fro in dismal habit, with hair loose about their shoulders, held torches in their hands. The Druids, those were their priests, of whom more in another place, with hands lifted up to heaven, uttering direful prayers, astonish'd the Romans ; who, at so strange a sight stood in amaze, tho' wounded : at length awak'd and encourag'd by their general, not to fear a barbarous and lunatick rout, fall on, and, beat them down scorch'd and rouling in their own fire. Then were they yok'd with garrisons, and the places consecrate to their bloody superstitions destroy'd. For whom they took in war they held it lawful to sacrifice ; and by the entrails of men us'd divination. While thus Paulinus had his thought still fix'd before, to go on winning, his back lay broad open to occasion of losing more behind. For the Britains urg'd and oppress'd with many unsufferable injuries, had all banded themselves to a general revolt. The particular causes are not all written by one author ; Tacitus, (Lib. 12.) who liv'd next those times of any to us extant, writes, that Prasutagus king of the Icenians, abounding in wealth, had left Cæsar coheir with his two daughters ; thereby hoping to have secur'd from all wrong both his kingdom and his house ; which fell out far otherwise. For under colour to oversee and take possession of the emperor's new inheritance, his kingdom became (61) a prey to centurions, his house to ravening officers, his wife Boadicea violated with stripes, his daughters with rape, the wealthiest of his subjects, as it were by the will and testament of their king, thrown out of their estates, his kindred made little better than slaves. The new colony also at Camalodunum took house or land from whom they pleas'd, terming them slaves and vassals ; the soldiers complying with the colony, out of hope hereafter to use the same licence themselves.[1] Moreover the temple erected to

---

[1] Boadicea Queen of the Britains, wars with the Romans.

Claudius, as a badge of their eternal slavery, stood a great eyesore; the priests whereof under pretext of what was due to the religious service, wasted and embezzled each man's substance upon themselves. And Catus Decianus, the procurator, endeavour'd to bring all their goods under the compass of a new confiscation, by disavowing the remitment (Dion. l. 62.) of Claudius. Lastly, Seneca, in his books, a philosopher, having drawn the Britains unwillingly to borrow of him vast sums upon fair promises of easie loan, and for repayment to take their own time, on a sudden compels them to pay in all at once with great extortion. Thus provok'd by heaviest sufferings, and thus invited by opportunities in the absence of Paulinus, the Icenians, and by their example the Trinobantes, and as many else as hated servitude, rise (Tac. in Vis. Agr. cap. 14.) up in arms. Of these ensuing troubles many foregoing signs appear'd: the image of victory at Camalodunum fell down of its self, with her face turn'd as it were to the Britons; certain women, in a kind of extasie, foretold of calamities to come; in the counsel-house were heard by night barbarous noises; in the theatre hideous howlings; in the creek horrid sights, betokening the destruction of that colony; hereto the ocean seeming of a bloody hue, and humane shapes, at a low ebb left imprinted on the sand, wrought in the Britains new courage, in the Romans unwonted fears. Camalodunum, where the Romans had seated themselves to dwell pleasantly, rather than defensively, was not fortify'd: against that therefore the Britains make first assault. The soldiers within were not very many. Decianus, the procurator, could send them but two hundred, those ill arm'd: and through the treachery of some among them, who secretly favour'd the insurrection, they had deferr'd both to entrench and to send out such as bore not arms; such as did, flying to the temple, which on the second day was forcibly taken, were put all to the sword, the temple made a heap, the rest rifled and burnt. Petilius Cerealls coming to his succour, is in his way met, and overthrown, his whole legion cut to pieces; he with his horse hardly escaping to the Roman camp. Decianus, whose rapine was the cause of all this, fled into Gallia. But Suetonius at these tidings not dismay'd, through the midst of his enemy's country, marches to London (though not term'd a colony, yet full of Roman inhabitants, and for the frequency of trade and other commodities, a town even then of principal note) with purpose to have made there the seat of war. But considering the smallness of his numbers, and the late rashness of Petilius, he chooses rather with the loss of one town to save the rest. Nor was he flexible to any prayers or weeping of them that besought him to tarry there; but taking with him such as were willing, gave signal to depart; they, who through weakness of sex or age, or love of the place, went not along, perish'd by the enemy; so did Verulam, a Roman free town. For the Britains omitting forts and castles, flew thither first where richest booty, and the hope of pillaging toal'd them on. In this massacree, about seventy thousand Romans, and their associates, in the places above-mention'd, of a certain, lost their lives. None might be spar'd, none ransom'd, but tasted all either a present or a lingring death; no cruelty that either outrage, or the insolence of success put into their heads, was (Dion. l. 62.) left unacted. The Romans, wives and virgins hang'd up all naked, had their breasts cut off, and sow'd to their mouths; that in the grimness of death they might seem to eat their own flesh; while the Britons fell to feasting and carousing in the temple of Andate their Goddess of Victory. Suetonius adding to his legion (the 14th) other old officers and soldiers thereabout, which gather'd to him, were near upon ten thousand; and purposing with those not to defer battle, had chosen a place narrow, and not to be overwing'd, on his rear a wood; being well inform'd, that his enemies were all in front on a plain unapt for ambush: the legionaries stood thick in order, impal'd with light-arm'd; the horse on either wing. The Britains in companies and squadrons were everywhere shouting and swarming, such a multitude as at other time never; no less reckon'd than two hundred and thirty thousand, so fierce and confident of victory, that their wives also came in waggons to sit and behold the sport, as they made full account, of killing Romans: a folly doubtless for the serious Romans to smile at, as a sure token of prospering that day: a woman also was their commander in chief. For Boadicea and her daughters ride about in a chariot, telling the tall champions, as a great encouragement, that with the Britains it was usual for women to be their leaders. A deal of other fondness they put into her mouth, not worth recital; how she was lash'd, how her daughters were handled, things worthier silence, retirement, and a veil, than for a woman to repeat, as done to her own person, or to hear repeated before an host of men. The Greek Historian (Dion.) sets her in the field on a high heap of turves, in a loose-body'd gown declaiming, a spear in her hand, a hare in her bosom, which after a long circumlocution she was to let slip among them for luck's sake; then praying to Andate, the British goddess, to talk again as fondly as before. And this they do out of a vanity, hoping to embelish and set out their history with the strangeness of our manners; not caring in the mean while to brand us with the rankest note of barbarism, as if in Britain women were men and men women. I affect not set speeches in a history, unless known for certain to have been so spoken in effect as they were written; nor then, unless worth rehearsal; and to invent such, though eloquently, as some historians have done, is an abuse of posterity, raising, in them that read, other conceptions of those times and persons than were true,

48 DEFEAT AND DEATH OF BOADICEA—SLAUGHTER OF HER PEOPLE.

Much less therefore do I purpose here or elsewhere to copy out tedious orations without decorum, though in their authors compos'd ready to my hand. Hitherto what we have heard of Cassibelan, Togadumnus, Venusius, and Caractacus, hath been full of magnanimity, soberness, and martial skill: but the truth is, that in this battle, and whole business, the Britains never more plainly manifested themselves to be right Barbarians; no rule, no foresight, no forecast, experience or estimation, either of themselves, or of their enemies: such confusion, such impotence, as seem'd likest not to a war, but to the wild hurry of a distracted woman, with as mad a crew at her heels. Therefore Suetonius contemning their unruly noises, and fierce looks, heartens his men but to stand close a while, and strike manfully this headless rabble that stood nearest, the rest would be a purchase rather than a toil. And so it fell out; for the legion, when they saw their time, bursting out like a violent wedge, quickly broke and dissipated what oppos'd them; all else held only out their necks to the slayer, for their own carts and waggons were so plac'd by themselves, as left them but little room to escape between. The Romans slew all; men, women, and the very drawing horses lay heap'd along the field, in a gory mixture of slaughter. About four-score thousand Britains are said to have been slain on the place; of the enemy scarce four hundred, and not many more wounded. Boadicea posyn'd her self, or, as others say, sicken'd and dy'd. She[1] was of stature big and tall, of vissage grim and stern, harsh of voice, her hair of bright colour, flowing down to her hips; she wore a plaited garment of divers colours, with a great golden chain, button'd over all a thick robe. Gildas calls her the crafty lioness, and leaves an ill fame upon her doings. Dion sets down otherwise the order of this fight, and that the field was not won without much difficulty, nor without intention of the Britains to give another battle, had not the death of Boadicea come between. Howbeit Suetonius, to preserve discipline, and to dispatch the relicks of war, lodg'd with all his army in the open field; which was supply'd out of Germany with a thousand horse and ten thousand foot; thence dispers'd to winter, and with incursions to waste those countries that stood out. But to the Britains famine was a worse affliction; having left off, during this uproar, to till the ground, and made reckoning to serve themselves on the provisions of their enemy. Nevertheless those nations, that were yet untam'd, hearing of some discord risen between Suetonius and the new procurator Classicianus, were brought but slowly to terms of peace; and the rigour us'd by Suetonius on them that yielded, taught them the better course to stand on their defence. For it is certain, that Suetonius, though else a worthy man (Tacit. Vit. Agric.), over-

[1] A full account of this war may be found in Tacitus, Annals lib. 14. cap. 31 to 37. and in his Vit. Agr. cap. 16.

proud of his victory, gave too much way to his anger against the Britains. Classician therefore sending such word to Rome, that these severe proceedings would beget an endless war; Polycletus,[1] no Roman, but a courtier, was sent by Nero to examine how things went. He admonishing Suetonius to use more mildness, aw'd the army, and to the Britains gave matter of laughter. Who so much even till then were nurs'd up in their native liberty, as to wonder that so great a general with his whole army should be at the rebuke and ordering of a court servitor. But Suetonius a while after having lost a few galleys on the shoar, was bid resign his command to Petronius Turpilianus, who not provoking the Britains, nor by them provok'd, was thought to have pretended the love of peace to what indeed was his love of ease and sloth. Trebellius Maximus follow'd his steps, usurping the name of gentle government to any remissness or neglect of discipline; which brought in first licence, next disobedience into his camp; incens'd against him, partly for his covetousness, partly by the incitement of Roscius Cœlius legate of a legion; with whom formerly disagreeing, now that civil war began in the empire, he fell to open discord; charging (Tacit. Hist. 8. 1. & vit. Agric.) him with disorder and sedition, and him Cœlius with peeling and defrauding the legions of their pay; insomuch that Trebellius hated and deserted of the soldiers, was content a while to govern by a base entreaty, and forc'd at length to fly the land. Which notwithstanding remain'd (69) in good quiet, govern'd by Cœlius, and the other legate of a legion, both faithful to Vitellius then emperor; who sent hither (Tacit. Hist. 2. & vit. Agric. 70) Vectius Bolanus; under whose lenity, though not tainted with other fault, against the Britains nothing was done, nor in their own discipline reform'd. Petilius Cercalis[2] by appointment of Vespasian succeeding, had to do with the populous Brigantines in many battles, and some of those, not unbloody. For as we heard before, it was Venusius who even to these times (Calvis, Tacit. Hist. 3, and vit. Agric. cap. 17) held them tack, both himself remaining to the end unvanquish'd, and some part of his country not so much as reach'd. It appears also by several passages in the histories of Tacitus, that no small number of British forces were commanded over sea the year before to serve in those bloody wars between Otho and Vitellius, Vitellius and Vespasian contending for the empire. To Cercalis succeeded (79) Julius Frontinus in the government of Britain, who by taming the Silures, a people warlike and strongly inhabiting, augmented much his reputation. But Julius Agricola,[3] whom Vespasian in his last year sent hither, train'd up from his youth in the British wars, extended with victories the Roman limit beyond all his predecessors. His coming was in the

[1] Nero's Freed Man. [2] One of consular dignity.
[3] Cornelius Tacitus, who wrote the life of Agricola, marry'd his daughter.

midst of summer; and the Ordovices to welcome the new general, had hewn in pieces a whole squadron of horse, which lay upon their bounds, few escaping. Agricola, who perceiv'd that the noise of this defeat had also in the province desirous of novelty, stirr'd up new expectations, resolves to be beforehand with the danger: and drawing together the choice of his legions with a competent number of auxiliars, not being met by the Ordovices, who kept the hills, himself in the head of his men hunts them up and down through difficult places, almost to the final extirpating of that whole nation. With the same current of success, what Paulinus had left unfinish'd he conquers in the Isle of Mona: for the islanders altogether fearless of his approach, whom they knew to have no shipping, when they saw themselves invaded on a sudden by the Auxiliars, whose country use had taught them to swim over with horse and arms, were compell'd to yield. This gain'd Agricola much opinion; who at his very entrance, a time which others bestow'd of course in hearing compliments and gratulations, had made such early progress into laborious and hardest enterprises. But by far not so famous was Agricola in bringing war to a speedy end, as in cutting off the causes from whence war arises. For he knowing that the end of war was not to make way for injuries in peace, began reformation from his own house; permitted not his attendants and followers to sway, or have to do at all in publick affairs: lays on with equality the proportions of corn and tribute that were impos'd; takes off exactions and the fees of encroaching officers, heavier than the tribute itself. For the countries had been compelled before, to sit and wait the opening of publick granaries, and both to sell and buy their corn at what rate the publicans thought fit; the purveyors also commanding when they pleas'd to bring it in, not to the nearest, but still to the remotest places, either by the compounding of such as would be excus'd, or by causing a dearth, where none was, made a particular gain. These grievances and the like, he in the time of peace removing, brought peace into some credit; which before, since the Romans coming, had as ill a name as war. The summer (80) following Titus then emperor, he so continually with inrodes disquieted the enemy over all the isle, and after terror so allur'd them with his gentle demeanour, that many cities which till that time would not bend, gave hostages, admitted garrisons, and came in voluntarily. The winter he spent all in worthy actions; teaching and promoting like a publick father, the institutes and customs of civil life. The inhabitants rude and scatter'd, and by that the proner to war, he so persuaded as to build houses, temples, and seats of justice; and by praising the forward, quick'ning the slow, assisting all, turn'd the name of necessity into an emulation. He caus'd moreover the noblemen's sons to be bred up in liberal arts; and by preferring the wits of Britain, before the studies of Gallia, brought them to affect the Latin eloquence, who before hated the language. Then were the Roman fashions imitated, and the gown; after a while the incitements also and materials of vice and voluptuous life, proud buildings, baths, and the elegance of banqueting[1]; which the foolisher sort call'd civility, but was indeed a secret art to prepare them for bondage. Spring appearing, he took the field, and with a prosperous expedition wasted as far northward as the frith of Taus all that obey'd not; with such a terror, as he went, that the Roman army, though much hinder'd by tempestuous weather, had the leisure to build forts and castles where they pleas'd, none daring to oppose them. Besides, Agricola had this excellence in him, so providently to chuse his places where to fortifie, as not another general then alive. No sconce, or fortress of his raising was ever known either to have been forc'd, or yielded up, or quitted. Out of these impregnable by siege, or in that case duely reliev'd, with continual irruptions he so prevail'd, that the enemy, whose manner was in winter to regain what in summer he had lost, was now alike in both seasons kept short, and straiten'd. For these exploits, then esteem'd so great and honourable (Dion. l. 66), Titus in whose reign they were achiev'd was the fifteenth time saluted Imperator; and of him Agricola receiv'd triumphal honours. The fourth summer, Domitian then ruling the empire, he spent in settling and confirming what the year before he had travail'd over with a running conquest: and had the valour of his soldiers been answerable, he had reach'd that year, as was thought, the utmost bounds of Britain. For Glota, and Bodotria, now Dunbritton, and the Frith of Edinborough; two opposite arms of the sea, divided only by a neck of land, and all the creeks and inlets on this side, were held by the Romans, and the enemy driven as it were into another island. In his fifth year (83) he pass'd over into the Orcades, as we may probably guess, and other Scotch isles: discovering and subduing nations till then unknown. He gain'd also with his forces that part of Britain which faces Ireland, as aiming also to conquer that island; where one of the Irish kings driven out by civil wars, coming to him, he both gladly receiv'd, and retain'd him as against a fit time. The summer ensuing on, mistrust that the nations beyond Bodotria would generally rise, and foreclay the passages by land, he caus'd his fleet, making a great shew, to bear along the coast, and up the friths and harbours; joining most commonly at night on the same shoar both land and sea forces, with mutual shouts and loud greetings. At sight whereof the Britains, not wont to see their sea so ridden, were much daunted. Howbeit, the Caledonians with great preparation, and by rumour, as of things unknown, much greater, taking arms, and of their own accord beginning war by the assault of sundry castles, sent back some of their fear to the Romans themselves: and there were of the commanders,

[1] *Tac. Quæ res Pars Servitutis erat.*

who cloaking their fear under shew of sage advice, counsell'd the general to retreat back on this side Bodotria. He in the meanwhile having intelligence, that the enemy would fall on in many bodies, divided also his army into three parts. Which advantage the Britains also spying, and on a sudden uniting what before they had disjoyn'd, assail by night with all their forces that part of the Roman army, which they knew to be the weakest; and breaking in upon the camp surpriz'd between sleep and fear, had begun some execution. When Agricola, who had learnt what way the enemies took, and follow'd them with all speed, sending before him the lightest of his horse and foot to charge them behind, the rest as they came on to affright them with clamour, so ply'd them without respite, that by approach of day the Roman ensigns glittering all about, had encompass'd the Britains: who now after a sharp fight in the very ports of the camp, betook them to their wonted refuge, the woods and fens, pursu'd a while by the Romans, that day else in all appearance had ended the war. The legions re-incourag'd by this event, they also now boasting, who but lately trembl'd, cry all to be led on as far as there was British ground. The Britains also not acknowledging the loss of that day to Roman valour, but to the policy of their captain, abated nothing of their stoutness, but arming their youth, conveying their wives and children to places of safety, in frequent assemblies, and by solemn covenants bound themselves to mutual assistance against the common enemy. About the same time (Dion. l. 66) a cohort of Germans having slain their centurion with other Roman officers in a mutiny, and for fear of punishment fled a shipboard, launch'd forth in three light gallies without pilot: and by tide or weather carried round about the coast, using piracy where they landed, while their ships held out, and as their skill serv'd them, with various fortune, were the first discoverers to the Romans that Britain was an island. The following summer (85), Agricola having before sent his navy to hover on the coast, and with sundry and uncertain landings to divert and disunite the Britains, himself with a power best appointed for expedition, wherein also were many Britains, whom he had long try'd both valiant and faithful, marches onward to the mountain Grampius,[1] where the British, above 30,000, were now lodg'd, and still increasing: for neither would their old men, so many as were yet vigorous and lusty, be left at home, long practis'd in war, and every one adorn'd with some badge, or cognisance of his warlike deeds long ago. Of whom Galgacus,[2] both by birth and merit the prime leader, to their courage, though of itself hot and violent, is by his rough oratory, in detestation of servitude and the Roman yoke, said to have added much more eagerness of fight; testified by their shouts and barbarous applauses. As much did on

---

[1] The Grainsbrane Hill in the county of Mar and other counties in Scotland.
[2] Known in the Scottish Histories by the name of Corbred II.

the other side Agricola exhort his soldiers to victory and glory: as much the soldiers by his firm and well grounded exhortations were all on fire to the onset. But first he orders them in this sort. Of 8,000 auxiliar foot he makes his middle ward, on the wings 3,000 horse, the legions as a reserve, stood in array before the camp; either to seize the victory won without their own hazard, or to keep the battle if it should need. The British powers on the hill side, as might best serve for shew and terrour, stood in their battalions; the first on even ground, the next rising behind, as the hill ascended. The field between rung with the noise of horsemen and chariots ranging up and down. Agricola doubting to be over-wing'd, stretches out his front, though somewhat with the thinnest, insomuch that many advis'd to bring up the legions; yet he not altering, alights from his horse, and stands on foot before the ensigns. The fight began aloof, and the Britains had a certain skill with their broad swashing swords and short bucklers either to strike aside, or to bear off the darts of their enemies; and withal to send back showers of their own. Until Agricola discerning that those little targets and unwieldy glaves ill pointed, would soon become ridiculous against the thrust and close, commanded three Batavian cohorts, and two of the Tungrians exercis'd and arm'd for close fight, to draw up, and come to handy strokes. The Batavians, as they were commanded, running in upon them, now with their long tucks thrusting at the face, now their piked targets bearing them down, had made good riddance of them that stood below; and for hast omitting farther execution, began apace to advance up hill, seconded now by all the other cohorts. Meanwhile the horsemen fly, the charioteers mix themselves to fight among the foot; where many of their horse also fall'n in disorderly, were now more a mischief to their own, than before a terror to their enemies. The battle was a confus'd heap; the ground unequal; men, horses, chariots crowded pelmel; sometimes in little room, by and by in large, fighting, rushing, felling, over-bearing, over-turning. They on the hill, which were not yet come to blows, perceiving the fewness of their enemies came down amain; and had enclos'd the Romans unawares behind, but that Agricola with a strong body of horse, which he reserv'd for such a purpose, repell'd them back as fast: and others drawn off the front, were commanded to wheel about and charge them on the backs. Then were the Romans clearly masters, they follow, they wound, they take, and to take more, kill whom they take: the Britains in whole troops with weapons in their hands, one while flying the pursuer, anon without weapons desperately running upon the slayer. But all of them, when once they got the woods to their shelter, with fresh boldness made head again, and the forwardest on a sudden they turn'd and slew, the rest so hamper'd, as had not Agricola, who was everywhere at hand, sent out his readiest cohorts, with part of his horse to alight and scower the woods, they had receiv'd a foil in the midst of victory; but following with a close and orderly pursuit, the Britains fled again, and were totally scatter'd; till night and weariness ended the chase. And of them that day 10,000 fell; of the Romans 340, among whom Aulus Atticus the leader of a cohort; carried with heat of youth and the fierceness of his horse too far on. The Romans jocond of this victory, and the spoil they got, spent the night; the vanquished wandring about the field, both men and women, some lamenting, some calling their lost friends, or carrying off their wounded; others forsaking, some burning their own houses; and it was certain enough that there were who with a stern compassion laid violent hands on their wives and children to prevent the more violent hands of hostile injury. Next day appearing manifest more plainly the greatness of their loss receiv'd; everywhere silence, desolation, houses burning afar off, not a man seen, and fled and doubtful whither: such words the scouts bringing in from all parts, and the summer now spent, not fit season to disperse a war, the Roman general leads his army among the Horestians (Highlanders);[1] by whom hostages being given, he commands his admiral with a sufficient navy to sail round the coast of Britain: himself with slow marches, that his delay in passing might serve to awe those new conquer'd nations, bestows his army in their winter-quarters. The fleet also having fetch'd a prosperous and speedy compass about the isle (Cambden. Juvenal, Sat. 2), put in at the haven Trutulensis, now Richborrow near Sandwich, from whence it first set out: and now likeliest, if not two years before (Eutrop. l. 7), as was mention'd, the Romans might discover and subdue the isles of Orkney; which others with less reason following Eusebius and Orosius, attribute to the deeds of Claudius. These perpetual exploits abroad won him wide fame; with Domitian, under whom great virtue was as punishable (Dion. l. 66), as open crime, won him hatred. For he maligning the renown of these his acts, in shew decreed him honours, in secret devis'd his ruin. Agricola therefore commanded (86) home for doing too much of what he was sent to do, left the province to his successor quiet and secure.[2] Whether he, as is conjectured, were Salustius Lucullus,[3] or before him some other, for Suetonius only

[1] These people have been plac'd about Eskdale, but the name does better answer the Mountaneers, or Highlanders; and Tacitus's relation of the matters of fact, agrees best to those people.
[2] The tyrant Domitian was so jealous of Agricola's glory, that he order'd him to make his entry into Rome at his return by night, that he might not receive those honours the citizens were ready to pay him.
[3] Salustius Lucullus was kill'd by Domitian, for calling his spears Lucullians.

Regem aliquem capies aut de Temone Brittanno   Exidet Arviragus —
— See the mighty ocean, see   He cries of some illustrious victory:
Some captive king thee his new lord shall own,
Or from his British chariot headlong thrown,
The proud Arviragus come humbling down.

The poet supposes this speech made by Fabricius Veien to flatter the emperor Domitian.

names him legate (87) of Britain under Domitian; but farther of him, or ought else done here until the time of Hadrian, is no where plainly to be found. Some gather by a preface in Tacitus to the book of his histories, that what Agricola won here, was soon after by Domitian either through want of valour lost, or through envy neglected. And Juvenal the poet speaks of Arviragus[1] in these days, and not before, king of Britain: who stood so well in his resistance, as not only to be talk'd of at Rome, but to be held matter of a glorious triumph, if Domitian could take him captive, or overcome him. Then also Claudia Rufina, the daughter of a Britain, and wife of Prudence a Roman senator, liv'd at Rome; famous by the verse of Martial for beauty, wit and learning. The next we hear of Britain, is that when Trajan was emperor, it revolted, and was subdu'd. Under Hadrian, Julius Severus, saith Dion, govern'd the island, a prime soldier of that age, but he being call'd away to suppress the Jews then in tumult, left things at such pass, as caus'd the emperor in person to take (122) a journey hither; where many things he reform'd, and, as Augustus and Tiberius counsell'd, to gird the empire within moderate bounds, he rais'd a wall with great stakes driven in deep, and fasten'd together, in a manner of a strong mound, eighty miles in length, to divide what was Roman from Barbarian: no ancient author names the place, but old inscriptions, and ruin itself yet testifies where it went along between Solway Frith, by Carlisle, and the mouth of Tine. Hadrian having quieted the island, took it for honour to be titl'd on his coin, the restorer of Britain. In his time also Priscus Licinius, as appears (Cambden) by an old inscription, was lieutenant here. Antonnius Pius reigning, the Brigantes ever least patient of foreign servitude, breaking in upon Genounia (which Cambden guesses to be Guinethia or North-Wales) part of the Roman province, were with the loss of much territory driven back by Lollius Urbicus, who drew another wall of turves (144. Graham's Dike), in likelihood much beyond the former, and as Cambden proves, between the Frith of Dunbritton, and of Edenborough, to hedge out incursions from the north. And Seius Saturninus, as is collected from the digest, had charge here of the Roman navy. With like success did Marcus Aurelius, next emperor, by his legate Calphurnius Agricola, finish (162. Digest. l. 36) here a new war: Commodius after him obtaining the empire in his time,[2] as among so many different accounts may seem most probable, Lucius a suppos'd (Beda) king in some part of Britain, the first of any king in Europe, that we read of, receiv'd the christian faith, and this nation the first by publick authority profess'd it: a high and singular grace from above, if sincerity and perseverance went along, otherwise an empty boast, and to be

[1] Arviragus dy'd, says Geoffrey, about the end of Domitian's reign, and was succeeded by his son Marius or Meurig, as the British historians call him. He is mention'd also by William of Malmsbury long before Geoffrey wrote.
All the circumstances of that story are fully discuss'd by the learned bishop of Worcester, in his Origines Brittannicæ, p. 67. &c. See also Bishop Usher's Primordia, p. 19, 23, &c.

fear'd the verify of that true sentence, the first shall be last. And indeed the praise of this action is more proper to king Lucius, than common to the nation; whose first professing by publick authority was no real commendation of their true faith; which had appear'd more sincere and praise-worthy, whether in this or other nation, first profess'd without publick authority, or against it, might else have been but outward conformity. Lucius in our Monmouth story is made the second by descent from Marius. Marius, the son of Arviragus, is there said to have overthrown the Picts, then first coming out of Scythia, slain Rodoric their king; and in sign of victory to have set up a monument of stone in the country, since call'd Westmaria; but these things have no foundation. Coilus, the son of Marius, all his reign, which was just and peaceable, holding great amity with the Romans, left it hereditary to Lucius. He (if Beda err not, living near five hundred years after, yet our antientest author of this report) sent (181) to Eleutherius, the bishop of Rome, an improbable letter, as some of the contents discover, desiring that by his appointment he and his people might receive christianity. From whom two religious doctors, nam'd in our chronicles Faganus and Deruvianus, forthwith sent (198) are said (Nennius) to have converted and baptized well nigh the whole nation: thence Lucius to have had the sirname of Lavermaur, that is to say, Great Light. Nor yet then first was the christian faith here known, but even from the latter days of Tiberius, as Gildas confidently affirms, taught and propagated, and as some say by Simon Zelotes, as others by Joseph of Arimathea,[1] Barnabas, Paul, Peter, and their prime disciples. But of these matters, variously written and believ'd, ecclesiastick historians can best determine: as the best of them do, with little credit given to the particulars of such uncertain relations.[2] As for Lucius, they (Geoff. Mon.) write, that after a long reign he was buried at Glocester; but dying without issue, left the kingdom in great commotion. By truer testimony (Dion. l. 72) we find, that the greatest war, which in those days busy'd Commodus, was in this island. For the nations northward, notwithstanding the wall rais'd to keep them out, breaking in upon the Roman province, wasted wide; and both the army, and the leader that came against them, wholly routed and destroy'd; which put the emperor in such a fear, as to dispatch (183) hither one of his best commanders, Ulpius Marcellus. He, a man endu'd with all nobleness of mind, frugal, temperate, mild and magnanimous, in war bold and watchful, invincible against lucre, and the assault of bribes, what with his valour,

[1] Bishop Stillingfleet has made it very probable, that a church was planted here in the apostles' times, by St. Paul himself. *Viz.* p. 35. Orig. Brit.
[2] Archbishop Usher in his Accl. Brit. Antiq. and bishop Stillingfleet in his Orig. Brit. allow the tradition of king Lucius: the archbishop says, that he had seen two coins, one of gold, and the other of silver, with the image of a king on them, and the letters L. U C, with a cross, which is plain proof, that there was such a king, and that he was a christian; but over what part of Britain he reign'd, is uncertain.

and these his other virtues, quickly ended this war that look'd so dangerous, and had himself like to have been ended by the peace he brought home, for presuming to be so worthy and so good under the envy of so worthless and so bad an emperor. After whose departure the Roman legions fell to sedition among themselves; 1500 of them went (Lamprid. in Comm. p. 273. 186) to Rome in name of the rest, and were so terrible to Commodus himself, as that to please them he put to death Perennius the captain of his guard. Notwithstanding which compliance they endeavour'd here to set up another emperor against him; and Helvius Pertinax[1] who succeeded governor, found it a work so difficult to appease them, that once in a mutiny he was left for dead among many slain; and was fain at length to seek a dismission from his charge. After him Clodius Albinus took the government; but he, for having to the soldiers made an oration against monarchy, by the appointment of Commodus was (193) bid resign to Junius Severus. But Albinus in those troublesome times ensuing, under a short reign of Pertinax and Didius Julianus, found means to keep in his hands the government of Britain; although Septinius Severus, who next held the empire, sent hither Heraclitus to displace him; but in vain, for Albinus, with all the British powers, and those of Gallia, met Severus about Lyons in France, and fought a bloody battle (Herod. l. 3) with him for the empire, though at last vanquish'd and slain.[2] The government of Britain, Severus divided between two deputies; till then one legate was thought sufficient; the north he committed to Virius Lupus. Where the Meatæ rising in arms, and the Caledonians, though they had promis'd the contrary to Lupus, preparing to defend them, so hard beset, he was compell'd (Digest. l. 28. tit. 6. Dion.) to buy his peace, and a few of prisoners with great sums of money. But hearing that Severus had now brought to an end his other wars, he writes (Herod. l. 3.) him plainly the state of things here, that the Britains of the north made war upon him, broke into the province, and harrass'd all the countries nigh them, that there needed suddenly either more aid, or himself in person. Severus, though now much weaken'd with age and the gout, yet desirous to leave some memorial of his warlike achievements here, as he had done in other places, and besides to withdraw by this means his two sons[3] from the pleasures of Rome, and his soldiers from idleness, with a mighty power, far sooner than could be expected, arrives (208) in Britain. The northern people much daunted with the report of so great forces brought over with him, and yet more preparing, send ambassadors to treat of peace, and to excuse their

---

[1] Pertinax was afterwards proclaimed emperor.
[2] His body was sent to Rome by Severus's order, to be set over the place of publick execution; and afterwards 'twas suffer'd to lie before the Pretorium till it stunk, and was devour'd by d_gs. [3] Bassianus and Geta.

former doings. The emperor now loth to return home without some memorable thing, whereby he might assume to his other titles the addition of Britannicus, delays his answer, and quickens his preparations; till in the end, when all things were in readiness to follow them, they are dismiss'd without effect. His principal care was to have many bridges laid over bogs and rotten moors, that his soldiers might have to fight on sure footing. For it seems, through lack of tillage, the northern parts were then, as Ireland is at this day; and the inhabitants in like manner wonted to retire, and defend themselves in such watry places half naked. He also being past Hadrian's wall, cut down woods, made way through hills (209), fasten'd and fill'd up unsound and plashy fens. Notwithstanding all this industry us'd, the enemy kept himself so cunningly within his best advantages, and seldom appearing, so opportunely found his times to make irruption upon the Romans, when they were most in straights and difficulties, sometimes training them on with a few cattle turn'd out, and drawn within ambush, cruelly handling them, that many a time enclos'd in the midst of sloughs and quagmires, they chose (Dion.) rather themselves to kill such as were faint and could not shift away, than leave them there a prey to the Caledonians. Thus lost Severus, and by sickness in those noisome places, no less than 50,000 men: and yet desisted not, though for weakness carry'd in a litter, till he had march'd through with his army to the utmost northern verge of the isle; and the Britains offering peace were compell'd to lose much of their country, not before subject to the Romans. Severus on the frontiers of what he had firmly conquer'd builds (210) a wall across the island from sea to sea; which one author judges the most magnificent of all his other deeds; and that he thence receiv'd the stile of Britannicus; in length[1] 132 miles. Orosius adds it fortifi'd (210) with a deep trench, and between certain spaces many towers or battlements. The place whereof some will have to be in Scotland,[1] the same (Eutropii Pean. Oros. l. 7) which Lollius Urbicus had wall'd before. Others affirm (Cassidor) it only Hadrian's work re-edified; both (Chro. Buchanan) plead authorities and the ancient tract yet visible: but this I leave among the studious of these antiquities to be discuss'd more at large. While peace held, the empress Julia meeting on a time certain British ladies, and discoursing with the wife of Argentocoxus a Caledonian, cast out a scoff against the looseness of our island women; whose manner then was to use promiscuously the company of divers men. Whom straight the British woman boldly thus answer'd: Much better do we Britains fulfil the work of nature, than you Romans; we with the best

---

[1] So Paulus Orosius; but Spartianus more truly, 80 or 82 miles; as is clearly prov'd in the new edition of Cambden, p. 845. and in archbishop Usher's Antiq. Eccl. Brit. cap. 4.
[2] Buchanan of that opinion, in which he is not only oppos'd by our English historians, but by Fordun and Major his own countrymen.

men accustom openly; you with the basest commit private adulteries. Whether she thought this answer might serve to justifie the practice of her country, as when vices are compar'd, the greater seems to justifie the less, or whether the law and custom wherein she was bred, had wip'd out of her conscience the better dictate of nature, and not convinc'd her of the shame; certain it is, that whereas other nations us'd a liberty not unnatural (Cæsar) for one man to have many wives, the Britains altogether as licentious, but more absurd and preposterous in their licence, had one or many wives in common among ten or twelve husbands; and those for the most part incestuously. But no sooner was Severus return'd into the province, than the Britains take arms again. Against whom Severus worn out with labours and infirmity, sends Antoninus his eldest son: expressly commanding him to spare neither sex nor age. But Antoninus who had his wicked thoughts taken up with the contriving of his father's death, a safer enemy than a son, did the Britains not much detriment. Whereat Severus more overcome with grief than any other malady, ended (211) his life at York. After whose decease Antoninus Caracalla his impious son, concluding peace with the Britains, took hostages and departed to Rome. The conductor of all this northern war, Scottish writers name Donaldus, he of Monmouth, Fulgenius; in the rest of his relation nothing worth. From hence the Roman empire declining apace, good historians growing scarce, or lost, have left us little else but fragments for many years ensuing. Under Gordian the Emperor (Cambd.) we find by the inscription of an altar-stone, that Nonius Philippus govern'd here. Under Galienus we read there was a (Eumen. Paneg. Const) strong and general revolt from the Roman legate. Of the thirty tyrants which not long after (267. Cambd.) took upon them the stile of Emperor, by many coins found among us, Lollianus, Victorinus, Posthumus, the Tetrici and Marius are conjectured to have risen or born great sway in this island. Whence (Gildas) Porphyrius, a philosopher, then living, said that Britain was a soil fruitful of tyrants; and is noted to be the first author that makes mention of the Scottish nation. While Probus was (282) Emperor, Bonosus the son of a rhetorician, bred up a Spaniard, though by descent a Britain, and a matchless drinker, nor much to be blam'd, if, as they write, he were still wisest in his cups, having attained in warfare to high honours, and lastly in his charge over the German shipping, willingly, as was thought, miscarried, trusting on his power with the western armies, and join'd with Proculus, bore himself a while for emperor; but (282) after a long and bloody fight at Cullen vanquish'd by Probus, he hang'd himself, and gave occasion of a ready jest made on him for his much drinking; here hangs a tankard not a man. After this, Probus with much wisdom prevented (Zozim. l. 1.) a new rising here in Britain, by the severe loyalty of Victorinus a Maur, at whose entreaty he had plac'd here that governor which rebelled. For the emperor upbraiding him with the disloyalty of whom he had commended, Victorinus undertaking to set all right again, hastes hither, and finding indeed the governor to intend sedition, by some contrivance not mention'd in the story, slew him, whose name some imagine to be Cornelius Lelianus. They (Cambd.) write also, that Probus gave leave to the Spaniards, Gauls, and Britains, to plant vines, and to make wine; and having subdu'd the Vandals and Burgundians in a great battle, sent over many of them hither to inhabit, where (Zozimus) they did good service to the Romans when any insurrection happen'd in the isle. After whom Carus emperor going (283. Vopisc. in Carin.) against the Persians, left Carinus, one of his sons, to govern among other western provinces this island with imperial authority; but him Dioclesian, saluted emperor by the eastern armies, overcame and slew. About which time (284. Aurel. Vict. de Cæsar) Carausius a man of low parentage, born in Menapia, about the parts of Cleves and Juliers, who through all military degrees was made at length admiral of the Belgic and Armoric seas, then much infested by the Franks and Saxons, what he took from the pirates, neither restoring to the owners, nor accounting to the publick, but enriching himself, and yet not scowring the seas, but conniving rather at those sea-robbers, was grown (285. Eutro. Oros.) at length too great a delinquent to be less than an emperor: for fear and guiltness in those days made emperors ofter than merit: and understanding that Maximianus Herculius, Dioclesian's adopted son, was come against him into Gallia, pass'd (Eumen Paneg. 2. 286.) over with the navy which he had made his own, into Britain, and possess'd the island. Where he built a new fleet after the Roman fashion, got into his power the legion that was left here in garrison, other outlandish cohorts detain'd, listed the very merchants and factors of Gallia, and with the allurement of spoil invited great numbers of other barbarous nations to his part, and train'd them to sea-service, wherein the Romans at that time were grown so out of skill, that Carausius with his navy did at sea what he listed, robbing on every coast; whereby Maximian, able to come no nearer than the shoar of Boloigne, was forc'd (Victor. Eutrop.) to conclude a peace with Carausius, and yield him Britain; as one fittest to guard the province there against inroads from the north. But not long after (291) having assum'd Constantius Chlorus to the dignity of Cæsar, sent him against Carausius: who in the mean while had made himself strong both within the land and without. Galfred of Monmouth, writes that he made the Picts his confederates; to whom lately come out of Scythia (Buchanan) he gave Albany to dwell in: and it is observ'd, that before his time the Picts are not known to have been any where mention'd,, and then first (Paneg. 2.) by Eumenius a rhetorician. He repair'd and fortified the wall of Severus with seven castles, and a round house of smooth stone on the bank of Carron, which river, saith Nennius, was of his name so call'd ; he built (291) also a triumphal arch in remembrance of some victory there obtain'd. In France he held Gessoriacum, or Boloigne ; and all the Franks which had by his permission seated themselves in Belgia, were at his devotion. But Constantius hasting into Gallia, besieges Boloigne, and with stones and timber obstructing the port, keeps out all relief that could be sent in by Carausius. Who, e'er Constantius with the great fleet which he had prepar'd, could arrive hither,[1] was (292) slain treacherously by Alectus, one of his friends, who long'd to step into his place ; when he seven years, and worthily, as some say, as others, tyrannically, had rul'd the island. So much the more did Constantius prosecute that opportunity (Cambd. ex Nin, Eume. Pan. 3.) before Alectus could well strengthen his affairs ; and though in ill weather, putting to sea with all urgency from several havens to spread the terror of his landing, and the doubt where to expect him, in a mist passing the British fleet unseen, that lay scouting near the Isle of Wight, no sooner got ashoar, but fires his own ships, to leave no hope of refuge but in victory. Alectus also, though now much dismaid, transfers his fortune to a battle on the shoar ; but encountered by Asclepiodotus captain of the Prætorian bands, and desperately rushing on unmindful both of ordering his men or bringing them all to fight, save the accessories of his treason, and his outlandish hirelings, is overthrown, and slain with little or no loss to the Romans, but great execution on the Franks. His body was found almost naked in the Field, for his purple robe he had thrown aside, lest it should descry him, unwilling to be found. The rest taking flight to London, and purposing with the pillage of that city to escape by sea, are met by another of the Roman army, whom the mist at sea disjoining, had by chance brought thither, and with a new slaughter chas'd through all the streets. The Britains, their wives also and children, with great joy go out to meet Constantius, as one whom they acknowledge their deliverer from bondage and insolence. All this seems by Eumenius, who then liv'd, and was of Constantius's household, to have been done in the course of our continu'd action ; so also thinks Sigonius a learned writer : though all other allow three years to the tyranny of Alectus.[2] In these days were great store of workmen, and excellent builders in this island, whom after the alteration of things here, the Æduans in Burgundy entertain'd to build their temples and publick edifices. Dioclesian having hitherto successfully

[1] Cambden in his Britannia Tit. Buckinghamshire, says Alectus kill'd him in battle, and thinks Cave-field to be the place where they fought. Caversfield stands on the Ouse, not far from Buckingham.
[2] See an account of Alectus and Carausius, and of the places nam'd from, Alcester and Caver-field in Oxford hire and Bucks : in a history of Alcester, printed from the M S. by Dr. Kennet in his Parochial antiquities.

us'd his valour against the enemies of his empire, uses now his rage in a bloody persecution (Gildas) against his obedient and harmless christian subjects: from the feeling whereof neither was this island, though most remote, far enough remov'd. Among them here who suffer'd gloriously,[1] Aron, and Julius of Caer-leon upon Usk, but chiefly Alban of Verulam, were most renown'd: the story of whose martyrdom soil'd, and worse martyr'd with the fabling zeal of some idle fancies, more fond of miracles, than apprehensive of truth, deserves not longer digression. Constantius after Dioclesian, dividing (303) the empire with Galerius, had Britain among his other provinces; where either preparing or returning with victory from an expedition against the Caledonians, he dy'd at York. His son Constantine, who happily came post from Rome to Boloigne just about the time, saith Eumenius, that his father was setting sail his last time hither, and not long before his death, was by him on his death-bed nam'd, (306. Eutrop. Eumen) and after his funeral, by the whole army saluted emperor.[2] There goes a fame, and that seconded by[3] most of our own historians, though not those the ancientest, that Constantine was born in this island, his mother Helena the daughter of[4] Coilus a British prince, not sure the father of king Lucius, whose sister she must then be, for that would detect her too old by an hundred years to be the mother of Constantine. But to salve this incoherence, another Coilus is feign'd to be then earl of Colchester. To this therefore the Roman authors give no testimony, except a passage or two in the Panegyrics, about the sense whereof much is argu'd: others (Euseb. Const.) nearest to those times clear the doubt, and write him certainly born of Helena, a mean woman at Naisus in Dardania. Howbeit, e'er his departure (307) hence he seems to have had some bickerings in the north, which by reason of more urgent affairs compos'd, he passes (Sigon) into Gallia; and after four years (311) returns either to settle or to alter the state of things here; until a new war against Maxentius call'd him back, leaving Pacatianus his vice-gerent.[5] He deceasing, Constantine his eldest son enjoy'd for his part of the empire, with all the provinces that lay on this side the Alps, this island also. But falling to civil war with Constans his brother, was by him slain; who with his third brother[6] Constantius

[1] A thousand martyr'd at Litchfield, thence call'd Licidfield, which Rouse of Warwick renders a field of carcasses, if Geoffrey of Monmouth's account is not forg'd.
[2] Eumenius, in his oration to Constantine, calls Britain the most bles't and fortunate of all lands, *quia Constantinum Cæsarem primum vidisti.* Which is not to be understood that he was born, but that he was first saluted emperor here, tho' Dr. Stillingfleet in his Orig. Brit. makes it probable, that Britain was the place of his birth.
[3] See Lipsius's epistle to Mr. Cambden, upon this point. Cambd. Ep. pag. 64., and Usher's Primordia, p. 93.
[4] Cambden in his Britan. says, Constantius Chlorus marry'd the daughter of Coilus or Cælus, a British prince, and by her had Constantine the great in Britain.
[5] Constantius, when he was last in Britain, divided the province into four parts. Britannica Prima & Secunda, the old division, to which he added Flavia and Maxima Cæsariensis.
[6] Constantius was in Asia when Constans came into Britain. Dr. Howell history.

coming into Britain, seiz'd it as victor. (340. Libanius.) Against him rose (343) Magnentius, one of his chief commanders, by some affirm'd the son of a Britain, he having gain'd on his side great forces, contested with Constantius in many battles for the sole empire; but vanquish'd, (350 Cambden) in the end slew himself. Somewhat before this time (353) Gratianus Funarius, the father of Valentinian, afterwards emperor, had chief comman*l* of those armies which the Romans kept here. And the Arrian doctrine which (Ammian) then divided christendom, wrought also in this island no small disturbance: a land, saith Gildas, greedy of every thing new, stedfast in nothing. At last Constantius appointed a Synod of more than 400 bishops to assemble at Ariminum on the emperor's charges, which the rest all refusing, three only of the British,[1] poverty constraining them, accepted; though the other bishops among them offer'd to have borne their charges: esteeming it more honourable to live on the publick, than to be obnoxious to any private purse. 'Doubtless an ingenious mind, and far above the presbyters of our age; who like well to sit in assembly on the publick stipend, but like not the poverty that caus'd these to do so.'[2] After this Martinus was deputy of the province; who being offended with the cruelty which Paulus, an inquisitor sent from Constantius, exercis'd in his inquiry after those military officers, who had conspir'd (354) with Magnentius, was himself laid hold on as an accessory; at which enrag'd, he runs at Paulus[3] with his drawn sword; but failing to kill him, turns it on himself. Next to whom, as may be guess'd, Alipius was made deputy. In the meantime Julian, whom Constantius had made Cæsar, having recover'd much territory about Rhine, where the German inrodes before had long insulted, to relieve those countries almost ruin'd, causes 800 pinaces to be built; and with them by frequent voyages, plenty of corn to be fetch'd in from Britain; which even then was the usual bounty of this soil to those parts, as oft as French and Saxon pirates hinder'd not the transportation. While Constantius yet reign'd, (Amm. l. 22. 360), the Scots and Picts breaking in upon the northern confines, Julian being at Paris sends over Lupicinus, a well try'd soldier, but a proud and covetous man; who with a power of light-arm'd Herulians, Batavians, and Mæsians, in the midst of winter sailing from Boloigne, arrives at Rutupiæ,[4] seated on the opposite shoar, and comes to London, to consult there about the war; but soon after was recall'd by Julian, then chosen emperor. Under whom we read not

---

[1] The British Church encreas'd mightily under Constantine the great, and in the year 314, sent deputy to the council of Arles, as also to the Œcumenical synod of Nice, Anno 225, and to the council of Sardica, in the year 347.
[2] This is spoken by the author with reference to the assembly of Presbyterian divines, who sat with daily wages.
[3] This Paulus was burnt alive afterwards by an order of Julian the apostate. Mr. Witen place Paul the notary's coming into England five years after the time.
[4] Richborrow near Sandwich in Kent. See Mr Sommer's discourse on the Roman port in Kent, p. 3, 4.

of ought happening here; only that Palladius, one of his great officers, was hither banish'd. This year (Amm. l. 26, 27), Valentinian being Emperor, the Attacots,[1] Picts, and Scots roving up and down; and last the Saxons, with perpetual landings and invasions, harry'd (367) the south coast of Britain; slew Nectaridius, who govern'd the sea borders, and Bulchobaudes with his forces by an ambush. With which news Valentinian, not a little perplex'd, sends first Severus, high steward of his house, and soon recalls him; then Jovinus, who intimating the necessity of greater supplies, he sends at length Theodocius, a man of try'd valour and experience, father to the first emperor of that name. He with selected numbers out of the legions and cohorts, crosses the sea from Boloigne to Rutupiæ: from whence with the Batavians, Herulians,[2] and other legions that arriv'd soon after, he marches to London; and dividing his forces into several bodies, sets upon the dispers'd and plundering enemy, laden with spoil; from whom recovering the booty which they led away, and were forc'd to leave there with their lives, he restores all to the right owners, save a small portion to his wearied soldiers, and enters London victoriously; which, before in many straights and difficulties, was now reviv'd as with a great deliverance. The numerous enemy, with whom he had to deal, was of different nations, and the war scatter'd; which Theodosius, getting daily some intelligence from fugitives and prisoners, resolves to carry on by sudden parties and surprisals, rather than set battles; nor omits he to proclaim indemnity to such as would lay down arms, and accept of peace, which brought in many. Yet all this not ending the work, he requires that Civilis, a man of much uprightness, might be sent him, to be as deputy of the island, and Dulcitius a famous captain. Thus was Theodosius busy'd, besetting with ambushes the roving enemy, repressing his roads, restoring cities and castles to their former safety and defence, laying every where the firm foundation of a long peace, when Valentius,[3] a Pannonian for some great offence banish'd into Britain, conspiring (368. Amm. l. 28. Zozim. l. 4) with certain exiles and soldiers against Theodosius, whose worth he dreaded as the only obstacle to his greater design of gaining the isle into his power, is discover'd, and with his chief accomplices deliver'd over to condign punishment: against the rest, Theodosius with a wise lenity suffer'd not inquisition to proceed too rigorously, lest the fear thereof appertaining to so many, occasion might arise of new trouble in a time so unsettled. This done, he applies himself to reform things out of order, raises on the confines many strongholds: and in them appoints due and diligent

---

[1] Dr. Gale supposes the Attacoti to be a barbarous sort of Britains, inhabiting the north of Scotland.
[2] The Jovii and Victores, the Batavi and the Heruli, which serv'd in this expedition, were the four best legions in the Roman armies.
[3] Should be Valentinus.

watches ; and so reduc'd all things out of danger, that the province, which but lately was under command of the enemy, became now wholly Roman, new nam'd Valentia of Valentinian, and the city of London, Augusta. Thus Theodosius nobly acquitting himself in all affairs, with general applause of the whole province, accompanied to the sea-side, returns to Valentinian. Who about five years after (373. Amm. l. 29.) sent hither Fraomarius, a king of the Almans, with authority of a tribune over his own country forces, which then both for number and good service were in high esteem. Against Gratian, who succeeded in the western empire, Maximus a Spaniard, and one who had serv'd in the British wars with younger Theodosius (for he also, either with his father, or not long after him, seems (Sozim, l. 4, Sigon.) to have done something in this island) and now general of the Roman armies here, either discontented that Theodosius was preferr'd before him to the empire, or constrain'd by the soldiers who hated Gratian, assumes the imperial purple, and having attain'd victory against the Scots and Picts, with the flower and strength of Britain, passes into France ; there (383) slays Gratian, and without much difficulty, in the space of five years, obtains his part of the empire, overthrown at length and slain by Theodosius. With whom perishing most of his followers, or not returning out of Armorica,[1] which Maximus had given them to possess, the south of Britain by this means exhausted of her youth, (Gildas. 388. Beda, Ninn.), and what there was of Roman soldiers on the confines drawn off, became a prey to savage invasions ; of Scots from the Irish seas, of Saxons from the German, of Picts from the north. Against them, first Chrysanthus the son of Marcian a Novatian bishop, made deputy of Britain by Theodosius, demean'd himself worthily : then Stilicho, a man of great power, whom Theodosius dying left protector of his son Honorius, either came in person, or sending over sufficient aid, repress'd them, and as it seems new fortify'd the wall against them. But that legion being call'd away, when the Roman armies from all parts hasted to relieve Honorius, then besieged in Asta of Piemont, by Alaric the Goth, Britain was left expos'd as before to those barbarous robbers.

Lest any wonder how the Scots came to infest Britain from the Irish sea, it must be understood, that the Scots not many years before had been driven all out of Britain by Maximus ; and their king Eugenius slain in fight, as their own annals report : whereby, it seems, wandring up and down, without certain seat, they liv'd by scumming those seas

[1] Geoffrey relates, that Maximus bestow'd Armorica, the province of Bretagne in France, on Conan a Britain. Lord of Denbyshire, whom he made duke of it ; as also that Dionotus, duke of Cornwall, sent his own daughter Ursula 11,000 noble virgins, and 60,000 others to duke Conan, for wives for himself and his Britains ; of whom part perish'd in a storm, the rest by the kings of the Hunns and the Picts, who either kill'd them, or made them slaves. The virgins are esteemed martyrs in the Roman legends : and Card. Baronius, from no better authority than Geoffrey of Monmouth, reports the same story, as if it had been matter of fact, though it carries so many improbabilities with it.

and shores as pirates. But more authentick writers confirm us, that the Scots, whoever they be originally, came first into Ireland, and dwelt there, and named it Scotia, long before the north of Britain took that name. About this time, though troublesome, Pelagius a Britain found the leisure to bring new and dangerous opinions into the Church, and is largely writ against by St. Austin. But the Roman powers which were call'd into Italy, when once the fear of Alaric was over, made return into several provinces: and perhaps Victorinus[1] of Tolosa, whom Rutilius the poet much commends, might be then prefect of the Island: if it were not he whom Stilicho sent hither.[2] Buchanan writes, that endeavouring to reduce the Picts into a province, he gave the occasion of their calling back Fergusius and the Scots, whom Maximus with their help had quite driven out of the island: and indeed the verses of that poet speak him to have been active in those parts. But the time which is assign'd him later Buchanan after Gratianus Municeps, by Cambden after Constantine the tyrant, accords not with that which follows in the plain course of history. For the Vandals having broke in and wasted all Belgia, even to those places from whence easiest passage is into Britain, the Roman forces here, doubting to be suddenly invaded, were all in uproar, and in tumultuous manner set up Marcus,[3] who it may seem was then deputy. But him not found agreeable to their heady courses, they as hastily kill: for the giddy favour of a mutining rout is as dangerous as their fury. The like they do by Gratian a British Roman, in four months advanc'd, ador'd, and destroy'd. There was among them a common soldier, whose name was Constantine, with him on a sudden so taken they are,[4] upon the conceit put in them of a luckiness in his name, as without other visible merit, to create him emperor.[5] It fortun'd that the man had not his name for nought; so well he knew to lay hold, and make good use of an unexpected offer. He therefore with a weaken'd spirit, to the extent of his fortune dilating his mind, which in his mean condition before lay contracted and shrunk up, orders with good advice his military affairs: and with the whole force of the province, and what of British was able to bear arms, he passes into France, aspiring at least to an equal share with Honorius in the

[1] Cambden calls the Roman general Victorinus, Broetius and Buchanan say his name was Maximinian.
[2] Claudius in his Panegyrick on Stilicho's first Consulship introduces Britannia speaking thus in his praise:

Scoti'ane Picta tremerem nec Littore toto
Prospicerem dubiis Venientem Saxona Ventis:
The Scots and Picts alike now dreadless are;
No longer on the coasts I quivering stand,
Nor fear a fleet of Saxons on the strand.

[3] Stilicho's succours were sent in his first consulship, Anno 395. and the Vandals did not break in the empire till the year 407, when Marcus was proclaim'd emperor in Britain, which very well agrees with the plain course of history. Dr. Howell's Vol. II.
[4] Hoping, says Cambden in his remains, he would prove another Constantinus Maximus.
[5] He was proclaim'd emperor at Silcester in Hampshire.

empire. Where by the valour of Edobecus a Frank, and Gerontius a Britain, and partly by persuasion gaining all in his way, he comes to Arles. With like facility by his son Constans, whom of a monk he had made a Cæsar, and by the conduct of Gerontius, he reduces all Spain to his obedience. But Constans after this displacing Gerontius, the affairs of Constantine soon went to wrack: for he by this means alienated, set up Maximus one of his friends against him in Spain; and passing into France took Vienna[1] by assault, and having slain Constans in that city, calls on the Vandals against Constantine; who by him incited, as by him before they had been repress'd, breaking forward, over-run most part of France. But when Constantius comes, the emperor's general, with a strong power came out of Italy, Gerontius deserted by his own forces, retires into Spain; where also growing into contempt with the soldiers, after his flight out of France, by whom his house in the night was beset, having first with a few of his servants defended himself valiantly, and slain above 300, though when his darts and other weapons were spent, he might have scap't at a private door, as all his servants did, not enduring to leave his wife Nonnichia, whom he lov'd, to the violence of an enraged crew, he first cuts off the head of his friend Alanus, as were agreed; next his wife though loth and delaying, yet by her entreated and importun'd, refusing to outlive her husband, he dispatches: for which her resolution, Sozomenus an ecclesiastick writer gives her high praise, both as a wife and as a christian. Last of all, against himself he turns his sword; but missing the mortal place, with the ponyard finishes the work. Thus far is pursu'd the story of a famous Britain,[2] related negligently by our other historians. As for Constantine, his ending was not answerable to his setting out: for he with his other son Julian besieg'd by Constantius in Arles, and mistrusting the change of his wonted success, to save his head, poorly turns priest; but that not availing him, is carried into Italy, and there put to death; having four years acted the emperor. While these things were doing, the Britains at home destitute of Roman aid, and the chief strength of their own youth, that went first with Maximus, then with Constantine, not returning home, vex'd and harass'd by their wonted enemies, had sent messages to Honorius; but he at that time not being able to defend Rome itself, which the same year was taken by Alaric, advises them by his letter to consult how best they might for their own safety, and acquits them of the Roman jurisdiction. They therefore thus relinquish'd, and by all right the government relapsing into their own hands, henceforth betook themselves to live after their own laws, defending their bounds as well as they were

[1] Vienne in Dauphine.
[2] Humphrey Lhuid, in his discourse concerning Britain, says, he was so famous, that the British bards celebrated him with several poems, part of which he recites.

able, and the Armoricans, who not long after were call'd the Britains of France, follow'd their example. Thus expir'd this great empire of the Romans; first in Britain, soon after in Italy itself: having born chief sway in this island, though never thoroughly subdued, or all at once in subjection, if we reckon from the coming in of Julius to the taking of Rome by Alaric, in which year Honorius wrote those letters of discharge into Britain, the space of 462 years.[1] And with the empire fell also what before in this western world was chiefly Roman; learning, valour, eloquence, history, civility, and even language itself, all these together, as it were, with equal pace diminishing, and decaying. Henceforth we are to steer by another sort of authors; near enough to the things they write, as in their own country, if that would serve; in time not much belated, some of equal age; in expression barbarous; and to say how judicious, I suspend awhile: this we must expect; in civil matters to find them dubious relaters, and still to the best advantage of what they term holy church, meaning indeed themselves: in most other matters of religion, blind, astonish'd, and struck with superstition, as with a planet; in one word, monks. Yet these guides, where can be had no better, must be follow'd; in gross it may be true enough; in circumstance each man as his judgement gives him, may reserve his faith, or bestow it. But so different a state of things requires a several relation.

BOOK III.

This third book having to tell of accidents as various and exemplary, as the intermission or change of Governmennt hath any where brought forth, may deserve attention more than common, and repay it with like benefit to them who can judiciously read: considering especially that the late civil broils had cast us into a condition not much unlike to what the Britains then were in, when the imperial jurisdiction departing hence, left them to the sway of their own councils; which times by comparing seriously with these latter, and that confused anarchy with this interreign, we may be able from two such remarkable turns of state, producing like events among us, to raise a knowledge of ourselves both great and weighty, by judging hence what kind of men the Britains generally are in matters of so high

[1] Julius Cæsar landed in Britain 53 years before our Saviour's birth, and in the year 473, according to Mr. Speed, the Romans hid their treasures in Britain, and despar'd of being able to defend it against the Scots and Picts. By this calculation, their dominion over the Britains lasted 490 years; and we read in the same Mr. Speed's Chronicle, that the Britain's ten years afterwards wrote to Ætius in his third consulate to assist them. Cambden in his Britannia Tit. The Romans in Britain, says the Roman empire expir'd here 476 years after Cæsar's first invasion. For Attila, the Hun, was so terrible at that time to the Romans, that they cou'd not spare any of their forces to succour the Britains.

enterprize, how by nature, industry, or custom fitted to attempt or undergo matters of so main consequence; for if it be a high point of wisdom in every private man, much more is it in a nation to know itself; rather than puft up with vulgar flatteries, and encomiums, for want of self-knowledge, to enterprise rashly, and come off miserably in great undertakings. The Britains, thus as we heard, being left without protection from the empire, and the land in a manner emptied of all her youth, consumed in wars abroad, or not caring to return home, themselves through long subjection, servile in mind, slothful of body, and with the use of arms unacquainted, sustain'd but ill for many years the violence of those barbarous invaders, who now daily grew upon them. For although at first greedy of change, and to be thought the leading nation to freedom from the empire, they seem'd a while to bestir them with a shew of diligence in their new affairs, some secretly aspiring to rule, others adoring the name of liberty, yet so soon as they felt by proof the weight of what it was to govern well themselves, and what was wanting within them, not stomach or the love of licence, but the wisdom, the virtue, the labour, to use and maintain true liberty, they soon remitted their heat, and shrunk more wretchedly under the burden of their own liberty, than before under a foreign yoke. Insomuch that the residue of those Romans which had planted themselves here, despairing of their ill deportment at home, and weak resistance in the field, by those few who had the courage, or the strength to bear arms, nine years after the sacking of Rome remov'd out of Britain into France, hiding for haste great part of their treasure, which was never after found. And now again the Britains, no longer able to support themselves against the prevailing enemy, solicit Honorius to their aid, with mournful letters, embassages and vows of perpetual subjection to Rome, if the northern foe were but repuls'd. He at their request spares them one Legion, which with great slaughter of the Scots and Picts drove (422) them beyond the borders, rescu'd the Britains, and advis'd them to build a wall across the island, between sea and sea, from[1] the place where Edenburgh now stands to the frith of Dunbritton, by the city Alcluith. But the material being only turf, and by the rude multitude unartificially built up without better direction, avail'd (Gildas) them little. For no sooner was the Legion departed, but the greedy spoilers returning, land in great numbers from their boats and pinaces, wasting, slaying, and treading down all before them. Then are messengers again posted to Rome in lamentable sort, beseeching that they would not suffer a whole province to be destroy'd, and the Roman name, so honourable yet among them, to become the subject of barbarian scorn and insolence. The emperor, at their sad complaint (423), with what speed was possible sends to their succour. Who coming suddenly on

[1 From Abercorn on the Forth to Danglass on the Clyde.—A. M.]

those ravenous multitudes that minded only spoil, surprise them with a terrible slaughter. They who escap'd, fled back to those seas, from whence yearly they were wont to arrive, and return laden with booties. But the Romans, who came not now to rule, but charitably to aid, declaring that it stood not longer with the ease of their affairs to make such laborious voyages in pursuit of so base and vagabond robbers, of whom neither glory was to be got, nor gain, exhorted them to manage their own warfare; and to defend like men their country, their wives, their children, and what was to be dearer than life, their liberty, against an enemy not stronger than themselves, if their own sloth and cowardice had not made them so; if they would but only find hands to grasp defensive arms, rather than basely stretch them (Bede.) out to receive bonds. They gave them also their help to build a new wall, not of earth as the former (Gildas), but of stone (both at the publick cost, and by particular contributions) traversing the isle in direct line from east to west, between certain cities placed there as frontiers to bear off the enemy, where Severus had wall'd once before. They rais'd it twelve foot high, eight broad. Along the south shoar,[1] because from thence also like hostility was fear'd, they place towers by the sea-side at certain distances, for safety of the coast. Withal, they instruct them in the art of war, leaving patterns of their arms and weapons behind them; and with animating words, and many lessons of valour to a faint-hearted audience, bid them finally farewell, without purpose to return. And these two friendly expeditions, the last of any hither by the Romans, were perform'd, as may be gather'd out of Beda and Diaconus, the two last years of Honorius. Their leader, as some modernly write, was Gallio of Ravenna; Buchanan, who departs not much from the fables of his predecessor Boethius, names him Maximianus, and brings against him to this battle Fergus first king of Scots, after their second suppos'd coming into Scotland, Durstus king of Picts, both there slain, and Dioneth an imaginary king of Britain, or duke of Cornwall, who improbably sided with them against his own country, hardly escaping. With no less exactness of particular circumstances, he (Buch. l. 5) takes upon him to relate all those tumultuary inroads of the Scots and Picts into Britain, as if they had but yesterday happen'd, their order of battle, manner of fight, number of slain, articles of peace, things whereof Gildas and Beda are utterly silent, authors to whom the Scotch writers have none to cite comparable in antiquity; no more thereof to be believ'd for bare assertion, however quaintly dressed, than our Geoffry of Monmouth when he varies most from authentick story. But either the inbred vanity of some, in that respect unworthily call'd historians, or the fond zeal of praising their nations above truth, hath so far transported them.

[1] The enemies, which they fear'd on that side, were the Saxon pirates, who hover'd upon the southern coast, and occasion'd the new officer, stil'd Comes Littoris Saxonici.

that where they find nothing faithfully to relate, they fall confidently to invent what they think may either best set ¡off their history, or magnifie their country. The ¡Scots and Picts in manners differing somewhat from each other, but still unanimous to rob and spoil, hearing that the Romans intended not to return from the Gorroghs, or leathern frigates, pour out themselves in swarms upon the land, more confident than ever : and from the north end of the isle to the very wall side, then first took possession, as (Gildas. Beda) inhabitants; while the Britains with idle weapons in their hands stand trembling on the battlements, till the half-naked barbarians with their long and formidable iron hooks pull them down head-long. The rest not only quitting the wall but towns and cities, leave them to the bloody pursuer, who follows killing, wasting, and destroying all in his way. From these confusions arose a famine, and from thence discord and civil commotion among the Britains : each man living by what he robb'd or took violently from his neighbour. When all stores were consumed and spent where men inhabited, they betook them to the woods, and liv'd by hunting, which was their only sustainment. To the heaps of their evils from without were (Beda. Constant) added new divisions within the church. For Agricola the son of Severianus, a Pelagian bishop, had spread his doctrine wide among the Britains not uninfected before. The sounder part neither willing to embrace his opinion to the overthrow of divine grace, nor able to refute him, crave assistance from the churches of France : who send (429) them Germanus bishop of Auxerre, and Lupus of Troyes. They by continual preaching (Prosp. Aquit.) in churches, in streets, in fields, and not without miracles, as is written, confirm'd some, regain'd others, and at Verulam in a public disputation put to silence their chief adversaries. This reformation (Matth. West. ad ann. 446) in the church was believ'd to be the cause of their success a while after in the field. For (430) the Saxons and Picts with joynt force, which was no new thing before the Saxons at least had any dwelling in this island, during this abode of Germanus here, had made a strong impression from the north. The Britains marching (Constant. vit. Germ.) out against them, and mistrusting their own power, send to Germanus and his colleague, reposing more in the spiritual strength of those two men, than in their own thousands arm'd. They came, and their presence in the camp was not less than if a whole army had come to second them. It was then the time of Lent, and the people instructed by the daily sermons of these two pastors, come flocking to receive baptism. There was a place in the camp set apart as a church, and trick'd up with boughs upon Easter-day. The enemy understanding this, and that the Britains were taken up with religion more than with feats of arms, advances, after the paschal feast, as to a certain victory. Germanus, who also had intelligence of their approach, undertakes to be captain that day: and riding out with selected troops to discover what advantages the place might offer, lights on a valley compass'd about with hills, by which the enemy was to pass. And placing there his ambush, warns them that what word they heard him pronounce aloud, the same they should repeat with universal shout. The enemy passes on securely, and Germanus thrice aloud cries Halleluia; which answered by the soldiers with a sudden burst of clamour, is from the hills and valleys redoubled. The Saxons and Picts on a sudden supposing it the noise of a huge host, throw themselves into flight, casting down their arms, and great numbers of them are drown'd in the river which they had newly pass'd. This victory, thus won without hands, left to the Britains plenty of spoil, and to the person and the preaching of Germanus greater authority and reverence than before. And the exploit might pass for current, if Constantius, the writer of his life in the next age had resolv'd us how the British army came to want baptizing; for of any Paganism at that time, or long before in the land, we read (Usher. Primord p. 333) not, or that Pelagianism was re-baptiz'd. The place of this victory, as is reported, was in Flintshire, by a town call'd Guid-cruk,[1] and the river Allen, where a field retains the Name of Maes German (Germains field) to this day. But so soon as Germanus was returned home (431. Prosp. Acquit.), the Scots and Picts, though now so many of them Christians, that Palladius a deacon was ordain'd and sent by Celestine the pope to be a bishop of them, were not so well reclaim'd (Ethelwerd. Florent. Gild. Bede.) or not so many of them as to cease from doing mischief to their neighbours, where they found no impeachment to fall in yearly as they were wont. They therefore of the Britains, who perhaps were not yet wholly ruin'd, in the strongest and south-west parts of the Isle, send letters to Ætius (Malmsbury l. 1. c. 1. p. 8.), then third time consul of Rome, with this superscription: To Altius thrice Consul, the groans of the Britains (446). And after a few words thus, The Barbarians drive us to the sea, the sea drives us back to the Barbarians; thus bandied up and down between two deaths we perish, either by the sword or by the sea. But the empire at that time overspread with Hunns and Vandals, was not in condition to lend them aid. Thus rejected and wearied out with continual flying from place to place, but more afflicted with famine, which then grew outrageous among them, many for hunger yielded to the enemy, others either more resolute, or less expos'd to wants, keeping within woods and mountainous places, not only defended themselves, but sallying out at length gave a stop to the insulting foe with many seasonable defeats; led by some eminent person, as may be thought, who exhorted them not to trust in their own strength, but in divine assistance. And perhaps no other is here meant than the foresaid deliverance by Germanus, if computation would

[1] Guiderac, in the British tongue, in the English, Mould in Flintshire.

permit, which Gildas either not much regarded, or might mistake; but that he tarried so long here, the writers of his life assent not. Finding therefore such opposition, the Scots or Irish robbers, for so they are indifferently term'd, without delay get them home. The Picts, as before was mention'd, then first began to settle in the utmost parts of the island, using now and then to make inroad upon the Britons. But they in the mean while thus rid of their enemies, begin afresh to till the ground; which after cessation yields her fruit in such abundance, as had not formerly been known for many ages. But wantonness and luxury, the wonted companions of plenty, grow up as fast; and with them, if Gildas deserve belief, all other vices incident to human corruption. That which he notes especially to be the chief perverting of all good in the land, and so continued in his days, was the hatred of truth, and all such as durst appear to vindicate and maintain it. Against them, as against the only disturbers, all the malice of the land was bent. Lies and falsities, and such as could best invent them, were only in request. Evil was embrac'd for good, wickedness honour'd and esteem'd as virtue: and this quality their valour had against a foreign enemy, to be ever backward and heartless; to civil broils eager and prompt. In matters of government, and the search of truth, weak and shallow; in falsehood and wicked deeds, pregnant and industrious. Pleasing to God, or not pleasing, with them weighed alike; and the worse, most an end, was the weightier. All things were done contrary to publick welfare and safety; nor only by secular men, for the clergy also, whose example should have guided others, were as vicious and corrupt. Many of them besotted with continual drunkenness, or swoll'n with pride and willfulness, full of contention, full of envy, indiscreet, incompetent judges to detemine what in the practice of life is good or evil, what lawful or unlawful. Thus furnish'd with judgment, and for manners thus qualify'd both priest and lay, they agree to choose them several kings of their own, as near as might be, likest themselves; and the words of my author import as much. Kings were anointed, saith he, not of God's anointing, but such as were cruellest, and soon after as inconsiderately without examining the truth, put to death by their anointers to set up others more fierce and proud. As for the election of their kings (and that they had not all one monarch, appears both in ages past and by the sequel) it began, as nigh as may be guess'd, either this year or the following, when they saw the Romans had quite deserted their claim. About which time also Pelagianism again prevailing by means of some few, the British clergy too weak it seems at dispute, intreat (447. Constant. Beda.) the second time, Germanus to their assistance. Who coming with Severus a disciple of Lupus that was his former associate, stands not now to argue, for the people generally continu'd right; but enquiring those authors of new disturbance, adjudges them to banishment. They therefore by consent of all who were deliver'd to Germanus; who (448. Sigon. Gildas.) carrying them over with him, dispos'd of them in such place, where neither they could infect others, and were themselves under cure of better instruction. But Germanus the same year dy'd in Italy; and the Britons not long after found themselves again in much perplexity, with no slight rumour that their old troublers the Scots and Picts had prepar'd a strong invasion, purposing to kill all, and dwell themselves in the land from end to end. But e'er their coming in, as if the instruments of divine justice had been at strife, which of them first should destroy a wicked nation, the pestilence forestalling the sword, left scarce alive whom to bury the dead; and for that time, as one extremity keeps off another, preserv'd the land from a worse incumbrance of those barbarous dispossessers (Malms. l. 1.), whom the contagion gave not leave now to enter far. And yet the Britains nothing better'd by these heavy judgments, the one threaten'd, the other felt, instead of acknowledging the hand of heaven, run to the palace of their king Vortigern with complaints and cries of what they suddenly fear'd from the Pictish invasion. Vortigern, who at that time was chief rather than sole king, unless the rest had perhaps left their dominions to the common enemy, is said by him of Monmouth to have procur'd the death first of Constantine, then of Constans his son, who of a monk was made king, and by that means to have usurp'd the crown. But they who can remember how Constantine with his son Constans the monk, the one made emperor, the other Cæsar, perish'd in France, may discern the simple fraud of this fable. But Vortigern however coming to reign (449), is decipher'd by truer stories a proud unfortunate tyrant, and yet of the people much belov'd, because his vices sorted so well with theirs. For neither was he skill'd in war nor wise in counsel, but covetous, lustful, luxurious, and prone to all vice; wasting the publick treasury in gluttony and riot, careless of the common danger, and through a haughty ignorance, unapprehensive of his own. Nevertheless importun'd and awak'd at length, by unusual clamours of the people, he summons a general council, to provide some better means than heretofore had been us'd against these continual annoyances from the north. Wherein by advice of all, it was determin'd, that the Saxons be invited into Britain against the Scots and Picts; whose breaking in they either shortly expected, or already found they had not strength enough to oppose. The Saxons were a barbarous and heathen nation, famous for nothing else but robberies and cruelties done to all their neighbours both by sea and land; in particular to this island, witness that military force which the Roman emperors maintain'd here purposely against them, under a special commander, whose title, as is foun[d] on good record (Notitiæ Imperii.), was Count of the Saxon-shoar in Britain; and the many mischiefs done by their

[1] Vortigern was chosen king in the year 447.

landing here, both alone and with the Picts, as above hath been related, witness as much. They were a people thought by good writers (Florent. Wigorn. ad. an. 370) to be descended of the Sacæ, a kind of Scythian in the north of Asia, thence call'd Sacasons, or sons of Sacæ, who with a flood of other northern nations came into Europe, toward the declining of the Roman empire; and using piracy from Denmark all along these seas, possess'd at length by intrusion all that coast of Germany and the Netherlands, which (Ethelwerd) took thence the name of Old Saxony, lying between the Rhine and Elbe, and from thence north as far as Fidora the river bounding Holsatia, tho' not so firmly or so largely, but that their multitude wander'd yet uncertain of habitation. Such guests as these the Britons resolve now to send for, and entreat into their houses and possessions, at whose very name heretofore they trembled afar off. So much do men through impatience count ever that the heaviest which they bear at present, and to remove the evil which they suffer, care not to pull on a greater; as if variety and change in evil also where acceptable. Or whether it be that men in the despair of better, imagine fondly a kind of refuge from one misery to another. The Britons (Ethelwerd, Malmsbur. Witichind, Gest. Sax. l. 1. p. 3.) therefore, with Vortigern, who was then accounted king over them all, resolve in full council to send ambassadors to their choicest men with great gifts, and, saith a Saxon writer in these words, desiring their aid; 'Worthy Saxons, hearing the fame of your prowess, the distress'd Britons wearied out, and overpress'd by a continual invading enemy, have sent us to beseech your aid. They have a land fertile and spatious,[1] which to your commands they bid us surrender. Heretofore we have liv'd with freedom under the obedience and protection of the Roman empire. Next to them we know none worthier than yourselves; and therefore become suppliants to your valour. Leave us not below our present enemies, and to aught by you impos'd, willingly we shall submit.' Yet Ethelwerd writes not that they promis'd subjection, but only amity and league. They therefore who had chief rule among them, hearing (Malms.) themselves entreated by the Britons, to that which gladly they would have wish'd to obtain of them by entreating to the British embassy, re-

[1] The bishop of Worcester will not agree with this opinion, because no rational account can be given how the Sacæ left their own country to people Saxony. Orig. Britann. p. 306. See also Cambden, English Edit. p. 124, and Sherington, De Anglorum Gentis Origine: Cambden derives them from the Saci, a people of Scythia, Sarhmatia or Asiatica; Sheringham does the same. Stillingfleet thinks they took their name from their Seaxes, or short swords. Julius Scaliger observes, that Fader, Moder, Broder, &c., are used in the same sense in the Persian language as in the Saxon, And Busbequius in his Epistles writes, that the inhabitants of the Taurick Chersonese have these words, Wind, Silver, Corn, Salt, Fish, Son, Apple; and forty others in the same signification as they are now in with us. From whence Mr. Cambden in his Remains, p. 22, argues that our Saxon Progenitors planted their colonies in the East as well as the West.

[2] I know not how liberal the Britains might be in this distress; but if they made such a frank surrender, 'tis strange why the Saxons (designing to make themselves masters of the kingdom) should insist upon the poor pretence of short diet and bad pay; and not rather urge the express promise of the Saxon-Ambassadors.

76 SETTLEMENT OF SAXONS IN ENGLAND.—HORDES OF THE NORTH.

turn this answer: 'Be assur'd henceforth of the Saxons, as of faithful friends to the Britons, no less ready to stand by them in their need, than in their best of fortune.' The ambassadors return joyful, and with news as welcome to their country, whose sinister fate had now blinded them for destruction. The Saxons, consulting (Gildas.) first their Gods (for they had answer, that the land whereto they went, they should hold 300 years, half that time conquering, and half quietly possessing) furnish out three long gallies, or kyules, with a chosen company (about 1500 men, Beda) of warlike youth, under the conduct of two brothers, Hengist and Horsa, descended in the fourth degree from Woden; of whom, deify'd for the fame of his acts, most kings, of those nations derive their pedigree. These, and either mix'd with these, or soon after by themselves, two other tribes, or neigbouring people,[1] Jutes and[2] Angles, the one from Jutland, the other from Anglen by the city of Sleswich, both provinces of Denmark, arrive in the first year of Martian the Greek emperor, from the birth of Christ, 450, receiv'd (Nennius. Malms.) with much good will of the people first, then of the king, who after some assurances giv'n and taken, bestows on them the Isle of Tanet, where they first landed, hoping they might be made hereby more eager against the Picts, when they fought as for their own country, and more loyal to the Britons, from whom they had receiv'd a place to dwell in, which before they wanted. The British Nennius writes, that these brethren were driven into exile out of Germany, and to Vortigern who reign'd in much fear, one while of the Picts, then of the Romans, and Ambrosius came opportunely into the haven. For it was the custom in old Saxony, when their numerous offspring overflow'd the narrowness of their bounds, to send them out by lot into new dwellings, wherever they found room, either vacant or to be forced. But whether sought, or unsought, they dwelt not here long without employment. For the Scots and Picts were now come down, some say, (Ethelwerd) as far as Stamford in Lincolnshire,[3] whom, perhaps not imagining to meet new opposition, the Saxons, though not till after a sharp encounter, put to flight; and that more than once: slaying in fight, as some Scotch writers affirm, their King Eugenius the son of Fergus. Hengist perceiving the island to be rich and fruitful, but her princes and other inhabitants given to vicious ease, sends word home, inviting others to a share of his good success: who returning with seventeen ships, were grown up now to a sufficient army, and enter-

[1] Vide Spelman Gloss. sub. Tit. Guti.
[2] See Cambden's Britannia, Engl. p. 125. The Jutes, so call'd from the Gutes, Getes, or Goths, inhabiting the Cymbrica Chersonesus, which the Danes to this day call Jutland. The Angles, says Beda, lib. 1, cap. 15, came out of the country call'd Angulus, which is said to lie between the Jutes and the Saxons. Holstein was the ancient seat of the Saxons, and in the country between Holstein and Jutland there is now a small province call'd Angel, under the jurisdiction of the city of Flensberg.
[3] Hengist, in this county, vanquish'd the Scots and Picts, and obtain'd of Vortigern as much land as he could encompass with an ox's hide cut into very small thongs; from which treaty, the town of Thongcaster in Lincolnshire was so call'd.

tain'd without suspicion on these terms, that they should bear the brunt of war against the Picts, receiving stipend and some place to inhabit. With these was brought over the daughter of Hengist, a virgin wondrous fair, as is reported, Rowen the British call her: she by commandment of her father, who had invited the king to a banquet, coming in presence with a bowl of wine to welcome him, and to attend on his cup till the feast ended, won so much upon his fancy, though already wiv'd, as to demand her in marriage upon any conditions. Hengist at first, though it fell out perhaps according to the drift, held off, excusing his meanness; then obscurely intimating a desire and almost a necessity, by reason of his augmented numbers, to have his narrow bounds of Tanet enlarged to the circuit of Kent,[1] had it straight by donation: though[2] Guorangonus till then was king of that place: and so, as it were overcome by the great munificence of Vortigern, gave his daughter. And still encroaching on the king's favour, got farther leave to call over Octa and Ebissa, his own and his brother's son; pretending that they, if the north were given them, would sit there as a continual defence against the Scots, while himself guarded the east. They therefore sailing with forty ships even to the Orcades, and every way curbing the Scots and Picts, possess'd that part of the isle which is now Northumberland. Notwithstanding this, they complain, that their monthly pay was grown much into arrear; which when the Britons found means to satisfie, though alledging withal, that they to whom promise was made of wages, were nothing so many in number; quieted with this a while, but still seeking occasion to fall off, they find fault next, that their pay is too small for the danger they undergo, threatning open war unless it be augmented. Guortimer, the king's son, perceiving his father and the kingdom thus betray'd, from that time bends his utmost endeavour to drive them out. They on the other side making league with the Picts and Scots, and issuing out of Kent, wasted without resistance almost the whole land even to the western sea, with such a horrid devastation, that towns and colonies overturn'd, priests and people slain, temples and palaces, what with fire and sword, lay altogether heaped in one mixt ruin. Of all which multitude, so great was the sinfulness that brought this upon them, Gildas adds, that few or none were likely to be other than lewd and wicked persons. The residue of these, part overtaken in the mountains, were slain; others subdu'd with hunger, preferr'd slavery before instant death; some getting to rocks, hills and woods inaccessible, preferr'd the fear and danger of any death before

---

[1] This, we know, is the common story: but the Saxon annals, as they say nothing of Rowena, so they seem to intimate that Hengist got it by force of arms: telling us, that he worsted the Britains in two pitched battles; and that, upon this, they quitted Kent, and betook themselves to London.
[2] Mr. Milton calls the name of this king of Kent, Guorangonus: whereas Camden in his Brit. says, the person who then govern'd Kent was Vortigern's vice-roy, or Guorong.

the shame of a secure slavery; many fled over sea into other countries; some into Holland, where yet remain the ruins of Brittenburgh, an old castle on the sea, to be seen at low water not far from Leiden; either built, as writers of their own affirm, or seiz'd on by those Britons in their escape from Hengist: others into Armorica, peopl'd, as some think, with Britons long before; either by gift of Constantine the Great, or else of Maximus, to those British forces which had serv'd them in foreign wars; to whom those also that miscarried not with the latter Constantine at Arles: and lastly, these exiles driven out by Saxons, fled for refuge. But the ancient chronicles of those provinces attest their coming thither to be then first when they fled the Saxons, and indeed the name of Britain in France is not read till after that time.[1] Yet how a sort of fugitives, who had quitted without stroke their own country, should so soon win another, appears not; unless joyn'd to some part of their own settled there before. Vortigern nothing better'd by these calamities, grew at last so obdurate as to commit incest with his daughter tempted or tempting him out of an ambition to the crown. For which being censur'd and condemn'd in a great synod of Clerks and Laics, and partly for fear of the Saxons, according to the counsel of his peers, he retir'd into Wales, and built him there a strong castle in Radnorshire, by the advice of Ambrosius a young prophet, whom others call Merlin. Nevertheless Faustus, who was the son thus incestuously begotten, under the instructions of Germanus, or some of his disciples, for Germanus was dead before, prov'd a religious man, and liv'd in devotion by the river Remnis in Glamorganshire. But the Saxons, though finding it so easy to subdue the isle, with most of their forces, uncertain for what cause, return'd home: when as the easiness of their conquest might seem rather likely to have call'd in more. Which makes more probable that which the British write of Guortimer. For he coming to reign instead of his father, depos'd for incest, is said to have thrice driv'n and besieg'd the Saxons in the isle of Tanet; and when they issu'd out with powerful supplies sent from Saxony, to have fought with them four other battles, whereof three are nam'd; the first on the river Darwent, the second at Episford, wherein Horsa the brother of Hengist fell, and on the British part Catigern, the other son of Vortigon.[2] The third in a field by Stonar[3], then call'd Lapis tituli in Tanet, where he beat them into their ships that bore them home, glad to have escap'd, and not venturing to land again for five

[1] Bishop Stillingfleet proves the contrary from several ancient authors, in his Antiquities of the British Church, cap. 5.
[2] A monument something like Stonehenge, to be seen near Ailsford, call'd by the country people Kith's Coty-house from Catigern.
[3] So Cambden and my lord primate of Armagh · induc'd by the resemblance of Lapis tituli to Stonar. But Mr. Somner discovering in some antient records, that this Stonar was writ formerly Estanore, implying no more than Ora Orientalis, remov'd it to Folkston, and is follow'd in that opinion by the bishop of Worcester. See Somner's forts and ports in Kent, p. 94, &c. Still. Orig. Brit. p. 322.

years after. In the space whereof Guortemir dying, commanded they should bury him in the port of Stonar; persuaded that his bones lying there would be terrour enough to keep the Saxons from ever landing in that place: they, saith Nennius, neglecting his command, buried him in Lincoln. But concerning these times, ancientest annals of the Saxons relate in this manner. In the year 445. Hengist and Horsa fought against Vortigern, in a place call'd Eglesthrip, now Ailsford in Kent; where Horsa lost his life, of whom Horsted, the place of his burial, took name. After this first battle and the death of his brother, Hengist with his son Esca took on him kingly title, and peopl'd Kent with Jutes; who also then or not long after possess'd the Isle of Wight, and part of Hampshire lying opposite. Two years after in a fight at Creganford, or Craford, Hengist and his son slew of the Britains four chief commanders,[1] and as many thousand men: the rest in great disorder flying to London, with the total loss of Kent. And eight years passing between, he made a new war on the Britains; of whom in a battle at Wepped-fleot, twelve princes were slain, and Wipped the Saxon earl, who left his name to that place, though not sufficient to direct us where it now stands. His last encounter was at a place not mention'd, where he gave them such an overthrow, that flying in great fear they left the spoil of all to their enemies. And these perhaps are the four battles, according to Nennius, fought by Guortemir, though by these writers far differently related and happening, besides many other bickerings, in the space of twenty years, as Malmsbury reckons. Nevertheless it plainly appears that the Saxons, by whomsoever, were put to hard shifts, being all this while fought withal in Kent, their own allotted dwelling, and sometimes on the very edge of the sea, which the word Wippeds-fleot seems to intimate. But Guortemir now (458) dead,[2] and none of courage left to defend the land, Vortigern, either by the power of his faction, or by consent of all, re-assumes the government: and Hengist thus rid of his grand opposer, hearing gladly the restorement of his old favourer, returns again with great forces; but to Vortigern whom he well knew how to handle without warring, as to his son-in-law, now that the only author of dissention between them was remov'd by death, offers nothing but all terms of new league and amity. The king, both for his wive's sake and his own sottishness, consulting also with his peers not unlike himself, readily yields; and the place of parly is agreed on: to which either side was to repair without weapons. Hengist, whose meaning was not peace but treachery, appointed his men to be secretly arm'd,[3]

[1] Florence of Worcester mentions 4000 men.
[2] Wortimer, says Mr. Tallent, was poyson'd by Rowena his mother-in-law, Anno 458, and the Saxon annals under the year 465, place the battel of Wippedes fleet then, which Mr. Milton puts in Anno 473.
[3] The return of Hengist, and the murder of the Briti h nobles happened according to Mr Tallens' chronology, Anno, 461, no authentick author places it so late as the year 473

and acquainted them to what intent. The watch-word was **Nemet cour Saxes**, that is, draw your daggers; which they observing, when the Britons were thoroughly heated with wine (for the treaty it seems not without cups) and provok'd, as was plotted, by some affront, dispatch'd with those poinards every one his next man, to the number of 300, the chief of those that could do ought against him either in counsel or in field. Vortigern they only bound and kept in custody, until he granted them for his ransom three provinces, which were called afterward Essex, Sussex, and Middlesex.[1] Who thus dismist, retiring (466) again to his solitary abode in his country of Guorthigirniaun,[2] so call'd by his name, from thence to the castle of his own building in North Wales by the river Tiebi; and living there obscurely among his wives, was at length burnt in his tower by fire from heaven, at the prayer, as some say, of Germanus, but that coheres not; as others, by Ambrosius Aurelian; of whom as we have heard at first, he stood in great fear, and partly for that cause invited in the Saxons. Who whether by constraint, or of their own accord, after much mischief done, most of them returning back into their own country, left a fair opportunity to the Britons of revenging themselves the easier on those that staid behind. Repenting therefore, and with earnest supplication imploring divine help to prevent their final rooting out, they gather from all parts, and under the leading of Ambrosius Aurelianus, a vertuous and modest man, the last here of Roman stock, advancing now onward against the late victors, defeat them in a memorable battle. Common opinion, but grounded chiefly on the British fables, makes this Ambrosius to be a younger son of that Constantine, whose eldest, as we heard, was Constans the monk: who both lost their lives abroad usurping the empire. But the express words both of Gildas and Bede, assures us that the parents of this Ambrosius having here born regal dignity, were slain in these Pictish wars and commotions in the island. And if the fear of Ambrose induc'd Vortigern to call in the Saxons, it seems Vortigern usurp'd his right. I perceive not that Nennius makes any difference between him and Merlin: for that child without father that prophecy'd to Vortigern, he names not Merlin but Ambrose, makes him the son of a Roman consul; but conceal'd by his mother, as fearing that the king therefore sought his life; yet the youth no sooner had confess'd his parentage, but Vortigern either in reward of his predictions, or as his right, bestow'd upon him all the west of Britain; himself retiring to a solitary life. Whose ever son he was, he was the first, according to the surest author, that led against the Saxons, and overthrew them; but whether before this time or after, none have written. This is certain, that in a time when most of the Saxon forces were de-

[1] In the county of Radnor. See Cambd. Brit.

parted home, the Britains gather'd strength; and either against those who were left remaining, or against their whole powers, the second time returning obtain'd this victory.[1] Thus Ambrose as chief monarch of the isle succeeded Vortigern; to whose third son Pascentius he permitted the rule of two regions in Wales,[2] Buelth and Guorthigirniaun. In his days, saith Nennius, the Saxons prevail'd not much: against whom Arthur, as being then chief general for the British kings, made great war; but more renown'd in songs and romances, than in true stories. And the sequel itself declares as much. For in the year 477, Ella the Saxon, with his three sons, Cymen, Pleting, and Cissa, at a place in Sussex, call'd Cymenshore, arrive in three ships, kill many of the Britains, chasing them that remain'd into the wood[3] Andreds-League. Another battle was fought (485) at Mercreds-Burnamsted, wherein Ella had by far the victory; but Huntingdon makes it so doubtful, that the Saxons were constrain'd to send home for supplies. Four years (489) after dy'd Hengist, the first Saxon king of Kent; noted to have attain'd that dignity by craft as much as valour, and giving scope to his own cruel nature, rather than proceeding by mildness and civility. His son Oeric, sirnam'd Oisc, of whom the Kentish kings were call'd Oiscings, succeeded him, and sat content with his father's winnings; more desirous to settle and defend, than to enlarge his bounds: he reign'd (492) twenty four-years. By this time Ella and his son Cissa besieging Andred-chester,[4] suppos'd now to be Newenden in Kent, take it by force, and all within it put to the sword. Thus Ella, three years after the death of Hengist, began his kingdom of the South-Saxons; peopling it with new inhabitants, from the country which was then Old Saxony, at this day Holstein in Denmark, and had besides at his command, all those provinces which the Saxons had won on this side Humber. Animated with these good successes, as if Britain were become now the field of fortune, Kerdic another Saxon prince, the tenth by lineage from Woden, an old and practis'd soldier, who in many prosperous conflicts against the enemy in those parts, had nurs'd up a spirit too big to live at home with equals, coming (495) to a[5] certain place, which from thence took the name of Kerdic-shoar, with five ships, and Kenric his son, the very same day overthrew the Britains that oppos'd him; and so effectually, that smaller skirmishes after that day were sufficient to drive them still farther off, leaving him a large territory. After him Porta another Saxon, with his two sons Bida and Megla, in two ships arrive (501) at

[1] Ambrosius commanded the Britains twenty years, as their general, and Anno 485 was chosen king. Vid. Dr. Powell's catalogue of the kings of Wales.
[2] Bualth in Brecknockshire, and Caer Guortigern in Radnorshire. Camb. Brit.
[3] The Weald in Sussex: call'd so from an ancient forest, which by the name Andreda. Vid. Glos. ad Chron. Sax. in Voc. Andreceaster. Andreadswald took in Sussex, Kent and Hampshire, 120 miles in length, and 30 in breadth.
[4] See Mr. Cambden; but Mr. Somner rather chuses Pemsey or Hastings. Ports and Forts, p. 104, 105.
[5] Sardichesora, quæ nunc vocatur Gernemeth, (says Brompton) or Yarmouth in Norfolk.

Portsmouth,[1] thence call'd, and at their landing slew a young British nobleman, with many others who unadvisedly set upon them. The Britains, (508) to recover what they had lost, draw together all their forces, led by Natanleod, or Nazaleod, a certain king in Britain, and the greatest, saith one; but him with 5000 of his men Kerdic puts to rout and slays. From whence the place in Hampshire, as far as Kirdicsford, now Chardford, was call'd of old Nazaleod. Who this king should be, hath bred much question; some think it to be the British name of Ambrose; others to be the right name of his brother, who for the terror of his eagerness in fight, became more known by the sirname of Uther, which in the Welch tongue signifies dreadful. And if ever such a king in Britain there were as Uther Pendragon,[2] for so also the Monmouth book surnames him, this in all likelihood must be he. Kirdic by so great a blow given to the Britons had made (508) large room about him; not only for the men he brought with him, but for such also of his friends as he desir'd to make great; for which cause, and withal the more to strengthen himself, his two nephews, Stuf and Withgar, in three vessels bring him (514) new levies to Kerdic-shoar. Who, that they might not come sluggishly to possess what others had won for them, either by their own seeking, or by appointment, are set in place where they could not but at their first coming give proof of themselves upon the enemy: and so well they did it, that the Britains after a hard encounter left them masters of the field. About the same time, Ella the first South-Saxon king dy'd; whom Cissa his youngest succeeded; the other two failing before him. Nor can it be much more or less than about this time, for it was before the West-Saxon kingdom, that Uffa the eighth from Woden made himself king of the East-Angels, who by their name testifie the country above-mention'd; from whence they came in such multitudes, that their native soil is said to have remain'd in the days of Beda uninhabited. Huntingdon defers the time of their coming in to the ninth year of Kerdic's reign: for, saith he, at first many of them strove for principality, seizing every one his province, and for some while so continu'd, making petty wars among themselves; till in the end Uffa, of whom those kings were call'd Uffings, overtopp'd them all in the year 571, then Titilus his son, the father of Redwald, who became potent. And not much after the East-Angels, began also the East-Saxons to erect a kingdom under Sleda the tenth from Woden. But Huntingdon, as before, will have it later by eleven years, (519) and Ercherwin to be the first king. Kerdic, the same in power, though not so fond of title, forbore the name twenty-four years after his arrival;

---

[1] Call'd so from its port, and not from Porta. Cambd.
[2] The story of Uther Pendragon is reckon'd a fable by all the British Antiquaries. Bishop Usher conjectures, that this Uther is the same person with Nazaleod, who for his valour was surnamed Uther, i.e. terrible.

but then founded so firmly the kingdom of West-Saxons, that it subjected all the rest at length, and became the sole monarchy of England. The same year he had a victory against the Britons at Kerdics-Ford, by the river Aven ; and after (527) eight years, another great fight at Kerdics-League,[1] but which won the day is not by any set down. Hitherto have been collected what there is of certainty, with circumstance of time and place, to be found register'd, and no more than barely register'd in annals of best note ; without describing after Huntingdon the manner of those battles and encounters, which they who compare and can judge of books, may be confident he never found in any current author whom he had to follow. But this disease hath been incident to many more historians; and the age whereof we now write hath had the ill hap, more than any since the first fabulous times, to be surcharg'd with all the idle fancies of posterity. Yet that we may not rely altogether on Saxon relaters, Gildas, in antiquity far before these, and every way more credible, speaks of these wars, in such a manner, though nothing conceited of the British valour, as declares the Saxons in his times and before, to have been foil'd not seldomer than the Britons. For besides that first victory of Ambrose, and the interchangeable success long after, he tells that the last overthrow which they receiv'd (527) at Badon-hill was not the least ; which they in their oldest annals mention not at all. And because the time of this battle, by any who could do more than guess, is not set down, or any foundation given from whence to draw a solid compute, it cannot be much wide to insert it in this place. For such authors as we have to follow give the conduct and praise of this exploit to Arthur ; and that this was the last of twelve great battles which he fought victoriously against the Saxons. The several places written by Nennius in their Welsh names, were many hundred years ago unknown, and so here omitted. But who Arthur was, and whether ever any such reign'd in Britain, hath been doubted heretofore, and may again with good reason.[1] For the monk of Malmesbury, and others whose credit hath sway'd most with the learneder sort, we may well perceive to have known no more of this Arthur five hundred years past, nor of his doings, than we now living : and what they had to say, transcrib'd out of Nennius, a very trivial writer yet extant, which hath already been related. Or out of a British book, the same which he of Monmouth set forth, utterly unknown to the world till more than six hundred

---

[1] Suppos'd to be Cherdsley in Buckinghamshire.
[2] Bishop Stillingfleet, in his fifth chapter of his Antiquities of the British Churches, justifies the History of King Arthur. He was born at Camelford, and dy'd at Tindagel in Cornwall. Camb. Brit. Tit. Corn. The story of this British hero is confirm'd by the Inscription on his coffin, which was dug up by command of Henry the Second, who had learn'd by the songs of the British bards, that he was bury'd at Glassenbury in Somersetshire, between two Pyramids ; where nine foot deep a coffin made of the trunk of an oak was found, with this Inscription on it in Gothic characters :
Hic jacet sepultus inclytus Rex Arturius in Insula Avalonia.
Cambd. Tit. Somersetsh,

years after the days of Arthur, of whom (as Sigebert in his chronicle confesses) all other histories were silent, both foreign and domestick, except only that fabulous book. Others of later time have sought to assert him by old legends and cathedral regests. But he who can accept of legends for good story, may quickly swell a volume with trash, and had need be furnish'd with two only necessaries, leisure and belief, whether it be the writer, or he that shall read. As to Arthur, no less is in doubt who was his father; for if it be true, as Nennius or his notist avers, that Arthur was call'd Mab-Uther, that is to say, a cruel son, for the fierceness that men saw in him of a child, and the intent of his name Arturus imports as much, it might well be that some in after-ages, who sought to turn him into a fable, wrested the word Uther into a proper name, and so fain'd him the son of Uther; since we read not in any certain story, that ever such person liv'd, till Geoffry of Monmouth set him off with the surname of Pendragon. And as we doubted of his parentage, so may we also of his puissance; for whether that victory at Baden-hill were his or no, is uncertain; Gildas not naming him, as he did Ambrose in the former. Next, if it be true as Caradoc relates, that Melvas king of that country, which is now Summerset, kept from him Gueniver his wife a whole year in the town of Glaston, and restor'd her at the entreaty of Gildas, rather than for any enforcement that Arthur with all his chivalry could make against a small town, defended only by a moory situation: had either his knowledge in war, or the force he had to make, been answerable to the fame they bear, that petty king had neither dar'd such an affront, nor he be so long, and at last without effect, in revenging it. Considering, lastly, how the Saxons gain'd upon him every where all the time of his suppos'd reign, which began, as some write, in the tenth year of Kerdic, who wrung from him by long war the countries of Summerset and Hampshire; there will remain neither place nor circumstance in story, which may administer any likelihood of those great acts that are ascribed him. This only is alledg'd by Nennius in Arthur's behalf, that the Saxons, tho' vanquish'd never so oft, grew still more numerous upon him by continual supplies out of Germany. And the truth is, that valour may be over-toil'd, and overcome at last with endless overcoming. But as for this battle of Mount Baden, where the Saxons were hemm'd in, or besieg'd, whether by Arthur won, or whensoever, it seems indeed to have given a most undoubted and important blow to the Saxons, and to have stopp'd their proceedings for a good while after. Gildas himself witnessing that the Britons having thus compell'd them to sit down with peace, fell thereupon to civil discord among themselves. Which words may seem to let in some light toward the searching out when this battle was fought. And we shall find no time since the first Saxon war, from whence a longer peace ensu'd, than from the fight of Kerdic's-League in the year 527, which all the chronicles mention, without victory to Kerdic; and gave us argument, from the custom they have of magnifying their own deeds upon all occasions, to presume here his ill speeding. And if we look still onward, even to the 44th year after, wherein Gildas wrote, if his obscure utterance be understood, we shall meet with very little war between the Britains and Saxons. This only remains difficult, that the victory first won by Ambrose was not so long before this at Badon siege, but that the same men living might be eye-witnesses of both; and by this rate hardly can the latter be thought won by Arthur, unless we reckon him a grown youth at least in the days of Ambrose, and much more than a youth, if Malmsbury be heard, who affirms all the exploits of Ambrose to have been done chiefly by Arthur as his general, which will add much unbelief to the common assertion of his reigning after Ambrose and Uther, especially the fight at Badon being the last of his twelve battles.[1] But to prove by that which follows, that the fight at Kerdics-League, though it differ in name from that of Badon, may be thought the same by all effects; Kerdic three years (530) after, not proceeding onward, as his manner was, on the continent, turns back his forces on the Isle of Wight, which with the slaying of a few only in[2] Withgarburgh, he soon masters; and not long surviving, left (534) it to his nephews by the mother's side, Stuff and Withgar; the rest of what he had subdu'd, Kenric his son held, and reign'd 26 years, in whose tenth year (544) Withgar was bury'd in the town of that island which bore his name. Notwithstanding all these unlikelihoods of Arthurs' reign and great achievements, in a narration crept in I know not how, among the laws of Edward the Confessor, Arthur the famous king of Britons, is said not only to have expell'd hence the Saracens, who were not then known in Europe, but to have conquer'd Freesland, and all the north-east isles as far as Russia, to have made Lapland the eastern bound of his empire, and Norway the chamber of Britain. When should this be done? From the Saxons, till after twelve battles, he had no rest at home: after those the Britains contented with the quiet they had from the Saxon enemies, were so far from seeking conquests abroad, that by report of Gildas above-cited, they fell to civil wars at home. Surely Arthur much better had made war in old Saxony, to repress their flowing hither, than to have won kingdoms as far as Russia, scarce able here to defend his own. Buchanan our neighbour historian reprehends him of Monmouth and others for fabling in the deeds of Arthur, yet what he writes thereof himself, as of better credit, shows not whence he had but from those fables; which he seems content to believe in part, on condition that the Scots

---

[1] This fight was fought, according to the best British Manuscripts, Anno. 520
[2] Suppos'd to be Carisbrook-Castle in the Isle of Wight. The town was then call'd Withgarisbyrig, from Withgar, Cerdic's nephew, to whom it was given.

and Picts may be thought to have assisted Arthur, in all his wars and achievements, whereof appears as little ground by any credible story as of that which he most counts fabulous. But not farther to contest about such uncertainties. In the year 547, Ida the Saxon sprang also from Woden in the tenth degree, began the kingdom of Bernicia in Northumberland; built the town Bebanburg, which was after wall'd; and had twelve sons, half by wives, and half by concubines. Hengist, by leave of Vortigern, we may remember, had sent Octa and Ebissa to seek them seats in the north, and there by warring on the Picts, to secure the southern parts. Which they so prudently effected, that what by force and fair proceeding, they well quitted those countries; and though so far distant from Kent, nor without power in their hands, yet kept themselves nigh 180 years within moderation; and as inferior governours they and their offspring gave obedience to the kings of Kent, as to the elder family. Till at length, following the example of that age; when no less than kingdoms were the prize of every fortunate commander, they thought it but reason, as well as others of their nation, to assume royalty. Of whom Ida was the first, a man in the prime of his years, and of parentage as we heard; but how he came to wear the crown, aspiring or by free choice, is not said. Certain enough it is, that his virtues made him not less noble than his birth, in war undaunted, and unfoil'd; in peace temp'ring the awe of magistracy, with a natural mildness: he reign'd about twelve years. In the meanwhile (552) Kenric in a fight at Scaresbirig, now Salisbury, kill'd and put to flight many of the Britains; and the fourth year after at Beranvirig, now Banbury, as some think, with Keaulin his son put them again to flight. Keaulin shortly after succeeded his father in the West-Saxons. And Alla descended also of Woden, but by another line, set up (560) a second kingdom in Deira the south part of Northumberland, and held it thirty years; while Adda the son of Ida and five more after him, reign'd without other memory in Bernicia: and in Kent, Ethelbert the next year began. For Esca the son of Hengist had left Otha, and he Emeric to rule after him; both which without adding to their bounds, kept what they had in peace fifty-three years. But Ethelbert in length of reign equall'd both his progenitors, and as Beda counts, three years exceeded. Young at his first entrance, and unexperienc'd, he was the first raiser of civil war among the Saxons; claiming from the priority of time wherein Hengist took possession here, a kind of right over the later kingdoms; and thereupon was troublesome to their confines: but by them twice defeated, he who but now thought to seem dreadful, became almost contemptible. For Keaulin and Cutha his son, pursuing him into his own territory, slew there (568) in battle, at Wibbandun (Wimbledon), two of his earls, Ostac, and Cnebban. By this means the Britains, but chiefly by this victory at Badon, for the space of forty-four years ending in 571, receiv'd no great annoyance from the Saxons : but the peace they enjoy'd, by ill using it, prov'd more destructive to them than war. For being rais'd on a sudden by two such eminent successes, from the lowest condition of thraldom, they whose eyes had beheld both those deliverances, that by Ambrose, and this at Badon, were taught by the experience of either fortune, both kings, magistrates, priests and private men, to live orderly. But when the next age, unacquainted with past evils, and only sensible of their present ease and quiet, succeeded, strait follow'd the apparent subversion of all truth and justice, in the minds of most men : scarce the least footstep, or impression of goodness left remaining through all ranks and degrees in the land ; except in some so very few, as to be hardly visible in a general corruption : which grew in short space not only manifest, but odious to all the neighbour nations. And first their kings, among whom also, the sons or grand children of Ambrose, were foully degenerated to all tyranny and vicious life. Whereof to hear some particulars out of Gildas will not be impertinent. They avenge, saith he, and they protect ; not the innocent, but the guilty : they swear oft, but perjure ; they wage war, but civil and unjust war. They punish rigorously them that rob by the highway ; but those grand robbers that sit with them at table, they honour and reward. They give alms largely, but in the face of their alms-deeds, pile up wickedness to a far higher heap. They sit in the seat of judgment, but go seldom by the rule of right; neglecting and proudly overlooking the modest and harmless ; but countenancing the audacious, though guilty of abominablest crimes ; they stuff their prisons but with men committed rather with circumvention, than any just cause. Nothing better were the clergy, but at the same pass or rather worse, than when the Saxons came first in ; unlearned, unapprehensive, yet impudent ; subtle prowlers, pastors in name, but indeed wolves ; intent upon all occasions, not to feed the flock, but to pamper and well line themselves : not call'd, but seizing on the ministry as a trade, nor as a spiritual charge ; teaching the people, not by sound doctrine, but by evil example ; usurping them the chair of Peter, but through the blindness of their own worldly lusts, they stumble upon the seat of Judas : deadly haters of truth, broachers of lies : looking on the poor christian with eyes of pride and contempt ; but fawning on the wickedest rich men without shame ; great promoters of other men's alms with their set exhortations ; but themselves contributing ever least ; slightly touching the many vices of the age, but preaching without end their own grievances, as done to Christ ; seeking after preferments and degrees in the church more than after heav'n ; and so gain'd, make it their whole study how to keep them by any tyranny. Yet lest they should be thought things of no use in their eminent places, they have their niceties and trivial points to keep in awe the superstitious multitude ; but in true saving knowledge leave them still as gross and stupid as themselves; bunglers at the scripture nay forbidding and silencing them that know; but in worldly matters, practis'd and cunning shifters; in that only art and simony, great clerks and masters, bearing their heads high, but their thoughts abject and low. He taxes them also as gluttonous, incontinent, and daily drunkards. And what shouldst thou expect from these, poor laity, so he goes on, these beasts, all belly? Shall these amend thee, who are themselves laborious in evil doings? Shalt thou see with their eyes, who see right forward nothing but gain? Leave them rather, as bids our saviour, lest ye fall both blind-fold into the same perdition. Are all thus? Perhaps not all, or not so grosly. But what avail'd it Eli to be himself blameless, while he connived at others that were abominable? Who of them hath been envy'd for his better life? Who of them hath been hated to consort with these, or withstood their entering the ministry, or endeavour'd zealously their casting out? Yet some of these perhaps by others are legended for great saints. This was the state of government, this of religion among the Britons, in that long calm of peace, which the fight at Badon hill had brought forth. Whereby it came to pass, that so fair a victory came to nothing. Towns and cities were not reinhabited, but lay ruin'd and waste; nor was it long e're domestick war breaking out, wasted them more. For Britain, as at other times, had then also several kings. Five of whom Gildas living then in Armorica, at a safe distance, boldly reproves by name; first Constantine (fabl'd the son of Cador, duke of Cornwall, Arthur's half brother by the mother's side) who then reign'd in Cornwall and Devon, a tyrannical and bloody king, polluted also with many adulteries: he got into his power, two young princes of the blood royal, uncertain whether before him in right, or otherwise suspected: and after solemn oath given of their safety, the year that Gildas wrote, slew them with their two governours in the church, and in their mother's arms, through the abbot's cope, which he had thrown over them, thinking by the reverence of his vesture to have withheld the murderer. These are commonly supposed to be the sons of Mordred, Arthur's nephew, said to have revolted from his uncle, given him in a battle his death's wound, and by him after to have been slain. Which things were they true, would much diminish the blame of cruelty in Constantine, revenging Arthur on the sons of so false a Mordred. In another part, but not express'd where, Aurelius Conanus was king: him he charges also with adulteries and parricide; cruelties worse than the former: to be a hater of his countrie's peace, thirsting after civil war and prey: his condition it seems, was not very prosperous; for Gildas wishes him, being now left alone, like a tree withering in the midst of a barren field, to remember the vanity, and arrogance of his father and elder brethren, who came all to untimely death in their youth. The third reigning in Demetia, or South Wales, was Vortipor, the son of a good father; he was when Gildas wrote, grown old, not in years only, but in adulteries, and in governing full of falsehood, and cruel actions. In his latter days, putting away his wife, who dy'd in divorce, he became, if we mistake not Gildas, incestuous with his daughter. The fourth was Cuneglas, imbru'd in civil war; he also had divorc'd his wife, and taken her sister, who had vow'd widowhood: he was a great enemy to the clergy, high-minded and trusting to his wealth. The last but greatest of all in power, was Maglocune, and greatest also in wickedness; he has driv'n out or slain many other kings, or tyrants; and was called the Island Dragon, perhaps having his seat in Anglesey: a profuse giver, a great warrior, and of a goodly stature. While he was yet young, he overthrew his uncle, though in the head of a complete army, and took from him the kingdom; then touch'd with remorse of his doings, not without deliberation took upon him the profession of a monk; but soon forsook his vow, and his wife also, which for that vow he had left, making love to the wife of his brother's son then living. Who not refusing the offer, if she were not rather the first that entic'd, found means both to dispatch her own husband, and the former wife of Maglocune, to make her marriage with him the more unquestionable. Neither did he this for want of better instructions, having had the learnedest and wisest man reputed of all Britain, the instituter of his youth. Thus much, the utmost that can be learnt by truer story, of what past among the Britons from the time of their useless victory at Badon, to the time that Gildas wrote, that is to say, as may be guessed from 527 to 571, is here set down all together; not to be reduced under any certainty of years. But now the Saxons, who for the most part all this while had been still, unless among themselves, began afresh to assault them, and e're long to drive them out of all which they yet maintain'd on this side Wales. For Cuthulf the brother of Keaulin, by a victory obtained (571) at Bedanford, now Bedford, took from them four good towns,[1] Liganburgh, Eglesburgh, Besington, now Benson in Oxfordshire, and Ignisham, but outliv'd not many months his good success.[2] And after six years more, Keaulin, and Cuthwin his son, gave them a great overthrow at Deorrham in Gloucestershire, slew three of their kings, Comail, Condidan, and Farinmail, and took three of their chief cities; Glocester, Cirencester, and Badencester. The Britons notwithstanding, after some space of time, judging to have out-grown their losses, gather to a head, and encounter Keaulin and Cutha his son, at Fethanlege; whom valiantly fighting, they slew among the

[1] Possibly Layton in Bedfordshire. See the Glossary to the Saxon Chronicle.
[2] Some authors place the founding of the kingdom of East-Angles by Ussa at this time. Anno. 575. Mr. Tallent is of this opinion in his chronological tables.

thickest, and as is said, forc'd the Saxons to retire. But Keaulin reinforcing the fight, put them to a main rout, and following his advantage, took many towns, and return'd laden with booty. The last of those Saxons who rais'd their own achievements to a monarchy, was Crida, much about this time,[1] first founder of the Mercian kingdom, drawing also his pedigree from Woden. Of whom all to write the several genealogies, though it might be done without long search, were, in my opinion, to encumber the story with a sort of barbarous names, to little purpose. This may suffice, that of Woden's three sons, from the eldest issu'd Hengist, and his succession; from the second, the kings of Mercia; from the third, all that reign'd in West Saxon, and most of the Northumbers, of whom Alla was one, the first king of Deira; which after his death (584) the race of Ida seiz'd, and made it one kingdom with Bernicia, usurping on the childhood of Edwin, Alla's son, whom Ethelric the son of Ida expell'd. Notwithstanding others write of him; that from a poor life, and beyond hope in his old age, coming to the crown, he could hardly by the access of a kingdom, have overcome his former obscurity, had not the fame of his son preserv'd him. Once more the Britons, ere they quitted all on this side the mountains, forgot not to shew some manhood; for meeting Keaulin at Wodens Beorth, that is to say, Wodens Mount[2] in Wiltshire, whether it were by their own forces, or assisted by the Angles, whose hatred Keaulin had incurr'd (592), they ruin'd his whole army, and chas'd him out of his kingdom, from whence flying, he dy'd the next year in poverty, who a little before was the most potent and indeed sole king of all the Saxons on this side Humber. But who was chief among the Britons in this exploit had been worth remembring, whether it were Maglocune, of whose prowess hath been spoken, or Teudric king of Glamorgan, whom the regest of Landaff recounts to have been always victorious in fight; to have reign'd about this time (592), and at length to have exchanged his crown for a hermitage; till in the aid of his son Mauric, whom the Saxons had reduc'd to extremes, taking arms again, he defeated them at Tinterne by the river Wye; but himself receiv'd a mortal wound. The same year with Keaulin, whom Keola the son of Cathulf, Keaulin's brother succeeded, Crida also the Mercian king deceas'd, in whose room Wibba succeeded; and in Northumberland, Ethelfred in the room of Ethelric, reigning twenty-four years. Thus omitting fables, we have the view of what with reason can be rely'd on for truth, done in Britain, since the Romans forsook it. Wherein we have heard the many miseries and desolations brought by divine hand on a perverse nation; driven, when nothing else would reform them, out of a fair

[1] Henry of Huntington and Matthew of Westminster, write that Crida founded the kingdom of Mercia in the year 585.
[2] 'Tis probably the same place with Wanburrow, on the borders of Wilts and Berks; or rather a little village between Marlborough and the Devizes, near Wansdike.

country, into a mountanous and barren corner,[1] by strangers and pagans. So much more tolerable in the eye of heaven is infidelity profess'd, than christian faith and religion dishonoured by unchristian works. Yet they also at length renounc'd their heathenism; which how it came to pass, will be the matter next related.

BOOK IV.

THE Saxons grown up now to seven absolute kingdoms, and the latest of them establish'd by succession, finding their power arrive well nigh at the utmost of what was to be gain'd upon the Britons, and as little fearing to be displanted by them, had time now to survey at leasure one another's greatness. Which quickly bred among them either envy or mutual jealousies; till the west kingdom at length grown overpowerful, put an end to all the rest. Meanwhile, above others, Ethelbert of Kent, who by this time had well ripen'd his young ambition, with more ability of years and experience in war, what before he attempted to his loss, now successfully attains; and by degrees brought all the other monarchies between Kent and Humber, to be at his devotion. To which design the kingdom of West-Saxons, being the firmest of them all, at that time sore shaken by their overthrow at Wodens-beorth, and the death of Keaulin, gave him no doubt a main advantage; the rest yielded not subjection, but as he earn'd it by continual victories. And to win him the more regard abroad, he marries Bertha the French king's daughter, though a christian, and with this condition, to have the free exercise of her faith, under the care and instruction of Letardus a bishop, sent by her parents along with her; the king notwithstanding and his people retaining their own religion. Beda out of Gildas lays it sadly to the Britons charge, that they never would vouchsafe their Saxon neighbours the means of conversion: but how far to blame they were, and what hope there was of converting in the midst of so much hostility, at least falsehood from their first arrival, is not now easie to determine. Howbeit not long after, they had the christian faith preach'd to them by a nation more remote, and (as report went, accounted old in Beda's time) upon this occasion. The Northumbrians had a custom at that time and many hundred years after not abolish'd, to sell their children for a small value into any foreign land. Of which number, two comely youths were brought to Rome, whose fair and honest countenance invited Gregory, archdeacon of that city, among others that beheld them, pitying their condition, to demand whence they were; it was answer'd by some that stood by, that they were Angli of the province of Deira, subjects to Alla king of Northumberland, and by religion Pagans.

[1] The British Chronicles put the total retreat of the Welsh into Wales, Anno. 517.

Which last Gregory deploring, fram'd, on a sudden this allusion to the three names he heard; that the Angli, so like to angels, should be snatch'd *de ira;* that is, from the wrath of God, to sing Hallelujah: and forthwith (593), obtaining licence of Benedict the pope, had come and preach'd here among them, had not the Roman people, whose love endur'd not the absence of so vigilant a pastor over them, recall'd him, then on his journey, though but deferr'd his pious intention. For a while after (596), succeeding in the papal seat, and now in his fourth year, admonish'd, saith Beda, by divine instinct, he sent Augustine, whom he had design'd for bishop of the English nation and other zealous monks with him, to preach to them the gospel, Who being now on their way, discouraged by some reports, or their own carnal fear, sent back Austin, in the name of all, to beseech Gregory they might return home, and not be sent a journey so full of hazard, to a fierce and infidel nation, whose tongue they understood not. Gregory with pious and apostolick persuasions, exhorts them not to shrink back from so good a work, but cheerfully to go on in the strength of divine assistance. The letter itself yet extant among our writers of ecclesiastick story, I omit here, as not professing to relate of those matters more than what mixes aptly with civil affairs. The Abbot Austin, for so he was ordain'd over the rest, reincourag'd by the exhortations of Gregory, and his fellows, by the letter which he brought them, came (597) safe to the isle of Tanet, in number about forty, besides some of the French nation, which they took along as interpreters. Ethelbert the king, to whom Austin at his landing had sent a new and wondrous message, that he came from Rome to proffer heaven and eternal happiness in the knowledge of another God than the Saxons knew, appoints them to remain where they landed, and necessaries to be provided for them, consulting in the meantime what was to be done. And after certain days coming into the island, chose a place to meet them under the open sky, possess'd with an old persuasion, that all spells, if they should use any to deceive him, so it were not within doors, would be unavailable. They on the other side, call'd to his presence, advancing for their standard a silver cross, and the painted image of our saviour, came slowly forward singing their solemn letanies; which wrought in Ethelbert more suspicion perhaps that they us'd enchantments; till sitting down as the king will'd them, they there preach'd to him, and all in that assembly, the tidings of salvation. Whom having heard attentively, the king thus answer'd: Fair indeed and ample are the promises which ye bring, and such things as have the appearance in them of much good; yet such as being new and uncertain, I cannot hastily assent to, quitting the religion which from my ancestors, with all the English nation, for so many years I have retain'd. Nevertheless because ye are strangers, and have endured so long a journey, to impart us the knowledge of things, which I persuade me you believe to be the truest and the best, ye may be sure we shall not recompence you with any molestation, but shall provide rather how we may friendliest entertain ye: nor do we forbid whom ye can by preaching gain to your belief. And accordingly their residence he allotted them in Deroverne or Canterbury his chief city, and made provision for their maintenance, with free leave to preach their doctrine where they pleased. By which, and by the example of their holy life, spent in prayer, fasting, and continual labour in the conversion of souls, they (597) won many; on whose bounty and the king's, receiving only what was necessary, they subsisted. There stood without the city, on the east side, an ancient church built in honour of St. Martin, while yet the Romans remain'd here: in which Bertha the queen went out usually to pray. Here they also began first to preach, baptize, and openly to exercise divine worship. But when the king himself, convinc'd by their good life and miracles, became christian, and was baptiz'd, which came to pass in the very first year (598) of their arrival; then multitudes[1] daily, conforming to their prince, thought it honour to be reckon'd among those of his faith: to whom Ethelbert indeed principally shewed his favour, but compell'd none. For so he had been taught by them, who were both the instructors and the authors of his faith, that christian religion ought to be voluntary, not compell'd. About this time (599) Kelwulf the son of Cutha, Keaulin's brother, reign'd over the West-Saxons, after his brother Keola or Kelric, and had continual war either with English, Welsh, Picts or Scots. But Austin, whom with his fellows, Ethelbert now (601), had endowed with a better place for their abode in the city, and other possessions necessary to livelihood, crossing into France, was by the archbishop of Arles, at the appointment of pope Gregory, ordain'd archbishop of the English: and returning, sent to Rome Laurence and Peter, two of his associates, to acquaint the pope of his good success in England, and to be resolv'd of certain theological, or rather levitical questions: with answers to which, not proper in this place, Gregory sends also to the great work of converting, that went on so happily, a supply of labourers, Mellitus, Justus, Paulinus, Rusinian, and many others; who what they were may be guess'd by the stuff which they brought with them, vessels and vestments for the altar, copes, relicks, and for the archbishop Austin a pall to say mass in: to such a rank superstition that age was grown, though some of them yet retaining an emulation of apostolick zeal. Lastly, to Ethelbert they brought a letter with many presents. Austin thus exalted to archiepiscopal authority, recover'd from the ruins and other profane uses, a christian church in Canterbury, built of old by the Romans; which he dedicated by the name of Christ's Church, and joining to it built a seat for himself and his successors; a monastery

[1] Ten thousand baptiz'd in the year 599. Tall. Tab.

also near the city eastward, where Ethelbert at his motion built St. Peter's, and enrich'd it with great endowments, to be a place of burial for the archbishops and kings of Kent: so quickly they step up into fellowship of pomp with kings. While thus Ethelbert and his people had their minds intent, Ethelfrid the Northumbrian king was not less busied in far different affairs: for being altogether warlike, and covetous of fame, he more wasted the Britons than any Saxon king before him: winning from them large territories, which either he made tributary, or planted with his own subjects. Whence Edan king of those Scots that dwelt in Britain, jealous of his successes, came (603) against him with a mighty army, to a place call'd Degsaston; but in the fight losing most of his men, himself with a few escap'd: only Theobald the king's brother, and the whole wing which he commanded, unfortunately cut off, made the victory to Ethelfrid less entire. Yet from that time no king of Scots in hostile manner durst pass into Britain for a hundred and more years after: and what some years before, Kelwulf of the West-Saxon is annal'd to have done against the Scots and Picts, passing through the Land of Ethelfrid a King so potent, unless in his aid and alliance, is not likely. Buchanan writes as if Ethelfrid, assisted by Keaulin, whom he mis-titles King of East-Saxons, had before this time a battle with Aidan, wherein Cutha Keaulin's son was slain. But Cutha, as is above written from better authority, was slain in fight against the Welsh twenty years before. The number of Christians began now (604) to increase so fast, that Augustine ordaining bishops under him, two of his assistants, Mellitus[1] and Justus, sent them out both to the work of their ministry. And Mellitus by preaching converted the East-Saxons, over whom Sebert the son of Sleda, by permission of Ethelbert, being born of his sister Ricula, then reigned. Whose conversion Ethelbert to gratulate, built them the great church of St. Paul in London to be their bishop's cathedral; as Justus also had his built at Rochester, and both gifted by the same king with fair possessions. Hitherto Austin labour'd well among Infidels, but not with like commendation soon after among Christians. For by means of Ethelbert summoning the Briton bishops to a place[2] on the edge of Worcestershire, call'd from that time Augustine's oak, he requires them to conform with him in the same day of celebrating Easter, and many other points wherein they differed from the rites of Rome: which when they refus'd to do, not prevailing by dispute, he appeals to a miracle, restoring to sight a blind man whom the Britons could not cure. At this something mov'd, though not minded to recede from their own opinions, without further consultation, they request a second

[1] Mellitus was made bishop of London, and Justus bishop of Rochester.
[2] Bede says, it was on the confines of Wiccians and West-Saxons; whereas Worcestershire doth not anywhere border upon the West-Saxons. By his account, it should have stood about that part of Gloucestershire, which joyns Somersetshire and Wiltshire.

meeting: To which came seven Brtisih bishops, with many other learned men especially from the famous monastery of Bangor, in which were said to be so many monks, living all by their own labour, that being divided under seven rectors, none had fewer than three hundred. One man there was who stayed behind, a hermit by the life he led, who by his wisdom effected more than all the rest who went; being demanded, for they held him as an oracle, how they might know Austin to be a man from God, that they might follow him, he answer'd, that if they found him meek and humble, they should be taught by him, for it was likeliest to be the yoke of Christ, both what he bore himself, and would have them bear; but if he bore himself proudly, that they should not regard him, for he was then certainly not of God. They took his advice, and hasted to the place of meeting. Whom Austin, being already there before them, neither arose to meet, nor received into any brotherly sort, but sat all the while pontifically in his chair. Whereat the Britons, as they were counsel'd by the holy man, neglected him, and neither hearken'd to his proposals of conformity, nor would acknowledge him for an arch-bishop: and in name of the rest, Dimothus then abbot of Bangor, is said, thus sagely to have answer'd him. 'As to the subjections which you require, be thus persuaded of us, that in the bond of love and charity we are all subjects and servants to the Church of God, yea to the pope of Rome, and every good Christian to help them forward, both by word and deed, to be the children of God: other obedience than this we know not to be due to him whom you term the pope; and this obedience we are ready to give both to him and to every Christian continually. Besides, we are govern'd under God by the bishop of Caerleon, who is to oversee us in spiritual matters.' To which Austin thus presaging, some say menacing, replies, 'Since ye refuse to accept of Peace with your brethren, ye shall have war from your enemies? and since ye will not with us preach the word of life, to whom ye ought, from their hands ye shall receive death.' This, though writers agree not whether Austin spake it as his prophecy, or as his plot against the Britons, fell out accordingly. For many years were not past, when Ethelfrid, whether of his own accord, or at the request of Ethelbert, incens'd by Austin, with a powerful host, came (607) to Westchester, then Caer-legion. Where being met by the British forces, and both sides in readiness to give the onset, he discerns a company of men, not habited for war, standing together in a place of some safety; and by them a squadron arm'd. Whom having learn'd upon some enquiry to be priests and monks, assembl'd thither after three days fasting to pray for the good success of the forces against them, therefore they first, saith he, shall feel our swords; for they who pray against us, fight heaviest against us by their prayers, and are our dangerousest enemies. And with that turns his first charge upon the monks. Brocmail, the captain, set to guard them, quickly turns his back, and leaves above 1200 monks to a sudden massacree, whereof scarce fifty 'scap'd : but not so easie work found Ethelfrid against another part of Britons that stood in arms, whom though at last he overthrew, yet with slaughter nigh as great to his own soldiers. To excuse Austin of this bloodshed, lest some might think it his revengeful policy, Beda writes that he was dead long before, although if the time of his sitting arch-bishop be right computed sixteen years, he must survive this action. Other just ground of charging him with this imputation appears not, save what evidently we have from Geoffrey Monmouth, whose weight we know. The same year Kelwulf made war on the South-Saxons, bloody, saith Huntingdon, to both sides, but most to them of the south :[1] and four years after (611) dying left the government of West-Saxons to Kineglis and Cuichelm the sons of his brother Keola. Others, as Florent of Worcester, and Matthew of Westminster, will have Cuichelm, son of Kineglis, but admitted to reign (614) with his father, in whose third year they are recorded with joynt forces or conduct to have fought against the Britons in [2] Beandune, now Bindon in Dorsetshire, and to have slain of them above two thousand. More memorable was (616) the second year following, by the death of Ethelbert the first Christian king of Saxons, and no less a favourer of all civility in that rude age.[3] He gave laws and statutes after the example of Roman emperors, written with the advice of his sagest counsellors, but in the English tongue, and observ'd long after. Wherein his special care was to punish those who had stoll'n aught from church or churchman, thereby shewing how gratefully he receiv'd at their hands the Christian faith, which, he no sooner dead (616), but his son Eadbald took the course as fast to extinguish ; not only falling back to heathenism, but that which heathenism was wont to abhor, marrying his father's second wife. Then soon was perceiv'd what multitudes for fear or countenance of the king had profess'd Christianity, returning now as eagerly to their old religion. Nor staid the apostasie within one province, but quickly spread over to the East-Saxons ; occasion'd there likewise, or set forward by the death of their Christian king Sebert : whose three sons of whom two are nam'd, Sexted and Seward, neither in his life-time would be brought to baptism, and after his decease re-establish'd the free exercise of idolatry ; nor so content, they set themselves in despight to do some open profanation against the other sacrament. Coming therefore into the church, where Mellitus the bishop was ministring, they requir'd him in abuse and scorn, to deliver to them unbaptiz'd the consecrated bread ; and

In this year 611, Sebert king of the East-Saxons founded St. Peter's church and abbey at Westminster, which was consecrated by Melitus first bishop of London.
[2] The Saxon chronical calls it Beamdune : and it is not unlikely, that 'twas Bampton in Devonshire, wh... e it borders upon Somersetshire, tho' Cambden in his Brit. Tit. Dorsetshire, says Beamdune is Byndon near Wareham in that county.
[3] He was the first English king who coin'd money. Cambd. Rem.

him refusing, drove disgracefully out of their dominion. Who cross'd forthwith into Kent, where things were in the same plight, and thence into France, with Justus bishop of Rochester. But divine vengeance deferr'd not long the punishment of men so impious; for Eadbald, vext with an evil spirit, fell often into foul fits of distraction; and the sons of Sebert, in a fight against the West-Saxons perish'd, with their whole army. But Eadbald, within the year, by an extraordinary means became penitent. For when Laurence the arch-bishop and successor of Austin was preparing to ship for France, after Justus and Mellitus, the story goes, if it be worth believing, that St. Peter, in whose church he spent the night before in watching and praying, appear'd to him, and to make the vision more sensible, gave him many stripes for offering to desert his flock; at sight whereof the king (to whom next morning he shewed the marks of what he had suffer'd, by whom and for what cause) relenting and in great fear dissolv'd his incestuous marriage, and apply'd himself to the christian faith more sincerely than before, with all his people. But the Londoners, addicted still to Paganism, would not be persuaded to receive again Mellitus their bishop, and to compel them was not in his power. Thus (617) much through all the south was troubl'd in religion, as much were the north parts disquieted through ambition. For Ethelfrid of Bernicia, as was touch'd before, having thrown Edwin out of Deira, and joyn'd that kingdom to his own, not content to have bereav'd him of his right, whose known vertues and high parts gave cause of suspicion to his enemies, sends messengers to demand him of Redwald king of East-Angles; under whose protection, after many years wandring obscurely through all the island, he had plac'd his safety. Redwald, though having promis'd all defence to Edwin as to his suppliant, yet tempted with continual and large offers of gold, and not contemning the puissance of Elthelfrid, yielded at length, either to dispatch him, or to give him into their hands; but earnestly exhorted by his wife, not to betray the faith and inviolable law of hospitality and refuge given, prefers his first promise as the more religious; nor only refuses to deliver him; but since war was thereupon denounc'd, determines to be beforehand with the danger; and with a sudden army rais'd, surprises Ethelfrid, little dreaming an invasion, and in a fight near to the east-side of the river Idle, on the Mercian border, now Nottinghamshire,[1] slays him, dissipating easily those few forces which he had got to march out over hastily with him; who yet has a testimony of his fortune, not his valour to be blam'd, slew first with his own hands Reiner the king's son. His two sons, Oswald and Oswi, by Acca, Edwin's sister, escap'd into Scotland. By this victory, Redwald became so far superior to the other Saxon kings, that Beda reckons him the next after Ella and Ethelbert; who besides this conquest of the north, had

[1] Near Markham.

likewise all on the hither-side Humber at his obedience. He had formerly in Kent receiv'd baptism, but coming home, and persuaded by his wife, who still it seems, was his chief counsellor to good or bad alike, relaps'd into his old religion ; yet not willing to forego his new, thought it not the worst way, lest perhaps he might err in either, for more assurance to keep them both : and in the same temple erected one altar to Christ, another to his idols. But Edwin, as with more deliberation he undertook, and with more sincerity retain'd the christian profession, so also in power and extent of dominion far exceeded all before him; subduing all, saith Beda, English or British, even to the isles, then call'd Mevanian, Anglesey, and Man ; settl'd in his kingdom by Redwald, he sought in marriage Edelburga, whom others call'd Tate, the daughter of Ethelbert. To whose embassadors, Eadbald her brother made answer, that to wed their daughter to a pagan, was not the christian law. Edwin reply'd, that to her religion he would be no hindrance, which with her whole household she might freely exercise. And moreover, that if examin'd it were found the better, he would imbrace it. These ingenious offers opening so fair a way to the advancement of truth, are accepted, and Paulinus (625) as a spiritual guardian sent along with the virgin. He being to that purpose made bishop by Justus, omitted no occasion to plant the gospel in those parts, but with small success, till the next year (626), Cuichelm, at that time one of the two West-Saxon kings, envious of the greatness which he saw Edwin growing up to, sent privily Eumerus a hir'd sword-man to assassin him ; who under pretence of doing a message from his master, with a poison'd weapon, stabs at Edwin, conferring with him in his house, by the river Derwent in Yorkshire, on an Easter-day : which Lilla, one of the king's attendants, at the instant perceiving, with a loyalty that stood not then to deliberate, abandon'd his whole body to the blow ; which notwithstanding made passage through to the king's person, with a wound not to be slighted. The murderer encompass'd now with swords, and desperate, fore-revenges his own fall with the death of another, whom his poinard reach'd home. Paulinus omitting no opportunity to win the king from mis-belief, obtain'd at length this promise from him ; that if Christ, whom he so magnify'd, would give him to recover of his wound, and victory of his enemies who had thus assaulted him, he would then become Christian, in pledge whereof he gave his young daughter Eanfled to be bred up in religion ; who with twelve others of his family, on the day of Pentecost was baptiz'd. And by that time well recover'd of his wound, to punish the authors of so foul a fact, he went with an army against the West-Saxons: whom having quell'd by war, and of such as had conspir'd against him, put some to death, others pardon'd, he return'd home victorious ; and from that time worshipp'd no more his idols, yet ventur'd not rashly into baptism, but first took care to be instructed rightly, what he learnt, examining and still considering with himself and others, whom he held wisest ; though Boniface the pope, by large letters of exhortation, both to him and his queen, was not wanting to quicken his belief. But while he still deferr'd, and his deferring might seem now to have past the maturity of wisdom to a faulty lingring ; Paulinus by revelation, as was believ'd, coming to the knowledge of a secret, which befel him strangely in the time of his troubles, on a certain day went in boldly to him, and laying his right hand on the head of the king, ask'd him if he remembered what that sign meant ? The king trembling, and in amaze rising up, straight fell at his feet : 'behold,' saith Paulinus, raising him from the ground, 'God hath deliver'd you from your enemies, and given you the kingdom, as you desir'd : perform now what long since you promis'd him, to receive his doctrine which I now bring you, and the faith, which if you accept, shall to your temporal felicity add eternal.' The promise claim'd of him by Paulinus, how and wherefore made, though favouring much of legend, is thus related : Redwald,[1] as we heard before, dazled with the gold of Ethelfrid, or by his threatning overaw'd, having promis'd to yield up Edwin, one of his faithful companions, of which he had some few with him in the court of Redwald, that never shrunk from his adversity, about the first hour of night comes in haste to his chamber, and calling him forth for better security, reveals to him his danger, offers him his aid to make escape : but that course not approv'd, as seeming dishonourable without more manifest cause to begin distrust towards one who had so long been his only refuge, the friend departs. Edwin left alone without the palace gate, full of sadness and perplext thoughts, discerns about the dead of night a man, neither by countenance nor by habit to him known, approaching towards him : who, after salutation, ask'd him, ' why at this hour, when all others were at rest, he alone so sadly sat waking on a cold stone ?' Edwin not a little misdoubting who he might be, ask'd him again, what his sitting within doors or without concern'd him to know ? To whom he again, 'think not that who thou art, or why sitting here, or what danger hangs over thee, is to me unknown : but what would you promise to that man, who ever would befriend you out of all these troubles, and persuade Redwald to the like ?' 'All that I am able,' answer'd Edwin. And he, ' what if the same man should promise to make you greater than any English king hath been before you ?' ' I should not doubt, quoth Edwin, ' to be answerably grateful.' 'And what if to all this he would inform you, said the other, in a way to happiness, beyond what any of your ancestors hath known ; would you hearken to his counsel ?' Edwin, without stopping, promis'd he would. And the other laying his right hand on Edwin's head, when this sign, saith he, shall next befall thee, remember this time of night, and this discourse, to perform

[1] 'Tis in Bede, and happen'd ten years before.

what thou hast promis'd;' and with these words disappearing, left Edwin much reviv'd, but not less fill'd with wonder who this unknown should be. When suddenly the friend who had been gone all this while to listen farther what was like to be decreed of Edwin, comes back, and joyfully bids him rise to his repose, for that the king's mind, tho' for a while drawn aside, was now fully resolv'd not only not to betray him, but to defend him against all enemies, as he had promis'd. This was said to be the cause why Edwin admonish'd by the bishop of a sign which had befallen him so strangely, and as he thought so secretly, arose to him with that reverence and amazement, as to one sent from heaven, to claim that promise of him which he perceiv'd well was due to a divine power that had assisted him in his troubles. To Paulinus therefore he makes answer, that the christian belief he himself ought by promise, and intended to receive; but would confer first with his chief peers and counsellers, that if they likewise could be won, all at once might be baptiz'd. They therefore being ask'd in council what their opinion was concerning this new doctrine, and well perceiving which way the king inclin'd, every one hereafter shap'd his reply. The chief priest speaking first, discover'd an old grudge he had against his gods, for advancing others in the king's favour above him their chief priest: another hiding his court compliance with a grave sentence, commended the choice of certain, before uncertain, upon due examination; to like purpose answer'd all the rest of his sages, none openly dissenting from what was likely to be the king's creed: whereas the preaching of Paulinus could work no such effect upon them, toiling till that time without success. Whereupon Edwin renouncing heathenism, became christian; and the pagan priest offering himself freely to demolish the altars of his former gods, made some amends for his teaching to adore them. With Edwin, his two sons, Osfrid and Eanfrid, born to him by Quenburga, daughter, as saith Beda, of Kearle king of Mercia, in the time of his banishment, and with them most of the people, both nobles and commons, easily converted, were (627) baptized;[1] he with his whole family at York, in a church hastily built up of wood, the multitude most part in rivers. Northumberland thus christen'd, Paulinus crossing Humber, converted (628) also the province of Linsey, and Blecca the governour of Lincoln, with his houshold and most of that city; wherein he built a church of stone, curiously wrought, but of small continuance: for the roof in Beda's time,[2] uncertain whether by neglect or enemies, was down, the walls only standing. Meanwhile in Mercia, Kearle a kinsman of Wibba, saith Huntingdon, not a son, having long withheld the kingdom from Penda, Wibba's son, left it now at length to the fiftieth year of his age: with whom Kinelis and Cuichelm, the West-Saxon kings, two years after (629), having by that time it seems re-

[1] On Easter-day, Anno 627.   [2] About eighty years afterwards.

cover'd strength, since the inroad made upon them by Edwin, fought at Cirencester, then made truce. But Edwin seeking every way to propagate the faith, which with so much deliberation he had receiv'd, persuaded Eorpwald[1] the son of Redwald, king of East-Angles, to embrace the same belief; willingly or in awe, is not known, retaining under Edwin the name only of a king. But Eorpwald not long surviv'd his conversion, slain in fight by Rickbert a pagan : whereby the people having lightly follow'd the religion of their king, as lightly fell back to their old superstitions for above three years after ; Edwin in the meanwhile, to his faith adding virtue, by the due administration of justice, wrought such peace over all his territories, that from sea to sea, man or woman might have travell'd in safety. His care also was of fountains by the wayside, to make them fittest for the use of travellers. And not unmindful of regal state, whether in war or peace, he had a royal banner carry'd before him. But having reign'd with much honour seventeen years, he was at length by Kedwalla, or Cadwallon, king of the Britains, who with aid of the Mercian Pinda,[2] had rebell'd against him, slain in a battle with his son Osfred, at a place call'd Hethfield,[3] and his whole army overthrown or dispers'd in the year 633, and the 47th of his age, in the eye of man worthy a more peaceful end. His head brought to York, was there bury'd in the church by him begun. Sad was this overthrow both to church and state of the Northumbrians : for Penda being a heathen, and the British king, though in name a christian, yet in deeds more bloody than the pagan, nothing was omitted of barbarous cruelty in the slaughter of sex or age ; Kedwalla threatning to root out the whole nation, though then newly christian. For the Britons, and as Beda saith, even to his days, accounted Saxon christianity no better than paganism, and with them held as little communion. From these calamities no refuge being left but flight, Paulinus taking with him Ethelburga the queen and her children, aided by Bassus, one of Edwin's captains made escape by sea to Eadbald king of Kent : who receiving his sister with all kindness, made Paulinus bishop of Rochester, where he ended his days. After Edwin, the kingdom of Northumberland became divided as before, each rightful heir seizing his part ; in Deira, Osric the son of Elfric, Edwin's uncle, by profession a christian, and baptiz'd by Paulinus ; in Bernicia, Eanfrid the son of Ethelfrid ; who all the time of Edwin, with his brother Oswald, and many of the young nobility, liv'd in Scotland exil'd, and had been there taught and baptis'd. No sooner had they gotten each a kingdom, but both turn'd recreant, sliding back into their old religion, and both

---

[1] On the death of Redwald the East-Angles would have bestow'd their kingdom on Edwin, but he out of gratitude to his benefactor Redwald permitted his son Eorpwald to reign as his tributary. Bede, ch. 15.   [2] Geoffrey says, he first conquer'd Penda.
[3] 'Tis probably Hatfield, in the bounds of Yorkshire and Lincolnshire. See the Glossary to the Saxon Chronicle.

were the same year slain ; Osric by a sudden eruption of Kedwalla, whom he in a strong town had unadvisedly besieged ; Eanfrid seeking peace, and inconsiderately with a few surrendring himself. Kedwalla now rang'd at will through both those provinces, using cruelly his conquest ; when Oswald,[1] the brother of Eanfrid, with a small, but christian army, unexpectedly coming on, defeated and destroy'd both him and his huge forces, which he boasted to be invincible, by a little river running into Tine, near the ancient Roman wall then call'd Denisburn,[2] the place afterwards Heavenfield, from the cross reported miraculous for cures, which Oswald there erected before the battle, in token of his faith against the great number of his enemies. Obtaining the kingdom, he took care to instruct again the people in christianity. Sending therefore to the Scotish elders, Beda so terms them, among whom he had receiv'd baptism, requested of them some faithful teacher, who might again settle religion in his realm, which the late troubles had impair'd ; they as readily hearkning to his request, send Aidan, a Scotch monk and bishop, but of singular zeal and meekness, with others to assist him, whom at their own desire he seated in Lindisfarne, as the episcopal seat, now Holy Island : and being the son of Ethelfrid, by the sister of Edwin, as right heir, others failing, easily reduc'd both kingdoms of Northumberland as before into one ; nor of Edwin's dominion lost any part, but enlarg'd it rather, over all the four British nations, Angles, Britons, Picts, and Scots, exercising regal authority. Of his devotion, humility, and almsdeeds, much is spoken ; that he disdain'd not to be the interpreter of Aidan, preaching in Scotch or bad English, to his nobles and houshold servants ; and had the poor continually serv'd at his gate, after the promiscuous manner of those times : his meaning might be upright, but the manner more ancient of private or of church contribution, is doubtless more evangelical. About this time the West-Saxons, anciently call'd Gevissi, by the preaching of Berinus a bishop, whom pope Honorius had sent, were converted to the faith with Kineglis their king : him Oswald receiv'd out of the font, and his daughter in marriage. The next year Cuichelm was baptiz'd in Dorchester,[3] but liv'd not to the year's end. The East-Angles also this year were reclaim'd to the faith of Christ, which for some years past they had thrown off. But Sigbert the brother of Eorpwald now succeeded in that kingdom, prais'd for a most christian and learned man : who while his brother yet reign'd, living in France an exile for some displeasure conceiv'd against him by Redwald his father, learn'd there the christian faith ; and reigning soon after, in the same instructed his people, by the preaching of

---

[1] Nephew to Edwin by his sister Occa.
[2] Diston, the seat and barony of the Earl of Darwentwater, call'd in old books Devilstone, by Bede, Devilsburn. Vid. Camb. Britan. Tit. Northumberland.
[3] By Byninus an Italian, the first bishop of Dorchester in Oxfordshire.

Felix[1] a Burgundian bishop. In the year 640, Eadbald deceasing, left to Ercombert his son by Emma the French king's daughter, the kingdom of Kent; recorded the first of English kings who commanded through his limits the destroying of idols; laudably, if all idols without exception; and the first to have establish'd Lent among us, under strict penalty, not worth remembring, but only to inform us, that no Lent was observ'd here till his time by compulsion; especially being noted by some to have fradulently usurp'd upon his elder brother Ermenred, whose right was precedent to the crown. Oswald having reign'd eight years, worthy also as might seem of longer life,[2] fell into the same fate with Edwin, and from the same hand, in a great battle overcome and slain by Penda, at a place call'd Maserfield, now Oswestre[3] in Shropshire, miraculous, as saith Beda, after his death. His brother Oswi succeeded him, reigning, tho' in much trouble, twenty-eight years; oppos'd either by Penda, or his son Alfred, or his brother's son Ethelwald. Next year Kinegils the West-Saxon dying (643), left his son Kenwalk in his stead, though as yet unconverted. About this time Sigebert, king of East-Angles, having learn'd in France, e'er his coming to reign, the manner of their schools, with the assistance of some teachers out of Kent, instituted a school here after the same discipline, thought to be the university of Cambridge then first founded:[4] and at length weary of his kingly office, betook him to a monastical life; commending the care of government to his kinsman Egric, who had sustain'd with him part of that burthen before. It happen'd some years after, that Penda made war on the East-Angles: they expecting a sharp encounter, besought Sigebert, whom they esteem'd an expert leader, with his presence to confirm the soldiery: and him refusing carried by force out of the monastery into the camp; where acting the monk rather than the captain, with single wand in his hand, he was slain with Egric, and his whole army put to flight. Anna of the royal stock, as next in right, succeeded; and hath the praise of a virtuous and most christian prince. But Kenwalk the West-Saxon having (645) married the sister of Penda, and divorc'd her, was by him with more appearance of a just cause vanquish'd in fight, and depriv'd of his crown: whence retiring to Anna king of the East-Angles, after three years abode in his court, he there became christian, and afterwards (646) regain'd his kingdom. Oswi in the former years of his reign, had sharer with him, Oswir nephew of Edwin, who rul'd in Deira seven years, commended much for his zeal in religion, and for comeliness of person, with other princely qualities, belov'd of all. Notwithstanding which, dissentions

[1] The first bishop of Dunwich in Suffolk.
[2] He liv'd 38 years only.   [3] Oswald-tre on the borders of Denbighshire.
[4] Bede say:, 'twas a little desolate city in his time, and takes no notice of it as an University. Anno 700. Robert of Remington writes, that in the reign of Edward the First, Grant-Bridge or Cambridge, from a school was made an University like Oxford. Caml Tit. Cambridge.

growing between them; it came to arms. Oswin seeing himself much exceeded in numbers, thought it more prudence, dismissing his army, to reserve himself for some better occasion. But committing his person with one faithful attendant to the loyalty of Hunwald an earl, his imagin'd friend, he was by him treacherously discover'd and (651) by command of Oswi slain. After whom within twelve days, and for grief of him whose death he foretold, dy'd bishop Aidan, famous for his charity, meekness, and labour in the gospel. The fate of Oswi was detestable to all; which therefore to expiate, a monastery was built in the place where it was done, and prayers there daily offer'd up for the souls of both kings, the slain and the slayer. Kenwalk by this time reinstall'd in his kingdom, kept it long, but with various fortune; for Beda relates him oft-times afflicted by his enemies with great losses: and in 652 by the annals, fought a battle (civil war Ethelward calls it) at Bradanford by the river Afene; against whom, and for what cause, or who had the victory, they write not. Cambden names the place Bradford in Wiltshire, by the river Avon, and Cuthred his near kinsman, against whom he fought, but cites no authority; certain it is, that Kenwalk four years before had given large possession to his nephew Cuthred, the more unlikely therefore now to have rebell'd. The next year (653) Penda, whom his father Penda, though a heathen, had for his princely virtues made prince of Middle-Angles, belonging to the Mercians, was with that people converted to the faith. For coming to Oswi with request to have in marriage Alfleda his daughter, he was deny'd her but on condition, that he with all his people should receive christianity. Hearing therefore not unwillingly what was preach'd to him of resurrection and eternal life, much persuaded also by Alfrid the king's son, who had his sister Kyniburg to wife, he easily assented, for the truth's sake only, as he profess'd, whether he obtain'd the virgin or no, and was baptiz'd with all his followers. Returning, he took with him four presbyters to teach the people of his province; who by their daily preaching won many. Neither did Penda, though himself no believer, probibit any in his kingdom to hear or believe the gospel, but rather hated and despis'd those, who professing to believe, attested not their faith by good works; condemning them for miserable and justly to be despis'd, who obey not that God in whom they chuse to believe. How well might Penda, this heathen, rise up in judgment against many pretending christians, both of his own and these days! Yet being a man bred up to war (as no less were others then reigning, and oft-times one against another, though both christian) he warr'd on Anna, king of the East-Angles, perhaps without cause, for Anna was esteem'd a just man, and at length (654) slew him. About this time the East-Saxons, who, as above hath been said, had expell'd their bishop Mellitus, and renounc'd the faith, were by the means of

Oswi thus reconverted. Sigebert, sirnam'd the Small, being the son of Seward, without other memory of his reign, left his son king of that province, after him Sigebert the second, who coming often to visit Oswi his great friend, was by him at several times fervently dissuaded from idolatry, and convinc'd at length to forsake it, was there baptiz'd; on his return home, taking with him Kedda a laborious preacher, afterwards made bishop; by whose teaching with some help of others, the people were again recover'd from misbelief. But Sigebert some years (661) after, though standing fast in religion, was by the conspiracy of two brethren in place near about him, wickedly murder'd; who being ask'd what mov'd them to do a deed so heinous, gave no other than this barbarous answer: 'That they were angry with him for being so gentle to his enemies, as to forgive them their injuries whenever they besought him.' Yet his death seems to have happen'd not without some cause by him given of divine displeasure. For one of those earls who slew him, living in unlawful wedlock, therefore excommunicated so severely by the bishop, that no man might presume to enter into his house, much less to sit at meat with him, the king not regarding this church censure, went to feast with him at his invitation. Whom the bishop meeting in his return, though penitent for what he had done, and fall'n at his feet, touch'd with the rod in his hand, and angerly thus foretold: 'Because thou hast neglected to abstain from the house of that excommunicate, in that house thou shalt die:' and so it fell out perhaps from that prediction, God bearing witness to his minister in the power of church discipline, spiritually executed, not juridically on the contemner thereof. This year 655 prov'd fortunate to Oswi, and fatal to Penda, for Oswi by the continual inroads of Penda, having long endur'd much devastation, to the endangering once by assault and fire Bebbanburg, his strongest city, now Banborrow castle, unable to resist him, with many rich presents offer'd to buy his peace. Which not accepted by the pagan, who intended nothing but destruction to that king, though more than once in affinity with him, turning gifts into vows, he implores divine assistance, devoting, if he were deliver'd from his enemy, a child of one year old, his daughter to be a nun, and twelve portions of land whereupon to build monasteries. His vows, as may be thought, found better success than his proffer'd gifts; for hereupon with his son Alfrid gathering a small power, he encounter'd and discomfited the Mercians, thirty times exceeding his in number, and led on by expert captains; at a place call'd Loydes, now Leeds in Yorkshire. Besides, this Ethelwald, the son of Oswald, who rul'd in Deira, took part with the Mercians, but in the fight withdrew his forces, and in a safe place expected the event: with which unseasonable retreat, the Mercians perhaps terrify'd and misdouting more danger, fled; their commanders, with Penda himself, most being slain, among whom Edelhere the brother of Anna, who rul'd after him the East-Angles, and was the author of this war; many more flying were drown'd in the river, which Beda calls Winved,[1] then swoll'n above his banks. The death of Penda, who had been the death of so many good kings, made general rejoicing, as the song witness'd. 'At the river Winwed, Anna was aveng'd.' To Edelhere succeeded Ethelwald his brother, in the East-Angles; to Sigebert in the East-Saxons, Suidelhelm the son of Sexbald, saith Bede, the brother of Sigebert, saith Malmsbury; he was baptiz'd by Kedda, then residing in the East-Angles, and by Ethelwald the king, receiv'd out of the font. But Oswi in the strength of his late victory, within (658) three years after subdu'd all Mercia, and of the Pictish nation greatest part at which time he gave to Peada his son-in-law the kingdom of South-Mercia, divided from the northern by Trent. But Peada the (659) spring following, as was said, by the treason of his wife the daughter of Oswi, married by him for a special christian, on the feast of Easter, not protected by the holy time, was slain. The Mercian nobles, Immin, Eaba, and Eadbert, throwing off the government of Oswi, set up Wulfer the other son of Penda to be their king, whom till then they had kept hid, and with him adhered to the christian faith. Kenwalk the West-Saxon, now settl'd at home, and desirous to enlarge his dominion, prepares against the Britons, joins battle with them at Pen in Somersetshire, and overcoming pursues them to Pedridan. Another fight he had with them before, at a place call'd Witgcornesbrug, barely mention'd by the monk of Malmsbury.' Nor was it long (661) e'er he fell at variance with Wulfer the son of Penda, his old enemy, scarce yet warm in his throne, fought with him at Possentesburg,[2] on the Easter holydays, and as Ethelwerd saith, took him prisoner; but the Saxon annals, quite otherwise, that Wulfer winning the field, wasted the West-Saxon country as far as Eskesdun;[3] nor staying there, took and wasted the isle of Wight, but causing the inhabitants to be baptiz'd, till then unbelievers, gave the island to Ethelwald king of the South-Saxons, whom he had receiv'd out of the font.[4] The year 664 a synod of Scotch and English bishops, in the presence of Oswi and Alfred his son, was held at a monastery in those parts, to debate upon what day Easter should be kept; a controversie which long before had disturb'd the Greek and Latin churches: wherein the Scots not agreeing with the way of Rome, not yielding to the disputants on that side, to whom the king most inclin'd, such as were bishops here, resign'd, and return'd home with their disciples. Another clerical question was there also much controverted, not so superstitious in my opinion as ridiculous, about the right shaving of crowns.

[1] Suppos'd to be the river Aire.
[3] Aston near Wallingford in Berkshire.
[2] Pontesbury in Shropshire.
[4] Bede agrees with the Saxon annals.

The same year was seen an eclipse of the sun in May, followed by a sore pestilence beginning in the south, but spreading to the north, and over all Ireland with great mortality. In which time the East Saxon after Swithelm's decease, being govern'd by Siger the son of Sigebert the Small, and Sebbi of Seward, though both subject to the Mercians. Siger and his people unsteady of faith, supposing that this plague was come upon them for renouncing their old religion, fell off the second time to infidelity. Which the Mercian king Wulfer understanding, sent Jerumanus a faithful bishop, who with other his fellow labourers, by sound doctrine and gentle dealing, soon recur'd them of their second relapse. In Kent, Ercombert expiring, was succeeded by his son Ecbert. In whose fourth (668) year by means of Theodore, a learned Greekish monk of Tarsus, whom pope Vitalian had ordain'd archbishop of Canterbury, the Greek and Latin tongue, with other liberal arts, arithmetick, musick, astronomy, and the like; began first to flourish among the Saxons; as did also the whole land, under potent and religious kings, more than ever before, as Bede affirms, till his own days. Two years after (670), in Northumberland dy'd Oswi, much addicted to Romish rites, and resolv'd, had his disease releas'd him, to have ended his days at Rome; Ecfrid the eldest of his sons begot in wedlock, succeeded him. After other three years (673), Ecbert in Kent deceasing, left nothing memorable behind him, but the general suspicion to have slain or conniv'd at the slaughter of his uncle's two sons,[1] Elbert and Egelbright. In recompence whereof, he gave to the mother of them part of Tanet, wherein to build an abbey; the kingdom fell to his brother Lothair. And much about this time, by best account it should be, however plac'd in Beda, that Ecfrid of Northumberland, having war with the Mercian Wulfer, won from him Lindsey, and the country there about. Sebbi having reign'd over the East Saxons thirty years, not long before his death, though long before desiring, took on him the habit of a monk; and drew his wife at length, though unwilling, to the same devotion. Kenwalk also dying, left the government to Sexbarga his wife, who out-liv'd him in it but one year, driven out (674), saith Mat. West, by the nobles, disdaining female government. After whom several petty kings, as Beda calls them, for ten years space divided the West Saxons; others name two, Escwin the nephew of Kinigils, and Kentwin the son, not petty by their deeds: for Escwin fought a battle with Wulfer, at Bedanhafde,[2] and about a year after (676) both deceas'd; but Wulfer not without a stain left behind him, of selling the bishoprick of London, to Wini the first simonist we read of in this story; Kenwalk had before expell'd him from his chair at Winchester; Ethelfred

[1] Matt. of Westminster calls them his cousins. [2] Suppos'd to be Bedwin in Wiltshire.

the brother of Wulfer obtaining next the kingdom of Mercia, not only recover'd Lindsey, and what besides in those parts Wulfer had lost to Ecfrid some years before, but found himself strong enough to extend his arms another way, as far as Kent, wasting that country without respect to church or monastery, much also endamaging the city of Rochester: notwithstanding what resistance Lothair could make against him. In August 678 was seen a morning comet for three months following, in manner of a fiery pillar. And the South-Saxons about this time were converted to the christian faith, upon this occasion. Wilfrid bishop of the Northumbrians entering into contention with Ecfrid the king, was by him depriv'd of his bishoprick, and long wandering up and down as far as Rome, return'd at length (679) into England, but not daring to approach the north, whence he was banish'd, bethought him where he might to best purpose elsewhere exercise his ministry. The south of all other Saxons remain'd yet heathen; but Edelwalk their king not long before had been baptiz'd in Mercia, persuaded by Wulfer, and by him, as hath been said, receiv'd out of the font. For which relation's sake he had the Isle of Wight, and a province of the Meanuari adjoining, given him on the continent about Meanesborow in Hantshire, which Wulfer had a little before gotten from Kenwalk. Thither Wilfrid takes his journey, and with the help of other spiritual labourers about him, in short time planted there the gospel. It had not rain'd, as is said, of three years before in that country, whence many of the people daily perish'd by famine; till on the first day of their publick baptism, soft and plentiful showers descending, restor'd all abundance to the summer following. Two years (681) after this, Kentwin the other West-Saxon king above-nam'd, chac'd the Welch-Britons, as is chronicl'd without circumstance to the very sea shoar. But in the year, by Beda's reck'ning, 683, Kedwalla a West-Saxon of the royal line (whom the Welch will have to be Cadwallader, last king of the Britons) thrown out by faction, return'd from banishment, and invaded both Kentwin, if then living, or whoever else had divided the succession of Kentwalk, slaying in fight Edelwalk the South-Saxon, who oppos'd him in their aid; but soon after was repuls'd by two of his captains, Bertune, and Andune, who for a while held the province in their power. But Kedwalla gathering new force, with the slaughter of Bertune, and also of Edric the successor of Edelwalk, won (684) the kingdom: but reduc'd the people to heavy thraldom. Then addressing to conquer the isle of Wight, till that time pagan, saith Beda (others otherwise, as above hath been related) made a vow, though himself yet unbaptiz'd, to devote the fourth part of that island, and the spoils thereof, to holy uses. Conquest obtain'd, paying his vow as then was the belief, he gave his fourth to bishop Wilfrid, by chance there present; and he to Bertwin a priest, his sister's son, with commission to baptize all the vanquish'd, who meant to save their lives. But the two young sons of Arwald, king of that island, met with much more hostility; for they at the enemies approach flying out of the isle, and betray'd where they were hid not far from thence, were led to Kedwalla, who lay then under cure of some wounds receiv'd, and by his appointment, after instruction and baptism, first given them, harshly put to death, which the youths are said above their age to have christianly suffer'd. In Kent, Lothair dy'd this year of his wounds receiv'd in fight against the South-Saxons, led on by Edric, who descending from Ermenred, it seems challeng'd the crown; and wore it, though not commendably, one year and a half: but coming to a violent death, left the land expos'd a prey either to home-bred usurpers, or neighbouring invaders. Among whom Kedwalla, taking advantage from their civil distempers, and marching easily through the South-Saxons, whom he had subdu'd, sorely harrass'd the country, untouch'd of long time by any hostile incursion. But the Kentish men, all parties uniting against a common enemy, with joynt power so oppos'd him, that he was constrain'd to retire back; his brother Mollo in the fight with twelve men of his company, seeking shelter in a house, was beset and therein burnt by the pursuers: Kedwalla much troubl'd at so great a loss, recalling and soon rallying his disordered forces, return'd (686) fiercely upon the chasing enemy: nor could be got out of the province, till both by fire and sword, he had aveng'd the death of his brother. At length Victred the son of Ecbert, attaining the kingdom, both settl'd at home all things in peace, and secur'd his borders from all outward hostility. While thus Kedwalla disquieted both west and east, after his winning the crown, Ecfrid the Northumbrian, and Ethelfred the Mercian, fought a sore battle by the river Trent; wherein Elfwin brother to Ecfrid, a youth of eighteen years, much belov'd, was slain; and the accident likely to occasion much more shedding of blood, peace was happily made by the grave exhortation of archbishop Theodore, a pecuniary fine only paid to Ecfrid, as some satisfaction for the loss of his brother's life. Another adversity befel Ecfrid in his family, by means of Ethildrith his wife, king Anna's daughter, who having taken him for her husband, and professing to love him above all other men, persisted twelve years in the obstinate refusal of his bed, thereby thinking to live the purer life. So perversly then was chastity instructed against the apostles rule. At length obtaining of him with much importunity her departure, she veil'd herself a nun, then made abbess of Ely, dy'd seven years after the pestilence; and might with better warrant have kept faithfully her undertaken wedlock, though now canoniz'd St. Audrey of Ely. In the mean while Ecfrid had sent Bertus with a power to subdue Ireland, a harmless nation, saith Beda, and ever friendly to the English; in both which they seem to have left a posterity much unlike them at this day: miserably wasted, without regard had to places hallowed or profane, they betook them partly to their weapons, partly to implore divine aid; and, as was thought, obtain'd it in their full avengement upon Ecfrid, for he the next year, against the mind and persuasion of his sagest friends, and especially of Cudbert, a famous bishop of that age, marching unadvisedly against the Picts, who long before had been subject to Northumberland, was by them, feigning flight, drawn unawares into narrow streights overtopt with hills, and cut off with most of his army. From which time, saith Bede, Military valour began among the Saxons to decay, not only the Picts till then peaceable, but some part of the Britons also recover'd by arms their liberty for many years after. Yet Alfred, elder but base brother to Ecfrid, a man said to be learned in the scriptures, recall'd from Ireland, to which place in his brother's reign he had retir'd, and now succeeding, upheld with much honour, though in narrower bounds, the residue of his kingdom. Kedwalla having now with great disturbance of his neighbours, reign'd over the West-Saxons two years, besides what time he spent in gaining it; weary'd perhaps with his own turbulence, went to Rome, desirous there to receive baptism, which till then his worldly affairs had deferr'd; and accordingly on Easter-day 689,[1] he was baptiz'd by Sergius the pope, and his name changed to Peter. All which notwithstanding, surpriz'd with a disease, he out-lived not the ceremony so far sought, much above the space of five weeks, in the thirtieth year of his age, and in the church of St. Peter was there bury'd, with a large epitaph upon his tomb. Him succeeded Ina of the royal family, and from the time of his coming in, for many years oppress'd the land with little grievances, as Kedwalla had done before him, insomuch that in those times there was no bishop among them. His first expedition was into Kent, to demand satisfaction for the burning of Mollo: Victred, loth to hazard all for the rash act of a few, deliver'd up thirty of those that could be found accessory; or, as others say, pacify'd Ina with a great sum of money.[2] Meanwhile, at the incitement of Ecbert, a devout monk, Wilbrod a priest, eminent for learning, pass'd over sea, having twelve others in company, with intent to preach the gospel in Germany. And coming (694) to Pepin, chief regent of the Franks, who a little before had conquer'd the hither Frisia, by his countenance and protection, promise also of many benefits to them who should believe, they found the work of conversion much the easier, and Wilbrod the first bishop in that

---

[1] Dr. Powell and Mr. Vaughan, in their notes on Caradoc's Welsh Chronicle, suppose that this Cadwalla was Edwal, surnam'd Ywrch, prince of Wales; who about this time went to Rome, and there dy'd. Other Welsh authors pretend, Cadwalla here mention'd was their king Cadwallader; who, according to Caradoc, publish'd by Dr. Powell, went to Rome, Anno 664, and dy'd there eight years afterwards.

[2] Ina in the year 693, held a great council of his bishops, elder men, and the antients of his people, by whom several laws were made, and is the first authentick great council, whose laws are come to us entire. Spelm. Brit. Counc.

nation.[1] But two priests, each of them Hewald by name, and for distinction surnam'd from the colour of their hair, the black and the white, by his example, piously affected to the souls of their countrymen the old Saxons, at their coming thither to convert them, met with much worse entertainment. For in the house of a farmer, who had promis'd to convey them, as they desir'd, to the governour of that country, discover'd by their daily ceremonies to be christian priests, and the cause of their coming suspected, they were by him and his heathen neighbours cruelly butcher'd; yet not unaveng'd, for the governor enrag'd at such violence offer'd to his strangers, sending arm'd men, slew all those inhabitants, and burnt their village. After three years in Mercia, Ostred the queen, wife to Ethelred, was kill'd (697) by her own nobles, as Beda's epitome records; Florence calls them Southimbrians, negligently omitting the cause of so strange a fact. And the year (698) following, Bertred, a Northumbrian general, was slain by the Picts. Ethelred, seven years (704) after the violent death of his queen, put on the monk, and resign'd his kingdom to Kenred the son of Wulfer his brother. The next year (700), Aldfrid in Northumberland dy'd, leaving Osred a child of eight years to succeed him. Four years (702) after which, Kenred having a while with praise govern'd the Mercian kingdom, went to Rome in the time of pope Constantine, and shorn a monk spent there the residue of his days. Kelred succeeded him, the son of Ethelred, who had reign'd the next before. With Kenred went Offa the son of Siger, king of East-Saxons, and betook him to the same habit, leaving his wife and native country; a comely person in the prime of his youth, much desir'd of the people; and such his virtue, by report, as might have otherwise been worthy to have reign'd. Ina the West-Saxon one year after (710) fought a battle, at first doubtful, at last successful, against[2] Gerent king of Wales. The next year (711) Bertfrid, another Northumbrian captain, fought with the Picts, and slaughter'd them, saith Huntingdon, to the full avengement of Ecfrid's death. The fourth year after, Ina had another doubtful and cruel battle at Wodnesburg in Wiltshire, with Kelred the Mercian, who dy'd the year following a lamentable death: for as he sat one day feasting with his nobles, suddenly possess'd with an evil spirit, he expir'd in despair, as Boniface archbishop of Mentz, an Englishman, who taxes him for a defiler of nuns, writes by way of caution to Ethelbald, his next of kin, who succeeded him. Osred also the young Northumbrian king, slain by his kindred in the eleventh of his reign, for his vicious life and incest committed with nuns; was by Kenred succeeded and aveng'd.

[1] His see was Weltaburgh, in the Gallick tongue Trajectum, now Utrecht.
[2] Supposed to be king of Cornwall, there being no such name in the catalogue of the kings of North or South-Wales.

He reigning two years, left Osric in his room. In whose seventh year (718), if Beda calculate right, Victred king of Kent deceas'd, having reign'd thirty four years, and some part of them with Suebhard, as Beda testifies. He left behind him three sons, Ethelbert, Eadbert, and Alric his heirs[1] (725). Three years after (728) which, appear'd two comets about the sun, terrible to behold, the one before him in the morning, the other after him in the evening, for the space of two weeks in January, bending their blaze towards the north; at which time the Saracens furiously invaded France, but were expell'd soon after with great overthrow. The same year in Northumberland, Osric dying or slain, adopted Kelwulf the brother of Kenrid his successor, to whom Beda dedicates his story; but writes this only of him, that the beginning and the process of his reign met with many adverse commotions, whereof the event was then doubtfully expected. Meanwhile Ina seven years before having slain Kenwulf, to whom Florent gives the addition of Clito, given usually to none but of the blood royal, and the fourth year after overthrown and slain Albright another Clito, driven from Taunton to the South-Saxons for aid, vanquish'd also the East-Angles in more than one battle, as Malmsbury writes, but not the year, whether to expiate so much blood, or infected with the contagious humour of those times, Malmsbury saith, at the persuasion of Ethelburga his wife, went to Rome, and there ended his days; yet this praise left behind him, to have made good laws, the first of Saxon that remain extant to this day, and to his kinsman Edelard, bequeath'd the crown: no less than the whole monarchy of England and Wales. For Ina, if we believe a digression in the laws of Edward the Confessor, was the first king crown'd of English and British, since the Saxon entrance; of the British by means of his second wife, some way related to Cadwallader last king of Wales, which I had not noted, being unlikely, but for the place where I found it.[2] After Ina, by a surer author, Ethelbald king of Mercia commanded all the provinces on this side Humber, with their kings; the Picts were in league with the English, the Scots peaceable within their bounds, and the Britons part were in their own government, part subject to the English. In which peaceful state of the land, many in Northumberland, both nobles and commons, laying aside the exercise of arms, betook them to the cloister : and not content so to do at home, many in the days of Ina, clerks and laicks, men and women, hasting to Rome in herds, thought themselves no where sure of eternal life, till they were cloister'd there. Thus representing the state of things in this island, Beda surceas'd to write. Out of whom chiefly hath been gather'd, since the Saxons arrival, such

---

[1] Peter-Pence was granted to the pope about the year 725, by Ina king of the West-Saxons.
[2] Among the laws of Edward the Confessor, 'tis inserted, that Ina marry'd Gaula, the daughter of Cadwallader king of Wales. Vid. Lambert's Archieves, cap. 17.

as hath been deliver'd, a scatter'd story pick'd out here and there, with some trouble and tedious work from among his many legends of visions and miracles; toward the latter end so bare of civil matters, as what can be thence collected may seem a kalendar rather than a history, taken up for the most part with succession of kings and computation of years, yet those hard to be reconcil'd with the Saxon annals. Their actions, we read of, were most commonly wars, but for what cause wag'd, or by what counsels carry'd on, no care was had to let us know: whereby their strength and violence we understand, of their wisdom, reason, or justice, little or nothing, the rest superstition and monastical affection; kings, one after another, leaving their kingly charge, to run their heads fondly into a monks cowle: which leaves us uncertain, whether Beda was wanting to matter, or his matter to him. Yet from hence to the Danish invasion it will be worse with us, destitute of Beda. Left only to obscure and blockish chronicles whom Malmsbury and Huntingdon, (for neither they than we had better authors of those times) ambitious to adorn the history, make no scruple oft-times, I doubt, to interline with conjectures and surmises of their own: them rather than imitate, I shall choose to represent the truth naked, though as lean as a plain journal. Yet William of Malmsbury must be acknowledg'd, both for style and judgment, to be by far the best writer of them all: but what labour is to be endur'd, turning over volumes of rubbish in the rest, Florence of Worcester, Huntingdon, Simeon of Durham, Hoveden, Matthew of Westminster, and many others of obscurer note, with all their monachisms, is a penance to think. Yet these are our only registers, transcribers one after another for the most part, and sometimes worthy enough for the things they register. This travel rather than not know at once what may be known of our ancient story, sifted from fables and impertinences, I voluntarily undergo; and to save others, if they please, the like unpleasing labour; except those who take pleasure to be all their life-time raking in the foundations of old abbies and cathedrals: but to my task now as it befalls. In the year 733, on the 17th kalends of September, was an eclipse of the sun about the third hour of day, obscuring almost his whole orb, as with a black shield.[1] Ethelbald of Mercia besieg'd and took the Castle or town of Somerton: and two years after (735), Beda our historian dy'd, some say the year before. Kelwulf in Northumberland three years after (738), became monk in Lindisfarne, yet none of the severest; for he brought those monks from milk and water, to wine and ale: in which doctrine no doubt but they were soon docile: and well might, for Kelwulf[2] brought with him good

---
[1] The next year, 734, the moon appear'd as it were stained with blood, which, says Simeon of Durham, lasted one whole hour, then follow'd a blackness, and then it return'd to its natural colour. In this or the next year Bede dy'd.
[2] To this Kelwulf Bede dedicated his history.

provision, great treasure and revenues of land, recited by Simeon, yet all under pretence of following (I use the author's words) poor Christ, by voluntary poverty: no marvel then if such applause were given by monkish writers to kings turning monks, and much cunning perhaps us'd to allure them. To Eadbert, his uncle's son, he left the kingdom, whose brother Ecbert, archbishop of York, built a library there. But two years after (740), while Eadbert was busy'd in war against the Picts, Ethebald the Mercian, by foul fraud, assaulted part of Northumberland in his absence, as the supplement of Beda's epitomy records. In the West-Saxons, Edelard who succeeded Ina, having been much molested in the beginning of his reign, with the rebellion of Oswald his kinsman, who contended with him for the right of succession; overcoming at last those troubles, dy'd in peace 741, leaving Cuthred one of the same lineage to succeed him: who at first had much war with Ethelbald the Mercian, and various success, but joining with him in league two years after (743) made war on the Welsh; Huntingdon doubts not to give them a great victory. And Simeon reports, another battle fought between Britons and Picts the year (744) ensuing. Now was the kingdom of East-Saxons drawing to a period: for Sigeard and Senfred, the sons of Sebbi, having reign'd a while and after them young Offa, who soon quitted his kingdom to go to Rome with Kenred, as hath been said, the government was conferr'd on Selred son of Sigebert the Good, who having rul'd thirty-eight years, (746) came to a violent death; how or wherefore, is not set down. After whom Swithred was the last king, driven out by Ecbert the West-Saxon: but London, with the countries adjacent, obey'd the Mercians till they also were dissolv'd. Cuthred had now (748) reign'd about nine years, when Kenric his son a valiant young prince, was in military tumult slain by his own soldiers. The same year Eadbert dying in Kent, his brother Edilbert reign'd in his stead. But after two years, (750) the other Eadbert in Northumberland, whose war with the Picts hath been above mention'd, made now such progress there, as to subdue Kyle,[1] so saith the auctary of Bede, and other countries thereabout, to his dominion; while Cuthred the West-Saxon had a fight with Ethelbun, one of his nobles, a stout warrier, envy'd by him in some matter of the commonwealth, as far as by the latin of Ethelwerd can be understood (others interpret it sedition), and with much ado over-coming, took Ethelbun for his valour into favour, by whom faithfully serv'd in the twelfth or thirteenth of his reign, he encounter'd in a set battle with Ethelbald the Mercian at Beorford, now Burford in Oxfordshire; one year after (753) against the Welsh, which was the last but one of his life. Huntingdon, as his manner is to comment upon the annal text, makes a terrible description of that fight between Cuthred and Ethelbald, and the prowess of Ethelbun, at

[1] Or Dumbritton-Frith, Dumbarton, Frith of Clyde, in Scotland.

Beorford, but so affectedly, and therefore suspiciously, that I hold it not worth rehearsal; and both in that and the latter conflict, gives victory to Cuthred; after whom Sigebert, uncertain by what right his kinsman, saith Florent, step'd (754) into the throne, whom hated for his cruelty and other evil doings, Kinwulf joyning with most of the[1] nobility, dispossess'd (755) of all but Hampshire, that province he lost also within a year, together with the love of all those who till then remain'd his adherents, by slaying Cumbram, one of his chief captains, who for a long time had faithfully serv'd, and now dissuaded him from incensing the people by such tyrannical practices. Thence flying for safety into Andreds wood, forsaken of all, he was at length slain by the swineherd of Cumbran in revenge of his master, and Kinwulf who had undoubted right to the crown, joyfully saluted king. The next year (756) Eadbert the Northumbrian joining forces with Unust king of the Picts, as Simeon writes, besieg'd and took by surrender the city Alcluith, now Dunbritton in Lenox, from the Britons of Cumberland; and ten days after, the whole army perish'd about Niwanbirig, but to tell us how, he forgets. In Mercia, Ethelbald was slain (757), at a place call'd Secandune, now Seckington in Warwickshire, the year following, in a bloody fight against Cuthred, as Huntingdon surmises, but Cuthred was dead two or three years before; others write him murder'd in the night by his own guard, and the treason, as some say, of Beornred, who succeeded him; but e're many months, was defeated and slain by Offa. Yet Ethelbald seems not without cause, after a long and prosperous reign, to have fallen by a violent death; not shaming on the vain confidence of his many alms, to commit uncleanness with consecrated nuns, besides laick adulteries, as the archbishop of Ments in a letter taxes him and his predecessors, and that by his example most of his peers did the like; which adulterous doings he foretold him were likely to produce a slothful off-spring, good for nothing but to be the ruin of that kingdom, as it fell out not long after. The next year (758) Osmund, according to Florence, ruling the South-Saxons, and Swithred the East, Eadbert in Northumberland, following the steps of his predecessor, got him into a monk's hood; the more to be wonder'd, that having reign'd worthily twenty-one years, with the love and high estimation of all, both at home and abroad, able still to govern, and much entreated by the kings his neighbours, not to lay down his charge; with offer on that condition to yield up to him part of their own dominion; he could not be mov'd from his resolution, but relinquish'd his regal office to Oswulf his son; who at the years end (759), though without just cause, was slain by his own servants. And the year after dy'd Ethelbert, son of Victred, the second of that name in Kent. After Oswulf, Ethelwald, otherwise call'd Mollo, was set up king; who in

[1] The Saxon annals call them the wise and noble men of the West-Saxons.

his third year (762) had a great battle at Eldune, by Melros, slew Oswin a great lord, rebelling, and gain'd the victory. But the third year (765) after, fell by the treachery of Alcred, who assum'd his place. The fourth year (769) after which,[1] Cataracta an ancient and fair city in Yorkshire, was burnt by Arnred a certain tyrant, who the same year came to like end. And after five years more, Alcred the king depos'd and forsaken of all his people, fled (774) with a few, first to Bebba, a strong city of those parts, thence to Kinot king of the Picts. Ethelred the son of Mollo, was crown'd in his stead. Mean while Offa the Mercian, growing powerful, had subdu'd a neighbouring people, by Simeon call'd Hestings ;[2] and fought successfully this year with Alric king of Kent, at a place call'd Ottanford : the annals also speak of wondrous serpents then seen in Essex. Nor had Kinwulf the West-Saxon given small proof of his valour in several battles against the Welsh heretofore, but this year 775, meeting with Offa, at a place call'd Besington, was put to the worse, and Offa won the town for which they contended. In Northumberland, Ethelred having caus'd three of his nobles, Aldwulf, Renwulf, and Ecca, treacherously to be slain by two other peers, was himself the next year driven into banishment,[3] Elfwald the son of Oswulf succeeding in his place, yet not without civil broils ; for in his second year (780) Osbald and Ethelheard, two noblemen, raising forces against him, routed Bearne his general, and pursuing, burnt him at a place call'd Seletune. I am sensible how wearisome it may likely be to read of so many bare and reasonless actions, so many names of kings one ofter another, acting little more than mute persons in a scene. What would it be to have inserted the long bead-roll of arch-bishops, bishops, abbots, abbesses, and their doings, neither to religion profitable, nor to morality ; swelling my authors each to a voluminous body, by me studiously omitted ; and left as their propriety, who have a mind to write the ecclesiastical matters of those ages ; neither do I care to wrinkle the smoothness of history with rugged names of places unknown, better harp'd at in Cambden, and other chorographers. Six years (786) therefore pass'd over in silence, as wholly of such argument, bring us to relate next the unfortunate end of Kinwulf the West-Saxon ; who having laudably reign'd about thirty-one years, yet suspecting that Kincard brother of Sigebert the former king, intended to usurp the crown after his decease, or revenge his brother's expulsion, had commanded him into banishment ; but he lurking here and there on the borders with a small company, having had intelligence that Kinwulf was in the country thereabout, at Merantun, or Merton in Surrey, at the house

---

[1] Catarick-bridge, of the antiquity whereof see the additions, in the late edition of Cambden's Britannia.
[2] Lambert in his glossary, at the end of the Decem Scriptores, thinks they were Danes.
[3] Roger Hovedon says he was depos'd by the common council, and consent of his own subjects.

of a woman whom he lov'd, went by night and beset the place. Kinwulf over-confident either of his royal presence, or personal valour, issuing forth with the few about him, runs fiercely at Kineard, and wounds him sore, but by his followers hemm'd in, is kill'd among them. The report of so great an accident soon running to a place not far off, where many more attendants awaited the king's return, Osric and Wivert, two earls, hasted with a great number to the house, where Kineard and his fellows yet remain'd. He seeing himself surrounded, with fair words and promise of great gifts, attempted to appease them; but those rejected with disdain, fights it out to the last, and is slain with all but one or two of his retinue, which were nigh a hundred. Kinwulf was succeeded by Birthric, being both descended of Kerdic the founder of that kingdom. Not better was the end of Elfwald in Northumberland, two years after (788) slain miserably by the conspiracy of Siggan, one of his nobles, others say of the whole people at Scilcester by the Roman wall; yet undeservedly, as his sepulchre at Hagulstald, now Hexam upon Tine, and some miracles there said to be done, are alledg'd to witness; and Siggan five years after laid violent hands on himself. Osred, son of Alcred, advanc'd into the room of Elfwald, and within one year driven out, left his seat vacant to Ethelred son of Mollo, who after ten years of banishment (imprisonment, saith Alcuin) had the scepter put again into his hand. The third year (789) of Birthric king of West-Saxons, gave beginning from abroad to a new and fatal revolution of calamity on this land. For three Danish ships, the first that had been seen here of that nation arriving in the west, to visit these, as was suppos'd, foreign merchants, the king's gatherer of customs taking horse from Dorchester,[1] found them spies and enemies. For being commanded to come and give account of their lading at the king's custom-house, they slew him and all who came with him; as an earnest of the many slaughters, rapines, and hostilities, which they return'd not long after to commit over all the island. Of this Danish first arrival, and on a sudden worse than hostile aggression, the Danish history far otherwise relates, as if their landing had been at the mouth of Humber, and their spoilful march far into the country; tho' soon repell'd by the inhabitants, they hasted back as fast to their ships: but from what cause, what reason of state, what authority or publick council the invasion proceeded, makes not mention, and our wonder yet the more, by telling us that Sigefrid then king in Denmark, and long after, was a man studious more of peace and quiet, than of warlike matters. These therefore seem rather to have been some wanderers at sea, who with publick commission, or without, through love of spoil, or hatred

---

[1] Cambden, in his Britania Tit. Devonshire, tells us, that the Danes first landed at Teignmouth in that county: now Tinmouth, a fisher-town, which was burnt by the French in the last war.

of christianity, seeking booties on any land of christians, came by chance or weather on this shoar. The next year (790) Osred in Northumberland, who driven out by his nobles had given place to Ethelred, was taken and forcibly shaven a monk at York. And the year (791) after, Oelf, and Oelfwin, sons of Elfwald, formerly king, were drawn by fair promises from the principal church of York, and after by command of Ethelred, cruelly put to death at Wonwaldremere, a village by the great pool in Lancashire, now call'd Winandermere. Nor was the third year less bloody; for Osred, who not liking a shaven crown, had desired banishment and obtain'd it, returning from the Isle of Man with small forces, at the secret but deceitful call of certain nobles, who by oath had promis'd to assist him, was also taken, and by Ethelred dealt with in the same manner; who the better to avouch his cruelties, thereupon married Elfled the daughter of Offa: for in Offa was found as little faith or mercy. He the same year having drawn to his palace Ethelbrite king of East-Angles, with fair invitations to marry his daughter, caus'd him to be there inhospitably beheaded, and his kingdom wrongfully seiz'd by the wicked counsel of his wife, saith Matt. West, annexing thereto a long unlikely tale. For which violence and bloodshed to make atonement, with fryars at least, he bestows (792) the reliques of St. Alban, in a shrine of pearl and gold. Far worse it far'd the next year (793) with the reliques in Lendisfarne; where the Danes landing, pillag'd that monastery, and of fryars kill'd some, carried away others captive, sparing neither priest nor lay: which many strange thunders and fiery dragons, with other impressions in the air seen frequently before, were judg'd to foresignifie. This year Alric third son of Victred, ended in Kent his long reign of thirty-four years. With him ended the race of Hengist: thenceforth whomsoever wealth or faction advanc'd, took on him the name and state of a king. The Saxon Annals of 784 name Ealmund then reigning in Kent; but that consists not with the time of Alric, and I find him no where else mention'd. The year (794) following was remarkable for the death of Offa the Mercian, a strenuous and subtle king; he had much intercourse with Charles the Great, at first enmity, to the interdicting of commerce on either side, at length much amity and firm league, as appears by the letter of Charles himself yet extant, procur'd by[1] Alcuin a learned and prudent man, though a monk, whom the kings of England in those days had sent orator into France, to maintain good correspondence between them and Charles the Great. He granted, saith Huntingdon, a perpetual tribute to the Pope, out of every house in his kingdom; for yielding perhaps to translate the primacy of Canterbury to Lichfield in his own dominion. He drew a trench[2] of wondrous

---

[1] He assisted Charlemagne in his founding the University of Paris.
[2] Call'd Offa's Dyke, about 90 miles long, says Mr. Cambden.

length[1] between Mercia and the British confines, from sea to sea. Ecferth the son of Offa, a prince of great hope, who also had been crown'd nine years before his father's decease, restoring to the church what his father had seiz'd on : yet within four months by a sickness ended his reign. And to Kenulf next in right of the same progeny bequeath'd his kingdom. Mean while the Danish pirates who still wasted Northumberland, venturing on shoar to spoil another monastery at the mouth of the river Don, were assail'd by the English, their chief captain slain on the place ; then returning to sea, were most of them ship-wreck'd ; others driven again on shoar, were put all to the sword. Simeon attributes this their punishment to the power of St. Cudbert, offended with them for the rifling of his convent. Two years (796) after this, dy'd Ethelred twice King, but not exempted at last from the fate of his many predecessors, miserably slain by his people, some say deservedly, as not inconscious with them who train'd Osred to his ruin. Osbald, a nobleman, exalted to the throne, and in less than a month, deserted and expelled, was forc'd to fly at last from Lindisfarne by sea to the Pictish king, and dy'd an abbot. Eardulf whom Ethelred six years before had commanded to be put to death at Ripun, before the abbey-gate, dead as was suppos'd, and with solemn dirge carried into the church, after midnight found there alive, I read not how, then banish'd, now recall'd, was in York created king. In Kent, Ethelbert or Pren, whom the annals call Eadbright (so different they often are one from another, both in timing and naming) by some means having usurp'd (796) regal power, after two years reign contending with Kenuif the Mercian, was by him taken prisoner, and soon after, out of pious commiseration, let go : but not receiv'd of his own, what become of him, Malmsbury leaves to doubt. Simeon writes, that Kenulf commanded to put out his eyes, and lop off his hands ; but whether the sentence were executed or not, is left as much in doubt by his want of expression. The second year (798) after this, they in Northumberland who had conspir'd against Ethelred, now also raising war against Eardulf, under Wada their chief captain, after much havock on either side at Langho, by Whaley in Lancashire, the conspirators at last flying, Eardulf return'd with victory. The same year (800) London with a great multitude of her inhabitants, by a sudden fire was consum'd. The year 800 made way for great alteration in England, uniting her seven kingdoms into one, by Ecbert the famous West-Saxon ; him Birthric, dying childless, left next to reign, the only survivor of that lineage descended from Inegild the brother of king Ina. And according to his birth, liberally bred, he began early from his youth to give signal hopes of more than ordinary worth

[1] From the mouth of Dee to that of the river Wye. Mr. Lloyd, in his additions to Wales in the late edition of Cambden) has set down the exact course of it, Pag. 587.

growing up in him ; which Birthric fearing, and withal his juster title to the crown, secretly sought his life, and Ecbert perceiving, fled to Offa the Mercian : but he having marry'd Eadburg his daughter to Birthric, easily gave ear to his ambassadors coming to require Ecbert. He again put to his shifts, escap'd thence into France : but after three years banishment there, which perhaps contributed much to his education, Charles the Great then reigning, he was call'd over by the publick voice (for Birthric was newly dead) and with general applause[1] created king of West-Saxons. The same day Ethelmund at Kinmeresford,[2] passing over with the Worcestershire men, was met by Weolstan another nobleman with those of Wiltshire, between whom happen'd a great fray, wherein the Wiltshire men overcame, but both dukes were slain ; no reason of their quarrel written. Such bickerings to recount, met often in these our writers ; what more worth is it than to chronicle the wars of kites or crows flocking and fighting in the air ? The year (801) following Eardulf the Northumbrian, leading forth an army against Kenulf the Mercian, for harbouring certain of his enemies, by the diligent mediation of other princes and prelates, arms were laid aside, and amity soon sworn between them. But Eadburga the wife of Birthric, a woman every way wicked, in malice especially cruel, could not or car'd not to appease (802) the general hatred justly conceiv'd against her ; accustom'd in her husband's days to accuse any whom she spighted ; and not prevailing to his ruin, her practice was by poison secretly to contrive his death. It fortun'd that the king her husband, lighting on a cup which she had temper'd, not for him, but for one of his great favourites, whom she could not harm by accusing, sipp'd thereof only, and in a while after still pining away, ended his days ; the favourite drinking deeper, found speedier the operation. She fearing to be question'd for these facts, with what treasure she had, pass'd over sea to Charles the Great, whom with rich gifts coming to his presence, the emperor courtly receiv'd with this pleasant proposal : 'Choose, Eadburga, which of us two thou wilt, me or my son (for his son stood by him) to be thy husband :' she, no dissembler of what she lik'd best, made easie answer : 'Were it in my choice, I should choose of the two your son rather, as the younger man.' To whom the emperor, between jest and earnest, 'Hadst thou chosen me, I had bestow'd on thee my son ; but since thou hast chosen him, thou shalt have neither him nor me.' Nevertheless he assign'd her a rich monastery to dwell in as abbess ; for that life, it may seem, she chose next to profess : but being a while after detected of unchastity with one of her followers, she was commanded to depart thence ; from that time wandring poorly up and down with one ser-

---

[1] Ethelwerd says, he was ordain'd king : Dr. Lloid bishop of Worcester, from Asser's Annals, Simeon of Durham, Roger Hoveden, and others, proves Egbert's accession to the throne to be two years forwarder, Anno 802.
[2] It seems to be Kempsford on the edge of Gloucestershire, next to Wiltshire.

vant, in Pavia a city of Italy, she finish'd at last in beggary her shameful life. In the year 805, Cuthred, whom Kenulf the Mercian had, instead of Pren, made king in Kent, having obscurely reign'd eight years, deceas'd. In Northumberland, Eardulf the year (806) following was driven out of his realm by Alfwold, who reign'd two years (808) in his room; after whom Eandred, son of Eardulf, thirty-three years. But I see not how this can stand with the sequel of story out of better authors: much less that which Buchanan relates the year (809) following of Acaius king of Scots, who having reign'd thirty-two years, and dying in 809, had formerly aided (but in what year of his reign tells not) Hungus king of Picts, with 10,000 Scots, against Athelstan a Saxon or Englishman, then wasting the Pictish borders; that Hungus, by the aid of those Scots, and the help of St. Andrew their patron, in a vision by night, and the appearance of his cross by day, routed the astonish'd English, and slew Athelstan in fight. Who this Athelstan was, I believe no man knows: Buchanan supposes him to have been some Danish commander, on whom king Alured, or Alfred, had bestow'd Northumberland: but of this I find no footstep in our ancient writers; and if any such thing were done in the time of Alfred, it must be little less than one hundred years after: this Athelstan therefore, and this great overthrow seems rather to have been the fancy of some legend, than any warrantable record. Meanwhile Ecbert having with much prudence, justice and clemency, a work of more than one year establish'd (813) his kingdom, and himself in the affections of his people, turns his first enterprise against the Britons, both them of Cornwall, and those beyond Severn, subduing both. In Mercia, Kenulf the sixth year after, having reign'd with great praise of his religious mind and virtues, both in peace and war, deceas'd. His son Kenelm, a child of seven years (819) was committed to the care of his eldest sister Quendred; who with a female ambition aspiring to the crown, hir'd one who had the charge of his nurture, to murder him, led into a woody place upon pretence of hunting. The murder, as is reported, was miraculously reveal'd; but to tell how, by a dove dropping a written note on the altar at Rome, is a long story told, tho' out of order, by Malmsbury; and under the year 821 by Matt. West. where I leave it to be sought by such as are more credulous than I with my readers. Only the note was to this purpose:

> Low in a mead of kine under a thorn,
> Of head bereaft li'th poor Kenelm king-born.

Keolwulf, the brother of Kenulf, after one year's reign (820), was driven out by one Bernulf an usurper: who in his third year (823), uncertain whether invading or invaded, was by Ecbert, though with great loss on both sides, overthrown and put to flight at Ellandune, or Wilton: yet Malmsbury accounts this battle fought in 806, a wide difference, but frequently found in their computations. Bernulf thence retiring to the East-Angles, as part of his dominion by the late seizure of Offa, was by them met in the field and slain: but they doubting what the Mercians might do in revenge hereof, forthwith yielded themselves, both king and people, to the sovereignty of Ecbert. As for the kings of East-Angles, our annals mention them not since Ethelwald; him succeeded his brother's sons, as we find in Malmsbury, Aldulf (a good king, well acquainted with Bede) and Elwold who left the kingdom to Beorn, he to Ethelred the father of this Ethelbrite, whom Offa perfidiously put to death. Simeon and Hoveden, in the year 749, write, that Elfwald king of East-Angles dying, Humbeanna and Albert shar'd the kingdom between them; but where to insert this among the former successions, is not easie, nor much material: after Ethelbrite none is nam'd of that kingdom till their submitting now to Ecbert: he from this victory against Bernulf sent part of his army under Ethelwulf his son, with Alstan bishop of Shirburn, and Wulfred a chief commander, into Kent. Who finding Baldred there reigning in his eighteenth year, overcame and drove him over the Thames; whereupon all Kent, Surrey, Sussex, and lastly Essex, with her king Swithred, became subject to the dominion of Ecbert. Neither were these all his exploits of this year, the first in order set down in Saxon annals, being his fight against the Devonshire Welsh, at a place call'd Gafulford, now Camelford in Cornwall. Ludiken the Mercian, after two years (825) preparing to avenge Bernulf his kinsman on the East-Angles, was by them with his five consuls, as the annals call them, surpriz'd and put to the sword: and Witlaf his successor first vanquish'd, then upon submission with all Mercia, made tributary to Ecbert. Meanwhile the Northumbrian kingdom of itself was fallen to shivers: their kings, one after another, so often slain by the people, no man daring, tho' never so ambitious, to take up the sceptre, which many had found so hot (the only effectual cure of ambition that I have read), for the space of thirty-three years after the death of Ethelred son of Mollo, as Malmsbury writes, there was no king: many noblemen and prelates were fled the country. Which misrule among them, the Danes having understood, oft-times from their ships entring far into the land, infested those parts with wide depopulation, wasting towns, churches, and monasteries, for they were yet heathen: the Lent before whose coming, on the north side of St. Peter's church in York, was seen from the roof to rain blood. The causes of these calamities, and the ruin of that kingdom, Alcuin, a learned monk living in those days, attributes in several epistles, and well may, to the general ignorance and decay of learning, which crept in among them after the death of Beda, and of Ecbert the archbishop; their neglect of breeding up youth in the scriptures, the spruce and gay apparel of their priests and nuns, discovering their vain and wanton minds; examples are also read, even in Beda's days, of their wanton deeds: thence altars defil'd with perjuries, cloisters violated with adulteries, the land polluted with blood of their princes, civil dissensions among the people, and finally all the same vices which Gildas alledg'd of old to have ruin'd the Britons. In this estate, Ecbert, who had now conquer'd all the south, finding them in the year 827 (for he was march'd thither with an army to complete his conquest of the whole island) no wonder if they submitted themselves to the yoke without resistance, Eandred their king becoming tributary. Thence turning his forces the year following (828), he subdu'd more thoroughly what remain'd of North Wales.

BOOK V.

THE sum of things in this island, or the best part thereof, reduc'd now (828) under the power of one man; and him one of the worthiest, which, as far as can be found in good authors, was by none attain'd at any time here before unless in fables; men might with some reason have expected from such union, peace and plenty, greatness, and the flourishing of all estates and degrees: but far the contrary fell out soon after, invasion, spoil, desolation, slaughter of many, slavery of the rest, by the forcible landing of a fierce nation; Danes commonly called, and sometimes Dacians by others, the same with Normans; as barbarous as the Saxons themselves were at first reputed, and much more; for the Saxons first invited came hither to dwell; these unsent for, unprovoked, came only to destroy. But if the Saxons, as is above related, came most of them from Jutland and Anglen, a part of Denmark, as Danish writers affirm, and that Danes and Normans are the same; then in this invasion, Danes drove out Danes, their own posterity: and Normans afterwards, none but ancienter Normans. Which invasion perhaps, had the heptarchy stood divided as it was, had either not been attempted, or not uneasily resisted; while each prince and people, excited by their nearest concernments, had more industriously defended their own bounds, than depending on the neglect of a deputed governor, sent oft-times from the remote residence of a secure monarch. Though as it fell out in those troubles, the lesser kingdoms revolting from the West-Saxon yoke, and not aiding each other, too much concern'd with their own safety, it came to no better pass; while severally they sought to repel the danger nigh at hand, rather than jointly to prevent it far off. But when God hath decreed servitude on a sinful nation, fitted by their own vices for no condition but servile, all estates of government are alike unable to avoid it. God had purpos'd to punish our instrumental punishers, though now christians, by other heathen, according to his divine retaliation, invasion for invasion, spoil for spoil, destruction for destruction. The Saxons were now full as wicked as the Britons were at their arrival, broken with luxury and sloth, either secular or superstitious; for laying aside the exercise of arms, and the study of all virtuous knowledge, some betook them to over worldly or vitious practice, others to religious idleness and solitude, which brought forth nothing but vain and delusive visions; easily perceiv'd such, by their commanding of things, either not belonging to the gospel, or utterly forbidden, ceremonies, reliques, monasteries, masses, idols, add to these ostentation of alms, got oft-times by rapine and oppression, or intermixt with violent and lustful deeds, sometimes prodigally bestow'd, as the expiation of cruelty and bloodshed. What longer suffering could there be, when religion itself grew so void of sincerity, and the greatest shews of purity were impur'd.

ECBERT in full height of glory, having now enjoy'd his conquest seven peaceful years, his victorious army long since disbanded, and the exercise of arms perhaps laid aside, the more was found unprovided against a sudden storm of Danes from the sea, who landing in the 32nd of his reign, wasted Shepey in Kent. Ecbert the next year gathering an army, for he had heard of their arrival in 35 ships, gave them battle by the river Carr[1] in Dorsetshire; the event whereof was, that the Danes kept their ground, and encamp'd where the field was fought; two Saxon leaders, Dudda and Osmund, and two bishops as some say, were there slain. This was the only check of fortune we read of, that Ecbert in all his time receiv'd. For the Danes returning two years (835) after with a great navy, and joyning forces with the Cornish, who had enter'd league with them, were overthrown and put to flight.[2] Of these invasions against Ecbert, the Danish history is not silent; whether out of their own records or ours, may be justly doubted; for of these times at home, I find them in much uncertainty, and beholding rather to outlandish chronicles than any records of their own. The victor Ecbert, as one who had done enough, seasonably now, after prosperous success, the next year (836) with glory ended his days, and was buried at Winchester.

ETHELWOLF the son of Ecbert succeeded; by Malmsbury describ'd a man of mild nature, not inclin'd to war, or delighted with much dominion; that therefore contented with the ancient West-Saxon bounds, he gave to Ethalstan his brother, or son, as some write, the kingdom of Kent and Essex. But (Mat. West.)

[1] Near Charmouth in Dorsetshire.
[2] At Henston in Cornwall: so call'd from Hengist the Saxon.

the Saxon annalist, whose authority is elder, saith plainly, that both these countries and Sussex, were bequeath'd to Ethelstan by Ecbert his father. The unwarlike disposition of Ethelwolf, gave encouragement no doubt, and easier entrance to the Danes, who came again. (837) the next year with thirty-three ships; but Wulfheard, one of the king's chief captains, drove them back at Southampton with great slaughter; himself dying the same year of age, as I suppose, for he seems to have been one of Ecbert's old commanders, who was sent with Ethelwulf to subdue Kent. Ethelhelm another of the king's captains with the Dorsetshire men, had at first like success against the Danes at Portsmouth;[1] but they reinforcing stood their ground, and put the English to rout. Worse was the success of earl Herbert at a place call'd Mereswar,[2] slain (839) with the most part of his army. The year following in Lindsey also, East-Angles, and Kent, much mischief was done by their landing; where the next year, imbolden'd by success, they come on as far as Canterbury, Rochester, and London itself, with no less cruel hostility: and giving no respite to the peaceable mind of Ethelwolf, they yet return'd with the next year (840) in thirty-five ships, fought with him, as before with his father, at the river Carr, and made good their ground. In Northumberland Eandred the tributary king deceasing, left the same tenure to his son Ethelred, driven out (844) in his fourth year, and succeeded by Readwulf, who soon after his coronation, hasting forth to battle against the Danes at Alvetheli, fell with the most part of his army; and Ethelred like in fortune to the former Ethelred, was re-exalted to his seat: and to be yet farther like him in fate, was slain the fourth year after. Osbert succeeded in his room. But more southerly, the Danes next year (845) after met with some stop in the full course of their outrageous insolencies. For Earnulf with the men of Somerset, Alstan the bishop, and Osric with those of Dorsetshire, setting upon them at the river's mouth of Pedridan, slaughter'd them in great numbers, and obtain'd a just victory.[3] This repulse quell'd them, for aught we hear, the space of six years; then (851) also renewing their invasion, with little better success. For Keorle an earl, aided with the forces of Devonshire, assaulted and overthrew them at Wigganbeorch[4] with great destruction; as prosperously were they fought with the same year at Sandwich, by king Ethelstan, and Ealker his general, their great army defeated, and nine of their ships taken, the rest driven off, however to ride out the winter on that shore, Asser saith, they then first winter'd in Shepey Isle. Hard it

---
[1] At Port now call'd Portland.
[2] On Merscwarum, says the Saxon chronicle, i.e., among the Marshers, or inhabitants of the marshes or fenns. The name does not denote any particular place, as Mr. Milton imagin'd.
[3] This battle is rather suppos'd to be fought at the mouth of the river Axe, on Bladen-Down in Somersetshire: the village being from the slaughter of that day, call'd Bleadon or Bloody-down.
[4] Thought to be Wenbury in Devonshire. [5] Okely in Surrey, upon the borders of Sussex.

is through the bad expression of these writers to define this fight, whether by sea or land; Hoveden terms it a sea-fight. Nevertheless, with fifty ships, (Asser and others add three hundred) they enter'd the mouth of Thames, and made excursions as far as Canterbury and London, and as Ethelwerd writes, destroy'd both; of London, Asser signifies only that they pillag'd it. Bertulf also the Mercian, successor of Withlaf, with all his army they forc'd to fly, and him beyond the sea. Then passing over Thames with their powers into Surrey, and the West-Saxons, and meeting there with king Ethelwolf and Ethelbald his son, at a place call'd Ak-Lea, or Oak-Lea,[1] they received a total defeat with memorable slaughter. This was counted a lucky year to England, and brought to Ethelwolf great reputation. Burhed therefore who after Bertulf held of him the Mercian kingdom, two years (853) after this, imploring his aid against the North-Welsh, as then troublesome to his confines, obtain'd it of him in person, and thereby reduc'd them to obedience. This done, Ethelwolf sent his son Alfrid, a child of five years, well accompanied to Rome, whom Leo the pope both consecrated to be king afterward, and adopted to be his son. At home Ealker with the forces of Kent, and Huda with those of Surrey, fell on the Danes at their landing in Tanet, and at first put them back; but the slain and drown'd were at length so many on either side, as left the loss equal on both: which yet hinder'd not the solemnity of a marriage[2] at the feast of Easter, between Burhed the Mercian, and Ethelswida king Ethelwolf's daughter. Howbeit the Danes next year (854) winter'd again in Shepey. Whom Ethelwolf not finding human health sufficient to resist, growing daily upon him, in hope of divine aid, register'd in a book, and dedicated to God, the tenth part of his own lands, and of his whole kingdom, eas'd of all impositions, but converted to the maintenance of masses and psalms weekly to be sung for the prospering of Ethelwolf and his captains, as appears at large by the patent itself, in William of Malmsbury. Asser saith, he did it for the redemption of his soul, and the soul of his ancestors. After which, as having done some great matter, to shew himself at Rome, and be applauded of the Pope, he takes a long and cumbersome journey (855) thither with young Alfrid again, and there stays a year, when his place requir'd him rather here in the field against pagan enemies left wintering in his land. Yet so much manhood he had, as to return thence no monk; and in his way home took to wife Judith daughter of Charles the Bald, king of France. But e'er his return, Ethelbard his eldest son, Alstan his trusty bishop, and Enulf earl of Somerset conspir'd against him; their complaints were, that he had taken with him Alfrid his youngest son to be there inaugurated king, and brought home with an out-landish wife; for which they

[1] Okely in Surrey, upon the borders of Sussex.   [2] At Chippenham in Wiltshire.

endeavour'd to deprive him of his kingdom. The disturbance was expected to bring forth nothing less than war: but the king abhorring civil discord, after many conferences tending to peace, condescended to divide the kingdom with his son: division was made, but the matter so carried, that the eastern and worst part was malignly afforded to the father: the western and best given to the son; at which many of the nobles had great indignation, offering to the king their utmost assistance for the recovery of all; whom he peacefully dissuading, sat down contented with his portion assign'd. In the East-Angles, Edmund, lineal from the ancient stock of those kings, a youth of fourteen years only, but of great hopes, was with consent of all but his own crown'd at Burie. About this time (857), as Buchanan relates, the Picts, who not long before had by the Scots been driven out (857) of their country, part of them coming to Osbert and Ella, then kings of Northumberland, obtain'd aid against Donaldus the Scottish king, to recover their ancient possession. Osbert, who in person undertook the expedition, marching into Scotland, was at first put to a retreat; but returning soon after on the Scots, over-secure of their suppos'd victory, put them to flight with great slaughter, took prisoner their king, and pursu'd his victory beyond Sterlingbridge. The Scots unable to resist longer, and by ambassadors intreating peace, had it granted them on these conditions: the Scots were to quit all they had possess'd within the wall of Severus: the limits of Scotland were beneath Sterlingbridge to be the river Forth, and on the other side Dunbritton-Frith; from that time so call'd of the British then seated in Cumberland, who had join'd with Osbert in this action, and so far extended on that side the British limits. If this be true, as the Scotch writers themselves witness (and who would think them fabulous to the disparagement of their own country?) how much wanting have been our historians to their country's honour, in letting pass unmention'd an exploit so memorable, by them remember'd and attested, who are wont ofter to extenuate than to amplify ought done in Scotland by the English? Donaldus on these conditions releas'd, soon after dies, according to Buchanan, in 858. Ethelwolf, chief king in England, had the year before ended his life, and was bury'd as his father at Winchester. He was from his youth much addicted to devotion; so that in his father's time he was ordain'd bishop of Winchester; and unwillingly, for want of other legitimate issue, succeeded him in the throne: managing therefore his greatest affairs by the activity of two bishops, Alstan of Sherburne, and Swithin of Winchester. But Alstan is noted of covetousness and oppression, by William of Malmsbury; the more vehemently, no doubt, for doing some notable damage to that monastery. The same author writes, that Ethelwolf at Rome paid a tribute to the Pope, continu'd to his days. However he were facile to his son and seditious nobles, in yielding up part of his kingdom; yet his queen he treated not the less honourably, for whomsoever it displeas'd. The West-Saxons had decreed, ever since the time of Eadburga, the infamous wife of Birthric, that no queen should sit in state with the king, or be dignify'd with the title of queen. But Ethelwolf permitted not that Judith his queen should lose any point of regal state by that law. At his death he divided the kingdom between his two sons, Ethelbald and Ethelbert; to the younger, Kent, Essex, Surrey, Sussex; to the elder, all the rest: to Peter and Paul certain revenues yearly, for what uses let others relate, who write also his pedigree from son to father, up to Adam.

ETHELBALD, unnatural and disloyal to his father, fell justly into another, though contrary sin, of too much love to his father's wife; and whom at first he oppos'd coming into the land, her now unlawfully marrying, he takes into his bed; but not long enjoying, dy'd at three years end, without doing aught more worthy to be remember'd; having reign'd two years with his father, impiously usurping, and three after him, as unworthily inheriting. And his hap was all that while to be unmolested by the Danes; not of divine favour doubtless, but to his great condemnation, living the more securely his incestuous life. Huntingdon on the other side much praises Ethelbald, and writes him bury'd at Sherburn (860), with great sorrow of his people, who miss'd him long after. Mat. West saith, that he repented of his incest with Judith, and dismiss'd her: but Asser an eye-witness of those times, mentions no such thing.

ETHELBALD by death remov'd, the whole kingdom came rightfully to Ethelbert his next brother. Who though a prince of great virtue and no blame, had as short a reign allotted him as his faulty brother, nor that so peaceful; once or twice invaded by the Danes. But they having landed in the west with a great army, and sack'd Winchester, were met by Osric earl of Southampton, and Ethelwolf of Barkshire, beaten to their ships, and forc'd to leave their booty. Five years after (865), about the time of his death, they set foot again in Tanet; the Kentishmen weary'd out with so frequent alarms, came to agreement with them for a certain sum of money; but e'er the peace could be ratify'd, and the money gather'd, the Danes impatient of delay by a sudden eruption in the night, soon wasted all the east of Kent. Meanwhile, or something before, Ethelbert deceasing was bury'd as his brother at Sherburn.

ETHELRED the third son of Ethelwolf, at his first coming (866) to the crown was entertain'd with a fresh invasion of Danes, led by Hinguar and Hubba, two brothers, who now had got footing among the East-

Angles; there they winter'd, and coming to terms of peace with the inhabitants, furnish'd themselves of horses, forming by that means many troops with riders of their own: these pagans, Asser saith, came from the river Danubius. Fitted thus for a long expedition, they ventur'd the next year (867) to make their way over land and over Humber, as far as York, them they found to their hands embroil'd in civil dissentions; their king, Osbert, they had thrown out, and Ella leader of another faction chosen in his room; who both, though late, admonish'd by their common danger, towards the year's end, with united powers made head against the Danes and prevail'd; but pursuing them over-eagerly into York, then but slenderly wall'd, the Northumbrians were everywhere slaughter'd, both within and without; their kings also both slain, their city burnt, saith Malmsbury, the rest as they could made their peace, over-run and vanquish'd as far as the river Tine, and Ecbert of English race appointed king over them. Brompton, no ancient author (for he wrote since Mat. West) nor of much credit, writes a particular cause of the Danes coming to York: that Bruern a nobleman, whose wife king Osbert had ravish'd, call'd in Hinguar and Hubba to revenge him. The example is remarkable, if the truth were as evident. Thence victorious, the Danes, next year (868) enter'd into Mercia towards Nottingham, where they spent the winter. Burhed, then king of that country, unable to resist, implores the aid of Ethelred and young Alfred his brother, they assembling (868) their forces and joining with the Mercians about Nottingham, offer battle: the Danes, not daring to come forth, kept themselves within that town and castle, so that no great fight was hazarded there; at length the Mercians, weary of long suspense, entered into conditions of peace with their enemies. After which the Danes returning back to York, made their abode there the space of one year, (869), committing, some say, many cruelties. Thence imbarking to Lindsey, and all the summer destroying that country, about September (870) they came with like fury into Kesteven, another part of Lincolnshire, where Algar, the Earl of Howland, now Holland, with his forces, and two hundred stout soldiers belonging to the abby of Croiland, three hundred from about Boston, Morcard lord of Brunne, with his numerous family, well train'd and arm'd, Osgot governor of Lincoln, with five hundred of that city, all joining together, gave battle to the Danes, slew of them a great multitude, with three of their kings, and pursu'd the rest to their tents: but the night following, Gothurn, Baseg, Osketil, Halfden, and Hamond, five kings; and as many earls, Frena, Hinguar, Hubba, Sidroc the elder and younger, coming in from several parts with great forces and spoils, great part of the English began to slink home. Nevertheless, Algar, with such as forsook him not, all next day in order of battle facing the Danes, and sustaining unmov'd the brunt of their assaults, could not withhold his men at last from pursuing their counterfeited flight; whereby open'd and disorder'd, they fell into the snares of their enemies, rushing back upon them. Algar, and those captains fore-nam'd with him, all resolute men, retreating to a hill-side, and slaying of such as followed them, manifold their number, dy'd at length upon heaps of dead which they had made round about them. The Danes thence passing on into the country of East-Angles, rifled and burnt the monastery of Ely, overthrew Earl Wulketul with his whole army, and lodg'd out the winter at Thetford; where king Edmund assailing them, was with his whole army put to flight, himself taken, bound to a stake, and shot to death with arrows, his whole country subdu'd. The next year (871), with great supplies, saith Huntingdon, bending their march toward the West-Saxons, the only people now left, in whom might seem yet to remain strength or courage likely to oppose them, they came to Reading, fortify'd there between the two rivers of Thames and Kennet; and about three days after, sent out wings of horse under two earls to forage the country; but Ethelwulf earl of Berkshire, at Englefield a village nigh, encounter'd them, slew one of their earls, and obtain'd a great victory. Four days after came the king himself and his brother Alfred with the main battle; and the Danes issuing forth, a bloody fight began, on either side great slaughter, in which earl Ethelwulf lost his life; but the Danes losing no ground, kept their place of standing to the end. Neither did the English for this make less haste to another conflict at Ecesdune, or Ashdown, four days after, where both armies with their whole forces on either side met. The Danes were imbattel'd in two great bodies, the one led by Bascai and Halfden their two kings, the other by such earls as were appointed. In like manner the English divided their powers, Ethelred the king stood against their kings; and though on the lower ground, and coming later into the battle from his orisons, gave a fierce onset, wherein Bascai (the Danish history names him Ivarus the son of Regnerus) was slain. Alfred was plac'd against the earls, and beginning the battle e're his brother came into the field, with such resolution charg'd them, that in the shock most of them were slain; they were nam'd, Sedroc, elder and younger, Osbern, Frean, Harald; at length in both divisions, the Danes turn'd their backs; many thousands of them cut off, the rest pursu'd till night. So much the more it may be wonder'd to hear next in the annals, that the Danes fourteen days after such an overthrow, fighting again with Ethelred and his brother Alfred at Basing, under conduct, saith the Danish history, of Agnerus and Hubbo, brothers of the slain Ivarus, should obtain the victory; especially since the new supply of Danes mention'd by Asser, arriv'd after this action. But after two months, the king and his brother fought with them again at Mertun, in Surrey, in two squadrons as before, in which fight hard it is to understand who had the better; so darkly do the

Saxon annals deliver their meaning with more than wonted infancy. Yet these I take (for Asser is here silent) to be the chief fountain of our story, the ground and basis upon which the monks later in time gloss and comment at their pleasure. Nevertheless it appears, that on the Saxon part, not Heamund the bishop only, but many valiant men lost their lives. This fight was follow'd by a heavy summer plague; whereof, as is thought, king Ethelred dy'd in the fifth of his reign, and was bury'd at Winburne, where his epitaph inscribes, that he had his death's wound by the Danes, according to the Danish history, 872.[1] Of all these terrible landings and devastations by the Danes, from the days of Ethelwolf till their two last battles with Ethelred, or of their leaders, whether kings, dukes, or earls, the Danish history of best credit saith nothing; so little wit or conscience it seems they had to leave any memory of their brutish, rather than manly actions; unless we shall suppose them to have come, as above was cited out of Asser, from Danubius, rather than from Denmark, more probably some barbarous nations of Prussia, or Livonia, not long before seated more northward on the Baltick sea.

ALFRED[2] the fourth son of Ethelwolf, had scarce perform'd his brother's obsequies, and the solemnity of his own crowning, when at the month's end in haste with a small power he encounter'd the whole army of Danes at Wilton, and most part of the day foil'd them; but unwarily following the chase, gave others of them the advantage to rally; who returning upon him now weary, remained masters of the field. This year (871), as is affirm'd in the annals, nine battles had been fought against the Danes on the south-side of Thames, besides innumerable excursions made by Alfred and other leaders; one king, nine earls were fall'n in fight, so that weary on both sides at the year's end (872) league or truce was concluded. Yet next year the Danes took their march to London, now expos'd their prey, there they winter'd, and thither came the Mercians to renew peace with them. The year (873) following they revok'd back to the parts beyond Humber, but winter'd at Torksey in Lincolnshire, where the Mercians now the third time made peace with them. Notwithstanding which, removing their camp to Rependuue in Mercia, now Repton upon Trent in Derbyshire, and there wint'ring (874), they constrain'd Burhead the king to fly into foreign parts, making seizure of his kingdom, he runing the direct way to Rome, with better reason than his ancestors,

---
[1] It appears by the inscription on his tomb, which may be read in Winbourn church, that he fell per manus Danorum Paganorum, by the hands of the pagan Danes, the 23d of April, Anno. 872.
[2] Asserius Menevensis, Asser bishop of St. David's, wrote the life of this prince, in who e reign he liv'd. The life of king Alfred was also written at large by Sir John Spelman, (sent to Sir Henry) the original manuscript whereof is now in the Bodleian library. It was translated into latin; and publish'd in folio, with Mr. Walker's notes, some years ago.

dy'd there, and was buried in a church by the English school. His kingdom the Danes farmed out to Kelfwulf, one of his houshold servants or officers, with condition to be resign'd them when they commanded. From Rependune they dislodg'd, Hafden their king, leading part of his army northward, winter'd (875) by the river Tine, and subjecting all those quarters, wasted also the Picts and British beyond: but Cuthrun, Oskitell, and Anwynd, other three of their kings moving from Rependune, came with a great army to Grantbridge (Cambridge), and remain'd there a whole year. Alfred that summer purposing to try his fortune with a fleet at sea (for he had found that the want of shipping and neglect of navigation, had expos'd the land to these piracies) met with seven Danish rovers, took one, the rest escaping; an acceptable success from so small a beginning: for the English at that time were but little experienc'd in sea affairs. The next year's (876) first motion of the Danes was towards Warham Castle: when Alfred meeting them, either by policy, or their doubt of his power; Ethelwerd saith, by money brought them to such terms of peace, as that they swore to him upon a hollow'd bracelet, others say upon certain reliques (a solemn oath it seems which they never vouchsafed before to any other nation) forthwith to depart the land; but falsifying that oath, by night with all the horse they had (Asser saith, slaying all the horsemen he had) stole to Exeter, and there winter'd. In Northumberland, Hafden their king began to settle, to divide the land, to till, and to inhabit. Mean while they in the west who were marched to Exeter, enter'd the city, coursing now and then to Warham; but their fleet the next year (877) sailing or rowing about the west, met with such a tempest near to Swanswich, or Gnavewic, as wrack'd 120 of their ships, and left the rest easie to be master'd by those gallies which Alfred had set there to guard the seas, and straiten Exeter of provision. He the while beleaguering them in the city; now humbled with the loss of their navy (two navies, saith Asser, the one at Gnavewic, the other at Swanwine) distress'd them so, as that they gave him as many hostages as he requir'd, and as many oaths, to keep their covenanted peace, and kept it. For the summer coming on, they departed into Mercia, whereof part they divided amongst themselves, part left to Kelwulf their substituted king. The twelfthtide following, all oaths forgotten, they came to Chippenham in Wiltshire dispeopling the countries round, dispossessing some, driving others beyond the sea; Alfred himself with a small company was forc'd to keep within woods and fenny places,[1] and for some time (878) all alone, as Florent saith, sojourn'd with Dunwulf a swine-herd, made afterwards for his devotion, and aptness to learning, bishop of Winchester. Hafden and the brother of Hinguar, coming with twenty-three ships from North-Wales, where they had made great spoil, landed in Devonshire, nigh

[1] Between the rivers Tone and Parrett in Somersetshire, about North-Petherton.

to a strong castle nam'd Kinwith; where by the garrison issuing forth unexpectedly, they were slain with twelve hundred of their men. Meanwhile the king about Easter, not despairing of his affairs, built a fortress at a place called Athelney in Somersetshire, therein valiantly defending himself and his followers, frequently sallying forth. The seventh week after, he rode out to a place call'd[1] Ecbryt-stone in the east part of Selwood: thither resorted to him with much gratulation, the Somerset and Wiltshire men, with many out of Hampshire, some of whom a little before had fled their country; with these marching to Ethandune now Edindon in Wiltshire, he gave battle to the whole Danish power, and put them to flight. Then besieging their castle, within fourteen days took it. Malmsbury writes, that in this time of his recess, to go a spy into the Danish camp, he took upon him with one servant the habit of a fidler; by this means gaining access to the king's table, and sometimes to his bed-chamber, got knowledge of their secrets, their careless encamping, and thereby this opportunity of assailing them on a sudden. The Danes by this misfortune broken, gave him more hostages, and renew'd their oaths to depart out of his kingdom. Their king Gytro, or Gothrum, offer'd willingly to receive baptism, and accordingly came with thirty of his friends, to a place call'd Aldra, or Aulre, near to Athelney, and were baptiz'd at Wedmore; where Alfred receiv'd him out of the font and nam'd him Athelstan. After which, they abode with him twelve days, and were dismissed with rich presents. Whereupon the Danes remov'd next year to Cirencester, thence peaceably to the East-Angles; which Alfred, as some write have bestow'd on Gothron to hold of him; the bounds whereof may be read among the laws of Alfred. Others of them went to Fulham on the Thames, and joining there with a great fleet newly come into the river, thence pass'd over into France and Flanders, both which they enter'd, so far conquering or wasting, as witness'd sufficiently, that the French and Flemish were no more able than the English, by policy or prowess to keep off that Danish inundation from their land. Alfred thus rid of them, and intending for the future to prevent their landing; three years after (882) (quiet the meanwhile) with more ships and better provided, puts to sea, and at first met with four of theirs, whereof two he took, throwing the men over-board, then with two others, wherein were two of their princes, and took them also, but not without some loss of his own. After three years (885) another fleet of them appear'd on these seas, so huge, that one part thought themselves sufficient to enter upon East-France, the other came to Rochester, and beleaguer'd it, they within stoutly defending themselves, till Alfred with great forces, coming down upon the Danes, drove them to their ships, leaving for haste all their horses behind them. The same year Alfred sent a fleet toward the East-Angles, then

[1] Possibly Brixton on the west-side of Wiltshire. See Glossary to the Saxon Chronicle.

inhabited by the Danes, which at the mouth of Stour,[1] meeting with sixteen Danish ships, after some fight took them all, and slew the soldiers aboard; but in the way home lying careless, were overtaken by another part of that fleet, and came off with loss; whereupon perhaps those Danes who were settled among the East-Angles, erected with new hopes, violated the peace which they had sworn to Alfred, who spent the next year (886) in repairing London (besieging, saith Huntingdon), much ruin'd and unpeopl'd by the Danes; the Londoners, all but those who had been led away captive, soon return'd to their dwellings, and Ethred duke of Mercia, was by the king appointed their governour.[2] But after thirteen years (893) respite of peace, another Danish fleet of 250 sail,[3] from the east part of France arriv'd at the mouth of a river in East-Kent, call'd Limen,[4] nigh to the great wood Andred,[5] famous for length and breadth; into that wood they drew up their ships four miles from the river's mouth, and built a fortress. After whom Haesten with another Danish fleet of eighty ships, entring the mouth of Thames, built a fort at Middleton, the former army remaining at a place call'd Apeltree. Alfred perceiving this, took of those Danes who dwelt in Northumberland, a new oath of fidelity, and of those in Essex, hostages, lest they should join, as they were wont, with their countrymen newly arriv'd. And by the next year (894), having got together his forces, between either army of the Danes, encamp'd so as to be ready for either of them, who first should happen to stir forth; troops of horse also he sent continually abroad, assisted by such as could be spar'd from strong places, wherever the countries wanted them, to encounter foraging parties of the enemy. The king also divided sometimes his whole army, marching out with one part by turns, the other keeping intrench'd. In conclusion, rowling up and down, both sides met at Farnham in Surry;[6] where the Danes by Alfred's horse troops were put to flight, and crossing the Thames to a certain island near Coln in Essex, or as Cambden thinks, by Colebroke, where besieg'd there by Alfred till provision fail'd the besiegers, another part staid behind with the king wounded. Meanwhile Alfred preparing to reinforce the siege at Colney, the Danes of Northumberland breaking faith, came by sea to the East-Angles, and with a hundred ships coasting southward, landed in Devonshire, and besieged Exeter; thither Alfred hasted with his powers, except a squadron of Welsh that came to London: with whom

[1] Not that in Kent, but that which runs by Harwich in Essex.
[2] In the year 886, 'tis said Alfred founded the university of Oxford, and in the next, he held that great council wherein all the laws were made that go under his name. Cambden Spelman.
[3] In 885 Mr. Milton says the Danes invaded England, and in 893 they came again: so there cou'd be but 8 years peace.
[4] The mouth of this river then ran into the sea near Romney, but 'tis now turn'd.
[5] The Weald of Kent, Sussex, and the wood-land part of Hampshire.
[6] Mr. Cambden writes, that the battle of Farnham, was fought in the year 893. Britania Tit. Surrey.

the citizens marching forth to Beamflet, where Haestan the Dane had built a strong fort, and left a garrison, while he himself with the main of his army was enter'd far into the country, luckily surprize the fort, master the garrison, make prey of all they find there; their ships also they burnt or brought away with good booty, and many prisoners, among whom, the wife and two sons of Heasten were sent to the king, who forthwith set them at liberty. Whereupon Heasten gave oath of amity and hostages to the king; he in requital, whether freely, or by agreement, a sum of money. Nevertheless, without regard of faith given, while Alfred was busied about Exeter, joyning with the other Danish army, he built another castle in Essex at Shoberie, thence marching westward by the Thames, aided with Northumbrians and East-Anglish Danes, they came at length to Severn, pillaging all in their way. . But, Ethred, Ethelm, and Ethelnoth, the king's captains, with united forces pitch'd nigh to them at Buttingtun, on the Severn bank in Montgomeryshire, the river running between, and there many weeks attended; the king meanwhile blocking up the Danes, who besieg'd Exeter, having eaten part of their horses, the rest urg'd with hunger broke forth to their fellows, who lay encamp'd on the east side of the river, and were all there discomfited, with some loss of valiant men on the king's party; the rest fled back to Essex and their fortress there. Then Laf, one of their leaders, gather'd before winter a great army of Northumbrian and East-Anglish Danes, who leaving their money, ships and wives with the East-Angles, and marching day and night, sat down before a city in the west call'd Wirheal[1] near to Chester, and took it e'er they could be overtaken. The English after two days siege, hopeless to dislodge them, wasted the country round to cut off from them all provision, and departed. Soon after which, next year (895) the Danes no longer able to hold Wirheal, destitute of victuals, enter'd North Wales; thence laden with spoils, part return'd into Northumberland, others to the East-Angles as far as Essex, where they seiz'd on a small island call'd Meresig. And here again the annals record them to besiege Exeter, but without coherence of sense or story. Others relate to this purpose, that returning by sea from the siege of Exeter, and in their way landing on the coast of Sussex, they of Chichester sallied out, and slew of them many hundreds, taking also some of their ships. The same year they who possess'd Meresig, intending to winter thereabouts, drew up their ships, some into the Thames, others into the river Lee, and on the bank thereof built a castle twenty miles from London; to assault which the Londoners aided with other forces, march'd out the summer following (896), but were soon put to flight, losing four of the king's captains. Huntingdon writes quite the contrary, that these four were

[1] Mr. Milton mistakes the name of the country for that of the city. H. Huntingdon says 'twas a certain city in Warheal call'd Legacester, now Chester, and the country that runs into the sea to the N. W. is by Mr. Cambden call'd Wirrall. Brit. Tit. Cheshire.

Danish captains, and the overthrow theirs; but little credit is to be plac'd in Huntingdon single. For the king thereupon with his forces, lay encamp'd nearer the city, that the Danes might not infest them in time of harvest; in the meantime, subtlely devising to turn Lee stream several ways; whereby the Danish bottoms were left on dry ground: which they soon perceiving march'd over the land to Quatbrig[1] on the Severn, built a fortress and winter'd there; while their ships left in Lee, were either broken or brought away by the Londoners; but their wives and children they had left in safety with the East-Angles. The next year was pestilent, and besides the common sort took away many great earls, Kelmond in Kent, Brithulf in Essex, Wulfred in Hampshire, with many others; and to this evil, the Danes of Northumberland and East-Angles ceas'd not to endamage the West-Saxons, especially by stealth, robbing on the south shoar in certain long galleys. But the king causing to be built others twice as long as usually were built, and some of sixty or seventy oars higher, swifter and steadier than such as were in use before either with Danes or Frisons, his own invention, some of these he sent out against six Danish pirates, who had done much harm in the Isle of Wight and parts adjoyning. The bickering was doubtful and intricate, part on the water, part on the sands; not without loss of some eminent men on the English side. The pirates at length were either slain or taken, two of them stranded; the men brought to Winchester, where the king then was, were executed by his command; one of them escap'd to the East-Angles, her men much wounded: the same year not fewer than twenty of their ships perish'd on the south coast with all their men. And Rollo the Dane or Norman landing here, as Mat. West. writes, though not in what part of the island, after an unsuccessful fight against those forces which first oppos'd him, sail'd into France, and conquer'd the country, since that time called Normandy. This is the sum of what pass'd in three years against the Danes, returning out of France, set down so perplexedly by the Saxon annalist, ill-gifted with utterance, as with much ado can be understood sometimes what is spoken, whether meant of the Danes or of the Saxons. After which troublesome time, Alfred enjoying three years of peace, by him spent, as his manner was, not idly or voluptuously, but in all vertuous employments both of mind and body, becoming a prince of his renown, ended his days in the year 900, the 51st of his age, the 30th of his reign, and was buried regally at Winchester: he was born (A.D. 849.) at a place call'd Wanading (Wantage) in Berkshire, his mother Osburga the daughter of Oslac the king's cup-bearer, a Goth[2] by nation, and of

---

[1] This is most like to be Bridgenorth in Shropshire. For what reasons, see the gloss of the Saxon chronicle, under the title of Cwathrigge. Suppos'd by others to be Cambridge, in Gloucestershire, now a village situated on the river Cam, where it falls into the Severn.

[2] A Saxon Lord descended from Withgar first prince of the isle of Wight.

noble descent. He was of person comelier than all his brethren, of pleasing tongue and graceful behaviour, ready wit and memory; yet through the fondness of his parents towards him, had not been taught to read till the twelfth year of his age; but the great desire of learning which was in him, soon appear'd, by his conning of Saxon poems day and night, which with great attention he heard by others repeated. He was besides, excellent at hunting, and the new art then of hawking, but more exemplary in devotion, having collected into a book certain prayers and psalms, which he carried over with him in his bosom to use on all occasions. He thirsted after all liberal knowledge, and oft complain'd that in his youth he had no teachers, in his middle age so little vacancy from wars, and the cares of his kingdom; yet leisure he found sometimes, not only to learn much himself, but to communicate thereof what he could to his people, by translating books out of Latin into English, Orosius, Boethius, Beda's history, and others, permitted none unlearn'd to bear office, either in court or commonwealth: at twenty years of age, not yet reigning, he took to wife Egelswitha the daughter of Ethelred a Mercian earl. The extremities which befel him in the sixth of his reign, Neothan abbot told him, were justly come upon him for neglecting in his younger days the complaints of such as injur'd and oppress'd repair'd to him, as then second person in the kingdom for redress; which neglect, were it such indeed, were yet excusable in his youth, through jollity of mind, unwilling perhaps to be detain'd long with sad and sorrowful narrations; but from the time of his undertaking regal charge, no man more patient in hearing causes, more inquisitive in examining, more exact in doing justice, and providing good laws, which are yet extant; more severe in punishing unjust judges or obstinate offenders. Thieves especially and robbers, to the terrour of whom in cross-ways were hung upon a high post certain chains of gold, as it were daring any one to take them thence; so that justice seem'd in his days not to flourish only, but to triumph: no man than he more frugal of two precious things in man's life, his time and his revenue; no man wiser in the disposal of both. His time, the day and night, he distributed by the burning of certain tapours into three equal portions: the one was for devotion, the other for publick or private affairs, the third for bodily refreshment: how each hour past, he was put in mind by one who had that office. His whole annual revenue, which his first care was should be justly his own, he divided into two equal parts; the first he employ'd to secular uses, and subdivided those into three, the first to pay his soldiers, houshold servants and guard, of which divided into three bands, one attended monthly by turn; the second was to pay his architects and workmen, whom he had got together of several nations; for he was also an elegant builder, above the custom and conceit of Englishmen in those days: the third he had in readiness to relieve or honour strangers according to their worth, who came from all parts to see him, and to live under him. The other equal part of his yearly wealth he dedicated to religious uses: those of four sorts; the first to relieve the poor, the second to building and maintenance of two monasteries, the third of a school, where he had persuaded the sons of many noblemen to study sacred knowledge and liberal arts, some say at Oxford:[1] the fourth was for the relief of foreign churches, as far as India to the shrine of St. Thomas, sending thither Sigelm bishop of Sherburn, who both return'd safe, and brought with him many rich gems and spices; gifts also, and a letter he receiv'd from the patriarch of Jerusalem, sent many to Rome, and for them receiv'd reliques. Thus far, and much more might be said of his noble mind, which render'd him the mirrour of princes; his body was diseas'd in his youth with a great soreness in the siege, and that ceasing of itself, with another inward pain of unknown cause, which held him by frequent fits to his dying day; yet not disenabl'd to sustain those many glorious labours of his life both in peace and war.

EDWARD the son of Alfred succeeded, in learning not equal, in power and extent of dominion, surpassing his father. The beginning of his reign had much disturbance by Ethelwald an ambitious young man, son of the king's uncle, or cousin-german, or brother, for his genealogy is variously deliver'd. He vainly avouching to have equal right with Edward of succession to the crown, possess'd himself of Winburne in Dorset, and another town diversly nam'd, giving out that there he would live or die; but encompass'd with the king's forces at Badburie, a place nigh, his heart failing him, he stole out by night, and fled to the Danish army beyond Humber. The king sent after him, but not overtaking, found his wife in the town, whom he had married out of a nunnery, and commanded her to be sent back thither.[2] About this time (902) the Kentish men, against a multitude of Danish pirates, fought prosperously at a place call'd Holme, as Hoveden records, Ethelwald aided by the Northumbrians with shipping, three years (905) after, failing to the East-Angles, persuaded the Danes there to fall into the king's territory, who marching with him as far as Creeklad, and passing the Thames there, wasted as far beyond as they durst venture, and laden with spoils return'd home. The king with his powers making speed after them, between the Dike[3] and Ouse, suppos'd to be Suffolk and Cambridgeshire, as far as the fens northward, laid waste all before

---

[1] The truth of it is so clearly made out by several authors, that he had no reason to mention it so suspiciously.
[2] Ran Higden, in his Polychron, says he took her out of the Monastery of Winburne, and went away with her to the Danes.
[3] The Devil's Ditch, which formerly divided the kingdoms of the Mercians and the East-Angles.

him. Thence intending to return, he commanding that all his army should follow him close without delay; but the Kentish men, though often call'd upon, lagging behind, the Danish army prevented them, and joyn'd battle with the king; where duke Sigulf and earl Sigelm, with many other of the nobles were slain; on the Danes part, Eoric their king, and Ethelwald the author of this war, with others of high note, and of them greater number, but with great ruin on both sides; yet the Danes kept in their power the burying of their slain. Whatever followed upon this conflict, which we read not, the king two years after (907) with the Danes, both of East-Angles and Northumberland, concluded peace, which continu'd three years (910), by whomsoever broken; for at the end thereof king Edward raising great forces out of West-Sex, and Mercia, sent them against the Danes beyond Humber; where staying five weeks, they made great spoil and slaughter. The king offer'd them terms of peace, but they rejecting all, enter'd with the next year (911) into Mercia, rendering no less hostility than they had suffer'd: but at Tetnal in Staffordshire, saith Florent, were by the English in a set battle overthrown. King Edward then in Kent, had got together of ships about a hundred sail, others gone southward, came back and met him. The Danes now supposing that his main forces were upon the sea, took liberty to rove and plunder up and down, as hope of prey led them, beyond Severn. The king guessing what might imbolden them, sent before him the lightest of his army to entertain them; then following with the rest, set upon them in their return over Cantbrig in Gloucestershire, and slew many thousands, among whom Ecwils, Hasden, and Hinguar their kings, and many other harsh names in Huntingdon; the place also of this fight is variously written by Ethelwerd and Florent, call'd Wodensfield. The year (912) following Ethred duke of Mercia, to whom Alfred had given London, with his daughter in marriage; now dying, king Edward resum'd that city, and Oxford, with the countries adjoyning into his own hands, and the year (913) after built, or much repair'd by his soldiers, the town of Hertford on either side Lee, and leaving a sufficient number at the work, march'd about middle summer with the other part of his forces into Essex, and encamp'd at Maldon, while his soldiers built Witham; where a good part of the country, subject formerly by the the Danes, yielded themselves to his protection.[1] Four years (917) after (Florent allows but one year) the Danes from Leister and Northampton, falling into Oxfordshire, committed much rapine, and in some towns thereof great slaughter; while another party wasting Hertfordshire, met with other fortune: for the country-people inur'd now to such kind of incursions, joyning stoutly together, fell upon the

---

[1] The next year 914, the Danes committed great outrages in Buckinghamshire about Bernwood, and destroy'd an ancient Roman burgh, which stood where now Briel stands.

spoilers, recover'd their own goods, with some booty from their enemies. About the same time Elfled the king's sister sent her army of Mercians into Wales, who routed the Welsh, took the castle of Bricenam-mere[1] by Brecknock, and brought away the king's wife of that country, with other prisoners. Not long after she took Derby from the Danes, and the castle by a sharp assault. But the year (918) ensuing brought a new fleet of Danes to Lidwic in Devonshire, under two leaders, Otter and Roald; who sailing thence westward about the island's end, came up to the mouth of Severn;[2] there landing wasted the Welsh Coast, and Irchenfield part of Hertfordshire; where they took Kuneleac a British Bishop, for whose ransome king Edward gave forty pounds, but the men of Hereford and Gloucestershire assembling, put them to flight; slaying Roald and the brother of Otter, with many more, pursu'd them to a wood, and there beset, compell'd them to give hostages of present departure. The king with his army sat not far off, securing from the south of Severn to Avon: so that openly they durst not, by night they twice ventur'd to land: but found such welcome, that few of them came back; the rest anchor'd by a small island, where many of them famish'd; then sailing to a place call'd Deomed,[3] they cross'd into Ireland. The king with his army went to Buckingham, staid there a month, and built two castles or forts on either bank of Ouse e'er his departing, and Turkitel a Danish leader, with those of Bedford and Northampton, yielded him subjection. Whereupon the next year (919) he came with his army to the town of Bedford, took possession thereof, staid there a month, and gave order to build another part of the town, on the south side of Ouse. Thence the year (920) following went again to Maldon, repair'd and fortifi'd the town. Turkitel the Dane having small hope to thrive here, where things with such prudence were manag'd against his interest, got leave of the king, with as many voluntaries as would follow him, to pass into France. Early the next year (921) King Edward re-edifi'd Tovechester, now Torchester; and another city in the annals call'd Wigingmere. Meanwhile (921) the Danes of Leister and Northamptonshire; not liking perhaps to be neighboured with strong towns, laid siege to Torchester, but they within, repelling the assault one whole day till supplies came, quitted the siege by night; and pursu'd close by the besieged, between Brinwood[4] and Ailsbury were surpris'd, many of them made prisoners, and

---

[1] Brecenanmere is the right name: in English Brecknock Mere.
[2] Where they besieg'd an island, which Florence of Worcester calls Reorie, suppos'd to be Stepholm; and when they had taken it, were almost starv'd with hunger. This island is now of no use nor defence, yielding nothing fit for human nourishment: it lies about two leagues from the shore, over-against Uphill in Somersetshire.
[3] Deomod the Saxon Annals call it. 'Tis no particular place, but a country: the same which the ancients call'd Demetæ, including Carmarthenshire, Pembrokeshire, and Cardiganshire.
[4] Forest of Bernwood. Kennet's Paroch. Antiquities of Ambrosden, &c

much of their baggage lost. Other of the Danes at Huntingdon, aided from the East-Angles, finding that castle not commodious, left it, and built another at Temsford, judging that place more opportune from whence to make their excursions; and soon after went forthwith to assail Bedford: but the garrison issuing out, slew a great part of them, the rest fled. After this, a great army of them gather'd out of Mercia and the East-Angles, came and besieg'd the city call'd Wingingamere a whole day; but finding it defended stoutly by them within, thence also departed, driving away much of their cattle: whereupon the English, from towns and cities round about joyning forces, laid siege to the town and castle of Temsford, and by assault took both; slew their king with Toglea a duke, and Mannan his son an earl, with all the rest there found; who chose to die rather than yield. Encourag'd by this, the men of Kent, Surrey, and part of Essex, enterprize the siege of Colchester, nor gave over till they won it, sacking the town, and putting to sword all the Danes therein, except some who escap'd over the wall. To the succour of these, a great number of Danes inhabiting ports and other towns in the East-Angles, united their forces; but coming too late, as in revenge beleaguer'd Maldon; but that town also timely reliev'd, they departed, not only frustrate of their design, but so hotly pursu'd, that many thousands of them lost their lives in the flight. Forthwith king Edward, with his West-Saxons, went to Pasham upon Ouse, there to guard the passage, while others were building a stone wall about Torchester; to him the earl Thursert, and other lord Danes, with their army there about as far as Woelud, came and submitted. Whereat the king's soldiers joyfully cry'd out to be dismiss'd home: therefore with another part of them he enter'd Huntingdon, and repair'd it, where breaches had been made; all the people thereabout returning to obedience. The like was done at Colnchester by the next remove of his army; after which both East and West-Angles, and the Danish forces among them, yielded to the king, swearing allegiance to him both by sea and land: the army also of Danes at Grantbrig, surrendering themselves, took the same oath. The summer (922) following he came with his army to Stamford, built a castle there on the south-side of the river, where all the people of those quarters acknowledg'd him supream. During his abode there, Elfled his sister a martial woman, who after her husband's death would no more marry, but gave her self to publick affairs, repairing and fortifying many towns, warring sometimes, dy'd at Tamworth the chief seat of Mercia, whereof by gift of Alfred her father, she was lady or queen; whereby that whole nation became obedient to king Edward, as did also North-Wales, with Howel, Cledaucus, and Jeothwell their kings. Thence passing to Nottingham, he enter'd and repair'd the town, plac'd there part English, part Danes, and receiv'd fealty from all in Mercia of

either nation. The next autumn (923) coming with his army into
Cheshire, he built and fortify'd Thelwel; and while he staid there,
call'd another army out of Mercia, which he sent to repair and fortifie
Manchester.[1] About Midsummer (924) following, he march'd again
to Nottingham, built a town over against it on the south-side of that
river, and with a bridge joyn'd them both; thence journeyed to a place
call'd Bedecanwillan in Pictland;[2] there also built and fenc'd a city
on the borders, where the king of Scots did him honour as to his sovereign, together with the whole Scotish nation; the like did Reginald
and the son of Eadulf, Danish princes, with all the Northumbrians,
both English and Danes. The king also of a people thereabout call'd
Streatgledwalli (the North-Welsh, as Cambden thinks, of Strat-Cluid
in Denbighshire, perhaps rather the British of Cumberland) did him
homage, and not undeserv'd. For Buchanan himself confesses, that
this king Edward, with a small number of men compar'd to his enemies, overthrew in a great battle, the whole united power both of Scots
and Danes, slew most of the Scotish nobility, and forc'd Malcolmb,
whom Constantine the Scotish king had made general, and design'd
heir of his crown, to save himself by flight, sore wounded. Of the
English he makes Athelstan the son of Edward chief leader; and so
far seems to confound times and actions, as to make this battle the
same with that fought by Athelstan, about twenty-four years after at
Bruneford, against Anlaf and Constantine, whereof hereafter. But
here Buchanan takes occasion to inveigh against the English writers,
upbraiding them with ignorance who affirm Athelstan to have been
supream king of Britain, Constantine the Scotish king with others to
have held of him; and denies that in the annals of Marianus Scotus,
any mention is to be found thereof; which I shall not stand much to
contradict; for in Marianus, whether by sirname or by nation
Scotus, will be found as little mention of any other Scotish affairs, till
the time of king Dunchand slain by Machetad or Mackbeth, in the
year 1040 which gives cause of suspicion, that the affairs of Scotland
before that time were so obscure as to be unknown to their own
countryman, who liv'd and wrote his chronicle not long after. But
king Edward thus nobly doing, and thus honour'd, the year (925) following dy'd at Farendon, a builder and restorer even in war, not a
destroyer of his land. He had by several wives many children; his
eldest daughter Edgith, he gave in marriage to Charles king of France,
grand-child of Charles the Bald above mention'd; of the rest in place
convenient. His laws are yet to be seen. He was buried at Win-

---

[1] This is an error which has been handed down to our historians by Marianus, who mistook the Saxon Annals. These do not tell us, that King Edward repair'd Manchester, but that he repair'd maniʒe ceaꞅteꞅ, i.e., many cities: which is certainly the sense of the place.

[2] The Cottonian Copy of the Saxon Annals relate, that he went from Nottingham into Peakland, the Peak in Darbyshire, and thence to Bedecanwell, suppos'd to be Bakewell in that county.

chester, in the monastery, by Alfred his father. And a few days after him dy'd (at Oxford) Ethelwerd his eldest son, the heir of his crown. He had the whole island in subjection, yet so as petty kings reign'd under him. In Northumberland, after Ecbert whom the Danes had set up, and the Northumbrians yet unruly under their yoke, at the end of six years had expell'd, one Ricsig was set up king, and bore the name three years, then another Ecbert, and Guthred, the latter if we believe legends, of a servant made king by command of St. Cudbert, in a vision; and enjoyn'd by another vision of the same saint, to pay well for his royalty many lands and privileges to his church and monastery. But now to the story.

ATHELSTAN next in age to Ethelward his brother, who deceas'd untimely few days before, though born of a concubine, yet for the great appearance of many virtues in him, and his brethren being yet under age, was (926) exalted to the throne,[1] at Kingstone upon Thames, and by his father's last will, saith Malmsbury, yet not without some opposition of one Alfred and his accomplices; who not liking he should reign, had conspir'd to seize on him after his father's death, and put out his eyes. But the conspiratours discover'd, and Alfred denying the plot, was sent to Rome to assert his innocence before the pope; where taking his oath on the altar, he fell down immediately, and carried out by his servants, three days after dy'd. Meanwhile beyond Humber, the Danes though much aw'd were not idle. Ingualed, one of their kings, took possession of York. Sitric, who some years before had slain Niel his brother, by force took Davenport in Cheshire; and however he defended these doings, grew so considerable, that Athelstan with great solemnity gave him his sister Edgith to wife: but he enjoy'd her not long, dying e're the year's end, nor his sons Anlaf and Guthfert the kingdom, driven out the next year (927) by Athelstan; nor unjustly saith Huntingdon, as being first raisers of the war. Simeon calls him Gudfrid a British king, whom Athelstan this year drove out of his kingdom; and perhaps they were both one, the name and time not much differing, the place only mistaken. Malmsbury differs in the name also, calling him Aldulf a certain rebel. Them also I wish as much mistaken, who write that Athelstan, jealous of his younger brother Edwin's towardly vertues, lest added to the right of birth, they might some time or other call in question his illegitimate precedence, caus'd him to be drown'd in the sea; expos'd, some say, with one servant in a rotten bark, without sail or oar; where the youth far off land, and in rough weather despairing, threw himself overboard; the servant more patient, got to land and reported the success. But this

[1] He was crown'd by Athelm bishop of Canterbury, on a scaffold erected for that purpose, in the midst of the town.

Malmsbury confesses to be sung in old songs, not read in warrantable authors: and Huntingdon speaks as of a sad accident to Athelstan, that he lost his brother Edwin by sea; far the more credible, in that Athelstan, as is written by all, tenderly lov'd, and bred up the rest of his brethren, of whom he had no less cause to be jealous. And the year (934) following he prosper'd better than from so foul a fact, passing into Scotland with great puissance, both by sea and land, and chasing his enemies before him by land as far as Dunfeoder, and Wertermore, by sea as far as Cathness. The cause of this expedition, saith Malmsbury, was to demand Gudfert the son of Sitric, thither fled, though not deny'd at length by Constantine, who with Eugenius king of Cumberland, at a place call'd Dacor or Dacre in that shire, surrender'd himself and each his kingdom to Athelstan, who brought back with him for hostage the son of Constantine. But Gudfert escaping in the meanwhile out of Scotland, and Constantine exasperated by this invasion, persuaded Anlaf the other son of Sitric then fled into Ireland, others write Anlaf king of Ireland and the Isles, his son-in-law, with 615 ships, and the king of Cumberland with other forces, to his aid. This within four years (938) effected, they enter'd England by Humber, and fought with Athelstan at a place call'd Wendune, others term it Brunanburg, others Bruneford, which Ingulf places beyond Humber, Cambden in Glendale of Northumberland on the Scotch borders: the bloodiest fight, say authors, that ever this island saw; to describe which, the Saxon annalist wont to be sober and succinct, whether the same or another writer, now labouring under the weight of his argument, and over-charg'd, runs on a sudden into such extravagant[1] fancies and metaphors, as bear him quite beside the scope of being understood. Huntingdon, though himself peccant enough in this kind, transcribes him word for word as a pastime to his readers. I shall only sum up what I can attain, in usual language. The battle was fought eagerly from morning till night; some fell of king Edward's old army, try'd in many a battle before; but on the other side great multitudes, the rest fled to their ships. Five kings, and seven of Anlaf's chief captains were slain on the place, with Froda a Norman leader; Constantine escap'd home, but lost his son in the fight, if I understand my author; Anlaf by sea to Dublin, with a small remainder of his great host. Malmsbury relates this war, adding many circumstances after this manner. That Anlaf joyning with Constantine and the whole power of Scotland, besides those which he brought with him out of Ireland, came on far southwards, till Athelstan who had retir'd on set purpose to be the surer of his enemies, enclosed from all succour and retreat, met him at Bruncford. Anlaf

---

[1] What he calls extravagant fancies, is nothing but a passage in imitation of Cædmon's verse, which was the standard of poetry among the Saxons. This Caedmon, says Mr. Cambden in his remains, about the year 680, became so divine a poet in our English tongue, that with his sweet verses he withdrew many from vice to virtue.

perceiving the valour and resolution of Athelstan, and mistrusting his own forces though numerous, resolv'd first to spy in what posture his enemies lay: and imitating perhaps what he heard attempted by king Alfred the age before, in the habit of a musician, got access by his lute and voice to the king's tent, there playing both the minstrel and the spy: then towards evening dismiss'd, he was observ'd by one who had been his soldier and well knew him, viewing earnestly the king's tent, and what approaches lay about it, then in the twilight to depart. The soldier forthwith acquaints the king, and by him blamed for letting go his enemy, answer'd, that he had given first his military oath to Anlaf, whom if he had betray'd, the king might suspect him of like treasonous mind towards himself; which to disprove, he advis'd him to remove his tent a good distance off; and so done, it happen'd that a bishop with his retinue coming that night to the army, pitch'd his tent in the same place, from whence the king had remov'd. Anlaf coming by night, as he had design'd to assault the camp, and especially the king's tent, finding there the bishop instead, slew him with all his followers. Athelstan took the alarm, and as it seems, was not found so unprovided, but that the day now appearing, he put his men in order, and maintain'd the fight till evening; wherein Constantine himself was slain, with five other kings and twelve earls, the annals were content with seven, in the rest not disagreeing. Ingulf abbot of Croyland, from the authority of Turketul a principal leader in this battle, relate it more at large to this effect: that Athelstan, about a mile distant from the place where execution was done upon the bishop and his supplies, alarm'd at the noise, came down by break of day, upon Anlaf and his army, overwatch'd and wearied now with the slaughter they had made, and something out of order, yet in two main battles. The king therefore in like manner dividing, led the one part, consisting most of West-Saxons, against Anlaf with his Danes and Irish, committing the other to his Chancellor Turketul, with the Mercians and Londoners against Constantine and the Scots. The shower of arrows and darts over-pass'd, both battles attack'd each other with a close and terrible engagement, for a long space neither side giving ground. Till the chancellor Turketul a man of great stature and strength, taking with him a few Londoners of select valour, and Singin who led the Worstershire men, a captain of undaunted courage, broke into the thickest, making his way first through the Picts and Orkeners, then through the Cumbrians and Scots, and came at length where Constantine himself fought, unhors'd him, and us'd all means to take him alive; but the Scots valiantly defending their king, and laying load upon Turketul, which the goodness of his armour well endur'd, he had yet been beaten down, had not Singin his faithful second at the same time slain Constantine; which once known, Anlaf and the whole army betook them to flight, whereof a huge multitude fell by the sword. This Turketul not long after leaving worldly affairs, became abbot of Croyland, which at his own cost he had repair'd from Danish ruins, and left there this memorial of his former actions. Athelstan with his brother Edmund victorious, thence turning into Wales, with much more ease vanquish'd Ludwal the king, and possest his land. But Malmsbury writes, that commiserating human chance, as he displac'd, so he restor'd both him and Constantine to their regal state; for the surrender of king Constantine hath been above spoken of. However the Welsh did him homage at the city of Hereford, and covenanted yearly payment of gold 20 pounds, of silver 300, of Oxen 25 thousand, besides hunting dogs and hawks. He also took Exeter from the Cornish Britons, who till that time had equal right there with the English, and bounded them with the river Tamar, as the other British with Wey. Thus dreaded of his enemies, and renown'd far and near, three years (941) after he dy'd at Gloster, and was buried with many trophies at Malmsbury, where he had caus'd to be laid his two cousin-germans, Elwin and Ethelstan, both slain in the battle against Anlaf. He was thirty years old at his coming to the crown, mature in wisdom from his childhood, comely of person and behaviour; so that Alfred his grandfather in blessing him was wont to pray he might live to have the kingdom, and put him yet a child into soldier's habit. He had his breeding in the court of Elfled his aunt, of whose vertues more than female we have related, sufficient to evince that his mother, though said to be no wedded wife, was yet such of parentage and worth, as the royal line disdain'd not, though the song went in Malmsbury's days (for it seems he refus'd not the authority of ballads for want of better) that his mother was a farmer's daughter, but of excellent feature; who dreamt one night she brought forth a moon that should enlighten the whole land : which the king's nurse hearing of, took her home and bred up courtly; that the king coming one day to visit his nurse, saw there this damsel, lik'd her, and by earnest suit prevailing, had by her this famous Athelstan, a bounteous, just and affable king, as Malmsbury sets him forth; nor less honour'd abroad by foreign kings, who sought his friendship by great gifts or affinity; that Harold king of Noricum sent him a ship, whose prow was of gold, sails purple, and other golden things, the more to be wonder'd at, sent from Noricum, whether meant Norway or Bavaria, the one place so far from such superfluity of wealth, the other from all sea : the embassadors were Helgrim and Offrid, who found the king at York. His sisters he gave in marriage to greatest princes, Elgif to Otho son of Henry the emperour, Egdith to a certain duke about the Alps, Edgiv to Ludwic king of Aquitain, sprung of Charles the great, Ethilda to Hugo king of France who sent Aldulf son of Baldwin, earl of Flanders, to obtain her. From all these great suitors especially from the emperour and king of France came rich presents, horses of excellent breed, gorgeous trappings and armour, reliques, jewels, odors, vessels of onyx, and other precious things, which I leave poetically describ'd in Malmsbury, taken, as he confesses, out of an old versifier, some of whose verses he recites. The only blemish left upon him, was the exposing of his brother Edwin, who disavow'd by oath the treason whereof he was accus'd, and implor'd an equal hearing. But these were songs, as before hath been said, which add also that Athelstan, his anger over, soon repented of the fact, and put to death his cup-bearer, who had induc'd him to suspect and expose his brother, put in mind by a word falling from the cup-bearer's own mouth, who slipping one day as he bore the king's cup, and recovering himself on the other leg, said aloud, fatally as to him it proved, one brother helps the other. Which words the king laying to heart, and pondering how ill he had done to make away his brother, aveng'd himself first on the adviser of that fact, took on him seven years penance, and as Mat. West. saith, built two monasteries for the soul of his brother. His laws are extant among the laws of other Saxon kings to this day.

EDMUND not above eighteen years old succeeded (942) his brother Athelstan, in courage not inferiour. For in the second of his reign he freed Mercia of the Danes that remain'd there, and took from them the cities of Lincoln, Nottingham, Stamford, Derby, and Leister, where they were plac'd by king Edward, but it seems gave not good proof of their fidelity. Simeon writes that Anlaf setting forth from York, and having wasted southward as far as Northampton, was met by Edmund at Leister; but that e're the battles joyn'd, peace was made between them by Odo and Wulstan the two arch-bishops, with conversion of Anlaf; for the same year Edmund receiv'd at the font-stone this or another Anlaf, as saith Huntingdon, not him spoken of before, who dy'd this year (so uncertain they are in the story of these times also) and held Reginald another king of the Northumbers, while the bishop confirm'd him : their limits were divided north and south by Watling-street. But spiritual kindred little avail'd to keep peace between them, whoever gave the cause ; for we read him two years 944) after driving Anlaf (whom the annals now first call the son of Sitric) and Suthfrid son of Reginald out of Northumberland, taking the whole country into subjection. Edmund the next year harass'd Cumberland, then gave it to Malcolm king of Scots, thereby bound to assist him in his wars, both by sea and land ; Mat. West. adds, that in this action Edmund had the aid of Leolin prince of North Wales, against Dunmail the Cumbrian king, him depriving of his kingdom, and his two sons of their sight.[1] But the year (946) after, he himself by strange accident, came to an untimely death, feasting with his nobles on St. Austin's Day at Puckle-kerke in Glostershire, to celebrate the memory of his first converting the Saxons. He spy'd Leof a noted thief whom he had banish'd, sitting among his guests; whereat transported with too much vehemence of spirit, though in a just cause, rising from the table he ran upon the thief, and catching his hair, pull'd him to the ground. The thief who doubted from such handling no less than his death intended, thought to die not unreveng'd; and with a short dagger struck the king, who still laid at him, and little expected such assassination, mortally into the breast. The matter was done in a moment, e're men set at table could turn them, or imagine at first what the stir meant, till perceiving the king deadly wounded, they flew upon the murderer, and hew'd him to pieces; who like a wild beast at bay, seeing himself surrounded, desperately laid about him, wounding some in his fall. The king was buried at Glaston, whereof Dunstan was then abbot; his laws yet remain to be seen among the laws of other Saxon kings.

EDRED the third brother of Athelstan, the sons of Edmund being yet but children, next (948) reign'd, not degenerating from his worthy predecessors, and crown'd at Kingston. Northumberland he thoroughly subdu'd, the Scots without refusal swore him allegiance; yet the Northumbrians, ever of doubtful faith, soon after chose to themselves one Eric, a Dane. Huntingdon still haunts us with this Anlaf (of whom we gladly would have been rid) and will have him before Eric recall'd once more and reign four years, then again put to his shifts. But Edred (950) entering into Northumberland, and with spoils returning, Eric the king fell upon his rear. Edred turning about, both shook off the enemy, and prepared to make a second inroad: which the Northumbrians dreading rejected Eric, slew Amancus the son of Anlaf, and with many presents appeasing Edred, submitted again to his government; nor from that time had kings, but were govern'd by earls, of whom Osulf was the first. About this time (953) Wulstan Archbishop of York, accused to have slain certain men of Thetford, in revenge of their abbot whom the townsmen had slain, was committed by the king to close custody; but soon after enlarg'd, was restor'd to his place. Malmsbury writes, that his crime was to have conniv'd at the revolt of his countrymen: But kind Edred two years after (955) sickning in the flower of his youth, dy'd much lamented, and was buried at Winchester.

EDWI the son of Edmund now come to age, after his uncle Edred's

[1] The Laudean copy of the Saxon annals, and Ethelwerd in his history, place the death of king Athelstane, Anno 898.

death took on him the government, and was crowned at Kingston. His lovely person sirnamed him the Fair: his actions are diversly reported, by Huntingdon not thought illaudable. But Malmsbury and such as follow him write far otherwise, that he married or kept as concubine, his near kinswoman, some say both her and her daughter; so inordinately given to his pleasure, that on the very day of his coronation, he abruptly withdrew himself from the company of his peers, whether in banquet or consultation, to sit wantoning in the chamber with this Algiva, so was her name, who had such power over him. Whereat his barons offended, sent Bishop Dunstan, the boldest among them, to request his return: he going to his chamber, not only interrupted his dalliance and rebuk'd the lady, but taking him by the hand, between force and persuasion brought him back to his nobles. The king highly displeased, and instigated perhaps by her, who was so prevalent with him, not long (956) after sent Dunstan into banishment, caus'd his monastery to be rifled, and became an enemy to all monks. Whereupon Odo archbishop of Canterbury pronounc'd a separation or divorce of the king from Algiva. But that which most incited William of Malmsbury against him, he gave that monastery to be dwelt in by secular priests, or, to use his own phrase made it a stable of clerks: at length these affronts done to the church were resented by the people, that the Mercians and Northumbrians revolted from him, and set up Edgar his brother (957), leaving to Edwi the West-Saxons only, bounded by the River Thames; with grief whereof, as is thought, he soon after ended his days, and was buried at Winchester. (958.) Meanwhile Elfsin bishop of that place after the death of Odo, ascending by simony to the chair of Canterbury, and going to Rome the same year for his pall, was frozen to death in the Alps.

EDGAR by his brother's death now (959) king of all England at sixteen years of age, called home Dunstan out of Flanders, where he liv'd in exile. This king had no war all his reign; yet always well prepar'd for war, govern'd the kingdom in great peace, honour and prosperity, gaining thence the sirname of Peaceable, much extoll'd for justice, clemency, and all kingly vertues, the more, ye may be sure, by monks, for his building so many monasteries; as some write, every year one: for he much favour'd the monks against secular priests, who in the time of Edwi had got possession in most of their convents. His care and wisdom was great in guarding the coasts round with stout ships, to the number of three thousand six hundred, Mat. West. reckons them four thousand eight hundred, divided into four squadrons, to sail to and fro about the four quarters of the land meeting each other; the first of one thousand two hundred sail from east to west, the second of as many from west to east, the third and fourth between north and south, himself in the summer time with his fleet. Thus he kept out wisely the force of strangers, and prevented foreign war; but by their two frequent resort hither in time of peace, and his too much favouring them, he let in their vices unaware. Thence the people, saith Malmsbury, learnt of the outlandish Saxons rudeness, of the Flemish daintiness and softness, of the Danes drunkenness; though I doubt these vices are as naturally home-bred here as in any other countries. Yet in the winter and spring time he usually rode the circuit as a judge itinerant through all his provinces, to see justice well administered, and the poor not oppress'd. Thieves and robbers he routed almost out of the land, and wild beasts of prey altogether ; enjoyning (961) Ludwal king of Wales to pay the yearly tribute of three hundred wolves, which he did for two years together, till the third year no more were to be found, nor ever after ; but his laws may be read yet extant. Whatever was the cause he was not crown'd till the 30th of his age, but then (973) with great splendor and magnificence at the city of Bath, in the feast of Pentecost.[1] This year (974) dy'd Swarling a monk of Croyland, in the 142nd year of his age, and another soon after him in the 115th, in that fenny and waterish air, the more remarkable. King Edgar the next year went to Chester, and summoning to his court there all the kings that held of him, took homage of them : Their names are Kened king of Scots, Malcolm of Cumberland. Maccuse of the isles, five of Wales, Duswil, Huwal, Grifith, Jacob, Judethil, these he had in such awe, that going one day into a gally, he caus'd them to take each man his oar, and row him down the river Dee, while he himself sat at the stern : which might be, done in merriment, easily obey'd ; if with a serious brow, discover'd rather vain glory, and insulting haughtiness, than moderation of mind. And that he did it seriously triumphing, appears by his words then utter'd, that his successors might then glory to be kings of England, when they had such honour done them. And perhaps the divine power was displeas'd with him for taking too much honour to himself ; since we read that the year (975) following he was taken out of this life by sickness in the heighth of his glory and the prime of his age, buried at Glaston Abbey. The same year, as Mat. West. relates, he gave to Kened the Scotish king, many rich presents, and the whole country of Laudain, or Lothein, to hold of him on condition that he and his successors should repair to the English Court at high festivals when the king sat crown'd ; gave him also many lodging places by the way, which till the days of Henry the second were still held by the kings of Scotland. He was of stature not tall, of body slender, yet so well made, that in strength he chose to contend with such as were thought strongest, and dislik'd nothing more than that they should spare him for respect or fear to hurt him. Kened king

---

[1] In an assembly of the Witena Gemos or counsel of wise men.

of Scots then in the court of Edgar, sitting one day at table was heard to say jestingly amongst his servants, he wonder'd how so many provinces could be held in subjection by such a little dapper man: his words were brought to the king's ear; he sends for Kened as about some private business, and in talk drawing him forth to a secret place, takes from under his garment two swords which he had brought with him, gave one of them to Kened; and now saith he, 'it shall be try'd which ought to be the subject; for it is shameful for a king to boast at table, and shrink in fight.' Kened much abash'd fell presently at his feet, and besought him to pardon what he had simply spoken, no way intended to his dishonour or disparagement: wherewith the king was satisfied. Cambden in his description of Ireland, cites a charter of king Edgar, wherein it appears, he had in subjection all the kingdoms of the isles as far as Norway, and had subdu'd the greatest part of Ireland, with the city of Dublin: but of this other writers make no mention. In his youth having heard of Elfrida, daughter to Ordgar Duke of Devonshire, much commended for her beauty, he sent earl Athelwold, whose loyalty he trusted most, to see her; intending, if she were found such as answer'd report, to demand her in marriage. He at the first view taken with her presence, disloyally, as it often happens in such employments, began to sue for himself; and with consent of her parents obtain'd her. Returning therefore with scarce an ordinary commendation of her feature, he easily took off the king's mind, soon diverted another way. But the matter coming to light how Ethelwald had forestall'd the king, and Elfrida's beauty more and more spoken of, the king now heated not only with a relapse of love, but with a deep sense of the abuse, yet dissembling his disturbance, pleasantly told the earl, what day he meant to come and visit him and his fair wife. The earl seemingly assur'd his welcome, but in meanwhile acquainting his wife, earnestly advis'd her to deform herself, what she might, either in dress or otherwise, lest the king, whose amorous inclination was not unknown, should chance be attracted. She who by this time was not ignorant, how Athelwold had step'd between her and the king, against his coming arrays herself richly, using whatever art she could devise might render her the more amiable; and it took effect. For the king inflam'd with her love, the more for that he had been so long defrauded and robbed of her, resolved not only to recover his intercepted right, but to punish the interloper of his destin'd spouse, and appointing with him, as was usual, a day of hunting, drawn aside in a forest, now call'd Harewood, smote him through with a dart. Some censure this act as cruel and tyrannical, but consider'd well, it may be judg'd more favourable, and that no man of sensible spirit, but in his place, without extraordinary perfection, would have done the like: for next to life, what worse treason could have been committed against him? It chanc'd that the earl's base son coming by upon the fact, the king stern'ly ask'd him, 'how he lik'd this game;' he submissively answering, that 'whatsoever pleas'd the king, must not displease him;' the king return'd to his wonted temper, took an affection to the youth, and ever after highly favour'd him making amends in the son for what he had done to the father. Ethelfrida forthwith he took to wife, who to expiate her former husband's death, though therein she had no hand, cover'd the place of his bloodshed with a monastery of nuns to sing over him. Another fault is laid to his charge, no way excusable, that he took a virgin Wilfrida by force out of the nunnery, where she was plac'd by her friends to avoid his pursuit, and kept her as his concubine; but liv'd not obstinately in the offence; for sharply reprov'd by Dunstan, he submitted to seven year's penance, and for that time to want his coronation: but why he had it not before, is left unwritten. Another story there goes of Edgar, fitter for a novel than a history; but as I find it in Malmsbury, so I relate it. While he was yet unmarried, in his youth he abstain'd not from women, and coming on a day to Andover, caus'd a duke's daughter there dwelling, reported of rare beauty to be brought to him. The mother not daring flatly to deny, yet abhorring that her daughter should be so deflower'd, at fit time of night sent in her attire one of her waiting maids: a maid it seems not unhandsome nor unwitty; who supplied the place of her young lady. Night pass'd, the maid going to rise, but daylight scarce yet appearing, was by the king ask'd, why she made such haste, she answer'd, to do the work which her lady had set her; at which the king wondring, and with much ado staying her to unfold the riddle, for he took her to be the duke's daughter, she falling at his feet besought him, that since at the command of her lady she came to his bed, and was enjoy'd by him, he would be pleased in recompence to set her free from the hard service of her mistress. The king a while standing in a study whether he had best be angry or not, at length turning all to a jest, took the maid away with him, advanc'd her above her lady, lov'd her, and accompanied with her only, till he married Elfrida. These only are his faults upon record, rather to be wonder'd how they were so few, and so soon left, he coming at sixteen to the licence of a scepter; and that his virtues were so many and so mature, he dying before the age wherein wisdom can in others attain to any ripeness: however with him dy'd all the Saxon glory. From henceforth nothing is to be heard of but their decline and ruin under a double conquest, and the causes foregoing; which, not to blur or taint the praises of their former actions and liberty well defended, shall stand severally related, and will be more than long enough for another book.

BOOK VI.

EDWARD the eldest son of Edgar by Egelsteda his first wife, the daughter of duke Ordmer, was according to right and his father's will, plac'd in the throne; Elfrida his second wife, and her faction only repining, who labour'd to have had her son Ethelred, a child of seven years, preferr'd before him; that she under that pretence might have rul'd all. Mean while comets were seen in heaven, portending not famine only, which follow'd the next year, but the troubl'd state of the whole realm not long after to ensue. The troubles began in Edwin's days, between monks and secular priests, now reviv'd and drew on either side many of the nobles into parties. For Elfere duke of the Mercians, with many other peers, corrupted as is said with gifts, drove the monks out of those monasteries where Edgar had plac'd them, and in their stead put secular priests with their wives. But Ethelwin duke of East-Angles, with his brother Elfwold, and earl Bretnoth oppos'd them, and gathering an army defended the abbies of East-Angles from such intruders. To appease these tumults, a synod was call'd at Winchester, and nothing there concluded, a general council both of nobles and prelates, was held (978) at Caln in Wiltshire, where while the dispute was hot, but chiefly against Dunstan, the room wherein they sat fell upon their heads, killing some, maiming others, Dunstan only escaping upon a beam that fell not, and the king absent by reason of his tender age. This accident quieted the controversie, and brought both parts to hold with Dunstan and the monks. Mean while the king addicted to a religious life, and of a mild spirit, simply permitted all things to the ambitious will of his stepmother and her son Ethelred: to whom she displeased that the name only of king was wanting, practis'd thenceforth to remove king Edward out of the way; which in this manner she brought about. Edward on a day wearied with hunting, thirsty and alone, while his attendants follow'd the dogs, hearing that Ethelred and his mother lodg'd at Corvesgate (Corfe-Castle, saith Cambden, in the isle of Purbeck) innocently went thither. She with all shew of kindness welcoming him, commanded drink to be brought forth, for it seems he lighted not from his horse; and while he was drinking, caus'd one of her servants, privately before instructed, to stab him with a poignard. The poor youth who little expected such unkindness there, turning speedily the reins, fled bleeding; till through loss of blood falling from his horse, and expiring, yet held with one foot in the stirrup, he was dragg'd along the way, trac'd by his blood, and buried without honour at Werham, having reigned about three years: but the place of his burial not long after grew famous for miracles. After which by duke Elfer (who, as

Malmsbury saith, had a hand in his death) he was royally interr'd at Skepton, or Shaftesbury. The murdress Elfrida at length repenting, spent the residue of her days in sorrow and great penance.

ETHELFRED second son of Edgar by Elfrida, (for Edmund dy'd a child) his brother Edward wickedly remov'd, was now (979) next in right to succeed, and accordingly crown'd at Kingston : reported by some, fair of visage, comely of person, elegant of behaviour ; but the event will shew, that with many sluggish and ignoble vices he quickly sham'd his outside ; born and prolong'd a fatal mischief of the people, and the ruine of his country ; whereof he gave early signs from his first infancy, bewraying the font and water while the bishop was baptizing him.[1] Whereat Dunstan much troubl'd, for he stood by and saw it, to them next him broke into these words, 'By God and God's mother this boy will prove a sluggard.' Another thing is written of him in his childhood, which argu'd no bad nature, that hearing of his brother Edward's cruel death, he made loud lamentation ; but his furious mother offended therewith, and having no rod at hand, beat him so with great wax candles, that he hated the sight of them ever after. Dunstan though unwilling to set the crown upon his head ; but at the same time foretold openly as is reported, the great evils that were to come upon him and the land, in avengement of his brother's innocent blood. And about the same time, one midnight, a cloud sometimes bloody, sometimes fiery, was seen over all England ; and within three years (982) the Danish tempest, which had long surceast, revolv'd again upon this island. To the more ample relating whereof, the Danish history, at least their latest and diligentest historian, as neither from the first landing of Danes, in the reign of West-Saxon Birthric, so now again from first to last, contributes nothing ; busied more than enough to make out the bare names and successions of their uncertain kings, and their small actions at home : unless out of him I should transcribe what he takes, and I better may, from our own annals ; the surer and the sadder witnesses of their doings here, not glorious, as they vainly boast, but most inhumanly barbarous. For the Danes well understanding that England had now a slothful king to their wish, first landing at Southampton from seven great ships, took the town, spoiled the country, and carried away with them great pillage ; nor was Devonshire nor Cornwall uninfested on the shoar ; pirates of Norway also harried the coast of West-Chester : and to add a worse calamity, the city of London was burnt, casually or not, is not written. It chanc'd four years after (986) that Ethelred besieg'd Rochester, some way or other offended by the bishop thereof. Dunstan not approving the cause, sent to warn him that he provoke not

---

[1] This seems to be a monkish fable, copy'd from the story of Constantine the VIth emperor of Constantinople, who is said to have done so, and was then called Copronymus.

St. Andrew the patron of that city, nor wast his lands ; an old craft of the clergy to secure their church-lands, by entailing them on some saint ; the king not hearkning, Dunstan on this condition that the siege might be rais'd, sent him a hundred pounds, the money was accepted and the siege dissolv'd. Dunstan reprehending his avarice, sent him again this word, because thou hast respected money more than religion, the evils which I foretold shall the sooner come upon thee ; but not in my days, for so God hath spoken. The next year (987) was calamitous, bringing strange fluxes upon men, and murrain upon cattle. Dunstan the year (988) following dy'd, a strenuous bishop, zealous without dread of person, and for aught appears, the best of many ages, if he busied not himself too much in secular affairs. He was chaplain at first to king Athelstan, and Edmund who succeeded, much imploy'd in court affairs, till envied by some who laid many things to his charge, he was by Edmund forbidden the court, but by the earnest mediation, saith Ingulf, of Turkitul the chancellor, receiv'd at length to favour, and made abbot of Glaston,[1] lastly by Edgar and the general vote, Archbishop of Canterbury. Not long after his death, the Danes arriving in Devonshire were met by Goda lieutenant of that country, and Strenwold a valiant leader, who put back the Danes, but with loss of their own lives. The third year following, under the conduct of Justin and Guthmund the son of Steytan, they landed and spoil'd Ipswich, fought with Brithnoth duke of the East-Angles about Maldon, where they slew him ; the slaughter else had been equal on both sides. These and the like depredations on every side, the English not able to resist, by counsel of Siric then Archbishop of Canterbury, and two dukes, Ethelward and Alfric ; it was thought best for the present to buy that with silver which they could not gain with their iron : and ten thousand pounds was paid to the Danes for peace. Which for a while contented ; but taught them the ready way how easiest to come by more. The next year (993) but one they took by storm and rifl'd Bebbanburgh an ancient city nigh Durham : sailing thence into the mouth of Humber, they wasted both sides thereof, Yorkshire and Lindsey, burning and destroying all before them. Against these went out three noblemen, Fræna, Frithegist, and Godwin, but being all Danes by the father's side, willingly began flight, and forsook their own forces betray'd to the enemy. No less treachery was at sea ; for Alfric the son of Elfer duke of Mercia, whom the king for some offence had banish'd, but now recall'd, sent from London with a fleet to surprize the Danes, in some place of disadvantage, gave them over-night intelligence thereof, then fled to them himself ; which his fleet, saith Florent, perceiving, pursu'd, took the ship, but miss'd of his person ; the Londoners by chance grappling with the East-Angles made them fewer, saith my author, by many thousands. Others say,

[1] Then bishop of Worcester.

that by this notice of Alfric, the Danes not only escap'd, but with a great fleet (994) set upon the English, took many of their ships, and in triumph brought them up the Thames, intending to besiege London: for Anlaf king of Norway, and Swane of Denmark, at the head of these, came with ninety-four gallies. The king for this treason of Alfric, put out his son's eyes; but the Londoners both by land and water, so valiantly resisted their besiegers, that they were forc'd in one day with great loss to give over. But what they could not on the city, they wreak'd themselves on the countries round about, wasting with sword and fire all Essex, Kent, and Sussex. Thence horsing their foot, diffus'd far wider their outrageous incursions, without mercy either to sex or age. The slothful king instead of warlike opposition in the field, sends ambassadors to treat about another payment; the sum promis'd was now 16000; till which paid, the Danes winter'd at Southampton; Ethelred inviting Anlaf to come and visit him at Andover; where he was royally entertain'd, some say baptiz'd, or confirm'd, adopted son by the king, and dismiss'd, with great presents, promising by oath to depart, and molest the kingdom no more; which he perform'd, but the calamity ended not, for after some intermission of their rage for three years (997), the other navy of Danes sailing about to the west, enter'd Severn, and wasted one while South-Wales, then Cornwall and Devonshire, till at length they winter'd about Tavistoc. For it were an endless work to relate how they wallow'd up and down to every particular place, and to repeat as oft what devastations they wrought, what desolations left behind them, easie to be imagin'd. In summer the next year (998), they afflicted Dorsetshire, Hamshire, and the isle of Wight; by the English many resolutions were taken, many armies rais'd, but either betray'd by the falshood, or discourag'd by the weakness of their leaders, they were put to rout, or disbanded themselves. For soldiers most commonly are as their commanders, without much odds of valour in one nation or other, only as they are more or less wisely disciplin'd and conducted. The following year (999) brought them back upon Kent, where they enter'd Medway, and besieg'd Rochester; but the Kentish men assembling, gave them a sharp encounter, yet that suffic'd not to hinder them from doing as they had done in other places. Against these depopulations, the king levied an army; but the unskilful leaders not knowing what to do with it when they had it, did but drive out time, burthening and impoverishing the people, consuming the publick treasure, and more emboldening the enemy, than if they had sat quiet at home. What cause mov'd the Danes next year (1000) to pass into Normandy, is not recorded; but that they return'd thence more outrageous than before. Meanwhile the king, to make some diversion, undertakes an expedition both by land and sea into Cumberland, where the Danes were most planted; there and in the isle of Man, or as Cambden saith, Anglesey, imitating his enemies in spoiling and unpeopling; the Danes from Normandy arriving (1001) in the river Ex, laid siege to Exeter; but the citizens, as those of London, valourously defending themselves, they wreak'd their anger, as before, on the villages round about. The country people of Somerset and Devonshire assembling themselves at Penho,[1] shew'd their readiness, but wanted a head; and besides, being then but few in number, were easily put to flight; the enemy plundering all at will, with loaded spoils pass'd into the isle of Wight; from whence all Dorsetshire, and Hamshire, felt again their fury. The Saxon annals write, that before their coming to Exeter, the Hamshire men had (1002) a bickering with them, wherein Ethelward the king's general was slain, adding other things hardly to be understood, and in one ancient copy; so end. Ethelred, whom no adversity could awake from his soft and sluggish life, still coming by the worse at fighting, by the advice of his peers not unlike himself, sends one of his gay courtiers, though looking loftily, to stoop basely and propose a third tribute to the Danes: they willingly hearken, but the sum is enhanc'd now to twenty-four thousand pounds, and paid: the Danes thereupon abstaining from hostility. But the king to strengthen his house by some potent affinity, marries Emma, whom the Saxons call Elgiva, daughter of Richard duke of Normandy. With him Ethelred formerly had war or no good correspondence, as appears by a letter of pope John the 15th, who made peace between them about eleven years before. Puft up now with his suppos'd access of strength by this affinity, he caus'd the Danes all over England, though now living peaceably, in one day perfidiously to be massacred, both men, women and children; sending private letters to every town and city, whereby they might be ready all at the same hour; which till the appointed time (being the 9th of July) was conceal'd with great silence, and perform'd with much unanimity; so generally hated were the Danes. Mat. West. writes, that this execution upon the Danes was ten years after; that Huna one of Ethelred's chief captains, complaining of the Danish insolencies in time of peace, their pride, their ravishing of matrons and virgins, incited the king to this massacre, which in the madness of rage made no difference of innocent or nocent. Among these, Gunhildis the sister of Swane was not spar'd, though much deserving not pity only, but all protection: she with her husband earl Palingus, coming to live in England, and receiving christianity, had her husband and young son slain before her face, herself then beheaded; foretelling and denouncing that her blood would cost England dear. Some say this was done by the traytor Edric, to whose custody she was committed; but the massacre was some years before Edric's advancement; and if it were done by him afterward, it seems to contradict the private correspondence

[1] Pen in Somersetshire, on the borders of Dorsetshire.

which he was thought to hold with the Danes. For Swane breathing
revenge, hasted the next year (1003) into England, and by the treason
or negligence of count Hugh, whom Emma had recommended to the
government of Devonshire, sack'd the city of Exeter, her wall from
east to west gate, broken down: after this wasting Wiltshire, the
people of that county, and of Hamshire, came together in great
numbers with resolution stoutly to oppose him; but Alfric their general,
whose son's eyes the king had lately put out, madly thinking to revenge himself on the king, by ruining his own country, when he should
have order'd his battle, the enemy being at hand, feign'd himself taken
with a vomiting; whereby his army in great discontent, destitute of a
commander, turn'd from the enemy; who straight took Wilton and
Salisbury,[1] carrying the pillage thereof to his ships. Thence the next
year (1004) landing on the coast of Norfolk, he wasted the country,[2]
and set Norwich on fire; Ulfketel duke of the East-Angles, a man of
great valour, not having space to gather his forces, after consultation had
thought it best to make peace with the Dane, which he breaking
within three weeks, issued silently out of his ships, came to Thetford,
staid there a night, and in the morning left it flaming. Ulfketel
hearing this, commanded some to go and break, or burn his ships;
but they not daring or neglecting, he in the meanwhile with what
secrecy and speed was possible, drawing together his forces, went out
against the enemy, and gave them a fierce onset retreating to their
ships; but much inferiour in number, many of the chief East-Angles
there lost their lives. Nor did the Danes come off without great
slaughter of their own; confessing that they never met in England
with so rough a charge. The next year (1005), whom war could not,
a great famine drove Swane out of the land. But the summer (1006)
following, another great fleet of Danes enter'd the port of Sandwich,
thence pour'd out over all Kent and Sussex, made prey of what they
found. The king levying an army out of Mercia, and the West-
Saxons, took on him for once the manhood to go out and face them;
but they who held it safer to live by rapine, than to hazard a battle,
shifting lightly from place to place, frustrated the slow motions of a
heavy camp, following their wonted course of robbery, then running to
their ships. Thus all autumn they wearied out the king's army, which
gone home to winter, they carried all their pillage to the isle of Wight,
and there staid till Christmas; at which time the king being in
Shropshire, and but ill employ'd (for by the procurement of Edric, he
caus'd, as is thought, Alfhelm a noble duke, treacherously to be slain,
and the eyes of his two sons to be put out), they came forth again,
over-running Hampshire, and Barkshire, as far as Reading and

---

[1] Old Sarum: for Salisbury, or New Sarum, was not built till the reign of Henry III., above 200 years afterwards.
[2] He came with his fleet to Norwich up the river Yare, which was then navigable.

Wallingford : thence to Ashdune, and other places thereabout, neither known nor of tolerable pronunciation ; and returning by another way, found many of the people in arms by the river Kenet ; but making their way through, they got safe with vast booty to their ships. The king and his courtiers wearied out with their last summer's (1007) jaunt after the nimble Danes to no purpose, which by proof they found too toilsome for their soft bones, more us'd to beds and couches, had recourse to their last and only remedy, their coffers ; and send now the fourth time to buy a dishonourable peace, every time still dearer, not to be had now under thirty-six thousand pounds (for the Danes knew how to milk such easie kine) in name of tribute and expences: which out of the people over all England, already half beggar'd, was extorted and paid. About the same time Etheldred advanc'd Edric, sirnam'd Streon, from obscure condition to be duke of Mercia, and marry Edgitha the king's daughter. The cause of his advancement, Florent of Worster, and Mat. West. attribute to his great wealth, gotten by fine policies and a plausible tongue : he proved a man accessory to the ruine of England, as his actions will soon declare. Ethelred the next year (1008), somewhat rousing himself, ordain'd that every three hundred and ten hides (a hide is so much land as one plow can sufficiently till) should set out a ship or galley, and every nine hides find a corslet and head-piece : new ships in every port were builded, victuall'd, fraught with stout mariners and soldiers, and appointed to meet all at Sandwich. A man might now think that all would go well, when suddenly a new mischief sprung up, dissention among the great ones ; which brought all this diligence to as little success as at other times before. Bithric the brother of Edric, falsly accus'd Wulnoth a great officer set over the South-Saxons, who fearing the potency of his enemies, with twenty ships got to sea, and practis'd piracy on the coast. Against whom, reported to be in a place where he might be easily surpriz'd, Bithric sets forth with eighty ships, all which driven back by a tempest, and wrack'd upon the shoar, were burnt soon after by Wulnoth. Dishearten'd with this misfortune, the king returns to London ; the rest of his navy after him ; and all this great preparation to nothing. Whereupon Turkill, a Danish earl, came with a navy to the isle of Tanet, and in August (1009) a far greater, led by Heming and Ilaf joyn'd with him. Thence coasting to Sandwich, and landed, they went onward and began to assault Canterbury, but the citizens and East-Kentish men, coming to composition with them for three thousand pounds, they departed thence to the isle of Wight, robbing and burning by the way. Against these the king levies an army through all the island, and in several quarters places them nigh the sea, but so unskilfully or unsuccessfully, that the Danes were not thereby hinder'd from exercising their wonted robberies. It happen'd that the Danes one day were gone up into the country, far from their ships; the king having notice thereof, thought to intercept them in their return; his men were resolute to overcome or die, time and place advantageous; but where courage and fortune was not wanting, there wanted loyalty among them. Edric with subtle arguments that had a shew of deep policy, disputed and persuaded the simplicity of his fellow counsellors, that it would be best consulted at that time to let the Danes pass without ambush or interception. The Danes where they expected danger, finding none, pass'd on with great joy and booty to their ships. After this, sailing about Kent, they lay that winter in the Thames, forcing Kent and Essex to contribution, oft-times attempting the city of London, but repuls'd as oft to their great loss. Spring (1010) begun, leaving their ships, they pass'd through Chiltern[1] wood into Oxfordshire, burnt the city, and thence returning with divided forces, wasted on both sides the Thames; but hearing, that an army from London was march'd out against them, they on the north side passing the river at Stanes, join'd with them on the south into one body, and, enrich'd with great spoils, came back through Surrey to their ships; which all the Lent time they repair'd. After Easter, sailing to the East-Angles, they arriv'd at Ipswich, and came to a place call'd Ringmere, where they heard that Ulfketel with his forces lay, who with a sharp encounter soon entertain'd them; but his men at length giving back, through the subtlety of a Danish servant among them who began the flight, lost the field, though the men of Cambridgeshire stood to it valiantly. In this battle Ethelstan the king's son-in-law, with many other noblemen, was slain; whereby the Danes, without more resistance, three months together had the spoiling of those countries and all the fenns, burnt Thetford and Grantbrig, or Cambridge; thence to a hilly place not far off, called by Huntingdon, Balesham, by Cambden, Gogmagog hills, and the villages thereabout they turn'd their fury, slaying all they met save one man, who getting up into a steeple, is said to have defended himself against the whole Danish army. They therefore so leaving him, their foot by sea, their horse by land through Essex, return'd back laden to their ships left in the Thames. But many days pass'd not between, when sallying again out of their ships as out of savage dens, they plunder'd over again all Oxfordshire, and added to their prey Buckingham, Bedford, and Hertfordshire; then like wild beasts glutted, returning to their caves. A third excursion they made into Northamptonshire, burnt Northampton, ransacking the country round; then as to fresh pasture betook them to the West-Saxons, and in like sort harassing all Wiltshire, return'd, as I said before, like wild beasts, or rather sea-monsters to their water-stables, accomplishing by Christmas the circuit of their

---

[1] The hill country of Hertfordshire, Bucks, and Oxfordshire; so call'd from Chilt or Cylt, in Saxon, chalk.

whole years good deeds; an unjust and inhumane nation, who receiving or not receiving tribute where none was owing them, made such destruction of mankind, and rapine of their livelihood, as is a misery to read. Yet here they ceas'd not, for the next year (1011) repeating the same cruelties on both sides the Thames, one way as far as Huntingdon, the other as far as Wiltshire and Southampton, solicited again by the king for peace, and receiving their demands both of tribute and contribution, they slighted their faith; and in the beginning of September laid siege to Canterbury. On the 20th day, by the treachery of Almere the Arch-deacon, they took part of it and burnt it, committing all sorts of massacre as a sport: some they threw over the wall, others into the fire; hung some by the privy members; infants pulled from their mother's breast, were either toss'd on spears, or carts drawn over them; matrons and virgins by the hair dragg'd and ravish'd. Alfage the grave Arch-bishop, above others hated of the Danes, as in all councils and actions to his might their known opposer, taken, wounded, imprison'd in a noisome ship; the multitude are tith'd, and every tenth only spar'd. Early the next year (1012) before Easter, while Ethelred and his peers were assembl'd at London, to raise now the fifth tribute, amounting to forty-eight thousand pounds, the Danes at Canterbury propose to the Arch-bishop, who had been now seven months their prisoner, life and liberty, if he pay them three thousand pounds; which he refusing, as not able of himself, and not willing to extort it from his tenants, is permitted till the next Sunday to consider; then hal'd before their council, of whom Turkill was chief, and still refusing, they rise, most of them being drunk, and beat him with the blunt side of their axes, then thrust forth, deliver him to be pelted with stones; till one Thrum a converted Dane, pitying him half dead, to put him out of pain, with a pious impiety, at one stroke of his ax on the head, dispatch'd him.[1] His body was carried to London, and there buried, thence afterwards remov'd to Canterbury. By this time the tribute paid and peace so often violated sworn again by the Danes, they dispersed their fleet; forty-five of them, and Turkill their chief, staid at London with the king, swore him allegiance to defend his land against all strangers, on condition only to be fed and cloath'd by him. But this voluntary friendship of Turkill was thought to be deceitful, that staying under this pretence he gave intelligence to Swane, when it would be most seasonable to come. In July therefore of the next year (1013), king Swane arriving at Sandwich, made no stay there, but sailing first to

---

[1] Alfage was kill'd not at Canterbury, but at Greenwich : to which place, the station of their ships, they had brought him prisoner. And therefore in the present church of Greenwich, on the top of the partition wall, between the nave of the church and the chancel is this inscription, "This church was erected and dedicated to the glory of God, and the memory of S. Alphage, arch-bishop of Canterbury, here slain by the Danes ; because he would not ransom his life by an unreasonable sum of money, An. 1012."

Humber, thence into Trent, landing and encamp'd at Gainsburrow: whither without delay repair'd to him the Northumbrians, with Uthred their earl; those of Lindsey also, then those of Fisburg, and lastly all on the north of Watling-street (which is a high-way from east to west sea) gave oath and hostages to obey him. From whom he commanded horses and provision for his army, taking with him besides bands and companies of their choicest men; and committing to his son Canute the care of his fleet and hostages; he marches towards the South Mercians, commanding his soldiers to exercise all acts of hostility; with the terror whereof fully executed, he took in few days the city of Oxford, then Winchester; thence tending to London, in his hasty passage over the Thames, without seeking bridge or ford, lost many of his men. Nor was his expedition against London prosperous; for assaying all means by force or wile to take the city, wherein the king then was, and Turkill with his Danes, he was stoutly beaten off as at other times. Thence back to Wallingford and Bath, directing his course, after usual havock made, he sat a while and refresh'd his army. There Ethelm an earl of Devonshire, and other great officers in the west, yielded him subjection. These things flowing to his wish, he betook him to his navy, from that time stil'd and accounted king of England, if a tyrant, saith Simeon, may be call'd a king. The Londoners also sent him hostages, and made their peace, for they fear'd his fury. Ethelred thus reduc'd to narrow compass, sent Emma his queen, with his two sons had by her, and all his treasure to Richard II. her brother, duke of Normandy; himself with the Danish fleet abode some while at Greenwich, then sailing to the Isle of Wight, pass'd after Christmas into Normandy; where he was honourably receiv'd at Roen by the duke, though known to have born himself churlishly and proudly towards Emma his sister, besides his dissolute company with other women. Meanwhile Swane ceas'd not to exact almost insupportable tribute of the people, spoiling them when he listed; besides, the like did Turkill at Greenwich. The next year (1014) beginning, Swane sickens and dies;[1] some say terrifi'd by an appearing shape of St. Edmund arm'd, whose church at Bury he had threaten'd to demolish; but the authority hereof relies only upon the legend of St. Edmund. After his death the Danish army and fleet made his son Canute their king; but the nobility and states[2] of England sent messengers to Ethelred, declaring that they preferr'd none before their native sovereign, if he would promise to govern them better than he had done, and with more clemency. Whereat the king rejoicing, sends over his son Edward with ambassadors to court both high and low, and win their love, promising largely to be their mild and devoted

[1] At Gainsborough in Lincolnshire.
[2] The wise and chief men as well of the clergy as the laity.

lord, to consent in all things to their will, follow their counsel, and whatever had been done or spoken by any man against him, freely to pardon, if they would loyally restore him to be their king. To this the people chearfully answer'd, and amity was both promis'd and confirm'd on both sides. An embassy of lords is sent to bring back the king honourably; he returns in Lent, and is joyfully receiv'd of the people, marches with a strong army against Canute; who having got horses, and joyn'd with the men of Lindsey, was preparing to make spoil in the countries adjoyning; but by Ethelred unexpectedly coming upon him, was soon driven to his ships, and his confederates of Lindsey left to the anger of their countrymen, executed without mercy by fire and sword. Canute in all haste sailing back to Sandwich, took the hostages given to his father from all parts of England, and with slit noses, ears cropp'd, and hands chopp'd off, setting them ashore, departed into Denmark. Yet the people were not disburthen'd, for the king rais'd out of them thirty thousand pounds to pay his fleet of Danes at Greenwich. To these evils the sea in October[1] pass'd his bounds, overwhelming many towns in England, and of their inhabitants many thousands. The year (1015) following, an assembly being at Oxford, Edric of Streon, having invited two noblemen, Sigeferth and Morcar, the sons of Earngrun of Seav'nburg[2] to his lodging, secretly murder'd them: the king, for what cause is unknown, seiz'd their estates, and caus'd Algith the wife of Sigeferth, to be kept at Maidulfsburg, now Malmsbury; whom Edmund the prince there married against his father's mind, then went and possess'd their lands, making the people there subject to him. Mat. West. saith, that these two were of the Danes, who had seated themselves in Northumberland, slain by Edric under colour of treason laid to their charge. They who attended them without, tumulting at the death of their masters, were beaten back; and driven into a church, and defending themselves, were burnt there in the steeple. Meanwhile Canute returning from Denmark with a great navy, two hundred ships richly gilded and adorn'd, well fraught with arms, and all provision; and, which Encomium Emmæ mentions not, two other kings, Lachman of Sweden, and Olav of Norway, arriv'd at Sandwich; and as the same author then living writes, sent out spies to discover what resistance on land was to be expected; who return'd with certain report, that a great army of English was in readiness to oppose them. Turkill, who upon the arrival of those Danish powers, kept faith no longer with the English, but joyning now with Canute, as it were to re-ingratiate himself after his revolt, whether real or complotted, counsell'd him (being yet young) not to land, but leave to him

[1] The Saxon annals tell us 'twas on the vigil of St. Michael in September.
[2] The same annals call the place Seafenburghs, i.e. seven towns, but where they lay we know not.

the management of this first battle; the king assented, and he with the forces which he had brought, and part of those which arriv'd with Canute, landing to their wish, encounter'd the English, though double in number, at a place call'd Scorastan,[1] and was at first beaten back with much loss. But at length animating his men with rage only and despair, obtain'd a clear victory, which won him great reward and possessions from Canute. But of this action no other writer makes mention. From Sandwich therefore sailing about to the river Frome, and there landing over all Dorset, Somerset, and Wiltshire, he spread wastful hostility. The king lay then sick at Cosham in this county; though it may seem strange how he could lie sick there in the midst of his enemies. Howbeit Edmund in one part, and Edric of Streon in another, rais'd forces by themselves; but so soon as both armies were united, the traytor Edric being found to practice against the life of Edmund, he remov'd with his army from him; whereof the enemy took great advantage. Edric easily enticing the forty ships of Danes to side with him, revolted to Canute, the West-Saxons also gave pledges and furnish'd him with horses. By which means the year (1016) ensuing, he with Edric the traytor, passing the Thames at Creclad, about twelftide, enter'd into Mercia, and especially Warwickshire, depopulating all places in their way. Against these, Prince Edmund, for his hardiness call'd Ironside, gather'd an army; but the Mercians refus'd to fight unless Ethelred with the Londoners came to aid them; and so every man return'd home. After the festival, Edmund gathering another army, besought his father to come with the Londoners, and what force besides he was able; they came with great strength gotten together, but being come, and in a hopeful way of great success, it was told the king, that unless he took the better heed, some of his own forces would fall off and betray him. The king daunted with this perhaps cunning whisper of the enemy, disbanded his army, returns to London. Edmund betook him into Northumberland, as some thought to raise fresh forces; but he with earl Uthred on the one side, and Canute with Edric on the other, did little else but waste the provinces; Canute to conquer them, Edmund to punish them who stood neuter; for which cause Stafford, Shropshire, and Lestershire, felt heavily his hand; while Canute, who was ruining the more southern shires, at length march'd into Northumberland; which Edmund hearing, dismiss'd his forces, and came to London. Uthred the earl hasted back to Northumberland, and finding no other remedy, submitted himself with all the Northumbrians, giving hostages to Canute. Nevertheless by his command or con-

---

[1] Sherston in Wiltshire. See the addit. to that county in the English edition of Cambden. The battle of Seorstan in the Saxon annals, comes under the year 1016, and after Ethelred's death. This Scorstan is suppos'd by others to be the place where four stones call'd Shirestones part the four counties of Oxford, Gloucester, Worcester, and Warwick.

nivance, and the hand of one Turebrand a Danish lord, Uthred was slain, and Eric another Dane made earl in his stead. This Uthred son of Waltcof, as Simeon writes, in his treatise of the siege of Durham, in his youth obtain'd a great victory against Malcolm son of Kened king of Scots, who with the whole power of his kingdom was fallen into Northumberland, and laid siege to Durham. Waltcof the old earl, unable to resist, had secur'd himself in Bebbanburg, a strong town ; but Uthred gathering an army rais'd the siege, slew most of the Scots, their king narrowly escaping, and with the heads of their slain, fixt upon poles, beset round the walls of Durham. The year of this exploit Simeon clears not, for in 969, and in the reign of Ethelred, as he affirms, it could not be. Canute by another way returning southward, joyful of his success, before Easter came back with all the army to his fleet. About the 23d of April ensuing, Ethelred after a long, troublesome, and ill-govern'd reign, ended his days at London, and was buried in the church of St. Paul.

AFTER the decease of Ethelred, they of the nobility who were then (1016) at London, together with the citizens, chose Edmund his son (not by Emma, but a former wife the daughter of carl Thored) in his father's room ; but the archbishops, abbots, and many of the nobles assembling together elected Canute ; and coming to Southampton where he then remain'd, renounc'd before him all the race of Ethelred, and swore him fidelity ; he also swore to them in matters both religious and secular, to be their faithful lord. But Edmund with all speed going to the West-Saxons, was joyfully receiv'd of them as their king, and of many other provinces by their example. Mean while Canute about mid May, came with his whole fleet up the river to London ; then causing a great dike to be made on Surrey side, turn'd the stream and drew his ships thither west of the bridge ; then begirting the city with a broad and deep trench, assail'd it on every side ; but repuls'd as before by the valourous defendants, and in despair of success at that time, leaving part of his army for the defence of his ships, with the rest sped him to the West-Saxons e'er Edmund could have time to assemble all his powers : who yet with such as were at hand invoking divine aid, encounter'd the Danes at Pen[1] by Gillingham in Dorsetshire, and put him to flight. After Midsummer, encreas'd with new forces, he[2] met with him at a place call'd Sherastan, now Sharstan ;[3] but Edric, Almar, and Algar, with the Hampshire and Wiltshire men, then siding with the Danes, he only maintain'd the fight, obstinately fought on both sides, till night and weariness parted them.

[1] P n i in S mer et hire.
[2] Can te was then at the Siege of Lond n, according to the annals we have often mention'd, did not c mmand the Danes in the fight at Pen, nor at Sherstan.
[3] Sher t n in Wiltshire, Cambden. Thought by others to be Shirestones on the borders of Oxfordshire.

Day-light returning renew'd the conflict; wherein the Danes appearing inferiour, Edric to dishearten the English, cut off the head of one Osmer, in countenance and hair somewhat resembling the king, and holding it up, cries aloud to the English, that Edmund being slain and this his head, it was time for them to flie; which fallacy Edmund perceiving, and openly shewing himself to his soldiers, by a spear thrown at Edric, that missing him yet slew one next him, and through him another behind, they recover'd heart, and lay sore upon the Danes till night parted them as before: for e'er the third morn, Canute sensible of his loss, march'd away by stealth to his ships at London, renewing there his leagre. Some would have this battle at Sherastan the same with that at Scorastan[1] beforemention'd, but the circumstance of time permits not that, having been before the landing of Canute, this a good while after, as by the process of things appears; from Sherastan, or Sharstan, Edmund return'd to the West-Saxons, whose valour Edric fearing, lest it might prevail against the Danes, sought pardon of his revolt, and obtaining it, swore loyalty to the king, who now the third time coming with an army from the West-Saxons to London rais'd the siege, chasing Canute and his Danes to their ships. Then after two days passing the Thames at Branford, and so coming on their backs, kept them so turn'd, and obtain'd the victory: then returns again to his West-Saxons, and Canute to his siege, but still in vain; rising therefore thence, he enter'd with his ships a river then call'd Arenne:[2] and from the banks thereof wasted Mercia; thence their horse by inland, their foot by ship came to Medway. Edmund in the mean while, with multiplied forces out of many shires, crossing again at Branford, came into Kent, seeking Canute; encountred him at Otford, and so defeated, that of his horse, they who escap'd fled to the isle of Sheppy; and a full victory he had gain'd, had not Edric still the traytor, by some wile or other detain'd his pursuit: and Edmund who never wanted courage, here wanted prudence to be so misled, ever after forsaken of his wonted fortune. Canute crossing with his army into Essex, thence wasted Mercia worse than before, and with heavy prey return'd to his ships: them Edmund with a collected army pursuing, overtook at a place call'd Assandune, or Asseshill,[3] now Ashdown in Essex; the battle on either side was fought with great vehemence; but perfidious Edric perceiving the victory to incline towards Edmund, with that part of the army which was under him,[4] fled, as he had promis'd Canute, and left the king over-match'd

---

[1] Mr Milton owns, that no other writer, but the author of Encomium Emæ, mentions the first battle of Scorastan; and 'tis much to be doubted, whether there was any such action.

[2] Mr. Gibson the editor of the Saxon Annals, supposes there is a mistake in the copy; and that it should be read to Waran or Ware, on the river Lee; or else that this Arenne is the river we now call Orwell, which divides Essex from Suffolk.

[3] Rather Assington, in that county: for the Saxon Annals have it Assandun: whereas the old Æscesdun is the word always turn'd by the moderns into Ashdown.

[4] The Mageæstons suppos'd by Cambden to be the Radnorshire Men.

with numbers: by which desertion the English were overthrown, duke Alfric, duke Godwin, and Ulfketel the valiant duke of East-Angles, with a great part of the nobility slain, so as the English of a long time had not receiv'd a greater blow. Yet after a while Edmund not absurdly call'd Ironside, preparing to try again his fortune in another field, was hinder'd by Edric and his faction, advising him to make peace and divide the kingdom with Canute. To which Edmund over-rul'd, a treaty appointed, and pledges mutually given, both kings[1] met at a place call'd Deorhirst in Gloucestershire; Edmund on the West-side of Severn, Canute on the East with their armies, then both in person wafted into an island, at that time call'd Olanege,[2] now Alney in the midst of the river; swearing amity and brotherhood; they parted the kingdom between them. Then interchanging arms and the habit they wore, assessing also what pay should be allotted to the navy; they departed each his way. Concerning this interview, and the cause thereof, others write otherwise; Malmsbury, that Edmund grieving at the loss of so much blood spilt for the ambition only of two men striving who should reign, of his own accord sent to Canute, offering him single combat, to prevent in their own cause the effusion of more blood than their own; that Canute though of courage enough, yet not unwisely doubting to adventure his body of small timber, against a man of iron sides, refus'd the combat, offering (1016) to divide the kingdom; this offer pleasing both armies, Edmund was not difficult to consent; and the decision was, that he as his hereditary kingdom should rule the West-Saxons, and all the South,[3] Canute the Mercians, and the north. Huntingdon follow'd by Mat. West. relates, that the peers on every side wearied out with continual warfare, and not refraining to affirm openly, that they two who expected to reign singly, had most reason to fight singly, the kings were content; the island was their lists, the combat knightly; till Knute finding himself too weak, began to parley, which ended as is said before. After which the Londoners bought their peace of the Danes, and permitted them to winter in the city. But king Edmund about the feast of St. Andrew, unexpectedly deceas'd at London, and was buried near to Edgar his grand-father at Glaston. The cause of his so sudden death is uncertain; common fame, saith Malmsbury, lays the guilt thereof upon Edric, who to please Canute, allur'd with promise of reward two of the king's privy chamber, though at first abhorring the fact, to assassinate him at the stool, by thrusting a sharp iron into his hinder parts. Huntingdon and Mat. West. relate it done at Oxford by the son of Edric, and something vary in the manner,[4]

[1] Bromton's Chronicle says, their Commissioners only met.
[2] Cambden writes it was call'd Alny by the Saxons; it now bears the name of the Eight, i.e. Isles; others say this island was betwixt Oversbridge and Maysmore. Brit. last Edit. p. 245.
[3] No mention made of the North or South by the authors that speak of the combat.
[4] He stabb'd him with a long knife in the same parts.

not worth recital. Edmund dead, Canute meaning to reign sole king of England, calls to him all the dukes, barons, and bishops of the land, cunningly demanding of them who were witnesses what agreement was made between him and Edmund dividing the kingdom, whether the sons and brothers of Edmund were to govern the West-Saxons after him, Canute living? They who understood his meaning, and fear'd to undergo his anger, timorously answered, that Edmund they knew had left no part thereof to his sons or brethren, living or dying; but that he intended Canute should be their guardian, till they came to age of reigning. Simeon affirms, that for fear or hope of reward they attested what was not true: notwithstanding which he put many of them to death not long after.

CANUTE having (1017) thus sounded the nobility, and by them understood, receiv'd their oath of fealty, they the pledge of his bare hand, and oath from the Danish nobles; whereupon the house of Edmund was renounc'd, and Canute crown'd. Then they enacted, that Edwi, brother of Edmund, a prince of great hope, should be banish'd the realm. But Canute not thinking himself secure while Edwi liv'd, consulted with Edric how to make him away; who told him of one Ethelward a decay'd nobleman, likeliest to do the work. Ethelward sent for, and tempted by the king in private, with largest rewards, but abhorring in his mind the deed, promis'd to do it when he saw his opportunity; and so still deferr'd it. But Edwi afterwards receiv'd into favour as a share, was by him or some other of his false friends, Canute contriving it, the same year (1017) slain.[1] Edric also counsel'd him to dispatch Edward and Edmund, the sons[2] of Ironside, but the king doubting that the fact would seem too foul done in England, sent them to the king of Sweden, with like intent; but he disdaining the office, sent them for better safety to Solomon king of Hungary; where Edmund at length dy'd, but Edward married Agatha daughter to Henry the German emperor. A digression in the laws of Edward Confessor, under the title of Lex Noricorum saith, that this Edward for fear of Canute, fled of his own accord to Malesclot king of the Rugians, who receiv'd him honourably, and of that country gave him a wife. Canute settl'd in his throne, divided the government of his kingdom into four parts; the West-Saxons to himself, the East-Angles to Earl Turkill, the Mercians to Edric, the Northumbrians to Eric; then made peace with all princes round about him, and his former wife being dead, in July married Emma the widow of king Ethelred. The Christmas following was an ill feast to Edric, of whose

---

[1] William of Malmsbury writes, that this prince having been long toss'd about by sea and land, return'd at last to England, where he lay conceal'd to his death, and was then bury'd at Tavistock.

By Algothe, widow of Sigeferth the Dane

treason, the king having now made use as much as serv'd his turn, and fearing himself to be the next betray'd, caus'd him to be slain at London in the palace, thrown over the city wall, and there to lie unburied; the head of Edric fix'd on a pole, he commanded to be set on the highest tower of London, as in a double sense he had promis'd him, for the murder of king Edmund to exalt him above all the peers of England. Huntingdon, Malmsbury, and Mat. West. write, that suspecting the king's intention to degrade him from his Mercian dukedom, and upbraiding him with his merits, the king enrag'd, caus'd him to be strangl'd in the room, and out at a window thrown into the Thames. Another writes, that Eric at the king's command struck off his head. Other great men though without fault, as duke Norman the son of Leofwin, Ethelward son of duke Agelmar,[1] he put to death at the same time, jealous of their power or familiarity with Edric: and notwithstanding peace, kept still his army; to maintain which, the next year (1018) he squeez'd out of the English, though now his subjects, not his enemies, seventy-two, some say eighty-two thousand pounds, besides fifteen thousand out of London.[2] Mean while great war arose at Carr, between Uthred son of Waldef, Earl of Northumberland, and Malcolm son of Kened king of Scots, with whom held Eugenius king of Lothian. But here Simeon the relater seems to have committed some mistake, having slain Uthred by Canute two years before, and set Eric in his place: Eric therefore it must needs be, not Uthred, who manag'd this war against the Scots. About which time in a convention of Danes[3] at Oxford, it was agreed on both parties to keep the laws of Edgar; Mat. West. saith of Edward the Elder. The next year (1019) Canute sail'd into Denmark, and there abode all winter. Huntingdon and Mat. West. say, he went thither to repress the Swedes, and that the night before a battle to be fought with them, Godwin stealing out of the camp with his English, assaulted the Swedes, and had got the victory e'er Canute in the morning knew of any fight. For which bold enterprize, though against discipline, he had the English in more esteem ever after. In the spring (1020), at his return into England, he held in the time of Easter a great assembly at Chirchester, and the same year was with Turkill the Dane at the dedication of a church by them built at Assendune, in the place of that great victory which won him the crown. But suspecting his greatness, the year (1021) following banish'd him the realm, and found occasion to do the like by Eric the Northumbrian earl upon the same jealousie.[4] Nor yet

[1] And Brithirio, son of Ælfger, Earl of Defenanseire or Devonshire.
[2] In the annals the tax is but 82,000 pounds in all; 11,000 pounds for London, and 71,000 pounds for the rest of England.
[3] And English. Bromton says, 'twas done in great council or parliament.
[4] In the year before, Canute founded the monastery of St. Edmundsbury, in honour of St. Edmund the king, and two years afterwards remov'd the reliques of St. Alphage, whom his countrymen had murder'd; both which were popular acts. The body of Alphage was translated to Canterbury.

(1028) content with his conquest of England, though now above ten years enjoy'd, he pass'd with fifty ships into Norway, dispossess'd Olave their king, and subdu'd the land, first with great sums of money sent the year before to gain him a party, then coming with an army to compel the rest.[1] Thence (1029) returning king of England, Denmark, and Norway, yet not secure in his mind, under colour of an embassy he sent into banishment Hacun a powerful Dane, who had married the daughter of his sister Gunildis, having conceiv'd some suspicion of his practices against him : but such course was taken, that he never came back ; either perishing at sea, or slain by contrivance the next year (1030) in Orkney. Canute therefore having thus establish'd himself by bloodshed and oppression, to wash away, as he thought the guilt thereof, sailing again into Denmark, went (1031) thence to Rome, and offer'd there to St. Peter great gifts of gold and silver, and other precious things ; besides the usual tribute of Romscot, giving great alms, by the way, both thither and back again, freeing many places of custom and toll with great expense, where strangers were wont to pay, having vow'd great amendment of life at the sepulchre of Peter and Paul, and to his whole people in a large[2] letter written from Rome yet extant. At his return (1032) therefore he built and dedicated a church to St. Edmund at Bury,[3] whom his ancestors had slain, threw out the secular priests who had intruded there, and plac'd monks in their stead ; then going into Scotland, subdu'd and receiv'd homage of Malcolm, and two other kings there, Melbeath and Jermare. Three years (1035) after having made[4] Swane his supposed son by Algiva of Northampton, duke Alfhelms's daughter (for others say the son of a priest whom Algiva, barren, had got ready at the time of her feigned labour) king of Norway, and Hardecnute his son by Emma, king of Denmark, and design'd Harold his son by Algiva of Northampton, king of England, dy'd at Shaftsbury, and was buried at Winchester in the old monastery. This king, as appears, ended better than he began; for tho' he seems to have had no hand in the death of Ironside, but detested the fact, and bringing the murderers, who came to him in hope of great reward, forth among his courtiers, as it were to receive thanks, after they had openly related the manner of their killing him; deliver'd them to deserved punishment, yet he spar'd Edric whom he

[1] Bromton writes, that he was in a manner expell'd by his own subjects, for his weakness and effeminacy : and returning a year afterwards, the people rose upon him and slew him. He was canoniz'd under the title of king Olaf the martyr.
[2] This letter was sent into England by Living Abbot of Tavistock. 'Twas address'd thus : To Æthelnoth bishop of Canterbury, to Alfric of York, with all the bishops and primates; and to the whole English nation, as well noblemen as plebeians, health, &c. is very kind and particular. 'Tis at large in William of Malmsb. Hist.
[3] This was done eleven years before, as appears by an old manuscript belonging to St. Edmundsbury ; also by the lord Coke, in the preface to the 8th book of his reports.
[4] Sweyne is suppos'd to be his son by some other woman, probably a Dane, before he was king of England : for 'tis not likely that Ælgiva, who 'tis said was barren, should be able to impose two sons upon him.

knew to be the prime author of that detestable fact; till willing to be rid of him, grown importune upon the confidence of his merits, and upbraided by him that he had first relinquish'd, then extinguish'd Edmund for his sake; angry to be so upbraided, therefore said he with a chang'd countenance, 'Traytor to God and to me, thou shalt die; thine own mouth accuses thee to have slain thy master my confederate brother, and the Lord's anointed.' Whereupon, although present and private execution was in rage done upon Edric, yet he himself in cool blood scrupl'd not to make away the brother and children of Edmund, who had better right to be the Lord's anointed here than himself. When he had obtain'd in England what he desir'd, no wonder if he sought the love of his conquer'd subjects for the love of his own quiet, the maintainers of his wealth and state, for his own profit. For the like reason he is thought to have married Emma, and that Richard duke of Normandy her brother might the less care what became of Elfred and Edward, her sons by king Ethelred. He commanded to be observ'd the ancient Saxon laws, call'd afterwards the laws of Edward the Confessor, not that he made them, but strictly observ'd them. His letter from Rome professes, if he had done aught amiss in his youth, though negligence or want of due temper, full resolution with the help of God to make amends, by governing justly and piously for the future; charges and adjures all his officers and viscounts, that neither for fear of him, or favour of any person, or to enrich the king, they suffer injustice to be done in the land; commands his treasurers to pay all his debts e'er his return home, which was by Denmark, to compose matters there; and what his letter profess'd, he perform'd all his life after. But it is a fond conceit in many great ones, and pernicious in the end, to cease from no violence till they have attain'd the utmost of their ambitions and desires; then to think God appeas'd by their seeking to bribe him with a share, however large, of their ill-gotten spoils, and then lastly to grow zealous of doing right, when they have no longer need to do wrong. Howbeit Canute was famous through Europe, and much honour'd of Conrade the emperour then at Rome, with rich gifts and many grants of what he there demanded for the freeing of passages from toll and custom. I must not omit one remarkable action done by him, as Huntingdon reports it, with great scene of circumstance, and emphatical expression, to shew the small power of kings in respect of God; which, unless to court-parasites, needed no such laborious demonstration. He caus'd his royal seat to be set on the shoar, while the tide was coming in: and with all the state that royalty could put into his countenance, said thus to the sea: 'Thou sea belong'st to me, and the land whereon I sit is mine; nor hath any one unpunish'd resisted my commands: I charge thee come no farther upon my land, neither presume to wet the feet of thy sovereign lord.' But the sea, as before, came rolling on, and without reverence both wet and dashed him. Whereat the king quickly rising, wish'd all about him to behold and consider the weak and frivolous power of a king, and that none indeed deserv'd the name of a king, but he whose eternal law, both heaven, earth, and sea obey. A truth so evident of itself, as I said before, that unless to shame his court flatterers, who would not else be convinc'd Canute needed not to have gone wet-shod home: the best is, from that time forth he never would wear a crown, esteeming earthly royalty contemptible and vain.

HAROLD for his swiftness surnam'd Harefoot, the son of Canute by Algiva of Northampton (though[1] some speak doubtfully as if she bore him not, but had him of a shoe-maker's wife, as Swane before of a priest: others of a maid servant, to conceal her barrenness) in a great assembly at Oxford, was by duke Leofric and the Mercians, with the[2] Londoners, according to his father's testament elected king; but without the regal habiliments, which Ælnot the arch-bishop having in his custody, refus'd to deliver up, but to the sons of Emma, for which Harold ever after hated the clergy; and (as the clergy are wont thence to infer) all religion. Godwin earl of Kent, and the West-Saxons with him, stood for Hardecnute. Malmsbury saith, that the contest was between Dane and English: that the Danes and Londoners grown now in a manner Danish, were all for Hardecnute; but he being then in Denmark, Harold prevail'd, yet so as that the kingdom should be divided between them; the west and south part reserv'd by Emma for Hardecnute, till his return. But Harold once advanc'd into the throne, banish'd Emma his mother-in-law, seiz'd on his father's treasure at Winchester, and there remain'd. Emma not holding it safe to abide in Normandy while duke William the bastard was yet under age, retir'd (1036) to Baldwin earl of Flanders.[3] In the meanwhile Alred and Edward, sons of Ethelred, accompanied with a small number of Norman soldiers in a few ships, coming to visit their mother Emma, not yet departed the land, and perhaps to see how the people were inclin'd to restore them their right; Elfred was sent for by the king then at London; but in his way met at Guilford by earl Godwin, who with all seeming friendship entertain'd him, was in the night surpris'd and made prisoner, most of his company put to various sorts of cruel death, decimated twice over, then brought to London, was by the king sent bound to Ely, had his eyes put out by the way, and deliver'd to the monks there, dy'd soon after in their custody. Malmsbury gives little credit to this story of Elfred,

[1] Radulph de diceto, who wrote in the reign of king John, says he was a shoemaker's son.
[2] The annals call them the seamen of London, whose citizens as William of Malmsbury observes, by their long conversation with the Danes, were become wholly Danish in their inclinations.
[3] The Saxon annals place her flight to earl Baldwin, under the year 1037.

as not chronicl'd in his time, but rumour'd only. Which Emma however hearing, sent away her son Edward, who by good hap accompanied not his brother, with all speed into Normandy. But the author of Encomium Emmæ, who seems plainly (though nameless) to have been some monk, yet liv'd, and perhaps wrote within the same year when these things were done : by his relation differing from all others, much aggravates the cruelty of Harold, that he not content to have practis'd in secret (for openly he durst not) against the life of Emma, sought many treacherous ways to get her son within his power; and resolv'd at length to forge a letter in the name of their mother, inviting them into England, the copy of which letter he produces written to this purpose.

'Emma in name only queen, to her sons Edward and Alfrid imparts motherly salutation. While we severally bewail the death of our lord the king, most dear sons, and while daily ye are depriv'd more and more of the kingdom, your inheritance; I admire what counsel ye take, knowing that your intermitted delay, is a daily strengthening to the reign of your usurper, who incessantly goes about from town to city, gaining the chief nobles to his party, either by gifts, prayers, or threats. But they had much rather one of you should reign over them, than to be held under the power of him who now over-rules them. I entreat therefore that one of you come to me speedily, and privately; to receive from me wholesome counsel, and to know how the business which I intend, shall be accomplish'd. By this messenger present, send back what you determine. Farewell, as dear both as my own heart.'

These letters were sent to the princes then in Normandy, by express messengers, with presents also, as from their mother; which they joyfully receiving, return word by the same messengers, that one of them will be with her shortly; naming both the time and place. Alfrid therefore the younger (for so it was thought best) at the appointed time, with a few ships and small numbers about him, appearing on the coast, no sooner came ashore but fell into the snare of earl Godwin, sent on purpose to betray him; as above was related. Emma greatly sorrowing for the loss of her son, thus cruelly made away, fled immediately with some of her nobles her faithfullest adherents into Flanders, had her dwelling assign'd at Bruges by the earl; where having remain'd about two years, she was (1039) visited out of Denmark by Hardecnute her son; and he not long had remain'd with her there, when Harold in England, having done nothing the while worth memory, save the taxing of every port at eight marks of silver to sixteen ships, dy'd (1040) at London, some say at Oxford, and was buried at Winchester. After which, most of the nobility, both Danes and English now agreeing, send embassadors to Hardecnute still at Bruges with his mother, entreating him to come and receive as his right, the scepter, who before midsummer came with sixty ships, and many soldiers out of Denmark.

HARDECNUTE receiv'd with acclamation, and seated in the throne, first call'd to mind the injuries done to him, or his mother Emma, in the time of Harold; sent Alfric archbishop of York, Godwin and others, with Troud his executioner, to London, commanding them to dig up the body of king Harold, and throw it into a ditch; but by a second order into the Thames. Whence taken up by a fisherman, and convey'd to a churchyard in London, belonging to the Danes, it was interr'd again with honour. This done, he levied a sore tax, that eight marks to every rower, and twelve to every officer in his fleet, should be paid throughout England;[1] by which time they who were so forward to call him over, had enough of him; for he, as they thought, had too much of theirs. After this he call'd to account Godwin earl of Kent, and Leving bishop of Worcester, about the death of Elfred his half brother, which Alfric the archbishop laid to their charge; the king depriv'd Leving of his bishoprick, and gave it to his accuser: but the year following, pacify'd with a round sum, restor'd it to Leving. Godwin made his peace by a sumptuous present, a galley with a gilded stem bravely rigg'd, and eighty soldiers in her, every one with bracelets of gold on each arm, weighing sixteen ounces, helmet, corslet, and hilts of his swords gilded; a Danish curtax listed with gold or silver hung on his left shoulder, a shield with boss and nails gilded in his left hand, in his right a launce: besides this he took his oath before the king, that neither of his own counsel or will, but by the command of Harold he had done what he did, to the putting out of Elfred's eyes. The like oath took most of the nobility for themselves, or in his behalf. The next year (1041), Hardecnute sending his housecarles,[2] so they call'd his officers, to gather the tribute impos'd; two of them, rigorous in their office, were slain at Worcester by the people; whereat the king enrag'd, sent Leofric duke of Mercia, and Seward of Northumberland,[3] with great forces and commission to slay the citizens, rifle and burn the city, waste the whole province. Affrighted with such news, all the people fled; the countrymen whither they could, the citizens to a small island in Severn, call'd Beverege, which they fortify'd and defended stoutly, till peace was granted them, and freely to return home: but their city they found sack'd and burnt; wherewith the king was appeas'd. This was commendable in him, however cruel to others, that towards his half brethren, tho' rivals of his crown, he shew'd himself always tenderly affection'd; as now towards Edward, who without

---

[1] Also 29029 pounds, and 11048 pounds for 32 sail of ships. This tax was the same as Danegelt, which was become a prerogative.
[2] Housecurles, in English, servants of the houshold.   [3] Earl Godwin went with them.

fear came to him out of Normandy, and with unfeigned kindness receiv'd, remain'd safely and honourably in his court.[1] But Hardecnute
the year (1042) following, at a feast wherein Osgod, a great Danish
lord, gave his daughter in marriage at Lambeth, to Prudon, another
potent Dane : in the midst of his mirth, sound and healthful to sight,
while he was drinking fell down speechless, and so dying, was buried
at Winchester beside his father. He was it seems a great lover of
good cheer; sitting at table four times a day, with great variety of
dishes, and superfluity to all comers. Whereas, saith Huntingdon, in
our time princes in their houses made but one meal a day.[2] He gave
his sister Gunildis, a virgin of rare beauty, in marriage to Henry the
Almain emperor; and to send her forth pompously, all the nobility
contributed their jewels and richest ornaments. But it may seem a
wonder, that our historians, if they deserve that name, should, in a
matter so remarkable, and so near their own time, so much differ.
Huntingdon relates, against the credit of all other records, that Hardecnute thus dead, the English rejoycing at this unexpected riddance of
the Danish yoke, sent over to Elfrid the eldest son of Emma by king
Ethelred, of whom we heard but now, that he dy'd prisoner at Ely,
sent thither by Harold six years before; that he came now out of
Normandy, with a great number of men to receive the crown ; that
earl Godwin aiming to have his daughter queen of England, by marrying her to Edward a simple youth, for he thought Elfred of a higher
spirit than to accept her, persuaded the nobles that Elfred had brought
over too many Normans, and promis'd them lands here, that it was
not safe to suffer a warlike and subtle nation to take root in the land ;
that these were to be so handled as none of them might dare for the
future to flock hither, upon pretence of relation to the king ; thereupon,
by common consent of the nobles, both Elfred and his company were
dealt with as was above related ; that they then sent for Edward out
of Normandy, with hostages to be left there, of their faithful intentions
to make him king, and their desires not to bring over with him many
Normans ; that Edward at their call, came then first out of Normandy ;
whereas all others agree, that he came voluntarily over to visit
Hardecnute, as is before said, and was remaining in the court at the
time of his death. For Hardecnute dead, saith Malmsbury, Edward
doubting greatly his own safety, determin'd to rely wholly on the
advice and favour of earl Godwin ; desiring therefore by messengers
to have private speech with him ; the earl a while deliberated : at
last assenting, prince Edward came, and would have fallen at his feet ;
but that not permitted, told him the danger wherein he thought himself
at present, and in great perplexity besought his help to convey him

[1] The Saxon annals tell us, he came into England the year before, 1040.
[2] John Rouse of Warwick, in his treatise *De Regibus Ang.*, relates, that the day of king
Hardecnute's death was kept by the English as a holy-day in his time, 400 years afterwards,
and was call'd Hoct Wednesday.

some whither out of the land. Godwin soon apprehending the fair occasion that now as it were prompted him how to advance himself and his family, cheerfully exhorted him to remember himself the son of Ethelred, the grandchild of Edgar, right heir to the crown, at full age; not to think of flying, but of reigning, which might easily be brought about, if he would follow his counsel: then setting forth the power and authority which he had in England, promis'd it should be all his to set him on his throne, if he on his part would promise and swear to be for ever his friend, to preserve the honour of his house, and to marry his daughter. Edward, as his necessity then was, consented easily, and swore to whatever Godwin requir'd. An assembly of states thereupon met at Gillingham, where Edward pleaded his right; and by the powerful influence of Godwin was accepted. Others, as Bromton, with no probability, write, that Godwin at this time was fled into Denmark, for what he had done to Elfred, return'd and submitted himself to Edward then king, was by him charg'd openly with the death of Elfred, and, not without much ado, by the intercession of Leofric, and other peers, receiv'd at length into favour.

GLAD were the English, deliver'd so unexpectedly from their Danish masters,[1] and little thought how near another conquest was hanging over them. Edward, the Easter following, crown'd at Winchester,[2] the same year (1043) accompanied with earl Godwin, Leofric, and Siward, came again thither on a sudden, and by their counsel seiz'd on the treasure of his mother Emma. The cause alleg'd is, that she was hard to him in the time of his banishment; and indeed she is said not much to have lov'd Ethelred her former husband, and thereafter the children by him; she was moreover noted to be very covetous, hard to the poor, and profuse to monasteries. About this time also, king Edward, according to promise, took to wife Edith or Egith, earl Godwin's daughter, commended much for beauty, modesty, and, beyond what is requisite in a woman, learning. Ingulf, then a youth, lodging in the court with his father, saw her oft, and coming from the school, was sometimes met by her and pos'd, not in grammar only, but in logick. Edward, the next year but one (1045), made ready a strong navy at Sandwich against Magnus king of Norway, who threaten'd an invasion: had not Swane king of Denmark diverted (1046) him by a war at home to defend his own land, not out of good will to Edward, as may be suppos'd, who at the same time express'd none to the Danes, banishing Gunildis the niece of Canute with her two sons, and Osgod,

---

[1] Brompton in his Chronicle tells us, that the great council, who elected Edward king, unanimously agreed and swore, that no Dane should reign over them any more. The Danes, insolence being become intolerable; an Englishman not daring to pass a bridge if he met a Dane, till the latter first pass'd it; and if he did not salute him, he was sure to be well beaten.

[2] By Archbishop Eadsige, who preach'd on this occasion; which is the first coronation-sermon mentioned in history.

by sirname Clapa, out of the realm. Swane overpower'd by Magnus, sent the next year (1047) to entreat aid of king Edward; Godwin gave counsel to send him fifty ships fraught with soldiers; but Leofric and the general voice gainsaying, none were sent.[1] The next year (1048) Harold Harvager king of Norway sending ambassadors, made peace with king Edward; but an earthquake at Worcester and Darby, pestilence and famine in many places, much lessen'd the enjoyment thereof. The next year (1049), Henry the emperor displeas'd with Baldwin earl of Flanders, had straiten'd him with a great army by land; and sending to king Edward, desir'd him with his ships to hinder what he might, his escape by sea. The king therefore with a great navy coming to Sandwich, there staid till the emperor came to an agreement with earl Baldwin. Meanwhile, Swane, son of earl Godwin, who not permitted to marry Edgiva the abbess of Chester, by him deflour'd, had left the land, came out of Denmark with eight ships, feigning a desire to return into the king's favour; and Beorn his cousin-german, who commanded part of the king's navy, promis'd to intercede that his earldom might be restor'd him. Godwin therefore and Beorn with a few ships, the rest of the fleet gone home, coming to Pevensey (but Godwin soon departing thence in pursuit of twenty-nine Danish ships, who had got much booty on the coast of Essex, and perish'd by tempest in their return) Swane with his ships comes to Beorn at Pevensey, guilefully requests him to sail with him to Sandwich, and reconcile him to the king, as he had promis'd. Beorn mistrusting no evil where he intended good, went with him in his ship, attended by three only of his servants: but Swane, set upon barbarous cruelty, not reconciliation with the king, took Beon, now in his power, and bound him; then coming to Dartmouth, slew and bury'd him in a deep ditch. After which, the men of Hastings took six of his ships, and brought them to the king at Sandwich; with the other two he escap'd into Flanders, there remaining, till Aldred bishop of Worcester, by earnest mediation, wrought his peace with the king. About this time king Edward sent to Pope Leo, desiring absolution from a vow, which he had made in his younger years to take a journey to Rome, if God vouchsaf'd him to reign in England; the pope dispenc'd with his vow, but not without the expence of his journey given to the poor, and a monastery built or re-edefy'd to St. Peter; who in a vision to a monk, as is said, chose Westminster, which king Edward thereupon rebuilding, endow'd with large privileges and revenues. The same year (1050), saith Florent of Worcester, certain Irish pirates with thirty-six ships enter'd the mouth of Severn, and with the aid of Griffin prince of South-Wales, did some hurt in those parts: then passing the river Wey, burnt Dunedham, and slew all the inhabitants

[1] The same author, Simeon of Durham, writes, that the king of Norway dying soon after Swane recover'd his kingdom.

they found. Against whom Aldred bishop of Worcester, with a few out of Glocester and Herefordshire, went out in haste; but Griffin, to whom the Welsh and Irish had privily sent messengers, came down upon the English with his whole power by night, and early in the morning suddenly assaulting them, slew many, and put the rest to flight. The next year (1051) but one, king Edward remitted the Danish tax, which had continu'd thirty-eight years heavy upon the land; since Ethelred first paid it to the Danes, and what remain'd thereof in his treasury he sent back to the owners; but through imprudence, laid the foundation of a far worse mischief to the English; while studying gratitude to those Normans,[1] who to him in exile had been helpful: he call'd them over to publick offices here, whom better he might have repaid out of his private purse; by this means exasperating either nation one against the other, and making way by degrees to the Norman conquest. Robert, a monk of that country, who had been serviceable to him there in time of need, he made bishop, first of London, then of Canterbury; William his chaplain, bishop of Dorchester. Then began the English to lay aside their own ancient customs, and in many things to imitate French manners, the great peers to speak French in their houses, in French to write their bills and letters, as a great piece of gentility, asham'd of their own; a presage of their subjection shortly to that people, whose fashions and language they affected so slavishly: but that which gave beginning to many troubles ensuing, happen'd this year, and upon this occasion. Eustace earl of Boloign, father of the famous Godfrey who won Jerusalem from the Saracens, and husband to Goda the king's sister, having been to visit king Edward, and returning by Canterbury to take ship at Dover, one of his harbingers insolently seeking to lodge by force in a house there, provok'd so the master thereof, as by chance, or heat of anger to kill him. The count with his whole train going to the house where his servant had been kill'd, slew both the slayer and eighteen more who defended him. But the townsmen running to arms, requited him with the slaughter of twenty-one more of his servants, wounded most of the rest; he himself with one or two hardly escaping, ran back with clamour to the king; whom seconded by other Norman courtiers, he stirr'd up to great anger against the citizens of Canterbury. Earl Godwin in haste is sent for, the cause related and much aggravated by the king against that city, the earl commanded to raise forces, and use the citizens thereof as enemies. Godwin, sorry to see strangers more favour'd of the king than his native people, answer'd, that it were better to summon first the chief men of the town into the king's court, to charge them with

---

[1] Ingulph says, William duke of Normandy, who was afterwards king of England, visited king Edward in this year; and some authors relate, that the king promis'd to make the duke his successor; but Ingulf affirms, no mention was then made of it.

sedition, where both parties might be heard, that not found in fault they might be acquitted, if otherwise, by fine or loss of life might satisfie the king whose peace they had broken, and the count whom they had injur'd : till this were done refusing to prosecute with hostile punishment them of his own country unheard, whom his office was rather to defend. The king displeased with his refusal, and not knowing how to compel him, appointed an assembly of all the peers to be held at Gloster, where the matter might be fully try'd ; the assembly was full and frequent according to summons ; but Godwin mistrusting his own cause, or the violence of his adversaries ; with his two sons, Swane and Harold, and a great power gathered out of his own and his sons earldoms, which contain'd most of the south-east and west parts of England, came no farther than Beverstan, giving out that their forces were to go against the Welsh, who intended an irruption into Herefordshire ; and Swane under that pretence lay with part of his army thereabout. The Welsh understanding this device, and with all diligence clearing themselves before the king, left Godwin detected of false accusation in great hatred to all the assembly. Leofric therefore and Siward dukes of great power, the former in Mercia, the other in all parts beyond Humber, both ever faithful to the king, send privily with speed to raise the forces of their provinces. Which Godwin not knowing, sent boldly to king Edward, demanding Count Eustace and his followers, together with those Boloignians, who as Simeon writes, held a castle in the jurisdiction of Canterbury. The king as then having but little force at hand, entertain'd him a while with treaties and delays, till his summon'd army drew nigh, then rejected his demands. Godwin thus match'd, commanded his sons not to begin fight against the king ; begun with, not to give ground. The king's forces were the flower of those counties whence they came, and eager to fall on ; but Leofric and the wiser sort, detesting civil war, brought the matter to this accord, that hostages given on either side, the whole cause should be again debated at London. Thither the king and lords coming with their army, sent to Godwin and his son (who with their powers were come as far as Southwark) commanding their appearance unarm'd, with only twelve attendants, and that the rest of their soldiers they should deliver over to the king. They to appear without pledges before an adverse faction deny'd ; but to dismiss their soldiers refus'd not, nor in aught else to obey the king as far as might stand with honour and the just regard of their safety. This answer not pleasing the king, an edict was presently issu'd forth, that Godwin and his sons within five days depart the land. He who perceiv'd now his numbers to diminish, readily obeyed, and with his wife and three sons, Tosti, Swane, and Gyrrha, with as much treasure as their ship could carry, embarking at Thorney,[1] sail'd into Flanders to Earl

[1] The annals say Bosenham in Sussex.

Baldwin, whose daughter Judith Tosti had married: for Wulnod his fourth son was then hostage to the king in Normandy; his other two, Harold and Leofwin, taking ship at Bristow, in a vessel that lay ready there belonging to Swane, passed into Ireland. King Edward pursuing his displeasure, divorc'd his wife Edith earl Godwin's daughter, sending her despoil'd of all her ornaments to Warewel with one waiting maid, to be kept in custody by his sister the abbess there. His reason of so doing was as harsh as his act, that she only, while her nearest relations were in banishment, might not, though innocent, enjoy ease at home. After this, William Duke of Normandy with a great number of followers coming into England, was by king Edward honourably entertain'd and led about the cities, and castles, as it were to shew him what e're long was to be his own (though at that time, saith Ingulf, no mention thereof pass'd between them) then after some time of his abode here, presented richly and dismiss'd, he return'd home. The next year (1052) queen Emma dy'd, and was buried at Winchester.[1] The chronicle attributed to John Brompton a Yorkshire abbot,[2] but rather of some nameless author living under Edward the Third, or later, reports that the year before, by Robert the archbishop, she was accused both of consenting to the death of her son Alfred, and of preparing poyson for Edward also; lastly, of too much familiarity with Alwin bishop of Winchester; that to approve her innocence, praying over-night to St. Swithune, she offer'd to pass blindfold between certain plow-shares red hot, according to the Ordalian Law, which without harm she perform'd; that the king thereupon receiv'd her to honour, and from her and the bishop, penance for his credulity; that the archbishop asham'd of his accusation, fled out of England. Which besides the silence of ancienter authors (for the bishop fled not till a year after) brings the whole story into suspicion, in this more probable, if it can be prov'd, that in the memory of this deliverance from the nine burning plow-shares, queen Emma gave to the abbey of St. Swithune nine manors, and bishop Alwin other nine. About this time, Griffin prince of South-Wales, wasted Herefordshire; to oppose whom the people of that country with many Normans, garrison'd in the castle of Hereford, went out in arms, but were put to the worse, many slain, and much booty driven away by the Welsh. Soon after which, Harold and Leofwin, sons of Godwin, coming into Severn with many ships, in the confines of Somerset and Dorsetshire, spoiled many villages, and resisted by those of Somerset and Devonshire, slew in fight more than thirty of their principal men, many of the common sort, and return'd with much booty to their fleet. King Edward on the other side made ready above sixty ships at Sandwich, well stor'd with men and provision, under the conduct of Odo and

---

[1] According to the Saxon Annals, Mr. Milton is out in his chronology: for the events of the last three years, the latest of them Earl Godwin's banishment, happen'd Anno. 1048.
[2] Henry of Knighton also mentions it in his history.

Radulf two of his Norman kindred, enjoyning them to find out Godwin, whom he heard to be at sea. To quicken them, he himself lay on ship-board, oft times watch'd and sail'd up and down in search of those Pirates. But Godwin, whether in a mist, or by other accident, passing by them, arrived in another part of Kent, and dispersing secret messengers abroad, by fair words allured the chief men of Kent, Sussex, Surrey, and Essex to his party; which news coming to the king's fleet at Sandwich, they hasted to find him out; but missing of him again, came up without effect to London. Godwin advertis'd of this, forthwith sail'd to the Isle of Wight; where at length his two sons Harold and Leofwin finding him, with their united navy lay on the coast, forbearing other hostility than to furnish themselves with fresh victual from land as they needed.[1] Thence as one fleet they set forwards to Sandwich, using all fair means by the way to encrease their numbers both of mariners and soldiers. The king then at London, startl'd at those tidings, gave speedy order to raise forces in all parts which had not revolted from him; but now too late, for Godwin within a few days after with his ships or galleys came up the river Thames to Southwark, and till the tide return'd had conference with the Londoners; whom by fair speeches, for he was held a good speaker in those times, he brought to his bent. The tide returning, and none upon the bridge hindring, he row'd up in his galleys along the south bank; where his land army, now come to him, in array of battle stood on the shore; then turning towards the north side of the river, where the king's galleys lay in some readiness, and land forces also not far off, he made shew as offering to fight; but they understood one another, and the soldiers on either side soon declar'd their resolution not to fight English against English. Thence coming to treaty, the king and the earl reconcil'd, both armies were dissolv'd, Godwin and his sons restor'd to their former dignities, except Swane, who touch'd in conscience for the slaughter of Beorn his kinsman, was gone barefoot to Jerusalem, and returning home, dy'd by sickness or Saracens in Lycia; his wife Edith, Godwin's daughter, king Edward took to him again, dignify'd as before. Then were the Normans, who had done many unjust things under the king's authority, and given him ill counsel against his people, banish'd the realm, some of them not blameable permitted to stay. Robert Archbishop of Canterbury, William of London, Ulf of Lincoln, all Normans, hardly escaping with their followers, got to sea. The Archbishop went with his complaint to Rome; but returning, dy'd in Normandy at the same monastery from whence he came. Osbern and Hugh surrender'd their castles, and by permission of Leofric passed through his countries with their Normans to Macbeth king of Scotland. The year (1053) follow-

[1] The Annals tell us, Godwin plunder'd it, and kill'd all before him at Porlock in Somersetshire.

ing Rhese, brother to Griffin, Prince of South Wales who by inrodes had done much damage to the English, taken at Bulendun, was put to death by the king's appointment, and his head brought to him at Gloster. The same year at Winchester, on the second holyday of Easter, earl Godwin sitting with the king at table, sunk down suddenly in his seat as dead: his three sons, Harold, Tosti, and Gytha, forthwith carried him to the king's chamber, hoping he might revive; but the malady had so seiz'd him, that the 5th day after he expir'd. The Normans, who hated Godwin, give out, saith Malmsbury, that mention happening to be made of Elfred, and the king thereat looking sowerly upon Godwin, he to vindicate himself, utter'd these words, 'Thou O king, at every mention made of thy brother Elfred, look'st frowningly upon me: but let God not suffer me to swallow this morsel, if I be guilty of aught done against his life or thy advantage;' that after these words, choak'd with the morsel taken, he sunk down and recover'd not. His first wife was the sister of Canute, a woman of much infamy for the trade she drove of buying up English youths and maids to sell in Denmark, whereof she made great gain; but e'er long was struck with thunder, and dy'd. The year (1054) ensuing, Siward, earl of Northumberland, with a great number of horse and foot, attended also by a strong fleet at the king's appointment, made an expedition into Scotland, vanquish'd the tyrant Macbeth, slaying many thousands of Scots, with those Normans that went thither, and plac'd Malcolm[1] son of the Cumbrian king in his stead; yet not without loss of his own son, and many other both English and Danes. Told of his son's death, he ask'd, whether he receiv'd his death's wound before or behind? When it was answer'd before, 'I am glad,' saith he; "and should not else have thought him, though my son, worthy of burial. In the mean while king Edward being without issue to succeed him, sent Aldred bishop of Winchester with great presents to the emperor, entreating him to prevail with the king of Hungary, that Edward the remaining son of his brother Edmund Ironside, might be sent into England. Siward but one year (1055) surviving his great victory, dy'd at York; reported by Huntingdon a man of giant-like stature, and by his own demeanour at point of death manifested, of a rough and mere soldierly mind: for much disdaining to die in bed by a disease, not in the field fighting with his enemies, he caus'd himself completely arm'd, and weapon'd with battle-ax and shield, to be set in a chair, whether to fight with death, if he could be so vain, or to meet him (when far other weapons and preparations were needful) in a martial bravery; but true fortitude glories not in feats of war, as they are such, but as they serve to end war soonest by a victorious peace. His earldom the king bestow'd on Tosti the son of earl Godwin: and

---

[1] Mat. Westminster writes, king Edward bestow'd the kingdom of Scotland on Malcolm, to be held of himself.

soon after a convention held at London, banish'd without visible cause, Huntingdon saith for treason, Algar the son of Leofric; who passing into Ireland, soon return'd with eighteen ships to Griffin prince of South-Wales, requesting his aid against king Edward. He assembling his powers, enter'd with him into Herefordshire; whom Radulf a timorous captain, son to the king's sister, not by Eustace, but a former husband, met two miles distant from Hereford; and having horsed the English who knew better to fight on foot, without stroke he with his French and Normans, beginning to flie, taught the English by his example. Griffin and Algar following the chase, slew many, wounded more, enter'd Hereford, slew seven Canons defending the minster, burnt the monastery and reliques, then the city; killing some, leading captive others of the citizens, return'd with great spoils; whereof king Edward having notice, gather'd (1055) a great army at Gloster under the conduct of Harold now earl of Kent; who strenuously pursuing Griffin, enter'd Wales, and encamp'd beyond Straddale. But the enemy, flying before him farther into the country, leaving there the greater part of his army with such as had charge to fight, if occasion were offer'd, with the rest he return'd, and fortifiy'd Hereford with a wall and gates. Meanwhile, Griffin and Algar dreading the diligence of Harold, after many messages to and fro, concluded a peace with him: Algar discharging his fleet with pay at Winchester, came to the king, and was restor'd to his carldom. But Griffin, with breach of faith, the next year (1056) set upon Leofgar, the bishop of Hereford, and his clerks, then at a place call'd Glastbrig, with Agelnoth viscount of the shire, and slew them; but Leofric, Harold, and king Edward, by force, as is likeliest, though it be not said how, reduc'd him to peace. The next year (1057), Edward son of Edmund Ironside, for whom his uncle king Edward had sent to the emperor, came out of Hungary, design'd successor to the crown; but within a few days after his coming, dy'd at London, leaving behind him Edgar Atheling his son Margaret and Christina his daughters. About the same time also dy'd earl Leofric in a good old age, a man of no less virtue than power in his time; religious, prudent, and faithful to his country, happily wedded to Godiva,[1] a woman of great praise. His son Algar found less favour with king Edward, again banish'd after his father's death; but he again (1058) by the aid of Griffin, and fleet from Norway, maugre the king, soon recover'd his carldom. The next year (1059) Malcolm king of Scots coming to visit king Edward, was brought on his way by Tosti the Northumbrian carl, to whom he swore brotherhood: yet the next year

---

[1] The lady who is famous in story for riding naked through Coventry, to gain some immunities for the citizens: the story is at large in Broniton's Chronicle. The pictures of earl Leofric, and his countess Godiva, were set up in the windows of Trinity church, with this inscription:

    Lurick, for the love of thee,   Do set Coventry toll-free.

but one (1061) while Tosti was gone to Rome with Aldred arch-bishop of York for his pall, this sworn brother taking advantage of his absence, roughly harrass'd Northumberland. The year passing to an end without other matter of moment, save the frequent inrodes and robberies of Griffin, whom no bonds of faith could restrain. king Edward sent (1062) against him after Christmas, Harold now duke of West-Saxons, with no great body of horse from Gloster; where he then kept his court; whose coming heard of, Griffin not daring to abide, nor in any part of his island holding himself secure, escap'd hardly by sea, e're Harold coming to[1] Rudeland, burnt his palace and ships there, returning to Gloster the same day: but by the middle of May (1063) setting out with a fleet from Bristow, he sail'd about the most part of Wales, and met by his brother Tosti with many troops of horse, as the king had appointed, began to waste the country; but the Welsh giving pledges, yielded themselves, promis'd to become tributary, and banish Griffin their prince; who lurking somewhere, was the next year (1064) taken and slain by Griffin prince of North-Wales; his head, with the head and tackle of his ship, sent to Harold, by him to the king, who of his gentleness made Blechgent and Rithwallon or Rivallon, his two brothers, princes in his stead: they to Harold, in behalf of the king, swore fealty and tribute.[2] Yet the next year (1065), Harold having built a fair house at a place call'd Portascith in Monmouthshire, and stor'd it with provision, that the king might lodge there in time of hunting; Caradoc the son of Griffin, slain the year before, came with a number of men, slew all he found there, and took away the provision. Soon after which, the Northumbrians in a tumult at York, beset the palace of Tosti their earl, slew more than two hundred of his soldiers and servants, pillaged his treasure, and put him to flie for his life. The cause of this insurrection they alledg'd to be, for that the queen Edith had commanded in her brother Tosti's behalf, Gospatric a Nobleman of that country to be treacherously slain in the king's court; and that Tosti himself the year before with like treachery had caus'd to be slain in his chamber Gamel and Ulf, two other of their noblemen, besides his intolerable exactions and oppressions. Then in a manner the whole country coming up to complain of their grievances, met with Harold at Northampton, whom the king at Tosti's request had sent to pacifie the Northumbrians; but they laying open the cruelty of his government, and their own birthright of freedom,[3] not to endure the tyranny of any

---

[1] By the agreement of the sound, and the nearness of the place to Glocester, it should be Ragland in Monmouthshire, which stands near the little river Usk; but the ships he burnt must be very small, or the river more navigable than 'tis at present.

[2] Florence of Worcester says, they swore fealty to earl Harold also.

[3] William of Malmsbury gives us the reason for which the Northumbrians declar'd they took arms, viz. that they were freemen born, and as freely educated, and that they wou'd not endure the insolence of an earl; for they had learnt from their ancestors to choose either liberty or death.

governour whatsoever, with absolute refusal to admit him again, and Harold hearing reason, all the accomplices of Tosti were expell'd the earldom. He himself banish'd the realm, went into Flanders; Morcar the son of Algar made earl in his stead. Huntingdon tells another cause of Tosti's banishment, that one day at Windsor, while Harold reach'd the cup to king Edward, Tosti envying to see his younger brother in greater favour than himself, could not forbear to run furiously upon him, catching hold of his hair; the scuffle was soon parted by other attendants rushing between, and Tosti forbidden the court. He with continu'd fury riding to Hereford, where Harold had many servants, preparing an entertainment for the king, came to the house and sat upon them with his followers; then lopping off hands, arms, legs of some, heads of others, threw them into butts of wine, meath or ale, which were laid in for the king's drinking: and at his going away charg'd them to send him this word, that of other fresh meats he might bring with him to his farm what he pleas'd, but of souse he should find plenty provided ready for him; that for his barbarous act the king pronounc'd him banish'd; that the Northumbrians taking advantage at the king's displeasure and sentence against him, rose also to be reveng'd of his cruelties done to themselves; but this no way agrees, for why then should Harold, or the king, so much labour with the Northumbrians to re-admit him, if he were a banish'd man for his crimes done before? About this time it happen'd, that Harold putting to sea one day for his pleasure, in a fisher-boat, from his mannor at Boseham in Sussex, caught with a tempest too far off land, was carry'd into Normandy; and by the earl of Pentiew, on whose coast he was driven, at his own request brought to duke William; who entertaining him with great curtesie, so far won him, as to promise the duke by oath of his own accord, not only the castle of Dover, then in his tenure, but the kingdom also after king Edward's death to his utmost endeavour; thereupon betrothing the duke's daughter, then too young for marriage; and departing richly presented. Others say, that king Edward himself, after the death of Edward his nephew, sent Harold thither, on purpose to acquaint duke William with his intention to bequeath him his kingdom: but Malmsbury accounts the former story to be the truer. Ingulf writes, that king Edward now grown old, and perceiving Edgar his nephew both in body and mind unfit to govern, especially against the pride and insolence of Godwin's sons, who would never obey him; duke William on the other side of high merit, and his kinsman by the mother, had sent Robert archbishop of Canterbury to acquaint the duke with his purpose, not long before Harold came thither. The former part may be true, that king Edward upon such considerations had sent one or other; but archbishop Robert was fled the land, and dead many years before. Eadmer and Simeon write, that Harold went of his own accord into Normandy, by the king's permission or connivance, to get free his brother Wulnod and nephew Hacun the son of Swane, whom the king had taken hostages of Godwin and sent into Normandy; that king Edward foretold Harold, his journey thither would be to the detriment of all England, and his own reproach; that duke William then acquainted Harold, how Edward e're his coming to the crown had promis'd, if he ever attain'd it, to leave duke William successor after him. Last of these Matthew Paris writes, that Harold to get free of Duke William, affirm'd his coming thither not to have been by accident or force of tempest, but on set purpose, in that private manner to enter with him into secret confederacy: so variously are these things reported. After this king Edward grew sickly, yet as he was able kept his Christmas at London, and was at the dedication of St. Peter's church in Westminster, which he had rebuilt; but on the eve of Epiphany, or Twelftide (1066), deceas'd much lamented, and in the church was entomb'd. That he was harmless and simple, is conjectur'd by his words in anger to a peasant, who had cross'd his game (for with hunting and hawking he was much delighted), 'By God and God's mother,' said he, ' I shall do you as shrewd a turn, if I can :' observing that law-maxim the best of all his successors, that the king of England can do no wrong. The softness of his nature gave growth to factions of those about him, Normans especially and English; these complaining, that Robert the arch-bishop was a sower of dissention between the king and his people, a traducer of the English; the other side, that Godwin and his sons bore themselves arrogantly and proudly towards the king, usurping to themselves equal share in the government; oft-times making sport with his simplicity, that thro' their power in the land they made no scruple to kill men, of whose inheritance they took a liking, and so to take possession. The truth is, that Godwin and his sons did many things boisterously and violently, much against the king's mind; which not able to resist, he had, as some say, his wife Edith, Godwin's daughter, in such aversation, as in bed never to have touch'd her; whether for this cause, or mistaken chastity, not commendable; to enquire farther, is not material. His laws held good and just, and long after desir'd by the English of their Norman kings, are yet extant. He is said to be at table not excessive, at festivals nothing puft up with the costly robes he wore, which his queen with curious art had woven for him in gold. He was full of almsdeeds, and exhorted the monks to like charity. He is said to be the first of English kings that cur'd the disease, call'd thence the king's evil; yet Malmsbury blames them who attribute that cure to his royalty, not to his sanctity; said also to have cur'd certain blind men with the water wherein he had wash'd his hands. A little before his death, lying speechless two days, the third day, after a deep sleep, he was heard to pray, that if it were a true vision, not an illusion which he had seen, God would give him strength to utter it, otherwise not. Then he related how he had seen two devout monks, whom he knew in Normandy, to have liv'd and dy'd well, who appearing, told him they were sent messengers from God to foretel, that because the great ones of England, dukes, lords, bishops, and abbots, were not ministers of God, but of the devil, God had deliver'd the land to their enemies ; and when he desir'd that he might reveal this vision, to the end they might repent, it was answer'd, they neither will repent, neither will God pardon them. At this relation others trembling, Stigand the Simonious archbishop, whom Edward much to blame had suffer'd many years to sit primate of the church, is said to have laugh'd, as at the feavourish dream of a doting old man ; but the event prov'd it true.

HAROLD, whether by king Edward a little before his death ordain'd successor to the crown, as Simeon of Durham, and others[1] affirm ; or by the prevalence of his faction, excluding Edgar the right heir, grandchild to Edmund Ironside, as Malmsbury and Huntingdon agree ; no sooner was the funeral of king Edward ended, but on the same day was elected and crown'd king : and no sooner plac'd in the throne, but began to frame himself by all manner of compliances to gain affection, endeavour'd to make good laws, repeal'd bad, became a great patron to church and churchmen, courteous and affable to all reputed good, a hater of evil-doers, charg'd all his officers to punish thieves, robbers, and all disturbers of the peace, while he himself by sea and land labour'd in the defence of his country : so good an actor is ambition. In the meanwhile a blazing star, seven mornings together, about the end of April, was seen to stream terribly, not only over England, but other parts of the world ; foretelling here, as was thought, the great changes approaching : plainliest prognosticated by Elmer a monk of Malmsbury, who could not foresee, when time was, the breaking of his own legs for soaring too high. He in his youth strangely aspiring, had made and fitted wings to his hands and feet ; with these on the top of a tower, spread out to gather air, he flew more than a furlong ; but the wind being too high, came fluttering down, to the maiming of all his limbs ; yet so conceited of his art, that he attributed the cause of his fall to the want of a tail, as birds have, which he forgot to make to his hinder parts. This story, tho' seeming otherwise too light in the midst of a sad narration, yet for the strangeness thereof, I thought worthy enough the placing as I found it plac'd in my author. But to digress no farther, Tosti the king's brother coming from Flanders, full of envy at his younger

---

[1] The annals says, he succeeded, as king Edward appointed. William of Malmsbury affirms, he extorted an oath of fidelity from the chief men — — all the bishops were for Harold.

brother's advancement to the crown, resolv'd what he might to trouble his reign; forcing therefore them of Wight-isle to contribution, he sail'd thence to Sandwich, committing piracies on the coast between. Harold then residing at London, with a great number of ships drawn together, and of horse troops by land, prepares in person for Sandwich: whereof Tosti having notice, directs his course with sixty ships towards Lindsey, taking with him all the seamen he found, willing or unwilling: where he burnt many villages, and slew many of the inhabitants; but Edwin the Mercian duke, and Morcar his brother, the Northumbrian earl, with their forces on either side, soon drove him out of the country. Who thence betook him to Malcolm the Scotish king, and with him abode the whole summer. About the same time Duke William sending ambassadors to admonish Harold of his promise and oath, to assist him in his plea to the kingdom, he made answer, that by the death of his daughter betroth'd to him on that condition, he was absolv'd of his oath, or not dead, he could not take her now an outlandish woman, without consent of the realm; that it was presumptuously done, and not to be persisted in, if without consent or knowledge of the states, he had sworn away the right of the kingdom; that what he swore was to gain his liberty, being in a manner then his prisoner; that it was unreasonable in the duke to require or expect of him the foregoing of a kingdom, conferr'd upon him with universal favour and acclamation of the people: to this flat denial he added contempt, sending the messengers back, saith Matthew Paris, on maim'd horses. The duke thus contemptuously put off, addresses himself to the Pope, setting forth the justice of his cause, which Harold, whether through haughtiness of mind or distrust, or that the ways to Rome were stop'd, sought not to do. Duke William, besides the promise and oath of Harold, alledg'd that king Edward by the advice of Seward, Godwin himself, and Stigand the arch-bishop, had given him the right of succession, and had sent him the son and nephew of Godwin, pledges of the gift; the Pope sent duke William, after this demonstration of his right, a consecrated banner. Whereupon he having with great care and choice got an army of tall and stout soldiers, under captains of great skill and mature age, came in August to the port of St. Valerie. Mean while Harold from London comes to Sandwich, there expecting his navy; which also coming, he sails to the Isle of Wight; and having heard of duke William's preparations and readiness to invade him, kept good watch on the coast, and foot forces every where in fit places to guard the shoar. But e'er the middle of September, provision failing when it was most needed, both fleet and army return home. When on a sudden, Harold Harvager king of Norway, with a navy of more than five hundred great ships, (others lessen them by two hundred, others augment them to a thousand) appears at the mouth of Tine; to whom earl Tosti with his ships came as was agreed between them ; whence both uniting, set sail with all speed, and enter'd the river Humber. Thence turning into Ouse, as far as Rical, landed ; and won York by assault. At these tidings, Harold with all his power hastes thitherward ; but e'er his coming, Edwin and Morcar at Fulford by York, on the north-side of Ouse, about the feast of St. Matthew had given them battle ; successfully at first, but overborn at length with numbers ; and forc'd to turn their backs, more of them perish'd in the river than in the fight. The Norwegians taking with them five hundred hostages out of York, and leaving there one hundred and fifty of their own, retir'd to their ships. But the fifth day after king Harold with a great and well appointed army, coming to York, and at Stamford bridge, or Battle bridge on Darwent, assailing the Norwegians, after much blood shed on both sides, cut off the greatest part of them with Harfager their king, and Tosti his own brother. But Olave the king's son, and Paul earl of Orkney, left with many soldiers to guard the ships, surrendering themselves with hostages, and oath given never to return as enemies, he suffer'd freely to depart with twenty ships, and the small remnant of their army. One man of the Norwegians is not to be forgotten, who with incredible valour keeping the bridge a long hour against the whole English army, with his single resistance delay'd their victory ; and scorning offer'd life, till in the end no man daring to grapple with him, either dreaded as too strong, or contemned as one desperate, he was at length shot dead with an arrow ; and by his fall open'd the passage of pursuit to a compleat victory. Wherewith Harold lifted up in mind, and forgetting now his former shews of popularity, defrauded his soldiers of their due and well deserved share of the spoils. While these things thus pass'd in Northumberland, duke William lay still at St. Valerie ; his ships were ready, but the wind serv'd not for many days ; which put the soldiery into much discouragement and murmur, taking this for an unlucky sign of their success ; at last the wind came favourable, the duke first under sail awaited the rest at anchor, till all coming forth, the whole fleet of nine hundred ships, with a prosperous gale arriv'd at Hastings. At his going out of the boat by a slip falling on his hands, to correct the omen, a soldier standing by said aloud, that their duke had taken scisin of England. Landed, he restrain'd his army from waste and spoil, saying, that they ought to spare what was their own. But these are things related of Alexander and Cæsar, and I doubt thence borrow'd by the monks to inlay their story. The duke for fifteen days after landing kept his men quiet within the camp, having taken the castle of Hastings, or built a fortress there. Harold secure the while, and proud of his new victory, thought all his enemies now under foot : but sitting jollily at dinner, news is brought him, that duke William of Normandy with a great multitude of horse and foot, slingers and archers, besides other choice auxiliaries which he had hir'd in France, was arriv'd at Pevensey. Harold who had expected him all the summer, but not so late in the year as now it was, for it was October; with his forces much diminish'd after two sore conflicts, and the departing of many others from him discontented, in great haste marches to London. Thence not tarrying for supplies which were on their way towards him, hurries into Sussex (for he was always in haste since the day of his coronation) and e'er the third part of his army could be well put in order, finds the duke about nine miles from Hastings, and now drawing nigh, sent spies before him to survey the strength and number of his enemies: them, discover'd such, the duke causing to be led about, and after well fill'd with meat and drink sent back. They not over-wise, brought word that the duke's army were most of them priests; for they saw their faces all over shaven; the English then using to let grow on their upper-lip large mustachio's, as did anciently the Britons. The king laughing, answer'd that they were not priests, but valiant and hardy soldiers. 'Therefore,' said Girtha his brother, a youth of noble courage and understanding above his age, 'forbear thou thy self to fight, who are obnoxious to duke William by oath; let us unsworn undergo the hazard of battle, who may justly fight in the defence of our country; thou reserved to fitter time, mayst either re-unite us flying, or revenge us dead.' The king not hearkning to this, lest it might seem to argue fear in him, or a bad cause, with like resolution rejected the offers of duke William sent to him by a monk before the battle, with this only answer hastily deliver'd, 'Let God judge between us.' The offers were these, that Harold would either lay down the scepter, or hold it of him, or try his title with him by single combat in the sight of both armies, or refer it to the Pope. These rejected, both sides prepar'd to fight the next morning, the English from singing and drinking all night, the Normans from confession of their sins, and communion of the host. The English were in a strait disadvantagous place,[1] so that many discourag'd with their ill ordering, scarce having room where to stand, slip'd away before the onset, the rest in close order with their battel-axes and shields, made an impenetrable squadron: the king himself with his brothers on foot, stood by the royal standard, wherein the figure of a man fighting was inwoven with gold and precious stones. The Norman foot, most bowmen, made the foremost front, on their side wings of horse somewhat behind. The duke arming, and his corslet given him on the wrong side, said pleasantly, 'The strength of my dukedom will be turn'd now into a kingdom.' Then the whole army singing the song of Rowland, the remembrance of whose exploits might hearten them, imploring lastly divine help, the battle began; and was fought sorely on either

---

[1] The battle was fought near Heathfield in Sussex, at the place where now stands the town of Battle, so call'd from this day's action.

side; but the main body of English foot by no means would be broken, till the duke causing his men to feign flight, drew them out with desire of pursuit into open disorder, then turn'd suddenly upon them so routed by themselves, which wrought their overthrow; yet so they dy'd not unmanfully, but turning oft upon their enemies, by the advantage of an upper ground, beat them down by heaps, and fill'd up a great ditch with their carcasses. Thus hung the victory wavering on either side, from the third hour of day to evening; when Harold having maintain'd the fight with unspeakable courage and personal valour, shot into the head with an arrow, fell at length, and left his soldiers without heart longer to withstand the unwearied enemy. With Harold, fell also his two brothers, Leofwin and Girtha, with them the greatest part of the English nobility. His body lying dead, a knight or soldier wounding it on the thigh, was by the Duke presently turn'd out of military service. Of Normans and French were slain no small number; the Duke himself also that day not a little hazarded his person, having had three choice horses kill'd under him. Victory obtain'd (Oct. 14th, 1066), and his dead carefully buried, the English also by permission, he sent the body of Harold to his mother without ransom, though she offer'd very much to redeem it, which having receiv'd, she buried at Waltham, in a church built there by Harold.[1] In the meanwhile, Edwin and Morca, who had withdrawn themselves from Harold, hearing of his death, came to London; sending Aldgith the queen their sister with all speed to West-Chester. Aldred archbishop of York, and many of the nobles, with the Londoners, would have set up Edgar the right heir, and prepar'd themselves to fight for him; but Morca and Edwin not liking the choice, who each of them expected to have been chosen before him, withdrew their forces and returned home. Duke William contrary to his former resolution, if Florent of Worster, and they who follow him say true, wasting, burning, and slaying all in his way, or rather, as saith Malmsbury, not in a hostile but in regal manner came up to London, met at Barcham by Edgar, with the nobles, bishops, citizens, and at length Edwin and Morca, who all submitted to him, gave hostages, and swore fidelity, he to them promis'd peace and defence; yet permitted his men the while, to burn and make prey. Coming to London with all his army, he was on Christmas day solemnly crown'd in the great church at Westminster, by Aldred archbishop of York, having first given his oath at the altar in presence of all the people, to defend the church, well govern the people, maintain right law; prohibit rapine and unjust judgment. Thus the English, while they agreed not about the choice of their native king, were constrain'd to take the yoke of an outlandish conquerour. With what minds, and

[1] Giraldus Cambrensis, and Henry de Knighton say, he was not slain in the Battle: but retiring privately out of it, liv'd and dy'd an Anchoret in a cell near St. John's church in Chester.—Which is against the report of all other authentick historians.

by what course of life they had fitted themselves for this servitude William of Malmsbury spares not to lay open. Not a few years before the Normans came, the clergy, though in Edward the Confessor's days, had lost all good literature and religion, scarce able to read and understand their Latin service : he was a miracle to others who knew his grammar. The monks went clad in fine stuffs, and made no difference what they eat ; which though in itself no fault, yet to their consciences was irreligious. The great men given to gluttony and dissolute life, made a prey of the common people, abusing their daughters whom they had in service, then turning them off to the stews ; the meaner sort tipling together night and day, spent all they had in drunkenness, attended with other vices, which effeminate men's minds. Whence it came to pass, that carried on with fury and rashness more than any true fortitude or skill of war, they gave to William their conquerour so easie a conquest. Not but that some few of all sorts were much better among them ; but such was the generality. And as the long suffering of God permits bad men to enjoy prosperous days with the good, so his severity oft-times exempts not good men from their share in evil times with the bad.

If these were the causes of such misery and thraldom to those our ancestors, with what better close can be concluded, that here in fit season to remember this age in the midst of her security, to fear from like vices without amendment, the revolution of like calamities.

[Many othes corrections and additions might be made to Mr. Milton's history, if collated with Mr. Sheringham's de Gentes Anglorum, Mr. Langhorn's Antiquitates Albionenses, and other industrious and learned writers : but we have noted what is most remarkable in them, wherein they differ from Mr. Milton, or he falls short of them.]

THE LIFE AND REIGN OF
EDWARD V. & RICHARD III.

KINGS OF ENGLAND.

BY SIR THOMAS MORE.

BY the death of king Edward IV, the first prince of the York line, the inheritance of the crown descended by the right of succession to his eldest son Edward, then prince of Wales, who from that day (April 9, 1483,) was stil'd king of England, and proclaim'd such by the name of Edward V., being then about 13 years of age.[1] In his father's sickness, which was something long, and tho' lingering was judg'd mortal, necessities of state, and the peace of the nation had oblig'd that king to separate his nobles and kindred from him; which gave them an opportunity of forming new contrivances and schemes among themselves to be put in execution after his death; which, notwithstanding the king's foresight and endeavours to prevent, prov'd fatal to his son. The prince of Wales himself was sent down to Ludlow in Shropshire, that by his presence he might compose the disorders of the Welsh; who, tho' not in actual rebellion, yet were grown so unruly, and disobedient to their governors and superiors, that the magistrates with all their power, were not able to suppress the dissentions and disorders, robberies and wrongs committed by them. The wisdom of this action appear'd in the present effect it had upon them: for the Welsh, who have always been very affectionate to those princes, who have born the title of their principality, as being memorials of their ancient liberty and dominion, shewed a wonderful respect to him; and tho' but a child, were more obedient to him, than ever they were known to their ancient magistrates. The queen, who had a mighty sway over the king's affections, and never more than at this time, had so framed matters, that for the security of her son, the prince, as well as for their honour and interest, all her own kindred and relations were placed in the greatest offices about him; by which contrivance she thought to secure his right and their power, against

[1] This unfortunate prince was born in Sept. 1470. His mother, queen Elizabeth, was delivered of him in sanctuary; whither she was escap'd from the earl of Warwick, who had driven her husband king Edward out of England. The abbot and prior of Westminster were his godfathers, the lady Scroop his godmother, and the whole ceremony of his christning as mean as a poor man's child.

all her and their enemies: for the queen's brother Anthony Woodvile Lord Rivers, a wise and valiant man, was appointed his governour; and Richard lord Grey, the queen's son by her former husband, with others of her friends and kin, had other offices about him; and that London the regal seat might be kept to her son's interests, in his absence, Thomas Grey her eldest son, being created marquess Dorset, was made governour of the tower, and not only the arms of that magazine, but the king's treasure put into his hands. These things the ancient nobility of the nation, of whom Henry Stafford duke of Buckingham, and William lord Hastings, chamberlain to king Edward, were the chief, bore with much indignation, as knowing, that if the queen and her kindred were so insolent and imperious when they had a king over them, who tho' too willing to yield to their humours and desires for the queen's sake, yet kept them within some bounds of modesty and subjection, they would grow most intolerable when they had a young prince under their command, and might abuse his power as they pleas'd, to fulfil their wills, and so they should be in greater danger and contempt under the new king, than they had been under the old; tho' even by him few of them were trusted, or regarded. These presages of unhappy times, made them entertain the thoughts and resolutions of getting the prince into their power, if the king should die, and to put him under the government of the duke of Gloucester, who might justly claim that place, as the next prince of the blood, and their uncle by the father's side, and would certainly put the affairs of the nation into the right current, by honouring and entrusting the ancient nobility more. But whether they had communicated their designs to the duke of Gloucester or no, is uncertain, because he was then at York, being lately return'd from his expedition to the borders of Scotland, whither he had been sent by his brother to repress the sudden invasions of those people, who, upon the breach with Lewis XI., the French king, were grown very troublesome neighbours to the English. This duke remaining here unemploy'd, began to cast his thoughts upon the succession to the crown, and to consider, how many things made for his title, tho' his brother's children stood between it and him, in the eye of the world: which yet ought to be no hindrance to his claim, if justice and right were on his side. And first, he call'd to mind, that in the attainder of his brother George duke of Clarence, it was (Anno 17, Edv. 4) alledg'd against him, 'that to advance himself to the kingdom, and for ever to disable the king, and his posterity from inheriting the crown, he had contrary to truth, nature, and religion, viper-like destroying her who gave him life, publish'd, that king Edward was a bastard, and so no way capable to reign; and that he himself therefore was true heir of the kingdom, and the royalty and crown belong'd to him and his heirs. As also that there was a report grounded upon vehement presumptions, that the duke of Clarence himself was a bastard.' Which malicious calumnies, tho' he did not believe, and was more loath to alledge against his mother as true, yet he thought they might be thus far serviceable to him, that since both his brothers were now dead, or dying, he was the only legitimate issue of Richard duke of York ; and so unquestionably the right heir to the crown, if the issue of his brothers were either thereby, or any other ways made incapable of it. And as to the children of the duke of Clarence, they were render'd incapable of the crown by the attainder of their father, and need not that bastardy be pleaded against them. The only bar of his title was then the children of his brother king Edward, by the lady Elizabeth Grey: the marriage with whom having at first begotten a great contest, and being violently opposed by his mother the duchess of York upon this ground, because he was before married to the lady Eleanour Butler, widow of Thomas lord Butler, baron of Sudesley, and daughter of John lord Talbot earl of Shrewsbury; he resolv'd to search narrowly into the truth of it, not only to vindicate his own right, but to keep the royal line from the foul plot of an illegitimate succession. This inquiry he made by men both diligent and faithful, by whose labour he got the depositions of several persons concerning it; and among others, (as Philip de Comines relates in vita Lud. XI. c. 112 and 122) the testimony of Dr. Thomas Stillington, bishop of Bath, to this effect, according to the words of the author; 'Le evesque de Bath (lequel avoit este counseiller du roy Edward) disoit, que le dit roy avoit promis foy de marriage a une dame de Angleterre, & que il avoit nomme dame Eleanor Talbot, & que le roy avoit fait la promise entre les mains du dict evesque, & dit aussi c'est evesque, qu'avoit apres espouse, & n'y avoit, que luy, & ceux deux.' Which is thus English'd : The bishop of Bath, a privy councellor of king Edward, said, that the said king had plighted his faith to marry a lady of England, whom the bishop named the lady Eleanour Talbot, and that this contract was made between the hands of the said bishop, who said that afterwards he married them, no persons being present but they two, and he the king charging him strictly not to reveal it.' These proofs the duke caused to be drawn up into an authentick form, and consulted the most eminent doctors and proctors of the civil law, who unanimously gave their judgments, that king Edward's children were bastards, the king having another wife before their mother; and consequently that Richard duke of Gloucester was the only undoubted heir to the lord Richard Plantagenet duke of York, who was adjudged to be the true heir to the crown of this realm by authority of parliament. And thus the duke of Gloucester having cleared up his title to the crown kept it secret, till he should have a fair opportunity after his brother's death to vindicate his own right, with as little disturbance to the peace of the nation, and dishonour to his nephews, as was possible; tho' it is probable, that one Potter of Redcross-street without Cripple-gate, a servant of the duke's, who was privy to the business, unwarily discover'd it, by telling one Mistlebronke, who brought him the news of king Edward's death: 'Then,' says he, 'will my master the duke of Gloucester be king': which words tho' startling to him, yet the grounds of them not being known, made little noise, till the duke of Gloucester was on the throne.

These foundations of discord being laid, tho' privately, in the life of the father, receiv'd a perfection immediately after his death, and began with the reign of the son; tho' to satisfie the king on his death-bed the two parties had shaken hands as friends, and promis'd to forget all former injuries. For the queen, as if she had been conscious that her pride had been too great to be forgiven, presently after her husband's death, writes down to her brother the earl of Rivers to raise such a body of men, as might be sufficient to defend him against the lords, and bring her son up to London to be crown'd, that it might not be in the power of her enemies to keep him from the actual possession of the throne; which order the said earl as carefully obey'd. On the other side, the duke of Buckingham, as zealous to carry on the design of himself and his party, to take the king out of the hands of his mother's kindred, sent a trusty servant of his, named Pursival, to the city of York, to propound their design to the duke of Gloucester, and to offer him, if need requir'd, a thousand stout fellows to assist him in the effecting of it. The duke of Gloucester looking upon this tender, as the first step to his greater design, willingly comply'd with the proposal, and sending the messenger back with many thanks to his master, and other private instructions, contrived a meeting soon after about Northampton; where the two dukes, with all the lords and gentlemen their friends, and 900 men in their retinue, came at the time agreed on. Here they entered into a consultation immediately upon their arrival, and the duke of Gloucester, who was the chief man in the action, communicated the necessity and reasonableness of the undertaking, to all the lords and gentlemen assembled, in words to this effect: 'That it was neither reasonable, nor tolerable, to leave the young king their master in the hands and custody of his mother's kindred; who to engross all honour to themselves, would exclude, the rest of the nobility from their attendance on him, tho' all of them were as ready and willing to perform all the services of a good subject to him, as themselves, and many of them a far more honourable part of his kindred, than those of his mother's side, whose blood (saving that it was the king's pleasure to have it so), was very unfit to be match'd with his. But granting it allowable for the king to do as he pleased; yet that all the ancient nobility should be remov'd from the king's presence, and only the least noble left about him, is neither honourable to his majesty, nor to us, and must in the issue be both dangerous to the nation in general, and unsafe to his majesty; for will not this strangeness make the king's most potent friends either turn his utter enemies, or become very indifferent to his service, when they see their inferiors both in birth and power in greatest authority and credit with him, and themselves likely to live in disgrace for ever, because the king, being in his youth framed to the love and liking of them, and to a distaste of others, will very hardly in his riper years alter his affections. They could not but remember, that the late king Edward himself, although he was a man of age and discretion, yet was often so over-ruled by his wife and her friends, that he did many things inconsistent with his own honour, our safety, and the nation's welfare, merely to advance them and establish their power. And if the friendship of some persons had not prevail'd more with the king, sometimes, than the suits of his kindred, they had before this brought some of us to ruin, as they did some of as great degree as any of us. And though indeed those dangers are now past, yet as great are growing, if we suffer the young king, still to remain in their hands, who, we see, value not the destruction of any that stand in the way of their designs, or the road to their greatness. Will they not engross all honours, and places of trust to themselves, and whenever they have occasion, abuse his name and authority to any of our destructions? Can we imagine, that their old resentments are so quite bury'd, that they will not remember to revenge them upon the least disgust, and, now their pride is arm'd with authority, become implacable to most of us, to whom they have ever had malice enough to ruin us, and wanted nothing but what they have now, authority to vent it upon us? That these things consider'd, it was their greatest wisdom to take the young king out of their enemies hands, and not suffer things to continue in the posture they are now in any longer: for tho' indeed there appears an outward friendship for the present, which was and is the effect more of the king's desire than their own; yet we shall find, that their old enmity will revive with their power, and their long accustom'd malice will be strengthen'd with their authority, in which if we endure them once to be settled, it will not be in all our powers to oppose them effectually; and therefore now's the time to prevent all mischiefs by taking away the cause of them.' These words and persuasions moved all present to engage heartily in the business; and the duke of Buckingham and lord Hastings, who were men both of great power and interest, shew'd such a forwardness in the attempt, that all the rest were encourag'd by their example to be assistants and followers of them; and many, which were not present, were drawn in by the duke of Gloucester's letters to promise their help in the same affair, if there were further occasion.

While the lords were thus consulting, and contriving to get the king into their hands, without the knowledge or privity of the queen and her friends, the duke of Gloucester receiv'd the news, that the lord Rivers had gather'd a strong body of armed men, and with them was ready to bring up the king to London to his coronation; which unexpected report surprised them much, because it broke all their measures at once, it being impossible for them, though they had a good number of attendants, to effect their design, if he were brought to London under a strong guard; especially considering, that as on the one hand the earl of Rivers was a valiant and experienc'd soldier, so if they should gain the king by force, besides the danger of the king's person, it would look like an open rebellion. Whereupon the duke of Gloucester, and his friends, rather chose to overturn force by policy, and to that end privately order'd some of his friends, who were about the queen, to represent to her, 'That as it was no ways necessary to bring the king to London with an army of attendants, as though he were to pass through an enemy's and not his own country, so it would be dangerous to the king's person and government; for whereas now all the lords seem'd to be perfect friends, and to study nothing but the honour of the king, and the triumph of his coronation, if they see the lords about his royal person, whom so lately they thought their enemies, to gather great numbers of men armed about them in the king's name, they will immediately suspect and fear, that those men are intended not so much for the king's safety as their destruction, and so they would take themselves obliged for their own defence to raise an equal force, and fill the nation with uproar and confusion, to the danger of the king and breach of the peace; and therefore such methods of action ought carefully to be avoided, especially since her son was a child, and in the beginning of his reign.' These reasons seem'd plausible to the queen, who was not suspicious of the evil designed, and very willing to submit to anything for the good of her son, and his quiet settlement on the throne; and therefore without delay wrote letters to her brother the lord Rivers, ordering him to dismiss all her son's extraordinary attendants and guards, and hasten to London with only his own household servants and usual retinue. The duke of Gloucester also, much about the same time, sent letters to the lord Rivers, with full assurances of duty and subjection to the king his nephew, and love and friendship to himself; so that he seeing all things calm and peaceable, concurred readily with the queen's desires, and leaving his armed men behind him, came up with no greater number of followers, than was necessary to shew the king's honour and greatness. In their way about Northampton, the dukes of Gloucester and Buckingham, with their retinues, had layn some days, and hearing of the king's arrival met him at Northampton; but because that town was not big enough to hold both their companies, they advised, that the king should go forward to Stony-Stratford to lodge there, and they would stay at Northampton, inviting the lord Rivers to lodge with them, that they might enjoy his company that evening. The lord Rivers, hoping to improve his friendship with them by compliance, dismissed his company, and took his lodgings with the dukes, who feasted him that night with all demonstrations of joy, and signs of friendship, till they parted with him to his lodgings. But as soon as he was gone, the two dukes with a select number of their friends enter'd into a consultation, and spent the greatest part of the night in it: what their resolutions were, the next day's actions shew. In the morning they got up very early, and by private orders had all their servants ready to attend them, before the lord Rivers or his servants were stirring. The keys of the inn, wherein they all were, they took into their own custody; and pretending that they themselves would be the first in the morning, who should be at Stony-Stratford to attend the king, they sent a certain number of their retinue to line the way, and suffer none to enter that town till they should arrive to wait on his majesty; for the dukes were resolv'd (as it was given out) to be the first that morning who should go to the king from Northampton. All this was done without lord Rivers' knowledge or advice, who therefore when he came to hear it, was very much surpris'd at the thing, and so much the more, because neither himself, nor servants were permitted to go out of the inn. His thoughts were in a great hurry, and what the reason should be, he could not conjecture. He easily saw thro' their weak pretences, and began to fear, that his last night's cheer might prove a bait to falshood and treachery. Fly he could not if he were guilty, but not being conscious of any wrong done them, which might provoke them to revenge, he resolv'd to go to the dukes, and demand of them the reason and cause of this action, which he accordingly did: but instead of giving him an answer, they quarrell'd with him, and told him with great passion, 'That he was one of them, who had labour'd all he could to alienate the king's mind from them, and stir up a dissension between the king and his nobles, that he might bring them and their families to confusion: but now they would take care that it should not lie in his power.' The lord Rivers was an eloquent and well-spoken man, and began to make his defence calmly and coolly; but they would hear no excuses, nor suffer him to make answer, and committing him to the custody of some of their servants, till they should give further orders concerning him, they mounted their horses, and rode in haste to the king at Stony-Stratford. When they were come into the royal presence (the king being ready to mount to leave room for their companies), they alighted from their horses with all their attendants, and saluted the king upon their knees, who received them freely and favourably, not mistrusting in the least what had been done. They pretended that they came only to wait on his majesty in his journey, and to that end the duke of Buckingham call'd aloud to the gentlemen and yeomen to keep their places, and march forward. But before the king was out of the town they pick'd a quarrel with the lord Richard Gray, the queen's son and the king's half brother, charging him in the king's presence, 'That he and the marquess Dorset, with his uncle the lord Rivers, had conspir'd together to rule the king and realm while the king was in his minority; and to that end had stirr'd up divisions among the nobles, that by subduing some of them, they might destroy the rest: and for the more effectual accomplishment of this their design, the Lord Marquess had entered into the Tower of London, and had taken from thence all the king's treasure, and sent several ships to sea with it, that none might be able to oppose him.' The king, who not only was young, and unexperienc'd in state-affairs, but having been absent some time, was ignorant of such matters of fact as his brother was charged with, yet gave a very judicious answer to the accusation, 'That he could not tell what his brother the marquess had done; but in good faith, he said, he dare well answer for his uncle Rivers, and his brother Richard, that they were both innocent of any such matter, having been continually with him.' The duke of Buckingham reply'd, 'That they had kept the knowledge of their actions from his good grace,' and forthwith they arrested the said lord Grey, with sir Thomas Vaughan and sir Richard Howse in the king's presence; and then instead of going forward, return'd back again with the king to Northampton; where they displaced all such persons, who had any offices about the king, as they could not confide in, and entered into serious consultation about their farther proceedings. The king was much troubled at these dealings, and wept because he had not power to defend himself or his friends, but the lords had now obtain'd their designs, and valu'd not who took, what they did, well or ill: yet they gave the king all the respect of good subjects; and promis'd the queen's kindred that all should be well; but when they left Northampton, they sent them to divers prisons in the north for a time, and at length, tho' they pretended they should have a fair trial to answer to several misdemeanours which they had to lay to their charge, they were all brought to Pomfract castle in order to their execution.

These actions of the lords being done under a shew of friendship and carrying in them something of violence and treachery, begat a great amazement in all places where they were known, and few men construed them, as the lord's wish'd, but look'd upon them as the prologues to the king's destruction. The queen, who was particularly certify'd of the same night, that the dukes of Gloucester and Buckingham, and others of their party, whom she look'd upon as her implacable enemies, had taken her son the king, and imprison'd her brother Rivers, and son Richard Grey, with other of her friends, in places remote and unknown, fell into a bitter passion of grief, and bewailed the destruction of her child, and other friends, cursing the hour in which she credulously harken'd to the persuasions of her false friends, and by ordering her son's guards to be dismiss'd, had expos'd him and her kindred to the malice and base designs of her enemies. But since to indulge herself in her just grief, and neglect a provision for her own; and those children's safety which she had with her, would make her case worse than it was at present; therefore she resolv'd to lay aside her sorrow for the present, and get herself, the duke of York, her second son, and her five daughters, with what goods were necessary for her use into the sanctuary at Westminster; and thereupon at midnight order'd her servants, and what help could be had, to remove them with all speed thither; where being receiv'd into the Abbot's lodgings, she and her children and all her company were immediately registered for sanctuary persons, and so look'd upon themselves, as in an inviolable fortress against their enemies power or malice. The lord Hastings, who was chamberlain, was at the same time at Court, and tho' a conspirator with the lords, yet made a quite different interpretation of the lords' actions, because he being truly loyal, and heartily desiring the welfare of the king, believed, that they had no further intent, than to take him out of the government of the queen's kindred, whose insolencies were intolerable, and from whom he himself in the late reign was often in danger of his life. He was therefore much pleas'd to see the queen and her friends in such a fright, and not doubting but the nation would be much better govern'd than before, and the king much happier in the hands of the ancient nobility, rejoyced to see the downfall of the queen, and her relations, whose pride they had felt long enough in the late king's reign ; but that he might give the nobility about the court a true information of the lords action, he dispatch'd a messenger the same night to Dr. Rotherham,[1] Archbishop of York, and then Lord Chancellor, who liv'd in York Place by Westminster, to assure him, ' That the lords intentions were honourable, and for the nations welfare ; and tho' the imprisonment of the queen's kindred, and the queen's fears, who was flying in great haste and confusion into sanctuary, had no good aspect ; yet he should find that all things would in the end prove well.' The archbishop, who was awakened out of his first sleep by his servants, and something amazed at the suddenness of the news, reply'd, ' Say'st thou, that all shall be well ? I can't see what good can be expected from such demeanour. Pray tell him, that be it as well as it will, it will never be so well as we have

[1] His name was Thomas Scot, he was call'd Rotherham from the place of his birth in Yorkshire.

seen it:' and so he sent the messenger back again to his master. But the archbishop was in too great a disturbance to return to his rest; and therefore immediately rose, and calling up all his servants, went with them arm'd to the queen at her palace, and carried the great seal along with him. He found all things there in a tumult, the servants removing trunks and houshold stuff to carry them into the sanctuary: the queen he saw sitting upon the floor on matts, lamenting her own and her children's miseries and misfortunes. The archbishop, who was no ways engaged in the conspiracy against her, much compassionated her case and grief; and endeavouring to comfort her, told her the message which he had received from the lord Hastings not an hour before, by which he was assured, that matters were nothing so bad as she imagin'd, that the king was in safe hands, and doubted not but all would be well. The queen, who had an invincible odium to Hastings, as soon as she heard his name, reply'd, 'That nothing was to be believ'd that came from him, being one of them that sought the destruction of herself and her blood.' The archbishop seeing her not thus to be comforted, assur'd her for himself, that he would be constant to her; and if the lords should deal ill with the prince, and crown any other person king besides her son, he would on the morrow crown his brother the duke of York, whom she had then in sanctuary with her; 'And that, madam, says he, you may be certain of my integrity, lo! here I leave with you the great seal of England, the badge of regal power, without which nothing of moment in state affairs can be done. His father your husband gave it me, and I here return it to you to keep it for his children, and secure their right; and if I could give you any greater testimony of my loyalty, I would do it;' and so he departed to his own house in the dawning of the morning, not considering what he had done in resigning the seal. The next day the city of London was in an uproar, and divers lords and gentlemen took arms, and assembled great companies of citizens and others for their own defence, till they should see what the lords intended; for the general report was, that what was done to the lord Rivers, and the others with him, was but a blind to the people: the real design of the nobility was to keep the king from his coronation, and deprive him of his right; and this they were the more confirm'd in, because great numbers of the duke of Gloucester's servants and friends were about the city and on the Thames, who examin'd all that passed, and kept any persons from taking sanctuary. In these tumults Archbishop Rotherham, fearing lest there should be a just occasion to shew his authority, and troubl'd that he had deliver'd up the great seal to the queen, to whom it did not belong, without the king's order, sent privately for the seal again and obtain'd it. In the meantime, the lord chamberlain Hastings, whose loyalty was not question'd, and who was suppos'd not to be ignorant of the lords' intentions, went into the city to appease the tumults, and calling the lords and gentlemen together who headed the commonalty, told them, 'That tho' the suddenness of the lords' actions was surprising, because the reasons were not generally known; yet he could assure them, that the duke of Gloucester was true and faithful to his prince, of which he had given many undeniable proofs in his brother's reign, and would continue the same to his son: that the lords Rivers and Grey, and the knights apprehended with them, were imprison'd for certain conspiracies plotted against the lives of the dukes of Gloucester and Buckingham, as would appear evidently at their trials, which was design'd shortly to be had before all the lords of his majesty's council: that their taking arms in such a riotous and seditious manner would prove of very dangerous consequence to themselves, if they did not speedily lay them down, as they had without just reason or cause taken them up; and therefore he advised them to depart to their dwellings, and not pretend to judge or censure the actions of their superiors, who meant nothing but the common good, till they knew the truth of their designs, lest they themselves should be the only damages to the publick, and hinder the king's coronation, which the lords were coming up to London to effect with all convenient speed.' With these words the chamberlain so pacify'd the discontents of the citizens, that all things were for the present at quiet.

By this time the lords, who seem'd as zealous for the king's coronation as his uncle had been, and behaved themselves with such wonderful reverence and respect to the king, even from the time that he came into their hands, that he suspected no ill designs in them, were upon their march to London, which caus'd the people to be the more easie, since they thought that now they should soon discern their intentions. By the way as they pass'd, the duke of Gloucester assum'd nothing upon the account of his birth or greatness, but demean'd himself as a dutiful subject; and that he might give a demonstration to the people of the treacherous and cruel designs of the lord Rivers, and the queen's friends, against himself and the duke of Buckingham, the duke's servants shew'd the barrels of harness which they had privily convey'd in their carriages to murder them; and tho' indeed some laugh'd at the weakness of the suggestion, because if they really intended to have so used them, their harness had better been on their backs than in barrels; yet they pretended they were seized before the plot was come fully to execution, and so aggravated matters, that the common people believ'd the truth of it, and cry'd out, 'That it would be a great charity to the nation to hang them.' When the king and dukes drew near the city of London, Edmund Shaw, goldsmith, then mayor, and William White and John Matthews, sheriffs, with all their brethren the aldermen in scarlet, and 500 commoners on horseback in purple-colour'd gowns met them at Harnsey Park, and with great honour and reverence conducted him thro' the city to the Bishop of London's palace, near St. Paul's church, on the 4th of May.

In this solemn cavalcade the behaviour of the duke of Gloucester to the king was very remarkable, for he rode bare-headed before him, and often with a loud voice said to the people, 'Behold your prince and sovereign;' giving them on all occasions such an example of reverence and duty as might teach them how to honour and respect their prince; by which actions he so won upon all the spectators, that they look'd on the late misrepresentations of him as the effects of his enemies malice, and he was on all hands accounted the best, as he was the first subject in the kingdom. At the bishop's palace he did the king homage, and invited all the nobility to do the same; by which he put his loyalty out of dispute with the nobles, as he had done before with the commons. Within a few days after, a great council of the nobility met to settle the government, and choose a protector according to the usual custom in the minority of their kings, and the duke of Gloucester was without the least contradiction appointed to manage that honourable station, not only as the king's uncle, and the next prince of the blood, and a person fit for that trust, as of eminent judgment and courage; but as one that was most loyal and loving to the king, and likely to prove the most faithful in that station. By this council was the Archbishop of York much blamed for delivering the great seal to the queen, and being deprived of his councellorship, the seal was given in the beginning of June to Dr. John Russel Bishop of Lincoln, a wise and good man, and of very great experience in state affairs. Several other inferior officers of the court were displaced, and others more fit put in their room. The lord chamberlain Hastings was continued in his office, with some others whom the protector and council had no great objections against; and so the council being dissolved, the protector betook himself to his double care: 1. Of the king to content and please him, as well as educate him and crown him. 2. Of the state and people, to rule so well as might be for the king's honour and general good and welfare of the nation.

King Edward, who was now under the sole care and government of his uncle Richard duke of Gloucester, made protector by the nobility, and general approbation of the people, being displeased at the violent actions of the lords towards his mother's relations, whom not only continual converse, but nature had endear'd to him, and seeing his mother and brother in sanctuary, as if she had fear'd the same hard usage, if not worse, was not contented with the present disposition of affairs; and tho' he being young could not help what was done, yet he could not willingly submit to it. The protector, who was a very sagacious person, and shew'd all readiness to satisfy the king's will, and discharge his station well, soon discern'd the causes of the king's uneasiness, and considering how much the reasons of the king's grief reflected upon his reputation, as well as hinder'd his designs in bringing the king to his coronation (for why should the queen with her children continue in sanctuary, unless it were that she was jealous of some wrong and injury from him, who having the supream power now in his hands could only hurt her? And what a lame ceremony would the coronation be, if the queen and the king's only brother bore not a part in it, but instead of that were deterred from it), he resolv'd to remove these rubs in the way of his government and designs; and to that end calling a council, he deliver'd himself to this purpose:[1] 'Let me perish for ever if it be not my greatest, my continual care to promote the happiness and welfare of the king my nephew, and all my brother's family; being sensible, that not only the nation's, but my own ruin is the unavoidable consequence of their misfortunes: and therefore since it hath pleased you, who are the nobles of the land, and to whom it belongs chiefly to provide for the good government of it in the minority of the king, to confer that weighty employment of ruling all upon myself, as I shall always look upon myself only as the king's and your deputy, so I shall, in all difficult matters of state, look upon you as my helpers and assistants, and not dare to move one step without your council and advice, that so I may have your approbation in all I do, that it is for the good of the king and welfare of all. In the management of the station you have placed me in, I do find, that the queen's continuance in the sanctuary with her children, is such an invincible impediment in the execution of my place, that I cannot but propound the manifest inconveniences of it: and so much the rather, because I expected, that so good a settlement as your lordships had made in the last council would have remov'd her womanish fears, and she would have return'd to court to the contentment of his majesty and us all: but since she persists in her mischievous purposes, it is evident, that if fear drove her into the sanctuary, 'tis nothing but malice that keeps her there; for she, who is no impolitick woman, sees several unavoidable mischiefs redounding to the publick, and to his majesty by this her action, which had she not some ill designs she would carefully avoid. And first, what greater affront can be offer'd to you of his majesty's council, than for the queen and children to remain in sanctuary? Will not the people upon so unexpected a resolution make these inferences from it, that doubtless they are in very great danger, and that you who are in power are her implacable enemies, since neither her son's authority, nor her own and children's greatness, are sufficient to secure them, but they are forc'd to seek protection from the church, which is the asylum of the greatest criminals? And what an intolerable injury is this to you? But if you shall think fit to pass this wrong over,

---

[1] This speech did not begin with a curse, according to the copy in Holinshead, nor is it entirely the same as in Holinshead, pag. 717.

yet his majesty's discontents are not to be overlook'd, who wanting the company of his brother, with whom chiefly he uses to recreate himself, leads a melancholy and discontented life, which doubtless if not timely prevented may endanger his health; for the good state of the body does not long last usually, when the mind is disturb'd. Sorrow of mind drieth up the bones, especially in youth, and want of moderate recreation and suitable company begets a dulness and pensiveness, which brings diseases and distempers on the body, which proves fatal. Wherefore since even kings themselves must have some company, and they are too great for their subjects generally, it seems necessary that his brother, who comes nearest an equality with him, should be sent for to him, that he may refresh himself with him. And thus we may hope that the king will not only be satisfy'd and pleas'd, but we shall be freed from the ill opinion which certainly all foreign princes have of us; for as long as he continues in sanctuary, they will either censure us as cruel or tyrannical, or deride us as impotent or weak. But besides, the coronation of the king being the main thing now in agitation, how can we proceed in it with any heart or earnestness, while the queen and duke of York are in sanctuary? What sort of men shall we be thought, who at the same time we crown one brother, so terrific the other; that he is forc'd to abide at the altar of the same church for his safety. Who can with satisfaction officiate at this great ceremony, while the duke of York, whose place is next to the king, is absent from it. It is therefore my opinion, these reasons and considerations being well weighed, that some honourable and trusty person, who cannot be doubted to tender the king's wealth, and reputation of the council, and is in credit with the queen, be sent to her to demand the release of the duke of York: and, for this office, I think no person better qualify'd than the most reverend father my lord Cardinal,[1] the archbishop of Canterbury, who may be the most prevailing mediator in this matter, if he pleases to take the trouble upon him, which of his great goodness, I do believe he will not refuse for the king's sake and ours, and the wealth of the young duke himself, the king's most honourable brother, and for the comfort of my sovereign lord himself, my most dearest nephew, considering that it will be a certain means to stop the mouths of our enemies abroad, and prevent the ill-constructions of censorious persons at home, and avoid the ill consequences which arise from it, both to his majesty, and the whole realm. And tho' the cardinal may go no further in treating with the queen, than to persuade her by the best arguments of reason and necessity to yield to our desires, which his wisdom knows best how to use and apply; yet if she prove so obstinate and wilful, and will yield to no advice and counsel which he

---

[1] Cardinal Thomas Bourchier descended of the noble family of the Bourchiers earls of Essex.

can give; then 'tis my opinion that we fetch the duke of York out of that prison by force, and bring him into the king's company and presence; in which he will take such care of him, and give him such honourable treatment, that all the world shall perceive, to our honour and her reproach, that it was nothing but her frowardness and groundless suspicion, that first carried, and then kept him there. This is my judgment in this affair; but if any of you, my lords, are of contrary sentiments, and find me mistaken, I never was, nor by God's grace ever shall be so wedded to my own opinion, but I shall be ready to change it upon better reasons and grounds.'

When the protector had thus deliver'd his mind to the council, they all approv'd of his motion, as a thing good and reasonable in itself, and honourable both to the king, and the duke his brother, agreeing with him, that the archbishop of Canterbury was the fittest person, in all respects, to be a mediator between the queen and them; not doubting, but by his candour and wisdom this business might easily be effected, and the queen without more ado persuaded to deliver him. Nor did the archbishop at all refuse the office, which much became his station, being to compose a growing difference among persons of the greatest quality; but he with the lords spiritual present told the council with submission,[1] 'That as he consented to the motion that the duke of York should be brought to the king's presence out of the sanctuary by persuasions, and would himself do his best to effect it, since they had pleas'd to impose that task upon him; yet he could not by any means consent to that proposition, that if the queen refus'd to deliver him, he should be taken out of sanctuary by force; because it would be a thing not only ungrateful to the whole nation, but highly displeasing to almighty God to have the privilege of sanctuary broken, in that church, which, being at first consecrated by S. Peter, who came down above 500 years ago in person accompany'd with many angels by night to do it, has since been adorn'd with the privilege of a sanctuary by many popes and kings; and therefore as no bishop ever dare attempt the consecration of that church, so no prince has ever yet been so fierce and indevout as to violate the privilege of it: and God forbid, that any man whatsoever shall at this time, or hereafter, upon any worldly advantages or reasons, attempt to infringe the immunities of that most holy place, that hath been the defence and safety of so many good men's lives. However, he said, he hop'd they should not be driven to use such extremities, and doubted not, when the queen, who was a person of known judgment and understanding, once heard their reasons, she would for her son's sake, the king, readily yield to their desires; and if it otherwise should happen, he

[1] In Sir Thomas More's History as printed in Holinshed, p. 717, 'tis as that the Archbishop of York made this speech; and for a proof of St. Peter's descending from heaven to consecrate the church of Westminster, the good prelate affirm'd St. Peter's cope was still to be seen in the abbey.

would so perform his part, that they should be convinc'd, that there wanted no good will, or endeavour in himself, but the queen's dread, and womanish fear was the only cause of it.' The duke of Buckingham, who impatiently heard the archbishop's objection against taking the duke out of sanctuary by force, immediately resumes the discourse, and in a passion replies with an oath; 'Womanish fear, say you my lord? Nay, womanish frowardness; for I dare take it upon my soul, that she knows she has no just occasion to fear any danger to her son or herself. But as to herself, here is no man that will contend with woman, and I would to God some of her kindred were so too, and then should the contest be soon at an end with them. Yet I dare be bold to say, that none of her kindred are the less belov'd for the relation they have to her, but because of their own demerits, and for joyning with her in her malicious designs. However let it be granted, that we love neither her nor her kindred; yet there can be no just ground to infer from thence that we hate the king's brother, who tho' her son, yet is also a-kin to us; and if she desir'd his honour, as we do, and had not more regard to her own will, than her son's welfare, she would not be so obstinate, but would be as unwilling to keep him from the king's presence, as any of us are. Some of whom at least she must acknowledge to have as much wit as herself, and can't doubt of their fidelity and love to the duke, who they would be as loath should come to any harm as she herself can be, and yet they would have him from her to continue with the king, if she will tarry there; but if she pleases to come out herself with him, and her other children, and take up her habitation in such a place where they may be with honour to herself and them, every man of us shall be better content than if she sends him alone. Now if upon these grounds she refuses to deliver him, denying to follow the wisdom of them, of whose ripe judgment and fidelity she hath had good experience, it is easie to discern that it is her frowardness, and not her fear, that is the cause of it. But we will suppose that her distrusts are invincible, thro' the greatness of her fears (as what can hinder her from fearing her own shadow, if she will so much indulge her passions) we have the greater reason to take heed, how we leave the duke in her hands: for if she causelessly fear his hurt out of sanctuary, she may also fear that he may be fetch'd from thence; (for 'tis easie for her to imagin, that if we be resolv'd to have him from her, we will not value the sacredness of the place she is in; as indeed I think good men without sin might somewhat less regard them than they do) and so for greater security convey him out of the realm, which if she should be so lucky as to effect (and without any great difficulty it may be done) all the world will scorn and deride us, saying, that we are a wise sort of counsellors about the king, to suffer his brother to be cast away under our noses. And therefore I assure you, for my part, I am for fetching him away against her will, rather than by humouring her fears and peevishness, give her an opportunity of conveying him away. And yet I shall be bold to assert, that I do not break any privilege of sanctuary, but rather rectify one of the abuses of it : for tho' indeed sanctuaries, as they were appointed and used under the Jewish law, were, and still may be of very good use in several cases, as to be a refuge for such men as the chance of sea, or their evil debtors have brought to poverty, to protect them from the cruelty of their creditors ; and because the title to the crown of these realms had often come in question, in which contests each side counts the other traitors, and the conquering side, tho' sometimes the worst rebels, treats the adverse party as such, it is necessary there should be a refuge in this case to the unfortunate : but as for thieves and murderers, whereof these places are full, and who seldom leave their trade when they have once begun, it is an horrid shame that any sanctuary should save them ; and especially wilful murderers, whom God himself commands to be taken from the altar, and put to death. Yet if we look into our sanctuaries, as now they are managed, how few are there whom necessity of their own defence, or their misfortunes, have driven to take shelter there ? But on the other side, what numbers are there in them of thieves, murderers, and malicious and heinous traitors, and especially in the two chief ones in this city, the one at the elbow, and the other in the very midst of it ? Insomuch that if the good they do were balanc'd with the evil, we shall find 'twere better for us to be without them, unless such as are in power would effectually correct their abuses, and amend them. And indeed, 'tis a gross shame not to be endur'd, to see St. Peter made a patron of thieves, prodigals, knaves, and whores ! Surely neither God, nor that apostle can approve of these abuses ; and therefore they may be reformed with thanks of both. Let sanctuaries then continue in God's name in their full force, as far as religion and reason will permit, and I am sure no lawful privilege granted to them can hinder us from fetching the duke of York from thence, where he neither is, nor can be a sanctuary-person. A sanctuary serveth to defend the body of man, who is in danger from not only some great, but unlawful hurt ? And what danger is that duke in ? Is not the king his brother, and all we his special friends ? As he has never done any man an injury, so no man designs him any wrong, and then what grounds can there be for him to be left in sanctuary ? Besides, men come not to a sanctuary, as to baptism by godfathers, but they must ask themselves if they will have it ; for none but such as can allege there just fears and dangers ought to be admitted thither. And how can the duke of York be justly entertain'd or kept there, who cannot thro' his infancy require it ; and if he were sensible of the place he is in, would rather desire to be released from it : so that I think with the clergy's leave, 'tis no breach of privilege, if he and many others be taken by force out of it. And to convince them of it more fully, let me ask them a few questions. If a man go into sanctuary with another man's goods, may not the king, leaving his body at liberty, take them out of the sanctuary, and restore them to the right owner? Can either pope or king privilege a man from paying debts that is able to pay them?' Several of the clergy present agreed, that by the laws of God and the church, a sanctuary-man may be deliver'd up to pay his debts, or restore stolen goods, his liberty being allow'd him to get his living by his labour. Then the duke said, 'There's the same reason to do it, if a man's wife ran from him to sanctuary, or a child take sanctuary because he will not go to school, and many like cases. And therefore I conclude, that since he can be no sanctuary-man who hath no discretion to desire it, (for I never yet heard of sanctuary-children) nor malice to deserve it, whose life and liberty can in no wise be in danger, he that taketh such an one out of sanctuary to do him good, breaks no privilege of that holy place.'

When the duke had finish'd this long discourse, it was generally agreed by all the lords, both spiritual and temporal,[1] that if the queen would not deliver up the duke by persuasions, he should be forced from her by the king's authority: but it being judg'd convenient that all fair means should be first try'd, the cardinal, with several lords to accompany him, was sent into the sanctuary to the queen; the protector, and the rest of the council going into the Star-Chamber at Westminster to expect the event. When the cardinal was come into the queen's presence, after all dutiful salutations, he deliver'd to her the cause of his coming, saying, 'That he was with those other lords, sent by the protector, and the privy council to her majesty, to let her know, how much her detaining of the duke of York in that place was scandalous to the publick, and dislik'd by the king his brother; it being an action that must needs produce ill effects: that the king himself was much grieved at it, and the council offended, because it look'd as if one brother was in danger from the other, and could not be preserved by the other's life: that it would be a very great comfort to his majesty to have his natural brother in company with him; nor would it be of less advantage to the young duke himself, because it would confirm and strengthen their loves to be brought up together, as well at their books, as sports: that in the king's court the duke could only live answerable to his state and condition: that it would much please the protector and council to send him to the king's presence, and in effect might prove of no small advantage to her friends, that were in prison. Upon which accounts, as he was sent by his majesty and council to demand the duke of her, to be brought to his brother; so

[1] Several of the bishops were against fetching him out by force.

he could not but earnestly entreat her to comply with a thing so very reasonable, and every way convenient.' The queen, who was of a sharp wit and graceful speech, answer'd the cardinal; and said, 'My lord, I cannot deny, but it is very convenient that my son, the duke, should be in the company of his brother the king as well for society, as love's-sake: but since they are both so young, as that it is the most suitable for them to be under the government of their mother; it is better for the king to be with me here, than that I should send the duke to him: tho' was it really otherwise, that duty obliged the duke to go to him, yet necessity in this case creates a dispensation, because he hath been of late so sorely afflicted with diseases, and being not perfectly recover'd is in so great a danger of a relapse (which generally physicians say is more fatal than the first sickness) that I dare trust no earthly person as yet with the care of him: for tho' I doubt not, but that he might have such about him as would do their best to preserve his health, yet since I have ordered him all along, and am his mother, it must be allow'd by all men, that as I am the most able, so I shall be the most affectionately careful and tender of him. And for these reasons, I hope both the king and his council will dispense with his absence awhile, till he is perfectly recovered, and in health; and before that, I can't endure to hear of parting with him.'

The cardinal hearing this reply, answer'd; 'No man, good madam, doth deny but that your majesty is the fittest person to take care of all your children, and I am sure the council will be very glad to hear that it is your pleasure so to do: yea, they would beg it of you, provided you would be contented to do it in such a place as is consistent with their, and your own honour; whereas, if you resolve to tarry in this place, then they judge it more convenient, that the duke should be with the king at liberty, to the comfort and satisfaction of them both, tho' with some small danger to his health; than to remain in sanctuary, to the dishonour of the king, duke himself, and the whole council: for it is not always so necessary that the child should be with the mother, but there may be reasons sometimes of taking him from her, and that for the best, as your majesty knows there was, when your eldest son, then prince of Wales, and now king, was sent to keep his court at Ludlow, for his own honour and the good order of the country, of which your majesty was so well convinced, that you seem'd contented with it.'

The queen grew a little warm, and smartly retorted, 'Not so very well contented neither at that separation; tho' the case is much different now: for the prince was in good health, the duke is now sick; for tho' the height of the distemper is past, yet he is weak, and not so fully recovered, but that without great care he may fall into a relapse; in which condition, while he remains, I wonder that the protector and council should be so earnest to have him from me, since if the child should grow sick again and miscarry, they would incur the censures of some ill-dealings with him. And whereas you say that it is dishonourable to my child, and to them, that he remain in this place, I think the contrary ; for certainly 'tis most for their honour to let him abide, where no man can doubt but he will remain safest, and that is here so long as I continue here : and I do not intend to leave this place and endanger my life with my friends, who, I would to God were rather in safety here with me, than I were in hazard with them.' 'Why, madam,' (saith the lord Howard) 'do you know any reason, that they are in danger?' 'No truly,' (said she roundly) 'nor why they should be in prison neither, as they now be : but I have great cause to fear, lest those, who have not scrupled to put them in prison without cause, will as little value to destroy them without law or right.' Upon these words, the cardinal wink'd upon the lord to put an end to that discourse ; and then added himself, 'That he did not doubt, but that those lords, who being of her kindred remained under arrest, would upon a due examination of matters, discharge themselves well enough of any accusation alleged against them : and as to her own royal person, there neither was, nor could be any kind of danger.' 'How shall I be certain of that (said the queen)? Is it, that I am innocent? It doth not appear that they are guilty. Is it, that I am better beloved of their enemies? No ; but rather, they are hated for my sake. Is it, that I am so nearly related to the king? They are not much further off : and therefore since it seems to me, that as I am in the same cause, so I am in like danger ; I do not intend to depart out of this place. And as for my son, the duke of York, I propose to keep him with me till I see how businesses will go ; for the more greedy and earnest some men are to have him into their hands without any substantial cause, the more fearful and scrupulous am I to deliver him.' 'And the more suspicious you are, madam,' (answer'd the cardinal) 'the more jealous are others of you, lest under a causeless pretence of danger, you should convey him out of the nation ; and so if they permit him to remain with you now, it shall not be in their power to have him for the future. Wherefore it is the opinion of many of the council, that there is a necessity of taking the duke of York immediately into their care and government, and since he can enjoy no privilege by sanctuary, who has neither will to require it, nor malice or offence to need it, they judge it no breach of sanctuary, if you finally refuse to deliver him by fair means, to fetch him out of it : and I assure you, madam, that the protector, who bears a most tender love to his nephews ; and the council, who have an equal care and respect for your children, will certainly set him at liberty, unless you resign him to us lest you should send him away.' 'Ay,' (says the queen) 'hath the protector his uncle such a love for him, that he fears nothing more than that he should escape his hands? I unfeignedly declare, that it never so much as entered into my thoughts to send him out of this place into any foreign parts, partly because his health will not bear any journeys, and partly because, tho' I should not scruple to send him into any part of the world, where I knew him out of all danger, yet I do not think any place more secure than this sanctuary, which there never was any tyrant so devilish, who dare violate ; and I trust that the Almighty God will so awe the minds of his, and my enemies, as to restrain them from offering violence to this holy place. But you tell me, that the lord protector and the council are of opinion that my son can't deserve a sanctuary, and therefore may not be allow'd the privileges of it : he hath found out a goodly gloss, as if that place which can protect a thief, or wicked person, is not of greater force to defend the innocent, because he is in no danger, and therefore can have no need of it ; which is an opinion as erroneous as hellish. But the child, you say, can't require the privilege of a sanctuary, and therefore since he has no will to choose it he ought not to have it : who told the protector so ? Ask him, and you shall here him require it. But suppose it were really so that he could not ask it, or if he could, would not, but would rather choose to go out ; I think it is sufficient that I do require it, and am registred a sanctuary person, to make any man guilty of breaking sanctuary to take my son out of it by force and against my will : for is not the sanctuary a protection in that case as well for my goods as myself? No man can lawfully take my horse from me, if I stole him not, or owe nothing ; and surely much less my child. Besides by law, as my learned council sheweth me, he is my ward, because he hath no lands by descent holden by knights service, but only by soccage, and then I being the guardian of my son by law, no man can take him by force from me without injustice in any place, and without sacrilege from hence. And upon this right I do insist, and require the privilege of sanctuary for him, as my pupil and infant, to whom alone by law the care of him belongs : and if this triple cord may be broken, I mean, the right which I have to keep him with me by the law of man, as his guardian ; by the law of nature, as his mother ; and by the law of God, as being in sanctuary with him ; if all this be not enough to secure him from any human force, I think nothing under heaven can : but I do not despair of safety where I have always found so much. Here was I brought to bed of my son who is now king, and tho' his enemy reigned, and might have used the same or like pretences to have taken us both from sanctuary, yet he did not ; and I hope no man will have the boldness to act contrary to all former precedents, but the place that protected one son, will be as great a security to the other : for to be plain with you, my lord, I fear to put him into the protector's hands, because he

.h his brother already, and since he pretends to be the next heir to the crown after them, notwithstanding his sisters, if they any ways miscarry, his way to the throne lies plain and easy to him. Now this is so just a cause of fear, that even the laws of the land teach me it, which as learned men tell me, forbids every man the guardianship of them, by whose death they become heirs to their inheritance ; and if the law is so careful of such as have the least inheritance, how much more ought I to be fearful that my children come not into his power, who by their death will have the kingdom for his inheritance. By these reasons I am confirmed in my resolution of keeping my son in sanctuary with me, and my right so to do, and think them so far to out-balance the protector's frivolous reasons of keeping his brother company, and being dishonourable to him, that I cannot alter my mind : for I have reason to think that whoever he proves a protector to, he will prove a destroyer to them, if they be once in his hands and power. I know the protector and council have power enough, if they have will, to take him and me from this place ; but whosoever he be that shall dare to do it, I pray God send him shortly need of a sanctuary, but no possibility to come to it.'

The cardinal seeing the queen grow more and more passionate by discoursing, and to reflect sharply upon the protector, which he was unwilling to hear, because he believed them inconsiderate effects of passion, thought it time to break off arguing with her, and therefore to bring all things to a conclusion, said unto her ; ' Madam, I will not dispute the matter longer with you : it is equal to me, whether you deliver him, or not. I am with these lords, but the messenger to know your resolution, and beg you will but tell us plainly, whether you will, or will not deliver him to us? For tho' if you resign him to us, I durst pawn my own body and soul to you for his safety ; yet if you deny it, I will immediately depart and finish my trust, resolving never to engage in the matter again, since I see you so resolute in your own judgment, as if you thought both me, and all others lack'd either wit or honesty ; wit, in that we, not perceiving the protector's ill designs, were made the tools of his wicked craft ; honesty, in that knowing his intentions we have labour'd to bring your son into the protector's hands to destroy him ; an execrable treason, which as ourselves abhor, so we dare boldly say was far from the protector's thoughts, and cannot be imputed to any in this case, but you must brand the whole council with short-sighted advice and disloyalty to their prince.'

These words of the cardinal's being peremptory and short, much amused the queen, being put to it on a sudden to resolve whether she would send him, or no. The cardinal she saw ready to depart, and the protector and council were near she knew ; what to do she could not tell: she fear'd that by delivering him, she cast him into the mouth of ruin; and by keeping him, she did but provoke the protector and council to be more rough and severe with them both. She saw there was no way to save him from the protector's hands, but by conveying him out of his knowledge or power; which tho' she wish'd, yet she had no way to effect it: wherefore she resolv'd to make the best use of necessity, and since the protector must have him, take the best way to secure him in his hands. She consider'd, that her fears were but grounded on vehement presumptions, and therefore hop'd things might not prove so bad as she imagin'd. She could not doubt of the cardinal's sincerity and loyalty to her son, and tho' she indeed fear'd he might be deceiv'd, yet she did not believe either he, or the lords present, would be any ways accessory to his destruction: and for these reasons she thought it better to deliver him to them, who were ready to pawn their honour and lives for his security, and would therefore look upon themselves engaged for his safety, than suffer him to be taken from her; and thereupon taking her son, the duke of York, in her hand, she led him to the cardinal and lords, and with great earnestness said to them, 'My lord cardinal, and you my lords, I am not so opinionated of myself, or ill-advised concerning you, as to mistrust either your wisdom or fidelity, as I shall prove to you by reposing such trust in you, as, if either of them be wanting in you, will redound to my inexpressible grief, the damage of the whole realm, and your eternal shame and disgrace: for lo! here is my son, the person whom you desire; and tho' I doubt not but that I could keep him safe in this sanctuary from all violence; yet here I resign him into your hands. I am sensible that I run great hazards in so doing, no whit less than my fears suggest; for I have some so great enemies to my blood, that if they knew where any of it lay in their own veins, they would presently let it out; and much more in others, and the nearer to me the more zealously. Experience also convinces us all, that the desire of a kingdom knows no kindred. The brother in that case hath been the destruction of the brother, and the son of his father; and have we any cause to think the uncle will be more tender of his nephews? Each of these children are the other's defence while they are asunder; if one be safe they are both secure; but being both together they are in great danger: and therefore as a wise merchant will never adventure all his goods in one ship, so it looks not so politickly in me to put them both under the same hazards. But notwithstanding all this (whether rightly foreseen or no, I leave you to think on, and prevent). I do here deliver him, and his brother in him to your keeping, of whom I shall ask him again at all times before God and the world. I am confident of your fidelity, and have no reason to distrust your wisdom, power, or ability to keep him, if you will make use of your resolution when it is required; and if you are unwilling to do that, then I pray you leave him still here with me:

and that you may not meet with more than you did expect, let me beg of you, for the trust which his father ever reposed in you, and for the confidence I now put in you, that as you think I fear too much, so you would be cautious that in this weighty case you fear not too little; because your credulity here may make an irrecoverable mistake.' Having thus spoken, she turn'd to the child, and said to him, 'Farewell, mine own sweet son, the Almighty be thy protector: let me kiss thee once more before we part, for God knows when we shall kiss again;' and then having kissed him, she blessed him, and turn'd from him and wept, and so went her way, leaving the child with the lords weeping also for her departure.

The cardinal and lords having obtain'd their desire thus, and gotten the duke of York from his mother, immediately led him to the Star-Chamber, where the protector and lords of the council staid in expectation of him. The protector receiv'd him with all the seeming kindness and respect that was due to him, as the king's brother and his nephew; and taking him in his arms kissed him, and said, 'Now welcome my lord with all my very heart;' and the same day carried him to the king his brother, who was at the bishop of London's palace near St. Paul's Church. Here he left them a few days together; and because all things were in a great forwardness for the coronation, which he was zealous to promote, he caused the king and the duke his brother to be remov'd to the Tower, the usual place from whence that solemnity began, with much pomp and state. But now the protector was at a stand how to proceed: he look'd upon himself as the lawful king of these realms, by the judgment of such as were best able to determine such doubts; but yet since his brother's children were generally presumed the true heirs, and their illegitimacy not understood, or disregarded, he was afraid to claim his right against the common opinion, and yet as loath to throw it up himself, as he must do by crowning his brother's son. There was almost a necessity the coronation should go forward; it had proceeded so far, that the nation would grumble extreamly at the expence if it were now laid aside; and on the other side, if his nephew were crown'd he must give up his right, and not only deprive himself but his children: wherefore he resolv'd with himself to seem as earnest as ever in carrying it on, and to that end, appointed a council of such lords as he knew to be most faithful to the king his nephew, of whom the lord Hastings the chamberlain, and lord Stanley were the chief, to assemble '*de die in diem*' at Baynard's Castle to consult and contrive the ways and ceremonies for the coronation of his nephew; but in the mean season he contriv'd secretly to make known his own title to certain persons that he could confide in, and by delaying the coronation try how far his own interests might be advanced, that he might obtain his right peaceably and quietly; but being sensible how great prejudices he was to encounter with on all hands, he knew he must proceed very warily in it. The duke of Buckingham in all his motions hitherto had been his chief friend and assistant. He in a manner had made him protector, and it would be such a disobligation if he should not make use of him in his councils, that he certainly would turn his enemy, and being of such mighty interest would pull him down, as he had set him up. And yet he could hardly hope for any encouragement from him; because tho' the duke was a malecontent in the days of the late king, yet he seemed very loyal to his son, as if he had buried the enmity to his father in his grave. But the protector knew old enmity is easily reviv'd, and to prepare the duke of Buckingham for his designs, he suborn'd certain persons about the duke to represent to him the king's displeasure for imprisoning his mother's kindred, and into what a miserable dilemma he had run himself by that action; for if they were released they'd bear him an immortal grudge, and if they were put to death, he was sure to incur the king's anger so much, that he could hope for nothing but misfortunes on all hands; for the king did not refrain from such expressions as shew'd, that whenever he had power he would revenge it upon him to the utmost. These relations struck him with a fear of danger, and predispos'd him to lay hold upon any opportunity of securing himself; which the duke of Gloucester, who laid the train, soon offer'd him; for a little after inviting him to a conference, he desired him to assist him in taking upon him the crown of England as his right, shewing him the judgment of the civil lawyers concerning the illegitimacy of his brother's children, and promising, as the reward of his faithful services to him, that his son should marry the duke's daughter; that he would give him the earldom of Hereford with all the appurtenances, which tho' his inheritance, yet had been unjustly kept from him by his brother; and lastly, that he would allow him a large share of king Edward's treasure, and so much of the wardrobe as should furnish his house, and settle upon him and his posterity the office of the high-constable of England, which his ancestors by descent for many generations had enjoy'd.

The duke of Buckingham was not hard to be won to engage in such an action as secur'd him from his present fears, and afforded a prospect of so much gain and advantage, and so became a zealous actor for the protector in making him king; for he soon brought many of his friends into the same design, and with the protector constituted a council, which sat at Crosbye's Place, the protector's mansion house, to contrive the most artificial and politick ways to settle the crown upon his head: but they were to meet very secretly and privately.

This council had not sat long, but both their persons and their actions were discerned: for cardinal Bourchier archbishop of Canterbury, Thomas Rotherham archbishop of York, John Morton bishop of Ely, the lord Stanley, lord Hastings, and other persons of quality, who were busie to order the coronation, perceiv'd that, notwithstanding their endeavours, matters mov'd slowly, and they saw cause to suspect contrary motions.

The common people began to murmur at the delays of the coronation, and talk'd as tho' there were some bad designs on foot, tho' no man could guess at what was really intended; but it was generally look'd upon as a bad omen that the protector took upon him a state and magnificence above his place, and would endure none but his own servants about the king, who gave an unkind welcome to all persons, that either desir'd to see the king out of curiosity, or wait on him out of duty; as tho' they would tell men that they must seek the king elsewhere, viz., at their master's palace, which was soon so well understood by such as expected any honours and preferments at court, that the protector was flatter'd and caress'd as king, while his nephew was little regarded, and bore only an insignificant name.

These actions increased the jealousie of the lords who sat at Baynard's Castle to direct the coronation; and the lord Stanley, who was a wise and sagacious man, began to declare openly to his brethren, 'That he much dislik'd these doings, and could not believe that two different councils could produce any good effects: we are conscious of the loyalty and integrity of our actions; but who knows what the cabal at Crosbye's Place talk of, and contrive? I fear, what we are building, they are plucking down; and unless we could unite, or know their councils, ours will be in vain.' 'Peace, my lord,' said the lord Hastings, 'never fear or misdoubt any thing; I durst assure you upon my life all's well, or at least nothing ill is intended against us: for while one man is there, who is never absent, I am sure there can be nothing propounded which shall sound ill to me, but it will be in my ears as soon as it is out of their mouths almost.' This the lord Hastings meant of one Catesby a lawyer, who was his special confident, and being put into a considerable trust in the counties of Leicester and Northampton, where this lord's interest and power lay, merely by his means, was reputed by him so faithful and grateful, that he would neither do, nor suffer to be done any things injurious to his patron: which indeed he had great reason to have done, but he much deceiv'd him, as will after appear, and so was the chief instrument of working the protector's will and aims; for the lords generally saw so many signs of distrust, that had they not rely'd entirely upon the lord Hastings's word, whom they knew firm and loyal, they had all departed every man to his own country and provided for their own safety, which had certainly broken all the protector's measures; for they were men of great power and interest with the people, and could easily have kept matters in the right current had they been at home; but Catesby carrying all fair to Hastings, and he persuading them that nothing could be done amiss till he should know it and advertise them of it, they trusted to him, and denying their own senses almost to construe all things for the best, laid themselves open to ruin, and made way to the protector's designs, which both himself and his council were vigilant to improve.

The former jealousies of the council at Baynard's Castle were soon known to the protector and the duke of Buckingham, and tho' they would not seem to be sensible of it, yet they took up resolutions with themselves either to win them over to their side, or if not, to secure them from being their enemies, and to this end they shew'd great favour to the lord Hastings, who much influenc'd the actions of all the rest, and kept him much in their company, hoping by familiarity and friendly endearments to dispose him to a compliance with their designs, which they not long after caus'd Catesby his familiar acquaintance to propound to him, but at some distance, lest his refusal should betray all; for if they could gain him, they were sure of the greater part of the rest. Catesby, who now had forgotten all former obligations, and was courting greater favours, readily undertook the employment, and coming to the lord Hastings, who had not yet the least mistrust of him, after much other discourse about the present circumstances of affairs, asks his opinion about the title and claim that the protector had to the crown; insinuating, that if it might lawfully be done, it would be better that an experienc'd person and a brave commander should rule than a child. The lord Hastings, who was firmly loyal to king Edward's children, presuming upon Catesby's fidelity, freely open'd his mind to him without any circumlocutions, and having shew'd him what jealousies the council had of the protector's actions, with indignation expressed his utter dislike of it in words to this effect: 'That he had rather see the death and destruction of the protector and duke of Buckingham, than the young king depriv'd of the crown; and that if he discern'd any designs that way in any persons whatsoever, he would engage his utmost power and ability against them.' These words, which 'tis believed the lord Hastings would never have spoke, had he suspected[1] either the mission, or treachery of Catesby, were carried to the protector immediately, and represented to him not with the mollifying terms of a friend, but aggravations of an enemy, because he hop'd by his death and the protector's favour, which for this ill office alone he had reason not to doubt of, to obtain most of the rule and trust, which that lord had in his country, and so his ruin would be his own making.

The protector received the account of Hastings aversion to his designs with much trouble and regret, not for the disappointment only, but because he had a great love for him, who had always been his friend, and had done him many kindnesses in his brother's days,

[1] Sir Thomas More makes it a doubt whether he spoke the words or not; or indeed, whether Catesby try'd him or not.

and therefore engaged Catesby to win him, if possible : but Catesby willing to see his downfall, represented him so irreconcilable to his proceedings, that he chang'd the protector's love into hatred to him, and made him lay hold upon any slight pretences to take away his life, without which he saw he must meet with a great impediment in the road of his ambition, and so the way was agreed upon in this manner. The protector call'd a great council at the Tower on Friday the 13th of June, on pretence of concluding all things for the coronation, which drew on apace, the pageants being making day and night at Westminster, and victuals killed ready for it. The lords of this council assembled early in the morning, and sat close to their business to settle everything for that solemnity.

The protector came about nine o'clock to them, and having saluted all the lords very courteously, excus'd himself for coming to them so late, saying merrily, that he had played the sluggard this morning. Then he sat down and discoursed a while with them about the business in hand, and was very pleasant and jocose in all his speeches. Among other things more serious he by the bye said to the bishop of Ely, 'My lord, you have very good strawberries in your garden at Holborn, I desire you to let us have a dish to dinner.' 'Gladly, my lord, will I do that, (quoth the bishop) I wish I had some better thing as ready for your service as they ;' and thereupon sent his servant in all haste for a dish of strawberries. A little after this, the protector obliging them to go on in their councils, requested them to dispense with his absence a-while, and so departed.

In the space of a little more than an hour he return'd again, but with such an angry countenance, knitting his brows, frowning and biting his lips, that the whole council were amaz'd at the sudden change. Being set down, he said nothing for a good while, but at length spoke with great concern, and ask'd them this question, 'What punishment do they deserve who had plotted his death, who was so near in blood to the king, and by office the protector of the king's person and realm ?' This question he had raised out of Catesby's account of the lord Hastings's words and discourse, which he so represented to him, as if he had wish'd and contriv'd his death. The lords of the council were much startled at it, and thinking with themselves of whom he meant it, return'd no answer. The lord Hastings who was always familiar with him, and thought this general silence not respectful, reply'd, 'That they deserv'd to be punish'd as heinous traitors, whosoever they were.' 'Then,' said the protector, 'and that hath that sorceress my brother's wife, (meaning the queen, but disdaining to call her so) with others her accomplices endeavour'd to do.' These words begat fresh fears and disturbances among them ; because they most of them favour'd the queen : but Hastings was well enough content that the crime was not laid upon any that he lov'd better, tho he lik'd not that the protector had not communicated it to him, as he had done his designs to put the queen's kindred to death: (which was by his advice and approbation to be done that day at Pomfret Castle.) The protector still went on in his complaints, and said, 'See, in what a miserable manner that sorceress, and Shore's wife, with others their associates have by their sorcery and witchcraft miserably destroy'd my body:' and therewith unbuttoning his left sleeve, shew'd them his arm fleshless, dry, and wither'd, saying, 'Thus would they by degrees have destroy'd my whole body, if they had not been discover'd and prevented, in a short time.' This proof, which the protector thought to give of his accusation, convinc'd the council that he had only a mind to quarrel with them, for they all knew that his arm was never otherwise, and that as the queen was too nice to engage in any such foolish enterprize, so if she had done it, she would not have made Shore's wife, whom of all women she most hated, because she was her husband's best-beloved concubine, one of her council.

The lord Hastings, who from king Edward's death had kept Shore's wife (for whom he had a great kindness in the king's life, but in reverence to him forbore her) was inwardly troubled to hear her, whom he lov'd, and knew to be innocent of any such thing, so highly and unjustly accused, and because he had made the first answer to the duke's question, he took himself obliged to return as modest an answer as he could to his accusation; and therefore said, 'Certainly my lord, if they have indeed done any such thing, they deserve to be both severely punish'd.' But this answer discover'd the lord Hastings's opinion so much, that he thought the accusation false and forged, that the protector in anger catch'd hold of his words and said, 'Do you answer me with ifs and ands as if I charg'd them falsely? I tell you, they have done it, and thou hast joyn'd with them in this villany;' and therewith clapped his fist down hard upon the board, at which sign several men in arms rush'd into the room, crying, 'treason, treason.' The protector seeing them come in, said to the lord Hastings, 'I arrest thee, traitor.' 'What me, my lord,' said Hastings? 'Yea, thou traitor,' said the protector. Whereupon he was taken into their custody. In this bustle, which was all before contriv'd, a certain person struck at the lord Stanley with a pole-ax, and had certainly cleft him down, had not he been aware of the blow and sunk under the table: yet he was wounded so on the head that the blood ran about his ears.

Then was the archbishop of York, bishop of Ely, and lord Stanley, with divers other lords who were thought averse to his designs, imprison'd in several places in the Tower: and the Lord Hastings order'd forthwith to confess and prepare himself for his death, for the protector had sworn by St. Paul that he would not dine till his head was off,

It was in vain to complain of severity, or demand justice, the protector's oath must not be broken: so he was forc'd to take the next priest that came, and make a short confession, for the common form was too long for the protector's stomach to wait on, and being immediately hurried to the green by the chappel within the Tower, his head was laid on a timber-logg which was provided for repairing the chappel, and there stricken off. His body and head was carried to Windsor, and there buried by his master king Edward IV. late deceased, it being very convenient that he should have a place next him at his death, who had lost his life for his unmovable loyalty to his children.

The death of this great lord, as it was sudden and unsuspected, so it may seem to have been particularly regarded by heaven, from whence he had many omens of it given him either to avoid it or prepare for it, if he had had but wisdom to take a due notice of them; which are worth a particular relation, that we may see the care providence has of men in imminent dangers.

The night before his death the Lord Stanley had a fearful dream, in which he thought that a wild boar with his tushes had so wounded his own and the lord chamberlain's head, that the blood ran about both their shoulders. This dream had more than an usual impression upon him, and because he interpreted the dream of the protector, who gave the boar for his arms, and the wounds and blood from their heads of some imminent danger of their lives, he resolv'd no longer to tarry within reach of his power, but ordering horses to be got ready, sent his chamberlain to the Lord Hastings at midnight to acquaint him with his dream, and encourage him to take horse as fast as he could, and with him secure himself, for with swift horses they could get near their friends by morning.

The lord Hastings, tho' awaked out of his sleep, yet being naturally a man neither melancholy nor superstitious, receiv'd the message with a smile; and said to him, 'Doth my lord, your master, give so much credit to such trifles as dreams, which are usually the effect of our fears or cares? Pray tell him, that it is plain witchcraft to believe in such dreams, which if they may be allowed foretellers of things to come, yet are so uncertain, that we may do ourselves more harm than good in following them: for who could assure him, that if there is any real danger to be feared from the boar, we shall not fall into it rather by flying than tarrying? For if we should be taken and brought back (as might very well happen) we should give the boar just occasion to goar us; for our flight would be such an argument of some guilt, that we could hardly avoid it, and to allege a dream as the cause, would make us ridiculous to all men: wherefore if there were danger, as indeed there is none unless in his causeless fears, it is rather in flying than tarrying; and if we must fall into it one way or other, I had rather that men should see it to be from others falsehood, than my guilt or cowardice: and therefore go to thy master, and commend me to him, and bid him be merry and fear nothing: for I can assure him, that there is as little danger from the man he means as from my own right hand.' 'God grant it may be so' (says the messenger) and so departed. The gentleman brought the message to his lord, and made him forget his resolution; tho' with what mischief to himself the event proved.

Other ominous presages he had of his death that morning, which his security would not suffer him to take notice of. Before he was up from his bed (where he had lain all night with Shore's wife) there came to him Sir Thomas Howard, son of the lord Howard, to call him as he pretended, and to accompany him to the council; but he was really sent by the protector to persuade him to come if he should not intend it, or if he design'd it to hasten him; which tho' he manag'd artificially enough, yet being of the protector's cabinet council he was suspicious, and in the way as they passed along, he gave the Lord Hastings such an odd interruption, in his discourse with a priest which he met by the way, by telling him, tho' merrily, 'That he wonder'd he would talk so long with a priest, he had no occasion for one, as yet,' that he might easily have suspected he knew that he should have need of one soon: but he was a loose and careless man, and regarded it not.

In the way also as he passed from his house to the Tower, his horse that he was accustom'd to ride, stumbled with him twice or thrice so dangerously that he had almost fallen; which thing, tho' it happens almost daily to persons who fall into no mischance, yet of old it was accounted a certain presage of some misfortune. Also when he came to the Tower-Wharf, within a stone's cast of the place where his head was cut off a few hours after, he met with a pursevant of his own name call'd Hastings, who having met him in the same place, when he lay under king Edward's displeasure thro' the accusation of the lord Rivers the queen's brother, and was in great danger of his life, put him in mind of his former danger, and thereupon he fell into a discourse with him about it and said, 'Ah Hastings! dost thou remember, when I once met thee in this place before with an heavy heart?' 'Yea, my lord,' (said he) 'very well, and thanks be to God, your enemies got no good and you no harm by it.' 'You would say so indeed' (said the lord Hastings), if you knew as much as I do now, or as you will shortly. I was never so afraid of my life, as I was then; but now matters are well mended with me: mine enemies are now in as great danger as I was then, (this he said, because he knew that the protector by his and others advice had given order for the execution of the lord Rivers, lord Grey, and sir Thomas Vaughan at Pomfret) and I was never merrier nor more secure in all my life.' With these words he parted and went into the Tower, whence he never came out again. Oh the uncertain confidence and short-sighted knowledge of man! When this lord was most afraid, he was most secure; and when he was secure, danger was over his head. By him we may see the truth of David's advice, 'Oh put not your trust in Princes!' and learn to leave all to God's providence who delivers us in dangers, and never leaves us but when we grow self-confident; of which this great man was a sad example, and ought to be a warning to us in the like case.

The protector having thus far proceeded to open himself a plain way to the crown, by removing all that appear'd in opposition to it, Hastings being dead, and the lords of his party in prison, was yet at a plunge, how to justify to the nation the severity of these proceedings against him. For the lord Hastings, tho' in himself no good man, as his publick keeping of Shore's wife for his concubine declared, yet was had in great esteem by the king's friends, as a person of approved loyalty and good affection to king Edward's line, and by the people as a lover of the common good, and he was sensible that the news of his death, which would fly into all parts from the city apace, would cause great discontents in all parts of the nation: whereupon he thought it his wisest course to send for the lord Mayor and chief citizens to him into the Tower, and give them a full account of the justice of the lord Hastings's sufferings; that so the murmurs of the city being appeased, the nation might have no cause to repine.

This contrivance he put in execution immediately after dinner the same day, and having put on old rusty armour, which lay neglected in the Tower, and commanded the duke of Buckingham to do the same, as if their sudden danger had caused them to take any thing that lay next for their defence, he and the duke stood ready to receive them.

When they were come, the protector told them, 'That the lord Hastings, and several other persons, had conspired and contrived together suddenly to kill him and the duke of Buckingham that day in council, for what cause, or for what design he could not guess, and had not yet time to search it out, because he had no certain knowledge of the intended treason before ten a-clock of the same day, so that he had enough to do to stand upon his own guard, and provide for his own defence; which tho' they had both done in an undecent manner, by putting on such filthy armour, yet necessity obliging them to it, they were forc'd to take what was next hand: that God had wonderfully protected them from the danger he hoped, now the lord Hastings was dead, against whom, tho' there might seem to be something of cruelty us'd in so sudden an execution without any legal tryal and hearing, yet there appearing to the king and the lords of his council many reasons to believe, that if he had been kept in prison, his accomplices would have made a formidable insurrection in the country to rescue him, and his guilt being very evident, they judg'd it best to inflict the deserved punishment of his crimes upon him immediately, that the peace of the nation might not be in danger. This is the real truth of the business, and we have therefore call'd you hither to inform you of it that you may, as you see cause, satisfie the people of the justice of the lord Hastings's sufferings, which tho' we were no ways oblig'd to do, yet out of our care to please them, we have condescended to it, and we require you thus to report it.' They all answer'd fair, and declar'd their readiness to obey, as if they really believed him, tho' in themselves they look'd upon his harangue as a plausible pretence for a foul fact, and so taking their leaves of him departed. But upon more mature deliberation this was not thought sufficient to appease the people's minds; and therefore soon after the mayor and citizens were gone, an herald of arms was sent into the city to publish a proclamation in all parts of it, to this effect:

'That the lord Hastings with divers other wicked conspirators, had traiterously contrived the same day to have slain the protector and duke of Buckingham sitting in council, with a purpose and design to take upon him the government of the king and kingdom, and rule all things at his pleasure, hoping that when they were dead, they should meet no opposition in their designs. And in how miserable a condition this nation had been, if God had left them in his hands, appear'd from the former actions of the said lord, who being so ill a man, could not make a good governour. For he it was, that by his ill advice enticed the king's father to many things much redounding to his dishonour and to the universal damage and detriment of the realm, leading him into debauchery by his examplary wickedness, and procuring lewd and ungracious persons to gratifie his lusts, and particularly Shore's wife, who was one of his secret council in this treason, by which lewd living, the said king not only shortned his days, but also was forced to oppress and tax his people, that he might have sufficient to gratify his expences. And since the death of the said king he hath lived in a continual incontinency with the said Shore's wife, and lay nightly with her, and particularly the very night before his death; so that it was no marvel if his ungracious life brought him to as unhappy a death, which he was put to by the special command of the king's highness, and of his honourable and faithful council, both for his own demerits, being so openly taken in his intended treason, and also lest any delay of his execution might have encourag'd other mischievous persons, who were engaged in the conspiracy with him, to make an insurrection for his deliverance, which being wisely foreseen, and as effectually prevented, was the only means under God's providence to preserve the whole realm in peace and quietness.'

This proclamation, which was very well indicted (as was thought by Catesby, who was a chief actor in this tragedy), and as fairly written on parchment, tho' the expedition of the publishing of it was look'd upon as politick and wise to prevent the discontents of the people, yet it did very little good: for when men came to compare things, and consider'd, that the proclamation was very elegantly composed, very fairly written, and being very long was yet publish'd two hours after the death of the lord Hastings, they began to suspect that that lord had foul dealings, and that his ruin being determin'd, it was composed and written before his death; for the time after was not sufficient, either to compose or write it in. And hence it was, that some spared not to reflect upon it. The school-master of Paul's sharply said,

Here's a very goodly cast,   Foully cast away for haste.

And a merchant that stood by him, answer'd him, it was written by prophecy. Thus did the protector endeavour to palliate his wickedness, in destroying the lord Hastings, but all was in vain; this action was too foul to receive any tolerable plea, which would pass with men of any thought at all.

The protector having done as much as cou'd be done, to excuse his cruelty to the lord Hastings, took himself oblig'd to proceed against Shore's wife, whom he had accus'd of the same treason; lest if he shou'd let her escape, he shou'd betray his plot; for if she were not guilty, no more was the lord Hastings; and if he deserved death, so did she. For this reason, he sent sir Thomas Howard to her house, with an order of council to apprehend her person, and seize her goods, as forfeited to the king by her treason; which were both accordingly done; and her goods, to the value of two or three thousand marks being taken from her, she was carry'd to prison into the Tower. Within a few days after, she was brought to her examination before the king's council, and the protector laid to her charge, 'That she had endeavour'd his ruin and destruction several ways; and particularly, by witchcraft had decay'd his body, and with the lord Hastings had contrived to assassinate him.' But she made so good a defence for herself, as that there appear'd not the least likelihood of her being guilty. Whereupon they, by the protector's order, fell upon her for her open and scandalous whoredom, which everybody knowing she cou'd not deny. And because they would do something to her to satisfy him, they deliver'd her over to the bishop of London, to do public penance for her sin in St. Paul's church, which she accordingly perform'd the next Sunday morning, after this manner: Mrs. Shore being depriv'd of all her ornaments, and cloath'd with a white sheet, was brought by way of procession, with the cross carried before her, and a wax taper in her hand, to the church of St. Paul's from the bishop's palace adjoyning, through great crowds of people gather'd together to behold her; and there standing before the preacher, acknowledg'd in a set form, her open wickedness, and declared her repentance for it: in all this action, she behav'd herself with so much modesty and decency, that such as respected her beauty more than her fault, never were in greater admiration of her, than now: for she being a beautiful and handsome woman, wanting nothing in her face but a little blush, this shameful act supply'd that so well, that she appear'd more lovely for it; and as to such, as were glad to see sin corrected, yet they pity'd her, because they knew, that the protector did it more out of hatred to her person, than sin; more out of malice, than a love to virtue. This woman was born in London, virtuously educated, and well married to a substantial and honest citizen; but being drawn to the match, rather by interest than affection, by her parents' judgment, than her own inclination, she never had that fondness for him, that joyns a wife inviolably to her husband's bed. This looseness to her husband, with that natural ambition, and affectation of gay cloathing and greatness, which is usually in women much above their fortunes, though almost never so great, dispos'd her to accept of the king's kindness, when offer'd: who, besides that he was a very handsome and lovely person, could easily gratify her desires, and by fulfilling his lusts, she knew she had mastery of his gifts and treasure; and for these reasons, she became his concubine. Her husband (tho' made unhappy by her lewdness) yet carried his resentments evenly; and after the king had abus'd her, never wou'd have anything to do with her, whether out of reverence to the king's person, or out of a principle of conscience, it is not easy to determine, tho' both might concur. She lived many years in king Edward's court, and though that king had many concubines, and some of them of much greater quality than herself, yet he loved her best for her merry and ingenious behaviour. In this great, tho' bad station, she demean'd herself with admirable prudence, and was not exalted by the king's favour, but always us'd it with as much benefit to others as to herself; for she never abus'd the king's kindness to any man's hurt, but always us'd it to their comfort and advantage: where the king took displeasure against any man, she would mitigate his anger and appease his mind; and such as were out of favour, she would reconcile. For many heinous offenders she obtain'd pardon, and got a relaxation, and sometimes a total remission of large fines; and tho' she was the only effectual suitor almost at court for such as wanted places and preferments, yet she made little advantage to herself by it; expecting none or very small reward, and that rather gay than rich; either because she was content with doing of a kindness, or delighted to be sought to; for wanton women and wealthy, be not always covetous. In fine, her lewdness was her only fault; and tho' that was great enough, yet to have a king for their bedfellow is such a mighty temptation, that if no woman would condemn her before they have the like trials, it's to be fear'd, she'd have few to cast a stone at her. She was affable and obliging, generous and charitable; and tho', indeed, she was after reduc'd to a miserable poverty in her old age, a just punishment for her sin, yet it was a reproach to many thousands, that she was so, whom she kept from beggary; and if they had been grateful to requite her for those kindnesses in her want, which she scorn'd to sell in her prosperity, she might have liv'd to her death, in a condition great enough for her birth and degree.

While the protector was thus busied at London, in making his way to the crown, and excusing himself for the death of the lord Hastings, his bloody order given for the execution of the queen's kindred, the lord Rivers and Richard lord Grey, with Richard Hause and sir Thomas Vaughan at Pomfract, was punctually executed by sir Richard Ratcliffe, a great favourite of the protector's, who was a man of a desperate courage, and forward to promote all his designs. It is thought, they suffer'd death at the same time the lord Hastings was beheaded in the Tower; who being a principal adviser in their deaths, may be a warning to us all, how we concur in the undeserved sufferings of innocent persons: for God often, and that justly, brings the evil we do to others upon our own heads. The lord Hastings, by advising the Protector to destroy the queen's kindred causelesly, shew'd him the way to do the like to himself. The manner of their execution was as barbarous as unjust. Great and heavy accusations were laid against them, but none prov'd. They had not so much as the formality of a tryal, but were brought to the scaffold on the day appointed; and being branded, in general, with the name of traitors, were beheaded. The lord Rivers would fain have declar'd his innocence to the people, but Ratcliffe wou'd not suffer him, lest his words shou'd lay open the protector's cruelty too much, and make both him and his party odious to the people; and so he died in silence. Sir Thomas Vaughan wou'd not endure his mouth to be stopp'd, but as he was going to the block he said aloud, 'A mischief take them that expounded the prophecy, which foretold that G should destroy king Edward's children, for George duke of Clarence, who for that suspicion is now dead; for there still remain'd Richard G. *i. e.* duke of Gloucester, who now I see is he that shall, and will, accomplish the prophecy, and destroy king Edward's children, and all his allies and friends, as appeareth by us this day; against whom I appeal to the high tribunal of God, for this wrongful murder, and our real innocency.' Sir Richard Ratcliffe heard this with regret, and putting it off, said to him in scorn. 'You have made a goodly appeal, lay down your head.' 'Yea,' saith sir Thomas, 'but I die in the right, take heed that you die not in the wrong:' and having this said, he was beheaded. He, with the other three, were buried naked in the monastery of St. John the evangelist at Pomfract.

Then the conspirators held councel among themselves, how they might bring about their wicked purposes. Their chief difficulty, was to engage the city; and having gain'd the Lord Mayor, Sir Edmund Shaw his brother, Dr. John Shaw a priest, and frier Pinker provincial of the Augustine friers, to their interest, they determin'd, that doctor Shaw should first break the matter in a sermon he was to preach at Paul's cross, and the main argument he was to use for the deposing of king Edward and the advancement of his uncle Richard, was resolv'd among them to be the bastardy of the two princes, sons to Edward the Fourth; which disabled them to inherit the imperial crown of this realm. Tho' this charge would bring the scandal of adultery on the queen, yet Richard and the conspirators did not consider much, that the whole royal family wou'd be defam'd by it, in the highest degree: on the contrary (rather than fail of the sovereignty to which he aspir'd), the duke of Gloucester, and his emissaries, intended to give out, that king Edward the Fourth was himself a bastard, tho' his mother was the parent of the protector, and in calling her an adultress, he prophaned the honour of the very person that brought him into the world. This accusation he would have at first only hinted, and spoken mysteriously, that if the people, in abhorrence of such an unnatural slander, shou'd have been set against the publisher of it, there might be room to put some other construction on the words. Shaw was order'd to declare to his auditory, that king Edward had promis'd marriage to the lady Elizabeth Lucy, by whom he had a child; and that the duchess of York had told him, he was her husband before God, to prevent his marrying the lady Elizabeth Grey, whose children, by king Edward, were consequently bastards. He was not to mention anything of that king's illegitimacy, unless he found his reflection on the queen's children would not take. The doctor was a famous preacher, and a vast number of persons, of all qualities us'd to flock to hear him: so they thought they had gone a great way in accomplishing their designs, when they had got him to their side. Shaw was not only ready to speak what the conspirators would have him, but turn'd his whole discourse against the legitimacy of the young king and his brother. He began his sermon with this expression, '*Spurea vitilamina non agent radices altas,*' 'bastard slips, shall never take deep root.' He shew'd the blessings that God bestow'd on the fruits of the marriage-bed, and the unhappiness of those children who were born out of wedlock. Several examples of both kinds he us'd to prove the truth of his assertion. He took occasion from what he had said, to shew the reason they had to fear, that the reign of the present king wou'd be unfortunate; and enlarg'd very much on the great things that they might hope for, from the government of a prince of the duke of York's illustrious qualities, the father of king Edward the Fourth, or rather, of the lord protector, who was the only lawful begotten son of the late duke of York, who was kill'd at the battle of Wakefield. He then declared, that king Edward was never legally married to the queen, being husband, before God, to the lady Elizabeth Lucy: besides, neither he, nor the duke of Clarence were thought legitimate by those of the duke of York's family, who were most acquainted with the duchess of York's intrigues with several persons of her husband's court, whom they resembled in the face: 'But my lord protector, that very noble prince, the pattern of all heroick deeds, represented the very face and mind of the great duke his father: he (says the false preacher) is the perfect image of his father; his features are the same, and the very express likeness of that noble duke.' At these words, 'twas design'd the protector should have enter'd, as if it had been by chance; and the conspirators hoped, that the multitude taking the doctor's words, as coming from the immediate inspiration of the holy ghost, wou'd have been induc'd to have cry'd out, 'God save king Richard.' Which artifice was prevented, either by the doctor's making too much haste to come to that part of his sermon, or the lord protector's negligence to come in at the instant when he was saying it; for it was over before he came, and the priest was enter'd on some other matter when the duke appear'd, which, however he left, and repeated again, abruptly, 'The lord protector, that very noble prince, the pattern of all heroick deeds, represents the very face and mind of the great duke his father; his features are the same, and the plain express likeness of that noble duke.' The protector, accompanied by the duke of Buckingham, passed thro' the multitude, as the priest said this: but the people were so far from saluting him king, that they were struck with indignation at the preacher's base flattery and treason; who, when he had clos'd his sermon, went home, hid himself for shame, and never after durst shew his face in the world. Being inform'd how odious he was become for what he had done, he fell, out of grief and remorse, into a consumption, of which he died in a short time. He preached this notable discourse, on a Sunday which was to be preparatory to the duke of Buckingham's oration, on the Tuesday following, to the lord mayor, aldermen, and council of the city of London, assembled for that purpose in the Guild-Hall; where that duke mounting the hustings, and silence being commanded in the lord protector's name, spoke to this effect, several lords, who were privy to the secret, attending him:

'Gentlemen, out of the zeal and sincere affection we have for your persons and interests, we are come to acquaint you with a matter of high importance, equally pleasing to God, and profitable to the Commonwealth, and to none more, than to you the citizens of this famous and honourable city. For the very thing, which we believe, you have a long while wanted and wish'd for, what you wou'd have purchas'd at any rate, and gone far to fetch, we are come hither to bring, without any labour, trouble, cost, or peril to you: and what can this be but your own safety, the peace of your wives and daughters, the security of your goods and estates, which were all in danger till now? Who, of you, cou'd call what he had his own, there were so many snares laid to deceive you? So many fines and forfeitures, taxes and impositions, of which there was no end, and often no necessity; or if there was, it was occasion'd by riots and unreasonable waste, rather than a just and lawful charge, for the defence and honour of the state. Your best citizens were plunder'd, and their wealth squander'd by profuse favourites: fifteenths, and the usual subsidies wou'd not do, but under the plausible name of benevolence, your goods were taken from you by the commissioners much against your will, as if by that name, was understood, that every man shou'd pay, not what he pleas'd, but what the king wou'd have him; who never was moderate in his demands, always exorbitant, turning forfeitures into fines, fines into ransoms; small offences into misprison of treason, and misprison into treason itself. We need not give you examples of it, Burdet's case will never be forgot; who for a word spoken in haste, was cruelly beheaded. Did not judge Markham resign his office, rather than joyn with his brethren, in passing that illegal sentence on that honest man? Were you not all witnesses of the barbarous treatment one of your own body, the worshipful alderman Cook, met with? And your own selves know, too well, how many instances of this kind I might name among you. King Edward gaining the crown by conquest, all that were any ways related to those that were his enemies, lay under the charge of treason: thus half of the kingdom became at once traytors; for half of the kingdom were either friends to king Henry, or relations or friends to some that were so. Tho' open war with invaders, is terrible and destructive to a nation, yet civil dissentions are much more fatal, and to be dreaded; with which his reign was more disturb'd, than the reigns of all his predecessors; but he is dead and gone, and God forgive his soul. It cost the people more blood and treasure to get the crown for this, than it had done to conquer France twice: half of the nobility of the realm lost their lives or estates in his quarrel; and when the dispute was over, the peace that follow'd was not much safer than the war: every rich and landed man was in danger; for whom cou'd he trust that distrusted his own brother? whom spare, that kill'd his own brother? or who cou'd perfectly love him, whom his own brother cou'd not love? We shall, in honour to the memory of one that was our sovereign, forbear to mention, who were the persons on which he was so lavish of his favours; only 'tis well known, that those that deserved them most, had least of them. Was not Shore's wife his chief minister? Was there not more court made to her than to all the lords in England; except those that were the strumpet's favourites? Who, poor woman, was herself chaste and of good reputation, till he deluded her to his lust, and tempted her from her husband, an honest substantial young man, whom you all know. Indeed I am ashamed to say it, the king's appetite in that point was insatiable and intolerable: no woman cou'd escape him, young or old, rich or poor, wife or virgin, all fell victims to his lust; by which means the most honourable houses were defil'd, and the most honest families were corrupted. You of this renown'd city suffer'd most: you who deserv'd most from him for your readiness to serve the house of York with your lives and fortunes, which tho' he ill requited, there is of that house, who, by God's grace shall reward you better. I shall not enlarge on this subject, you have heard it from one, whom you will hearken to more, as you ought to do; for I am not so vain as to think, what I can say, will have so great authority with you, as the words of a preacher; a man so wise and so pious, that he wou'd not utter a thing, in the pulpit especially, which he did not firmly believe 'twas his duty to declare. You remember, I doubt not, how he set forth the last Sunday, the right of the most excellent prince Richard, duke of Gloucester, unto the crown of this realm: for, as he prov'd to you, the children of king Edward the Fourth were never lawfully begotten, the king leaving his lawful wife, the lady Lucy, to contract an illegal marriage with the queen: my noble lord the protector's reverence to the duchess his mother, will not permit me to say anything further concerning what the worthy doctor alledg'd of her familiarity with others besides her own husband, for fear of offending the duke of Gloucester her son: tho' for these causes, the crown of England is devolv'd to the most excellent prince, the lord protector, as the only lawfully begotten son of the right noble duke of York. This, and the consideration of his many high qualities, has prevail'd with the lords and commons of England, of the northern counties especially, who have declared they will not have a bastard reign over them, to petition that high and mighty prince, to take on him the sovereign power for the good of the realm, to which he has so rightful and lawful a title: we have reason to fear he will not grant our request, being a prince whose wisdom foresees the labour both of mind and body that attends the supreme dignity: which office is not a place for a child? as that wise man observ'd, who said, '*Væ Regno cujus Rex Puer est*,' ' Wo is that realm that has a child to their king.' Wherefore we have reason to bless God that the prince whose right it is to reign over us is of so ripe age, so great wisdom and experience, who tho' he is unwilling to take the government upon himself, yet the petition of the lords and gentlemen will meet with the more favourable acceptance if you the worshipful citizens of the metropolis of the kingdom will joyn with us in our request; which for your own welfare we doubt not but you will. However, I heartily entreat you to do it for the common good of the people of England, whom you will oblige by choosing them so good a king, and his majesty by shewing early your ready disposition to his election. In which my most dear friends, I require you in the name of myself and these lords, to shew us plainly your minds and intentions.' The duke stop'd here, expecting the assembly would have cry'd out, 'God save king Richard,' but all were hush'd and silent, as if the auditory was confounded with the extravagance of the proposal; at which the duke was extremely surpriz'd, and taking aside the mayor, with some others of the conspirators, said to them softly, ' How comes it the people are so still?' ' Sir,' says the mayor, 'it may be they don't understand you well.' The duke to help the matter repeated his speech with a little variation, and with such grace and eloquence, that never so ill a subject was handled with so much oratory. However the assembly continu'd silent. Then the mayor told the duke, 'The citizens had not been accustom'd to hear any one but the recorder, and perhaps they wou'd take the thing better from him who is the mouth of the city.' Upon which the recorder Fitz-Williams, much against his will spoke to the same purpose at the mayor's command; and yet he manag'd his speech so well as to be understood to speak the duke's sense, and not his own. The people being still as before, the duke mutter'd to the lord mayor, saying, ' They are wonderfully obstinate in their silence.' And turning to the assembly, he said, ' Dear friends, we came to acquaint you with a thing which we needed not have done, had it not been for the affections we bear you. The lords and commons could have determin'd the matter without you, but would gladly have you joyn with us, which is for your honour and profit, tho' you do not see it nor consider it: we require you therefore to give your answer one way or another, whether you are willing, as the lords are, to have the most excellent prince the lord protector to be your king or not.' The assembly then began to murmur, and at last some of the protector's and the duke's servants, some of the city apprentices, and the rabble that had crouded into the hall, cry'd out, 'king Richard, king Richard !' and threw up their hats in token of joy. The duke perceiv'd easily enough who they were that made the noise; yet, as if the acclamation had been general, he took hold of it; saying, ' 'Tis a goodly and a joyful cry to hear every man with one voice agree to it, and nobody say no; since therefore, dear friends, we see you are all as one man inclin'd to have this noble prince to be your king, we shall report the matter so effectually to him, that we doubt not 'twill be much for your advantage. We require you to attend us to-morrow with our joynt petition to his grace; as has been already agreed on between us.' Then the duke and the lords came down from the hustings and the assembly broke up, the most part of them with weeping eyes and aching hearts; tho' they were forc'd to hide their tears and their sorrows as much as possible for fear of giving offence, which had been dangerous.

The next day the lord mayor, the aldermen, and the chief of the common-council resorted to Baynard's-castle, where the protector then lay; and the duke of Buckingham, attended by several lords and gentlemen, came thither also. The duke sent word to the protector that a great company attended to move a business of the highest importance to him, and desir'd audience of his grace. The duke of Gloucester made some difficulty of coming forth, as if he was jealous whether their errand was good or was not.

The duke of Buckingham took this occasion to shew the lord mayor and citizens how little the protector was conscious of their design; and then he sent another messenger with so humble and so earnest a request to be heard, that his grace came forth; yet with so much affected diffidence, that he seem'd unwilling to draw near them till he knew their business. Then the duke of Buckingham very submissively beg'd pardon for himself and his company, and liberty to propose to him what they had to offer, without which they durst not proceed; tho' 'twas for his grace's honour and the good of the realm. The protector gave them leave to propose what they would, saying, 'He believ'd none of 'em meant him any harm.' The duke then set forth elegantly and pathetically 'the grievances of the people, and pray'd him to redress them by assuming the sovereign authority, which of right belong'd to him, and which the whole kingdom with unusual unanimity desired he would take to himself for the benefit of the commonwealth, as much as for his grace's honour.' The protector seemed mightily surpriz'd; and answer'd, 'That tho' he knew the things he alleg'd to be true, yet he lov'd king Edward and his children above any crown whatsoever, and therefore cou'd not grant their request. However he pardon'd their petition, and thank'd them for their love, but desir'd them to be obedient to the prince under whom himself and they liv'd at that time, and whom he would advise to the best of his capacity, as he had already done to the satisfaction of all parties.' The duke of Buckingham murmur'd at this reply, and after having ask'd and obtain'd pardon a second time for what he was about to say, he declar'd aloud to the protector, 'That they were all agreed not to have any of king Edward's line to reign over them: that they were gone too far to go back; for which reason if his grace wou'd be pleas'd to take the crown upon him, they humbly beseech him to do it: or if he would give them a resolute answer to the contrary, which they should be loath to hear; they must and wou'd look out for some worthy person that would accept of their proposal.' At these words, the protector began to comply a little, and at last he spoke thus to them : 'Since we perceive that the whole realm is bent upon it not to have king Edward's children to govern them, of which we are sorry, and knowing that the crown can belong to no man so justly as to ourself, the right heir, lawfully begotten of the body of our most dear father Richard late duke of York; to which title is now joyn'd your election the nobles and commons of this realm, which we, of all titles possible, take for the most effectual : we are content and agree favourably to receive your petition and request, and according to the same take upon us the royal estate, pre-eminence and kingdoms of the two noble realms England and France; the one from this day forward by us and our heirs, to rule, govern and defend; the other by God's grace, and your good help, to get again, subdue, and establish for ever in due obedience unto this realm of England ; and we ask of God to live no longer than we intend to procure its advancement.' At the close of his speech there was a great shout of 'God save king Richard.' The lords went up to the king, and the people departed every man talking for or against the revolution, as he was inclin'd by humour or interest. 'Twas easie to perceive that however the thing appear'd strange to king Richard, 'twas acted by concert with him, and what was done, was only to preserve decency and order.

THE LIFE AND REIGN OF RICHARD III.

THE next day he went to Westminster, sat himself down in the court of king's-bench, made a very gracious speech to the assembly there present, and promis'd them halcyon days from the beginning of his reign.

To shew his forgiving temper, he order'd one Hog whom he hated, and who fled to sanctuary for fear of him, to be brought before him, took him by the hand and spoke favourably to him, which the multitude thought was a token of his clemency, and the wise men of his vanity. In his return home, he saluted every one he met.

From this mock election in June he commenc'd his reign, and was crown'd in July with the same provision that was made for the coronation of his nephew. But to be sure of his enemies he sent for 5000 men out of the north, who came up to town ill cloath'd and worse harness'd, their horses poor and their arms rusty; who being muster'd in Finsbury-Fields were the contempt of the spectators. The appearance of these rude fellows in arms, gave cause to the people to suspect, that as he was conscious of his guilt, he was apprehensive of its punishment.

On the 4th of July he came to the Tower by water, with his wife Ann daughter to Richard earl of Warwick; and the next day he created Thomas lord Howard duke of Norfolk, sir Thomas Howard his son earl of Surrey, William lord Berkly earl of Nottingham, Francis lord Lovell, viscount Lovell, and lord Chamberlain of the household, and the lord Stanley was set at liberty and made lord Steward of the household: the king being afraid of the lord Strange who was raising men in Lincolnshire, as was reported. The archbishop of York was releas'd from his imprisonment, and bishop Morton deliver'd to the charge of the duke of Buckingham, who engag'd to keep him in safe custody at his manour of Brecknock. King Richard also created seventeen knights of the Bath, and his son Edward prince of Wales. The same day he and his queen rode through the city of London to Westminster, and the next day they were both crown'd in the Abby-Church with extraordinary pomp. What is most observable in the procession is, that the countess of Richmond, mother to king Henry the seventh, bore up the queen's train. After the ceremony was over, the king dismiss'd all the lords who attended his coronation except the lord Stanley, whom he retain'd till he heard that the lord Strange, his son, was quiet in the country. He gave the lords a strict charge to see their several counties were well govern'd and none of his subjects wrong'd. He liberally rewarded his northern men, who valu'd themselves so much on the king's favour, that presuming to commit many acts of injustice and oppression upon it, he was forc'd to take a journey into the north to reclaim them. What is ill got is never well kept; which king Richard soon shew'd by the murder of his two innocent nephews, the young king and his tender brother; whose death has however been much doubted of since, whether 'twas in his time or not; Perkin Warbeck, thro' the malice of some and the folly of others, having a long time abus'd the world, and impos'd himself upon princes as well as people, for the younger of king Edward the fourth's sons. King Richard contriv'd the destruction of the two young princes in a progress he made to Gloucester, to honour the town, which gave him the title of duke, with a visit: he imagin'd that while his nephews liv'd, his right to the crown wou'd be call'd in question: wherefore he resolv'd to rid himself of them, and to that end sent John Green, a creature of his, to sir Robert Brackenbury, constable of the tower with a letter, desiring him one how or other to make away with the two children whom he had in keeping. Brackenbury refus'd to do it, and Green return'd to king Richard, who then lay at Warwick, with the constable's answer; at which the king was so displeas'd, that he said to a page of his the same night, 'Alas! who is there that a man can trust? Those that I have brought up myself, those that I thought wou'd be most ready to serve me, even those fail me, and will not do what I command them.' The page reply'd, 'Sir, there lyes a man on the pallat in the outer chamber, who I am sure will think nothing too hard that you shall require him to do.' Meaning sir James Tyrrell, a brave handsome man, who deserv'd a better master, and wou'd have merited the esteem of all men had his virtue been as great as his valour. He was ambitious, and with regret saw sir Richard Ratcliff soar above him in his master's favour. The king knowing how aspiring he was, imagin'd the page had hit upon the person who was for his purpose, believing Tyrrell wou'd do anything in hopes of further preferment; so he went out into the chamber where he found sir James and sir Thomas Tyrrell his brother on a pallat bed, to whom he said merrily, 'What are you a bed so soon, gentlemen?' and calling sir James to him, told him his mind and what he wanted of him; whom he found ready to do whatever he commanded him. The next day therefore he sent him with a letter to sir Robert Brackenbury, requiring him to deliver sir James the keys of the Tower, to the end that he might accomplish the king's pleasure in certain things he had given him commandment about. Sir Robert having restor'd the keys to this assassin, he resolv'd to murder the two princes in the ensuing night. When the elder, who was call'd king Edward the fifth, was told that his uncle was crown'd king; he sigh'd and said, 'Ah! wou'd my uncle let me have my life, he might take my kingdom.' The person that told him so, comforted him as well as he could, and for a little while the king and his brother were well us'd; but afterwards they were shut up close, and one servant only allow'd to attend them. Then the young king apprehended what would be his fate, gave himself over to sorrow and despair; and the prince his brother was the companion of his grief as well as of his misfortune. Sir James Tyrrell contriv'd to have them murder'd in their beds, and appointed one Miles Forrest, a noted ruffian, and John Dighton his groom a lusty fellow, to see execution done. Those that waited near the prince's lodgings were removed, and way made for Forrest and Dighton, to enter their chamber, unperceiv'd of anyone, at midnight. The poor youths were asleep in their beds, whom the two assassins wrap'd up in the blankets and coverlaid of the bed, clapt the feather bed and pillows upon them, stopt their mouths and smother'd them to death. When the ruffians perceiv'd by their struggling that they were dying, and afterwards by their lying still that they were dead, they laid their bodies out naked upon the bed, and fetch'd sir James Tyrrell to see them, who ordered the murderers to bury them at the stair foot deep in the ground under a heap of stones. Then Tyrrell rode to the king, and gave him a full account of the murder, with which he was so well pleased, that 'tis said, he knighted him at that time; tho' he seem'd not to approve of their being buried in so vile a corner, they being the sons of a king: upon which, sir Robert Brackenbury's chaplain took their bodies up, and buried them privately in a place, that, by occasion of his death, never came to light. Sir James Tyrrell, when he was afterwards in the reign of king Henry the seventh, committed to the Tower for treason, confess'd the murder in the manner we have related it: so did Dighton, and both the master and the man, and Forrest the warder came to miserable ends, thro' the just judgment of God, the avenger of innocent blood. Dighton and Forrest, tho' they were not executed by the hangman, died in a most horrible manner, rotting away by degrees. Sir James Tyrrell was beheaded, and king Richard himself, slain by his enemies, and his body ignominiously used by the rabble. He could never after be at rest; his guilt haunted him like a spectre; he was afraid of his own shadow when he went abroad, his eyes roll'd in his head; his limbs trembled, and his hand was always on his dagger; his sleep was ever disturb'd by frightful dreams; he would suddenly start up, leap out of his bed, and run about the chamber. Nor did he long enjoy the fruits of his bloody policy; for tho' the princes were remov'd, new enemies arose from time to time, that kept him in continual fear thro' the course of his short reign. The first that conspired against him, was the very person who had been most instrumental in his advancement, the duke of Buckingham, whose intimacy with him, commenced from the death of king Edward the fourth.

We must look a little backward into the beginning of their confederacy, the better to clear the history of this duke's misfortunes. On the death of king Edward he sent a trusty servant of his to the duke of Gloucester, to offer him his service, and that he wou'd attend him with a thousand men, whenever he pleas'd to command him. The duke of Gloucester return'd him thanks, and informed the duke of Buckingham with his secret designs. At Northampton, Buckingham met the duke of Gloucester, at the head of three hundred horse, and joyn'd with him in all his undertakings; he accompanied him to London, and stay'd with him till after the coronation: he went with him to Gloucester, and there he took his leave of him to return home; where he was no sooner arrived, than he began to repent of what he had done; and to think he had not been sufficiently rewarded for it by the usurper. The reason of his first discontent, is said to be this: some time before the usurper was crown'd, 'twas agreed between him and the duke of Buckingham, that the latter should have all the lands belonging to the duke of Hereford, to which he pretended to have a title, by his descent from the house of Lancaster; his mother being the daughter of Edmund Beaufort, duke of Somerset, brother to John duke of Somerset, father to Margaret countess of Richmond, mother to king Henry VII. But this title having some relation to that of the crown, the usurper would not hear of restoring him to the duke of Hereford's estate, and rejected his petition with indignation and threats, when he was in possession of the sovereignty; which the duke of Buckingham so highly resented, that from that time forward he contrived how he might pull him down from the throne upon which he had set him. We are told he feign'd himself sick, and excused his attendance at the coronation, and that king Richard should send him word, if he would not come and ride he would make him be carried.

This circumstance of the duke of Buckingham's discontent is not given credit to, by those who consider the natures of the usurper and of the duke, being both of them the greatest dissemblers in the world: The one would not so rashly have provok'd a powerful enemy, nor the other have given a jealous tyrant occasion to suspect his fidelity: the truth is, the duke of Buckingham was a high spirited man, and envied the glory of another so much, that when he saw the crown set upon king Richard's head, he cou'd not endure the sight, but turn'd his head away. Others write, that they continu'd good friends till after his return home, and that the usurper dismiss'd him at Gloucester with rich gifts and extraordinary marks of his favour and affection; when he came to Brecknock, he convers'd much with Dr. Moreton, bishop of Ely, whom he had there in keeping. This prelate was a very wise politic person, a man of learning and of a winning behaviour. He had been always faithful to king Henry; and when he fell in with the party of king Edward, on king Henry's death, he serv'd him as faithfully, and was one of the lords whom the usurper seiz'd at the council in the tower. The bishop perceiving the duke of Buckingham was pleas'd with his company and discourse, thought he might improve the favour he had obtain'd of him to the advantage of the common-wealth, by getting him to joyn in a conspiracy against king Richard, towards whom, he found, he was not very well inclin'd; yet he managed the matter so warily, that he rather seem'd to follow than to lead him, and brought him by degrees to open his whole mind to him, and to engage in prosecuting a design which he had form'd, to bring about a match between Henry earl of Richmond, and the lady Elizabeth, eldest daughter to king Edward, by which marriage, the two houses of York and Lancaster wou'd be united, and an end put to the long and bloody disputes between the two factions. He durst not come to the point presently, but advanced to it step by step, as he saw the duke of Buckingham prepared to hearken to it.

When that lord came to Brecknock first, he prais'd the king, and boasted what great things the nation might expect from such a prince: the bishop reply'd ; 'My lord, 'twould be folly in me to lye, and if I should swear the contrary, your lordship wou'd not, I suppose, believe me ; had things gone as I would have had them, king Henry's son had been king, and not king Edward. But when by God's providence, he was deprived of the crown, and king Edward advanced to the throne, I was not so mad, as to bring a dead man in competition with a living one : so I became king Edward's faithful chaplain, and should have been glad that his son had succeeded him : however, since God has otherwise order'd it, I shall not kick against the pricks, nor labour to set up whom the Almighty has pull'd down : as for the late protector, the king that now is ——. Here he stopt short, as if he had said too much already, to heighten the duke's curiosity to know what he had to say more. The duke earnestly desired him to proceed, promising him, upon his honour, 'That never any hurt should come of it ; and perhaps, it might produce more good than he was aware of ; saying, he intended to consult him, and to be govern'd by his advice ; for which cause only, he had procured of the king to have him in his custody, where he might reckon himself at home ; otherwise, he had been deliver'd to those that would not have been so kind to him.' The bishop humbly thank'd him, and said, 'Indeed, my lord, I don't care to talk much of princes, as a thing which is dangerous, tho' the words may be innocent ; for if they be not taken in good part, they may be fatal to him that speaks them, the prince, putting what construction he pleases upon them : I often think of the fable in Esop, when the lyon proclaim'd, 'That no horn'd beast should stay in the wood, on pain of death ; one that had a bunch of flesh in his forehead, fled away in haste : the fox meeting him, ask'd him, whither so fast? The beast answer'd, troth I don't know nor don't care, provided I was out of the wood, as the proclamation commands all horned beasts to be gone. You fool, says the fox, thou mayest stay, the lyon does not mean thee ; it is not a horn that grows in thy head ; no, quoth the beast, I know that well enough, but what if he should call it a horn, where am I then?" The duke laugh'd at the tale, and answered, 'I warrant you, my lord, neither the lyon nor the boar, shall resent anything that is said here, it shall never go any further I assure you.' The bishop reply'd, 'If it did, were the thing that I was about to say, understood as I meant it, I should deserve thanks ; but taken as I suppose it wou'd be, it might perhaps turn to your prejudice and mine.' This raised the duke's curiosity still higher ; upon which the bishop proceeded thus : 'As for the late protector, since he is now king, I don't intend to dispute his title ; however, for the good of the realm he governs (of which I am a poor member) I was about to wish, that to the good qualities he possesses, it had pleased God to have added some of those excellent virtues, requisite for the governing a kingdom, which are so conspicuous in the person of your grace.'

[*Here ends Sir Thomas More. What follows, is taken from Hall and Hollinshead's Chronicles.*]

The duke wondering why the bishop made such frequent pauses, was the more eager to have him speak his mind freely, and reply'd ; 'I cannot but take notice of your stopping so often in the midst of your discourse, which hinders my making any judgment of your opinion of the king, or your goodwill towards me. As for any good qualities in me, I pretend to none, and expect no praise on account of my merit. I plainly perceive you have some hidden meaning which you reserve from me, either out of fear or shame. You may be bold and free with me who am your friend ; I assure you on my honour, that I will be as secret in this case, as the deaf and dumb person is to the singer, or the tree to the hunter.'

The bishop grew bolder on the duke's promise of secrecy, in which he was encouraged, by the discoveries he made of Buckingham's hatred to the king, he resolv'd therefore to come to the point, and to propose to the duke, that either out of ambition, or his love to his country, he should attempt to destroy the tyrant.

To this end, he resumed his former conversation in this manner : ' My singular good lord; since I have been your grace's prisoner, I have not known what it is to be depriv'd of liberty ; and to avoid idleness, the mother and nurse of vice, I have spent my time in reading. I have read in some of my books, that no man was born for himself only : he owes a duty to his parents that begat him ; to his relations and friends for proximity of blood and good offices : but above all to the country, whose air he first breath'd : and this duty is never to be forgotten : for which reason, I consider the present state of this realm, wherein I was born, and in these considerations, I cannot help making reflections on what a governor we now have, and what a ruler we might have. In the present circumstances of affairs, the kingdom must soon decay : confusion and destruction will certainly be the sudden end of disorder and misrule. All my hope is in your grace : when I reflect on your valour, your justice, impartiality, your zeal for the public welfare, your learning, your sense and eloquence, I rejoyce at the happiness of England, that possesses so good and so great a prince, worthy the highest dignities : but when I on the other side consider the good qualities of the late protector (now call'd king) how they are violated and subverted by tyranny, eclipsed by blind and insatiate ambition, and changed from mild and human, to cruel and bloody ; I cannot forbear declaring openly to you, that he is neither fit to be a king of so noble a realm, nor so noble a realm fit to be govern'd by such a tyrant, whose kingdom, were it larger than it is, could not long continue: God will overthrow those that are thirsty of blood; he will bring horrible slaughter upon them: how many brave and virtuous persons were murder'd to make way for him to the throne? did he not accuse his own mother, an honourable and religious princess, of adultery? Which, if it had been true, a dutiful child would have past it over in silence. Did he not declare his two brothers and his two nephews bastards? And what is still more barbarous, did he not cause those two poor innocent princes, whose blood cries aloud for vengeance, to be cruelly murdered? My heart melts when I think of their untimely fate; and my soul, with horror, remembers this bloody butcher, this inhumane monster. What man can be sure of his own life, under the dominion of a prince, who spared not his own blood? Especially if at any time he is suspicious of his fidelity to him, and that he is carrying on ill designs against him, as every thing will be term'd, that tends to the good of the publick: all will be reckon'd guilty by him, that are great and rich. 'Tis enough for persons to have large possessions to provoke his wrath. Now, my lord, to conclude this discourse with what I have to say to your grace; I conjure you by your love to God, your illustrious line, and your native country to take the imperial crown of this realm upon you, to restore this kingdom to its ancient splendour, and deliver it from the violence of the oppressor. I dare affirm, if the Turk stood in competition with this bloody tyrant, this killer of infants, the people of England would prefer him to Richard, who now sits on the throne. How much more then would they rejoice to live under the government of so excellent a prince as your grace? Despise not, neither lose so fair an occasion of saving your self and your dear country: but if you will not your self accept of the sovereignty of this kingdom; if the toils and hazards of a crown, prevail over you more than the charms of power, I intreat you, by the faith you owe to God, and your oath to St. George, patron of the honourable garter, (of which order you are a companion) by your affection to the place that gave you birth, and to the English nation; that you will in your high and princely wisdom, think of some means of advancing such a good governour, as you shall appoint to rule and govern them. All the hopes of the people of England are in you, and to you only can they fly for succour. If you could set up the house of Lancaster once more, or marry the eldest daughter of king Edward to some great and potent prince, the new king would not long enjoy his usurped empire: all civil war would cease, domestick discord would sleep, and universal peace and profit would be the blessings of this noble realm.'

When the bishop had done speaking, the duke continued silent for some time: the bishop chang'd colour, and was very much concern'd at it, expecting his proposal would have been receiv'd with joy and greediness.

The duke perceiving the fright he was in, said, 'Fear nothing, my lord, I will keep my word with you; to morrow we'll talk more of the matter, let us now go to supper.'

The duke the next day sent for the bishop, who had not all that while been very easy, for fear how his last conversation would be taken. Buckingham repeated almost all the bishop of Ely had said to him, and when he had done, he pull'd off his hat and made this sort of a prayer, 'O Lord God! creator of all things; how much is thy kingdom of England and the English nation indebted to thy goodness? Tho' we are now oppress'd by an evil governour, yet I hope e're long, by thy help, to provide such a ruler, as shall be to thy pleasure and the security of the common-wealth.' He then put on his hat, and apply'd himself thus to the bishop; 'My lord of Ely, I have always found you faithful and affectionate to me, and especially in your last free confidence in me: I acknowledge you to be a sure friend, a trusty counsellor, a vigilant statesman, and a true lover of your country; for which I return you hearty thanks now, and shall recompence you more effectually, if life and power serve. Since, when we were last together, you open'd your mind freely, touching the duke of Gloucester, who has usurp'd the crown; and hinted a little, the advancement of the two noble families of York and Lancaster; I shall also, with as much freedom, communicate to you what I have done, and what I intend to do. I declare therefore, that when king Edward died, to whom I thought I was very little oblig'd, (tho' he and I had married two sisters) because he neither promoted nor prefer'd me as I thought I deserv'd, by my birth, and the relation I had to him. I did not much value his children's interest, having their father's hard usage still in my mind. I call'd an old proverb to remembrance, which says, 'Wo be to that kingdom where children rule and women govern.' I thought it of very ill consequence to the people of England, to suffer the young king to govern, or the queen his mother to be regent; considering that her brothers and her children by her first husband, though of no high descent, would be at the head of all affairs by their favour with the queen, and have more share in the government than the king's relations, or any person of the highest quality in the kingdom. For this reason I thought it to be for the publick welfare and my private advantage to side with the duke of Gloucester, whom I took to be as sincere and merciful as I now find him to be false and cruel. By my means, as you, my lord, know well, he was made protector of the king and kingdom. After which, partly by fair words and partly by threats, he persuaded me and other lords, as well spiritual as temporal, to consent that he might assume the crown till the young king was four and twenty yea of age. I stuck at it first, and he produced instruments witness'd doctors, proctors, and notaries, whose depositions I then thought to be true, testifying that king Edward's children were bastards. When these testimonials were read before us, he stood up bare-headed and said, 'Well, my lords, even as I and you (sage and discreet councellors) wou'd that my nephew shoul'd have no wrong, so I pray you to do me nothing but right, these depositions being true, I am the undoubted heir to lord Richard Plantagenet duke of York, who by act of parliament was adjudged the true heir to the crown of this realm.'

'Upon which, my self and others took him really for our rightful prince and sovereign lord; the duke of Clarence's son by reason of his father's attainder cou'd not inherit. The duke was also suspected to be a bastard. Thus by my assistance and friendship he was made king: at which time he promis'd me at Baynard's-Castle, laying his hand on mine, that the two young princes shou'd live and shou'd be provided for to mine and every one's satisfaction: how he perform'd his promises, we all know to our sorrow. When he was in possession of the throne, he forgot his friends and the assurances he had given them: he deny'd to grant my petition for part of the earl of Hereford's lands, which his brother wrongfully detain'd from me: he refused me in such a manner as made the affront much more intolerable. I have born his ingratitude hitherto with patience; I have conceal'd my resentments I had with him afterwards, carry'd it outwardly fair, tho' I inwardly repented that I had been accessory to his advancement. But when I was certainly inform'd of the death of the two innocent princes; to which (God be my judge) I never consented; my blood curdled at his treason and barbarity, I abhor'd the sight of him, and his company much more; and pretending an excuse to leave the court retir'd to Brecknock. In my way home, I meditated how I might dethrone this unnatural uncle. I thought if I wou'd take the soveraignty on my self, now was the time. The temporal lords I saw hated the tyrant: he was odious alike to the gentlemen and people of England; and had I assum'd the supream power, I thought there was no body so likely to carry it as myself. Flattering my ambition with those vain imaginations, I staid two days at Tewksbury. As I travell'd further homewards, I consider'd that to pretend to seat my self on the throne as a conqueror would not do; which wou'd be to subject the whole constitution of the government, and entitle the conqueror to all the noblemens' possessions, which wou'd ruin my design: at last I remember'd that Edmund duke of Somerset my grandfather, was with king Henry VI. in two or three degrees from John duke of Lancaster lawfully begotten; my mother being duke Edmund's eldest daughter, I look'd on my self as the next heir to Henry VI. of the House of Lancaster: but as I travel'd homewards, between Worcester and Bridgenorth I met the lady Margaret countess of Richmond, at present wife to the lord Stanley, who is the rightful and sole heir of John duke of

Somerset, my grandfather's elder brother, whose title I had forgot till I saw her in my way, and then I remember'd that both her claim and her son the earl of Richmond's were bars to mine, and forbad my pretending to the imperial crown of England.

'I had some discourse with her about her son, and then we parted, she for Worcester and I for Shrewsbury. As I proceeded in my journey, I consider'd with my self, whether since I cou'd not pretend to the crown by descent, I might not have recourse to the election of the lords and gentry of the realm, the usurper being generally hated by them; but then I began to reflect on the dangers and difficulties of the enterprize; that the late king's daughters and friends, and the earl of Richmond's relations, whose interest is very considerable, wou'd certainly oppose me to the utmost: and if the houses of Lancaster and York shou'd joyn against me, I shou'd soon lose the vain power I might obtain: wherefore I resolv'd to flatter my self no more with chimæra's of my imaginary right to the royal diadem, but only to revenge mine and the people's wrongs on the common enemy.

'The countess of Richmond propos'd in the conversation we had on the road, that her son might marry one of king Edward's daughters; and she conjur'd me by the memory of duke Humphrey my grandfather, that I wou'd procure the king's favour for her son, and get him to consent to the match. I took no notice of her proposal then; which when I weigh'd in my mind, I found of so great advantage to the commonwealth, that I thought it was an inspiration of the holy spirit for the benefit of the kingdom; and I came to a resolution in my self to spend my life and fortune in endeavouring to accomplish so glorious a design, to marry the princess Elizabeth to the earl of Richmond, the heir of the house of Lancaster, in whose quarrel my father and grandfather lost their lives in battle. If the mothers of the princes and the earl can come to an agreement concerning the marriage, I doubt not but the proud boar, whose tusks have goar'd so many innocent persons, shall soon be brought to confusion. The rightful and indubitate heir shall enjoy the crown, and peace be restor'd to this distracted kingdom.'

The bishop rejoyced extremely at this free declaration of the duke: and that he might not slacken his zeal in so righteous a cause, he endeavour'd to fire him the more, and hasten him to the execution of his designs; 'My lord,' says the bishop, 'since by the providence of God and your grace's incomparable wisdom this happy alliance is set on foot, 'tis convenient or rather necessary that we shou'd consult whom to trust in so important and perilous an undertaking. To whom shall we first apply towards effecting it?' 'To whom,' reply'd the duke, 'but to the countess of Richmond; who knows where her son is, and how to send to him.' The bishop answer'd, 'if you begin there, I have an old friend in her service, one Reginald Bray, a man of probity and judgment, for whom I will send to attend your grace and receive your commands, if you think proper so to do.' The duke consenting to it, the bishop wrote to Mr. Bray to come to him to Brecknock; which he did immediately, believing there was something to be done for his lady's and her son's service. The duke told him what he intended to attempt in favour of the earl of Richmond, no less than to seat him in the royal throne of England, if he swore to marry the lady Elizabeth; and by that allowance put an end to the long and bloody dispute between the white rose and the red.

In order to this, he said, the countess must manage the business with the queen dowager and the princess her daughter, and when they were engaged, send to her son in Britain, and get him to swear he wou'd perform the articles, agreed on between his mother and the princess Elizabeth in both their names. Bray gladly undertook to carry this message to his mistress, and now they were embark'd in so great an affair, the bishop who long'd to be at liberty, desir'd the duke to let him go to Ely, where the number of his friends wou'd secure him against all the force king Richard cou'd send to destroy him. The duke loath to lose so able and experienced a counsellor, excus'd his detaining him a little longer; saying, 'He should go in a few days, and so well accompanied that he need fear no enemy.'

The bishop impatient of confinement, stole away from Brecknock to Ely in disguise, rais'd money there, and pass'd over into Flanders. The good prelate thought he had done enough in setting the duke at work on so hazardous a business, in which it seems he did not care to venture further. Whether he thought he could be more serviceable to the earl of Richmond abroad, or was afraid of his person at home; or whatever reason he had to leave the duke of Buckingham, he does not appear to be excusable in history: for knowing the duke was too apt to open his mind freely, he might have imagin'd that his indiscretion wou'd ruin him, and 'twas to sacrifice a person of his high quality, to put him upon an enterprize he was not fit to manage, and then forsake him in the execution of it; at which the duke was very much concern'd.

In the mean time Reginald Bray return'd to his mistress, inform'd her of what had been concerted between the duke and the bishop, for the advancement of her son; and the countess with great joy intended to play her part as soon as possible. The first thing she was to do, was to engage the queen dowager and the princess; to which purpose she dispatch'd one Lewis, a Welshman who was her physician, with instructions to attend the queen at Westminster, and break the matter to her. Lewis's message was not in the least suspected, because he came as a doctor, to advise her about her health. When he was admitted into her presence, and every body withdrawn, he gave her to understand what errand he was sent upon. He set forth the wrongs she, her children, and the whole nation had suffered by the tyranny of Richard, what miseries had befalen the kingdom by the civil war between the houses of York and Lancaster, and what advantages wou'd accrue to her, her children, and the commonwealth, by the uniting the two houses in marrying her daughter Elizabeth, the only true heir of the house of York, to his mistress's son the only true heir of the house of Lancaster. The queen heard him with attention, agreed to the proposals, and bad him tell his lady, 'That all king Edward's friends and dependants should joyn with her for the earl of Richmond, on condition he took his corporal oath to marry the lady Elizabeth her eldest daughter, or in case she were not living, the lady Cecilia, her second daughter.' Dr. Lewis cary'd this pleasing answer to his mistress; from whom he went frequently to the queen as a physician, and from her to the countess, till matters were fully concluded between them. While these things were transacting by the two princesses, Reginald Bray was employ'd to engage as many persons of quality as he could in the earl's interest; accordingly, he procur'd Sir Charles Daubeney, Sir John Cheyney, Richard Guilford and Thomas Rame esquires, and others, to promise their utmost assistance, taking an oath of secrecy and fidelity of all of them. The queen dowager on her part made the earl many friends, and the business in a short time was so ripe, that 'twas thought proper to send an account of it to the earl, and give him notice to prepare for his return to England, Christopher Ursewick her chaplain, was first sent, and soon after follow'd by Hugh Conway, esq.; with money to provide men and other necessaries for his voyage, and a full account of the disposition the nobility and commonalty were in to receive him favourably. She advis'd him to land in Wales, that principality being most inclin'd to him, as well for his descent being Welsh, as for the great estate she had there. For fear Mr. Conway should miscarry in his voyage, Mr. Rame was despatch'd away with the same instructions : the former sail'd from Plimoth, the latter from Kent; and tho' they took different routes they arriv'd at the duke of Britain's court both within an hour of each other. They communicated the subject of their commission to him. For which he render'd thanks to the Almighty, being such joyful news as he wou'd not have given light credit to ; but it came so circumstantiated, and by such trusty messengers, that he did not doubt of the truth of it. He imparted the secret to the duke of Bretagne, informing him what a fair prospect he had of obtaining the crown of England, desiring him to assist him, and promising to return all his acts of generosity and friendship as soon as it was in his power. The duke gave him hopes of assistance, and accordingly he lent him money and troops for his intended expedition ; though Thomas Hutton, king Richard's ambassador, offer'd large sums. and earnestly solicited the duke and his ministers to put the earl's person in safe custody. The earl having receiv'd so good incouragement in Bretagne, sent Mr. Conway and Mr. Rame back again to gave his friends an account of his intentions and preparations, and to desire them to provide everything necessary for his reception.

The messengers returning, satisfy'd the queen dowager by Dr. Lewis of the earl's readiness to comply with the terms she propos'd, and inform'd the conspirators of the duke of Bretagne's promising to lend him men and money: upon which they all repair'd to their several posts to make provision for joyning him with sufficient strength to accomplish their designs when he arriv'd. With these, all such as had any grudge against, or quarrel with king Richard, fell in, by which means the party encreas'd daily, and so many persons could not act zealously in such an affair without giving umbrage of their intentions to the usurper.

King Richard endeavour'd by his spies to find out the bottom of their conspiracies, but he had to deal with men of equal cunning and secrecy, and he cou'd not fix the matter on any one, tho' he did not doubt but there was a plot carrying on to dethrone him and advance the earl of Richmond. The duke of Buckingham's avoiding the court, made him jealous that he was in it; and to get him into his power he made use of his dissimulation, a quality that had been very serviceable to him in his usurpation, and wrote him very kind obliging letters to come to London; but the duke pretending indisposition excus'd himself. The king enrag'd to find his artifices unsuccessful, sent him a letter in a rougher stile commanding him on his allegiance to attend him. The duke answer'd as roughly, 'That he wou'd not expose himself to his mortal enemy whom he neither lov'd nor wou'd serve:' he knew this answer was a declaration of war, and to lose no time took arms. The same did Thomas Marquess of Dorset, who had escap'd out of sanctuary, in Yorkshire. Sir Edward Courtney and Peter Bishop of Exeter his brother in Devonshire and Cornwall; and others in other places. The king hearing of these insurrections was not at all dishearten'd, but must'ring all his forces march'd against the duke of Buckingham, the head and heart of the conspirators; whom if he suppress'd he suppos'd the others wou'd fall of course, or if not, he might easily reduce them. The duke rather by the influence he had over the Welshmen who were his tenants, than out of any inclination they had to follow him, got a great multitude of them together, with whom he march'd through the forrest of Dean towards Gloucester, intending to pass the Severn there, and thence to proceed into the west to joyn the Courtneys; which if he cou'd have effected, king Richard's reign had not been so long as it was by a year. But it happen'd that the river Severn was so swoln by a continual rain for ten days together, that it over-flow'd all the neighbouring country, did abundance of damage, and 'twas so remarkable, that for a hundred years after, that inundation was call'd, the Great Water, or Buckingham's water, by the inhabitants of those parts. These floods as it hinder'd the duke's passing the Severn to joyn his friends in Devonshire; so it prevented his friends on the other side of the river passing over to him: in which extremity the Welshmen deserted by degrees, till at last the duke had none left about him but his domestick servants. Nor prayers nor threats cou'd keep them together, so he was forc'd to fly with the rest, and in despair fled to the house of one Humphrey Banister near Shrewsbury, designing to hide himself there till he cou'd raise more forces, or escape thence to the earl of Richmond in Bretagne. He trusted this Banister as a man who had so many obligations to him, that he did not think it cou'd be almost possible for human nature to be so ungrateful, as to betray a master who had been so kind to a servant as the duke had been to Banister; having bred him up, provided for him honourably, and put entire confidence in him on many occasions. Yet upon king Richard's proclamation to apprehend the duke, with the promise of a thousand pounds reward to the man that should discover him, this faithless wretch betray'd his master to John Milton esq., sheriff of Shropshire, who surrounded his house with a party of the county militia, seiz'd the duke, and carried him to the king, who then kept his court at Salisbury. Banister and his whole family were destroy'd by the surprizing judgments of the Almighty. The usurper refus'd to pay him the thousand pounds promis'd in the proclamation; saying, 'He that wou'd betray so good a master, wou'd be false to any other.' The duke earnestly desir'd to be admitted to the king's presence, but whether he was or not, we cannot determine. Some writers affirm he was, and that he attempted to stab him with a dagger. 'Tis certain he confess'd the whole conspiracy, and without any further tryal was beheaded in the market-place at Salisbury, on the 2nd of November. Such was the fate of Henry Stafford, whom most authors call Edward duke of Buckingham: he married Katherine the daughter of Richard Woodville, sister to queen Elizabeth wife to Edward IV. by whom he had Edward duke of Buckingham, Henry earl of Wiltshire, and two daughters; the one married George lord Hastings, and the other Richard Ratcliffe lord Fitz-Waters The duke of Bucks was hereditary constable of England, and his estate and revenues were so great, that king Richard had reason to be jealous of him; for no subject in England was so powerful either in the number of his tenants and dependants, or in his vast riches.

By the dispersing of the Welshmen the western army was so discouraged, that every man shifted for himself. Some fled to sanctuary, others took shipping and sail'd to Bretagne to the earl of Richmond. Among these were Peter Courtney bishop of Exeter, sir Edward

Courtney his brother, afterwards created earl of Devonshire by Henry the seventh, Thomas marquess Dorset, John lord Welles, sir John Bourchier, sir Edward Woodville the queen dowager's brother, sir Robert Willoughby, sir Giles Daubeney, sir John Cheyney and his two brothers, sir Thomas Arundel, sir William Berkley, sir William Branden, Thomas Branden esq., and Capt. Edward Poynings, a famous soldier, whom Henry VII. highly preferr'd. King Richard did all that a wise prince cou'd think of to prevent their getting off. Knowing what an addition to the earl's power, the presence of so many persons of quality wou'd make, he set guards on most of the ports of England; but those in the west being in the hands of the malecontents, they escap'd the cruel vengeance which was prepar'd for them. The usurper fitted out a fleet to cruise off the coasts of Bretagne, and prevent the earl of Richmond's landing any forces in England; but the earl not hearing of the duke's misfortune, set sail the 12th of October with a fleet of forty ships having 5000 Bretons aboard. They had not been long at sea before they met with a storm that scatter'd their fleet. The ship in which was the earl in person was driven on the coast of England to the mouth of the Haven of Pool in Dorsetshire; where finding the shoar was crouded with troops to oppose his descent, he forbad any of his men to land till the whole navy came up. However, he sent out his boat with some officers to demand of the men, who stood on the shoar, whether they were friends or enemies? These traytors instructed by king Richard answer'd, they were friends posted there by the duke of Bucks, to receive the earl of Richmond. The earl suspecting the deceit, and perceiving he was alone, the rest of his fleet not appearing, weigh'd anchor and return'd to France. He landed in Normandy, where he refresh'd himself and his men two or three days, and then sent a gentleman to Charles the eighth, the French king, desiring passports thro' his territories into Bretagne; which was readily granted by Charles. However the earl did not stay for the return of his courier, but trusting to the French king's generosity continu'd his journey thro' Normandy to Vannes, where the duke of Bretagne resided. When he arriv'd there he heard of the duke of Buckingham's death, and found the marquess Dorset, and the other English gentlemen who had made their escape. They all swore allegiance to him, and he took his corporal oath, on the same day the 25th of December, that he would marry the princess Elizabeth when he had suppress'd the usurper Richard, and was in possession of the crown.

The zeal which these gentlemen shewed in his cause, and the consideration of the great interest they had in England, lessen'd the earl's sorrow for the misfortune of his friends in their first attempts against the tyrant, and encouraged him to refit his fleet and prepare for a new voyage to England, where many of his friends were seiz'd and executed; as sir George Brown and sir Roger Clifford who were beheaded at London; and sir Thomas St. Leger, who had married the king's own sister the Duchess of Exeter, Thomas Rame, esq., and several of his own servants; the two former were executed at Exon; the latter, whom he condemn'd on bare suspicion, at London, and other places. The usurper made a progress to Devonshire and Cornwall to settle the peace of those countries, where the earl's party was very numerous. The mayor, aldermen, and citizens of Exeter presented him with a purse of gold to obtain his favour: he receiv'd it graciously, lay in the city one night, and the next day went about it to take a view of it: when he came to the castle, and was inform'd 'twas called Rugemont, he seem'd very melancholy, and said, 'I find I shall not live long.' He thought that name was foretold by an old prophecy which he had heard relating to him, that his end would be nigh when he came to Richmond: which prediction was fulfill'd at the battle of Bosworth. In his western journey, he found the gentlemen of those parts were almost all concern'd in the conspiracy to depose him and raise the earl of Richmond to the throne. All that had made their escape were out-law'd, and those that fell into his hands were put to death; for he knew not what mercy and humanity meant.

In the beginning of the following year (1484) he summon'd a parliament, in which the earl of Richmond and his followers were attainted, and the people burthen'd with severe taxes and impositions. The money so collected was wasted on his creatures, or squander'd away prodigally on such as knew anything of his guilt in the death of his nephews, to stop their mouths. He obliged the lord Stanley to confine his wife the countess of Richmond, so that she should have no means of holding correspondence with any one to his prejudice. He ordered William Collingburne of Lydiard in Wiltshire to be hang'd, drawn and quarter'd, for aiding and assisting the earl of Richmond and his followers, and writing a satyrical dystich upon him and his favourites, the lord viscount Lovel, Sir Richard Ratcliffe, and sir William Catesby.

  The cat, the rat, and Lovell the dog,
  Rule all England under a hog.

Alluding by the hog to the usurper's arms, one of his supporters being a wild boar. Yet these executions did not ease him of his fears: he heard by his emissaries abroad, that Dr. Moreton, bishop of Ely, and Ursewich, the countess of Richmond's chaplain, who liv'd in Flanders, had carried on a close correspondence with many of the chief persons in his kingdom; and that the duke of Bretagne still continu'd to protect and support the earl Henry. He saw the storm that had been lately gathering over him was not dispers'd by the duke of Buckingham's death, and the flight of the Courtneys; the clouds grew darker still, and the tempest that threatened him was such as requir'd all his arts and all his power to provide against. He secur'd his dominions on the side of Scotland, by entring into an alliance with the Scots king, to whose eldest son the duke of Rothsay he married the lady Anne de la Pool, daughter to John duke of Suffolk, by Anne the usurper's best belov'd sister. Her son John he proclaim'd heir apparent to the crown, without having regard to king Edward the Fourth's daughters: yet all his negotiations and successes abroad and at home were ineffectual, and he perceiv'd that nothing would entirely secure him against the earl and his friends' contrivances, unless he cou'd get his person into his power. To this purpose he sent over other ambassadors to the duke of Bretagne, with instructions to apply themselves to Peter Landeise the duke's chief minister and favourite, and by immense sums of money to endeavour to tempt him to betray the earl. They were to offer him for the duke his master the clear profits of all the earl's estate in England, and for himself whatever he cou'd ask of them. The treacherous Breton hearken'd to the proposals made by Richard's ambassadors, and promis'd to deliver the earl of Richmond to them. But the bishop of Ely who had intelligence in king Richard and the duke of Bretagne's courts, understood what designs were forming against earl Henry, of which he sent him notice by Ursewich; and the earl giving credit to his information, escap'd in disguise with his principal officers into the French king's dominions. Landeise intended a day or two after to have seiz'd him, and when he miss'd him sent couriers into all parts of the duchy in search of him. He was scarce got into the French territories when one of the parties that was sent out after him came within an hour's riding of him, but he had prevented Landeise his treachery, who acted without his master's privity. The duke of Bretagne being at that time dangerously ill, and leaving all things to his management. The English refugees that remain'd in Bretagne expected all to be delivered up to the fury of king Richard, when they heard of the earl's escape, and the reasons of it: and had not the duke of Bretagne recover'd and took on him the administration of affairs, the traytor Landeise wou'd have seiz'd them, and yielded them up to the usurper's ambassadors. The duke inquiring into the causes of the earl's flight into France, was very much displeas'd with Landeise and sent for sir Edward Woodvill and Capt. Poynings, to whom he excus'd the treachery of his minister, disowning the knowledge of it, and gave them a considerable sum of money to conduct them and all the Englishmen who were at Vannes, thro' Bretagne into France to their master the earl of Richmond: for which generous act the earl sent him thanks by a messenger on purpose. Himself went to Loinges on the Loire, where Charles VIII., the French king, kept his court, and from thence accompanied him to Montargis. Charles entertain'd him and his followers very magnificently, but was not very forward to lend him any assistance.

While the earl was in the French court, John earl of Oxford repair'd to him with James Blunt captain of the castle of Haumes, in which the Lord Oxford had been confin'd several years, and had engag'd the governour in the interest of the earl of Richmond; with them came Sir John Fortescue, porter of the tower of Calais. James Blunt had reinforc'd his garrison, supply'd it with all sorts of provisions for a vigorous defence, and left a trusty officer to command there in his absence. The arrival of the earl of Oxford, and the revolt of the garrison of Haumes, animated afresh earl Henry and his friends, whose spirits began to sink, seeing the little hopes they had of help in France. Their company increas'd after this daily: most of the English gentlemen who were students in the university of Paris did homage to the earl, among whom was Mr. Richard Fox, afterwards bishop of Winchester; and as their numbers grew greater abroad, their interest at home was consequently enlarged.

The usurper, who by his spies had a full account of all their proceedings, knew that the hopes of the party were founded on the earl's promise to marry the princess Elizabeth, which he resolv'd by some means or other to prevent; and to that end he did his utmost to ingratiate himself with her mother queen Elizabeth. He sent several flattering messages to her in sanctuary, promised to advance the marquess Dorset and all her relations, and won upon her so much by his fair speeches, that forgetting the many affronts he had cast on the memory of her husband, on her own honour and the legitimacy of her children, and even the murder of her dear sons, she comply'd with him, and promis'd to bring over her son, and all the late king's friends from the party of the earl of Richmond. She went so far, as to deliver up her five daughters into his hands; whom as soon as king Richard had got in his custody, he resolv'd to order the matter so, that he might be in a condition to take the eldest of them to be his wife; which was a sure way of defeating the earl of Richmond's purposes. Queen Elizabeth was so charm'd by his false promises, that she wrote to her son the marquis Dorset to leave earl Henry and hasten to England, where she had procur'd him a pardon, and provided all sorts of honours for him. What success her letters had, we shall see in the course of this history.

We have already observed, that king Richard had cast his eyes upon his brother Edward the Fourth's daughter, the princess Elizabeth: he had been guilty of treason and murder, and almost all the crimes that are to be found in the infernal rolls: incest seem'd only wanting to make him a compleat monster of mankind, the horror of his people, and the shame of the whole world. As he was master of the art of dissimulation, and had lately put on the mask of piety, so he was a little at a loss how to remove his wife out of the way, to make room for his niece in his bed. He began his lewd design, by shewing an aversion to his wife's company and embraces. He complain'd to several lords of the council, of her barrenness; especially to Thomas Rotherham, archbishop of York, whom he had lately released out of prison. He told him of some private defects in the queen, which had render'd her person disagreeable to him, and hop'd the bishop would tell her of it, who being a woman of a meek temper, he thought would take it so much to heart, that she would not live long after it. Dr. Rotherham said to some of his most intimate friends, the queen's days are but few; for he perceiv'd by the usurper's discourse, that he was weary of her and wanted another wife, and he knew him so well, that he could not suppose he would scruple to add one murder more to the many bloody cruelties he had been guilty of to satisfy his lust and ambition. To prepare the way for her death, he order'd a report to be spread among the people that she was dead: which he did with an intention, that the rumour coming to her ears, it might alarm her with fear of her sudden fate, and those fears throw her into a disease which might carry her off. The queen no sooner heard of what was reported against her, but she believ'd it came originally from her husband; and thence concluding, that her hour was drawing nigh, she ran to him in a most sorrowful and deplorable condition, and demanded of him 'What she had done to deserve death?' The tyrant answer'd her with fair words and false smiles, bidding her 'Be of good chear, for to his knowledge she had no other cause.' But whether her grief, as he design'd it should, struck so to her heart, that it broke with the mortal wound, or he hasten'd her end, as was generally suspected, by poison, she died in a few days afterwards. She was daughter to the famous earl of Warwick; and when Richard married her, widow to prince Edward, heir to Henry VI. The usurper affected to show an extraordinary sorrow at her death, and was at the expense of a pompous funeral for her. Notwithstanding all his pretended mourning, before she was scarce cold in the grave, he made his addresses to the princess Elizabeth, who had his love in abhorrence, and the whole kingdom appear'd averse to so unnatural a marriage. His affairs were in such an ill posture, that he durst not provoke the queen and the people further, by putting a violence on the princess's inclinations; so he deferr'd his courtship till he was better settl'd in the throne. The nobility daily past over into France: the gentry and commonalty everywhere, shew'd an affection to the earl of Richmond, as far as they durst do it, without bringing themselves under the lash of the tyrant's laws. He was most jealous of Thomas Lord Stanley, his brother sir William Stanley, and Gilbert Talbot. He obliged the

Lord Stanley to leave his son George Stanley, lord Strange, at court, as an hostage of his old fidelity. He commanded the governour of Calais to attack the castle of Haumes : (1485) The earl of Oxford and Captain Blunt immediately hasten'd to the relief of it, but before they could arrive near it, the garrison was reduced to the last extremity, and the besiegers, on the report of the earl of Oxford's approach, offering them to march out with bag and baggage, they surrender'd the fort, and joyn'd the earl, who led them to Paris, where they were entertain'd by the earl of Richmond. The reduction of Haumes, and the small hopes of assistance which earl Henry had in the French court, made the usurper so secure, that he recall'd the squadron of men of war, which he had order'd to cruise in the channel and prevent the earl's making a descent in England, and contented himself with commanding the lords and gentlemen, who liv'd near the coasts to be on their guard to defend them.

In the mean time the earl of Richmond continued his negotiations in the court of France for succours; but Charles VIII. being in his minority, he was forced to apply to the Regents, or ministers of state, who being divided among themselves, had no inclination to unite in his favour. The chiefest of them was Lewis, duke of Orleans, who afterwards was king: but by their civil dissensions, the affairs of his supplies were spun on to so great a length, that the usurper flattered himself 'twould never take effect. For this reason he grew more pleasant than before, his joy increased as his care lessen'd, and lull'd him at last into a fatal security.

The queen dowager, to oblige the king, who lately appear'd very ready to serve her and her daughters, continued to write to her son the marquess of Dorset, to leave earl Henry. The marquis fearing the earl wou'd not succeed in his enterprize, gave way to his mother's persuasions, and king Richard's flattering promises, left the earl, and stole away from Paris by night, intending to escape to Flanders: but as soon as the earl had notice of his flight, he apply'd to the French court, for leave to apprehend him in any part of his dominions; for both himself and his followers were afraid of his discovering all their designs, to their utter destruction if he got to England. Having obtain'd licence to seize him, the earl sent messengers every way in search of him, and among the rest, Humphrey Cheyney, esq., who overtook him near Champaigne, and by arguments and fair promises prevail'd with him to return. By the marquess's disposition to leave him, the earl began to doubt that if he delay'd his expedition to England longer, many more of his friends might grow cool in their zeal for him; so he earnestly solicited the French court for aid, desiring so small a supply of men and money, that Charles cou'd not in honour refuse him; yet for what he lent him, he would have hostages, that satisfaction should be made. The earl made no scruple of that, so leaving the lord marquess

Dorset (whom he still mistrusted) and sir John Bourchier as his pledges at Paris, he departed for Roan, where the few men that the French king had lent him, and all the English that follow'd his fortunes rendezvous'd.

When he arriv'd there, he was inform'd of the usurper's intentions to marry the princess Elizabeth himself, and her sister, the princess Cecilia, to a man of mean condition. This was mortifying news to him, for he imagin'd if his alliance with the house of York was by that means broken, their friends would all fall off from him: however he resolv'd to push for the crown, as heir to the house of Lancaster, but then it was necessary for him to encrease his strength and interest; wherefore he dispatch'd away a messenger to sir Walter Herbert, a man of great power in Wales, to get him to espouse his quarrel, by an offer of marrying his sister, a beautiful young lady. The earl of Northumberland had married another of sir Walter's sisters, and the earl of Richmond's agent had instructions to address himself also to him, and persuade him to forward the marriage. The messenger found the ways so narrowly watch'd, that he cou'd not proceed on his journey: and 'twas well for the earl that he did no more in it; for had any such treaty been proposed and known, his friends, who were so on the princess Elizabeth's account, had all forsaken him. The messenger being thus disappointed, the earl receiv'd one out of England, Morgan Kidwellie, esq., a lawyer, who brought him advice, that sir Rice ap Thomas, a gentleman who was as powerful in Wales as sir Walter Herbert, and capt. John Savage, a famous soldier, had made great preparations to assist him; that Reginald Bray had collected large sums of money to pay his troops, and earnestly entreated him to hasten his voyage and direct his course to Wales. The earl rejoycing at this good news, order'd all his forces to embark and sail from Harfleet in Normandy in August, with about two thousand men, in a few ships, just enough to transport them. After seven days' sail, he arriv'd in the haven of Milford, and landed at a place call'd Dalle, from whence he march'd the next day to Haverford West, whence he was receiv'd with joy by the townsmen. Having refresh'd his men, and sent notice, by trusty messengers, to his mother, the lord Stanley, and Sigilbert Talbot, that he intended to direct his march towards London, desiring them to meet him on the way with their powers, he advanced to Shrewsbury, where sir Gilbert Talbot joyn'd him with the earl of Shrewsbury's tenants, as sir Rice ap Thomas and Richard Griffith, esq. had done before, with a body of Welsh-men; by which his army became so strong, that he easily reduced all the towns to which he came in his march. Sir Rice ap Thomas wou'd not come unto him, till he had promised to make him governour of Wales, in case he got the crown; which the earl agreed to and perform'd as soon as 'twas in his power, sir Rice having been very faithful and serviceable to him.

In the meanwhile, the lord Stanley and his brother sir William Stanley rais'd men, but did not declare whom they would side with; sir William advanced with his army into Staffordshire, and waited on the earl of Richmond at Stafford, attended only by twenty or thirty persons. The lord Stanley lay at Litchfield with 5000 men; yet neither he nor his brother joyn'd the earl. Sir William having had a short conference with him, return'd to his forces; and when the earl approach'd near Litchfield, the lord Stanley return'd to Atherstone, to prevent king Richard's having any suspicion of him; being afraid that the tyrant would murder his son the lord Strange, whom he had in his custody, if he sided openly with the earl of Richmond.

The usurper at first despised the earl's attempt, hearing he had brought so few men with him, he did not doubt but sir Walter Herbert would easily suppress him with the militia in Wales, which he order'd him to raise, but when he heard that sir Walter had suffered him to pass, and so many gentlemen had joyn'd him with their friends and dependants, that his army would be as numerous as his own, if the Lancashire men, under the Stanley's, declar'd for him, he resolved to oppose him in person. He commanded Henry earl of Northumberland, sir Thomas Bourchier, and sir Walter Hungerford, and other gentlemen whose loyalty he suspected, to attend him in arms, and sent for the duke of Norfolk, the earl of Surrey, sir Robert Brackenbury, lieutenant of the Tower, and others, to bring their whole strength with them, to enable him to give the earl battle before he receiv'd further assistance. When all his troops were arriv'd at Nottingham, where he kept his court, he put himself at their head and led them to Leicester. Sir Thomas Bourchier, sir Walter Hungerford, and several others, found means to desert to the earl; which tho' it was a great discouragement to Richard, yet it did ease earl Henry of his discontent, for that the lord Stanley had not joyn'd him. His army proceeded from Litchfield to Tamworth, himself bringing up the rear with about twenty horse.

As he was musing on the difficulties of his enterprize, he lagg'd behind his company, and it growing dark, they march'd on and enterd Tamworth before they missed him. His care was increased, by a report, that king Richard was at hand; whose coming up before the lord Stanley had joyn'd him, threatned his whole army with destruction; yet his men were not discourag'd, they trusted in their own valour and the goodness of their cause, and proceeded with great resolution.

The earl having insensibly lost his companions, and the high-way to Tamworth, turn'd aside to a little village three miles from Tamworth, where he stay'd all night, not daring to discover himself, or ask a guide to the town. His followers were much surprized at his absence, and afraid what was become of him. He was also apprehensive of the ill effects of their missing him, and not a little fearful of falling into the hands of some of the usurper's parties. Early in the morning he left the village, and happily arriv'd at the town, to the unspeakable joy of his army: he excus'd his absence by pretending he had been to consult with some private friends of his who durst not yet appear for him. He was unwilling his companions shou'd think him guilty of such a blunder as to lose his way, when he had so many guides about him, and made that a piece of policy, which was indeed downright ignorance: so easie 'tis for princes to impose upon their people who are ready to judge favourably of all their actions.

He just shew'd himself to his soldiers, and then left them again to go to Atherstone, where he first saw and saluted the lord Stanley, his father in law; he held a conference with him and sir William Stanley in a little field, where they consulted how they should give the tyrant battle to the best advantage. In the evening sir John Savage, sir Bryan Sanford, and sir Simon Digby, came unto him with all their friends and followers from king Richard, who was advanc'd to Leicester, and his army encamp'd not far off, on a hill call'd Arme Beame, in Bosworth parish. The next day after king Richard arriv'd at Leicester, he went to the camp and drew up his men in order of battle on the plain. He plac'd his archers in front under the command of the duke of Norfolk, and the earl of Surrey his son; himself led the main body, with two wings of cavalry on each flank. The earl leaving the lord Stanley return'd to his army, and march'd them out of Tamworth towards the enemy, resolving to fight king Richard. The lord Stanley also march'd from Atherstone, and halted in a place between the two armies. The earl sent to him to come and help to set his men in order of battle; but the lord Stanley even now was so cautious, that he excus'd his appearing among the earl's followers: he bad him draw up his soldiers, he wou'd do the same by his, and joyn him at supper time. Tho' this answer vext the earl of Richmond inwardly, he seem'd as well satisfy'd as if he had come, and cheerfully put his men in order: his front was thin, and consisted of archers, commanded by John earl of Oxford; sir Gilbert Talbot led the right wing, and sir John Savage the left, attended by a troop of young fellows well arm'd, clad in white coats and hoods, who made a gallant figure, terrible to the enemy. The earl of Richmond accompanied by the earl of Pembroke led the main body; his whole strength did not amount to six thousand men, Stanley's forces which were seven or eight thousand strong excepted: and king Richard had twice that number. In the order we have mention'd, the two armies advanced towards each other; the lord Stanley moving aside off as the earl of Richmond mov'd; and when the usurper was come farther into the plain where he expected the earl's approach, he made a speech to his army to this purpose.

'MY FRIENDS AND FELLOW SOLDIERS,

'By your valour and conduct I got and have enjoy'd the crown in spite of all the wicked designs of your and my enemies. I have govern'd this nation as a good prince ought to do for the benefit of my subjects, and done nothing without the advice and consent of my councellors, whose fidelity and wisdom I have often prov'd ; and your loyalty to me makes me believe that you have an opinion of me as I have of myself, that I am your rightful and lawful king. Tho' at my accession to the throne I was guilty of a wicked detested crime, yet my repentance of it has been so severe and so sincere that I hope you will forget it, as I shall never cease to deplore and lament it. Considering the danger we are in at this time, what a gracious prince I have been to you, and what good subjects you have been to me, we are bound by the strictest bonds of obligation and duty mutually to defend one another in so great peril. To keep what we have got is as glorious as to get it : and as by your assistance I was advanced to the throne, so I hope by the same help to continue in it. I doubt not you have heard of the traiterous devices of an obscure Welshman (whose father I never knew, and whom I never saw) against our crown and dignity. You hear who they are that he depends upon, a company of traytors, thieves, outlaws and fugitives ; mean beggarly Bretons, and cowardly Frenchmen : whose aim is the destruction of you, your wives and children, as 'tis their leaders to dispossess me of the imperial crown of this realm. Let us therefore joyn heartily in our common defence, fight like lions, and fear not to die like men : indeed there is nothing for you to be afraid of. The hare never fled faster from before the hound, nor the lark from the kite, nor the sheep from the wolf, than these boasting adversaries of ours shall quit the field at the sight of such brave soldiers. Nor do I promise you victory without reason : for let us think a little who it is that we have to deal with. And first for the earl of Richmond, captain of the rebels, a Welsh boy, of little courage and less experience in war ; bred up in the duke of Britain's court like a bird in a cage, who never saw an army, and consequently is not capable to lead one. The soldier's success is owing in a great measure to the captain's conduct and valour. What can his men hope from him ? What from themselves ? a crew of vagabonds and rebels, who will tremble when they see us advancing with banners display'd to chastise them. They will either fly before us, or conscious of divine vengeance for the breach of many oaths of allegiance they have sworn to us, throw down their arms, and at our feet implore our royal mercy. As for the Frenchmen and Bretons, our noble ancestors have often triumph'd over them. What are they ? Boasters, drunkards, ravishers, cowards, the most effeminate and lewd wretches that ever offer'd themselves in front of battle.

Since such are the enemies we are to fight with, come on, my friends and fellow soldiers, and dauntless try if they dare dispute this matter with us by dint of sword. Come on my captains and champions, in whose wisdom and courage I trust for me and my people. What is a handful to a whole nation? Let me conjure you all by your love to your country, your duty to your king, and your affection to your families, to behave yourselves like good subjects and soldiers this day, when I resolve to be victorious or crown my death with immortal fame. Remember, that as I promise those who do well riches and honours; so I shall severely punish such as deserve it by their cowardice or treachery. And now in the name of St. George, let us meet our enemies.'

Whether this speech was made by him or for him, we cannot decide; the author from whom we took it says it was his own, and that it had not so good an effect on the minds of his soldiers as he intended it should have. He had many gentlemen, and others in his army, who follow'd him more out of fear than affection; and wish'd well to his adversary. The earl of Richmond receiving by his scouts, that the usurper's army was drawn up in battalia a little distance off on the plain, rode from rank to rank and wing to wing to encourage his men. He was arm'd at all points (his helmet excepted) and got up on an eminence to be the better seen by his soldiers: for tho' he was handsome and well-proportion'd, yet he was short. Having kept silence some time to consider of what he was about to say to them, he began his speech thus:

'If ever God appear'd in a just cause, and gave a blessing to their arms who warr'd for the good of their country: if ever he aided such as ventur'd their lives for the relief of the innocent, and to suppress malefactors and publick criminals; we may now, my friends and fellow soldiers, be sure of victory over our proud and insolent enemies. Just and righteous is our cause, and we cannot be so wicked as to imagine God will leave us, to assist those that fear neither him nor his laws, nor have any regard to honesty or justice. We have the laws divine and civil on our side; we fight against a parricide stain'd with his own blood, a destroyer of the nobility, and an oppressor of the poor commons of this realm; and against a horrid band of murderers, assassins, rebels and usurpers: for he that stiles himself king wears the crown which of right only belongs to me. His favourites and followers seize your estates, cut down your woods, ruin and lay waste your mannours and mansions, and turn your wives and children to wander in the wide world without succour and relief: the cause of all these mischiefs, the cruel tyrant Richard, rest assur'd that God will this day give into our hands to be punish'd according to his demerits. His followers wounded by the stings of their guilty consciences, will not dare to look justice in the face: and believe not that yon numerous army are your adversaries; many of them, if not the most part of that multitude, are forc'd into the tyrant's service, have his crimes in abhorrence, and wait only for an opportunity to joyn us. You have often heard from the pulpit, that 'tis the greatest of virtues to bring down the oppressor, and to help those who are in distress. Is not the usurper, Richard duke of Gloucester, a violator of God's laws and man's? Who can have the least good thought of one that so injur'd his own brother's memory, and murder'd his nephews? Who can hope for mercy from him who delights in blood? Who trust in him who mistrusts all men. Tarquin the proud, so infamous in history, whom the Romans banish'd their city for ever, was less guilty than this usurper. Nero, who slew his own mother, and open'd the womb that bare him to see the place of his conception, was not more a monster of mankind than Richard. In him you have at once a Tarquin and a Nero, behold there, a tyrant worse than even him that murder'd his mother, and set his imperial city in a flame. One, who has not only slain his own nephew, his king and sovereign lord, bastardiz'd his noble brothers, affronted his mother's honour, but try'd all the arts his and his creatures cunning cou'd invent to defile his own niece, under the specious pretence of a marriage, a princess I have sworn to marry, as you all know and believe. If this cause is not just, let God the giver of all victory judge and determine. We have (thanks be to Jesus our saviour) escap'd the treasons form'd in Bretagne, and the snares laid by our subtle adversaries to destroy us; we have pass'd the seas, travers'd a spacious country in safety to search for the boar, whom we have at last found. Let us not therefore fear to begin the bloody chase. Let us put our confidence in the Almighty, and verily believe that this is the hour we have long'd and pray'd for, which will put an end to the many miseries we have hitherto endur'd. Think what a glorious prize is before us. The wealth and spoil of the tyrant and his followers is yours if we conquer, and conquer we must or die; for we are now come so far that there is no retreat left us. Let us one and all resolve to end our labours now by death or victory. Let courage supply want of number, and as for me, I purpose to live with glory hereafter, or perish with glory here. Come on then, let us meet these traytors, murderers, usurpers; let us be bold and we shall triumph: we are utterly destroy'd if we fly; if we are victorious there's an end of all our perils and dangers. In the name of God, and St. George, come on and prosper.'

These words so encourag'd his men, that they demanded to be led immediately against the enemy. There was a morass between the two armies, the earl left it on his right hand, by which he not only hinder'd king Richard's attacking him on that side, but had the sun in his back, and it shone full in the faces of his enemies. The usurper seeing his army was approaching, order'd his trumpets to sound and the archers to let fly their arrows: the earl's bowmen return'd their shot, and when that dreadful storm was over, the foot joyn'd and came to close fight. 'Twas then that the lord Stanley came in to the earl's assistance. The earl of Oxford fearing his men might be surrounded by the multitude of the enemy, commanded none should stir above ten foot from the standard: the soldiers presently closed their ranks and ceas'd the combat, expecting further orders. King Richard's troops being jealous of some stratagem, stood still to observe them; and indeed they did not fight with a very good will at all. The earl of Oxford led his men again to the charge. The duke of Norfolk, the usurper's fast friend, chang'd the order of his battle, widen'd his first line, but clos'd and enlarg'd his second; and then renew'd the combat. King Richard hearing the earl of Richmond was not far off, attended with a few of his guards only, sought him amidst his enemies, and having spy'd him, set spurs to his horse and ran towards him; the earl perceiv'd him, and prepar'd to receive him as a man shou'd his mortal foe. The king meeting with sir William Branden the earl's standard bearer in his way, overthrew and slew him. This knight was father of Charles Branden duke of Suffolk, famous in the reign of Henry VIII. Richard then fought sir John Cheyney, dismounted him, and forc'd his way up to the earl; who kept him off at swords point till assistance came in, and he was reliev'd by his followers. At the instant sir William Stanley, who had been as wary as the lord Stanley his brother, joyn'd the earl with three thousand chosen men, upon which king Richard's soldiers turn'd their backs and fled; himself fighting manfully in the midst of his enemies was slain. The earl of Oxford made a terrible slaughter in the van of the usurper's army. The duke of Norfolk, the lord Ferrars of Chartley, sir Richard Ratcliffe, and sir Robert Brackenbury dy'd on the spot, together with about a thousand of their men. The greatest part of those in the main body of Richard's army watching their opportunity, while the van was hotly engag'd with the earl's, left the field and departed every man to his home; having been by force taken from their habitations to fight for a prince whose government was odious to them. The duke of Norfolk was warn'd, by a dystich in the meeter of those times which was fix'd on the gate of the house where he lodg'd, not to venture farther in the tyrant's quarrel; for he was betray'd, and all those that engag'd with him would be ruin'd. The Rhimes were these:

> Jack of Norfolk, be not too bold;
> For Dicken, thy master, is bought and sold.

But as John Howard duke of Norfolk owed his advancement to the usurper, who made him a duke, he thought his own title to the honours he held wou'd be precarious, if Richard cou'd not defend his crown; so he follow'd his fortune, and fell a victim to his ambition.

Sir William Catesby a judge, who had been a main instrument of the usurper's tyranny, and several other offenders were taken, and two days afterwards beheaded at Leicester. The lord viscount Lovell, Humphrey Stafford, esq., and Thomas Stafford his brother, made their escapes. Many gentlemen and private soldiers threw down their arms, submitted to the earl, and were graciously receiv'd. Among those was Henry earl of Northumberland, who did not engage in the late battle, he and his men standing neuter; for which he was immediately taken into the earl of Richmond's favour and sworn of his privy-council. Thomas earl of Surrey was sent to the Tower, as having been more zealous than the rest in the tyrant's cause: however he was releas'd soon after, and preferr'd to places of the greatest trust and honour. Earl Henry had scarce a hundred men killed on his part, and no person of quality besides sir William Branden. The engagement lasted in all about two hours, and happen'd on the 22nd day of August. The usurper there finish'd his evil course after he had reign'd two years, two months and one day, reckoning from the time of his coronation, which was the day after his election. Had he liv'd with as much glory as he dy'd, his character wou'd have shone bright in the English annals. But tho' he wanted not personal bravery, yet that quality as shining as it is, was sully'd and obscur'd by his cruelty, and thirst of blood. He might have sav'd his life had not despair hurried him on to death. In the beginning of the battle, he perceiv'd, by his men's fighting with an ill-will and others leaving him, that the day was lost. Some of his creatures advised him to fly, and brought him a swift horse to carry him off; but knowing how generally he was hated by the whole kingdom, and that his crimes were such as deny'd him all hopes of pardon, he thought the longer he liv'd his misery wou'd be the longer, and that at last he shou'd dye with infamy; wherefore he rush'd desperately into the thickest of the enemy, and met a more glorious fate than he deserved.

After the battle was over and the victory entirely gain'd, the earl of Richmond fell down on his knees in the open field, thank'd the Almighty for the blessing he had given to his arms, pray'd for the catholick church, and his subjects which now he had the charge of. He then rode up to an eminence, and from thence gave his soldiers thanks for behaving themselves so well in the late fight, promising them all rewards answerable to their deserts. The army shouting clapped their hands and saluted him king, crying out with one voice, king Henry, king Henry! And the lord Stanley taking king Richard's crown, which was found among the spoils of the field, put it on the earl's head, who from that time assum'd the title and power of king. We must not omit to inform the reader of the lord Strange's escape. King Richard hearing his father had raised five thousand men and was advancing towards the earl of Richmond, sent to him to join him, and swore by God's death, if he refus'd it, he wou'd order his son's head to be cut off before he died. The lord Stanley answer'd, he had more sons, and cou'd not promise to come to him at that time. The tyrant as he swore to do, order'd the lord Strange to be beheaded at the instant when the two armies were to engage: but some of his council abhorring that the innocent young gentleman should suffer for his father's offence, told the usurper, 'Now was a time to fight, and not to execute;' advising him to keep him prisoner till the battle was over; the tyrant hearken'd to their advice, broke his oath, and commanded the keepers of his tents to take him into custody, till he return'd from the combat. By this means the lord Strange escaped the king's revenge, equally bloody and unjust. The keepers of his tents deliver'd him to his father the lord Stanley after the fight; and for saving him, were taken into the new king's favour, and preferr'd. In the evening king Henry march'd to Leicester. Where king Richard's body stripped stark naked was brought in a shameful manner to be buried. Blanch Sanglier, a pursuivant at arms threw it upon a horse, like a calf; his head and arms hanging on one side and his legs on the other, his whole carcass besmear'd with dirt and blood. The pursuivant rode with it to the Grey-Fryers Church at Leicester, where it was expos'd a filthy spectacle to the view of the people, who us'd it ignominiously, and afterwards 'twas buried in that abbey-church; where king Henry in respect to his family, order'd a tomb to be erected over his grave. We shall not trouble the reader with a long account of his person and manners: he has doubtless by this time seen enough of him, and the picture shewn at a nearer view wou'd rather frighten than divert him. He was short and little, crooked or hump-back'd, one shoulder higher than the other: his face was little: he had a cruel look; and what confess'd the malice and deceit of his heart, he often mus'd, and musing bit his nether lip: he wore a dagger always about him, and frequently would draw it up and down the scabbard: he was cunning, and false, proud and valiant; and in a word, by the history sir Thomas More has left us of him, the greatest tyrant that ever sat on the British throne; where no tyrant did ever sit long.

The reigns of king Edward V. and his successor Richard III. were so short, that there were few remarkable occurrences in their times: and the most illustrious persons, both in war and the arts and sciences, will more properly come under that of Henry the VIIth.

In the first part of Richard III's reign, there happen'd such a flood in Gloucestershire, that all the country was overflow'd by the Severn, several persons were drown'd in their beds, children in cradles swam about the fields, and beasts were drown'd even on the hills : the waters did not abate in ten days ; which hinder'd the duke of Buckingham's passing that river into Wales to joyn the Welshmen who were risen against king Richard, and occasion'd his misfortune and death.—Hollinshed 743.

Banister, who betray'd the duke of Buckingham his master, was severely afflicted with God's secret judgments : his eldest son went mad, and died raving in a hog-sty. His eldest daughter who was very beautiful, was suddenly stricken with a foul leprosy. His second son was taken lame in his limbs. His younger son was suffocated in a puddle of filthy water ; and himself in an extreme old age found guilty of murder, but sav'd by his clergy.—Hol. 644.

John duke of Norfolk ;

Sir Robert Brackenbury, lieutenant of the Tower ;

The Lord Ferrars, and Sir Richard Ratcliff, lost their lives fighting valiantly for king Richard at Bosworth battle ;

Sir William Brandon, and sir John Cheyney, signaliz'd themselves in the same fight, on the side of the earl of Richmond.

Of men of learning, there were some in the reign of Richard III. of note : as,

John Penketh an Augustine frier, of Warrington in Lancashire, one of Scotus's followers ; he preach'd an infamous sermon in favour of king Richard : the same did Dr. Shaw, an eminent preacher, sir Edmund Shaw's brother, an alderman of London.

John Kent, or Caileie, born in South-Wales, rhetorician.

George Ripley, a Carmelite frier of Boston, a great mathematician and poet.

Dr. John Spine, a Carmelite frier of Bristol, &c.

THE LIFE AND REIGN OF KING HENRY VII.

BY THE RIGHT HON. FRANCIS LORD VERULAM,
VISCOUNT ST. ALBANS.

AFTER that Richard the third of that name, king in fact only, but tyrant both in title and regiment, and so commonly termed and reputed in all times since, was by the divine revenge, favouring the design of an exil'd man, overthrown and slain at Bosworth field: there succeeded in the kingdom the earl of Richmond, thenceforth styl'd Henry the seventh. The king immediately after the victory, as one that had been bred under a devout mother, and was in his nature a great observer of religious forms, caused *Te Deum Laudamus* to be solemnly sung in the presence of the whole army upon the place, and was himself with general applause and great cries of joy, in a kind of military election or recognition, saluted king. Meanwhile the body of Richard after many indignities and reproaches (the dirgies and obsequies of the common people towards tyrants) was obscurely buried. For tho' the king of his nobleness gave charge unto the fryars of Leicester to see an honourable interrment to be given to it, yet the religious people themselves (being not free from the humours of the vulgar) neglected it; wherein nevertheless they did not then incur any man's blame or censure. No man thinking any ignominy or contumely unworthy of him, that had been the executioner of king Henry VI. (that innocent prince) with his own hands; the contriver of the death of the duke of Clarence, his brother; the murderer of his two nephews (one of them his lawful king in the present, and the other in the future, failing of him), and vehemently suspected to have been the impoisoner of his wife, thereby to make vacant his bed, for a marriage within the degrees forbidden. And altho' he were a prince in military vertue approv'd, jealous of the honour of the English nation, and likewise a good law maker, for the ease and solace of the common people: yet his cruelties and parricides in the opinion of all men, weigh'd down his vertues and merits; and in the opinion of wise men, even those vertues themselves were conceived to be rather feign'd, and affected things to serve his ambition, than true qualities ingenerate in his judgment or nature. And therefore it was noted by men of great understanding (who seeing his after-acts, look'd back upon his former proceedings) that even in the time of king Edward his brother, he was not without secret trains and mines to turn envy and hatred upon his brother's government; as having an expectation and a kind of divination, that the king, by reason of his many disorders, could not be of long life, but was like to leave his sons of tender years; and then he knew well how easie a step it was from the place of a protector, and first prince of the blood, to the crown. And that out of this deep root of ambition it sprang, that as well at the treaty of peace that passed between Edward IV. and Lewis XI. of France, concluded by interview of both kings at Piqueny, as upon all other occasions, Richard then Duke of Gloucester, stood ever upon the side of honour, raising his own reputation to the disadvantage of the king his brother, and drawing the eyes of all (especially of the nobles and soldiers), upon himself; as if the king by his voluptuous life and mean marriage, were become effeminate and less sensible of honour and reason of state, than was fit for a king. And as for the politick and wholesome laws which were enacted in his time, they were interpreted to be but the brocage of an usurper, thereby to woo and win the hearts of the people, as being conscious to himself, that the true obligations of sovereignty in him failed, and were wanting. But king Henry in the very entrance of his reign, and the instant of time, when the kingdom was cast into his arms, met with a point of great difficulty and knotty to solve, able to trouble and confound the wisest king in the newness of his estate; and so much the more, because it could not endure a deliberation, but must be at once deliberated and determined.

There were fallen to his lot, and concurrent to his person, three several titles to the imperial crown; the first, the title of the lady Elizabeth, with whom, by precedent pact with the party that brought him in, he was to marry. The second, the ancient and long disputed title (both by plea and arms) of the house of Lancaster, to which he was inheritor in his own person. The third, the title of the sword, or conquest, for that he came in by victory of battle, and that the king in possession was slain in the field. The first of these was fairest, and most like to give contentment to the people, who by two and twenty years reign of king Edward IV. had been fully made capable of the clearness of the title of the white rose, or house of York; and by the mild and plausible reign of the same king toward his later time, were become affectionate to that line. But then it lay plain before his eyes, that if he relied upon that title, he could be but a king at courtesy; and have rather a matrimonial than a regular power; the right remaining in his queen; upon whose decease, either with issue, or without issue, he was to give place and be removed. And tho' he should obtain by parliament to be continued, yet he knew there was a very great difference between a king that holdeth his crown by a civil act of estates, and one that holdeth it originally by the law of nature and descent of blood. Neither wanted there even at that time, secret rumours and whisperings (which afterwards gather'd strength, and turn'd to great troubles) that the two young sons of king Edward IV., or one of them (which were said to be destroy'd in the Tower) were not indeed murder'd, but convey'd secretly away, and were yet living: which if it had been true, had prevented the title of the lady Elizabeth. On the other side, if he stood upon his own title of the house of Lancaster, inherent in his person, he knew it was a title condemn'd by parliament, and generally prejudg'd in the common opinion of the realm, and that it tended directly to the disinherison of the line of York, held then the indubiate heirs of the crown. So that if he should have no issue by the lady Elizabeth, which should be descendents of the double line, then the ancient flames of discord and intestine wars upon the competition of both houses, would again return and revive.

As for conquest, notwithstanding sir William Stanley, after some acclamations of the souldiers in the field, had put a crown of ornament (which Richard wore in the battle, and was found among the spoils) upon king Henry's head, as if there were his chief title; yet he remembr'd well upon what conditions and agreements he was brought in; and that to claim as conqueror, was to put as well his own party, as the rest, into terror and fear; as that which gave him power of disannulling of laws, and disposing of men's fortunes and estates, and the like points of absolute power, being in themselves so harsh and odious, as that William himself, commonly call'd the conqueror, howsoever he used and exercised the power of a conqueror to reward his Normans, yet he forbare to use that claim in the beginning, but mixt it with a titulary pretence, grounded upon the will and designation of Edward the confessor. But the king, out of the greatness of his own mind, presently cast the die, and the inconveniencies appearing unto him on all parts; and knowing there could not be any inter-reign, or suspension of title; and preferring his affection to his own line and blood; and liking that title best that made him independent; and being in his nature and constitution of mind not very apprehensive or forecasting of future events afar of, but an entertainer of fortune by the day, resolv'd to rest upon the title of Lancaster as the main, and to use the other two, that of marriage and that of battle, but as supporters; the one to appease secret discontents, and the other to beat down open murmur and dispute; not forgetting that the same title of Lancaster had formerly maintain'd a possession of three descents in the crown, and might have proved a perpetuity, had it not ended in the weakness and inability of the last prince. Whereupon the king presently, that very day, being the 22nd of August, assumed the stile of king in his own name, without mention of the lady Elizabeth at all, or any relation thereunto ; in which course he ever after persisted, which did spin him a thread of many seditions and troubles. The king full of these thoughts, before his departure from Leicester, dispatch'd sir Robert Willoughby to the castle of sheriff Hutton in Yorkshire, where were kept in safe custody, by king Richard's commandment, both the lady Elizabeth, daughter of king Edward, and Edward Plantagenet, son and heir to George duke of Clarence. This Edward was, by the king's warrant deliver'd from the constable of the castle to the hand of sir Robert Willoughby, and by him, with all safety and diligence, convey'd to the tower of London ; where he was shut up close prisoner : which act of the king's (being an act merely of policy and power) proceeded not so much from any apprehension he had of doctor Shaw's tale at Paul's Cross, for the bastarding of Edward the fourth's issues, in which case this young gentleman was to succeed (for that fable was ever exploded) but upon a settled disposition to depress all eminent persons of the line of York ; wherein, still the king out of strength or will, or weakness of judgment, did use to shew a little more of the party than of the king.

For the lady Elizabeth she received also a direction to repair with all convenient speed to London, and there to remain with the queen dowager her mother ; which accordingly she soon after did, accompanied with many noblemen and ladies of honour. In the mean season the king set forwards by easy journeys to the city of London, receiving the acclamations and applauses of the people as he went, which indeed were true and unfeigned, as might well appear in the very demonstrations and fullness of the cry : for they thought generally, that he was a prince as ordain'd and sent down from heaven, to unite and put an end to the long dissention of the two houses ; which altho' they had in the times of Henry IV., Henry V., and part of Henry VI. on the one side, and the times of Edward IV. on the other, lucid intervals and happy pauses ; yet they did ever hang over the kingdom, ready to break forth into new perturbations and calamities. And as his victory gave him the knee, so his purpose of marriage with the lady Elizabeth gave him the heart ; so that both knee and heart did truly bow before him.

He on the other side with great wisdom (not ignorant of the affections and fears of the people) to disperse the conceit and terror of a conquest, had given order that there should be nothing in his journey like unto a warlike march or manner, but rather like unto the progress of a king in full peace and assurance.

He enterd into the city upon a Saturday, as he had also obtain'd the victory upon a Saturday, which day of the week, first upon an observation, and after upon memory and fancy, he accounted and chose as a day prosperous unto him.

The mayor and companies of the city receiv'd him at Shoreditch; whence, with great and honourable attendance and troops of noblemen, and persons of quality he enterd the city; himself not being on horseback, or in any open chair, or throne, but in a close chariot, as one that having been sometimes an enemy to the whole state, and a proscrib'd person, chose rather to keep state, and strike a reverence into the people than to fawn upon them.

He went first into St. Paul's church, where not meaning that the people should forget too soon that he came in by battle, he made offertory of his standards, and had Orizons and Te Deum again sung, and went to his lodging prepared in the bishop of London's palace, where he stay'd for a time.

During his abode there, he assembled his council and other principal persons, in presence of whom he did renew again his promise to marry with the lady Elizabeth. This he did the rather, because, having at his coming out of Brittaine given artificially, for serving of his own turn, some hopes, in case he obtain'd the kingdom, to marry Anne inheritress to the duchy of Brittaine, whom Charles the eighth of France soon after married; it bred some doubt and suspicion amongst divers that he was not sincere, or at least not fix'd in going on with the match of England so much desir'd : which conceit also, tho' it were but talk and discourse, did much afflict the poor lady Elizabeth herself. But, howsoever he both truly intended it, and desired also it should be so believ'd, (the better to extinguish envy and contradiction to his other purposes) yet was he so resolv'd in himself not to proceed to the consummation thereof till his coronation and a parliament were past; the one, least a joynt coronation of himself and his queen might give any countenance of participation of title; the other, lest in the entailing of the crown to himself, which he hoped to obtain by parliament, the votes of the parliament might any ways reflect upon her.

About this time, in autumn, towards the end of September, there began and reign'd in the city and other parts of the kingdom, a disease then new; which of the accidents and manner thereof, they call'd the sweating sickness. This disease had a swift course both in the sick body, and in the time and period of the lasting thereof: for they that were taken with it, upon four and twenty hours escaping, were thought almost assured: and as to the time of the malice and reign of the disease e're it ceased; it began about the 21st of September, and clear'd up before the end of October; insomuch as it was no hindrance to the king's coronation, which was the last of October; nor (which was more) to the holding of the parliament, which began but seven days after. It was a pestilent fever, but as it seemed not seated in the veins of humours, for that there follow'd no carbuncle, no purple or livid spots, or the like, the mass of the body being not tainted, only a malign vapour flew to the heart, and seized the vital spirits; which stirr'd nature to strive to send it forth by an extreme sweat. And it appear'd by experience that this disease was rather a surprize of nature than obstinate to remedies, if it were in time look'd unto: for if the patient were kept in an equal temper, both for cloaths, fire, and drink moderately warm, with temperate cordials, whereby nature's work were neither irritated by heat, nor turn'd back by cold, he commonly recover'd. But infinite persons died suddenly of it, before the manner of the cure and attendance was known. It was conceiv'd not to be an epidemick disease, but to proceed from a malignity in the constitution of the air, gathered by the pre-dispositions of seasons; and the speedy cessation declared as much.

On Simon and Jude's even the king dined with Thomas Bourchier, archbishop of Canterbury and cardinal; and from Lambeth went by land over the bridge to the tower, where the morrow after he made twelve knight bannerets. But for creations he dispensed them with a sparing hand: for notwithstanding a field so lately fought, and a coronation so near at hand, he only created three. Jasper earl of Pembroke (the king's uncle) was created duke of Bedford; Thomas the lord Stanley (the king's father-in-law) earl of Derby; and Edward Courtney earl of Devon; tho' the king had then nevertheless a purpose in himself to make more in time of parliament, bearing a wise and decent respect to distribute his creations, some to honour his coronation, and some his parliament.

The coronation follow'd two days after, upon the 30th day of October, in the year of our Lord 1485; at which time Innocent the eighth was pope of Rome; Frederick the third, emperor of Almaine; and Maximilian his son, newly chosen king of the Romans; Charles the eighth king of France; Ferdinando and Isabella kings of Spain; and James the third, king of Scotland; with all which kings and states, the king was at that time at good peace and amity. At which day also (as if the crown upon his head had put perils into his thoughts) he did institute, for the better security of his person, a band of fifty archers under a captain to attend him, by the name of yeomen of his guard; and yet that it might be thought to be rather a matter of dignity, after the imitation of that he had known abroad, than any matter of diffidence appropriate to his own case, he made it to be understood for an ordinance not temporary, but to hold in succession for ever after.

The seventh of November the king held his parliament at Westminster, which he had summon'd immediately after his coming to London. His ends in calling a parliament (and that so speedily) were chiefly three; first, to procure the crown to be intail'd upon himself: next, to have the attainders of all his party (which were in no small number) reversed, and all acts of hostility by them done in his quarrel, remitted and discharged; and on the other side, to attaint by parliament the heads and principles of his enemies. The third, to calm and quiet the fears of the rest of that party by a general pardon: not being ignorant in how great danger a king stands from his subjects, when most of his subjects are conscious in themselves that they stand in his danger. Unto these three special motives of a parliament, was added, that he, as a prudent and moderate prince made this judgment; that it was fit for him to hasten to let his people see that he meant to govern by law, howsoever he came in by the sword; and fit also to reclaim them to know him for their king, whom they had so lately talk'd of as an enemy or banish'd man. For that which concern'd the entailing of the crown, (more than that he was true to his own will, that he wou'd not endure any mention of the lady Elizabeth, no not in the nature of special entail) he carried it otherwise with great wisdom and measure: for he did not press to have the act penn'd by way of declaration or recognition of right; as on the other side he avoided to have it by new law or ordinance; but chose rather a kind of middle-way, by way of establishment, and that under covert and indifferent words; that the inheritance of the crown should rest, remain, and abide in the king, &c., which words might equally be apply'd; that the crown should continue to him; but whether as having former right to it (which was doubtful), or having it then in fact and possession (which no man denied) was left fair to interpretation either way. And again, for the limitation of the entail, he did not press it to go further than to himself and to the heirs of his body, not speaking of his right heirs; but leaving that to the law to decide: so as the entail might seem rather a personal favour to him and his children, than a total dis-inherison to the house of York. And in this form was the law drawn and pass'd; which statute he procured to be confirm'd by the Pope's bull the year following, with mention, nevertheless (by way of recital), of his other titles, both of descent and conquest: so as now the wreath of three was made a wreath of five; for to the three first titles of the two houses, or lines, and conquest, were added two more, the authorities parliamentary and papal.

The king likewise in the reversal of the attainders of his partakers, and discharging them of all offences incident to his service and succour, had his will, and acts did pass accordingly: in the passage whereof, exception was taken to divers persons in the house of commons for that they were attainted, and thereby not legal, nor habilitate to serve in parliament, being disabled in the highest degree: and that it should be a great incongruity to have them to make laws, who themselves were not inlaw'd. The truth was, that divers of those which had in the time of king Richard been strongest and most declared for the king's party, were return'd knights and burgesses for the parliament, whether by care or recommendation from the state, or the voluntary inclination of the people; many of them which had been by Richard III. attainted by outlawries, or otherwise. The king was somewhat troubled with this: for tho' it had a grave and specious shew, yet it reflected upon his party. But wisely not shewing himself at all moved therewith, he would not understand it but as a case in law, and wish'd the judges to be advised thereupon; who, for that purpose, were forthwith assembled in the Exchequer-chamber (which, is the council-chamber of the judges) and upon deliberation, they gave a grave and safe opinion and advice, mix'd with law and convenience; which was, that the knights and burgesses attainted by the course of law, should forbear to come into the House till a law were made for the reversal of their attainders.

It was at that time incidently moved among the judges in their consultation, what should be done for the king himself, who likewise was attainted? But it was with unanimous consent resolv'd 'That the crown takes away all defects and stops in blood; and that from the time the king did assure the crown the fountain was clear'd, and all attainders and corruption of blood discharged.' But nevertheless, for honour's sake, it was ordain'd by parliament, that all records wherein there was any memory or mention of the king's attainder, should be defaced, cancel'd, and taken off the file.

But on the part of the king's enemies, there were by parliament attainted the late duke of Gloucester, calling himself Richard the third; the duke of Norfolk, the earl of Surrey, viscount Lovel, the lord Ferrers, the lord Zouch, Richard Ratcliffe, William Catesby, and many others of degree and quality.[1] In which bills of attainders nevertheless there were contain'd many just and temperate clauses savings, and proviso's, well shewing and fore-tokening the wisdom, stay, and moderation of the king's spirit of government. And for the pardon of the rest, that had stood against the king; the king, upon a second advice, thought it not fit it should pass by parliament, the better (being matter of grace) to impropriate the thanks to himself, using only the opportunity of a parliament time the better to disperse it into the veins of the kingdom : therefore during the parliament, he publish'd his royal proclamation, offering pardon and grace of restitution to all such as had taken arms, or been participant of any attempts against him; so as they submitted themselves to his mercy by a day, and took the oath of allegiance and fidelity to

---

[1] Amongst whom was John Buck, a relation of George Buck the author of the life of king Richard III. which perhaps was the reason why that historian, in opposition to other writers on the same subject, endeavours to have it believed, that king Richard was both a great and a good man. This John Buck was a creature of the duke of Norfolk, a fast friend to king Richard III. Buck lost his head at Bosworth.

him: whereupon many came out of sanctuary, and many more came out of fear, no less guilty than those that had taken sanctuary.

As for money or treasure, the king thought it not seasonable, or fit to demand any of his subjects at this parliament; both because he had received satisfaction from them in matters of so great importance, and because he could not remunerate them with any general pardon, being prevented therein by the coronation pardon, pass'd immediately before; but chiefly, for that it was in every man's eye, what great forfeitures and confiscations he had at that present to help himself; whereby those casualties of the crown, might in reason spare the purses of the subject, especially in a time when he was in peace with all his neighbours. Some few laws pass'd at that parliament, almost for form sake; amongst which, there was one to reduce aliens, being made denizens, to pay stranger's customs; and another, to draw to himself the seisures and compositions of Italian goods, for not imployment, being points of profit to his coffers, whereof from the very beginning he was not forgetful, and had been more happy at the latter end, if his early providence (which kept him from all necessity of exacting upon his people) could likewise have attemp'red his nature therein. He added, during parliament, to his former creations, the innoblement or advancement in nobility of a few others: the Chandos of Brittain was made earl of Bath; and sir Giles Daubeny was made lord Dawbeny; and sir Robert Willoughby lord Brooke.

The king did also with great nobleness and bounty (which virtues at that time had their turns in his nature) restore Edward Stafford, eldest son to Henry duke of Buckingham, attainted in the time of king Richard) not only to his dignities, but to his fortunes and possessions, which were great; to which he was moved also by a kind of gratitude, for that the duke was the man that mov'd the first stone against the tyranny of king Richard, and indeed made the king a bridge to the crown upon his own ruins. Thus the parliament brake up.

The parliament being dissolv'd, the king sent forthwith money to redeem the marquess Dorset, and sir John Bouchier, whom he had left as his pledges at Paris, for money which he had borrow'd when he made his expedition for England. And thereupon he took a fit occasion to send the lord treasurer and Mr. Bray (whom he used as counsellor) to the lord mayor of London, requiring of the city a prest of six thousand marks: but after many parleys, he could obtain but two thousand pounds. Which nevertheless the king took in good part; as men use to do that practice to borrow money when they have no need. About this time, the king called unto his privy council John Moreton and Richard Fox, the one bishop of Ely, the other bishop of Exeter, vigilant men and secret, and such as kept watch with him almost upon all men else. They had been both vers'd in his affairs, before he came to the crown, and were partakers of his adverse fortune. This Moreton soon after upon the death of Bouchier, he made archbishop of Canterbury. And for Fox, he made him lord keeper of his privy-seal, and afterwards advanc'd him by degrees, from Exeter to Bathe and Wells, thence to Durham, and last to Winchester. For altho' the king lov'd to employ and advance bishops, because having rich bishopricks, they carried their reward upon themselves: yet he did use to raise them by steps, that he might not lose the profit of the first-fruits, which by that course of gradation was multiplied.

At last upon the 18th of January, 1486, was solemnized the so long expected and so much desir'd marriage, between the king and the lady Elizabeth: which day of marriage was celebrated with greater triumph and demonstrations (especially on the people's part) of joy and gladness, than the days either of his entry or coronation; which the king rather noted than liked. And it is true, that all his lifetime, whilst the lady Elizabeth liv'd with him, (for she died before him) he shew'd himself no very indulgent husband towards her, tho' she was beautiful, gentle, and fruitful. But his aversion to the house of York was so predominant in him, as it found place, not only in his wars and counsels, but in his chamber and bed.

Towards the middle of the spring, the king full of confidence and assurance, as a prince that had been victorious in battle, and had prevail'd with his parliament in all that he desir'd, and had the ring of acclamations fresh in his ears, thought the rest of his reign should be but play, and the enjoying of a kingdom. Yet as a wise and watchful king, he would not neglect any thing for his safety; thinking nevertheless to perform all things now, rather as an exercise, than as a labour. So he being truly inform'd that the northern parts were not only affectionate to the house of York, but particularly had been devoted to king Richard the third; thought it would be a summer well spent to visit those parts, and by his presence and application of himself to reclaim and rectifie those humours. But the king in his accompt of peace and calms, did much overcast his fortunes; which proved for many years together full of broken seas, tides and tempests. For he was no sooner come to Lincoln, where he kept his Easter, but he receiv'd news, that the lord Lovel, Humphrey Stafford, and Thomas Stafford (who had formerly taken sanctuary at Colchester) were departed out of sanctuary; but to what place, no man could tell. Which advertisement the king despised, and continued his journey to York. At York there came fresh and more certain advertisement, that the lord Lovel was at hand with a great power of men, and that the Staffords were in arms in Worcestershire, and had made their approaches to the city of Worcester to assail it. The king, as a prince of great and profound judgment, was not much mov'd with it; for that he thought it was but a rag or remnant of Bosworth-field, and had nothing in it of the main party of the house of York. But he was more doubtful of the raising of forces to resist the rebels, than of the resistance itself; for that he was in a core of people whose affections he suspected. But the action enduring no delay, he did speedily levy and send against the lord Lovel to the number of three thousand men, all arm'd, but well assur'd (being taken some few out of his own train, and the rest out of the tenants and followers of such as were safe to be trusted) under the conduct of the duke of Bedford. And as his manner was to send his pardons rather before the sword than after, he gave commission to the duke to proclaim pardon to all that would come in: which the duke, upon his approach to the lord Lovel's camp, did perform. And it fell out as the king expected; the heralds were the great ordnance. For the lord Lovel upon proclamation of pardon, mistrusting his men, fled into Lancashire, and lurking for a time with sir Thomas Broughton, after sail'd over into Flanders to the lady Margaret: and his men, forsaken of their captain, did presently submit themselves to the duke. The Staffords likewise, and their forces, hearing what had happen'd to the lord Lovel (in whose success their chief trust was) despair'd and dispers'd. The two brothers taking sanctuary at Colnham, a village near Abingdon; which place upon view of their priviledge in the king's-bench, being judged no sufficient sanctuary for traitors, Humphrey was executed at Tyburn; and Thomas, as being led by his elder brother, was pardon'd. So this rebellion prov'd but a blast, and the king having by his journey purg'd a little the dregs and leaven of the northern people, that were before in no good affection towards him, return'd to London.

In September following;[1] the queen was deliver'd of her son, whom the king (in honour of the British race, of which himself was) nam'd Arthur, according to the name of that ancient worthy king of the Britains; in whose acts there is truth enough to make him famous besides that which is fabulous. The child was strong and able, tho' he was born in the eighth month, which the physicians do prejudge.

There follow'd this year, being the second of the king's reign, a strange accident of state, whereof the relations which we have are so naked, as they leave it scarce credible; not for the nature of it (for it hath fallen out oft) but for the manner and circumstance of it, especially in the beginnings. Therefore we shall make our judgment upon the things themselves, as they give light one to another, and (as we can) dig truth out of the mine. The king was green in his estate; and, contrary to his own opinion and desert both, was not without

---

[1] Holinshead writes, the queen was deliver'd at Winchester, in September, 1488, which is more probable than that she should be deliver'd now; for she was married but on the 18 of January in this year.

much hatred throughout the realm. The root of all, was the discountenancing of the house of York, which the general body of the realm still affected. This did alienate the hearts of the subjects from him daily more and more, especially when they saw, that after his marriage, and after a son born, the king did nevertheless not so much as proceed to the coronation of the queen, not vouchsafing her the honour of a matrimonial crown; for the coronation of her was not till almost two years after, when danger had taught him what to do. But much more when it was spread abroad (whether by errour, or the cunning of malecontents) that the king had a purpose to put to death Edward Plantagenet closely in the Tower; whose case was so nearly parallel'd with that of Edward the fourth's children, in respect of the blood, like age, and the very place of the Tower, as it did refresh and reflect upon the king a most odious resemblance, as if he would be another king Richard. And all this time it was still whisper'd everywhere, that at least one of the children of Edward IV. was living. Which bruit was cunningly fomented by such as desir'd innovation. Neither was the king's nature and customs greatly fit to disperse these mists; but contrariwise he had a fashion rather to create doubts than assurance. Thus was fuel prepar'd for the spark; the spark that afterwards kindled with such a fire and combustion was at the first contemptible.

There was a subtil priest call'd Richard Simon, that liv'd in Oxford, and had to his pupil a baker's son nam'd Lambert Simnell, of the age of some fifteen years; a comely youth, and well favour'd, not without some extraordinary dignity and grace of aspect. It came into this priest's fancy (hearing what men talk'd, and in hope to raise himself to some great bishoprick) to cause this lad to counterfeit and personate the second son of Edward IV. suppos'd to be murder'd; and afterward (for he chang'd his intention in the menage) the lord Edward Plantagenet, then prisoner in the Tower, and accordingly to frame him and instruct him in the part he was to play. This is that which (as was touch'd before) seemeth scarce credible; not that a false person should be assum'd to gain a kingdom, for it hath been seen in ancient and late times; nor that it should come into the mind of such an abject fellow, to enterprize so great a matter; for high conceits do sometimes come streaming into the imaginations of base persons, especially when they are drunk with news and talk of the people But here is that which hath no appearance; that this priest being utterly unacquainted with the true person, according to whose pattern he should shape his counterfeit, should think it possible for him to instruct his player, either in gesture and fashions, or in recounting past matters of his life and education; or in fit answers to questions, or the like, any ways to come near the resemblance of him whom he was to represent. For this lad was not to personate one that had been long before taken out of his cradle, or convey'd away in his infancy, known to few; but a youth that till the age almost of ten years had been brought up in a court, where infinite eyes had been upon him. For king Edward touch'd with remorse of his brother the duke of Clarence's death would not indeed restore his son (of whom we speak) to be duke of Clarence; but yet created him earl of Warwick, reviving his honour on the mother's side, and used him honourably during his time, tho' Richard III. afterwards confin'd him. So that it cannot be, but that some great person that knew particularly and familiarly Edward Plantagenet, had a hand in the business, from whom the priest might take his aim. That which is most probable, out of the precedent and subsequent acts, is, that it was the queen dowager, from whom this action had the principal source and motion: for certain it is, she was a busy negociating woman, and in her withdrawing chamber had the fortunate conspiracy for the king against king Richard the third been hatch'd; which the king knew, and remembred perhaps but too well; and was at this time extremely discontent with the king, thinking her daughter (as the king handled the matter) not advanced but depressed: and none could hold the book so well to prompt and instruct this stage-play, as she could. Nevertheless it was not her meaning, nor no more was it the meaning of any of the better and sager sort that favour'd this enterprize, and knew the secret, that this disguised idol should possess the crown; but at his peril to make way to the overthrow of the king: and that done, they had their several hopes and ways. That which doth chiefly fortifie this conjecture is, that as soon as the matter brake forth in any strength, it was one of the king's first acts to cloister the queen dowager in the nunnery of Bermondsey, and to take away all her lands and estate; and this by close council without any legal proceeding, upon far-fetch'd pretences; that she had deliver'd her two daughters out of sanctuary to king Richard contrary to promise. Which proceeding being even at that time taxed for rigorous and undue, both in matter and manner, makes it very probable there was some great matter against her, which the king upon reason of policy, and to avoid envy would not publish. It is likewise no small argument that there was some secret in it, and some suppressing of examinations; for that the priest Simon himself, after he was taken, was never brought to execution; no not so much as to publick trial (as many clergymen were upon less treasons) but was only shut up close in a dungeon. Add to this, that after the earl of Lincoln (a principal person of the house of York) was slain in Stoke field, the king open'd himself to some of his council, that he was sorry for the earl's death, because by him (he said) he might have known the bottom of his danger.

But to return to the narration itself; Simon did first instruct his

scholar for the part of Richard duke of York, second son to king
Edward IV. and this was at such time as it was voiced that the king
purposed to put to death Edward Plantagenet prisoner in the Tower,
whereat there was great murmur. But hearing soon after a general
bruit that Plantagenet had escap'd out of the Tower, and thereby
finding him so much beloved amongst the people, and such rejoycing
at his escape, the cunning priest chang'd his copy, and chose now
Plantagenet to be the subject his pupil should personate, because he
was more in the present speech and votes of the people ; and it pieced
better, and follow'd more close and handsomely upon the bruit of
Plantagenet's escape. But yet doubting that there would be too near
looking and too much perspective into his disguise, if he should shew
it here in England: he thought good (after the manner of scenes in
stage plays and masks) to shew it afar off; and therefore sail'd with
his scholar into Ireland, where the affection to the house of York was
most in height. The king had been a little improvident in the
matters of Ireland, and had not remov'd officers and councellors, and
put in their places, or at least intermingled persons, of whom he stood
assured, as he should have done, since he knew the strong bent of
that country towards the house of York ; and that it was a ticklish
and unsettled state, more easy to receive distempers and mutations
than England was. But trusting to the reputation of his victories and
successes in England, he thought he should have time enough to extend his cares afterwards to that second kingdom.

Wherefore through this neglect, upon the coming of Simon with his
pretended Plantagenet into Ireland, all things were prepar'd for revolt
and sedition, almost as if they had been set and plotted beforehand.
Simon's first address was to the lord[1] Thomas Fitzgerard, earl of
Kildare, and deputy of Ireland : before whose eyes he did cast such a
mist (by his own insinuation, and by the carriage of his youth, that
express'd a natural princely behaviour) as joyn'd perhaps with some
inward vapours of ambition and affection in the earl's own mind, left
him fully possess'd that it was the true Plantagenet. The earl presently communicated the matter with some of the nobles[2] and others
there, at the first secretly. But finding them of like affection to himself, he suffer'd it of purpose to vent and pass abroad ; because they
thought it not safe to resolve, till they had a taste of the people's inclination. But if the great ones were in forwardness, the people were
in fury, entertaining this airy body or phantasm with incredible affec-

[1] The lord Thomas Fitzgerald was Lord Chancellor of Ireland, and brother to Gerald, earl
of Kildare, deputy to Jasper, duke of Bedford, Lord Lieutenant of Ireland.—Sir James
Ware, Annals of Hen. VII. cap. 1.
[2] His brother the Lord Chancellor and the lord Portlester Lord Treasurer, who were
devoted to the house of York, the king had written to the lord deputy to come over to England some time before, suspecting his fidelity ; but he excus'd himself till some matters of
great consequence then depending were finish'd, and the lords spiritual and temporal sign'd
a letter to the king to desire he might stay. The lord Heath advis'd him of it.—Sir J.
Ware, cap. 11.

tion ; partly, out of their great devotion to the house of York ; partly out of a proud humour in the nation, to give a king to the realm of England. Neither did the party in this heat of affection much trouble themselves with the attainder of George duke of Clarence ; having newly learn'd by the king's example, that attainders do not interrupt the conveying of title to the crown. And as for the daughters of king Edward IV. they thought king Richard had said enough for them ; and took them to be but as of the king's party, because they were in his power and at his disposing. So that with marvellous consent and applause, this counterfeit Plantagenet was brought with great solemnity to the castle of Dublin, and there saluted, serv'd and honour'd as king ; the boy becoming it well, and doing nothing that did bewray the baseness of his condition. And within a few days after he was proclaim'd king in Dublin, by the name of king Edward the sixth ; there being not a sword drawn in king Henry's quarrel.

The king was much mov'd with this unexpected accident, when it came to his ears ; both because it struck upon that string which ever he most fear'd, as also because it was stirred in such a place, where he could not with safety transfer his own person to suppress it. For partly thro' natural valour, and partly thro' an universal suspicion (not knowing whom to trust) he was ever ready to wait upon all his achievements in person. The king therefore first called his council together at the Charterhouse at Shæne ; which council was held with great secrecy ; but the open decrees thereof which presently came abroad were three.

The first was, that the queen dowager, for that she, contrary to her pact and agreement with those that had concluded with her concerning the marriage of her daughter Elizabeth with king Henry, had nevertheless deliver'd her daughters out of sanctuary into king Richard's hands ; should be cloister'd in the nunnery of Bermondsey, and forfeit all her lands and goods.

The next was, that Edward Plantagenet then close prisoner in the Tower, should be in the most publick and notorious manner, that could be devised, shew'd unto the people : in part to discharge the king of the envy of that opinion and bruit, how he had been put to death privily in the Tower ; but chiefly to make the people see the levity and imposture of the proceedings of Ireland, and that thei Plantagenet[1] was indeed but a puppit, or a counterfeit.

The third was, that there should be again proclaim'd a general pardon to all that would reveal their offences, and submit themselves by a day. And that this pardon should be conceiv'd in so ample and liberal a manner, as no high treason (no not against the king's own person) should be excepted. Which tho' it might seem strange, yet

[1] In Ireland the impostor was retorted on the king, as if he had impos'd a counterfeit earl of Warwick on the people.—Sir J. Ware.

was it not so to a wise king, that knew his greatest dangers were not from the least treasons, but from the greatest. These resolutions of the king and his council were immediately put in execution. And first, the queen dowager was put into the monastery of Bermondsey, and all her estate seiz'd into the king's hands, whereat there was much wondering; that a weak woman, for the yielding to the menaces and promises of a tyrant, after such a distance of time (wherein the king had shew'd no displeasure nor alteration) but much more after so happy a marriage, between the king and her daughter, blessed with issue-male, should upon so sudden mutability or disclosure of the king's mind be so severely handled.

This lady was amongst the examples of great variety of fortune. She had first from a distressed suitor and desolate widow, been taken to the marriage bed of a batchelor-king, the goodliest personage of his time; and even in his reign she had endur'd a strange eclipse by the king's flight, and temporary depriving from the crown. She was also very happy, in that she had by him a fair issue, and continu'd his nuptial love (helping herself by some obsequious bearing and dissembling of his pleasures) to the very end. She was much affectionate to her own kindred, even unto faction; which did stir great envy in the lords of the king's side, who counted her blood a disparagement to be mingled with the king's. With which lords of the king's blood, joyn'd also the king's favourite the lord Hastings; who, notwithstanding the king's great affection to him, was thought at times, through her malice and spleen, not to be out of danger of falling. After her husband's death, she was matter of tragedy, having liv'd to see her brother beheaded, and her two sons deposed from the crown, bastarded in their blood, and cruelly murdered. All this while nevertheless she enjoy'd her liberty, state, and fortunes. But afterwards again, upon the rise of the wheel, when she had a king to her son-in-law, and was made grandmother to a grandchild of the best sex; yet was she (upon dark and unknown reasons, and no less strange pretences) precipitated and banish'd the world into a nunnery; where it was almost thought dangerous to visit her, or see her; and where not long after she ended her life: but was by the king's commandment buried with the king her husband at Windsor. She was foundress of Queen's College in Cambridge. For this act the king sustain'd great obloquy, which nevertheless (besides the reason of state) was somewhat sweetened to him by a great confiscation.

About this time also Edward Plantagenet was upon a Sunday brought throughout all the principal streets of London, to be seen of the people. And having pass'd the view of the streets, was conducted to Paul's church in solemn procession, where great store of people were assembled. And it was provided also in good fashion, that divers of the nobility, and others of quality (especially of those that the king most suspected, and knew the person of Plantagenet best) had communication with the young gentleman by the way, and entertain'd him with speech and discourse; which did in effect mar the pageant in Ireland with the subjects here, at least with so many as out of error, and not out of malice, might be misled. Nevertheless, it wrought little or no effect. But contrariwise, in Ireland (where it was too late to go back) they turn'd the imposture upon the king, and gave out, that the king, to defeat the true inheritor, and to mock the world and blind the eyes of simple men, had trick'd up a boy in the likeness of Edward Plantagenet, and shewed him to the people, not sparing to prophane the ceremony of a procession, the more to countenance the fable brought forward.

The general pardon likewise near the same time came forth; and the king therewithal omitted no diligence, in giving straight order for the keeping of the ports; that fugitives, malecontents, or suspected persons might not pass over into Ireland and Flanders.

Meanwhile the rebels in Ireland had sent privy messengers both into England and into Flanders, who in both places had wrought effects of no small importance. For in England they won to their party John earl of Lincoln, son of John de la Pole, duke of Suffolk, and of Elizabeth, king Edward IV.'s eldest sister. This earl was a man of great wit and courage, and had his thoughts highly rais'd by hopes and expectations for a time. For Richard III. had a resolution, out of hatred to both his brethren, king Edward and the duke of Clarence, and their lines (having had his hand in both their bloods), to disable their issues upon false and incompetent pretexts; the one of attainder, the other of illegitimation; and to design this gentleman (in case himself should dye without children) for inheritor of the crown. Neither was this unknown to the king, who had secretly an eye upon him. But the king having tasted of the envy of the people, for his imprisonment of Edward Plantagenet, was doubtful to heap up any more distastes of that kind, by the imprisonment of de la Pole also; the rather thinking it policy to conserve him as a co-rival unto the other. The earl of Lincoln was induced to participate with the action of Ireland, not lightly upon the strength of the proceedings there, which was but a bubble, but upon letters from the lady Margaret of Burgundy, in whose succours and declaration for the enterprize, there seemed to be a more solid foundation, both for reputation and forces. Neither did the earl refrain the business, for that he knew the pretended Plantagenet to be but an idol: but contrariwise he was more glad it should be the false Plantagenet than the true; because the false being sure to fall away of himself, and the true to be made sure of by the king; it might open and pave a fair and prepar'd way to his own title. With this resolution he sail'd secretly into Flanders, where was a little before arriv'd the lord Lovel,[1] leaving a correspondence here in England with sir Thomas Broughton, a man of great power and dependencies in Lancashire. For before this time, when the pretended Plantagenet was first receiv'd in Ireland, secret messengers had been also sent to the lady Margaret, advertising her what was pass'd in Ireland, imploring succours in an enterprize (as they said) so pious and just, and that God had so miraculously prosper'd the beginning thereof; and making offer, that all things should be guided by her will and direction, as the sovereign patroness and protectress of the enterprize. Margaret was second sister to king Edward IV., and had been second wife to Charles, sirnam'd the Hardy, duke of Burgundy; by whom having no children of her own, she did with singular care and tenderness intend the education of Philip and Margaret, grandchildren to her former husband; which won her great love and authority among the Dutch. This princess (having the spirit of a man, and malice of a woman) abounding in treasure, by the greatness of her dower, and her provident government, and being childless, and without any nearer care, made it her design and enterprize to see the majesty royal of England once again replaced in her house, and had set up king Henry as a mark, at whose overthrow all her actions should aim and shoot; insomuch as all the counsels of his succeeding troubles came chiefly out of that quiver. And she bare such a mortal hatred to the house of Lancaster, and personally to the king, as she was no ways mollify'd by the conjunction of the houses in her niece's marriage, but rather hated her niece, as the means of the king's ascent to the crown, and assurance therein. Wherefore with great violence of affection she embraced this overture. And upon counsel taken with the earl of Lincoln and the lord Lovel, and some other of the party, it was resolv'd with all speed, the two lords assisted with a regiment of two thousand Almains, being choice and veteran bands, under the command of Martin Swart (a valiant and experimented captain) should pass over into Ireland to the new king. Hoping, that when the action should have the face of a received and settled regality (with such a second person, as the earl of Lincoln and the conjunction and reputation of foreign succours) the fame of it would embolden and prepare all the party of the confederates and malecontents within the realm of England, to give them assistance, when they should come over there. And for the person of the counterfeit, it was agreed, that if all things succeeded well, he should be put down, and the true Plantagenet received: wherein nevertheless the earl of Lincoln had his particular hopes. After they were come into Ireland, and that the party took courage, by seeing themselves together in a body, they grew very confident of success, conceiving and discoursing amongst themselves, that they went in upon far better cards to over-

[1] Francis Viscount Lovell, lord chamberlain to Richard III.

throw king Henry, than king Henry had to overthrow king Richard. And that if there were not a sword drawn against them in Ireland, it was a sign the swords in England would be soon sheath'd, or beaten down. And first, for a bravery upon this accession of power, they crown'd their new king in the cathedral church of Dublin;[1] who formerly had been but proclaim'd only; and then sate in council what should further be done. At which council, tho' it were propounded by some, that it were the best way to establish themselves first in Ireland, and to make that the seat of the war, and to draw king Henry thither in person, by whose absence they thought there would be great alterations and commotions in England; yet because the kingdom there was poor, and they should not be able to keep their army together, nor pay their German soldiers, and for that also the sway of the Irishmen, and generally of the men of war, which (as in such cases of popular tumults is usual) did in effect govern their leaders, was eager, and in affection to make their fortunes upon England: it was concluded with all possible speed to transport their forces into England. The king in the meantime, who at the first when he heard what was done in Ireland, tho' it troubled him, yet thought he should be well enough able to scatter the Irish as a flight of birds, and rattle away this swarm of bees, with their king; when he heard afterwards that the earl of Lincoln was embarked in the action, and that the lady Margaret was declared for it, he apprehended the danger in a true degree as it was, and saw plainly that his kingdom must again be put to the stake, and that he must fight for it. And first he did conceive before he understood of the earl of Lincoln's sailing into Ireland out of Flanders, that he should be assail'd both upon the east-parts of the kingdom of England by some impression from Flanders, and upon the north-west out of Ireland. And therefore having order'd musters to be made in both parts, and having provisionally design'd two generals, Jasper earl of Bedford, and John earl of Oxford (meaning himself also to go in person where the affairs should most require it), and nevertheless not expecting any actual invasion at that time (the winter being far on) he took his journey himself towards Suffolk and Norfolk, for the confirming of those parts. And being come to St. Edmondsbury, he understood that Thomas Marquess of Dorset (who had been one of the pledges in France) was hastning towards him, to purge himself of some accusations which had been made against him. But the king, tho' he kept an ear for him, yet was the time so doubtful, that he sent the earl of Oxford to meet him, and forthwith to carry him to the Tower; with a fair message nevertheless, that he should

---

[1] He was crown'd with a crown taken from a statue of the Virgin Mary in our lady's church near Damesgate. Dr. Payn bishop of Meath preach'd his coronation sermon; and the deputy, lord chancellor, lord treasurer, earl of Lincoln, lord Lovel, and many more persons of quality assisted at the ceremony; the archbishop of Armagh refus'd to attend at it. —Sir James Ware, cap iii.

bear that disgrace with patience, for that the king meant not his hurt, but only to preserve him from doing hurt, either to the king's service, or to himself; and that the king should always be able (when he had cleared himself) to make him reparation.

From St. Edmonds-bury he went to Norwich, where he kept his Christmas. And from thence he went (in a manner of pilgrimage) to Walsingham, where he visited our ladies church, famous for miracles, and made his prayers and vows for help and deliverance. And from thence he return'd by Cambridge to London. Not long after, the rebels, with their king (under the leading of the earl of Lincoln, the earl of Kildare, the lord Lovel, and colonel Swart), landed at Fouldrey in Lancashire, whither there repair'd to them sir Thomas Broughton with some small company of English. The king by that time (knowing now the storm would not divide, but fall in one place) had levied forces in good number: and in person (taking with him his two designed generals, the duke of Bedford and the earl of Oxford) was come on his way towards them as far as Coventry, whence he sent forth a troop of light horsemen for discovery, and to intercept some stragglers of the enemies, by whom he might the better understand the particulars of their progress and purposes, which was accordingly done; tho' the king otherwise was not without intelligence from his espials in the camp.

The rebels took their way towards York, without spoiling the country, or any act of hostility, the better to put themselves into favour of the people, and to personate their king: who (no doubt of a princely feeling) was sparing and compassionate towards his subjects. But their snow-ball did not gather as it went: for the people came not into them; neither did any rise or declare themselves in other parts of the kingdom for them, which was caused partly by the good taste that the king had given his people of his government, joyned with the reputation of his felicity; and partly for that it was an odious thing to the people of England to have a king brought into them upon the shoulders of Irish and Dutch, of which their army was in substance compounded. Neither was it a thing done with any great judgment on the party of the rebels, for them to take way towards York: considering that howsoever those parts had formerly been a nursery of their friends; yet it was there where the lord Lovel had so lately disbanded, and where the king's presence had a little before qualify'd discontents. The earl of Lincoln deceived of his hopes of the countries concourse unto him (in which case he would have temporized) and seeing the business past retract resolv'd to make on where the king was, and to give him battle; and thereupon march'd towards Newark, thinking to have surprized the town. But the king was somewhat before this time come to Nottingham, where he call'd a council of war, at which was consulted, whether it were best to protract time, or speedily to set upon the rebels. In which council the king himself (whose continual vigilancy did suck in sometimes causeless suspicions which few else knew) inclined to the accelerating a battle. But this was presently put out of doubt by the great aids that came in to him in the instant of this consultation; partly upon missives, and partly voluntaries from many parts of the kingdom.

The principal persons that came then to the king's aid, were the earl of Shrewsbury and the lord Strange, of the nobility; and of knights and gentlemen to the number of at least threescore and ten persons, with their companies making in the whole at the least six thousand fighting men, beside the forces that were with the king before. Whereupon the king, finding his army so bravely re-enforced, and a great alacrity in all his men to fight, was confirm'd in his former resolution, and march'd speedily, so as he put himself between the enemies camp and Newark; being loth their army should get the commodity of that town. The earl nothing dismay'd, came forwards that day unto a little village call'd Stoke, and there encamp'd that night upon the brow or hanging of a hill. The king the next day [1] presented him battle upon the plain, the fields there being open and champion. The earl courageously came down and joynd battle with him. Concerning which battle, the relations that are left unto us are so naked and negligent (though it be an action of so recent memory) as they rather declare the success of the day, than the manner of the fight. They say, that the king divided his army into three battles; whereof the van-guard only, well strengthen'd with wings, came to fight. That the fight was fierce and obstinate, and lasted three hours, before the victory inclined either way; save that judgment might be made, by that the king's van-guard of it self maintain'd fight against the whole power of the enemies, (the other two battles remaining out of action) what the success was like to be in the end. That Martin Swart with his Germans perform'd bravely; and so did those few English that were on that side; neither did the Irish fail in courage or fierceness, but being almost naked men, only arm'd with darts and skeins, it was rather an execution, than a fight upon them; insomuch as the furious slaughter of them was a great discouragement and appalement to the rest; that there died upon the place all the chieftains; that is, the earl of Lincoln, the earl of Kildare,[2] Francis lord Lovel, Martin Swart, and Sir Thomas Broughton; all making good the fight without any ground given. Only of the Lord Lovel there went a report, that he fled and swam over Trent on horseback, but could not recover the further side, by reason of the steepness of the bank, and so was

---

[1] Polydore Virgil places this battle in the year 1485. But that is not one of the least mistakes in his history.
[2] 'Twas the lord Thomas Fitzgerald, whom, says sir James Ware, 'some do erroneously call the earl of Kildare. There fell also Maurice Fitz-Thomas a Geraldine, and Plunket the baron of Kelleny's son.

drown'd in the river. But another report leaves him not there, but that he liv'd long after in a cave or vault. The number that was slain in the field, was of the enemies part four thousand at the least; and of the king's part one half of his van-guard, besides many hurt, but none of name. There were taken prisoners amongst others, the counterfeit Plantagenet (now Lambert Simnell again) and the crafty priest his tutor. For Lambert, the king would not take his life, both out of magnanimity, taking him but as an image of wax that others had temper'd and moulded; and likewise out of wisdom, thinking that if he suffer'd death he would be forgotten too soon; but being kept alive, he would be a continual spectacle, and a kind of remedy against the like inchantments of people in time to come. For which cause he was taken into service in his court to a base office in his kitchin; so that (in a kind of mattacina of human fortune) he turn'd a broach that had worn a crown. Whereas fortune commonly doth not bring in a comedy or farce after a tragedy. And afterwards he was preferred to be one of the king's falconers. As to the priest, he was committed close prisoner, and heard of no more; the king loving to seal up his own dangers.[1]

After the battle the king went to Lincoln where he caused supplications and thanksgivings to be made for his deliverance and victory; and that his devotions might go round in circle, he sent his banner to be offer'd to our lady of Walsingham where before he made his vows. And thus deliver'd of this so strange an engine and new invention of fortune, he return'd to his former confidence of mind; thinking now, that all his misfortunes had come at once: but it fell out unto him according to the speech of the common people in the beginning of his reign, that said, 'It was a token he should reign in labour, because his reign began with a sickness of sweat.' But howsoever the king thought himself now in a haven, yet such was his wisdom, as his confidence did seldom darken his foresight, especially in things near hand. And therefore awaken'd by so fresh and unexpected dangers, he entered into due consideration, as well how to weed out the partakers of the former rebellion, as to kill the seeds of the like in time to come; and withal to take away all shelters and harbours for discontented persons, where they might hatch and foster rebellions, which afterwards might gather strength and motion. And first, he did yet again make a progress from Lincoln to the northern parts, though indeed it were rather an itinerary circuit of justice, than a progress: for all along as he went, with much severity and strict inquisition,

---

[1] The king wrote to the mayor and citizens of Waterford in Ireland, to commend their fidelity, which he next year rewarded with new privileges and immunities. The earl of Kildare and the lord who had sided with Lambert, sent over letters to the king and begg'd pardon; which he not only granted them, but continued the earl of Kildare lord deputy. —Sir J. Ware. Cap. 111.

In the year following, sir Richard Edgcomb was sent over to Ireland with 500 men to take new oaths of allegiance of the nobility, and king Henry order'd them to come to England; where he feasted them all, and gave the Lord Heath 300*l*. in gold.

partly by martial law, and partly by commission, were punished, the adherents and aiders of the late rebels: not all by death, for the field had drawn much blood) but by fines and ransoms which spared life and raised treasure. Amongst other crimes of this nature, there was diligent inquiry made of such as had raised and dispersed a bruit and rumour, a little before the field fought, that the rebels had the day, and that the king's army was overthrown and the king fled: whereby it was supposed, that many succours, which otherwise would have come unto the king, were cunningly put off and kept back. Which charge and accusation, though it had some ground, yet was industriously embraced and put on by divers, who having been in themselves not the best affected to the king's part, nor forward to come to his aid, were glad to apprehend this colour to cover their neglect and coldness, under the pretence of such discouragements. Which cunning nevertheless the king would not understand, tho' he lodg'd it, and noted it in some particulars, as his manner was.

But for the extirpating of the roots and causes of the like commotions in time to come, the king began to find where his shoe did wring him, and that it was his depressing of the house of York, that did rancle and fester the affections of his people. And therefore being now too wise to disdain perils any longer, and willing to give some contentment in that kind (at least in ceremony) he resolv'd at last to proceed to the coronation of his queen. And therefore at his coming to London, where he entered in state, and in a kind of triumph, and celebrated his victory with two days of devotion, (for the first day he repair'd to Paul's and had the hymn of Te Deum sung, and the morrow after he went in procession, and heard the sermon at the Cross) the queen was with great solemnity crown'd at Westminster, the five and twentieth of November, in the third year of his reign, which was about two years after the marriage; like an old christning, that had stayed long for godfathers. Which strange and unusual distance of time, made it subject to every man's note, that it was an act against his stomach, and put upon him by necessity and reason of state. Soon after, to shew that it was now fair weather again, and that the imprisonment of Thomas marquess Dorset, was rather upon suspicion of the time than of the man, he the said marquess was set at liberty without examination, or other circumstance. At that time also the king sent an ambassadour unto Pope Innocent, signifying unto him this his marriage, and that now (like another Æneas) he had passed through the floods of his former troubles and travels, and was arriv'd unto a safe haven: and thanking his holiness that he had honour'd the celebration of his marriage with the presence of his ambassador; and offering both his person and the forces of his kingdom upon all occasions to do him service.

The ambassador making his oration to the Pope, in the presence of the cardinals, did so magnifie the king and queen, as was enough to glut the hearers. But then he did again so extol and deify the Pope, as made all that he had said in praise of his master and mistress seem temperate and passable. But he was very honourably entertain'd, and extremely much made on by the Pope : who knowing himself to be lazy and unprofitable to the christian world, was wonderfully glad to hear that there were such echoes of him sounding in remote parts. He obtain'd also of the Pope a very just and honourable bull, qualifying the privileges of sanctuary (wherewith the king had been extremely gauled) in three points.

The first, that if any sanctuary-man did by night, or otherwise, get out of sanctuary privily and commit mischief and trespass, and then come in again, he should lose the benefit of sanctuary for ever after. The second, that howsoever the person of the sanctuary-man was protected from his creditors, yet his goods out of sanctuary should not. The third, that if any took sanctuary for case of treason the king might appoint him keepers to look to him in sanctuary.

The king also for the better securing of his estate, against mutinous and malecontented subjects (whereof he saw the realm was full) who might have their refuge into Scotland, which was not under key, as the ports were ; for that cause, rather than for any doubt of hostility from those parts, before his coming to London (when he was at Newcastle) had sent a solemn embassage unto James III. king of Scotland, to treat and conclude a peace with him. The ambassadors were Richard Fox bishop of Exeter, and sir Richard Edgcomb, comptroller of the king's house, who were honourably receiv'd and entertain'd there. But the king of Scotland labouring of the same disease that king Henry did (tho' more mortal, as afterwards appear'd) that is, discontented subjects, apt to rise and raise tumult, altho' in his own affection he did much desire to make a peace with the king ; yet finding his nobles averse, and not daring to displease them, concluded only a truce for seven years ; giving nevertheless promise in private, that it should be renew'd from time to time, during the two kings lives.

Hitherto the king had been exercis'd in setting his affairs at home. But about this time brake forth an occasion that drew him to look abroad, and to hearken to foreign business. Charles VIII. the French king, by the vertue and good fortune of his two immediate predecessors, Charles VII. his grandfather, and Lewis XI. his father, receiv'd the kingdom of France in more flourishing and spreading estate than it had been of many years before ; being redintegrate in those principal members which anciently had been portions of the crown of France, and were after dissevered, so as they remain'd only in homage, and not in sovereignty (being govern'd by absolute princes of their own) Anjou, Normandy, Provence, and Burgundy. There remain'd only Brittainy to be re-united, and so the monarchy of France to be reduced to the ancient terms and bounds.

King Charles was not a little inflamed with an ambition to re-purchase and re-annex that duchy. Which his ambition was a wise and well weigh'd ambition; not like unto the ambitions of his succeeding enterprizes of Italy. For at that time being newly come to the crown, he was somewhat guided by his father's councils (councils, not counsellors) for his father was his council, and had few able men about him. And that king (he knew well) had ever distasted the designs of Italy, and in particular had an eye upon Brittainy. There were many circumstances that did feed the ambition of Charles, with pregnant and apparent hopes of success. The duke of Brittainy old, and entred into a lethargy, and serv'd with mercenary counsellors, father of two only daughters, the one sickly and not like to continue. King Charles himself in the flower of his age, and the subjects of France at that time well train'd for war, both for leaders and soldiers; men of service being not yet worn out since the wars of Lewis against Burgundy. He found himself also in peace with all his neighbour princes. As for those that might oppose to his enterprize, Maximilian king of Romans, his rival in the same desires (as well for the duchy, as the daughter), feeble in means; and king Henry of England as well somewhat obnoxious to him for his favours and benefits, as busy'd in his particular troubles at home. There was also a fair and specious occasion offer'd him to hide his ambition and to justify his warring upon Britainy, for that the duke had receiv'd and succour'd Lewis duke of Orleans, and other of the French nobility, which had taken arms against their king. Wherefore king Charles being resolv'd upon that war, knew well he could not receive any opposition so potent, as if king Henry should either upon policy of state, in preventing the growing greatness of France: or upon gratitude unto the duke of Britainy, for his former favours in the time of his distress, espouse that quarrel, and declare himself in aid of the duke. Therefore he no sooner heard that king Henry was settled by his victory, but forthwith he sent ambassadors unto him to pray his assistance, or at the least that he would stand neutral. Which ambassadors found the king at Leicester, and deliver'd their embassage to this effect. They first imparted unto the king the success that their master had had a little before against Maximilian, in recovery of certain towns from him; which was done in a kind of privacy, and inwardness towards the king; as if the French king did not esteem him for an outward or formal confederate, but as one that had part in his affections and fortunes, and with whom he took pleasure to communicate his business. After this compliment, and some gratulation for the king's victory, they fell to their errand; declaring to the king, that their master was enforc'd to enter into a just and necessary war with the duke of Britainy, for that he had receiv'd and succour'd those that were traytors, and declared enemies unto his person and state. That they were no mean, distressed and calamitous persons that fled to him for refuge, but of so great quality, as it was apparent that they came not thither to protect their own fortune, but to infest and invade his; the head of them being the duke of Orleans, the first prince of the blood, and the second person of France. That therefore, rightly to understand it, it was rather on their master's part a defensive war than an offensive; as that, that could not be omitted or forborn, if he tendred the conservation of his own estate; and that it was not the first blow that made the war invasive; (for that no wise prince would stay for) but the first provocation, or at least the first preparation. Nay, that this war was rather a suppression of rebels, than a war with a just enemy, where the case is; that his subjects, traytors, are receiv'd by the duke of Britainy his homager. That king Henry knew well what went upon it in example, if neighbour-princes should patronize and comfort rebels, against the law of nations and of leagues. Nevertheless that their master was not ignorant, that the king had been beholden to the duke of Britainy in his adversity; as on the other side, they knew he would not forget also the readiness of their king, in aiding him when the duke of Britainy, or his mercenary councellors fail'd him and would have betray'd him; and that there was a great difference between the courtesies receiv'd from their master and the duke of Britainy; for that the duke's might have ends of utility and bargain; whereas their masters could not have proceeded but out of entire affection. For that, if it had been measur'd by a politick line, it had been better for his affairs, that a tyrant should have reign'd in England, troubled and hated, than such a prince, whose vertues could not fail to make him great and potent, whensoever he was come to be master of his affairs. But howsoever it stood for the point of obligation which the king might owe to the duke of Britainy, yet their master was well assur'd, it would not divert king Henry ot England from doing that that was just, nor ever embark him in so ill-grounded a quarrel. Therefore, since this war which their master was now to make, was but to deliver himself from imminent dangers, their king hop'd the king would shew the like affection to the conservation of their master's estate, as their master had (when time was) shew'd to the king's acquisition of his kingdom. At the least, that according to the inclination which the king had ever professed of peace, he would look on, and stand neutral; for that their master could not with reason press him to undertake part in the war, being so newly settled and recover'd from intestine seditions.

But touching the mystery of re-annexing of the duchy of Britainy to the crown of France, either by war, or by marriage with the daughter of Britainy; the ambassadors bear aloof from it, as from a rock, knowing that it made most against them. And therefore by all means declined any mention thereof, but contrariwise interlaced in their conference with the king, the assured purpose of their master, to match with the daughter of Maximilian: and entertain'd the king also with some wandring discourses of their king's purpose to recover by arms his right to the kingdom of Naples, by an expedition in person; all to remove the king from all jealousy of any design in these hither parts upon Britainy, otherwise than for quenching of the fire, which he fear'd might be kindled in his own estate.

The king after advice taken with his council, made answer to the ambassadors. And first returned their compliment, shewing he was right glad of the French king's reception of those towns from Maximilian. Then he familiarly related some particular passages of his own adventures and victory passed. As to the business of Britainy, the king answer'd in few words; that the French king and the duke of Britainy were the two persons to whom he was most obliged of all men; and that he should think himself very unhappy if things should go so between them, as he should not be able to acquit himself in gratitude towards them both; and that there was no means for him as a christian king and a common friend to them, to satisfy all obligations both to God and man, but to offer himself for a mediator of an accord and peace between them; by which course he doubted not but their king's estate and honour both, would be preserv'd with more safety and less envy than by war, and that he would spare no costs or pains, not if it were to go on pilgrimage for so good an effect: and concluded, that in this great affair, which he took so much to heart, he would express himself more fully by an embassage, which he would speedily dispatch unto the French king for that purpose. And in this sort the French ambassadors were dismissed; the king avoiding to understand any thing touching the re-annexing of Britainy, as the ambassadors had avoided to mention it; save that he gave a little touch of it in the word, envy. And so it was, that the king was neither so shallow, nor so ill advertis'd, as not to perceive the intention of the French king, for the investing himself of Britainy. But first he was utterly unwilling (howsoever he gave out) to enter into war with France. A fame of a war he liked well, but not an achievement; for the one he thought would make him richer, and the other poorer: and he was possessed with many secret fears touching his own people, which he was therefore loth to arm, and put weapons into their hands. Yet notwithstanding (as a prudent and couragious prince) he was not so averse from a war, but that he was resolv'd to choose it, rather than to have Britainy carried by France, being so great and opulent a duchy, and situate so opportunely to annoy England, either for coast, or trade. But the king's hopes were, that partly by negligence, commonly imputed to the French (especially in the court of a young king) and partly by the native power of Britainy it self, which was not small; but chiefly in respect of the great party that the duke of Orleans had in the kingdom of France, and thereby means to stir up civil troubles, to divert the French king from the enterprize of Britainy. And lastly, in regard of the power of Maximilian, who was co-rival to the French king in that pursuit, the enterprize would either bow to a peace, or break in it self. In all which, the king measur'd and valued things amiss, as afterwards appear'd. He sent therefore forthwith to the French king, Christopher Urswicke his chaplain, a person by him much trusted and imploy'd: choosing him the rather, because he was a churchman, as best sorting with an embassy of pacification; and giving him also a commission, that if the French king consented to treat, he would thence repair to the duke of Britainy, and ripen the treaty on both parts. Urswicke made declaration to the French king, much to the purpose of the king's answer to the French ambassadors here; instilling also tenderly some overture of receiving to grace the duke of Orleans, and some taste of conditions of accord. But the French king on the other side proceeded not sincerely, but with a great deal of art and dissimulation, in this treaty; having for his end to gain time, and so put off the English succours, under hope of peace, till he had got good footing in Britainy, by force of arms. Wherefore he answer'd the ambassador, that he would put himself into the king's hands, and make him arbiter of the peace; and willingly consented, that the ambassador should straightways pass into Britainy, to signify this his consent, and to know the duke's mind likewise; well foreseeing, that the duke of Orleans, by whom the duke of Britainy was wholly led, taking himself to be upon terms irreconcileable with him, would admit of no treaty of peace. Whereby he should in one, both generally abroad veyl over his ambition, and win the reputation of just and moderate proceedings; and should withal endear himself in the affections of the king of England, as one that had committed all to his will: nay, and (which was yet more fine) make faith in him, that altho' he went on with the war, yet it should be but with his sword in his hand to bend the stiffness of the other party to accept of peace; and so the king should make no umbrage of his arming and prosecution; but the treaty to be kept on foot, till the very last instant, till he were master of the field.

Which grounds being by the French king wisely laid, all things fell out as he expected. For when the English ambassador came to the court of Britainy, the duke was then scarcely perfect in his memory, and all things were directed by the duke of Orleans; who gave audience to the chaplain Urswicke, and, upon his ambassage deliver'd, made answer in somewhat high terms: that the duke of Britain having been an host, and a kind of parent or fosterfather to the king, in his tenderness of age and weakness of fortune, did look for at this time from king Henry (the renowned king of England) rather brave troops for his succours, than a vain treaty of peace. And if the king could forget the good offices of the duke done unto him aforetime; yet he knew well, he would in his wisdom consider of the future, how much it imported his own safety and reputation, both in foreign parts and with his own people, not to suffer Britainy (the old confederates of England) to be swallowed up by France, and so many good ports and strong towns upon the coast be in the command of so potent a neighbour-king, and so ancient an enemy. And therefore humbly desired the king to think of this business as his own; and therewith brake off, and denyed any further conference for treaty.

Urswicke return'd first to the French king, and related to him what had passed. Who finding things to sort to his desire, took hold of them, and said, that the ambassador might perceive now that which he for his part partly imagined before. That considering in what hands the duke of Britainy was, there would be no peace, but by a mixed treaty of force and persuasion. And therefore he would go on with the one, and desired the king not to desist from the other. But for his own part, he did faithfully promise to be still in the king's power to rule him in the matter of peace. This was accordingly represented unto the king by Urswicke at his return, and in such a fashion as if the treaty were in no sort desperate, but rather stay'd for a better hour, till the hammer had wrought, and beat the party of Britainy more pliant. Whereupon there passed continually packets and dispatches between the two kings, from the one out of desire, and from the other out of dissimulation, about the negociation of peace. The French king mean while invaded Britainy with great forces, and distress'd the city of Nantes with a straight siege, and (as one, who tho' he had no great judgment, yet had that, that he could dissemble home) the more he did urge the prosecution of the war, the more he did at the same time urge the solicitation of the peace. Insomuch as during the siege of Nantes, after many letters and particular messages, the better to maintain his dissimulation, and to refresh the treaty; he sent Bernard Daubigney (a person of good quality) to the king, earnestly to desire him to make an end of the business howsoever.

The king was no less ready to revive and quicken the treaty: and thereupon sent three commissioners, the abbot of Abington, sir Richard Tunstall, and chaplain Urswicke formerly imploy'd, to do their endeavours, to manage the treaty roundly and strongly.

About this time the lord Woodvile (uncle to the queen), a valiant gentleman and desirous of honour, sued to the king, that he might raise some power of voluntaries under hand, and without licence or pasport (wherein the king might any ways appear) go to the aid of the duke of Britainy. The king denyed his request (or at least seemed so to do) and lay'd strait commandment upon him, that he should not stir; for that the king thought his honour would suffer therein during a treaty, to better a party. Nevertheless this lord (either being unruly, or out of conceit that the king would not inwardly dislike that which he would not openly avow) sail'd secretly over into the Isle of Wight, whereof he was governour, and levied a fair troop of four hundred men, and with them passed over into Britainy, and joyned himself with the duke's forces. The news whereof when it came to the French court, put divers young bloods into such a fury, as the English ambassadors were not without peril to be outraged. But the French king both to preserve the privilege of ambassadors, and being conscious to himself that in the business of peace, he himself was the greater dissembler of the two, forbad all injuries of fact or word against their persons, or followers. And presently came an agent from the king, to purge himself touching the lord Woodvile's going over, using for a principal argument, to demonstrate that it was without his privity, for that the troops were so small, as neither had the face of a succour by authority; nor could much advance the Bretagne affairs. To which message, although the French king gave no full credit, yet he made fair weather with the king, and seem'd satisfied: soon after the English ambassadors returned, having two of them been likewise with the duke of Britainy, and found things in no other terms, than they were before. Upon their return, they inform'd the king of the state of the affairs, and how far the French king was from any true meaning of peace; and therefore he was now to advise of some other course. Neither was the king himself led all this while with credulity merely, as was generally supposed. But his error was not so much facility of belief, as an ill measuring of the forces of the other party.

For (as was partly touch'd before) the king had cast the business thus with himself. He took it for granted in his own judgment, that the war of Britainy, in respect of the strength of the towns and of the party, could not speedily come to a period. For he conceiv'd that the counsels of a war, that was undertaken by the French king, then childless, against an heir-apparent of France, would be very faint and slow. And besides, that it was not possible, but that the state of France should be embroil'd with some troubles and alterations in favour of the duke of Orleans. He conceived likewise, that Maximilian, king of the Romans, was a prince, warlike and potent; who (he made account) would give succours to the Britains roundly. So then judging it would be a work of time, he laid his plot, how he might best make use of that time, for his own affairs. Wherein first he thought to make his vantage upon his parliament; knowing that they being affectionate unto the quarrel of Britainy, would give treasure largely. Which treasure, as a noise of war might draw forth; so a peace succeeding might coffer up. And because he knew his people were hot upon the business, he chose rather to seem to be deceiv'd, lull'd asleep by the French, than to be backward in himself; considering his subjects were not so fully capable of the reasons of state, which made him hold back. Wherefore to all these purposes he saw no other expedient, than to set and keep on foot a continual treaty of peace; laying it down, and taking it up again, as the occurrence requir'd. Besides, he had in consideration the point of honour in bearing the blessed person of a pacificator. He thought likewise to make use of the envy, that the French king met with, by occasion of this war of Britany, in strengthening himself with new alliances; as namely that of Ferdinando of Spain, with whom he had ever a consent even in nature and customs; and likewise with Maximilian, who was particularly interested. So that in substance he promised himself money, honour, friends, and peace in the end. But those things were too fine to be fortunate, and succeed in all parts; for that great affairs are commonly too rough and stubborn to be wrought upon by the finer edges, or points of wit. The king was likewise deceived in his two main grounds. For although he had reason to conceive, that the counsel of France would be wary to put the king into a war against the heir-apparent of France; yet he did not consider, that Charles was not guided by any of the principal of the blood or nobility, but by mean men, who would make it their masterpiece of credit and favour, to give venturous counsels, which no great or wise man durst, or would. And for Maximilian, he was thought then a greater matter than he was; his unstable and necessitous courses being not then known.

After consultation with the ambassadors, who brought him no other news, than he expected before (though he would not seem to know it till then) he presently summoned his parliament, and in open parliament propounded the cause of Britainy to both houses, by his chancellor Moreton Archbishop of Canterbury, who spake to this effect.

'My lords and masters; the king's grace our soverain lord, hath commanded me to declare unto you the causes that have mov'd him at this time to summon this his parliament; which I shall do in few words, craving pardon of his grace, and you all, if I perform it not as I would.

'His grace doth first of all let you know, that he retaineth in thankful memorie the love and loyalty shewed to him by you, at your last meeting, in establishment of his royaltie; freeing and discharging of his partakers, and confiscation of his traytors and rebels; more than which could not come from subjects to their soveraign, in one action. This he taketh so well at your hands, as he hath made it a resolution to himself, to communicate with so loving and well approved subjects, in all affairs that are of publick nature, at home or abroad.

'Two therefore are the causes of your present assembling; the one, a foreign business; the other, matter of government at home.

'The French king (as no doubt ye have heard) maketh at this present hot war upon the duke of Britain. His army is now before Nantes, and holdeth it straightly beseig'd, being the principal city (if not in ceremonie and pre-eminence, yet in strength and wealth) of that duchie. Ye may guess at his hopes, by his attempting of the hardest part of the war first. The cause of this war he knoweth best. He alledgeth the entertaining and succouring of the duke of Orleance, and some other French lords, whom the king taketh for his enemies. Others divine of other matters. Both parts have by their ambassadors divers times prayed the king's aids : the French king's aids, or neutrality ; the Britons aids simply ; for so their case requireth. The king, as a christian prince, and blessed son of the holy church hath offered himself as a mediator to treat a peace between them. The king yeildeth to treat, but will not stay the prosecution of the war. The Britons, that desire peace most, hearken to it at least; not upon confidence or stiffness, but upon distrust of true meaning, seeing the war goes on. So as the king, after as much pains and care to effect a peace, as ever he took in any business, not being able to remove the prosecution on the one side, nor the distrust on the other, caused by that prosecution, hath let fall the treatie ; not repenting of it, but despairing of it now, as not likely to succeed. Therefore by this narrative you now understand the state of the question, whereupon the king prayeth your advice ; which is no other, but whether he shall enter into an auxiliary and defensive war for the Britons against France.

'And the better to open your understandings in this affair, the king hath commanded me to say somewhat to you from him, of the persons that do intervene in this business ; and somewhat of the consequence thereof, as it hath relation to this kingdom ; and somewhat of the example of it in general : making nevertheless no conclusion or judgment of any point, until his grace hath received your faithful and politick advices.

'First, for the king our soveraign himself, who is the principal person you are to eye in this business ; his grace doth profess, that he truly and constantly desireth to reign in peace. But his grace saith, he will neither buy peace with dishonour, nor take it up at interest of danger to ensue ; but shall think it a good change, if it please God to change the inward troubles and seditions, wherewith he hath been hitherto exercised into an honourable foreign war. And for the other two persons in this action, the French king, and the duke of Britain, his grace doth declare unto you, that they be the men, unto whom he is of all other friends and allies most bounden ; the one having held over him his hand of protection from the tyrant ; the other having reached forth unto him his hand of help, for the recovery of his kingdom. So that his affection toward them in his natural person, is upon equal terms. And whereas you may have heard, that his grace was enforced to flie out of Brittain into France, for doubts of being betrayed; his grace would not in any sort have that reflect upon the duke of Brittain, in defacement of his former benefits: for that he is thoroughly informed, that it was but the practice of some corrupt persons about him, during the time of his sickness, altogether without his consent or privity.

'But howsoever these things do interest his grace in his particular, yet he knoweth well, that the higher bond that tyeth him to procure by all means the safety and welfare of his loving subjects, doth disinterest him of these obligations of gratitude, otherwise than thus: that if his grace be forced to make a war, he do it without passion, or ambition.

'For the consequence of this action towards this kingdom, it is much as the French king's intention is. For if it be no more, but to range his subjects to reason, who bear themselves stout upon the strength of the duke of Brittain, it is nothing to us. But if it be in the French king's purpose, or if it should not be in his purpose, yet if it shall follow all one as if it were sought, that the French king shall make a province of Brittain, and joyn it to the crown of France; then it is worthy the consideration, how this may import England, as well in the increasement of the greatness of France, by the addition of such a country, that stretcheth his boughes unto our seas, as in depriving this nation, and leaving it naked of so firm and assured confederates, as the Brittains have always been. For then it will come to pass, that whereas not long since, this realm was mighty upon the continent, first in territory, and after in alliance, in respect of Burgundy and Brittain, which were confederates indeed, but dependant confederates; now the one being already cast, partly into the greatness of France, and partly into that of Austria, the other is like wholly to be cast into the greatness of France, and this island shall remain confined in effect within the salt waters, and girt about with the coast-countries of two mighty monarchs.

'For the example, it resteth likewise upon the same question, upon the French king's intent. For if Brittain be carried and swallow'd up by France, as the world abroad (apt to impute and construe the actions of princes to ambition) conceive it will; then it is an example very dangerous and universal, that the lesser neighbour estate should be devoured of the greater. For this may be the case of Scotland towards England; of Portugal, towards Spain; of the smaller estates of Italy, towards the greater; and so of Germany; or as if some of you of the commons, might not live and dwell lately, besides some of these great lords. And the bringing in of this example, will be chiefly laid to the king's charge, as to him that was most interested and most able to forbid it. But then on the other side, there is so fair a pretext on the French king's part (and yet pretext is never wanting to power) in regard the danger imminent to his own estate is such, as may make this enterprize seem rather a work of necessity, than of ambition, as doth in reason correct the danger of the example. For that the example of that which is done in a man's own defence, cannot be dangerous; because it is in another's power to avoid it. But in all this business, the king remits himself to your grave and mature advice, whereupon he purposeth to rely.'

This was the effect of the lord chancellor's speech touching the cause of Brittain: for the king had commanded him to carry it so, as to affect the parliament towards the business; but without engaging the king in any express declaration.

The chancellor went on:

'For that which may concern the government at home, the king hath commanded me to say unto you; that he thinketh there was never any king (for the small time that he hath reign'd) had greater and juster cause of the two contrary passions of joy, and sorrow, than his grace hath joy, in respect of the rare and visible favours of Almighty God in girting the imperial sword upon his side, and assisting the fame of his sword against all his enemies; and likewise in blessing him with so many good and loving servants and subjects, which have never fail'd to give him faithful counsel, ready obedience, and couragious defence. Sorrow, for that it hath not pleased God to suffer him to sheath his sword (as he greatly desired otherwise than for administration of justice) but that he hath been forced to draw it so oft, to cut off traiterous and disloyal subjects, whom (it seems) God hath left (a few amongst many good) as the Canaanites among the people of Israel, to be thorns in their sides to tempt and try them; tho the end hath been always (God's name be blessed therefore) that the destruction hath faln upon their own heads.

'Wherefore his grace saith, that he seeth that it is not the blood spilt in the field, that will save the blood in the city; nor the marshal's sword, that will set this kingdom in perfect peace: but that the true way is, to stop the seeds of sedition and rebellion in their beginnings; and for that purpose to devise, confirm, and quicken good and wholsom laws, against riots and unlawful assemblies of people, and all combinations and confederacies of them, by liveries, tokens, and other badges of factious dependance; that the peace of the land may by these ordinances, as by bars of iron, be soundly bound in and strengthened, and all force both in court, country, and private houses, be suppress'd. The care hereof, which so much concerneth your selves, and which the nature of the times doth instantly call for, his grace commends to your wisdoms.

'And because it is the king's desire, that this peace, wherein he hopeth to govern and maintain you, do not bear only unto you leaves for you to sit under the shade of them in safety: but also should bear you fruit of riches, wealth and plenty: therefore his grace prays you, to take into consideration matter of trade, as also the manufactures of the kingdom, and to repress the bastard and barren imployment of moneys, to usury and unlawful exchanges, that they may be (as their natural use is) turned upon commerce, and lawful and royal trading. And likewise, that our people be set on work in arts and handicrafts; that the realm may subsist more of it self; that idleness be avoided, and the drawing out of our treasure for foreign manufactures stopped. But you are not to rest here only, but to provide further, that whatsoever merchandize shall be brought in from beyond the seas, may be imploy'd upon the commodities of this land; whereby the kingdom's stock of treasure may be sure to be kept from being diminished, by any over-trading of the foreigner.

'And lastly, because the king is well assured, that you would not have him poor, that wishes you rich; he doubteth not, but that you will have care, as well to maintain his revenues, of customs, and all other natures, as also to supply him with your loving aids, if the case shall so require. The rather, for that you know the king is a good husband, and but a steward in effect for the publick; and that what comes from you is but as moisture drawn from the earth, which gathers into a cloud, and falls back upon the earth again. And you know well, how the kingdoms about you grow more and more in greatness, and the times are stirring; and therefore not fit to find the king with an empty purse. More I have not to say to you; and wish, that what hath been said, had been better express'd: but that your wisdoms and good affections will supply. God bless your doings.'

It was no hard matter to dispose and affect the parliament in this business; as well in respect of the emulation between the nations, and the envy at the late growth of the French monarchy; as in regard of the danger, to suffer the French to make their approaches upon England, by obtaining so goodly a maritime province, full of sea-towns, and havens, that might do mischief to the English either by invasion or by interruption of traffick. The parliament was also moved with the point of oppression; for altho' the French seem'd to speak reason, yet arguments are ever with multitudes too weak for suspitions. Wherefore they did advise the king, roundly to embrace the Britons' quarrel, and to send them speedy aids, and with much alacrity and forwardness granted to the king a great rate of subsidy, in contemplation of these aids. But the king, both to keep a decency towards the French king, to whom he profess'd himself to be obliged, and indeed desirous rather to shew war, than to make it, sent new solemn ambassadors to intimate unto him the decree of his estates and to iterate his motion, that the French would desist from hostility; or if war must follow, to desire him to take it in good part, if at the motion of his people, who were sensible of the cause of the Britons as their ancient friends and confederates, he did send them succours ; with protestation nevertheless, that to save all treaties and laws of friendship, he had limited his force to proceed in aid of the Britons, but in no wise to war upon the French, otherwise than as they maintain'd the possession of Britain. But before this formal embassage arriv'd, the party of the duke had receiv'd a great blow, and grew to manifest declination. For near the town of St. Alban in Britain, a battle had been given where the Britons were overthrown, and the duke of Orleans, and the prince of Orange taken prisoners, there being slain on the Britons, part six thousand men, and amongst them the lord Woodvile, and almost all his soldiers valiantly fighting. And of the French part one thousand two hundred, with their leader James Galeot, a great commander.

When the news of the battle came over into England, it was time for the king (who now had no subterfuge to continue further treaty, and saw before his eyes, that Britain went so speedily for lost, contrary to his hopes, knowing also that with his people and foreigners both, he sustained no small envy and disreputation for his former delays) to dispatch with all possible speed his succours into Britain ; which he did under the conduct of Robert Lord Brook, to the number of eight thousand choice men, and well arm'd ; who having a fair wind, in few hours landed in Britain, and joyned themselves forthwith to those Briton forces, that remain'd after the defeat, and march'd straight on to find the enemy, and incamped fast by them. The French wisely husbanding the possession of a victory, and well acquainted with the courage of the English, especially when they are fresh, kept themselves within their trenches, being strongly lodged, and resolved not to give battle. But mean while, to harrass and weary the English, they did upon all advantages set upon them with their light horse ; wherein nevertheless they received commonly loss, especially by means of the English archers.

But upon these achievements Francis, duke of Britain, deceased ; an accident that the king might easily have foreseen, and ought to have reckon'd upon, and provided for ; but that the point of reputation, when news first came of the battle lost (that somewhat must be done) did over-bear the reason of war.

After the duke's decease, the principal persons of Britain, partly bought, partly through faction, put all things into confusion ; so as the English not finding head or body with whom to joyn their forces, and being in jealousy of friends, as well as in danger of enemies, and the winter begun, return'd home five months after their landing. So the battle of St. Alban, the death of the duke, and the retire of the English succours were (after some time) the causes of the loss of that duchy ; which action some accounted as a blemish of the king's judgment ; but most as the misfortune of his times.

But howsoever the temporary fruit of the parliament in their aid and advice given for Britain, took not, nor prospered not ; yet the lasting fruit of parliament, which is good and wholesome laws, did prosper, and doth yet continue to this day. For according to the lord chancellor's admonition, there were that parliament divers excellent laws ordained concerning the points which the king recommended.

First, the authority of the Star-Chamber, which before subsisted by the ancient common laws of the realm, was confirme ̣ in certain cases by act of parliament. This court is one of the sagest and noblest institutions of this kingdom. For in the distribution of courts of ordinary justice (besides the high court of parliament) in which distribution the king's-bench holdeth the pleas of the crown, the common-place pleas civil, the exchequer pleas concerning the king's revenue, and the chancery the prætorian power for mitigating the rigour of law, in case of extremity, by the conscience of a good man ; there was nevertheless always reserv'd a high and pre-eminent power to the king's council, in causes that might in example, or consequence, concern the state of the commonwealth, which if they were criminal, the council used to sit in the chamber, call'd the Star-Chamber ; if civil in the White-chamber, or White-hall. And as the chancery had the prætorian power for equity : so the Star-Chamber had the censorian power for offences, under the degree of capital. This court of Star-Chamber is compounded of good elements ; for it consisteth of four kinds of persons : councellors, peers, prelates, and chief judges. It discerneth also principally of four kinds of causes ; forces, frauds, crimes various of stellionate, and the inchoations or middle acts towards crimes capital, or heighnous, not actually committed or perpetrated. But that which was principally aimed at by this act was force, and the two chief supporters of force, combination of multitudes, and maintenance or head ship of great persons.

From the general peace of the country, the king's care went on to the peace of the king's house, and the security of his great officers and counsellors. But this law was somewhat of a strange composition and temper. That if any of the king's servants under the degree of a lord, do conspire the death of any of the king's council, or lord of the realm, it is made capital. This law was thought to be procur'd by the lord chancellor, who being a stern and haughty man, and finding he had some mortal enemies in court, provided for his own safety ; drowning the envy of it in a general law, by communicating the priviledge with all other councellors and peers, and yet not daring to extend it further, than to the king's servants in check-roll, lest it should have been too harsh to the gentlemen, and other commons of the kingdom ; who might have thought their ancient liberty, and the clemency of the laws of England invaded, if the will in any case of felony should be made the deed. And yet the reason which the act yieldeth (that is to say, that he that conspireth the death of councellors may be thought indirectly, and by a mean, to conspire the death of the king himself) is indifferent to all subjects, as well as to servants in court. But it seemeth this sufficed to serve the lord chancellor's turn at this time. But yet he lived to need a general law, for that he grew afterwards as odious to the country, as he was then to the court.

From the peace of the king's house, the king's care extended to the peace of private houses and families. For there was an excellent moral law moulded thus; the taking and carrying away of women forcibly, and against their will (except female-wards and bondwomen) was made capital. The parliament wisely and justly conceiving, that the obtaining of women by force into possession (howsoever afterwards assent might follow by allurements) was but a rape drawn forth in length, because the first force drew on all the rest.

There was made also another law for peace in general, and repressing of murders and man-slaughters, and was in amendment of the common laws of the realm, being this: that whereas by the common law, the king's suit in case of homicide, did expect, the year and the day, allowed to the parties suit by way of appeal; and that it was found by experience, that the party was many times compounded with, and many times wearied with the suit, so that in the end such suit was let fall, and by that time the matter was in a manner forgotten, and thereby prosecution at the king's suit by indictment (which is ever best, *flagrante crimine*) neglected; it was ordain'd, that the suit by indictment might be taken as well at any time within the year and the day, as after, not prejudicing nevertheless the parties suit.

The king began also then, as well in wisdom as in justice, to pare a little the privilege of clergy, ordaining, that clerks convict should be burn'd in the hand; both because they might taste of some corporal punishment, and that they might carry a brand of infamy. But for this good act's sake, the king himself was after branded by Perkin's proclamation, for an execrable breaker of the rites of holy church.

Another law was made for the better peace of the country; by which law the king's officers and farmers were to forfeit their places and holds, in case of unlawful retainer, or partaking in routs and unlawful assemblies.

These were the laws that were made for repressing of force, which those times did chiefly require; and were so prudently framed, as they are found fit for all succeeding times, and so continue to this day.

There were also made good and politick laws that parliament against usury, which is the bastard use of money: and against unlawful chievances and exchanges, which is bastard usury: and also for the security of the king's customs; and for the imployment of the procedures of foreign commodities, brought in by merchant-strangers, upon the native commodities of the realm: together with some other commodities of the realm ; together with some other laws of less importance.

But howsoever the laws made in that parliament did bear good and wholesome fruit; yet the subsidy granted at the same, bare a fruit that proved harsh and bitter. All was inned at last into the king's barn; but it was after a storm. For when the commissioners entred into the taxation of the subsidy in Yorkshire, and the bishoprick of Duresme; the people upon a suddain grew into great mutiny, and said openly that they had endured of late years a thousand miseries, and neither could nor would pay the subsidy. This (no doubt) proceeded not simply of any present necessity, but much by reason of the old humour of those countries, where the memory of king Richard was so strong, that it lies like lees in the bottom of men's hearts; and if the vessel was but stirred, it would come up. And (no doubt) it was partly also by the instigation of some factious malecontents, that bare principal stroke amongst them. Hereupon the commissioners being somewhat astonished, deferr'd the matter unto the earl of Northumberland, who was the principal man of authority in those parts. The earl forthwith wrote unto the court, signifying to the king plainly enough in what flame he found the people of those countries, and praying the king's direction. The king wrote peremptorily. That he would not have one penny abated of that which had been granted to him by Parliament, both because it might encourage other countries to pray the like release or mitigation, and chiefly because he would never endure that the base multitude should frustrate the authority of the parliament, wherein their votes and contents were concluded. Upon this dispatch from court, the earl assembled the principal justices and freeholders of the country, and speaking to them in that imperious language wherein the king had written to him, which needed not (save that an harsh business was unfortunately fallen into the hands of a harsh man) did not only irritate the people, but made them conceive, by the stoutness and haughtiness of delivery of the king's errand, that himself was the author or principal persuader of that counsel. Whereupon the meaner sort routed together, and suddenly assaying the earl in his house, slew him and divers of his servants. And rested not there, but creating for their leader Sir John Egremond, a factious person, and one that had of a long time born an ill talent towards the king; and being animated also by a base fellow, called John a Chamber, a very Boutescu, who bare much sway amongst the vulgar and popular, entered into open rebellion, and gave out in flat terms they would go against king Henry, and fight with him for the maintenance of their liberties.

When the king was advertised of this new insurrection (being almost a fever, that took him every year) after his manner little troubled therewith, he sent Thomas earl of Surrey (whom he had a little before not only released out of the Tower, and pardoned, but also received to special favour) with a competent power against the rebels; who fought with the principal band of them, and defeated them, and took alive John a Chamber, their firebrand. As for sir John Egremond, he fled into Flanders, to the lady Margaret of Burgundy; whose palace was the Sanctuary and receptacle of all traitors against the king. John a Chamber was executed at York in great state; for he was hanged upon a gibbet raised a stage higher in the midst of a square gallows, as a traitor paramount, and a number of his men that were his chief complices, were hanged upon the lower story round about him; and the rest were generally pardoned. Neither did the king himself omit his custom, to be first or second in all his warlike exploits; making good his word, which was usual with him when he heard of rebels; that he desired but to see them. For immediately after he had sent down the earl of Surrey, he marched towards them himself in person. And although in his journey he heard news of the victory, yet he went on as far as York, to pacify and settle those countries. And that done, returned to London, leaving the earl of Surrey for his lieutenant in the northern parts, and sir Richard Tunstall for his principal commissioner, to levy the subsidy, whereof he did not remit a denier.

About the same time that the king lost so good a servant as the earl of Northumberland, he lost likewise a faithful friend and allie of James the third king of Scotland, by a miserable disaster. For this unfortunate prince, after a long smother of discontent, and hatred of many of his nobility and people, breaking forth at times into seditions and alterations at court, was at last distressed by them, having taken arms, and surprised the person of prince James his son, partly by force, partly by threats, that they would otherwise deliver up the kingdom to the king of England, to shadow their rebellion, and to be the titular and painted head of those arms. Whereupon the king (finding himself too weak) sought unto king Henry as also unto the pope, and the king of France, to compose those troubles between him and his subjects. The kings accordingly interposed their mediation in a round and princely manner: not only by way of request and persuasion, but also by way of protestation of menace; declaring, that they thought it to be the common cause of all kings, if subjects should be suffer'd to give laws unto their sovereign; and that they would accordingly resent it, and revenge it. But the rebels that had shaken off the greater yoke of obedience, had likewise cast away the lesser tye of respect. And fury prevailing above fear, made answer, that there was no talking of peace, except the king would resign his crown. Whereupon (treaty of accord taking no place) it came to a battle, at Bannocksbourn by Strivelin. In which battle the king transported with wrath and just indignation, inconsiderately fighting and precipitating the charge, before his whole numbers came up to him, was (notwithstanding the contrary express and straight commandment of the prince his son) slain in the pursuit, being fled to a mill, situate in the field, where the battle was fought.

As for the pope's embassy, which was sent by Adrian de Castello an Italian legate (and perhaps as those times were might have preval'd more) it came too late for the ambassy, but not for the ambassador. For passing through England, and being honourably entertained, and received of king Henry; (who ever applied himself with much respect to the see of Rome) he fell into great grace with the king, and great familiarity and friendship with Moreton the chancellor. Insomuch as the king taking a liking to him, and finding him to his mind preferr'd him to the bishoprick of Hereford, and afterwards to that of Bath and Wells, and imployed him in many of his affairs of state, that had relation to Rome. He was a man of great learning, wisdom and dexterity in business of state; and having not long after ascended to the degree of cardinal, paid the king large tribute of his gratitude, in diligent and judicious advertisement of the occurrences of Italy. Nevertheless in the end of his time, he was partaker of the conspiracy, which cardinal Alphonso Petrucci, and some other cardinals had plotted against the life of pope Leo And this offence in itself so hainous, was yet in him aggravated by the motive thereof; which was not malice or discontent, but an aspiring mind to the papacy. And in this height of impiety there wanted not an intermixture of levity and folly; for that (as was generally believed) he was animated to expect the papacy, by a fatal mockery, the prediction of a sooth-sayer, which was; that one should succeed pope Leo, whose name should be Adrian, an aged man of mean birth, and of great learning and wisdom. By which character and figure, he took himself to be describ'd, though it were fulfilled of Adrian the Flemming, son of a Dutch brewer, cardinal of Tortosa, and preceptor unto Charles the fifth; the same that not changing his christian name was afterwards called Adrian the sixth.

But these things happened in the year following, which was the fifth of this king. But in the end of the fourth year the king had called again his parliament, not as it seemeth for any particular occasion of state. But the former parliament being ended somewhat suddenly, in regard of the preparations for Britain, the king thought he had not renumerated his people sufficiently with good laws, which ever more was his retribution for treasure. And finding by the insurrection in the north, there was discontentment abroad in respect of the subsidy, he thought it good to give his subjects yet further contentment, and comfort in that kind. Certainly his times for good common-wealth laws did excel. So as he may justly be celebrated for the best law giver to this nation, after king Edward the first. For his laws (who so marks them well) are deep, and not vulgar; not made upon the spur of a particular occasion for the present, but out of providence of the future, to make the estate of his people still more and more happy; after the manner of the Legislators in ancient and heroical times.

First therefore he made a law, suitable to his own acts and times. For as himself had in his person and marriage made a final concord in the great suit and title for the crown; so by this law he settled the like peace and quiet in the private possessions of the subjects. Ordaining, that fines thenceforth should be final, to conclude all strangers rights; and that upon fines levied, and solemnly proclaim'd the subject should have his time of watch for five years after his title accrued; which if he fore-passed, his right should be bound for ever after; with some exception nevertheless, of minors, married women and such incompetent persons.

This statute did in effect but restore an ancient statute of the realm, which was itself also made but in affirmance of the common law. The alteration had been by a statute commonly called the statute of non-claim, made in the time of Edward the third. And surely this law was a kind of prognostic of the good peace, which since his time hath (for the most part) continued in this kingdom, until this day. For statutes of non-claim are fit for times of war, when men's heads are troubled, that they cannot intend their estates; but statutes, that quiet possessions, are fittest for times of peace, to extinguish suits and contentions, which is one of the banes of peace

Another statute was made of singular policy, for the population apparently, and (if it be thoroughly considered) for the soldiery, and military forces of the realm.

Inclosures at that time began to be more frequent, whereby arable land (which could not be manured without people and families) was turned into pasture, which was easily rid by a few herdsmen; and tenancies for years, lives, and at will (whereupon much of the yeomanry lived) were turned into demesnes. This bred a decay of people, and (by consequence) a decay of towns, churches, tithes, and the like. The king likewise knew full well, and in no wise forgot, that there ensued withal upon this a decay and diminution of subsidy and taxes; for the more gentlemen, ever the larger books of subsidies. In remedying of this inconvenience, the king's wisdom was admirable, and the parliament's at that time. Inclosures they would not forbid, for that had been to forbid the improvement of the patrimony of the kingdom; nor tillage they would not compel, for that was to strive with nature and utility. But they took a course to take away depopulating inclosures, and depopulating pasturage, and yet not by that name, or by any imperious express prohibition, but by consequence. The ordinance was, 'That all houses of husbandry, that were used with twenty acres of ground, and upwards, should be maintained and kept up for ever; together with a competent proportion of land to be used and occupied with them;' and in no wise to be severed from them, as by another statute, made afterwards in his successor's time, was more fully declared. This upon forfeiture to be taken; not by way of popular action, but by seizure of the land itself, by the king and lords of the fee, as to half the profits, till the houses and lands were restored. By this means the houses being kept up, did of necessity inforce a dweller; and the proportion of land for occupation being kept up, did of necessity inforce that dweller not to be a beggar or cottager, but a man of some substance, that might keep hinds and servants, and set the plough on going. This did wonderfully concern the might and mannerhood of the kingdom, to have farms, as it were of a standard sufficient to maintain an able body out of penury, and did in effect amortize a great part of the lands of the kingdom unto the hold and occupation of the yeomanry or middle people, of a condition between gentlemen, and cottagers and peasants. Now, how much this did advance the military power of the kingdom, is apparent by the true principles of war, and the examples of other kingdoms. For it hath been held by the general opinion of men of best judgment in the wars (howsoever some few have varied, and that it may receive some distinction of case) that the principal strength of an army consisteth in the infantry or foot. And to make good infantry, it requireth men bred, not in a servile or indigent fashion, but in some free and plentiful manner. Therefore if a state run most to noblemen and gentlemen, and that the husband-men and plough-men be but as their work-folks and labourers, or else mere cottagers, (which are but hous'd beggars) you may have a good cavalry, but never good stable bands of foot; like to coppice-woods, that if you leave in them staddles too thick, they will run to bushes and briars, and have little clean underwood. And this is to be seen in France, and Italy, and some other parts abroad, where in effect all is noblesse, or peasantry. I speak of people out of town, and no middle people; and therefore no good forces of foot: insomuch, as they are inforced to imploy mercenary bands of Switzers and the like, for their battalions of foot: whereby also it comes to pass, that those nations have much people. and few soldiers. Whereas the king saw, that contrariwise it would follow, that England, though much less in territory, yet should have infinitely more soldiers of their native forces, than those other nations have. Thus did the king secretly sow Hydra's teeth, whereupon (according to the poets fiction) should rise up armed men for the service of this kingdom.

The king also (having care to make his realm potent, as well by sea as by land) for the better maintenance of the navy, ordained; that wines and woods from the parts of Gascoyn and Languedock should not be brought but in English bottoms, bowing the ancient policy of this estate, from consideration of plenty, to consideration of power. For that almost all the ancient statutes incite by all means merchant-strangers, to bring in all sorts of commodities ; having for end cheapness, and not looking to the point of state concerning the naval power.

The king also made a statute in that parliament monitory and minatory, towards justices of peace, that they should duly execute their office, inviting complaints against them, first to their fellow-justices, then to the justices of assise, then to the king or chancellor ; and that a proclamation, which he had published of that tenor, should be read in open sessions four times a year, to keep them awake. Meaning also to have his laws executed, and thereby to reap either obedience or forfeitures ; (wherein towards his latter times he did decline too much to the left hand) he did ordain remedy against the practice that was grown in use, to stop and damp informations upon penal laws, by procuring informations by collusion to be put in by the confederates of the delinquents, to be faintly prosecuted, and let fall at pleasure, and pleading them in bar of the informations, which were prosecuted with effect.

He made also laws for the correction of the mint, and counterfeiting of foreign coyn currant. And that no payment in gold should be made to any merchant-stranger, the better to keep treasure within the realm, for that gold was the metal that lay in the least room.

He made also statutes for the Maintenance of drapery, and the keeping of wools within the realm ; and not only so, but for stinting, and limiting the prices of cloth, one for the finer, and another for the coarser sort. Which I note, both because it was a rare thing to set prices by statute, especially upon our home-commodities ; and because of the wise model of this act, not prescribing prices, but stinting them not to exceed a rate, that the clothier might drape according as he might afford.

Divers other good statutes were made that parliament, but these were the principal. And here I do desire those, into whose hands this work shall fall, that they do take it in good part my long insisting upon the laws that were made in this king's reign. Whereof I have these reasons; both because it was the pre-eminent vertue and merit of this king, to whose memory I do honour; and because it hath some correspondence to my person ; but chiefly because (in my judgment) it is some defect even in the best writers of history, that they do not often enough summarily deliver and set down the most memorable laws that passed in the times whereof they write, being indeed the principal acts of peace. For though they may be had in the original books of law themselves, yet that informeth not the judgments of kings and councellors, and persons of estate, so well as to see them describ'd, and enterd into the table and pourtrait of the times.

About the same time, the king had a loan from the city of four thousand pounds; which was double to that they lent before,[1] and was duly and orderly paid back at the day, as the former likewise had been. The king ever choosing rather to borrow too soon, than to pay too late, and so keeping up his credit.

Neither had the king yet cast off his cares and hopes touching Britain, but thought to master the occasion by policy, though his arms had been unfortunate, and to bereave the French king of the fruit of his victory. The sum of his design was, to encourage Maximilian to go on with his suit, for the marriage of Ann, the heiress of Britain, and to add him to the consummation thereof. But the affairs of Maximilian were at that time in great trouble and combustion, by a rebellion of his subjects in Flanders, especially those of Bruges and Gaunt; whereof the town of Bruges (at such time as Maximilian was there in person) had suddenly arm'd in tumult, and slain some of his principal officers, and taken himself prisoner, and held him in durance, till they had enforced him, and some of his councellors, to take a solemn oath, to pardon all their offences, and never to question and revenge the same in time to come. Nevertheless Frederick the emperor would not suffer this reproach and indignity offer'd to his son to pass, but made sharp war upon Flanders, to reclaim and chastise the rebels. But the lord Ravenstein, a principal person about Maximilian, and one that had taken the oath of abolition with his master, pretending the religion thereof, but indeed upon private ambition, and (as it was thought) instigation and corrupted from France, forsook the emperor and Maximilian his lord, and made himself an head of the popular party, and seiz'd upon the towns of Ipre and Sluce, with both the castles. And forthwith sent to the lord Cordes, governour of Picardy under the French king, to desire aid, and to move him, that he on the behalf of the French king would be protector of the united towns, and by force of arms reduce the rest. The lord Cordes was ready to embrace the occasion, which was partly of his own setting, and sent forthwith greater forces, than it had been possible for him to raise on the sudden, if he had not look'd for such a summons before, in aid of the lord Ravenstein, and the Flemmings with instructions to invest the towns between France and Bruges. The French forces besieged a little town called Dixmue, where part of the Flemmish forces joyned with them. While they lay at this siege, the king of England, upon pretence of the safety of the English pale about Calice, but in truth being loth that Maximilian should become contemptible, and thereby be shaken off by the states of Britain about this marriage,

---

[1] The king borrowed of every alderman 200*l.* and of the Chamber of London 908*l.* 17*s.* 4*d.* —Hollingshed.

sent over the lord Morley with a thousand men unto the lord Daubigny, then deputy of Callice, with secret instructions to aid Maximilian, and to raise the siege of Dixmue. The lord Daubigny (giving it out that all was for the strengthening of the English marches) drew out of the garisons of Calice, Hammes, and Guines, to the number of two thousand men more. So that with the fresh succours that came under the conduct of the lord Morley, they made up to the number of two thousand, or better. Which forces joining with some companies of Almains, put themselves into Dixmue, not perceived by the enemies ; and passing through the town with some re-enforcement (from the forces that were in the town) assail'd the enemies camp ; negligently guarded, as being out of fear ; where there was a bloody fight, in which the English and their partakers obtain'd the victory, and slew to the number of eight thousand men, with the loss on the English part of a hundred or thereabouts ; amongst whom were the lord Morley. They took also their great ordnance, with much rich spoils which they carried to Newport, whence the lord Daubigny return'd to Calice, leaving the hurt men, and some other voluntiers in Newport. But the lord Cordes being at Ipre with a great power of men, thinking to recover the loss and disgrace of the fight at Dixmue, came presently on, and sate down before Newport and besieg'd it ; and after some days siege, he resolv'd to try the fortune of an assault : which he did, one day, and succeeded therein so far, that he had taken the principal tower and fort in that city, and planted upon it the French banner. Whence nevertheless they were presently beaten forth by the English, by the help of some fresh succours of archers arriving by good fortune (at the instant) in the Haven at Newport. Whereupon the lord Cordes discouraged, and measuring the new succours (which were small) by the success (which was great) levied his siege. By this means, matters grew more exasperate between the two kings of England and France, for that in the war of Flanders, the auxiliary forces of French and English were much blooded one against another. Which blood rankled the more by the vain words of the lord Cordes, that declared himself an open enemy of the English, beyond that appertain'd to the present service : making it a common by-word of his, that he could be content to lie in hell seven years, so he might win Calice from the English.

The king having thus upheld the reputation of Maximilian, advised him now to press on his marriage with Britain to a conclusion. Which Maximilian accordingly did, and so far forth prevail'd both with the young lady, and with the principal persons about her, as the marriage was consummate by proxy, with a ceremony at that time in these parts new. For she was not only publickly contracted, but stated as a bride, and solemnly bedded ; and after she was laid, there came in Maximilian's ambassador with letters of procuration, and in the presence of sundry noble personages, men and women, put his leg (stript naked to the knee) between the espousal sheets; to the end, that that ceremony might be thought to amount to a consummation and actual knowledge. This done, Maximilian (whose property was to leave things then, when they were almost come to perfection, and to end them by imagination; like ill archers, that draw not their arrows up to the head; and who might as easily have bedded the lady himself, as to have made a play and disguise of it) thinking now all assured, neglected for a time his further proceeding, and intended his wars. Meanwhile, the French king (consulting with his divines, and finding that this pretended consummation was rather an invention of court, than any ways valid by the laws of the church) went more really to work, and by secret instruments and cunning agents, as well matrons about the young lady as councellors, first sought to remove the point of religion and honour out of the mind of the lady herself, wherein there was a double labour. For Maximilian was not only contracted unto the lady, but Maximilian's daughter was likewise contracted to king Charles. So as the marriage halted upon both feet, and was not clear on either side: but for the contract with king Charles, the exception lay plain and fair; for that Maximilian's daughter was under years of consent, and so not bound by law, but a power of disagreement left to either part. But for the contract made by Maximilian with the lady herself, they were harder driven: having nothing to alledge, but that it was done without the consent of her sovereign lord king Charles, whose ward and client she was, and he to her in place of a father; and therefore it was void, and of no force, for want of such consent. Which defect (they said) tho' it would not evacuate a marriage, after cohabitation, and actual consummation, yet it was enough to make void a contract. For as for the pretended consummation, they made sport with it, and said, that it was an argument, that Maximilian was a widower, and a cold wooer, that could content himself to be a bridegroom by deputy, and would not make a little journey, to put all out of question. So that the young lady, wrought upon by these reasons, finely instilled by such as the French king (who spared for no rewards or promises) had made on his side; and allured likewise by the present glory and greatness of king Charles, (being also a young king, and a batchelor) and loth to make her country the seat of a long and miserable war; secretly yielded to accept of king Charles. But during this secret treaty with the lady, the better to save it from blasts of opposition and interruption, king Charles resorting to his wonted arts, and thinking to carry the marriage as he had carried the wars, by entertaining the king of England in vain belief, sent a solemn ambassage by Francis lord of Luxemburg, Charles Marignian, and Robert Gaguien, general of the order of the Bonnes Hommes of the Trinity, to treat a peace and league with the king; accoupling it with an article in the nature of a request, that the French king might with the king's good-will (according to his right of seigniority and tutelage) dispose of the marriage of the young duchess of Britain, as he should think good; offering by a judicial proceeding to make void the marriage of Maximilian by proxy. Also all this while, the better to amuse the world, he did continue in his court and custody the daughter of Maximilian, who formerly had been sent unto him, to be bred and educated in France; not dismissing or renvoying her, but contrariwise professing and giving out strongly, that he meant to proceed with that match. And that for the duchess of Britain, he desired only to preserve his right of seigniory, and to give her in marriage to some such allie, as might depend upon him.

When the three commissioners came to the court of England, they deliver'd their ambassage unto the king, who remitted them to his council; where some days after they had audience, and made their proposition by the prior of the trinity (who tho' he were third in place, yet was held the best speaker of them) to this effect.

'My lords, the king our master, the greatest and mightiest king that reigned in France since Charles the Great (whose name he beareth), hath nevertheless thought it no disparagement to his greatness, at this time to propound a peace, yea, and to pray a peace with the king of England. For which purpose he hath sent us his commissioners, instructed and enabled with full and ample power, to treat and conclude; giving us further in charge, to open in some other business the secrets of his own intentions. These be indeed the precious love tokens between great kings, to communicate one with another the true state of their affairs, and to pass by nice points of honour, which ought not to give law unto affection. This I do assure your lordships, it is not possible for you to imagine the true and cordial love that the king our master beareth to your sovereign, except you were near him, as we are. He useth his name with so great respect; he remembreth their first acquaintance at Paris with so great contentment; nay, he never speaks of him, but that presently he falls into discourse of the miseries of great kings, in that they cannot converse with their equals, but with their servants. This affection to your king's person and vertues, God hath put into the heart of our master, no doubt for the good of Christendom, and for purposes yet unknown to us all. For other root it cannot have, since it was the same to the earl of Richmond, that it is now to the king of England. This is therefore the first motive that makes our king to desire peace, and league with your sovereign: good affection, and somewhat that he finds in his own heart. This affection is also arm'd with reason of estate. For our king doth in all candour and frankness of dealing open himself unto you; that having an honourable, yea, and a holy purpose to make a voyage and war in remote parts, he considereth that it will be of no small effect, in point of reputation to his enterprize, if it be known abroad, that he is in good peace with all his neighbour princes, and specially with the king of England, whom for good causes he esteemeth most.

'But now (my lords) give me leave to use a few words to remove all scruples and misunderstandings between your sovereign and ours, concerning some late actions; which, if they be not cleared, may perhaps hinder this peace. To the end, that for matter past, neither king may conceive unkindness of other, nor think the other conceiveth unkindness of him. The late actions are two; that of Britain, and that of Flanders. In both which, it is true, that the subjects swords of both kings have encountred and stricken, and the ways and inclinations also of the two kings, in respect of their confederates and allies, have severed.

'For that of Britain; the king your sovereign knoweth best what hath passed. It was a war of necessity on our master's part. And tho' the motives of it were sharp and piquant as could be, yet did he make that war rather with an olive-branch, than a laurel-branch in his hand, more desiring peace than victory. Besides from time to time he sent (as it were) blank-papers to your king, to write the conditions of peace. For tho' both his honour and safety went upon it, yet he thought neither of them too precious, to put into the king of England's hands. Neither doth our king on the other side make any unfriendly interpretation of your king's sending of succours to the duke of Britain; for the king knoweth well, that many things must be done of kings for satisfaction of their people, and it is not hard to discern what is a king's own. But this matter of Britain is now (by the act of God) ended and passed; and (as the king hopeth) like the way of a ship in the sea, without leaving any impression in either of the kings minds; as he is sure for his part it hath not done in his.

'For the action of Flanders; as the former of Britain was a war of necessity, so this was war of justice, which with a good king is of equal necessity, with a danger of estate, for else he should leave to be a king. The subjects of Burgundy are subjects in chief to the crown of France, and their duke the homager and vassal of France. They had wont to be good subjects, howsoever Maximilian hath of late distemper'd them. They fled to the king for justice and deliverance from oppression. Justice he could not deny; purchase he did not seek. This was good for Maximilian, if he could have seen it in people mutined to arrest fury, and prevent despair. My lords, it may be this I have said is needless, save that the king our master is tender in any thing, that may but glance upon the friendship of England. The amity between the two kings (no doubt) stands entire and inviolate. And that their subjects swords have clashed, it is nothing unto the publick peace of the crowns: it being a thing very usual in auxiliary forces of the best and straitest confederates, to meet and draw blood in the field. Nay, many times there be aids of the same nation on both sides, and yet not (for all that) a kingdom divided in itself.

'It resteth (my lords) that I impart unto you a matter, that I know your lordships all will much rejoyce to hear; as that which importeth the christian commonweal more than any action that hath hapned of a long time. The king our master hath a purpose and determination, to make war upon the kingdom of Naples; being now in the possession of a bastardship of Arragon, but appertaining unto his majesty, by clear and undoubted right; which if he should not by just arms seek to recover, he could neither acquit his honour, nor answer it to his people. But his noble and christian thoughts rest not here. For his resolution and hope is, to make the re-conquest of Naples, but as a bridge to transport his forces into Grecia; and not to spare blood or treasure (if it were to the impawning of his crown, and dispeopling of France) till either he hath overthrown the empire of the Ottomans, or taken it in his way to paradise. The king knoweth well, that this is a design, that could not arise in the mind of any king, that did not steadfastly look up unto God, whose quarrel this is, and from whom cometh both the will and the deed. But yet it is agreeable to the person that he beareth (tho' unworthy) of the thrice christian king, and the eldest son of the church. Whereunto he is also invited by the example (in more ancient time) of king Henry IV. of England (the first renown'd king of the house of Lancaster; ancestor, tho' not progenitor, to your king), who had a purpose towards the end of his time (as you know better) to make an expedition into the Holy Land; and by the example also (present before his eyes) of that honourable and religious war which the king of Spain now maketh, and hath almost brought to perfection, for the recovery of the realm of Granada from the Moors. And altho' this enterprize may seem vast and unmeasur'd, for the king to attempt that by his own forces, wherein heretofore a conjunction of most of the christian princes hath found work enough: yet his majesty wisely considereth, that sometimes smaller forces being united under one command, are more effectual in proof (tho' not so promising in opinion and fame) than much greater forces, variously compounded by associations and leagues; which commonly in a short time after their beginnings, turn to dissociations and divisions. But (my lords) that which is as a voice from heaven that called the king to this enterprize, is a rent at this time in the house of the Ottomans. I do not say, but there hath been brother against brother in that house before, but never any that had refuge to the arms of the christians, as now hath Gemes (brother unto Bajazeth, that reigneth) the far braver man of the two ; the other being between a monk and a philosoper, and better read in the Alcoran and Averroes, than able to wield the sceptre of so warlike an empire. This therefore is the king our master's memorable and heroical resolution for an holy war. And because he carrieth in this the person of a christian soldier, as well as of a great temporal monarch ; he beginneth with humility, and is comtent for this cause to beg peace at the hands of other christian kings. There remaineth only rather a civil request, than any essential part of our negotiation, which the king maketh to the king your sovereign. The king (as the world knoweth) is lord in chief of the duchy of Britain. The marriage of the heir belongeth to him as guardian. This is a private patrimonial right, and no business of estate ; yet nevertheless (to run a fair course with your king ; whom he desires to make another himself, and to be one and the same thing with him) his request is, that with the king's favour and consent, he may dispose of her marriage, as he thinketh good, and make void the intruded and pretended marriage of Maximilian, according to justice. This (my lords) is all that I have to say, desiring your pardon for my weakness in the delivery.'

Thus did the French ambassadors with great show of their king's affection, and many sugar'd words seek to adulce all matters between the two kings, having two things for their ends ; the one, to keep the king quiet till the marriage of Brittain was past, and this was but a summer fruit, which they thought was almost ripe and would soon be gathered. The other was more lasting ; and that was to put him into such a temper as he might be no disturbance or impediment to the voyage for Italy. The lords of the council were silent ; and said only, that they knew the ambassadors would look for no answer, till they had reported to the king ; and so they rose from council. The king could not tell what to think of the marriage of Brittain. He saw plainly the ambition of the French king was to impatronize himself of the duchy ; but he wondred he would bring into his house a litigious marriage, especially considering who was his successor. But weighing one thing with another, he gave Brittain for lost ; but resolv'd to make his profit of this business of Brittain, as a quarrel for war ; and that of Naples, as a wrench and mean for peace ; being well advertised how strongly the king was bent upon that action. Having therefore conferred divers times with his council, and keeping himself somewhat close ; he gave a direction to the chancellor, for a formal answer to the ambassadors, and that he did in the presence of his council. And after calling the chancellor to him apart, bade him speak in such language as was fit for a treaty that was to end in a breach ; and gave him also a special caveat, that he should not use any words, to discourage the voyage of Italy. Soon after the ambassadors were sent for to the council, and the lord chancellor spake to them thus.

'My lords ambassadors, I shall make answer by the king's commandment, unto the eloquent declaration of you my lord prior, in a brief and plain manner. The king forgetteth not his former love and acquaintance with the king your master. But of this there needeth no repetition. For if it be between them as it was, it is well; if there be any alteration, it is not words that will make it up.

'For the business of Britain, the king findeth it a little strange that the French king maketh mention of it, as matter of well deserving at his hand. For that deserving was no more, but to make him his instrument, to surprise one of his best confederates. And for the marriage, the king would not meddle in it if your master would marry by the book, and not by the sword.

'For that of Flanders, if the subjects of Burgundy had appeal'd to your king, as their chief lord, at first, by way of supplication; it might have had a shew of justice. But it was a new form of process, for subjects to slay their prince first, and to slay his officers, and then to be complainants. The king saith, that sure he is, when the French king and himself sent to the subjects of Scotland (they had taken arms against their king) they both spake in another stile, and did in princely manner signifie their detestation of popular attentates upon the person or authority of princes. But my lords ambassadors, the king leaveth these two actions thus: that on the one side, he hath not received any manner of satisfaction from you concerning them; and on the other, that he doth not apprehend them so deeply, as in respect of them, to refuse to treat of peace, if other things may go hand in hand. As for the war of Naples, and the design against the Turks; the king hath commanded me expresly to say, that he doth wish with all his heart, to his good brother the French king, that his fortunes may succeed according to his hopes, and honourable intentions. And whensoever he shall hear, that he is prepared for Grecia, as your master is pleased now to say, that he beggeth a peace of the king, so the king will then beg of him a part in that war.

'But now my lords ambassadors, I am to propound unto you somewhat on the king's part. The king your master hath taught our king what to say and demand. You say (my lord prior) that your king is resolv'd to recover his right to Naples, wrongfully detained from him. And that if he should not thus do, he could not acquit his honour, nor answer it to his people. Think (my lords) that the king our master saith the same thing over again to you touching Normandy, Guien, Angeou, yea and the kingdom of France it self. I cannot express it better than in your own words: if therefore the French king shall consent, that the king our master's title to France (at least tribute for the same) be handled in the treaty, the king is content to go on with the rest; otherwise he refuseth to treat.'

The ambassadors being somewhat abashed with this demand;

answered in some heat ; 'That they doubted not but the king their sovereign's sword would be able to maintain his scepter ! And they assured themselves, he neither could nor would yield to any diminution of the crown of France either in territory or regality. But howsoever, they were too great matters for them to speak of, having no commission.' It was replied ; 'that the king looked for no other answer from them ; but would forthwith send his own ambassadors to the French king. There was a question also asked at the table, 'Whether the French king would agree to have the disposing of the marriage of Britain with an exception and exclusion, that he should not marry her himself ?' To which the ambassadors answered ; 'that it was so far out of the king's thoughts, as they had received no instructions touching the same.' Thus were the ambassadors dismissed, all save the prior ; and were followed immediately by Thomas earl of Ormond, and Thomas Goldenston prior of Christ-church in Canterbury ; who were presently sent over into France. In the mean space Lionell, bishop of Concordia, was sent as Nuntio from pope Alexander the sixth to both kings, to move a peace between them. For pope Alexander finding himself pent and lockt up, by a league and association of the principal states of Italy, that he could not make his way for the advancement of his own house (which he immoderately thirsted after) was desirous to trouble the waters in Italy, that he might fish the better ; casting the net, not out of Saint Peter's, but out of Borgia's bark. And doubting lest the fears from England might stay the French King's voyage into Italy, dispatch'd this bishop to compose all matters between the two kings, if he could. Who first repaired to the French king, and finding him well inclin'd (as he conceiv'd) took on his journey towards England, and found the English ambassadors at Calice, on their way towards the French king. After some conference with them, he was in honourable manner transported over into England, where he had audience of the king. But notwithstanding he had a good ominous name to have made a peace, nothing followed. For in the mean time, the purpose of the French king to marry the duchess could be no longer dissembled. Wherefore the English ambassadors (finding how things went) took their leaves and returned. And the prior also was warned from hence, to depart out of England. Who when he turned his back (more like a pedant than an ambassador) dispersed a bitter libel, in Latin verse, against the king (though he had nothing of a pedant) yet was content to cause an answer to be made in like verse ; and that as speaking in his own person, but in a style of scorn and sport. About this time also was born the king's second son Henry who afterwards reigned. And soon after followed the solemnization of the marriage between Charles and Ann duchess of Britain, with whom he received the duchy of Britain as her dowry : the daughter of Maximilian being a little before sent home. Which when it came to the ears of Maximilian, who could never believe it till it was done, being ever the principal in deceiving himself, though in this the French king did very handsomely second it, and tumbling it over and over in his thoughts that he should at one blow (with such a double scorn) be defeated, both of the marriage of his daughter, and his own (upon both which he had fixed high imaginations); he lost all patience, and casting off the respects fit to be continued between great kings (even when their blood is hottest, and most risen) fell to bitter invectives against the person and actions of the French king. And (by how much he was less able to do, talking so much the more) spake all the injuries he could devise of Charles, saying, that he was the most perfidious man upon the earth, and that he had made a marriage compounded between an advoutry and a rape; which was done (he said) by the just judgment of God, to the end that (the nullity thereof being so apparent to all the world) the race of so unworthy a person might not reign in France. And forthwith he sent ambassadors as well to the king of England, as to the king of Spain, to incite them to war, and to treat a league offensive against France, promising to concur with great forces of his own. Hereupon the king of England (going nevertheless his own way) called a parliament, it being the seventh year of his reign; and the first day of opening thereof (sitting under his cloth of estate) spake himself unto his lords and commons in this manner.

'My lords, and you the commons; when I purposed to make a war in Britain by my lieutenant, I made declaration thereof to you by my chancellor. But now that I mean to make a war upon France in person, I will declare it to you my self. That war was to defend another man's right, but this is to recover our own; and that ended by accident, but we hope this shall end in victory.

'The French king troubles the christian world. That which he hath, is not his own, and yet he seeketh more. He hath invested himself of Britain. He maintaineth the rebels in Flanders; and he threateneth Italy. For ourselves, he hath proceeded from dissimulation to neglect; and from neglect to contumely. He hath assayled our confederates: he denyeth our tribute: in a word, he seeks war. So did not his father, but sought peace at our hands; and so perhaps will he, when good council or time shall make him see as much as his father did.

'Meanwhile; let us make his ambition our advantage; and let us not stand upon a few crowns of tribute, or acknowledgment, but (by the favour of Almighty God) try our right to the crown of France it self: remembring there hath been a French king prisoner in England, and a king of England crowned in France. Our confederates are not diminished. Burgundy is in a mightier hand than ever, and never more provoked. Britain cannot help us, but it may hurt them.

New acquests are more burthen than strength. The malecontents of his own kingdom have not been base, popular, nor titulary impostors, but of an higher nature. The king of Spain (doubt ye not) will join with us, not knowing where the French king's ambition will stay. Our holy father the Pope likes no Tramontanes in Italy. But howsoever it be, this matter of confederates, is rather to be thought on than reckoned on. For God forbid, but England should be able to get reason of France, without a second.

'At the battles of Cressy, Poictiers, Agent-Court, we were of ourselves. France hath much people and few soldiers. They have no stable bands of foot. Some good horse they have; but those are forces which are least fit for a defensive war, where the actions are in the assailant's choice. It was our disorders only, that lost France; and (by the power of God) it is the good peace which we now enjoy, that will recover it. God hath hitherto blessed my sword. I have in this time that I have reigned, weeded out my bad subjects, and tried my good. My people and I know one another; which breeds confidence. And if there should be any bad blood left in the kingdom, an honourable foreign war will vent it, or purify it. In this great business, let me have your advice, and aid. If any of you were to make his son knight, you might have aid of your tenants by law. This concerns the knighthood and spurs of the kingdom, whereof I am father; and bound not only to seek to maintain it, but to advance it. But for matter of treasure, let it not be taken from the poorest sort; but from those, to whom the benefit of the war may redound. France is no wilderness: and I, that profess good husbandry, hope to make the war (after the beginnings) to pay itself. Go together in God's name, and lose no time; for I have called this parliament wholly for this cause.'

Thus spake the king; but for all this, though he showed great forwardness for a war, not only to his parliament and court, but to his privy council likewise (except the two bishops and a few more) yet nevertheless in his secret intentions, he had no purpose to go through with any war upon France. But the truth was, that he did but traffick with that war, to make his return in money. He knew well that France was now entire, and at unity with itself, and never so mighty many years before. He saw by the tast that he had of his forces sent into Britain, that the French knew well enough how to make war with the English; by not putting things to the hazard of a battle but wearying them by long sieges of towns, and strong fortified encampings. James the III. of Scotland, (his true friend and confederate) gone; and James the IV. (that had succeeded) wholly at the devotion of France, and ill affected towards him. As for the conjunctions of Ferdinando of Spain, and Maximilian; he could make no foundation upon them. For the one had power and not will; and the other hath will, and not power. Besides that, Ferdinando had but newly taken breath, from the war with the Moors; and merchanded at this time with France, for the restoring of the counties of Russignon and Perpignan, oppignorated to the French. Neither was he out of fear of the discontents, and ill blood within the realm ; which having used always to repress and appease in person, he was loth they should find him at a distance beyond sea, and engaged in war. Finding therefore the inconveniences and difficulties in the prosecution of a war, he cast with himself how to compass two things. The one, how by the declaration and inchoation of a war, to make his profit. The other, how to come off from the war, with saving of his honour. For profit, it was to be made two ways ; upon his subjects for the war, and upon his enemies for the peace ; like a good merchant, that maketh his gain, both upon the commodities exported and imported back again. For the point of honour, wherein he might suffer, for giving over the war ; he considered well, that as he could not trust upon the aids of Ferdinando and Maximilian for supports of war : so the impuissance of the one, and the double proceeding of the other, lay fair for him for occasions to accept peace. These things he did wisely foresee, and did as artificially conduct, whereby all things fell into his lap, as he desired.

For as for the parliament, it presently took fire, being affectionate (of old) to the war of France ; and desirous afresh to repair the dishonour they thought the king sustained by the loss of Britain. Therefore they advised the king (with great alacrity) to undertake the war of France : and although the parliament consisted of the first and second nobility (together with principal citizens and townsmen) yet worthily and justly respecting more the people (whose deputies they were) than their own private persons, and finding by the lord chancellor's speech the king's inclination that way ; they consented that commissioners should go forth, for the gathering and levying a benevolence, from the more able sort. This tax (called benevolence) was devised by Edward the fourth for which he sustained much envy. It was abolished by Richard the third by Act of Parliament, to ingratiate himself with the people : and it was now revived by the king, but with consent of parliament, for so it was not in the time of king Edward the fourth. But by this way he raised exceeding great sums. Insomuch as the city of London (in those days) contributed nine thousand pounds and better ; and that chiefly levied upon the wealthier sort. There is a tradition of a dilemma that bishop Moreton the chancellor used, to raise up the benevolence to higher rates ; and some called it his fork, and some his crutch. For he had couch'd an article in the instructions to the commissioners, who were to levy the benevolence ; 'That if they met with any that were sparing, they should tell them, that they must needs have, because they laid up; and if they were spenders, they must needs have, because it was seen in their port, and manner of living.' So neither kind came amiss.

This parliament was merely a parliament of war; for it was in substance, but a declaration of war against France and Scotland, with some statutes conducing thereunto; as the severe punishing of mort-pays, and keeping back of soldiers wages and captains. The like severity for the departure of soldiers without licence; strengthening of the common-law in favour of protections, for those that were in the king's service; and the setting the gate open and wide, for men to sell or mortgage their lands without fines for alienation, to furnish themselves with money for the war; and lastly, the voiding of all Scottish men out of England. There was also a statute for the dispersing of the standard of the exchequer, throughout England; thereby to size weights and measures; and two or three more of less importance.

After the parliament was broken up (which lasted not long) the king went on with his preparations for the war of France; yet neglected not in the meantime the affairs of Maximilian, for the quieting of Flanders, and restoring him to his authority amongst his subjects. For at that time, the lord of Ravenstein being not only a subject rebell'd, but a servant revolted (and so much the more malicious and violent, by the aid of Bruges and Gaunt) had taken the town and both the castles of Sluice; as we said before.

And having (by the commodity of the haven) gotten together certain ships and barks, fell to a kind of pyratical trade; robbing and spoyling, and taking prisoners the ships and vessels of all nations, that passed alongst that coast, towards the mart of Antwerp, or into any part of Brabant, Zeland, or Freezeland; being ever well victualled from Picardie, besides the commodity of victuals from Sluice, and the country adjacent, and the avails of his own prizes. The French assisted him still under-hand; and he likewise (as all men do, that have been of both sides) thought himself not safe, except he depended upon a third person.

There was a small town some two miles from Bruges, towards the sea, called Dam; which was a fort and approach to Bruges, and had a relation also to Sluice. This town the king of the Romans had attempted often, (not for any worth of the town in itself, but because it might choak Bruges, and cut it off from the sea) and ever fail'd. But therewith the duke of Saxony came down into Flanders, taking upon him the person of an umpire, to compose things between Maximilian and his subjects; but being (indeed) fast and assured to Maximilian. Upon this pretext of neutrality and treaty, he repaired to Bruges; desiring of the states of Bruges, to enter peaceably into their town, with a retinue or some number of men of arms, fit for his estate ; being somewhat the more (as he said) the better to guard him in a country, that was up in arms ; and bearing them in hand, that he was to communicate with them of divers matters of great importance, for their good. Which having obtained of them, he sent his carriages and harbingers before him, to provide his lodging. So that his men of war enterd the city in good array, but in peaceable manner, and he followed. They that went before, enquired still for inns and lodgings, as if they would have rested there all night, and so went on, till they came to the gate, that leadeth directly towards Dam ; and they or Bruges only gazed upon them and gave them passage. The captains and inhabitants of Dam also suspected no harm, from any that passed through Bruges ; and discovering forces afar off, supposed they had been some succours, that were come from their friends, knowing some dangers, towards them. And so perceiving nothing but well, till it was too late, suffered them to enter their town. By which kind of sleight rather than stratagem, the town of Dam was taken and the town of Bruges shrewdly blockt up, whereby they took great discouragement.

The duke of Saxony having won the town of Dam, sent immediately to the king to let him know that it was Sluice chiefly, and the lord Ravenstein, that kept the rebellion of Flanders in life ; and that if it pleased the king to besiege it by sea, he also would besiege it by land, and so cut out the core of those wars.

The king willing to uphold the authority of Maximilian (the better to hold France in awe) and being likewise sued unto by his merchants, for that the seas were much infested by the barks of the lord Ravenstein ; sent straightways sir Edward Poynings a valiant man, and of good service, with twelve ships, well furnished with souldiers and artillery, to clear the seas, and to besiege Sluice on that part. The Englishmen did not only coop up the lord Ravenstein, that he stirred not, and likewise held in strait siege the maritime part of the town ; but also assail'd one of the castles, and renewed the assault so for twenty days space (issuing still out of their ships at the ebb) as they made great slaughter of them of the castle ; who continually fought with them to repulse them, though of the English part also were slain a brother of the earl of Oxford's and some fifty more.

But the siege still continuing more and more strait, and both the castles (which were the principal strength of the town) being distressed, the one by the duke of Saxony, and the other by the English ; and a bridge of boats, which the lord Ravenstein had made between both castles, whereby succours and relief might pass from the one to the other, being on a night set on fire by the English, he despairing to hold the town, yielded (at the last) the castles to the English, and the towns to the duke of Saxony, by composition. Which done, the duke of Saxony and sir Edward Poynings treated with them of Bruges, to submit themselves to Maximilian their lord ; which after some time they did, paying (in some good part) the charge of the war, whereby the Almains and foreign succours were dismissed. The example of Bruges other of the revolted towns followed; so that Maximilian grew to be out of danger, but (as his manner was to handle matters) never out of necessity. And sir Edward Poynings (after he had continued at Sluice some good while, till all things were settled) returned unto the king, being then before Bulloigne.

Somewhat about this time came letters from Ferdinando, and Isabella, king and queen of Spain; signifying the final conquest of Granada from the Moors; which action in itself so worthy, king Ferdinando (whose manner was never to lose any vertue for the shewing) had expressed and displayed in his letters at large, with all the particularities, and religious punctoes and ceremonies, that were observed in the reception of that city and kingdom: shewing amongst other things, that the king would not by any means in person enter the city, until he had first aloof seen the cross set up upon the greater tower of Granada, whereby it became Christian ground: that likewise before he would enter, he did homage to God above, pronouncing by an herald from the height of that tower, that he did acknowledge to have recovered that kingdom, by the help of God Almighty and the glorious virgin, and the vertuous apostle Saint James, and the holy father Innocent the eight, together with the aids and services of his prelates, nobles, and commons: that yet he stirred not from his camp, till he had seen a little army of martyrs, to the number of seven hundred and more christians (that had lived in bonds and servitude as slaves to the Moors) pass before his eyes, singing a psalm for their redemption, and that he had given tribute unto God by alms and relief extended to them all, for his admission into the city. These things were in the letters, with many more ceremonies of a kind of holy ostentation.

The king ever willing to put himself into the consort or quire of all religious actions, and naturally affecting much the king of Spain, (as far as one king can affect another) partly for his virtues, and partly for a counterpoise to France; upon the receipt of these letters, sent all his nobles and prelates, that were about the court, together with the mayor and aldermen of London, in great solemnity to the church of Pauls; there to hear a declaration from the lord chancellor, now cardinal. When they were assembled, the cardinal (standing up on the uppermost step, or half-pace before the quire; and all the nobles, prelates, and governours of the city at the foot of the stairs) made a speech to them; letting them know, that they were assembled in that consecrate place to sing unto God a new song: 'For that' (said he) 'these many years the christians have not gained new ground or territory upon the infidels, nor enlarged and set further the bounds of the christian world: but this is now done by the prowess and devotion of Ferdinando and Isabella, kings of Spain ; who have (to their immortal honour) recover'd the great and rich kingdoms of Granada, and the populous and mighty city of the same name, from the Moors, having been in possession thereof by the space of seven hundred years, and more. For which, this assembly and all christians are to render laud and thanks unto God, and to celebrate this noble act of the king of Spain ; who in this is not only victorious, but apostolical, in the gaining new provinces to the christian faith. And the rather, for that this victory and conquest is obtain'd, without much effusion of blood. Whereby it is to be hoped, that there shall be gained, not only new territory but infinite souls to the church of Christ ; whom the Almighty (as it seems) would have live to be converted.' Herewithall Cardinal Moreton did relate some of the most memorable particulars of the war and victory. And after his speech ended, the whole assembly went solemnly in procession, and Te Deum was sung.

Immediately after the solemnity, the king kept his May-day at his palace of Sheine, now Richmond : where to warm the blood of his nobility and gallants, against the war, he kept great triumphs of justing and tourney, during all that month. In which space it so fell out, that sir James Parker and sir Hugh Vaughan, (one of the king's gentlemen ushers) having had a controversy touching certain arms, that the king at arms had given Vaughan, were appointed to run some courses one against another ; and by accident of a faulty helmet, that Parker had on, he was stricken into the mouth at the first course, so that his tongue was born unto the hinder-part of his head, in such sort that he died presently upon the place. Which because of the controversy precedent and the death that follow'd, was accounted amongst the vulgar, as a combate of tryal of right. The king towards the end of this summer, having put his forces, wherewith he meant to invade France, in readiness, (but so as they were not yet met or mustered together) sent Urswick (now made his Almoner) and sir John Risley to Maximilian ; to let him know, that he was in arms, ready to pass the seas into France, and did but expect to hear from him, when and where he did appoint to joyn with him, according to his promise made unto him by Countebalt, his ambassador.

The English ambassadors having repaired to Maximilian, did find his power and promise at a very great distance ; he being utterly unprovided of men, money, and arms for any such enterprize. For Maximilian having neither wing to fly on (for that his patrimony of Austria was not in his hands, his father being then living : and on the other side, his matrimonial territories of Flanders being partly in dower to his mother-in-law, and partly not serviceable, in respect of the late rebellions) was thereby destitute of means to enter into war. The ambassadors saw this well, but wisely thought fit to advertise the king thereof, rather than to return themselves till the king's further pleasure were known : the rather, for that Maximilian himself spake as great as ever he did before, and entertain'd them with dilatory answers ; so as the formal part of their ambassage might well warrant and require their further stay. The king hereupon (who doubted as much before, and saw thro' his business from the beginning) wrote back to the ambassadors, commending their discretion in not returning, and willing them to keep the state wherein they found Maximilian, as a secret, till they heard further from him ; and meanwhile went on with his voyage royal for France, suppressing for a time this advertisement touching Maximilian's poverty and disability.

By this time was drawn together a great and puissant army into the city of London, in which were Thomas marquess of Dorset, Thomas earl of Arundel, Thomas earl of Derby, George earl of Shrewsbury, Edmond earl of Suffolk, Edward earl of Devonshire, George earl of Kent, the earl of Essex, Thomas earl of Ormond, with a great number of barons, knights, and principal gentlemen ; and amongst them Richard Thomas, much noted for the brave troops that he brought out of Wales; the army rising in the whole to the number of five and twenty thousand foot, and sixteen hundred horse. Over which, the king (constant in his accustom'd trust and imployment) made Jasper duke of Bedford, and John earl of Oxford, generals under his own person. The 9th of September, in the eighth year of his reign, he departed from Greenwich towards the sea ; all men wondering that he took that season (being so near winter) to begin the war ; and some thereupon gathering it was a sign that the war would not be long. Nevertheless, the king gave out the contrary, thus : 'That he intended not to make a summer business of it, but a resolute war (without term prefixed) until he recover'd France ; it skilled not much when he began it ; especially having Calice at his back ; where he might winter, if the reason of the war so required.' The sixth of October, he imbark'd at Sandwich ; and the same day took land at Calice ; which was the rendezvous where all his forces were assigned to meet. But in this his journey towards the sea side (wherein, for the cause that we shall now speak of, he hover'd so much the longer) he had receiv'd letters from the lord Cordes ; who the hotter he was against the English in time of war, had the more credit in a negociation of peace, and besides was held a man open, and of good faith. In which letters there was made an overture of peace from the French king, with such conditions, as were somewhat to the king's taste : but this was carried at the first with wonderful secrecy. The king was no sooner come to Calice, but the calm winds of peace began to blow. For, first, the English ambassadors return'd out of Flanders from Maximilian; and certified the king, that he was not to hope for any aid from Maximilian, for that he was altogether unprovided : his will was good ; but he lacked money. And this was made known and spread through the army. And altho' the English were therewithal nothing dismay'd ; and that it be the manner of soldiers, upon bad news to speak the more bravely; yet nevertheless it was a kind of preparative to a peace. Instantly in the neck of this (as the king had laid it) came news that Ferdinando and Isabella, kings of Spain, had concluded a peace with king Charles ; and that Charles had restor'd unto them the counties of Roussignon and Perpignian, which formerly were mortgaged by John king of Arragon (Ferdinando's father) unto France, for three hundred thousand crowns : which debt was also upon this peace, by Charles clearly released. This came also handsomely to put on the peace : both because so potent a confederate was fallen off, and because it was a fair example of peace bought ; so as the king should not be the sole merchant in this peace. Upon these airs of peace, the king was content, that the bishop of Exeter and the lord Daubigney, (governour of Calice) should give a meeting unto the lord Cordes, for the treaty of a peace. But himself nevertheless, and his army, the fifteenth of October removed from Calice, and in four days march sat down before Bulloigne.

During this siege of Bulloigne (which continued near a month) there passed no memorable accident of war ; only sir John Savage, a valiant captain was slain, riding about the walls of the town to take a view. The town was both well fortify'd and well mann'd ; yet it was distressed, and ready for an assault. Which if it had been given (as was thought) would have cost much blood ; but yet the town would have been carried in the end. Meanwhile, a peace was concluded by the commissioners, to continue for both the kings lives. Where there was no article of importance ; being in effect rather a bargain than a treaty. For, all things remained as they were ; save that there should be paid to the king seven hundred and forty five thousand ducats (£186,250 sterling) in present, for his charges in that journey ; and five and twenty thousand crowns yearly, for his charges sustained in the aids of the Britons. For which annual, tho' he had Maximilian bound before for those charges ; yet he counted the alteration of the hand, as much as the principal debt. And besides, it was left somewhat indefinitely, when it should determine or expire : which made the English esteem it as a tribute carried under fair terms. And the truth is, it was paid both to the king, and to his son king Henry VIII. longer than it could continue upon any computation of charges. There were also assign'd by the French king, unto all the king's principal counsellors great pensions, besides rich gifts for the present. Which whether the king did permit to save his own purse from rewards, or to communicate the envy of a business that was displeasing to his people, was diversly interpreted. For certainly, the king had no great fancy to own this peace. And therefore, a little before it was concluded, he had under-hand procur'd some of his best captains, and men of war, to advise him to a peace under their hands, in an earnest manner, in the nature of a supplication. But the truth is, this peace was welcome to both kings. To Charles, for that it assured unto him the possession of Brittain, and freed the enterprize of Naples. To Henry, for that it fill'd his coffers; and that he foresaw at that time a storm of inward troubles coming upon him; which presently after brake forth. But it gave no less discontent to the nobility, and principal persons of the army; who had many of them sold or engaged their estates upon the hopes of the war. They stuck not to say, 'That the king cared not to plume his nobility and people, to feather himself.' And some made themselves merry with that the king had said in parliament: 'That after war was once begun, he doubted not but to make it pay itself;' saying he had kept promise.

Having risen from Bulloigne, he went to Calice, where he stay'd some time. From whence also he wrote letters, (which was a courtesy that he sometimes used) to the mayor of London, and aldermen his brethren; half bragging, what great sums he had obtain'd for the peace; knowing well, that full coffers of the king is ever good news to London. And better news it would have been, if their benevolence had been but a loan. And upon the seventeenth of December following, he return'd to Westminster, where he kept his Christmas.

Soon after the king's return, he sent the order of the garter, to Alphonso duke of Calabria, eldest son to Ferdinando king of Naples; an honour sought by that prince, to hold him up in the eyes of the Italians; who, expecting the arms of Charles, made great account of the amity of England for a bridle to France. It was received by Alphonso with all the ceremony and pomp that could be devised; as things use to be carried, that are intended for opinion. It was sent by Urswick; upon whom the king bestow'd this ambassage, to help him, after many dry employments.

At this time (1492) the king began again to be haunted with sprites, by the magick and curious arts of the lady Margaret: who raised up the ghost of Richard duke of York, second son to king Edward IV. to walk and vex the king. This was a finer counterfeit stone than Lambert Symnel, better done, and worn upon greater hands; being graced after with the wearing of a king of France, and a king of Scotland, not of the duchess of Burgundy only. And for Symnell, there was not much in him, more than that he was a handsome boy, and did not shame his robes. But this youth (of whom we are now to speak) was such a mercurial, as the like hath seldom been known, and could make his own part if at any time he chanc'd to be out. Wherefore, this being one of the strangest examples of a personation that ever was in elder or later times ; it deserveth to be discovered, and related at the full : altho' the king's manner of shewing things, by pieces and by dark lights, hath so muffled it, that it hath left it almost as a mystery to this day.

The lady Margaret (whom the king's friends call'd Juno, because she was to him as Juno was to Æneas, stirring both heaven and hell to do him mischief) for a foundation of her particular practices against him, did continually, by all means possible, nourish, maintain, and divulge the flying opinion, that Richard duke of York (second son to Edward IV.) was not murder'd in the Tower (as was given out) but saved alive : for that those who were employ'd in that barbarous fact, having destroy'd the elder brother, were stricken with remorse and compassion towards the younger, and set him privily at liberty to seek his fortune. This lure she cast abroad, thinking that this fame and belief (together with the fresh example of Lambert Simnell) would draw at one time or other some birds to strike upon it. She used likewise a further diligence, not committing all to chance. For, she had some secret espials (like to the Turks commissioners for children of tribute) to look abroad for handsome and graceful youths to make Plantagenets, and dukes of York. At the last she did light on one, in whom all things met, as one could wish, to serve her turn, for a counterfeit of Richard duke of York.

This was Perkin Warbeck, whose adventures we shall now describe. For, first, the years agreed well. Secondly, he was a youth of fine favour and shape; but more than that, he had such a crafty and bewitching fashion, both to move pity and to induce belief, as was like a kind of fascination and enchantment to those that saw him, or heard him. Thirdly, he had been from his childhood such a wanderer, or (as the king called him) such a land-loper, as it was extreme hard to hunt out his nest and parents. Neither again could any man, by company or conversing with him, be able to say or detect well what he was ; he did so flit from place to place. Lastly, there was a circumstance (which is mentioned by one that wrote in the same time) that is very likely to have made somewhat to the matter, which is, that king Edward IV. was his god-father. Which, as it is somewhat suspicious, for a wanton prince to become gossip in so mean a house ; and might make a man think that he might indeed have in him some base blood of the house of York ; so at the least (tho' that were not) it might give the occasion to the boy, in being call'd king Edward's godson, or perhaps in sport, king Edward's son, to entertain such thoughts into his head. For, tutor he had none (for ought that appears) as Lambert Simnell had, until he came unto the lady Margaret, who instructed him.

Thus therefore it came to pass : there was a townsman of Tourney that had born office in that town, whose name was[1] John Osbeck a convert Jew, married to Catherine de Faro; whose business drew him to live for a time with his wife at London, in king Edward IV's days. During which time he had a son by her; and being known in court, the king either out of a religious nobleness, because he was a convert, or upon some private acquaintance, did him the honour as to be godfather to his child, and named him Peter. But afterwards proving a dainty and effeminate youth, he was commonly call'd by the diminutive of his name, Peter-kin, or Perkin. For, as for the name of Warbecke it was given him when they did but guess at it, before examinations had been taken. But yet he had been so much talk'd on by that name, as it stuck by him after his true name of Osbecke was known. While he was a young child, his parents return'd with him to Tourney. Then was he placed in a house of a kinsman of his, call'd John Stenbeck at Antwerp; and so roved up and down between Antwerp and Tourney, and other towns of Flanders, for a good time; living much in English company, and having the English tongue perfect. In which time being grown a comely youth, he was brought by some of the espials of the lady Margaret unto her presence. Who viewing him well, and seeing that he had a face and personage, that would bear a noble fortune: and finding him otherwise of a fine spirit and winning behaviour, thought she had now found a curious piece of marble, to carve out an image of a duke of York. She kept him by her a great while; but with extreme secrecy. The while, she instructed him, by many cabinet conferences, First, in princely behaviour and gesture; teaching him how he should keep state, and yet with a modest sense of his misfortunes. Then she inform'd him of all the circumstances and particulars that concern'd the person of Richard duke of York, which he was to act: describing unto him the personages, lineaments, and features of the king and queen his pretended parents; and of his brother, and sisters, and divers others that were nearest him in his childhood; together with all passages, some secret, some common, that were fit for a child's memory, until the death of king Edward. Then she added the particulars of the time, from the king's death, until he and his brother were committed to the Tower, as well during the time he was abroad, as while he was in sanctuary. As for the times while he was in the tower, and the manner of his brother's death, and his own escape; she knew they were things that a very few could controul. And therefore she taught him only to tell a smooth and likely tale of those matters; warning him not to vary from it. It was agreed likewise between them, what account he should give of his peregrination abroad; intermixing many things

[1] His true name was Peter Osbeck; he was not unlike Richard duke of York, both in body and countenance; he was born at Tournay in Flanders. Whose father, John Osbeck, was controuler of that city, and his mother Catherine de Faro, who could speak English.—Sir J Ware, Ann. Hen. VII. Cap. 6.

which were true, and such as they knew others could testifie, for the credit of the rest; but still making them hang together, with the part he was to play. She taught him likewise how to avoid sundry captious and tempting questions, which were like to be asked of him. But, in this she found him of himself so nimble and shifting, as she trusted much to his own wit and readiness; and therefore labour'd the less in it. Lastly, she raised his thoughts with some present rewards, and further promises; setting before him chiefly the glory and fortune of a crown, if things went well; and a sure refuge to her court, if the worst should fall. After such time as she thought he was perfect in his lesson, she began to cast with herself from what coast this blazing star should first appear, and at what time it must be upon the horizon of Ireland; for there had the like meteor strong influence before: the time of the apparition to be, when the king should be engaged into a war with France. But well she knew, that whatsoever should come from her, would be held suspected. And therefore, if he should go out of Flanders immediately into Ireland, she might be thought to have some hand in it. And besides, the time was not yet ripe; for that the two kings were then upon terms of peace. Therefore she wheel'd about; and to put all suspicion afar off, and loth to keep him any longer by her (for that she knew secrets are not long liv'd) she sent him unknown into Portugal, with the lady Brampton,[1] an English lady, that embark'd for Portugal at that time; with some privado of her own, to have an eye upon him; and there he was to remain, and to expect her further directions. In the meantime, she omitted not to prepare things for his better welcome, and accepting, not only in the kingdom of Ireland, but in the court of France. He continued in Portugal about a year; and by that time, the king of England called his parliament (as hath been said) and declared open war against France. Now did the sign reign, and the constellation was come, under which Perkin would appear. And therefore he was straight sent unto by the duchess to go for Ireland, according to the first designment. In Ireland he did arrive at the town of Cork. When he was come thither, his own tale was (when he made his confession afterwards) that the Irishmen, finding him in good clothes, came flocking about him, and bare him down, that he was the duke of Clarence, that had been there before: and after, that he was Richard the IIIrd's base son: and lastly, that he was Richard duke of York, second son to Edward IV.: but that he (for his part) renounced all these things, and offered to swear upon the holy evangelists, that he was no such man: till at last they forced it upon him and bad him fear nothing, and so forth. But the truth is, that immediately upon his coming into Ireland, he took upon him the said person of the duke of York, and drew unto him accomplices, and par-

[1] Sir Richard Brampton's wife.

takers, by all the means he could devise; insomuch, as he wrote his letters unto the earls of Desmond and Kildare, to come in to his aid, and be of his party; the originals of which letters are extant.

Somewhat before this time, the duchess had gained unto her, a near servant of king Henry's own, one Stephen Frion, his secretary for the French tongue; an active man, but turbulent and discontented. This Frion had fled over to Charles the French king, and put himself into his service, at such time as he had began to be in open enmity with the king. Now king Charles, when he understood of the person and attempts of Perkin (ready of himself to embrace all advantages against the king of England; instigated by Frion, and formerly prepared by the lady Margaret) forthwith dispatch'd one Lucas, and this Frion, in the nature of ambassadors to Perkin; to advertise him of the king's good inclination to him, and that he was resolved to aid him to recover his right against king Henry, an usurper of England, and an enemy of France; and wish'd him to come over unto him at Paris. Perkin thought himself in heaven now that he was invited by so great a king, in so honourable a manner: and imparting unto his friends in Ireland for their encouragement, how fortune called him, and what great hopes he had, sail'd presently into France. When he was come to the court of France, the king received him with great honour; saluted, and stiled him by the name of the duke of York; lodged him, and accommodated him in great state: and the better to give him the representation and the countenance of a prince, assign'd him a guard for his person, whereof the lord Congresall was captain. The courtiers likewise (tho' it be ill mocking with the French) applied themselves to the king's bent, seeing there was reason of state of it. At the same time there repair'd unto Perkin divers Englishmen of quality; sir George Nevile, sir John Taylor, and about one hundred more; and amongst the rest, this Stephen Frion, of whom we spake; who follow'd his fortune both then and for a long time after, and was indeed his principal counsellor, and instrument in all his proceedings. But all this, on the French king's part, was but a trick; the better to bow king Henry to a peace. And therefore upon the first grain of incense that was sacrificed upon the altar of peace at Bulloigne, Perkin was smoked away. Yet would not the French king deliver him up to king Henry (as he was laboured to do) for his honour's sake, but warned him away and dismissed him. And Perkin on his part was ready to be gone, doubting he might be caught up underhand. He therefore took his way into Flanders, unto the Duchess of Burgundy; pretending, that having been variously toss'd by fortune, he directed his course thither, as to a safe harbour: no ways taking knowledge that he had ever been there before, but as if that had been his first address. The duchess, on the other part, made it as new and strange to see him: pretending (at the first) that she was taught and made wise by the example of Lambert Simnell, how she did admit of any counterfeit stuff; tho' even in that (she said) she was not fully satisfied. She pretended at the first (and that was ever in the presence of others) to pose and sift him, thereby to try whether he were indeed the very duke of York, or no. But seeming to receive full satisfaction by his answers, she then feign'd herself to be transported with a kind of astonishment, mixt of joy and wonder, at his miraculous deliverance; receiving him, as if he were risen from death to life; and inferring, that God, who had in such wonderful manner preserv'd him from death, did likewise reserve him for some great and prosperous fortune. As for his dismission out of France, they interpreted it not, as if he were detected or neglected for a counterfeit deceiver; but contrariwise, that it did shew manifestly unto the world, that he was some great matter; for that it was his abandoning, that (in effect) made the peace: being no more but the sacrificing of a poor distressed prince unto the utility and ambition of two mighty monarchs. Neither was Perkin for his part wanting to himself, either in gracious or princely behaviour, or in ready and apposite answers, or in contenting and caressing those that did apply themselves unto him, or in pretty scorn and disdain to those that seem'd to doubt of him; but in all things did notably acquit himself: insomuch as it was generally believed (as well amongst great persons, as amongst the vulgar) that he was indeed duke Richard. Nay, himself, with long and continual counterfeiting, and with oft telling a lye, was turn'd by habit almost into the thing he seem'd to be; and from a lyer to a believer. The duchess therefore (as in a case out of doubt) did him all princely honour, calling him always by the name of her nephew, and giving him the delicate title of the white rose of England; and appointed him a guard of thirty persons, halberdiers, clad in a partycoloured livery of murrey and blew, to attend his person. Her court likewise, and generally the Dutch and strangers in their usage towards him, expressed no less respect.

The news hereof came blazing and thundering over into England, that the duke of York was sure alive. As for the name of Perkin Warbeck, it was not at that time come to light, but all the news ran upon the duke of York; that he had been entertained in Ireland, bought and sold in France, and was now plainly avowed, and in great honour in Flanders. These fames took hold of divers; in some upon discontent, in some upon ambition, in some upon levity and desire of change, and in some few upon conscience and belief, but in most upon simplicity: and in divers out of dependence upon some of the better sort, who did in secret favour and nourish these bruits. And it was not long, ere these rumours of novelty had begotten others of scandal and murmur against the king and his government; taxing him for a great taxer of his people, and discountenancer of his nobility. The loss of Brittain, and the peace with France were not forgotten. But chiefly they fell upon the wrong that he did his queen, in that he did not reign in her right. Wherefore they said, that God had now brought to light a masculine-branch of the house of York, that would not be at his curtesy, howsoever he did depress his poor lady. And yet (as it fareth in things which are current with the multitude, and which they affect) these fames grew so general, as the authors were lost in the generality of speakers. They being like running weeds, that have no certain root; or like footings up and down, impossible to be traced. But after a while, these ill humours drew to an head, and settled secretly in some eminent persons; which were sir William Stanley, lord chamberlain of the king's houshold, the lord Fitzwalter, sir Simon Mountfort, sir Thomas Thwaites. These entred into a secret conspiracy to favour duke Richard's title. Nevertheless none engaged their fortunes in this business openly, but two; sir Robert Clifford and master William Barley, who sail'd over into Flanders, sent indeed from the party of the conspirators here, to understand the truth of those things that passed there, and not without some help of monies from hence; provisionally to be deliver'd, if they found and were satisfied that there was truth in these pretences. The person of sir Robert Clifford (being a gentlemen of fame and family) was extremely welcome to the lady Margaret. Who after she had conference with him, brought him to the sight of Perkin, with whom he had often speech and discourse. So that in the end won either by the duchess to affect, or by Perkin to believe, he wrote back into England, that he knew the person of Richard duke of York, as well as he knew his own; and that this young man was undoubtedly he. By this means all things grew prepared to revolt and sedition here, and the conspiracy came to a correspondence between Flanders and England.

The king on his part was not asleep; but to arm or levy forces yet, he thought would but shew fear, and do this idol too much worship. Nevertheless the ports he did shut up, or at least kept a watch on them, that none should pass to or fro that was suspected. But for the rest, he chose to work by countermine. His purposes were two: the one, to lay open the abuse; the other, to break the knot of the conspirators. To detect the abuse, there were but two ways: the first, to make it manifest to the world that the duke of York was indeed murdered: the other to prove, that were he dead or alive, yet Perkin was a counterfeit. For the first, thus it stood. There were but four persons that could speak upon knowledge to the murder of the duke of York: sir James Tirrel (the employ'd man from king Richard), John Dighton, and Miles Forrest, his servants (the two butchers or tormentors), and the priest of the Tower, that buried them. Of which four, Miles Forrest, and the priest were dead, and there remain'd alive only sir James Tirrel and John Dighton. These two the king caused to be committed to the Tower, and examined touching the manner of the death of the two innocent princes. They agreed both in a tale (as the king gave out), to this effect: that king Richard having directed his warrant for the putting of them to death by Brackenbury the lieutenant of the Tower, was by him refused. Whereupon the king directed his warrant to sir James Tirrel, to receive the keys of the Tower from the lieutenant (for the space of a night) for the king's special service. That sir James Tirrel accordingly repair'd to the Tower by night, attended by his two servants aforenam'd, whom he had chosen for that purpose. That himself stood at the stair-foot, and sent these two villains to execute the murder. That they smother'd them in their bed; and that done, call'd up their master to see their naked bodies, which they had laid forth. That they were buried under the stairs, and some stones cast upon them. That when the report was made to king Richard, that his will was done, he gave sir James Tirrel great thanks, but took exception to the place of their burial, being too base for them that were king's children. Whereupon another night, by the king's warrant renew'd, their bodies were remov'd by the priest of the Tower, and buried by him in some place, which (by means of the priest's death soon after) could not be known. Thus much was then delivered abroad, to the effect of those examinations. But the king nevertheless made no use of them in any of his declarations; whereby (as it seems) those examinations left the business somewhat perplex'd. And as for sir James Tirrel, he was soon after beheaded in the Tower-yard, for other matters of treason. But John Dighton (who it seemeth spake best for the king) was forthwith set at liberty, and was the principal means of divulging this tradition. Therefore this kind of proof being left so naked, the king used the more diligence in the latter, for the tracing of Perkin. To this purpose, he sent abroad into several parts, and especially into Flanders, divers secret and nimble scouts and spies; some feigning themselves to fly over unto Perkin, and to adhere unto him; and some under other pretences, to learn, search, and discover all the circumstances and the particulars of Perkin's parents, birth, person, travels up and down; and in brief, to have a journal (as it were) of his life and doings. He furnish'd these his employ'd men liberally with money, to draw on and reward intelligences: giving them also in charge, to advertise continually what they found, and nevertheless still to go on. And ever as one advertisement and discovery call'd up another, he employ'd other new men, where the business did require it. Others he employ'd in a more special nature and trust, to be his pioneers in the main counter-mine. These were directed to insinuate themselves into the familiarity and confidence of the principal persons of the party in Flanders, and so to learn what associates they had, and correspondents, either here in England, or abroad; and how far every one engaged, and what new ones they meant afterwards to try, or board. And as this for the persons; so for the actions themselves, to discover to the bottom (as they could) the utmost of Perkin and the conspirators, their intentions, hopes, and practices. These latter best-be-trust spies had some of them further instructions, to practice and draw off the best friends and servants of Perkin, by making remonstance to them, how weakly his enterprise and hopes were built, and with how prudent and potent a king they had to deal; and to reconcile them to the king, with promise of pardon, and good conditions of reward. And (above the rest) to assail, sap, and work into the constancy of sir Robert Clifford, and to win him (if they could), being the man that knew most of their secrets, and who being won away, would most appall and discourage the rest, and in a manner break the knot.

There is a strange tradition; that the king being lost in a wood of suspicions, and not knowing whom to trust, had both intelligence with the confessors and chaplains of divers great men, and for the better credit of his espials abroad with the contrary side, did use to have them cursed at Pauls (by name) amongst the bead-roll of the king's enemies, according to the custom of those times. Those espials plied their charge so roundly, as the king had an anatomy of Perkin alive; and was likewise well informed of the particular correspondent conspirators in England, and many other mysteries were reveal'd; and sir Robert Clifford in especial won to be assured to the king, and industrious and officious for his service. The king therefore (receiving a rich return of his diligence, and great satisfaction touching a number of particulars) first divulged and spread abroad the imposture and juggling of Perkin's person and travels, with the circumstances thereof throughout the realm. Not by proclamation (because things were yet in examination, and so might receive the more or the less) but by court-fames, which commonly print better than printed proclamations. Then thought he it also time to send an ambassage unto archduke Philip into Flanders, for the abandoning and dismissing of Perkin. Herein he employ'd sir Edward Poynings and sir Will. Warham, doctor of the canon-law. The archduke was then young, and governed by his council: before whom the ambassadors had audience, and Dr. Warham spake in this manner.

'My lords, the king our master is very sorry, that England and your country here of Flanders having been counted as man and wife for so long time, now this country of all others should be the stage, where a base counterfeit should play the part of a king of England; not only to his grace's disquiet and dishonour, but to the scorn and reproach of all sovereign princes. To counterfeit the dead image of a king in his coyn, is an high offence by all laws: but to counterfeit the living image of a king in his person, exceedeth all falsifications, except it should be that of Mahomet, or an antichrist, that counterfeit divine honour. The king hath too great an opinion of this sage council, to think that any of you is caught with this fable (though way may be given by you to the passion of some) the thing in it self is so improbable. To set testimonies aside of the death of duke Richard, which the king hath upon record, plain and infallible (because they may be thought to be in the king's own power) let the thing testify for it self. Sense and reason no power can command. Is it possible (trow you) that king Richard should damn his soul, and foul his name with so abominable a murder, and you not mend his case? Or do you think, that men of blood (that were his instruments) did turn to pity in the midst of their execution? Whereas in cruel and savage beasts, and men also, the first draught of blood doth yet make them more fierce, and enraged. Do you not know, that the bloody executioners of tyrants do go to such errands, with an halter about their neck: so that if they perform not, they are sure to dye for it? And do you think, that these men would hazard their own lives, for sparing anothers? Admit they should have saved him: what should they have done with him? Turn him into London streets, that the watch-men or any passenger that should light upon him, might carry him before a justice, and so all come to light? Or should they have kept him by them secretly? That surely would have required a great deal of care, charge, and continual fears. But (my lords) I labour too much in a clear business. The king is so wise, and hath so good friends abroad, as now he knoweth duke Perkin from his cradle. And because he is a great prince, if you have any good poet here, he can help him with notes to write his life, and to parallel him with Lambert Simnel, now the king's faulconer. And therefore (to speak plainly to your lordships) it is the strangest thing in the world, that the lady Margaret (excuse us if we name her, whose malice to the king is both causeless and endless) should now when she is old, at the time when other women give over childbearing, bring forth two such monsters; being not the birth of nine or ten months, but of many years. And whereas other natural mothers bring forth children weak, and not able to help themselves; she bringeth forth tall striplings, able soon after their coming into the world, to bid battle to mighty kings. My lords, we stay unwillingly upon this part. We would to God, that lady would once taste the joys, which God Almighty doth serve up unto her, in beholding her niece to reign in such honour, and with so much royal issue, which she might be pleased to accompt as her own. The king's request unto the arch-duke, and your lordships might be; that according to the example of king Charles, who hath already discarded him, you would banish this unworthy fellow out of your dominions. But because the king may justly expect more from an ancient confederate, than from a new reconciled enemy; he maketh his request unto you, to deliver him up into his hands. Pirates and impostures of this sort, being fit to be accounted the common enemies of mankind, and no ways to be protected by the laws of nations.

After some time of deliberation, the ambassadors received this short answer.

'That the archduke, for the love of king Henry, would in no sort aid or assist the pretended duke, but in all things conserve the amity he had with the king. But for the duchess dowager, she was absolute in the lands of her dowry, and that he could not let her to dispose of her own.'

The king, upon the return of the ambassadors, was nothing satisfied with this answer. For well he knew, that a patrimonial dowry carried no part of sovereignty, or command of forces. Besides, the ambassadors told him plainly, that they saw the duchess had a great party in the arch-duke's council; and that howsoever it was carried in a course of connivance, yet the arch-duke under hand gave aid and furtherance to Perkin. Wherefore (partly out of courage, and partly out of policy) the king forthwith banished all Flemings (as well their persons as their wares) out of his kingdom; commanding his subjects likewise (and by name his merchant-adventurers) which had a resiance in Antwerp, to return; translating the mart (which commonly followed the English cloth) under Calice, and embarred also all further trade for the future. This the king did, being sensible in point of honour, not to suffer a pretender to the crown of England to affront him so near at hand, and he to keep terms of friendship with the country where he did set up. But he had also a further reach: for that he knew well, that the subjects of Flanders drew so great commodity from the trade of England as by this embargo they would soon wax weary of Perkin, and that the tumults of Flanders had been so late and fresh, as it was no time for the prince to displease the people. Nevertheless for form's sake, by way of requital, the archduke did likewise banish the English out of Flanders; which in effect was done to his hand.

The king being well advertised, that Perkin did more trust upon friends and partakers within the realm, than upon foreign arms thought it behoved him to apply the remedy where the disease lay; and to proceed with severity against some of the principal conspirators here within the realm; thereby to purge the ill humours in England, and to cool the hopes in Flanders. Wherefore he caused to be apprehended (almost at an instant) John Ratcliff, lord Fitzwalter, sir Simon Mountford, sir Thomas Thwaites, William Dawbigney, Robert Ratcliff, Thomas Chressenor, and Thomas Astwood. All these were arraigned, convicted, and condemned for high treason, in adhering, and promising aid to Perkin. Of these, the lord Fitz-walter was conveyed to Calice, and there kept in hold and in hope of life, until soon after (either impatient, or betrayed) he dealt with his keeper to have escaped, and thereupon was beheaded; but sir Simon Mountford, Robert Ratcliff, and William Dawbigney were beheaded immediately after their condemnation. The rest were pardoned, together with many other clerks and laikes, amongst which were two Dominican friers, and William Worseley, dean of Pauls : which latter sort passed examination, but came not to publick trial.

The lord chamberlain at that time was not touched : whether it were, that the king would not stir too many humours at once but (after the manner of good physicians) purge the head last ; or that Clifford (from whom most of these discoveries came) reserved that piece for his own coming over ; signifying only to the king in the mean time, that he doubted there were some greater ones in the business, whereof he would give the king further accompt, when he came to his presence.

Upon Al-hallows-day-even, being now the tenth year of the king's reign, the king's second son Henry was created duke of York ; and as well the duke, as divers others, noblemen, knights batchellours, and gentlemen of quality were made knights of the bath, according to the ceremony. Upon the morrow after twelfth-day, the king removed from Westminster (where he had kept his Christmas) to the Tower of London. This he did as soon as he had advertisement, that sir Robert Clifford (in whose bosom or budget most of Perkin's secrets were layed up) was come into England. And the place of the Tower was chosen to that end, that if Clifford should accuse any of the great ones, they might without suspicion, or noise, or sending abroad of warrants, be presently attached ; the court and prison being within the cincture of one wall. After a day or two, the king drew unto him a selected council, and admitted Clifford to his presence ; who first fell down at his feet, and in all humble manner craved the king's pardon, which the king then granted, though he were indeed secretly assured of his life before. Then commanded to tell his knowledge, he did amongst many others (of himself, not interrogated) appeach sir William Stanley, the lord chamberlain of the king's household.

The king seemed to be much amazed at the naming of this lord, as if he had heard the news of some strange and fearful prodigy. To hear a man that had done him service of so high a nature, as to save his life, and set the crown upon his head ; a man that enjoyed by his favour and advancement so great a fortune, both in honour and riches ; a man, that was tied unto him in so near a band alliance, his brother having married the king's mother ; and lastly, a man, to whom he had committed the trust of his person, in making him his chamberlain. That this man, no ways disgraced, no ways discontent, no ways put in fear, should be false unto him. Clifford was required to say over again, and again, the particulars of his accusation, being warned, that in a matter so unlikely, and that concerned so great a servant of the king's, he should not in any wise go too far. But the king finding that he did sadly and constantly (without hesitation or varying, and with those civil protestations that were fit) stand to that that he had said, offering to justifie it upon his soul and life; he caused him to be removed. And after he had not a little bemoaned himself unto his council there present, gave order that sir William Stanley should be restrained in his own chamber, where he lay before, in the square tower. And the next day he was examined by the lords. Upon his examination he denied little of that wherewith he was charged, nor endeavoured much to excuse or extenuate his fault. So that (not very wisely) thinking to make his offence less by confession, he made it enough for condemnation. It was conceived, that he trusted much to his former merits, and the interest that his brother had in the king. But those helps were over-weighed by divers things that made against him, and were predominant in the king's nature and mind. First, an over-merit; for convenient merit, unto which reward may easily reach, doth best with kings: next the sense of his power; for the king thought, that he that could set him up, was the more dangerous to pull him down. Thirdly, the glimmering of a confiscation; for he was the richest subject for value in the kingdom: there being found in his castle of Holt forty thousand marks in ready money, and plate, besides jewels, householdstuff, stocks upon his grounds, and other personal estate, exceeding great. And for his revenue in land and fee, it was three thousand pounds a year of old rent, a great matter in those times. Lastly, the nature of the time: for if the king had been out of fear of his own estate, it was not unlike he would have spared his life. But the cloud of so great a rebellion hanging over his head, made him work sure. Wherefore after some six weeks distance of time, which the king did honourably interpose, both to give space to his brother's intercession, and to show to the world, that he had a conflict with himself what he should do; he was arraigned of high-treason, and condemned, and presently after beheaded.

Yet it is to this day but in dark memory, both what the case of this noble person was, for which he suffered, and what likewise was the ground and cause of his defection, and the alienation of his heart from the king. His case was said to be this; that in discourse between sir Robert Clifford and him, he had said; 'That if he were sure, that that young man were king Edward's son, he would never bear arms against him.' This case seems somewhat an hard case, both in respect of the conditional, and in respect of the other words. But for the conditional, it seems the judges of that time (who were learned men, and the three chief of them of the privy council) thought it was a dangerous thing to admit ifs and ands, to qualifie words of treason; whereby every man might express his malice, and blanch his danger. And it was like to the case (in the following times) of Elizabeth Barton the holy maid of Kent; who had said, 'That if king Henry the eighth did not take Katherine his wife again, he should be deprived of his crown, and die the death of a dog.' And infinite cases may be put of like nature. Which (it seemeth) the grave judges taking into consideration, would not admit of treasons upon condition. And as for the positive words, that he would not bear arms against king Edward's son; though the words seem calm, yet it was a plain and direct over-ruling of the king's title, either by the line of Lancaster, or by act of parliament. Which (no doubt) pierced the king more, than if Stanley had charged his launce upon him in the field. For if Stanley would hold that opinion, that a son of king Edward had still the better right, he being so principal a person of authority, and favour about the king; it was to teach all England to say as much. And therefore (as those times were) that speech touched the quick. But some writers do put this out of doubt: for they say, that Stanley did expressly promise to aid Perkin, and sent him some help of treasure.

Now for the motive of his falling off from the king; it is true, that at Bosworth field the king was beset, and in a manner inclosed round about by the troops of king Richard, and in manifest danger of his life; when this Stanley was sent by his brother, with three thousand men to his rescue, which he performed so, that king Richard was slain upon the place. So as the condition of mortal men is not capable of a greater benefit, than the king received by the hands of Stanley; being like the benefit of Christ, at once to save and crown. For which service the king gave him great gifts, made him his councellour and chamberlain; and (somewhat contrary to his nature) had winked at the great spoils of Bosworth field, which came almost wholly to this man's hands, to his infinite enriching. Yet nevertheless blown up with the conceit of his merit, he did not think he had received good measure from the king, at least not prest down and running over, as he expected. And his ambition was so exorbitant, and unbounded, as he became suitor to the king for the earldom of Chester. Which ever being a kind of appendage to the principality of Wales, and using to go to the king's son; his suit did not only end in a denial, but in a distaste. The king perceiving thereby, that his desires were intemperate, and his cogitations vast, and irregular, and that his former benefits were but cheap, and lightly regarded by him. Wherefore the king began not to brook him well. And as a little leaven of new distast doth commonly sour the whole lump of former merit, the king's wit began to suggest unto his passion that Sir William Stanley, at Bosworth field, though he came time enough to save his life, yet he stayed long enough to endanger it. But yet having no matter against him, he continued him in his places until this his fall.

After him was made lord chamberlain, Giles lord Dawbeny, a man of great sufficiency and valour; and the more, because he was gentle and moderate.

There was a common opinion, that sir Robert Clifford (who now was become the state-informer) was from the beginning an emissary, and spie of the king's; and that he fled over into Flanders with his consent and privity. But this is not probable; both because he never recovered that degree of grace, which he had with the king before his going over; and chiefly, for that the discovery which he had made touching the lord chamberlain (which was his great service) grew not from anything he learn'd abroad, for that he knew it well before he went there.

These executions (and especially that of the lord chamberlain, which was the chief strength of the party, and by means of sir Robert Clifford, who was the most inward man of trust amongst them) did extremely quail the design of Perkin, and his accomplices, as well through discouragement, as distrust. So that they were now (like sand without lime) ill bound together; especially as many as were English: who were at a gaze, looking one upon another, not knowing who was faithful to their side; but thinking that the king (what with his baits, and what with his nets) would draw them all unto him, that were anything worth. And indeed it came to pass, that divers came away by the thred, sometimes one, and sometimes another. Barley (that was joint commissioner with Clifford) did hold out one of the longest, till Perkin was far worn; yet made his peace at the length. But the fall of this great man, being in so high authority and favour (as was thought) with the king; and the manner of carriage of the business, as if there had been secret inquisition upon him, for a great time before; and the cause for which he suffered, which was little more, than for saying in effect, that the title of York was better than the title of Lancaster; which was the case almost of every man (at the least in opinion;) was matter of great terror amongst all the king's servants and subjects: insomuch, as no man almost thought himself secure; and men durst scarce commune or talk one with another. But there was a general diffidence every where. Which nevertheless made the king rather more absolute, than more safe. For, bleeding inwards and shut vapours strangle soonest, and oppress most.

Hereupon presently came out swarms and vollies of libels (which are the gusts of liberty of speech restrained, and the females of sedition) containing bitter invectives and slanders against the king, and some of the council. For the contriving and the dispersing whereof (after great diligence and enquiry) five mean persons were caught, and executed.

Meanwhile, the king did not neglect Ireland, being the soil where the mushromes and upstart-weeds (that spring up in a night) did chiefly prosper. He sent therefore from hence (for the better settling of his affairs there) commissioners of both robes: the prior of Lanchony,[1] to be his chancellour in that kingdom; and sir Edward Poynings with a power of men[2] and a marshal commission, together with a civil power of his lieutenant, with a clause, that the earl of Kildare, then deputy, should obey him. But, the Wild-Irish (who were the principal offenders) fled into the woods and bogs, after their manner: and those that knew themselves guilty, in the pale, fled to them. So that sir Edward Poynings was enforced to make a wild chase upon the Wild-Irish: where (in respect of the mountains and fastnesses) he did little good. Which (either out of a suspicious melancholy upon his bad success, or the better to save his service from disgrace) he would needs impute unto the comfort, that the rebels should receive under-hand from the earl of Kildare that was in the action of Lambert Simnel, slain at Stokefield.[3] Wherefore he caused the earl to be apprehended, and sent into England; where, upon examination, he declared himself so well, as he was re-placed in his government. But, Poynings (the better to make compensation of the meagerness of his service in the wars by acts of peace) called a parliament; where was made that memorable act, which at this day is called Poynings' law, whereby all the statutes of England were made to be of force in Ireland.[4] For, before they were not: neither are any now in force in Ireland, which were made in England since that time; which was the tenth year of the king.

About this time, began to be discovered in the king that disposition, which, afterward nourished and whet on by bad councellours and ministers, proved the blot of his times? which was the course he took, to crush treasure out of his subjects purses, by forfeitures upon penal laws. At this, men did startle the more at this time, because it appeared plainly to be in the king's nature, and not out of his necessity, he being now in float for treasure; for that he had newly received the peace-money from France, the benevolence-money from his subjects, and great casualties upon the confiscations of the lord chamberlain, and divers others. The first noted case of this kind was that of sir

[1] Sir Henry Dean Hol. Sir James Ware calls him Henry Dean bishop of Bangor in Wales. Sir Edward Poynings was made lord deputy. Dean lord chancellour, and sir Hugh Conway lord treasurer. They arriv'd in Ireland the 13th of September in the year before.
[2] Not 1000 men, sir James Ware, An. Hen. VII. Cap. X.
[3] 'Twas not the earl of Kildare, but his brother the lord Thomas Howard that was slain at the battle of Stokefield. Ibid. Cap. III.
[4] The English statutes were admitted in Ireland in old times. Those laws that were now made did not in a long time pass beyond the English pale. Ibid. Cap. X. Poynings arrested the earl of Kildare, and sent him prisoner to England.

William Capel, alderman of London: who, upon sundry penal laws, was condemned in the sum of seven and twenty hundred pounds, and compounded with the king for sixteen hundred: and yet after, Empson would have cut a chop out of him, if the king had not died in the instant.

The summer following, the king, to comfort his mother (whom he did always tenderly love and revere) and to make demonstration to the world, that the proceedings against sir William Stanley (which was imposed upon him by necessity of state) had not in any degree diminished the affection he bore to Thomas his brother; went in progress to Latham, to make merry with his mother, and the earl, and lay there divers days.

During this progress, Perkin Warbeck finding, that time and temporizing, which (whilst his practices were covert and wrought well in England) made for him; did now, when they were discovered and defeated, rather make against him (for that when matters once go down the hill they stay not without a new force) resolved to try his adventure in some exploit upon England; hoping still upon the affections of the common people towards the house of York. Which body of common people he thought was not to be practised upon, as persons of quality are; but, that the only practice upon their affections, was, to set up a standard in the field. The place where he should make his attempt, he chose to be the coast of Kent.

The king by this time was grown to such an height of reputation for cunning and policy, that every accident and event, that went well, was laid and imputed to his foresight, as if he had set it before: as, in this particular of Perkin's design upon Kent. For, the world would not believe afterwards, but the king, having secret intelligence of Perkin's intention for Kent, (the better to draw it on) went of purpose into the north, afar off, laying an open side unto Perkin, to make him come to the close, and so to trip up his heels, having made sure in Kent before hand.

But so it was, that Perkin had gather'd together a power of all nations, neither in number, nor in the hardiness and courage of the persons, contemptible; but in their nature and fortunes, to be feared as well of friends as enemies; being bankrupts, and many of them felons, and such as liv'd by rapine. These he put to sea, and arriv'd upon the coast of Sandwich and Deal in Kent, about July.

There he cast anchor; and to prove the affections of the people, sent some of his men to land, making great boast of the power that was to follow. The Kentish men (perceiving that Perkin was not followed by any English of name or account, and that his forces consisted but of strangers born, and most of them base people, and free booters, fitter to spoil a coast than to recover a kingdom) resorting unto the principal gentlemen of the country, professed their loyalty to the king, and desired to be directed and commanded for the best of the king's service. The gentlemen, entring into consultation, directed some forces in good number, to shew themselves upon the coast ; and some of them to make signs, to entice Perkin's soldiers to land, as if they would join with them : and some others to appear from some other places, and to make semblance as if they fled from them ; the better to encourage them to land. But Perkin, (who, by playing the prince, or else taught by secretary Frion had learned thus much, that people under command do use to consult, and after to march in order ; and rebels contrariwise run upon an head together in confusion) considering the delay of time, and observing their orderly, and not tumultuary arming, doubted the worst. And therefore the wily youth would not set one foot out of his ship till he might see things were sure. Wherefore the king's forces, perceiving that they could draw on no more than those that were formerly landed, set upon them, and cut them in pieces, ere they could fly back to their ships. In which skirmish (besides those that fled and were slain) there were taken about an hundred and fifty persons. Which, for that the king thought that to punish a few for example was gentleman's play, but for rascal people, they were to be cut off every man, especially in the beginning of an enterprize ; and likewise for that he saw that Perkin's forces would now consist chiefly of such rabble, and scum of desperate people ; he therefore hang'd them all for the greater terrour. They were brought to London, all rail'd in ropes, like a team of horses in a cart ; and were executed some of them at London, and Wapping, and the rest at divers places upon the sea-coast of Kent, Sussex, and Norfolk, for sea-marks, or light-houses, to teach Perkin's people to avoid the coast. The king being advertised of the landing of the rebels, thought to leave his progress ; but being certify'd the next day that they were partly defeated, and partly fled, he continued his progress, and sent sir Richard Guilford into Kent in message. Who, calling the country together, did much commend (from the king) their fidelity, manhood, and well-handling of that service ; and gave them all thanks, and (in private) promis'd reward to some particulars.

Upon the sixteenth of November (this being the eleventh year of the king) was holden the serjeants-feast at Ely-Place ; there being nine serjeants of that call. The king, to honour the feast, was present with his queen at the dinner ; being a prince, that was ever ready to grace and countenance the professors of the law ; having a little of that, that as he governed his subjects by his laws, so he governed his laws by his lawyers.

This year also the king entred into league with the Italian potentates, for the defence of Italy against France. For king Charles had conquer'd the realm of Naples, and lost it again, in a kind of felicity of a dream. He pass'd the whole length of Italy without resistance: so that it was true which pope Alexander was wont to say; 'That the Frenchmen came into Italy, with chalk in their hands, to mark up their lodgings, rather than with swords to fight.' He likewise entred and won, in effect, the whole kingdom of Naples itself, witnout striking stroke. But presently thereupon he did commit and multiply so many errors, as was too great a task for the best fortune to overcome. He gave no contentment to the barons of Naples, of the faction of the Angeovines; but scatter'd his rewards according to the mercenary appetites of some about him. He put all Italy upon their guard by the seizing and holding of Ostia, and the protecting of the liberty of Pisa; which made all men suspect that his purposes look'd further than his title of Naples. He fell too soon at difference with Ludovico Sfortia; who was the man that carried the keys which brought him in, and shut him out. He neglected to extinguish some relicks of the war. And lastly, in regard of his easy passage through Italy without resistance, he entered into an overmuch despising of the arms of the Italians: whereby he left the realm of Naples at his departure so much the less provided. So that not long after his return, the whole kingdom revolted to Ferdinando the younger, and the French were quite driven out. Nevertheless, Charles did make both great threats and great preparations to re-enter Italy once again. Wherefore at the instance of divers of the states of Italy (and especially of pope Alexander) there was a league concluded between the said pope, Maximilian king of Romans, Henry king of England, Ferdinando and Isabella king and queen of Spain (for so they are constantly placed in the original treaty throughout) Augustissimo Barbadico, duke of Venice, and Ludovico Sfortia, duke of Milan, for the common defence of their estates. Wherein though Ferdinando of Naples was not named as principal; yet no doubt, the kingdom of Naples was tacitly included, as a fee of the church.

There died also this year Cecile duchess of York, mother to king Edward IV. at her castle of Berkhamsted, being of extreme years; and who had liv'd to see three princes of her body crown'd, and four murder'd. She was buried at Foderingham by her husband.

This year also the king call'd his parliament: where many laws were made, of a more private and vulgar nature, than ought to detain the reader of an history. And it may be justly suspected by the proceedings following, that as the king did excel in good commonwealth laws; so nevertheless he had, in secret, a design to make use of them, as well for the collecting of treasure, as for the correcting of manners; and meaning thereby to harrow his people, did accumulate them the rather.

The principal law that was made this parliament, was a law of a strange nature: rather just, than legal; and more magnanimous than provident. This law did ordain, that no person, that did assist in arms, or otherwise, the king for the time being, should after be impeached therefore, or attainted, either by the course of the law, or by act of parliament: but, if any such act of attainder did happen to be made, it should be void and of none effect; for that it was agreeable to reason of estate, that the subject should not enquire of the justness of the king's title, or quarrel; and it was agreeable to good conscience, that (whatsoever the fortune of the war were) the subject should not suffer for his obedience. The spirit of this law was wonderful pious and noble: being like in matter of war, unto the spirit of David in matter of plague, who said, 'If I have sinned, strike me; but what have these sheep done?' Neither wanted this law parts of prudent and deep foresight. For, it did the better take away occasion for the people to busie themselves, to pry into the king's title; for that howsoever it fell, their safety was already provided for. Besides it could not but greatly draw unto him the love and hearts of the people, because he seemed more careful for them than for himself. But yet nevertheless, it did take off from his party, that great tie and spur of necessity, to fight and go victors out of the field; considering their lives and fortunes were put in safety, and protected, whether they stood to it or ran away. But the force and obligation of this law was in itself illusory, as to the latter part of it; by a precedent act of parliament, to bind or frustrate a future. For a supreme and absolute power cannot conclude itself, neither can that which is in nature revocable be made fixt, no more than if a man should appoint or declare by his will, that if he made any latter will, it should be void. And for the case of the act of parliament, there is a notable precedent of it in king Henry the VIII.'s time; who doubting he might dye in the minority of his son, procur'd an act to pass, 'That no statute made during the minority of the king should bind him or his successors, except it were confirmed by the king under his great seal, at his full age.' But the first act that passed in king Edward the VI.'s time, was an act of repeal of that former act; at which time nevertheless the king was minor. But things that do not bind, may satisfie for the time.

There was also made a shoaring or under-propping act for the benevolence; to make the sums which any person had agreed to pay, and nevertheless were not brought in, to be leviable by course of law. Which act did not only bring in the arrears, but did indeed countenance the whole business, and was pretended to be made at the desire of those that had been forward to pay.

This parliament also was made that good law, which gave the attaint upon a false verdict between party and party, which before was a kind of evangile, irremediable. It extends not to causes capital, as well because they are for the most part at the king's suit; as because in them (if they be follow'd in course of indictment) there passeth a double jury, the indictors, and the triers; and so not twelve men, but four and twenty. But it seemeth that was not the only reason; for this reason holdeth not in the appeal. But the great reason was, lest it should tend to the discouragement of jurors in cases of life and death; if they should be subject to suit and penalty, where the favour of life maketh against them. It extendeth not also to any suit, where the demand is under the value of forty pounds; for that in such cases of petty value, it would not quit the charge to go about again.

There was another law made against a branch of ingratitude in women, who having been advanced by their husbands, or their husbands' ancestors, should alien, and thereby seek to defeat the heirs, or those in remainder, of the lands, whereunto they had been so advanced. The remedy was, by giving power to the next, to enter for a forfeiture.

There was also enacted that charitable law, for the admission of poor suitors *in forma pauperis*, without fee to counsellor, attorney, or clerk, whereby poor men became rather able to vex than unable to sue. There were divers other good laws made that parliament, as we said before. But we still observe our manner, in selecting out those, that are not of a vulgar nature.

The king this while, tho' he sate in parliament, as in full peace, and seem'd to account of the designs of Perkin (who was now return'd into Flanders) but as a May-game; yet having the composition of a wise king (stout without, and apprehensive within) had given order for the watching of beacons upon the coasts, and erecting more where they stood too thin, and had a careful eye where this wandring cloud would break. But Perkin advised to keep his fire (which hitherto burn'd as it were upon green wood) alive, with continual blowing; sail'd again into Ireland, whence he had formerly departed, rather upon the hopes of France, than upon any unreadiness or discouragement he found in that people. But in the space of time between, the king's diligence and Poyning's commission had so settled things there, as there was nothing left for Perkin, but the blustring affection of wild and naked people. Wherefore he was advis'd by his council, to seek aid of the king of Scotland; a prince young and valorous, and in good terms with his nobles and people, and ill-affected to king Henry. At this time also both Maximilian and Charles of France began to bear no good will to the king. The one being displeased with the king's prohibition of commerce with Flanders: the other holding the king for suspect, in regard of his late entry into league with the Italians. Wherefore besides the open aids of the duchess of Burgundy, which did with sails and oars put on and advance Perkin's designs, there wanted not some secret tides from Maximilian and Charles, which did further his fortunes. Insomuch as they, both by their secret letters and messages, recommended him to the king of Scotland.

Perkin therefore coming into Scotland upon those hopes, with a well appointed company, was by the king of Scots (being formerly well prepared) honourably welcom'd and soon after his arrival admitted to his presence in a solemn manner. For the king received him in state in his chamber of presence, accompany'd with divers of his nobles. And Perkin well attended, as well with those that the king had sent before him, as with his own train, entred the room where the king was, and coming near to the king, and bowing a little to embrace him, he retired some paces back, and with a loud voice (that all that were present might hear him) made his declaration in this manner:

'High and mighty king, your grace, and these your nobles here present, may be pleased benignly to bow your ears, to hear the tragedy of a young man, that by right ought to hold in his hand the ball of a kingdom; but by fortune is made himself a ball, tossed from misery to misery, and from place to place. You see here before you the spectacle of a Plantagenet, who hath been carried from the nursery to the sanctuary; from the sanctuary to the direful prison; from the prison to the hand of the cruel tormentor; and from that hand to the wide wilderness (as I may call it), for so the world hath been to me. So that he that is born to a great kingdom, hath not ground to set his foot upon, more than this where he now standeth, by your princely favour. Edward the fourth, late king of England (as your grace cannot but have heard), left two sons; Edward and Richard duke of York, both very young. Edward the eldest, succeeded their father in the crown, by the name of king Edward V. But Richard duke of Gloucester, their unnatural uncle, first thirsting after the kingdom, through ambition, and afterwards thirsting for their blood, out of desire to secure himself, employed an instrument of his (confident to him, as he thought) to murder them both. But this man that was employ'd to execute that execrable tragedy, having cruelly slain king Edward, the eldest of the two, was moved partly by remorse, and partly by some other means, to save Richard his brother; making a report nevertheless to the tyrant, that he had perform'd his commandment for both brethren. This report was accordingly believ'd, and publish'd generally. So that the world hath been possessed of an opinion that they both were barbarously made away, tho' ever truth hath some sparks that fly abroad until it appear in due time, as this hath had. But Almighty God, that stoppeth the mouth of the lion, and saved little Joas from the tyranny of Athaliah, when she massacred the king's children; and did save Isaac, when the hand was stretch'd forth to sacrifice him, preserv'd the second brother. For I myself, that stand here in your presence, am that very Richard duke of York, brother of that unfortunate prince, king Edward V., now the most rightful surviving heir-male to that victorious and most noble Edward, of that name the fourth, late king of England. For the manner of my escape, it is fit it should pass in silence, or (at least) in a more secret relation: for that it may concern some alive, and the memory of some that are dead. Let it suffice to think, that I had then a mother living, a queen, and one that expected daily such a commandment from the tyrant, for the murdering of her children. Thus in my tender age escaping by God's mercy out of London, I was secretly convey'd over sea. Where, after a time, the party that had me in charge, (upon what new fears, change of mind, or practice God knoweth) suddenly forsook me. Whereby I was forced to wander abroad, and to seek mean conditions for the sustaining of my life. Wherefore distracted between several passions, the one of fear to be known, lest the tyrant should have a new attempt upon me; the other of grief and disdain to be unknown, and to live in that base and servile manner that I did; I resolved with myself to expect the tyrant's death, and then to put my self into my sister's hands, who was next heir to the crown. But in this season, it happen'd one Henry Tudder, son to Edmond Tudder, earl of Richmond, to come from France and enter into the realm, and by subtle and foul means to obtain the crown of the same, which to me rightfully appertain'd. So that it was but a change from tyrant to tyrant. This Henry, my extream and mortal enemy, so soon as he had knowledge of my being alive, imagined and wrought all the subtle ways and means he could, to procure my final destruction. For my mortal enemy hath not only falsely surmised me to be a feign'd person, giving me nick-names, so abusing the world; but also to defer and put me from entry into England, hath offer'd large sums of money, to corrupt the princes and their ministers, with whom I have been retained; and made importune labours to certain servants about my person, to murder or poison me, and others to forsake and leave my righteous quarrel and to depart from my service; as sir Robert Clifford, and others. So that every man of reason may well perceive that Henry, calling himself king of England, needed not to have bestow'd such great sums of treasure, nor so to have busy'd himself with importune and incessant labour and industry, to compass my death and ruin, if I had been such a feign'd person. But the truth of my cause being so manifest, moved the most christian king Charles and the lady duchess dowager of Burgundy, my most dear aunt, not only to acknowledge the truth thereof, but lovingly to assist me. But it seemeth that God above (for the good of this whole island, and the knitting of these two kingdoms of England and Scotland in a strait concord and amity, by so great an obligation) had reserv'd the placing of me in the imperial throne of England, for the arms and succours of your grace. Neither is it the first time that a king of Scotland hath supported them that were bereft and spoiled of the kingdom of England; as of late (in fresh memory) it was done in the person of Henry VI. Wherefore for that your grace hath given clear signs, that you are in no noble quality inferiour to your royal ancestors; I, so distressed a prince, was hereby moved to come and put my self in your royal hands, desiring your assistance to recover my kingdom of England; promising faithfully to bear my self towards your grace no otherwise, than if I were your own natural brother, and will upon the recovery of mine inheritance, gratefully do you all the pleasure that is in my utmost power.'

After Perkin had told his tale, king James answered bravely and wisely, 'That whatsoever he were he should not repent him of putting himself into his hands.' And from that time forth, tho' there wanted not some about him, that would have persuaded him, that all was but an illusion; yet notwithstanding, either taken by Perkin's amiable and alluring behaviour, or inclining to the recommendation of the great princes abroad, or willing to take an occasion of a war against king Henry, he entertain'd him in all things, as became the person of Richard duke of York; embraced his quarrel: and (the more to put it out of doubt, that he took him to be a great prince, and not a representation only) he gave consent, that this duke should take to wife the lady Katharine Gordon, daughter to the earl of Huntley, being a near kinswoman to the king himself, and a young virgin of excellent beauty and vertue.

Not long after,[1] the king of Scots in person, with Perkin in his company, entred with a great army (though it consisted chiefly of borderers, being raised somewhat suddenly) into Northumberland. And Perkin, for a perfume before him as he went, caused to be publish'd a proclamation of this tenor following, in the name of Richard duke of York, true inheritor of the crown of England.

'It hath pleased God, who putteth down the mighty from their seat, and exalteth the humble, and suffereth not the hopes of the just to perish in the end, to give us means at the length, to show ourselves armed unto our lieges and people of England. But far be it from us, to intend their hurt and damage, or to make war upon them, otherwise than to deliver our self and them from tyranny and oppression. For our mortal enemy Henry Tudder, a false usurper of the crown of England, (which to us by natural and lineal right appertaineth) knowing in his own heart our undoubted right, (we being the very Richard duke of York, younger son, and now surviving heir-male of the noble and victorious Edward IV. late king of England) hath not only deprived us of our kingdom, but likewise by all foul and wicked means sought to betray us, and bereave us of our life. Yet if his tyranny only extend to it self to our person (altho' our royal blood teacheth us to be ... le of injuries) it should be less to our grief. But this Tudder, who bo... teth himself to have overthrown a tyrant, hath

---

[1] Ma... in t... Charles the English, king of France, and Margaret, duchess of Burgundy, wrote to the ... king in favour of this counterfeit.—Sir J. W. cap. 9.

ever since his first entrance into his usurped reign, put little in practice but tyranny and the feats thereof.

'For king Richard, our unnatural uncle, altho' desire of rule did bind him, yet in his other actions (like a true Plantagenet) was noble, and lov'd the honour of the realm, and the contentment and comfort of his nobles and people. But this our mortal enemy (agreeable to the meanness of his birth) hath trodden under foot the honour of this nation ; selling our best confederates for money, and making merchandize of the blood, estates, and fortunes of our peers and subjects, by feigned wars and dishonourable peace, only to enrich his coffers. Nor unlike hath been his hateful misgovernment, and evil deportments at home. First, he hath (to fortify his false quarrel) caused divers nobles of this our realm (whom he held suspect, and stood in dread of) to be cruelly murder'd ; as our cousin sir William Stanley lord chamberlain, sir Simon Mountfort, sir Robert Ratcliffe, William Dawbeney, Humphry Stafford, and many others, besides such as have dearly bought their lives with intolerable ransoms. Some of which nobles are now in the sanctuary. Also he hath long kept, and yet keepeth in prison, our right entirely well-beloved cousin Edward, son and heir to our uncle duke of Clarence, and others ; with-holding from them their rightful inheritance, to the intent they should never be of might and power to aid us and assist us at our need, after the duty of their liegances. He also married by compulsion certain of our sisters, and also the sister of our said cousin the earl of Warwick, and divers other ladies of the royal blood, to certain of his kinsmen and friends of simple and low degree ; and putting apart all well-disposed nobles, he hath none in favour and trust about his person, but bishop Fox, Smith, Bray, Lovel, Oliver King, David Owen, Riseley, Turbervile, Tiler, Cholmley, Empson, James Hobart, John Cut, Garth, Henry Wyat, and such other caitiffs and villains of birth, which by subtle inventions and pilling of the people, have been the principal finders, occasioners, and counsellors of the misrule and mischief now reigning in England.

'We remembring these premisses, with the great and execrable offences daily committed, and done by our foresaid great enemy, and his adherents, in breaking the liberties and franchises of our mother the holy church, upon pretences of wicked and heathenish policy, to the high displeasure of Almighty God ; besides the manifold treasons, abominable murders, manslaughters, robberies, extortions, the daily pilling of the people, by dismes, taxes, tallages, benevolences, and other unlawful impositions, and grievous exactions, with many other heinous effects, to the likely destruction and desolation of the whole realm : shall by God's grace, and the help and assistance of the great lords of our blood, with the counsel of other said persons, see that the commodities of our realm be employ'd to the most advantage of the same; the entercourse of merchandize betwixt realm and realm, to be ministred and handled, as shall more be to the common-weal and prosperity of our subjects; and all such dismes, taxes, tallages, benevolences, unlawful impositions, and grievous exactions, as be above rehearsed, to be fore-done and laid apart, and never from henceforth to be called upon, but in such cases as our noble progenitors, kings of England, have of old time been accustom'd to have the aid, succour, and help of their subjects and their true liege-men.

'And further, we do out of our grace and clemency, hereby as well publish and promise to all our subjects remission and free pardon of all by-past offences whatsoever, against our person, or estate, in adhering to our said enemy, by whom (we know well) they have been mis-led, if they shall within time convenient submit themselves unto us. And for such as shall come with the foremost, to assist our righteous quarrel, we shall make them so far partakers of our princely favour and bounty, as shall be highly for the comfort of them and theirs, both during their life, and after their death. As also we shall by all means, which God shall put into our hands, demean ourselves to give royal contentment to all degrees and estates of our people, maintaining the liberties of holy church in their entire, preserving the honours, privileges, and preeminences of our nobles from contempt or disparagement, according to the dignity of their blood. We shall also unyoak our people from all heavy burthens and endurances, and confirm our cities, boroughs, and towns, in their charters and freedoms, with inlargement, where it shall be deserv'd; and in all points give our subjects cause to think, that the blessed and debonaire government of our noble father king Edward (in his last times) is in us revived.

'And for as much as the putting to death, or taking alive of our said mortal enemy, may be a means to stay much effusion of blood, which otherwise may ensue, if by compulsion or fair promises, he shall draw after him any number of our subjects to resist us; which we desire to avoid (though we be certainly informed that our said enemy is purposed and prepared to fly the land, having already made over great masses of the treasure of our crown, the better to support him in foreign parts) we do hereby declare, that whosoever shall take or distress our said enemy (though the party be of never so mean a condition) he shall be rewarded with a thousand pound in money, forthwith to be laid down to him, and an hundred marks by he year of inheritance: besides that he may otherwise merit, both towards God and all good people, for the destruction of such a tyrant.

'Lastly, we do all men to wit, and herein we take also God to witness, that whereas God hath moved the heart of our dearest cousin, the king of Scotland, to aid us in person, in this our righteous quarrel; it is altogether without any pact or promise, or so much as demand of any thing, that may prejudice our crown or subjects: but contrariwise with promise on our said cousin's part, that whensoever he shall find us in sufficient strength to get the upper hand of our enemy (which we hope will be very suddenly) he will forthwith peaceably return into his own kingdom; contenting himself with only the glory of so honourable an enterprise, and our true and faithful love and amity. Which we shall ever (by the grace of Almighty God) so order, as shall be to the great comfort of both our kingdoms.

But Perkin's proclamation did little edifie with the people of England; neither was he the better welcome for the company he came in. Wherefore the king of Scotland seeing none came into Perkin, nor none stirred any where in his favour, turned his enterprise into a raid; and wasted and destroyed the county of Northumberland with fire and sword. But hearing that there were forces coming against him, and not willing that they should find his men heavy and laden with booty, he returned into Scotland with great spoils, deferring further prosecution, till another time. It is said that Perkin acting the part of a prince handsomly, when he saw the Scottish fell to wast the country, came to the king in a passionate manner, making great lamentation, and desir'd, that that might not be the manner of making the war; for that no crown was so dear to his mind, as that he desired to purchase it with the blood and ruin of his country. Whereunto the king answered half in sport: that he doubted much, he was careful for that that was none of his, and that he should be too good a steward for his enemy, to save the country to his use.

By this time, being the eleventh year of the king, the interruption of trade between the English and the Flemmish, began to pinch the merchants of both nations very sore. Which moved them, by all means they could devise, to affect and dispose their sovereigns respectively, to open the entercourse again. Wherein, time favoured them. For the arch-duke and his council began to see, that Perkin would prove but a runnagate, and citizen of the world; and that it was the part of children to fall out about babies. And the king on his part, after the attempts upon Kent and Northumberland, began to have the business of Perkin in less estimation; so as he did not put it to account, in any consultation of state. But that that moved him most, was, that being a king that loved wealth and treasure, he could not endure to have trade sick, nor any obstruction to continue in the gate-vein, which dispersed that blood. And yet he kept state so far, as first to be sought unto. Wherein the merchant-adventurers likewise (being a strong company at that time, and well underset with rich men, and good order), did hold out bravely; taking off the commodities of the kingdom, though they lay dead upon their hands for want of vent. At the last, commissioners met at London, to treat. On the king's part; bishop Fox lord privy-seal, viscount Wells, Kendal prior of saint John, Warham master of the rolls, who began to gain much upon the king's opinion ; Urswick, who was almost ever one ; and Riseley. On the arch-duke's part, the lord Bevers his admiral, the lord Verunsel president of Flanders, and others. These concluded a perfect treaty, both of amity and intercourse, between the king and the arch-duke ; containing articles both of state, commerce, and freefishing. This is that treaty, which the Flemmings call at this day, *Intercursus Magnus;* both because it is more compleat, than the precedent treaties, of the third and fourth years of the king ; and chiefly to give it a difference from the treaty that followed in the one and twentieth year of the king ; which they call *Intercursus Malus.* In this treaty, there was an express article against the reception of the rebels of either prince by other ; purporting, that if any such rebel should be required by the prince whose rebel he was, of the prince confederate, that forthwith the prince confederate should by proclamation command him to avoid the country. Which if he did not within fifteen days, the rebel was to stand proscrib'd, and put out of protection. But nevertheless in this article, Perkin was not named, neither perhaps contained, because he was no rebel. But by this means his wings were clipt of his followers, that were English. And it was expresly comprised in the treaty, that it should extend to the territories of the duchess dowager. After the intercourse thus restored, the English merchants came again to their mansion at Antwerp, where they were received with procession and great joy.

The winter following, being the twelfth year of his reign, the king called again his parliament : where he did much exaggerate both the malice, and cruel predatory war lately made by the king of Scotland ; that that king, being in amity with him, and no ways provok'd, should so burn in hatred towards him, as to drink of the lees and dregs of Perkin's intoxication, who was every where else detected and discarded : and that when he perceived it was out of his reach, to do the king any hurt, he had turned his arms upon unarmed and unprovided people to spoil only and depopulate, contrary to the laws both of war and peace : concluding, that he could neither with honour, nor with the safety of his people, to whom he did owe protection, let pass these wrongs unrevenged. The parliament understood him well, and gave him a subsidy, limited to the sum of one hundred and twenty thousand pounds, besides two fifteens. For his wars were always to him as a mine of treasure, of a strange kind of ore ; iron at the top, and gold and silver at the bottom. At this parliament (for that there had been so much time spent in making laws the year before, and for that it was called purposely in respect of the Scottish war) there were no laws made to be remembered. Only there passed a law at the suit of the merchant-adventurers of England, against the merchant-adventurers of London, for monopolizing and exacting upon the trade: which it seemeth they did, a little to save themselves, after the hard time they had sustained by want of trade. But those innovations were taken away by parliament.

But it was fatal to the king, to fight for his money. And though he avoided to fight with enemies abroad, yet he was still enforced to fight for it with rebels at home. For no sooner began the subsidy to be levied in Cornwall, but the people there began to grudge and murmur. The Cornish being a race of men, stout of stomach, mighty of body and limb, and that lived hardly in a barren country, and many of them could (for a need) live under ground, that were tinners; they muttered extreamly, that it was a thing not to be suffered, that for a little stir of the Scots, soon blown over, they should be thus grinded to powder with payments: and said, it was for them to pay, that had too much, and lived idly. But they would eat the bread they got with the sweat of their brows, and no man should take it from them. And as in the tides of people once up, there want not commonly stirring winds to make them more rough: so this people did light upon two ringleaders, or captains of the rout. The one was Michael Joseph, a blacksmith or farrier of Bodmin; a notable talking fellow, and no less desirous to be talked of. The other was Thomas Flammoch, a lawyer; who by telling his neighbours commonly upon any occasion, that the law was on their side, had gotten great sway amongst them. This man talked learnedly, and as if he could tell how to make a rebellion, and never break the peace. He told the people, that subsidies were not to be granted, nor levied in this case; that is, for wars of Scotland (for that the law had provided another course, by service of escuage, for those journeys) much less when all was quiet, and war was made but a pretence to poll and pill the people: and therefore that it was good they should not stand now like sheep before the shearers, but put on harness, and take weapons in their hands: yet to do no creature hurt; but go and deliver the king a strong petition, for the laying down of those grievous payments, and for the punishment of those that had given him that counsel, to make others beware how they did the like in time to come: and said, for his part he did not see how they could do the duty of true Englishmen, and good liege men, except they did deliver the king from such wicked ones that would destroy both him and the country. Their aim was at archbishop Moreton, and sir Reginald Bray, who were the king's skreens in this envy.

After that these two, Flammock and the blacksmith, had by joint and several pratings found tokens of consent in the multitude, they offer'd themselves to lead them, until they should hear of better men to be their leaders; which they said would be e'er long: telling them further, that they would be but their servants, and first in every danger; but doubted not but to make both the west end and the east end of England to meet in so good a quarrel; and that all (rightly understood) was but for the king's service. The people, upon these seditious instigations, did arm (most of them with bows and arrows, and bills, and such other weapons of rude and country people), and forthwith under the command of their leaders (which in such cases is ever at pleasure), march'd out of Cornwall, thro' Devonshire, and Taunton in Somersetshire, without any slaughter, violence, or spoil of the country. At Taunton they killed, in fury, an officious and eager commissioner for the subsidy, whom they called the provost of Perin. Thence they marched to Wells; where the lord Audley (with whom their leaders had, before, some secret intelligence), a nobleman of an ancient family, but unquiet and popular, and aspiring to ruin, came in to them, and was by them (with great gladness and cries of joy) accepted as their general; they being now proud, that they were led by a nobleman. The lord Audley led them on from Wells to Salisbury, and from Salisbury to Winchester. Thence the foolish people, who (in effect) led their leaders, had a mind to be led into Kent; fancying, that the people there would joyn with them, contrary to all reason or judgment; considering the Kentish men had shewed great loyalty and affection to the king so lately before. But the rude people had heard Flammock say, that Kent was never conquer'd, and that they were the freest people of England. And upon these vain noises, they look'd for great matters at their hands, in a cause which they conceited to be for the liberty of the subject. But when they were come into Kent, the country was so well settled, both by the king's late kind usage towards them, and by the credit and power of the earl of Kent, the lord Abergavenny, and the lord Cobham, as neither gentleman nor yeoman came in to their aid; which did much damp and dismay many of the simpler sort : insomuch as divers of them did secretly fly from the army, and went home. But the sturdier sort, and those that were most engaged, stood by it, and rather waxed proud, than fail'd in hopes and courage. For as it did somewhat appall them, that the people came not in to them; so it did no less encourage them, that the king's forces had not set upon them, having march'd from the west unto the east of England. Wherefore they kept on their way, and encamp'd upon Blackheath, between Greenwich and Eltham; threatning either to bid battle to the king (for now the seas went higher than to Moreton and Braie), or to take London within his view; imagining within themselves, there to find no less fear than wealth.

But to return to the king. When first he heard of this commotion of the Cornishmen, occasioned by the subsidy, he was much troubled therewith : not for itself, but in regard of the concurrence of other dangers, that did hang over him at that time. For he doubted lest a war from Scotland, a rebellion from Cornwall, and the practices and conspiracies of Perkin and his partakers, would come upon him at once ; knowing well, that it was a dangerous triplicity to a monarchy, to have the arms of a foreigner, the discontents of subjects, and the title of a pretender, to meet. Nevertheless, the occasion took him in some part well provided. For as soon as the parliament had broken up, the king had presently raised a puissant army, to war upon Scotland. And king James of Scotland likewise, on his part, had made great preparations either for defence, or for new assailing of England. But as for the king's forces, they were not only in preparation, but in readiness presently to set forth, under the conduct of Dawbeney, the lord chamberlain. But as soon as the king understood of the rebellion of Cornwall, he stayed those forces, retaining them for his own service and safety. But therewithal he dispatch'd the earl of Surrey into the north, for the defence and strength of those parts, in case the Scots should stir. But for the course he held towards the rebels, it was utterly differing from his former custom and practice ; which was ever full of forwardness and celerity, to make head against them, or to set upon them as soon as ever they were in action. This he was wont to do. But now, besides that he was attemper'd by years, and less in love with dangers, by the continued fruition of a crown, it was a time when the various appearance to his thoughts of perils of several natures, and from divers parts, did make him judge it his best and surest way to keep his strength together, in the seat and centre of his kingdom ; according to the ancient Indian emblem, in such a swelling season, to hold the hand upon the middle of the bladder, that no side might rise. Besides, there was no necessity put upon him, to alter this counsel. For neither did the rebels spoil the country ; in which case it had been dishonour to abandon his people : neither on the other side, did their forces gather or increase, which might hasten him to precipitate and assail them, before they grew too strong. And lastly, both reason of estate and war seem'd to agree with this course : for that insurrections of base people are commonly more furious in their beginnings. And by this means also he had them the more at vantage, being tired and harrassed with a long march ; and more at mercy, being cut off far from their country, and therefore not able by any sudden flight to get to retreat, and to renew the troubles.

When therefore the rebels were encamped on Blackheath, upon the hill, whence they might behold the city of London, and the fair valley about it ; the king knowing well, that it stood him upon, by how much the more he had hitherto protracted the time in not encountring them, by so much the sooner to dispatch with them, that it might appear to have been no coldness in foreslowing, but wisdom in chusing his time, resolved with all speed to assail them, and yet with that providence and surety, as should leave little to venture or fortune. And having very great and puissant forces about him, the better to master all events and accidents, he divided them into three parts. The first was led by the earl of Oxford in chief, assisted by the earls of Essex and Suffolk. These noblemen were appointed, with some cornets of horse, and bands of foot, and good store of artillery wheeling about, to put themselves beyond the hill, where the rebels were encamped; and to beset all the skirts and descents thereof, except those that lay towards London; whereby to have these wild beasts (as it were) in a toil. The second part of his forces (which were those that were to be most in action, and upon which he relied most for the fortune of the day) he did assign to be led by the lord chamberlain, who was appointed to set upon the rebels in front, from that side which is toward London. The third part of his forces (being likewise great and brave forces) he retained about himself, to be ready upon all events, to restore the fight, or consummate the victory: and meanwhile to secure the city. And for that purpose he encamped in person in St. George's fields, putting himself between the city and the rebels. But the city of London (especially at the first) upon the near encamping of the rebels, was in great tumult: as it useth to be with wealthy and populous cities (especially those, which, for greatness and fortune, are queens of their regions) who seldom see out of their windows, or from their towers, an army of enemies. But that which troubled them most, was the conceit, that they dealt with a rout of people with whom there was no composition or condition, or orderly treating, if need were; but likely to be bent altogether upon rapin and spoil. And although they had heard, that the rebels had behaved themselves quietly and modestly, by the way as they went, yet they doubted much that would not last, but rather made them more hungry, and more in appetite, to fall upon spoil in the end. Wherefore there was great running to and fro of people, some to the gates, some to the walls, some to the water side; giving themselves alarms and panic fears continually. Nevertheless, both Tate the lord mayor, and Shaw and Haddon the sheriffs, did their parts stoutly and well, in arming and ordering the people. And the king likewise did adjoin some captains of experience in the wars, to advise and assist the citizens. But soon after, when they understood that the king had so ordered the matter, that the rebels must win three battles, before they could approach the city, and that he had put his own person between the rebels and them, and that the great care was rather how to impound the rebels, that none of them might escape, than that any doubt was made to vanquish them; they grew to be quiet and out of fear. The rather, for the confidence they reposed (which was not small) in the three leaders Oxford, Essex, and Dawbeny, all men famed and loved amongst the people. As for Jasper duke of Bedford, whom the king used to employ with the first in his wars, he was then sick, and died soon after.

It was the two and twentieth of June, and a Saturday (which was the day of the week the king fancied) when the battle was fought; though the king had, by all the art he could devise, given out a false day, as if he prepared to give the rebels battle on the Monday following, the better to find them unprovided, and in disarray. The lords that were appointed to circle the hill, had some days before planted themselves (as at the receipt) in places convenient. In the afternoon, towards the decline of the day, (which was done the better to keep the rebels in opinion that they should not fight that day) the lord Dawbeny marched on towards them, and first beat some troops of them from Deptford-bridge, where they fought manfully; but being in no great number were soon driven back, and fled up to their main army upon the hill. The army at that time hearing of the approach of the king's forces, were putting themselves in array, not without much confusion. But neither had they placed upon the first high ground towards the bridge any forces to second the troops below, that kept the bridge; neither had they brought forwards their main battle (which stood in array far into the heath) near to the assent of the hill. So that the earl with his forces mounted the hill, and recovered the plain without resistance. The lord Dawbeny charged them with great fury; insomuch, as it had like (by accident) to have brandled the fortune of the day. For, by inconsistent forwardness in fighting in the head of his troops, he was taken by the rebels, but immediately rescued and delivered. The rebels maintained the fight for a small time, and for their persons shewed no want of courage; but being ill armed, and ill led, and without horse and artillery, they were with no great difficulty cut in pieces, and put to flight. And for their three leaders, the lord Audley, the Blacksmith and Flammock, (as commonly the captains of commotions are but half-couraged men) suffered themselves to be taken alive. The number slain on the rebels part were some two thousand men; their army amounting (as it is said) unto the number of sixteen thousand. The rest were (in effect) all taken; for that the hill, as was said, was encompassed with the king's forces round about. On the king's part there died about three hundred; most of them shot with arrows which were reported to be about the length of a taylor's yard: so strong and mighty a bow the Cornish men were said to draw.

The victory thus obtained, the king created divers bannerets, as well upon Blackheath, where his lieutenant had won the field, (whither he rode in person to perform the said creation) as in St. George's fields, where his own person had been encamped. And for matter of liberality, he did (by open edict) give the goods of all the prisoners unto those that had taken them; either to take them in kind, or compound for them as they could. After matter of honour and liberality, followed matter of severity and execution. The lord Audley was led from Newgate to Tower-Hill, in a paper coat painted with his own arms; the arms reversed, and the coat torn, and he at Tower-Hill beheaded. Flammock and the blacksmith were hanged, drawn, and quartered at Tyburn; the blacksmith taking pleasure upon the hurdle (as it seemeth by words that he uttered) to think that he should be famous in after-times. The king was once in mind to have sent down Flammock and the blacksmith to have been executed in Cornwall, for the more terror; but being advertised, that the country was yet unquiet and boiling, he thought better not to irritate the people further. All the rest were pardoned by proclamation, and to take out their pardons under seal, as many as would. So that, more than the blood drawn in the field, the king did satisfy himself with the lives of only three offenders, for the expiation of this great rebellion.

It was a strange thing, to observe the variety and inequality of the king's executions and pardons. And a man would think it, at the first, a kind of lottery or chance. But, looking into it more nearly, one shall find there was reason for it: much more perhaps, than (after so long a distance of time) we can now discern. In the Kentish commotion (which was but a handful of men) there were executed to the number of one hundred and fifty; and, in this so mighty a rebellion, but three; whether it were, that the king put to accompt the men that were slain in the field: or that he was not willing to be severe in a popular cause; or that the harmless behaviour of this people (that came from the west of England, to the east, without mischief almost, or spoil of the country) did somewhat mollify him, and move him to compassion; or lastly, that he made a great difference between people, that did rebel upon wantonness, and them that did rebel upon want.

After the Cornish men were defeated, there came from Calice to the king, an honourable ambassage from the French king, which had arrived at Calice a month before, and there was stayed in respect of the troubles; but honourably entertained and defrayed.

The king, at their first coming, sent unto them, and prayed them to have patience, till a little smoak, that was raised in his country, were over; which would soon be: slighting (as his manner was) that openly, which nevertheless he intended seriously.

This ambassage concerned no great affair; but only the prolongation of days for payment of monies, and some other particulars of the frontiers. And it was (indeed) but a wooing ambassage; with good respects to entertain the king in good affection: but nothing was done or handled, to the derogation of the king's late treaty with the Italian princes.

But, during that time that the Cornish men were in their march towards London, the king of Scotland (well advertised of all that passed, and knowing himself sure of war from England, whensoever those stirs were appeased) neglected not his opportunity; but thinking the king had his hands full, enterd the frontiers of England again with an army, and besieged the castle of Norham in person, with part of his forces, sending the rest to forrage the country. But Fox, bishop of Duresme (a wise man, and one that could see through the present, to the future) doubting as much before, had caused his castle of Norham to be strongly fortified and furnished, with all kind of munition: and had mann'd it likewise with a very great number of tall soldiers, more than for the proportion of the castle; reckoning rather upon a sharp assault, than a long siege. And for the country likewise, he had caused the people to withdraw their cattle and goods into fast places, that were not of easie approach; and sent in post to the earl of Surrey (who was not far off in Yorkshire) to come in diligence to the succour. So as the Scottish king both failed of doing good upon the castle, and his men had but a catching harvest of their spoils. And when he understood that the earl of Surrey was coming on with great forces, he returned back into Scotland. The earl finding the castle freed, and the enemies retired, pursued with all celerity into Scotland; hoping to have overtaken the Scottish king, and to have given him battle; but not attaining him in time, sat down before the castle of Aton (one of the strongest places then esteemed, between Berwick and Edenburgh) which in a small time he took. And soon after, the Scottish king retiring further into his country, and the weather being extraordinary foul and stormy, the earl of Surrey returned into England. So that the expeditions on both parts were (in effect) but a castle taken, and a castle distressed; not answerable to the puissance of the forces, nor to the heat of the quarrel, nor to the greatness of the expectation.

Amongst these troubles both civil and external, came into England from Spain Peter Hialas, some call him Elias (surely he was the forerunner of the good hap, that we enjoy at this day. For, his ambassage set the truce between England and Scotland; the truce drew on the peace; the peace the marriage; and the marriage the union of the kingdoms) a man of great wisdom, and (as those times were) not unlearned; sent from Ferdinando and Isabella kings of Spain unto the king, to treat a marriage between Katherine their second daughter, and prince Arthur. This treaty was by him set in a very good way, and almost brought to perfection. But it so fell out by the way, that upon some conference which he had with the king touching this business, the king (who had a great dexterity in getting suddenly into the bosom of ambassadors of foreign princes, if he liked them; insomuch as he would many times communicate with them of his own affairs, yea and employ them in his service) fell into speech and discourse incidently, concerning the ending of the debates and differences with Scotland. For the king naturally did not love the barren wars with Scotland, though he made his profit of the noise of them. And he wanted not in the council of Scotland, those that would advise their king to meet him at the half way, and to give over the war with England; pretending to be good patriots, but indeed favouring the affairs of the king. Only his heart was too great to begin with Scotland for the motion of peace. On the other side, he had met with an ally of Ferdinando of Arragon, as fit for his turn as could be. For after that king Ferdinando had, upon assured confidence of the marriage to succeed, taken upon him the person of a fraternal allie to the king, he would not let (in a Spanish gravity) to counsel the king in his own affairs. And the king on his part not being wanting to himself, but making use of every man's humours, made his advantage of this in such things as he thought either not decent, or not pleasant to proceed from himself; putting them off as done by the council of Ferdinando. Wherefore he was content that Hialas (as in a matter moved and advised from Hialas himself) should go into Scotland, to treat of a concord between the two kings. Hialas took it upon him : and coming to the Scottish king, after he had with much art brought king James to hearken to the more safe and quiet counsels, wrote unto the king, that he hoped that peace would with no great difficulty cement and close, if he would send some wise and temperate counsellor of his own, that might treat of the conditions. Whereupon the king directed bishop Fox (who at that time was at his castle of Norham) to confer with Hialas, and they both to treat with some commissioners deputed from the Scottish king. The commissioners on both sides met. But after much dispute upon the articles and conditions of peace, propounded upon either part, they could not conclude a peace. The chief impediment thereof was the demand of the king to have Perkin deliver'd into his hands, as a reproach to all kings, and a person not protected by the law of nations. The king of Scotland on the other side peremptorily denied so to do; saying, that he (for his part) was no competent judge of Perkin's title; but that he had received him as a suppliant, protected him as a person fled for refuge, espoused him with his kinswoman, and aided him with his arms, upon the belief that he was a prince; and therefore that he could not now with his honour so unrip and (in a sort) put a lye upon all that he had said and done before, as to deliver him up to his enemies. The bishop likewise (who had certain proud instructions from the king, at the least in the front, tho' there were a pliant cause at the foot, that remitted all to the bishop's discretion, and requir'd him by no means to break off in ill terms) after that he had failed to obtain the delivery of Perkin, did move a second point of his instructions: which was, that the Scottish king would give the king an enterview in person at Newcastle. But this being reported to the Scottish king, his answer was, 'That he meant to treat a peace, and not to go a begging for it.' The bishop also (according to another article of his instructions) demanded restitution of the spoils taken by the Scottish, or damages for the same. But the Scottish commissioners answered, 'That it was but as water spilt upon the ground, which could not be gotten up again; and that the king's people were better able to bear the loss, than their master able to repair it.' But in the end (as persons capable of reason) on both sides they made rather a kind of recess, than a breach of treaty, and concluded upon a truce for some months following. But the king of Scotland, tho' he would not formally retract his judgment of Perkin, wherein he had engaged himself so far; yet in his private opinion, upon often speech with the Englishmen, and divers other advertisements, began to suspect him for a counterfeit. Wherefore in a noble fashion he call'd him unto him, and recounted the benefits and favours that he had done him, in making him his ally, and in provoking a mighty and opulent king by an offensive war in his quarrel, for the space of two years together. Nay more, that he had refused an honourable peace, whereof he had a fair offer, if he would have deliver'd him; and that to keep his promise with him, he had deeply offended both his nobles and people, whom he might not hold in any long discontent. And therefore requir'd him to think of his own fortunes, and to choose out some fitter place for his exile: telling him withal, that he could not say, but the English had forsaken him before the Scottish; for that upon two several trials, none had declar'd themselves on his side. But nevertheless he would make good what he said to him at his first receiving; which was, 'That he should not repent him, for putting himself into his hands;' for that he would not cast him him off, but help him with shipping and means to transport him where he should desire. Perkin, not descending at all from his stage-like greatness, answered the king in few words, 'That he saw his time was not yet come; but whatsoever his fortunes were, he should both think and speak honour of the king.' Taking his leave, he would not think on Flanders, doubting it was but hollow ground for him, since the treaty of the arch-duke concluded the year before; but took his lady, and such followers as would not leave him, and sail'd over into Ireland.

This twelfth year of the king, a little before this time, pope Alexander (who loved best those princes that were furthest off, and with whom he had least to do) taking very thankfully the king's late entrance into league for the defence of Italy, did remunerate him with an hallow'd sword, and cap of maintenance sent by his nuncio. Pope Innocent had done the like, but it was not received in that glory.

For the king appointed the mayor and his brethren to meet the pope's orator at London-Bridge, and all the streets between the bridge-foot and the palace of Paul's (where the king then lay) were garnish'd with the citizens, standing in their liveries. And the morrow after (being All-Hallow's day) the king, attended with many of his prelates, nobles, and principal courtiers, went in procession to Paul's, and the cap and sword were born before him. And after the procession, the king himself remaining seated in the quire, the lord archbishop upon the Greece of the quire, made a long oration, setting forth the greatness and eminency of that honour, which the pope (in these ornaments and ensigns of benediction) had done the king; and how rarely, and upon what high deserts they used to be bestowed. And then recited the king's principal acts and merits, which had made him appear worthy in the eyes of his holiness the pope of this great honour.

All this while the rebellion of Cornwall (whereof we have spoken) seem'd to have no relation to Perkin; save that perhaps Perkin's proclamation had stricken upon the right vein, in promising to lay down exactions and payments, and so had made them now and then have a kind thought on Perkin. But now these bubbles by much stirring began to meet, as they use to do upon the top of water. The king's lenity (by that time the Cornish rebels, who were taken and pardon'd, and (as it was said) many of them sold by them that had taken them, for twelve-pence and two shillings apiece, were come down into their country) had rather imbolden'd them, than reclaim'd them. Insomuch, as they stuck not to say to their neighbours and countrymen, ' That the king did well to pardon them, for that he knew he should leave few subjects in England, if he hang'd all that were of their mind:' and began whetting and inciting one another to renew the commotion. Some of the subtillest of them, hearing of Perkin's being in Ireland,[1] found means to send to him to let him know, that if he would come over to them, they would serve him.

When Perkin heard this news, he began to take heart again, and advis'd upon it with his council which were principally three; Horne a mercer, that fled for debt; Skelton a taylor, and Astley a scriviner; for secretary Frion was gone. These told him that he was mightily overseen, both when he went into Kent, and when he went into Scotland; the one being a place so near London, and under the king's nose; and the other, a nation so distasted with the people of England, that if they had lov'd him never so well, yet they would never have

[1] He arriv'd at Cork the 26th of July; where some out of affection, others for desire of change flock'd to him; among whom, 'tis said, was Maurice earl of Desmond. The mayor and citizens of Waterford notify'd his arrival to the king, and as they had bravely defended themselves against Simnel's adherents, so they did the same now against Perkin; for which they were taken into the king's especial favour.—Sir J. W., Cap. XIII.

taken his part in that company. But if he had been so happy as to have been in Cornwall at the first when the people began to take arms there, he had been crown'd at Westminster before this time. For, these kings (as he had now experience) would sell poor princes for shoes: but he must rely wholly upon people; and therefore advised him to sail over with all possible speed into Cornwall. Which accordingly he did; having in his company four small barks, with some sixscore or sevenscore fighting men.[1] He arrived in September at Whitsand-bay, and forthwith came to Bodmin, the blacksmith's town: where there assembled unto him to the number of three thousand men of the rude people. There he set forth a new proclamation, stroaking the people with fair promises, and humouring them with invectives against the king and his government. And, as it fareth with smoke, that never loseth itself till it be at the highest; he did now before his end raise his stile, intituling himself no more Richard duke of York, but Richard the IVth, king of England. His council advised him by all means, to make himself master of some good walled town; as well to make his men find the sweetness of rich spoils, and to allure to him all loose and lost people, by like hopes of booty; as to be a sure retreat to his forces, in case they should have any ill day, or unlucky chance in the field. Wherefore they took heart to them, and went on, and besieged the city of Exeter, which was the principal town for strength and wealth in those parts.

When they were come before Exeter, they forbare to use any force at the first; but made continual shouts and outcries, to terrifie the inhabitants. They did likewise in divers places call and talk to them from under the walls, to joyn with them, and be of their party; telling them, that the king would make them another London, if they would be the first town that should acknowledge him. But they had not the wit to send to them, in any orderly fashion, agents or chosen men to tempt them, and to treat with them. The citizens on their part shew'd themselves stout and loyal subjects. Neither was there so much as any tumult or division amongst them: but all prepar'd themselves for a valiant defence, and making good the town. For well they saw that the rebels were of no such number or power, that they needed to fear them as yet: and well they hoped, that before their numbers increased, the king's succours would come in. And, howsoever, they thought it the extremest of evils, to put themselves at the mercy of those hungry and disorderly people. Wherefore setting all things in good order within the town, they nevertheless let down with cords, from several parts of the walls privily, several messengers (that, if one came to mischance, another might pass on) which should advertise the king of the state of the town, and implore

[1] His wife came also with him.

his aid. Perkin also doubted that succours would come ere long ; and therefore resolved to use his utmost force to assault the town ; and for that purpose, having mounted scaling-ladders in divers places upon the walls, made at the same instant an attempt to force one of the gates : but having no artillery nor engines, and finding that he could do no good by ramming with logs of timber, nor by the use of iron bars and iron crows, and such other means at hand, he had no way left him but to set one of the gates on fire : which he did. But the citizens, well perceiving the danger, before the gate could be fully consumed, block'd up the gate, and some space about it on the inside with faggots and other fuel : which they likewise set on fire, and so repuls'd fire with fire : and in the meantime, raised up rampiers of earth, and cast up deep trenches, to serve instead of wall and gate. And for the escalades, they had so bad success, as the rebels were driven from the walls, with the loss of two hundred men.

The king when he heard of Perkin's siege of Exeter, made sport with it, and said to them that were about him, ' That the king of Rake-hells was landed in the west, and that he hoped now to have the honour to see him, which he could never yet do.' And it appear'd plainly to those that were about the king, that he was indeed much joy'd with the news of Perkin's being in English ground, where he could have no retreat by land ; thinking now that he should be cured of those privy stitches which he had long had about his heart, and had sometimes broken his sleeps in the midst of all his felicity. And to set all men's hearts on fire, he did by all possible means let it appear, that those, who should now do him service to make an end of these troubles, should be no less accepted of him, than he that came upon the eleventh hour and had the whole wages of the day. Therefore now (like the end of a play) a great number came upon the stage at once. He sent the lord chamberlain and the lord Brook, and sir Rice ap Thomas, with expedite forces to speed to Exeter, to the rescue of the town, and to spread the fame of his own following in person with a royal army. The earl of Devonshire and his son, with the Caroes, and the Fulfordes, and other principal persons of Devonshire (uncall'd from the court, but hearing that the king's heart was so much bent upon this service) made hast with troops, that they had raised, to be the first that should succour the city of Exeter, and prevent the king's succours. The duke of Buckingham likewise, with many brave gentlemen, put themselves in arms, not staying either the king's or the lord chamberlain's coming on, but making a body of forces of themselves, the more to endear their merit ; signifying to the king their readiness, and desiring to know his pleasure, So that according to the proverb, ' In the coming down every saint did help.'

Perkin hearing this thunder of arms and preparations against him from so many parts, raised his seige, and marched to Taunton; beginning already to squint one eye upon the crown, and another upon the sanctuary: tho' the Cornishmen were become, like metal often fir'd and quench'd, churlish, and that would sooner break than bow; swearing and vowing not to leave him, till the uttermost drop of their blood were spilt. He was at his rising from Exeter between six and seven thousand strong, many having come unto him after he was set before Exeter, upon fame of so great an enterprise, and to partake of the spoil; tho' upon the raising of his siege, some did slip away. When he was come near Taunton, he dissembled all fear, and seemed all the day to use diligence in preparing all things ready to fight. But about midnight, he fled with threescore horse to Bewley in the new-forest, where he and divers of his company registered themselves sanctuary-men, leaving his Cornish men to the four winds: but yet thereby easing them of their vow, and using his wonted compassion, 'Not to be by when his subjects' blood should be spilt.' The king, as soon as he heard of Perkin's flight, sent presently five hundred horse to pursue and apprehend him, before he should get either to the sea, or to that same little island, call'd a sanctuary. But they came too late for the latter of these. Therefore all they could do, was to beset the sanctuary, and to maintain a strong watch about it, till the king's pleasure were further known. As for the rest of the rebels, they (being destituted of their head) without stroke stricken, submitted themselves unto the king's mercy. And the king, who commonly drew blood (as physicians do) rather to save life than to spill it, and was never cruel when he was secure; now he saw the danger was past, pardon'd them all in the end, except some few desperate persons which he reserv'd to be executed, the better to set off his mercy towards the rest. There were also sent with all speed some horse to St. Michael's Mount in Cornwall, where the lady Katharine Gordon was left by her husband, whom in all fortunes she entirely loved; adding the vertues of a wife to the vertues of her sex. The king sent in the greater diligence, not knowing whether she might be with child; whereby the business would not have ended in Perkin's person. When she was brought to the king, it was commonly said, that the king receiv'd her not only with compassion, but with affection; pity giving more expression to her excellent beauty. Wherefore comforting her (to serve as well his eye as his fame) he sent her to his queen to remain with her; giving her very honourable allowance for the support of her estate: which she enjoy'd both during the king's life and many years after. The name of the white-rose (which had been given to her husband's false title) was continued in common speech to her true beauty.

The king went forwards on his journey, and made a joyful entrance into Exeter, where he gave the citizens great commendations and thanks; and taking the sword he wore from his side, he gave it to the mayor, and commanded it should be ever after carried before him. There also he caused to be executed some of the ringleaders of the Cornish-men, in sacrifice to the citizens, whom they had put in fear, and trouble. At Exeter the king consulted with his council, whether he should offer life to Perkin if he would quit the sanctuary, and voluntarily submit himself. The council were divided in opinion. Some advised the king to take him out of the sanctuary perforce, and to put him to death, as in a case of necessity, which in it self dispenseth with consecrated places and things. Wherein they doubted not also, but the king should find the pope tractable to ratify his deed, either by declaration, or (at least) by indulgence. Others were of opinion (since all was now safe, and no further hurt could be done) that it was not worth the exposing of the king to new scandal and envy. A third sort fell upon the opinion that it was not possible for the king ever, either to satisfie the world well touching the imposture, or to learn out the bottom of the conspiracy, except by promise of life and pardon, and other fair means, he should get Perkin into his hands. But they did all in their preambles much bemoan the king's case, with a kind of indignation at his fortune. That a prince of his high wisdom and vertue should have been so long and so oft exercis'd and vex'd with idols. But the king said, that it was the vexation of God Almighty himself, to be vex'd with idols, and therefore that that was not to trouble any of his friends. And that for himself, he always despised them; but was griev'd that they had put his people to such trouble and misery. But (in conclusion) he lean'd to the third opinion, and so sent some to deal with Perkin. Who seeing himself prisoner, and destitute of all hopes, having try'd princes and people, great and small, and found all either false, faint, or unfortunate, did gladly accept of the condition. The king did also (while he was at Exeter) appoint the lord Darcy and others, commissioners, for the fining all such as were of any value, and had any hand or partaking in the aid or the comfort of Perkin or the Cornish-men, either in the field or in the flight.

These commissioners proceeded with such strictness and severity, as did much obscure the king's mercy in sparing of blood, with the bleeding of so much treasure. Perkin was brought unto the king's court, but not to the king's presence; tho' the king (to satisfie his curiosity) saw him sometimes out of a window, or in passage. He was in shew at liberty, but guarded with all care and watch that was possible, and willed to follow the king to London. But from his first appearance upon the stage, in his new person of a sycophant or juggler, instead of his former person as a prince, all men may think how he was exposed to the derision, not only of the courtiers, but also of the common people, who flock'd about him as he went along; that one might know afar off where the owl was by the flight of birds. Some mocking, some wondring, some cursing, some prying and picking matter out of his countenance and gesture to talk of. So that the false honour and respects which he had so long enjoy'd, was plentifully repay'd in scorn and contempt. As soon as he was come to London, the king gave also the city the solace of this May game. For he was conveigh'd leisurely on horseback (but not in any ignominious fashion) through Cheapside and Cornhill to the Tower; and from thence back again unto Westminster, with the charm of a thousand taunts and reproaches. But to amend the show, there followed a little distance of Perkin, an inward councellor of his, one that had been serjeant-farrier to the king. This fellow, when Perkin took sanctuary, chose rather to take an holy habit than a holy place, and clad himself like a hermit, and in that weed wander'd about the country till he was discover'd and taken. But this man was bound hand and foot upon the horse, and came not back with Perkin, but was left at the Tower, and within few days after executed. Soon after, now that Perkin, could tell better what himself was, he was diligently examined; and after his confession taken, an extract was made of such parts of them, as were thought fit to be divulged, which was printed and dispers'd abroad. Wherein the king did himself no right. For as there was a laboured tale of particulars, of Perkin's father, and mother, and grandsire, and grandmother, and uncles, and cousins, by names and sirnames, and from what places he travell'd up and down; so there was little or nothing to purpose of anything concerning his designs, or any practices that had been held with him; nor the duchess of Burgundy her self (that all the world did take knowledge of, as the person that had put life and being into the whole business) so much as nam'd or pointed at. So that men missing of that they look'd for, look'd about for they knew not what, and were in more doubt than before. But the king chose rather not to satisfie, than to kindle coals. At that time also it did not appear by any new examinations or commitments, that any other person of quality was discover'd or appeach'd, tho' the king's closeness made that a doubt-dormant.

About this time, a great fire in the night-time suddenly began at the king's palace of Shyne, near unto the king's own lodgings, whereby a great part of the building was consumed, with much costly household stuff; which gave the king occasion of building from the ground that fine pile of Richmond, which is now standing.

Somewhat before this time also there fell out a memorable accident: there was one Sebastian Gabato, a Venetian, dwelling in Bristow, a man seen and expert in cosmography and navigation. This man seeing the success, and emulating perhaps the enterprize of Christopherus Columbus in that fortunate discovery towards the southwest, which had been by him made some six years before; conceited with himself, that lands might likewise be discover'd towards the northwest. And surely it may be he had more firm and pregnant conjectures of it, than Columbus had of this at the first. For the two great islands of the old and new world, being (in the shape and making of them) broad towards the north, and pointed towards the south; it is likely, that the discovery first began where the lands did nearest meet. And there had been before that time a discovery of some lands, which they took to be islands, and were indeed the continent of America towards the northwest. And it may be, that some relation of this nature coming afterwards to the knowledge of Columbus, and by him suppress'd, (desirous rather to make his enterprize the child of his science and fortune, than the follower of a former discovery) did give him better assurance, that all was not sea, from the west of Europe and Africk unto Asia, than either Seneca's prophecy, or Plato's antiquities, or the nature of the tides, and land-winds, and the like, which were the conjectures that were given out, whereupon he should have rely'd. Tho' I am not ignorant that it was likewise laid unto the casual and wind beaten discovery (a little before) of a Spanish pilot, who died in the house of Columbus. But this Gabato bearing the king in hand, that he would find out an island endued with rich commodities, procur'd him to man and victual a ship at Bristol, for the discovery of that island; with whom ventur'd also three small ships of London merchants, fraught with some gross and slight wares fit for commerce with barbarous people. He sail'd (as he affirm'd at his return, and made a card thereof) very far westwards, with a quarter of the north, on the north-side of Terra de Labrador, until he came to the latitude of sixty-seven degrees and a half, finding the seas still open. It is certain also, that the king's fortune had a tender of that great empire of the West Indies. Neither was it a refusal on the king's part, but a delay by accident, that put by so great an acquest. For Christóphorus Columbus refused by the king of Portugal (who would not embrace at once both east and west) imploy'd his brother Bartholomeus Columbus unto king Henry, to negotiate for his discovery. And it so fortun'd, that he was taken by pirates at sea; by which accidental impediment he was long ere he came to the king. So long, that before he had obtain'd a capitulation with the king for his brother; the enterprize by him was achieved, and so the West Indies by providence were then reserv'd for the crown of Castilia. Yet this sharpen'd the king so, that not only in this voyage, but again in the 16th year of his reign, and likewise in the 18th thereof, he granted forth new commissions, for the discovery and investing of unknown lands.

In this fourteenth year also (by God's wonderful providence, that boweth things unto his will, and hangeth great weights upon small wyers) there fell out a trifling and untoward accident, that drew on great and happy effects. During the truce with Scotland, there were certain Scottish young gentlemen that came into Norham town, and there made merry with some of the English of the town. And having little to do, went sometimes forth, and would stand looking upon the castle. Some of the garrison of the castle, observing their doing twice or thrice, and having not their minds purg'd of the late ill blood of hostility, either suspected them, or quarrelled them for spies. Whereupon they fell at ill words, and from words to blows; so that many were wounded of either side, and the Scottish-men (being strangers in the town) had the worst. In so much as some of them were slain, and the rest made haste home. The matter being complained on, and often debated before the wardens of the marches of both sides, and no good order taken, the king of Scotland took it to himself, and being much kindled, sent a herald to the king to make protestation, that if reparation were not done, according to the conditions of the truce, his king did denounce war. The king (who had often try'd fortune, and was inclin'd to peace) made answer, 'That what had been done, was utterly against his will, and without his privity. But if the garrison soldiers had been in fault, he would see them punish'd, and the truce in all points to be preserv'd.' But this answer seem'd to the Scottish king but a delay to make the complaint breath out with time; and therefore it did rather exasperate him, than satisfie him. Bishop Fox, understanding from the king, that the Scottish king was still discontent and impatient, being troubled that the occasion of breaking of the truce should grow from his men, sent many humble and deprecatory letters to the Scottish king to appease him. Whereupon king James, mollify'd by the bishop's submiss and eloquent letters, wrote back unto him, 'That tho' he were in part moved by his letters, yet he should not be fully satisfied, except he spake with him, as well about the compounding of the present differences as about other matters, that might concern the good of both kingdoms.' The bishop advising first with the king, took his journey for Scotland. The meeting was at Melrosse, an abbey of the Cestercians, where the king then abode. The king first roundly utter'd unto the bishop his offence conceiv'd for the insolent breach of truce, by his men of Norham castle. Whereunto Bishop Fox made such an humble and smooth answer, as it was like oil into the wound, whereby it began to heal. And this was done in the presence of the king and his council. After the king spake with the bishop apart, and opened himself unto him, saying, 'That these temporary truces and peaces were soon made and soon broken: but that he desir'd a straiter amity with the king of England,' discovering his mind; that if the king would give him in marriage the lady Margaret, his eldest daughter, that indeed might be a knot indissoluble. That he knew well what place and authority the bishop deservedly had with his master. Therefore if he would take the business to heart, and deal in it effectually, he doubted not but it would succeed well. The bishop answered soberly, 'That he thought himself rather happy, than worthy, to be an instrument in such a matter; but would do his best endeavour.' Wherefore the bishop returning to the king, and giving account what had passed, and finding the king more than well-disposed in it, gave the king advice; first to proceed to a conclusion of peace, and then to go on with the treaty of marriage, by degrees. Hereupon a peace was concluded, which was published a little before Christmas, in the fourteenth year of the king's reign, to continue for both the king's lives, and the outliver of them, and a year after. In this peace there was an article contained, that no English man should enter into Scotland, and no Scottish man into England, without letters commendatory from the kings of either nation. This at the first sight might seem a means to continue a strangeness between the nations; but it was done, to lock in the borderers.

This year there was also born to the king a third son, who was christened by the name of Edmund, and shortly after dyed. And much about the same time came news of the death of Charles the French king; for whom were celebrated solemn and princely obsequies.

It was not long, but Perkin (who was made of quick-silver, which is hard to hold or imprison) began to stir. For deceiving his keepers, he took him to his heels, and made speed to the sea coasts. But presently all corners were laid for him, and such diligent pursuit and search made, as he was fain to turn back, and get him to the house of Bethleem, called the priory of Shyne (which had the privilege of sanctuary), and put himself into the hands of the prior of that monastery. The prior was thought an holy man, and much reverenced in those days. He came to the king, and besought the king for Perkin's life only; leaving him otherwise to the king's discretion. Many about the king were again more hot than ever, to have the king to take him forth, and hang him. But the king (that had an high stomach, and could not hate any that he despised) bid, 'Take him forth, and set the knave in the stocks.' And so promising the prior his life, he caused him to be brought forth. And within two or three days after, upon a scaffold, set up in the palace court at Westminster, he was fettered and set in the stocks, for the whole day. And the next day after, the like was done by him at the cross in Cheapside, and in both places he read his confession, of which we made mention before; and was from Cheapside, conveyed and laid up in the Tower. Notwithstanding all this, the king was (as was partly touch'd before) grown to be such a partner with fortune, as nobody could tell what actions the one, and what the other owned. For it was believed generally, that Perkin was betrayed, and that this escape was not without the king's privity, who had him all the time of his flight in a line; and that the king did this to pick a quarrel with him to put him to death, and to be rid of him at once. But this is not probable. For that the same instruments who observed him in his flight, might have kept him from getting into sanctuary.

But it was ordained, that this winding ivy of a Plantagenet, should kill the true tree itself. For Perkin, after he had been a while in the Tower, began to insinuate himself into the favour and kindness of his keepers, servants to the lieutenant of the tower, sir John Digby, being four in number; Strangways, Blewet, Astwood, and Long-Roger. These varlets, with mountains of promises, he sought to corrupt, to obtain his escape. But knowing well, that his own fortunes were made so contemptible, as he could feed no man's hopes (and by hopes he must work, for rewards he had none), he had contrived with himself a vast and tragical plot; which was, to draw into his company Edward Plantagenet earl of Warwick, then prisoner in the Tower; whom the weary life of a long imprisonment, and the often and renewing fears of being put to death, had softened to take any impression of counsel for his liberty. This young prince he thought these servants would look upon, though not upon himself. And therefore after that by some message by one or two of them, he had tasted of the earl's consent; it was agreed, that these four should murder their master the lieutenant, secretly in the night, and make their best of such money and portable goods of his, as they should find ready at hand, and get the keys of the Tower, and presently let forth Perkin and the earl. But this conspiracy was revealed in time, before it could be executed. And in this again the opinion of the king's great wisdom did surcharge him with a sinister fame, that Perkin was but his bait, to entrap the earl of Warwick. And in the very instant while this conspiracy was in working (as if that also had been the king's industry), it was fatal, that there should break forth a counterfeit earl of Warwick, a cordwainer's son, whose name was Ralph Wilford; a young man, taught and set on by an Augustine frier, called Patriarck. They both from the parts of Suffolk, came forwards into Kent, where they did not only privily and underhand give out, that this Wilford was the true earl of Warwick, but also the frier finding some light credence in the people, took the boldness in the pulpit to declare as much, and to incite the people to come into his aid. Whereupon they were both presently apprehended, and the young fellow executed, and the frier condemned to perpetual imprisonment. This also happening so opportunely, to represent the danger to the king's estate, from the earl of Warwick, and thereby to colour the king's severity that followed: together with the madness of the frier, so vainly and desperately to divulge a treason, before it had gotten any manner of strength; and the saving of the frier's life, which nevertheless was (indeed) but the privilege of his order; and the pity in the common people (which, if it run in a strong stream, doth ever cast up scandal and envy) made it generally rather talked, than believed, that all was but the king's device. But howsoever it were, hereupon Perkin (that had offended against grace now the third time) was at the last proceeded with, and by commissioners of Oyer and Determiner, arraigned at Westminster, upon divers treasons committed and perpetrated after his coming on land within this kingdom (for so the judges advised, for that he was a foreigner), and condemned, and a few days after executed at Tyburn. Where he did again openly read his confession, and take it upon his death to be true. This was the end of this little cockatrice of a king, that was able to destroy those that did not espy him first. It was one of the longest plays of that kind, that hath been in memory; and might perhaps have had another end, if he had not met with a king both wise, stout, and fortunate.

As for Perkin's three counsellors, they had registred themselves sanctuary-men when their master did. And whether upon pardon obtained, or continuance within the privilege, they came not to be proceeded with.

There was executed with Perkin, the mayor of Cork and his son,[1] who had been principal abettors of his treasons. And soon after were likewise condemned eight other persons, about the Tower conspiracy, whereof four were the lieutenant's men. But of those eight but two were executed. And immediately after was arraigned before the earl of Oxford (then for the time high steward of England) the poor prince the earl of Warwick; not for the attempt to escape simply (for that was not acted; and besides, the imprisonment not being for treason, the escape by law could not be treason), but for conspiring with Perkin to raise sedition, and to destroy the king. And the earl confessing the inditement had judgment, and was shortly after beheaded on Tower-hill.

This was also the end not only of this notable and commiserable person Edward the earl of Warwick, eldest son to the duke of Clarence, but likewise of the line male of the Plantagenets, who had flourished in great royalty and renown, from the time of the famous king of England king Henry the second. Howbeit it was a race often dipped in their own blood. It hath remained since only transplanted into other names, as well of the imperial line, as of other noble houses. But it was neither guilt of crime, nor reason of state, that could quench the envy that was upon the king for this execution. So that he thought good to export it out of the land, and to lay it upon his new allie Ferdinando king of Spain. For these two kings understanding one another at half a word, so it was that there were letters shewed out of Spain, whereby in the passages concerning the treaty of the

[1] As for Philip, John Water's son, he was afterwards pardoned by the king's clemency. The citizens of Cork were also pardoned.—Sir J. Ware., Cap. xv.

marriage, Ferdinando had written to the king in plain terms, that he saw no assurance of his succession, as long as the earl of Warwick lived; and that he was loth to send his daughter to troubles and dangers. But hereby, as the king did in some part remove the envy from himself; so he did not observe, that he did withall bring a kind of malediction and installing upon the marriage, as an ill prognostick. Which in event so far proved true, as both prince Arthur enjoyed a very small time after the marriage, and the lady Katherine herself (a sad and a religious woman) long after, when king Henry the eight, his resolution of a divorce from her was first made known to her, used some words; 'That she had not offended: but it was a judgment of God, for that her former marriage was made in blood;' meaning that of the earl of Warwick.

This fifteenth year of the king there was a great plague, both in London and in divers parts of the kingdom. Wherefore the king, after often change of places (whether to avoid the danger of the sickness, or to give occasion of an enterview with the arch-duke, or both) sail'd over with his queen to Calice. Upon his coming thither, the arch-duke sent an honourable ambassage unto him, as well to welcome him into those parts, as to let him know, that (if it pleased him) he would come and do him reverence. But it was said withal; 'That the king might be pleased to appoint some place, that were out of any walled town or fortress, for that he had denied the same upon like occasion to the French king. And though he said he made a great difference between the two kings, yet he would be loth to give a precedent, that might make it after to be expected at his hands, by another whom he trusted less. The king accepted of the courtesie, and admitted of his excuse, and appointed the place to be at St. Peter's church without Calice. But withall he did visit the arch-duke with ambassadors sent from himself, which were the lord Saint John, and the secretary; unto whom the arch-duke did the honour, as (going to mass at Saint Omers) to set the lord Saint John on his right hand, and the secretary on his left, and so to ride between them to church. The day appointed for the enterview, the king went on horseback some distance from St. Peter's church to receive the arch-duke. And upon their approaching, the arch-duke made hast to light, and offered to hold the king's stirrup at his alighting; which the king would not permit, but descending from horseback, they embraced with great affection, and withdrawing into the church to a place prepared, they had long conference, not only upon the confirmation of former treaties, and the freeing of commerce, but upon cross marriages, to be had between the duke of York the king's second son, and the arch-duke's daughter; and again between Charles the arch-duke's son and heir, and Mary the king's second daughter. But these blossoms of unripe marriages, were but friendly wishes, and the airs of loving entertainment; though one of them came afterwards to conclusion in treaty, though not in effect. But during the time that the two princes conversed and communed together in the suburbs of Calice, the demonstrations on both sides were passing hearty and affectionate, especially on the part of the arch-duke. Who (besides that he was a prince of an excellent good nature) being conscious to himself, how dryly the king had been used by his counsel in the matter of Perkin, did strive by all means to recover it in the king's affection. And having also his ears continually beaten with the counsels of his father and father-in-law, who (in respect of their jealous hatred against the French king) did always advise the arch-duke to anchor himself upon the amity of king Henry of England: was glad upon this occasion, to put in use and practice their precepts, calling the king patron, and father, and protector (these very words the king repeats; when he certified of the loving behaviour of the arch-duke to the city), and what else he could devise, to express his love and observance to the king. There came also to the king the governour of Picardy, and the bailiff of Amiens, sent from Lewis the French king to do him honour, and to give him knowledge of his victory and winning of the duchy of Milan. It seemeth the king was well pleased with the honours he received from those parts, while he was at Calice. For he did himself certify all the news and occurrences of them in every particular, from Calice, to the mayor and aldermen of London, which (no doubt) made no small talk in the city. For the king, though he could not entertain the good will of the citizens, as Edward the fourth did; yet by affability and other princely graces, did ever make very much of them, and apply himself to them.

This year also died John Moreton, archbishop of Canterbury, chancellor of England, and cardinal. He was a wise man, and an eloquent, but in his nature harsh, and haughty; much accepted by the king, but envied by the nobility, and hated of the people. Neither was his name left out of Perkin's proclamation for any good will, but they would not bring him amongst the king's casting-counters, because he had the image and superscription upon him of the pope, in his honour of cardinal. He won the king with secrecy and diligence, but chiefly because he was his old servant in his less fortunes; and also for that (in his affections) he was not without an inveterate malice against the house of York, under whom he had been in trouble. He was willing also to take envy from the king, more than the king was willing to put upon him. For the king cared not for subterfuges, but would stand envy, and appear in any thing that was to his mind; which made envy still grow upon him more universal, but less daring. But in the matter of exactions, time did after shew, that the bishop in feeding the king's humour, did rather temper it. He had been by Richard the third committed (as in custody) to the duke of Buckingham, whom he did secretly incite to revolt from king Richard. But after the duke was engaged, and thought the bishop should have been his chief pilot in the tempest, the bishop was gotten into the cock-boat and fled over beyond seas. But whatsoever else was in the man, he deserveth a most happy memory, in that he was the principal mean of joyning the two roses. He died of great years, but of strong health and powers.

The next year, which was the sixteenth year of the king, and the year of our lord one thousand five hundred, was the year of jubilee at Rome. But pope Alexander, to save the hazeard and charges of men's journeys to Rome, thought good to make over those graces by exchange, to such as would pay a convenient rate, seeing they could not come to fetch them. For which purpose was sent into England Jasper Pons, a Spaniard, the pope's commissioner, better chosen than were the commissioners of pope Leo, afterwards employ'd for Germany; for he carried the business with great wisdom, and semblance of holiness. In so much as he levied great sums of money within this land to the pope's use, with little or no scandal. It was thought the king shared in the money. But it appeareth by a letter which cardinal Adrian, the king's pensioner, wrote to the king from Rome some few years after, that this was not so. For this cardinal, being to perswade pope Julius on the king's behalf, to expedite the bull of dispensation for the marriage between prince Henry and the lady Katherine, finding the pope difficile in granting thereof, doth use it as a principal argument concerning the king's merit towards that see, that he had touched none of those deniers, which had been levied by Pons in England. But that it might the better appear (for the satisfaction of the common people) that this was consecrate money, the same nuntio brought unto the king a brief from the pope, wherein the king was exhorted and summoned to come in person against the Turk. For that the pope (out of the care of an universal father) seeing almost under his eyes the successes and progresses of that great enemy of the faith, had had in the conclave, and with the assistance of the ambassadors of foreign princes, divers consultations about an holy war, and a general expedition of christian princes against the Turk. Wherein it was agreed, and thought fit, that the Hungarians, Polonians, and Bohemians should make a war upon Thracia; the French and Spaniards upon Grecia; and that the pope (willing to sacrifice himself in so good a cause) in person and in company of the king of England, the Venetians, and such other states as were great in maritime power, would sail with a puissant navy through the Mediterrane unto Constantinople. And that to this end, his holiness had sent nuncio's to all christian princes; as well for a cessation of all quarrels and differences amongst themselves, as for speedy preparations and contributions of forces and treasure for this sacred enterprize.

To this the king, (who understood well the court of Rome) made an answer rather solemn, than serious; signifying,

'That no prince on earth should be more forward and obedient, both by his person, and by all possible forces, and fortunes, to enter into this sacred war, than himself. But that the distance of place was such, as that no forces he should raise for the seas, could be levied or prepared, but with double the charge, and double the time (at the least) that they might be from the other princes, that had their territories nearer adjoining. Besides, that neither the manner of his ships (having no gallies) nor the experience of his pilots and mariners could be so apt for those seas as theirs. And therefore that his holiness might do well, to move one of those other kings, who lay fitter for the purpose, to accompany him by sea. Whereby both all things would be sooner put in readiness, and with less charge, and the emulation and division of command, which might grow between those kings of France and Spain, if they should both join in the war by land upon Grecia, might be wisely avoided. And that for his part, he would not be wanting in aids and contribution. Yet notwithstanding if both these kings should refuse, rather than his holiness should go alone, he would wait upon him, as soon as he could be ready. Always provided, that he might first see all differences of the christian princes amongst themselves, fully laid down and appeased (as for his own part he was in none.) And that he might have some good towns upon the coasts in Italy put into his hands, for the retreat and the safeguard of his men.'

With this answer Jasper Pons returned, nothing at all discontented. And yet this declaration of the king (as superficial as it was) gave him that reputation abroad, as he was not long after elected by the knights of Rhodes, protector of their order; all things multiplying to honour in a prince, that had gotten such high estimation for his wisdom and sufficiency.

There were these two last years some proceedings against hereticks, which was rare in the king's reign, and rather by penances, than by fire. The king had (though he were no good schoolman) the honour to convert one of them by dispute at Canterbury.

This year also, though the king were no more haunted with spirits, for that by the sprinkling partly of blood, and partly of water, he had chased them away; yet nevertheless he had certain apparitions, that troubled him, still shewing themselves from one region, which was the house of York. It came so to pass, that the earl of Suffolk, son to Elizabeth eldest sister to king Edward the fourth, by John duke of Suffolk, her second husband, and brother to John earl of Lincoln, that was slain at Stock-field, being of an hasty and cholerick disposition, had killed a man in his fury; whereupon the king gave him his pardon. But either willing to leave a cloud upon him, or the better to make him feel his grace, produced him openly to plead his pardon. This wrought in the earl, as in a haughty stomach it useth to do ; for the ignominy printed deeper than the grace, wherefore he being discontent, fled secretly into Flanders unto his aunt the duchess of Burgundy. The king startled at it. But being taught by troubles, to use fair and timely remedies, wrought so with him by messages, (the lady Margaret of Burgundy also growing by often failing in her alchymie, weary of her experiments, and partly being a little sweetned, for that the king had not touched her name in the confession of Perkin) that he came over again upon good terms, and was reconciled to the king.

In[1] the beginning of the next year, being the seventeenth of the king, the lady Catherine, fourth daughter of Ferdinando and Isabella, king and queen of Spain, arrived in England, at Plymouth, the second of October, and was married to prince Arthur in Pauls, the fourteenth of November following. The prince being then about fifteen years of age,[2] and the lady about eighteen. The manner of her receiving, the manner of her entry into London, and the celebrity of the marriage were performed with great and true magnificence, in regard of cost, shew, and order, The chief man that took the care was bishop Fox ; who was not only a grave counsellor for war or peace, but also a good surveyor of works, and a good master of ceremonies, and any thing else that was fit for active part, belonging to the service of court, or state of a great king. This marriage was almost seven years in treaty ; which was in part caused by the tender years of the marriage couple, especially of the prince. But the true reason was, that these two princes, being princes of great policy and profound judgment, stood a great time looking one upon another's fortunes, how they would go ; knowing well that in the meantime, the very treaty itself gave abroad in the world a reputation of a strait conjunction, and amity between them ; which served on both sides to many purposes, that their several affairs required, and yet they continued still free. But in the end, when the fortunes of both princes did grow every day more and more prosperous and assured, and that looking all about them, they saw no better conditions, they then shut it up.

The marriage money the princess brought (which was turned over to the king by act of renunciation) was two hundred thousand ducats. Whereof one hundred thousand were payable ten days after the solemnization, and the other hundred thousand at two payments annual ; but part of it to be in jewels and plate, and a due course set

---

[1] She arrived as Stow says on the fourth of October, which is not the beginning of the year, she was married the 14th of November.—Sir J. Ware.
[2] He was born according to the lord Bacon, p. 8, in September 1486, and so he must be 15 years and 2 months old. According to Hollinshead he was born in September 1488, and then he was but 13 years and 2 months.—See Hol. p. 769.

down to have them justly and indifferently prized. The joynture or advancement of the lady, was the third part of the principality of Wales, and of the dukedom of Cornwall, and the earldom of Chester, to be after set forth in severalty. And in case she came to be queen of England, her advancement was less indefinite, but thus; that it should be as great, as ever any former queen of England had been.

In all the devices and conceits of the triumphs of this marriage, there was a great deal of astronomy. The lady being resembled to Hesperus, and the prince to Arcturus, and the old king Alphonsus (that was the greatest astronomer of kings, and was ancestor to the lady) was brought in to be the fortune-teller of the match. And whosoever had those toys in compiling, they were not altogether pedantical. But you may be sure that king Arthur, the Britton, and the descent of the lady Catherine from the house of Lancaster, was in no wise forgotten. But (as it should seem) it is not good to fetch fortunes from the stars. For this young prince (that drew upon him at that time not only the hopes and affections of his country, but the eyes and expectation of foreigners) after a few months, in the beginning of April, 1502, deceased at Ludlow castle, where he was sent to keep his residence and court, as prince of Wales. Of this prince in respect he dyed so young, and by reason of his father's manner of education, that did cast no great lustre upon his children, there is little particular memory. Only thus much remaineth, that he was very studious and learned, beyond his years, and that beyond the custom of great princes.

There was a doubt ripped up in the times following, when the divorce of king Henry the eighth from the lady Catherine did so much busie the world, whether Arthur was bedded with his lady or no, whereby that matter in fact (of carnal knowledge) might be made part of the case. And it is true, that the lady herself denied it, or at least her council stood upon it, and would not blanch that advantage, although the plenitude of the pope's power of dispensing was the main question. And this doubt was kept long open, in respect of the two queens that succeeded, Mary and Elizabeth, whose legitimations were incompatible one with another, though their succession was settled by act of parliament. And the times that favoured queen Mary's legitimation would have it believed, that there was no carnal knowledge between Arthur and Katherine. Not that they would seem to derogate from the pope's absolute power to dispense even in that case; but only in point of honour, and to make the case more favourable and smooth. And the times that favoured queen Elizabeth's legitimation (which were the longer, and the latter) maintained the contrary. So much there remaineth in memory, that it was half a year's time between the creation of Henry prince of Wales, and prince Arthur's death; which was construed to be, for to expect a full time, whereby it might appear, whether the lady Catherine were with child by prince Arthur, or no. Again, the lady her self procured a bull, for the better corroboration of the marriage, with a clause of (*vel forsan cognitam*) which was not in the first bull. There was given in evidence also, when the cause of the divorce was handled, a pleasant passage, which was; that in a morning prince Arthur, upon his up-rising from bed with her, called for drink, which he was not accustomed to do, and finding the gentleman of his chamber that brought him the drink to smile at it, and to note it, he said merrily to him; 'That he had been in the midst of Spain, which was an hot region, and his journey had made him dry, and that if the other had been in so hot a clime, he would have been drier than he.' Besides, the prince was upon the point of sixteen years of age when he died, and forward and able in body.

The February following, Henry duke of York was created prince of Wales, and earl of Chester and Flint. For the dukedom of Cornwall devolved to him by statute. The king also being fast handed, and loth to part with a second dowry, but chiefly being affectionate, both by his nature and out of politick considerations, to continue the alliance with Spain, prevailed with the prince (though not without some reluctation, such as could be in those years, for he was not twelve years of age) to be contracted with the princess Katherine. The secret providence of God ordaining that marriage to be the occasion of great events and changes.

The same year (1503) were the espousals of James king of Scotland, with the lady Margaret, the king's eldest daughter; which was done by proxy, and published at Paul's Cross, the five and twentieth of January, and Te Deum solemnly sung. But certain it is, that the joy of the city thereupon shewed, by ringing of bells, and bonfires, and such other incense of the people, was more than could be expected, in a case of so great and fresh enmity between the nations; especially in London, which was far enough off from feeling any of the former calamities of the war. And therefore might be truly attributed to a secret instinct and inspiring (which many times runneth not only in the hearts of princes, but in the pulse and veins of people) touching the happiness thereby to ensue in time to come. This marriage was in August following consummate at Edenburgh. The king bringing his daughter as far as Colli-Weston on the way, and then consigning her to the attendance of the earl of Northumberland; who with a great troop of lords and ladies of honour, brought her into Scotland, to the king her husband.

This marriage had been in treaty by the space of almost three years, from the time that the king of Scotland did first open his mind to bishop Fox. The sum given in marriage by the king was ten thousand pounds. And the jointure and advancement assured by the king of Scotland, was two thousand pounds a year after king James his death, and one thousand pounds a year in present, for the lady's allowance or maintenance. This to be set forth in lands, of the best and most certain revenue. During the treaty, it is reported, that the king remitted the matter to his council; and that some at the table in the freedom of councellors (the king being present) did put the case; that if God should take the king's two sons without issue, that then the kingdom of England would fall to the king of Scotland, which might be prejudice to the monarchy of England. Whereupon the king himself replied; 'That if that should be, Scotland would be but an accession to England, and not England to Scotland, for that the greater would draw the less. And that it was a safer union for England, than that of France.' This passed as an oracle, and silenced those that moved the question

The same year was fatal, as well for deaths, as marriages, and that with equal temper. For the joys and feasts of the two marriages, were compensed with the mournings and funerals of prince Arthur (of whom we have spoken) and of queen Elizabeth, who died in child bed in the Tower, and the child lived not long after. There dyed also that year sir Reginald Bray who was noted to have had with the king the greatest freedom of any councellor; but it was but a freedom, the better to set off flattery. Yet he bare more than his just part of envy, for the exactions.

At this time the king's estate was very prosperous, secured by the amity of Scotland, strengthened by that of Spain, cherished by that of Burgundy, all domestick troubles quenched, and all noise of war (like a thunder afar off) going upon Italy. Wherefore nature, which many times is happily contained, and refrained by some bands of fortune, began to take place in the king; carrying (as with a strong tide) his affections and thoughts unto the gathering and heaping up of treasure. And as kings do more easily find instruments for their will and humour, than for their service and honour; he had gotten for his purpose, or beyond his purpose, two instruments, Empson and Dudley, (whom the people esteemed as his horse-leeches and shearers) bold men, and careless of fame, and took toll of their master's grist. Dudley was of a good family, eloquent, and one that could put hateful business into good language. But Empson, that was the son of a sieve-maker, triumphed always upon the deed done, putting off all other respects whatsoever. These two persons being lawyers in science, and privy councellors in authority (as the corruption of the best things is the worst) turned law and justice into wormwood and rapine. For first, their manner was to cause divers subjects to be indicted of sundry crimes, and so far forth to proceed in form of law; but when the bills were found, then presently to commit them. And nevertheless not to produce them in any resonable time to their answer, but to suffer them to languish long in prison, and by sundry artificial devices and terrors, to extort from them great fines and ransoms, which they termed compositions and mitigations.

Neither did they (towards the end) observe so much as the half face of justice, in proceeding by indictment; but sent forth their precepts to attach men, and convent them before themselves and some others, at their private houses, in a court of commission, and there used to shuffle up a summary proceeding by examination without trial of jury; assuming to themselves there, to deal both in pleas of the crown, and controversies civil.

Then did they also use to enthrall and charge the subjects lands with tenures in capite, by finding false offices, and thereby to work upon them for wardships, liveries, primier seisines, and alienations, (being the fruits of those tenures) refusing upon divers pretexts and delays, to admit men to traverse those false offices, according to the law. Nay, the king's wards, after they had accomplished their full age, could not be suffered to have livery of their lands, without paying excessive fines, far exceeding all reasonable rates. They did also vex men with informations of intrusion upon scarce colourable titles.

When men were out-lawed in personal actions, they would not permit them to purchase their charters of pardon, except they paid great and intolerable sums; standing upon the strict point of law, which upon outlawries giveth forfeiture of goods. Nay, contrary to all law and colour, they maintained, the king ought to have the half of men's lands and rents, during the space of full two years, for a pain in case of out-lawry. They would also ruffle with jurors, and inforce them to find as they would direct, and (if they did not) convent them, imprison them, and fine them.

These and many other courses, fitter to be buried than repeated, they had of preying upon the people; both like tame hawks for their master, and like wild hawks for themselves; in so much as they grew to great riches and substance. But their principal working was upon penal laws, wherein they spared none, great nor small; nor considered whether the law were possible, or impossible, in use or obsolete: but raked over all old and new statutes, though many of them were made with intention rather of terror, than of rigour; having ever a rabble of promoters, questmongers, and leading jurors at their command, so as they could have any thing found either for fact or for valuation.

There remaineth to this day a report, that the king was on a time entertained by the earl of Oxford (that was his principal servant, both for war and peace) nobly and sumptuously, at his castle at Heningham. And at the king's going away, the earl's servants stood (in a seemly manner) in their livery coats, with cognisances, ranged on both sides, and made the king a lane. The king called the earl unto him and said 'My lord, I have heard much of your hospitality, but I see it is greater than the speech. These handsome gentlemen and yeomen, which I see on both sides of me, are sure your menial servants.' The earl smiled and said ; 'It may please your grace, that were not for mine ease. They are most of them my retainers, that are come to do me service at such a time as this, and chiefly to see your grace.' The king started a little, and said ; 'By my faith (my lord) I thank you for my good chear, but I may not endure to have my laws broken in my sight. My attorney must speak with you.' And it is part of the report, that the earl compounded for no less than fifteen thousand marks. And to shew further the king's extreme diligence ; I do remember to have seen long since a book of accompt of Empson's, that had the king's hand almost to every leaf, by way of signing, and was in some places postilled in the margent with the king's hand likewise, where was this remembrance.

'Item, received of such a one, five marks, for the pardon to be procured ; and if the pardon do not pass, the money to be repaid ; except the party be some other ways satisfied.'

And over against this memorandum (of the king's own hand)
'Otherwise satisfied.'

Which I do the rather mention, because it shews in the king a nearness, but yet with a kind of justness. So these little sands and grains of gold and silver (as it seemeth) helped not a little to make up the great heap and bank.

But mean while (to keep the king awake) the earl of Suffolk having been too gay at prince Arthur's marriage, and sunk himself deep in debt, had yet once more a mind to be a knight errant, and to seek adventures in foreign parts. And taking his brother with him, fled again into Flanders. That (no doubt) which gave him confidence, was the great murmur of the people against the government. And being a man of a light and rash spirit, he thought every vapour would be a tempest. Neither wanted he some party within the kingdom. For the murmurs of people awakes the discontents of nobles, and again, that calleth up commonly some head of sedition. The king resorting to his wonted and tried arts, called sir Robert Curson, captain of the castle at Hammes (being at that time beyond sea, and therefore less likely to be wrought upon by the king) to fly from his charge, and to fain himself a servant of the earl's. This knight having insinuated himself into the secrets of the earl, and finding by him upon whom chiefly he had either hope or hold, advertised the king thereof in great secrecy. But nevertheless maintained his own credit and inward trust with the earl. Upon whose advertisements, the king attached William Courtney, earl of Devonshire, his brother-in-law, married to the lady Katherine, daughter to king Edward the fourth ; William

De-la-Pole, brother to the earl of Suffolk; sir James Tirrel, and sir John Windham, and some other meaner portions, and committed them to custody. George lord Abergavennie, and sir Thomas Green, were at the same time apprehended; but as upon less suspicion, so in a freer restraint, and were soon after delivered. The earl of Devonshire, being interested in the blood of York, that was rather feared than nocent· yet as one, that might be the object of other plots and designs, remained prisoner in the Tower, during the king's life. William De-la-pole was also long restrained though not so straitly. But for Sir James Tirrel (against whom the blood of the innocent princes, Edward the fifth, and his brother, did still cry from under the altar), and Sir John Windham, and the other meaner ones, they were attainted and executed; the two knights beheaded. Nevertheless, to confirm the credit of Curson (who belike had not yet done all his feats of activity) there was published at Paul's Cross about the time of the said executions, the pope's bull of excommunication and curse, against the Earl of Suffolk, and sir Robert Curson, and some others by name, and likewise in general against all the abettors of the said earl. Wherein it must be confessed, that heaven was made too much to bow to earth, and religion to policy. But soon after, Curson (when he saw time) returned into England, and withall into wonted favour with the king, but worse fame with the people. Upon whose return the earl was much dismayed and seeing himself destitute of hopes (the lady Margaret of Burgundy also by tract of time, and bad success, being now become cool in those attempts) after some wandering in France, and Germany, and certain little projects, no better than squibbs of an exiled man, being tired out, retired again into the protection of the archduke Philip in Flanders, who by the death of Isabella, was at that time king of Castile, in the right of Joan his wife.

This year (being the nineteenth of his reign) the king called his parliament. Wherein a man may easily guess, how absolute the king took himself to be with his parliament, when Dudley that was so hateful, was made Speaker of the House of Commons. In this parliament, there were not made any statutes memorable, touching publick government. But those that were, had still the stamp of the king's wisdom and his policy.

There was a statute made for the disannulling of all patents of lease, or grant, to such as came not upon lawful summons, to serve the king in his wars, against the enemies or rebels, or that should depart without the king's licence; with an exception of certain persons of the long robe. Providing nevertheless, that they should have the king's wages, from their house, till their return home again. There had been the like made for officers, and by this statute it was extended to lands. But a man may easily see by many statutes made in this king's time, that the king thought it safest, to assist martial law by the law of parliament.

Another statute was made, prohibiting the bringing in of manufactures of silk wrought by itself, or mixt with any other thread. But it was not of stuffs of whole piece (for that the realm had of them no manufacture in use at that time) but of knit silk, or texture of silk; as ribbands, laces, caules, points, and girdles, &c., which the people of England could then well skill to make. This law pointed at a true principle: that where foreign materials are but superfluities foreign manufactures should be prohibited. For that will either banish the superfluity or gain the manufacture.

There was a law also of resumption of patents of gaols, and the reannexing of them to the sherifwicks; privileged officers being no less an interuption of justice, than privileged places.

There was likewise a law to restrain the by-laws or ordinances of corporations, which many times were against the prerogative of the king, the common-law of the realm, and the liberty of the subject, being fraternities in evil. It was therefore provided, that they should not be put in execution, without the allowance of the chancellor, treasurer, and the two chief-justices, or three of them, or of the two justices of circuit where the corporation was.

Another law was (in effect) to bring in the silver of the realm to the mint, in making all clipped, minished, or impaired coins of silver, not to be current in payments; without giving any remedy of weight, but with an exception only of a reasonable wearing, which was nothing in respect of the incertainty; and so (upon the matter) to set the mint on work, and to give way to new coins of silver, which should be then minted.

There likewise was a long statute against vagabonds, wherein two things may be noted; the one the dislike the parliament had of gaoling of them, as that which was chargeable, pesterous, and of no open example. The other, that in the statutes of this king's time, (for this of the nineteenth year is not the only statute of that kind) there are ever coupled, the punishment of vagabonds, and the forbidding of dice, and cards, and unlawful games unto servants and mean people, and the putting down and suppressing of ale-houses, as strings of one root together, and as if the one were unprofitable, without the other.

As for riot and retainers, there passed scarce any parliament in this time without a law against them, the king ever having an eye to might, and multitude.

There was granted also that parliament a subsidy, both for the temporalty and the clergy. And yet, nevertheless, ere the year expired, there went out commissions for a general benevolence, though there were no wars; no fears. The same year the city gave five thousand marks, for confirmation of their liberties; a thing fitter for the beginnings of king's reigns, than the latter ends. Neither was it a smal matter, that the mint gained upon the late statute, by the recoinage of groats and half-groats, now twelve-pences and six-pences. As for Empson and Dudley's mills, they did grind more than ever. So that it was a strange thing, to see what golden showers poured down upon the king's treasury at once. The last payments of the marriage money from Spain; the subsidy; the benevolence; the recoinage; the redemption of the citie's liberties; the casualties. And this is the more to be marvelled at, because the king had then no occasions at all of wars or troubles. He had now but one son, and one daughter unbestowed. He was wise; he was of an high mind; he needed not to make riches his glory. He did excel in so many things else; save that certainly avarice doth ever find in itself matter of ambition. Belike he thought to leave his son such a kingdom, and such a mass of treasure, as he might choose his greatness where he would.

This year was also kept the serjeants' feast, which was the second call in this king's days.

About this time Isabella, queen of Castile, deceased; a right noble lady, and an honour to her sex, and times, and the corner-stone of the greatness of Spain that hath followed. This accident the king took not for news at large, but thought it had a great relation to his own affairs; especially in two points. The one for example; the other for consequence. First, he conceived that the case of Ferdinando of Arragon, after the death of queen Isabella, was his own case, after the death of his own queen: and the case of Joan the heir unto Castile, was the case of his own son prince Henry. For if both of the kings had their kingdoms, in the right of their wives, they descended to the heirs, and did not accrew to the husbands. And although his own case had both steel and parchment, more than the other (that is to say, a conquest in the field, and an act of parliament) yet notwithstanding, that natural title of descent in blood, did (in the imagination even of a wise man) breed a doubt, that the other two were not safe nor sufficient. Wherefore he was wonderful diligent, to inquire and observe what became of the king of Arragon, in holding and continuing the kingdom of Castile. And whether he did hold it in his own right, or as administrator to his daughter; and whether he were like to hold it in fact, or to be put out by his son in law. Secondly, he did revolve in his mind, that the state of Christendom might by this late accident have a turn. For whereas before time himself, with the conjunction of Arragon and Castile (which then was one) and the amity of Maximilian and Philip his son the arch-duke, was far too strong a party for France; he began to fear, that now the French king (who had great interest in the affections of Philip the young king of Castile) and Philip himself, now king of Castile (who was in ill terms with his father in law about the present government of Castile). And thirdly, Maximilian, Philip's father (who was ever variable, and upon whom the surest aim that could be taken, was that he would not be long, as he had been last before) would, all three being potent princes, enter into some strait league and confederation amongst themselves. Whereby, though he should not be endangered, yet he should be left to the poor amity of Arragon. And whereas he had been heretofore a kind of arbiter of Europe, he should now go less, and be over-topped by so great a conjunction. He had also (as it seems) an inclination to marry, and bethought himself of some fit conditions abroad. And amongst others, he had heard of the beauty and virtuous behaviour of the young queen of Naples, the widow of Ferdinando the younger, being then of matronal years of seven and twenty. By whose marriage he thought that the kingdom of Naples (having been a gaol for a time between the king of Arragon, and the French king, and being but newly settled) might in some part be deposited in his hands who was so able to keep the stakes. Therefore he sent in ambassage or message three confident persons; Francis Marsin, James Bray-brook, and John Stile, upon two several inquisitions rather than negotiations. The one touching the person and condition of the young queen of Naples. The other touching all particulars of estate, that concerned the fortunes and intentions of Ferdinando. And because they may observe best who themselves are observed least, he sent them under colourable pretexts; giving them letters of kindness and complement from Katherine the princess, to her aunt, and niece, the old and young queen of Naples, and delivering to them also a book of new articles of peace; which notwithstanding it had been delivered unto doctor de Puebla, the legier ambassador of Spain here in England, to be sent; yet for that the king had been long without hearing from Spain, he thought good those messengers, when they had been with the two queens, should likewise pass on to the court of Ferdinando, and take a copy of the book with them. The instructions touching the queen of Naples were so curious and exquisite, being as articles whereby to direct a survey, or framing a particular of her person, for complexion, favour, feature, stature, health, age, customs, behaviour, conditions, and estate, as if the king had been young, a man would have judged him to be amorous; but being ancient, it ought to be interpreted, that sure he was very chaste, for that he meant to find all things in one woman, and so to settle his affections, without ranging. But in this match he was soon cooled, when he heard from his ambassadors, that this young queen had had a goodly jointure in the realm of Naples, well answered during the time of her uncle Frederick, yea, and during the time of Lewis the French king, in whose division her revenue fell; but since the time that the kingdom was in Ferdinando's hands, all was assigned to the army, and garrisons there, and she received only a pension or exhibition out of his coffers.

The other part of the inquiry had a grave and diligent return, informing the king at full of the present state of king Ferdinando. By this report it appeared to the king, that Ferdinando did continue the government of Castile as administrator unto his daughter Joan, by the title of queen Isabella's will, and partly by the custom of the kingdom, as he pretended. And that all mandates and grants were expedited in the name of Joan his daughter, and himself as administrator, without mention of Philip, her husband. And that king Ferdinando, howsoever he did dismiss himself of the name of king of Castile, yet meant to hold the kingdom, without accompt, and in absolute command.

It appeareth also, that he flattered himself with hopes, that king Philip would permit unto him the government of Castile during his life; which he had laid his plot to work him unto, both by some counsellors of his about him, which Ferdinando had at his devotion, and chiefly by promise, that in case Philip gave not way unto it, he would marry some young lady, whereby to put him by the succession of Arragon and Granada, in case he should have a son. And lastly, by representing unto him that the government of the Burgundians, till Philip were by continuance in Spain made as natural of Spain, would not be endured by the Spaniards. But in all those things (though wisely laid down and consider'd) Ferdinando fail'd; but that Pluto was better to him, than Pallas.

In the same report also, the ambassadors being mean men, and therefore the more free, did strike upon a string which was somewhat dangerous. For they declared plainly, that the people of Spain, both nobles and commons, were better affected unto the part of Phillip (so he brought his wife with him) than to Ferdinando; and expressed the reason to be, because he had imposed upon them many taxes, and tallages, which was the king's own case, between him and his son.

There was also in this report a declaration of an overture of marriage, which Amason the secretary of Ferdinando had made unto the ambassadors in great secret, between Charles prince of Castile and Mary the king's second daughter; assuring the king, that the treaty of marriage then on foot, for the said prince and the daughter of France, would break; and that she the said daughter of France should be married to Angolesme, that was the heir apparent of France.

There was a touch also of a speech of marriage between Ferdinando and Madam de Fois, a lady of the blood of France, which afterwards indeed succeeded. But this was reported as learned in France, and silenced in Spain.

The king by the return of this ambassage, which gave great light unto his affairs, was well instructed, and prepared how to carry himself between Ferdinando king of Arragon, and Philip his son-in-law, king of Castile; resolving with himself, to do all that in him lay to keep them at one within themselves; but howsoever that succeeded, by a moderate carriage and bearing the person of a common friend, to lose neither of their friendships; but yet to run a course more entire with the king of Arragon, but more laboured and officious with the king of Castile. But he was much taken with the overture of marriage with his daughter Mary; both because it was the greatest marriage of Christendom, and for that it took hold of both allies.

But to corroborate his alliance with Philip the winds gave him an interview. For Philip choosing the winter season, the better to surprise the king of Arragon, set forth with a great navy out of Flanders for Spain in the month of January, the one and twentieth year of the king's reign. But himself was surprised with a cruel tempest, that scatter'd his ships upon the several coasts of England. And the ship wherein the king and queen were (with two other small barks only) torn, and in great peril to escape the fury of the weather, thrust into Weymouth. King Philip himself, having not been used (as it seems) to sea, all wearied and extreme sick, would needs land to refresh his spirits, tho' it was against the opinion of his council, doubting it might breed delay, his occasions requiring celerity.

The rumour of the arrival of a puissant navy upon the coast, made the country arm. And sir Thomas Trenchard with forces suddenly raised, not knowing what the matter might be, came to Weymouth, Where understanding the accident, he did in all humbleness and humanity invite the king and queen to his house; and forthwith dispatched posts to the court. Soon after came sir John Caroe likewise, with a great troop of men well arm'd; using the like humbleness and respect towards the king, when he knew the case. King Philip doubting that they, being but subjects, durst not let him pass away again, without the king's notice and leave, yielded to their entreaties, to stay till they heard from the court. The king as soon as he heard the news, commanded presently the earl of Arundel, to go to visit the king of Castile, and let him understand, that as he was very sorry for his mishap, so he was glad that he had escaped the dangers of the seas, and likewise of the occasion himself had to do him honour; and desiring him, to think himself as in his own land; and that the king made all haste possible to come and imbrace him. The earl came to him in great magnificence, with a brave troop of three hundred horse; and (for more state) came by torch-light. After he had done the king's message, king Philip seeing how the world went, the sooner to get away, went upon speed to the king at Windsor, and his queen follow'd by easy journeys. The two kings at their meeting us'd all the caresses, and loving demonstrations that were possible. And the king of Castile said pleasantly to the king, 'That he was now punished, for that he would not come within his walled town of Calice, when they met last.' But the king answer'd, 'That walls and seas were nothing, where hearts were open; and that he was here no otherwise, but to be served.' After a day or two's refreshing, the kings entered into speech of renewing the treaty : the king saying, 'That tho' king Philip's person were the same, yet his fortunes and state were raised. In which case a renovation of treaty was used amongst princes.' But while these things were in handling, the king choosing a fit time, and drawing the king of Castile into a room, where they two only were private, and laying his hand civilly upon his arm, and changing his countenance a little from a countenance of intertainment, said to him; 'Sir, you have been saved upon my coast, I hope you will not suffer me to wrack upon yours.' The king of Castile ask'd him, 'What he meant by that speech?' 'I mean it (saith the king) by that same harebrain wild fellow, my subject, the earl of Suffolk, who is protected in your country, and begins to play the fool, when all others are weary of it.' The king of Castile answer'd, 'I had thought (sir) your felicity had been above those thoughts. But if it trouble you, I will banish him.' The king reply'd, Those hornets were best in their nest, and worst when they did fly abroad, that his desire was, to have him delivered to him.' The king of Castile herewith a little confused, and in a study, said, 'That can I not do with my honour, and less with yours ; for you will be thought to have used me as a prisoner.' The king presently said, 'Then the matter is at an end. For I will take that dishonour upon me, and so your honour is saved.' The king of Castile, who had the king in great estimation, and besides remembered where he was, and knew not what use he might have of the king's amity, for that himself was new in his estate of Spain, and unsettled, both with his father in law, and with his people, composing his countenance, said, 'Sir, you give law to me ; but so will I to you. You shall have him, (but upon your honour) you shall not take his life.' The king embracing him, said, 'Agreed. Saith the king of Castile, 'Neither shall it dislike you if I send to him in such a fashion as he may partly come with his own good will.' The king said, 'It was well thought of; and if it pleased him, he would joyn with him, in sending to the earl a message to that purpose.' They both sent severally, and mean while they continued feastings and pastimes. The king being (on his part) willing to have the earl sure before the king of Castile went ; and the king of Castile being as willing to seem to be inforced. The king also with many wise and excellent perswasions, did advise the king of Castile to be ruled by the council of his father in law Ferdinando ; a prince so prudent, so experienced, so fortunate. The king of Castile (who was in no very good terms with his said father in law) answer'd, ' That if his father in law would suffer him to govern his kingdom, he should govern him.'

There were immediately messengers sent from both kings to recall the earl of Suffolk : who upon gentle words used to him was soon charmed, and willing enough to return ; assur'd of his life, and hoping of his liberty. He was brought through Flanders to Calice, and thence landed at Dover, and with sufficient guard delivered and received at the Tower of London. Mean while king Henry (to draw the time) continued his feastings and entertainments, and after he had receiv'd the king of Castile into the fraternity of the Garter, and for a reciprocal his son the prince admitted to the order of the Golden-Fleece, he accompany'd king Philip and his queen to the city of London; where they were entertain'd with the greatest magnificence and triumph, that could be upon no greater warning. And as soon as the earl of Suffolk had been convey'd to the Tower (which was the serious part) the jollities had an end, and the kings took leave. Nevertheless during their being here, they in substance concluded that treaty, which the Flemings term *Intercursus malus*, and bears date at Windsor; for that there be some things in it more to the advantage of the English, than of them; especially, for that the free-fishing of the Dutch upon the coasts and seas of England, granted in the treaty of *Undecimo*, was not by this treaty confirmed. All articles that confirm former treaties being precisely and warily limited and confirm'd to matter of commerce only, and not otherwise.

It was observed, that the great tempest which drove Philip into England, blew down the golden eagle from the spire of Paul's, and in the fall it fell upon a sign of the black eagle, which was in Paul's Church-yard, in the place where the school-house now standeth, and batter'd it, and brake it down. Which was a strange stooping of a hawk upon a fowl. This the people interpreted to be an ominous prognostick upon the imperial house, which was (by interpretation also) fulfill'd upon Philip the emperor's son, not only in the present disaster of the tempest, but in that that follow'd. For Philip arriving into Spain, and attaining the possession of the kingdom of Castile without resistance (insomuch as Ferdinando, who had spoke so great before, was with difficulty admitted to the speech of his son in law), sickned soon after, and deceased. Yet after such time as there was an observation by the wisest of that court, that if he had liv'd his father would have gain'd upon him in that sort, as he would have govern'd his council and designs, if not his affections. By this all Spain return'd into the power of Ferdinando in state as it was before; the rather, in regard of the infirmity of Joan his daughter, who loving her husband (by whom she had many children) dearly well, and no less belov'd of him (howsoever her father to make Philip ill beloved of the people of Spain, gave out that Philip us'd her not well) was unable in strength of mind to bear the grief of his decease, and fell distracted of her wits. Of which malady her father was thought no ways to endeavour the cure, the better to hold his regal power in Castile. So that as the felicity of Charles VIII. was said to be a dream; so the adversity of Ferdinando was said likewise to be a dream, it passed over so soon.

About this time the king was desirous to bring into the house of Lancaster celestial honour, and became suitor to Pope Julius, to canonize king Henry VI. for a saint; the rather in respect of that his famous prediction of the king's own assumption to the crown. Julius referred the matter (as the manner is) to certain cardinals,[1] to take the verification of his holy acts and miracles. But it died under the reference. The general opinion was that Pope Julius was too dear, and that the king would not come to his rates. But it is more probable, that that pope (who was extremely jealous of the dignity of the see of Rome, and of the acts thereof), knowing that king Henry VI. was reputed in the world abroad but for a simple man, was afraid it would but diminish the estimation of that kind of honour, if there were not a distance kept betwixt innocents and saints.

The same year likewise there proceeded a treaty of marriage between the king and the lady Margaret duchess dowager of Savoy, only daughter to Maximilian, and sister to the king of Castile; a lady wise, and of great good fame. This matter had been in speech between the two kings at their meeting, but was soon after resumed; and therein was employ'd for his first piece the king's then chaplain, and after the great prelate Thomas Wolsey. It was in the end concluded, with great and ample conditions for the king, but with promise *de futuro* only. It may be the king was the rather induced unto it, for that he heard more and more of the marriage to go on between his great friend and ally Ferdinando of Arragon, and madam de Fois, whereby that king began to piece with the French king, from whom he had been always before severed. So fatal a thing it is, for the greatest and straitest amities of kings, at one time or other to have a little of the wheel. Nay, there is a further tradition (in Spain tho' not with us), that the king of Arragon, after he knew that the marriage between Charles, the young prince of Castile, and Mary the king's second daughter went roundly on (which tho' it was first moved by the king of Arragon, yet it was afterwards wholly advanced and brought to perfection by Maximilian, and the friends on that side), entered into a jealousy, that the king did aspire to the government of Castilia, as administrator during the minority of his son-in-law; as if there should have been a competition of three for that government; Ferdinando, grandfather on the mother's side; Maximilian, grandfather on the father's side; and king Henry, father-in-law to the young prince. Certainly, it is not unlike, but the king's government (carrying the young prince with him) would have been perhaps more welcome to the Spaniards, than the other two. For the nobility of Castilia, that so lately put out the king of Arragon, in favour of king

---

The pope by his bull committed the examination of this matter to the Archbishop of Canterbury, the bishops of London, Winchester, and Durham; the bull is in the Collomais library.—Sir J. Ware, Kn. Henry VII., Cap. xx.

Philip, and had discover'd themselves so far, could not be but in a secret distrust and distaste of that king. And as for Maximilian, upon twenty respects he could not have been the man. But this purpose of the king's seemeth to me (considering the king's safe courses, never found to be enterprising or adventurous) not greatly probable, except he should have had a desire to breathe warmer, because he had ill lungs. This marriage with Margaret was protracted from time to time, in respect of the infirmity of the king, who now in the two and twentieth of his reign began to be troubled with the gout. But the defluxion taking also into his breast, wasted his lungs, in that thrice in a year (in a kind of return, and especially in the spring) he had great fits and labours of the tissick. Nevertheless, he continued to intend business with as great diligence, as before in his health. Yet so, as upon this warning, he did likewise now more seriously think of the world to come, and of making himself a saint, as well as king Henry the sixth, by treasure better employ'd, than to be given to Pope Julius. For this year he gave greater alms than accustomed, and discharged all prisoners about the city, that lay for fees or debts under forty shillings. He did also make haste with religious foundations; and in the year following (which was the three and twentieth) finished that of the Savoy. And hearing also of the bitter cries of his people against the oppressions of Dudley and Empson, and their accomplices; partly by devout persons about him, and partly by publick sermons (the preachers doing their duty therein) he was touch'd with great remorse for the same. Nevertheless, Empson and Dudley, tho' they could not but hear of these scruples in the king's conscience; yet as if the king's soul and his money were in several offices, that the one was not to intermeddle with the other, went on with as great rage as ever. For the same three and twentieth year was there a sharp prosecution against sir William Capel now the second time; and this was for matters of misgovernment in his mayoralty. The great matter being, that in some payments he had taken knowledge of false moneys, and did not his diligence to examine and bear it out who were the offenders. For this and some other things laid to his charge, he was condemn'd to pay two thousand pounds; and being a man of stomach, and harden'd by his former troubles, refused to pay a mite; and belike used some untoward speeches of the proceedings, for which he was sent to the Tower, and there remain'd till the king's death. Knesworth likewise, that had been lately mayor of London, and both his sheriffs, were for abuses in their offices, question'd, and imprison'd, and deliver'd upon one thousand four hundred pounds paid. Hawis an alderman of London, was put in trouble, and died with thought and anguish before his business came to an end. Sir Lawrence Ailmer, who had likewise been mayor of London, and his two sherifis, were put to the fine of one thousand pounds. And sir Lawrence, for refusing to make payment, was committed to prison, where he stay'd till Empson himself was committed in his place.

It is no marvel (if the faults were so light and the rates so heavy) that the king's treasure of store that he left at his death, most of it in secret places under his own key and keeping, at Richmond, amounted (as by tradition it is reported to have done) unto the sum of near eighteen hundred thousand pounds sterling; a huge masse of money, even for these times.

The last act of state that concluded this king's temporal felicity, was the conclusion of a glorious match between his daughter Mary, and Charles prince of Castile, afterwards the great emperor, both being of tender years. Which treaty was perfected by bishop Fox, and other his commissioners at Calice, the year before the king's death. In which alliance, it seemeth he himself took so high contentment, as in a letter which he wrote thereupon to the city of London (commanding all possible demonstrations of joy to be made for the same) he expresseth himself, as if he thought he had built a wall of brass about his kingdom. When he had for his sons in law, a king of Scotland, and a prince of Castile and Burgundy. So as now there was nothing to be added to this great king's felicity, being at the top of all worldly bliss (in regard of the high marriages of his children, his great renown throughout Europe, and his scarce credible riches, and the perpetual constancy of his prosperous successes), but an opportune death, to withdraw him from any future blow of fortune. Which certainly (in regard of the great hatred of his people, and the title of his son being then come to eighteen years of age, and being a bold prince, and liberal, and that gained upon the people by his very aspect and presence) had not been impossible to have even come upon him.

To crown also the last year of his reign as well as his first, he did an act of piety, rare and worthy to be taken into imitation. For he granted forth a general pardon, as expecting a second coronation in a better kingdom. He did also declare in his will, that his mind was, that restitution should be made of those sums, which had been unjustly taken by his officers.

And thus this Solomon of England (for Solomon also was too heavy upon his people in exactions) having lived two and fifty years, and thereof reigned three and twenty years, and eight months, being in perfect memory, and in a most blessed mind, in a great calm of a consuming sickness passed to a better world, the two and twentieth of April, 1508,[1] at his palace of Richmond, which himself had built.

[1] Reckoning from the day of his victory at Bosworth, when Sir William Stanley crown'd him in the field, which was the 22nd day of August, 1485, to the 22nd of April 1508, is but 22 years and 8 months; whereas he reigned 23 years and 8 months, and dy'd the 22nd of April, 1509.

'This king (to speak of him in terms equal to his deserving) was one of the best sort of wonders: a wonder for wisemen. He had parts (both in his virtues, and his fortune) not so fit for a common place, as for observation. Certainly he was religious, both in his affection and observance. But as he could see clear (for those times) through superstition, so he would be blinded (now and then) by human policy. He advanced churchmen; he was tender in the privilege of sanctuaries, tho' they wrought him much mischief. He built and endowed many religious foundations, besides his memorable hospital of the Savoy. And yet was he a great alms-giver in secret; which shewed that his works in public were dedicated rather to God's glory, than his own. He professed always to love and seek peace; and it was his usual preface, in his treaties; 'That when Christ came into the world, peace was sung; and when he went out of the world, peace was bequeath'd.' And this virtue could not proceed out of fear or softness; for he was valiant and active, and therefore (no doubt) it was truly christian and moral. Yet he knew the way to peace, was not to seem to be desirous to avoid wars. Therefore would he make offers, and fames of wars, till he had mended the conditions of peace. It was also much, that one that was so great a lover of peace, should be so happy in war. For his arms (either in foreign or civil wars) were never unfortunate; neither did he know what a disaster meant. The war of his coming in, and the rebellions of the earl of Lincoln, and the lord Audley were ended by victory. The wars of France and Scotland by peaces sought at his hand. That of Brittain, by accident of the duke's death. The insurrection of the lord Lovel, and that of Perkin at Exeter, and in Kent, by flight of the rebels before they came to blows. So that his fortune of arms was still inviolate. The rather sure, for that in the quenching of the commotions of his subjects, he ever went in person. Sometimes reserving himself to back and second his lieutenants, but ever in action; and yet that was not merely forwardness, but partly distrust of others.

'He did much maintain and countenance his laws. Which (nevertheless) was no impediment to him to work his will. For it was so handled, that neither prerogative, nor profit went to diminution. And yet as he would sometimes strain up his laws to his prerogative, so would he also let down his prerogative to his parliament. For mint and wars, and martial discipline (things of absolute power), he would nevertheless bring to parliament. Justice was well administered in his time, save where the king was party: save also that the counciltable intermedled too much with *meum* and *teum*. For it was a very court of justice during his time, especially in the beginning. But in that part both of justice and policy, which is the durable part, and cut (as it were) in brass or marble (which is the making of good laws), he did excel. And with his justice, he was also a merciful prince. As in whose time there were but three of the nobility that suffer'd ; the earl of Warwick, the lord chamberlain, and the lord Audley. Though the first two were instead of numbers, in the dislike and obloquy of the people. But there were never so great rebellions expiated with so little blood, drawn by the hand of justice, as the two rebellions of Blackheath and Exeter. As for the severity used upon those which were taken in Kent, it was but upon a scum of people. His pardons went ever both before and after his sword. But then he had withal a strange kind of interchanging of large and inexpected pardons, with severe executions. Which (his wisdom consider'd) could not be imputed to any inconstancy, or inequality ; but either to some reason which we do not now know, or to a principle he had set unto himself, ' That he would vary, and try both ways in turn.' But the less blood he drew, the more he took of treasure. And (as some constru'd it) he was the more sparing in the one, that he might be the more pressing in the other ; for both would have been intolerable. Of nature assuredly he coveted to accumulate treasure, and was a little poor in admiring riches. The people (into whom there is infused, for the preservation of monarchies, a natural desire to discharge their princes, tho' it be with the unjust charge of their counsellors and ministers) did impute this unto cardinal Moreton, and sir Reginald Bray. Who (as it afterwards appear'd) as counsellors of ancient authority with him, did so second his humours, as nevertheless they did temper them. Whereas Empson and Dudley that follow'd, being persons that had no reputation with him (otherwise than by the servile following of his bent), did not give way only (as the first did), but shape him way to those extremities, for which himself was touch'd with remorse at his death, and which his successor renounc'd and sought to purge. This excess of his had at that time many glosses and interpretations. Some thought the continual rebellions wherewith he had been vexed, had made him grow to hate his people. Some thought it was done to pull down their stomachs, and to keep them low. Some, for that he would leave his son a golden fleece. Some suspected he had some high design upon foreign parts. But those perhaps shall come nearest the truth, that fetch not their reasons so far off ; but rather impute it to nature, age, peace, and a mind fixed upon no other ambition or pursuit. Whereunto I should add, that having every day occasion to take notice of the necessities and shifts for money of other great princes abroad, it did the better (by comparison) set off to him the felicity of full coffers. As to his expending of treasure, he never spar'd charge which his affairs requir'd ; and in his buildings was magnificent, but his rewards were very limited. So that his liberality was rather upon his own state and memory, than upon the deserts of others.

' He was of an high mind, and lov'd his own will, and his own way ; as one that revered himself, and would reign indeed. Had he been a private man he would have been termed proud. But in a wise prince, it was but keeping of distance, which indeed he did towards all; not admitting any near or full approach, neither to his power or to his secrets. For he was govern'd by none. His queen (notwithstanding she had presented him with divers children, and with a crown also, tho' he would not acknowledge it) could do nothing with him. His mother he reverenced much, heard little. For any person agreeable to him for society (such as was Hastings to king Edward IV., or Charles Brandon after to king Henry VIII.) he had none : except we should account for such persons, Fox, and Bray, and Empson; because they were so much with him; but it was but as the instrument is much with the workman. He had nothing in him of vain glory, but yet kept state and majesty to the height ; being sensible, that majesty maketh the people bow, but vain glory boweth to them.

'To his confederates abroad he was constant and just, but not open. But rather such was his inquiry, and such his closeness, as they stood in the light towards him, and he stood in the dark to them. Yet without strangeness, but with a semblance of mutual communication of affairs. As for little envies, or emulations upon foreign princes (which are frequent with many kings) he had never any ; but went substantially to his own business. Certain it is that though his reputation was great at home yet it was greater abroad. For foreigners that could not see the passage of affairs, but made their judgments upon the issues of them, noted that he was ever in strife, and ever a loft. It grew also from the airs which the princes and states abroad receiv'd from their ambassadors and agents here ; which were attending the court in great number. Whom he did not only content with courtesy, reward, and privateness ; but (upon such conferences as passed with them) put them in admiration, to find his universal insight into the affairs of the world. Which tho' he did suck chiefly from themselves ; yet that which he had gather'd from them all, seemed admirable to every one. So that they did write ever to their superiors in high terms, concerning his wisdom and art of rule, nay, when they were return'd, they did commonly maintain intelligence with him. Such a dexterity he had to impropriate to himself all foreign instruments.

'He was careful and liberal to obtain good intelligence from all parts abroad. Wherein he did not only use his interest in the liegers here, and his pensioners which he had both in the court of Rome, and other the courts of Christendom ; but the industry and vigilancy of his own ambassadors in foreign parts. For which purpose, his instructions were ever extream, curious, and articulate ; and in them more articles touching inquisition, than touching negotiation. Requiring likewise from his ambassadors an answer, in particular distinct articles, respectively to his questions.

'As for his secret spialls, which he did employ both at home and abroad, by them to discover what practices and conspiracies were against him, surely his case required it: he had such moles perpetually working and casting to undermine him. Neither can it be reprehended. For if spialls be lawful against lawful enemies, much more against conspirators and traytors. But indeed to give them credence by oaths or curses, that cannot be well maintained; for those are too holy vestments for a disguise. Yet surely there was this further good in his employing of these flies and familiars; that many conspiracies were revealed, so the fame and suspicion of them kept (no doubt) many conspiracies from being attempted.

'Towards his queen he was nothing uxorious, nor scarce indulgent; but companiable and respective, and without jealousy towards his children[1] he was full of paternal affection, careful of their education, aspiring to their high advancement, regular to see that they should not want of any due honour and respect, but not greatly willing to cast any popular lustre upon them.

'To his council he did refer much, and oft in person; knowing it to be the way to assist his power, and inform his judgment. In which respect also he was fairly patient of liberty, both of advice, and of vote, till himself were declar'd. He kept a strait hand on his nobility, and chose rather to advance clergymen and lawyers, which were more obsequious to him, but had less interest in the people; which made for his absoluteness, but not for his safety. In so much as (I am persuaded) it was one of the causes of his troublesome reign: for that his nobles, tho' they were loyal and obedient, yet did not co-operate with him, but let every man go his own way. He was not afraid of an able man, as Lewis XI. was. But contrariwise, he was serv'd by the ablest men that were to be found; without which his affairs could not have prosper'd as they did. For war, Bedford, Oxford, Surrey, Dawbeny, Brooke, Poynings. For other affairs, Moreton, Fox, Bray, the prior of Lanthony, Warham, Urswick, Hussey, Frowick, and others. Neither did he care how cunning they were, that he did employ; for he thought himself to have the master-reach: and as he chose well, so he held them up well. For it is a strange thing, that tho' he were a dark prince, and infinitely suspicious, and his times full of secret conspiracies and troubles; yet in twenty-four years reign, he never put down, or discomposed counsellor, or near servant, save only Stanley, the lord chamberlain. As for the disposition of his subjects in general towards him, it stood thus with him; that of the three affections, which naturally tie the hearts of the

[1] He had by his queen, Elizabeth Daughter to Edward the fourth; four sons and four daughters. Arthur who died five months after his marriage to the princess Katherine of Spain. Henry who married his brother's widow, and succeeded his father, by the name of Henry the eighth, Edmund and another son, who died young; Margaret queen of the Scots, and Mary, who married the French king Lewis the twelfth, and afterwards Charles Brandon, duke of Suffolk. The other two daughters died in their childhood.

subjects to their sovereigns; love, fear, and reverence; he had the last in height, the second in good measure, and so little of the first, as he was beholding to the other two.

' He was a prince sad, serious, and full of thoughts and secret observations, and full of notes and memorials of his own hand, especially touching persons. As whom to employ, whom to reward, whom to enquire of, whom to beware of, what were the dependencies, what were the factions and the like; keeping (as it were) a journal of his thoughts. There is to this day a merry tale; that his monkey (set on as it was thought by one of his chamber) tore his principal note book all to pieces, when by chance it lay forth. Whereat the court (which liked not those pensive accompts) was almost tickled with such sport.

' He was indeed full of apprehensions and suspicions. But as he did easily take them, so he did easily check them, and master them: whereby they were not dangerous, but troubled himself more than others. It is true, his thoughts were so many, as they could not well always stand together; but that which did good one way, did hurt another. Neither did he at some times weigh them aright in their proportions. Certainly that rumour which did him so much mischief (that the duke of York should be saved, and alive) was (at the first) of his own nourishing; because he would have more reason not to reign in the right of his wife. He was affable, and both well and fair spoken; and would use strange sweetness and blandishment of words, where he desired to effect or persuade any thing that he took to heart. He was rather studious than learned; reading most books that were of any worth, in the French tongue. Yet he understood the Latin, as appeareth in that cardinal Hadrian, and others, who could very well have written French, did use to write to him in Latin.

' For his pleasures, there is no news of them. And yet by his instruction to Marsin and Stile touching the queen of Naples, it seemeth he could interrogate well touching beauty. He did by pleasures, as great princes do by banquets, come and look a little upon them, and turn away. For never prince was more wholly given to his affairs, nor in them more of himself. In so much, as in triumphs of justs, and tourneys, and balls, and masks (which they then called disguises) he was rather a princely and gentle spectator, than seemed much to be delighted with them.

' No doubt, in him as in all men (and most of all in kings) his fortune wrought upon his nature, and his nature upon his fortune. He attained to the crown, not only from a private fortune, which might endow him with moderation; but also from the fortune of an exiled man, which had quickened in him all seeds of observation and industry. And his times being rather prosperous, than calm, had raised his confidence by success, but almost marred his nature by troubles. His wisdom, by often evading from perils, was turned rather into a dexterity to deliver himself from dangers, when they press'd him, than into a providence to prevent and remove them afar off. And even in nature, the sight of his mind was like some sights of eyes; rather strong at hand, than to carry afar off. For his wit increased upon the occasion; and so much the more if the occasion were sharpened by danger. Again, whether it were the shortness of his foresight, or the strength of his will, or the dazling of his suspicions, or what it was; certain it is, that the perpetual troubles of his fortunes (there being no more matter out of which they grew) could not have been without some great defects, and main errors in his nature, customs, and proceedings, which he had enough to do to save and help, with a thousand little industries and watches. But those do best appear in the story itself. Yet take him with all his defects, if a man should compare him with the kings his concurrents, in France and Spain, he shall find him more politick than Lewis the twelfth of France, and more entire and sincere that Ferdinando of Spain. But if you shall change Lewis the twelfth, for Lewis the eleventh, who lived a little before; then the consort is more perfect. For that Lewis the eleventh, Ferdinando, and Henry, may be esteemed for the *tres magi* of kings of those ages. To conclude, if this king did no greater matters, it was long of himself; for what he minded, he soon compassed.

' He was a comely personage, a little above just stature, well and straight limmed, but slender. His countenance was reverend, and a little like that of a churchman: and as it was not strange or dark, so neither was it winning or pleasing, but as the face of one well disposed. But it was to the disadvantage of the painter; for it was best when he spake.

' His worth may bear a tale or two, that may put upon him somewhat that may seem divine. When the lady Margaret, his mother had divers great suitors for marriage, she dream'd one night, that one in the likeness of a bishop, in pontifical habit, did tender her Edmund earl of Richmond (the king's father) for her husband. Neither had she ever any child but the king, though she had three husbands. One day when king Henry the sixth (whose innocency gave him holiness) was washing his hands at a great feast, and cast his eye upon king Henry, then a young youth, he said; 'This is the lad, that shall possess quietly that, that we now strive for.' But that that was truly divine in him, was, that he had the fortune of a true christian, as well as of a great king, in living exercis..d, and dying repentant. So as he had an happy warfare in both conflicts, both of sin and the cross.

' He was born at Pembroke castle, and lyeth buried at Westminster, in one of the stateliest and daintiest monuments of Europe, both for the chappel, and for the sepulcher. So that he dwelleth more richly dead, in the monument of his tomb, than he did alive in Richmond, or any of his palaces. I could wish he did the like, in this monument of his fame.'

THE REMARKABLE OCCURRENCES IN THE REIGN OF HENRY VII.

IN his second year, John Percival, the lord mayor's carver, was chosen one of the sheriffs of London in this manner: sir Henry Collet the lord mayor, took a cup of wine, and drank to John Percival, who waited then at his table standing bare, the lord mayor drinking to him and stiling him sheriff of London for the ensuing year, so far made use of his privilege of election that way, as to cause Percival to put on his hat, and sit down at the table; accordingly the carver sat down, took on him the office of sheriff, and was afterwards lord mayor himself, and knighted.

In his seventh year, Robert Fabian was elected an alderman and sheriff of London. He wrote a history of England and France, from the creation of the world to the third year of the reign of king Henry the VIII.

In his ninth year, on the 28th of April, Joan Broughton a widow was burnt in Smithfield for heresie and professing Wickliff's opinions. In this year wheat was sold in London for four shillings a quarter, and Bordeaux wine or Claret, for thirty shillings a hogshead.

In the tenth year of his reign, the body of one Alice Hackney, which had been buried 175 years, ever since the beginning of the reign of Edward the II, was accidently dug up in the church of St. Mary Hill, London: the skin of the corpse was whole, and the joynts of the arms were pliable.

In his fifteenth year, a pestilence rag'd in England, which swept away no less than 30,000 men, women and children in one year in the city of London.

In the seventeenth year of his reign, sir John Shaw, then Lord Mayor, first caus'd his brethren the aldermen to ride to the water side when he went to the exchequer-bar by water to be sworn. He was also the first that had the mayor's feast in Guild-Hall, which was before done at Grocer's or Merchant Taylor's Hall. Also this year Sebastian Cabot brought three Indians into England. They were cloath'd in beasts skins, and eat raw flesh. Two of these Indians were seen two years after dress'd like Englishmen, and not to be distinguish'd from them.

In the year following, on the 18th day of January, the first stone of the chappel known by the name of Henry the seventh's chappel was laid within the monastry of Westminster by John Islip the abbot, sir Reginal Bray knight of the garter, Dr. Barnes master of the rolls, sir Edward Stanhope, and others, assisting at the ceremonies. The charges of this building amounted to no more than fourteen thousand pounds, if we may believe our author.

In the 22nd year of his reign, the sweeting sickness which happen'd in his first year return'd; but the cure being known, it was not so mortal as the first was.

Besides the famous captains mention'd by the noble author of this reign, in his discoursing of king Henry VII. he had other officers of great valour and conduct, as

George earl of Shrewsbury, George lord Strange, Edward lord Woodville, sir Rice ap Thomas, the lord Morley, and sir John Cheyney. Those that we name hereafter were men of courage and experience; but being enemies to the house of Lancaster, and taking hold of all opportunities to disturb king Henry's government, they perished all of them as traytors.

John de la Pool earl of Lincoln, James Touchet lord Audley, the lord Lovel, sir Humphey Stafford, sir John Broughton, sir John Egremond, and sir Simon Monfort.

The writers in king Henry VII. time, were

George Ripley a Carmelite fryer of Boston. He wrote several mathematical treatises, and was after his death reckoned a conjurer by the populace.

Dr. John Ergham a black fryer born in York, professor of divinity at Oxford: he was fond of prophecies.

John Percival a Carthusian monk.

Thomas Maillorie a Welshman. He wrote of king Arthur and the knights of the round table.

Thomas Scroop of the noble family of the Scroops: he affected to preach in sackcloth and bare-foot. He was sometimes a Benedictine, sometimes a Dominican, and sometimes a Carmelite fryer. He was at last made a bishop in Ireland, and liv'd to be near a hundred years old. The latter part of his life he spent like an anchorite.

John Tonneis an Augustine fryer, wrote a grammar, which was printed by Richard Pinson one of the first printers in England.

Geffery, sirnamed the grammarian.

INDEX.

Adda succeeds his father Ida in the Kingdom of Bernicia, 86. Adminius, banish'd his country, flies to the Emp. Caligula, and stirs him up against it, 38.

Aganippus, a Gaulish king, marries Cordelia, the daughter of king Leir, 19. Agricola, son of Severianus, spreads the Pelagian doctrine in Britain, 70.

Aidan, a Scottish bp., sent for by Oswald to settle religion, 102.

Alaric takes Rome from the Emp. Honorius, 64. Alban of Verulam with others, suffers martyrdom under Dioclesian, 62. Albanact, one of the three sons of Brutus, has Albania, now Scotland, for his share in the kingdom, 17, defeated and slain by Humber king of the Huns, 17. Albina, said to be the eldest of Dioclesian's fifty daughters, 11, from her the name of Albion deriv'd, 11. Albion, the ancient name of this island, 11, from whence deriv'd, 11. Alcred, slaying Ethelwald, usurps the kingdom of the Northumbrians, 116. Aldfrid recall'd from Ireland, succeeds his brother Ecfrid in the Northumbrian kingdom, 110. He leaves Osred a child, to succeed him, 111. Aldulf, the nephew of Ethelwald, succeeds king of the East-Angles, 122. Alectus treacherously slays his friend Caurausius, to get the dominion, 61, overthrown by Asclepiodotus, and slain, 61. Alemannus, reported one of the four sons of Histion, descended from Japhet, and of whom the Alemanni or Germans, 12. Alsage, Abp. of Canterbury, inhumanly us'd by the Danes, 161, kill'd out-right by Thrum a Dane, in pity of his misery, 161.

Alfred, the fourth son of Ethelwolfe, succeeds his brother Ethelred, encounters the Danes at Wilton, 131. Gives battle to the whole Danish power at Edindon, and totally routing them, brings them to terms, 133. Said to have bestowed the East-Angles on Gytro a Danish king, who had been lately baptiz'd, 133. A long war afterwards maintain'd between him and the Danes, 134, 136, dies in thirtieth year of his reign, and is bury'd at Winchester, 136, his noble character, 136. Alfwold, driving out Eardulfe, usurps the kingdom of Northumberland, 121. Algar earl of Howland, Morcard lord of Brunne, and Osgot gov. of Lincoln, slaughter a great multitude of the Danes in battle with three of their kings, 129. Overpower'd with numbers, and drawn into a snare, Algar dies valiantly fighting, 130. Algar the son of Leofric banish'd by king Edward, joins with Griffin prince of South Wales, 183. Unable to withstand Harold earl of Kent, he submits to the king, 183. Banish'd, again he recovers his earldom by force, 184. Alipius made deputy of the Briti-h province, in the room of Martinus, 63. Alla begins the kingdom of Deira in the south part of Northumberland, 86. Alric king of Kent after Ethelbert II., 116. With him dying ends the race of Hengist, 118.

Ambrosius Aurelianus, dreaded by Vortimer, 80, defeats the Saxons in a memorable battle, 80, uncertain whether the son of Constantine the usurper, or the same with Merlin, and son of a Roman Consul, 80 succeeds Vortigern, as chief monarch of the isle, 80.

Anacletus, the friend of king Pandrasus, is taken in fight by Brutus, 14, forc'd by Brutus to betray his own countrymen, 14. Andragius, one in the catalogue of ancient British kings, 25. Androgeus, one of Lud's sons, has London assigned him, and Kent, 26. Forsakes his claim to the kingdom, and follows Cæsar's fortune, 38. Anlaff the Dane, with his army of Irish, and Constantine king of Scotland, utterly discomfited by king Athelstan, 145. Anna succeeds Sigebert in the kingdom of East-Angles, 103. Slain in war by Penda the Mercian, 103. Anne, heiress of Bretagne, marry'd by proxy to Maximilian king of the Romans, 311. Antigonius, brother of king Pandrasus, taken in fight by Brutus, 14. Antonius, sent against the Caledonians, 59, after the death of his father Severus, he takes hostages, and departs to Rome, 59. Antwerp, joyful reception of the English merchants there after treaty of peace and commerce, 355.

Archigallo depos'd for his tyranny, 24, being restor'd by his brother, he becomes a new man, and reigns worthily, 24. Archimailus one in the number of ancient British king 25. Armorica in France, peopled by Britains that fled from the Saxons, 78. Arthur, victory at Bad on-hill by some ascribed to him, by others attributed to Ambrose, 83, who he was, and whether the author of such famous acts as are related of him, 83. Lord Verulam's saying of him, 276. Arthur, eldest son of Hen. VII. born, 276, marry'd to Kath. of Spain, 380. Dies, 381. Character of, 381. Dispute whether he had carnal knowledge of the princess, 381, 382. Arviragus, engaging against Claudius, keeps up the battle to a victory by personating his slain brother Guiderius, 40.

Assaracus, a Trojan prince, joyns with Brutus against Pandrasus, 13. Another of that name, together with his brothers, conquer and settle in Germany, 18.

INDEX. 407

Athelstan, the son of king Edward the elder, by a concubine, solemnly crowned at Kingston upon Thames, 143, conspiracy of Alfred and his accomplices against him discovered, 143, gives his sister Edgith to Sitric the Dane, but drives Anlaf and Guthfred out of their kingdom, 143, the story of his dealing with his brother Edwin question'd as improbable, 143. Overthrows a vast army of Scots and Irish under Anlaff and Constantine king of Scotland, 144. Dies at Glocester, and is buried at Malmsbury, character, 146.

Audley, lord, heads the Cornish rebels, 357. Routed, taken, and ignominiously beheaded, 361. Aulus Plantius sent against this island by the Emperor Claudius, 39, overthrows Caractacus and Togodumnus, 39, very much put to it by the Britains, 39. Sends to Claudius to come over and joyn with him, 40, leaves the country quiet, and returns triumphant to Rome, 40. Aurelius Conanus, a British king, one of the five said to have reign'd towards the beginning of the Saxon heptarchy, 88. Austin, with others, sent over from Rome to preach the gospel to the Saxons, 92, receiv'd by king Ethelbert, who hears him in a great assembly, 92. Ordain'd Abp. of the English, 93, his seat at Canterbury, 93. Summons together the British bps., requiring them to conform with him in points wherein they differ'd, 94, upon their refusal he stirs up Ethelfred against them, to the slaughter of 1200 monks, 94, 95.

Baldred the last king of Kent, submits to Ecbert, 121. Banocksbourn, battle at, 305. Bardus, one of the first race of kings fabled to have reign'd in this island, 11, descended from Samothes, 11. Battel of Bosworth, 260, 263. Of Stokefield, 286. Of St. Albans in Bretagne, 301. Of Dixmuyde, 311.
Beda, his death, 112. Bedford, Jasper Tudor Earl of Pembroke, created duke of, 271. General against the earl of Lincoln and Simnel's army, 284. At Hen. VII.'s French expedition, 326. Death, 359. Benevolence, tax so called, granted to Hen. VII. by act of parliament, 321. Another, 388. Beorn precedes Ethelred in the kingdom of the East-Angles, 122. Berinus a bp., sent by Pope Honorius, converts the West-Saxons and their kings to christianity, 102.
· Bernulfe, usurping the kingdom of Mercia from Kealwulf, is overthrown by Ecbert at Ellandune, 121. Flying to the East-Angles, is by them slain, 122.
Birthric, king of the West Saxons, after Kinwulf, 117. Secretly seeks the life of Ecbert, 120, poyson'd by a cup which his wife had prepared for another, 120. Bishops, Scots and English disagree about the time of keeping Easter, 106, Saxon bps. zealous for the Romish discipline, 106.
Bladud, son of Rudhudibras, builds Caerbadus or Bath, 18 Bleadon in Somersetshire, why so call'd, 125. Bleduno, one of the ancient British kings, 25. Blegadebus, his excellency in musick, 25.
Boadicea, wife of Prasutagus, together with

her daughters, abus'd by the Roman soldiers, 43. Commands in chief the British army against the Romans, 47. Vanquish'd by Suetonius, thought to have poyson'd herself, 48. Bonosus, a Britain by descent, endeavouring to make himself Emp., is vanquish'd by Probus, hangs himself, 59. Bourchier, Thos., speech to the lords against violating sanctuaries, in relation to their taking thence Rich. duke of York, brother to Edw. V., 206. Goes to the queen to persuade her to deliver him up, 209, conference with her, 210, 216.
Brackenbury, sir Rob., lieut. of the Tower, refuses to be concern'd in the murder of Edw. V. and his brother the duke of York, 237. Kill'd at the battle of Bosworth, in Richard's army, 261. Brampton, lady, carries Perkin Warbeck to Portugal, 330. Brandon, sir Will., kill'd at the battle of Bosworth, by king Richard himself, 261. Bray, Reginald, chief agent in managing the conspiracy to dethrone Rich. III. and advance Hen. VII., 246. Complain'd of, when in favour with Henry VII., 356. Brennus and Belinus, sons of Dunwallo Mulmutius, contend about the kingdom, 22, after various conflicts, they are reconcil'd by their mother Conuvenna, turn 22, their united forces against foreign parts but Belinus returns, and reigns long in peace, 22. Bretagne, Francis, duke of, duchy like to be torn from him by Chas. VIII. of France in his old age, 291. 292. Death, 301. Causes of the loss of his duchy to the French, 301.
Britain, the history of its affairs altogether obscure and uncertain till the coming of Julius Cæsar, 9. By whom first peopled, 11, nam'd first Samothea from Samothes; next, Albion, and from whence, 11. Britains stoutly oppose Cæsar at his landing in this island, 29. Offer him terms of peace, 30. Manner of fighting, 31. Are defeated by Cæsar, 33. Brought anew to terms of peace, 35. Sharp dispute between the Britains and Romans near the Stour in Kent, 35. Nature and customs, 37. Cruel massacre of the Romans, 46. Are acquitted of the Roman jurisdiction by the Emp. Honorius, not able to defend them against their enemies, 66. Again supplicate Honorius for aid, who spares them a Roman legion, 68, and again, at their new request, another supply, 68. Their submissive letters to Ætius the Roman consul, 72. Luxury and wickedness, corruption of the clergy, 73. Embassy to the Saxons for their aid against the Scots and Picts, the Saxons answer 74. Miserably harrass'd by the Saxons, whom they call'd in, 77. Routed by Kerdic, 81. By Kenric and Keaulin, 85. By Cuthulf, 89. Totally vanquish Keaulin, 89. Are put to flight by Kenwalk, 106. Brito, nam'd among the four sons of Histion, sprung of Japhet, from him the Britains said to be deriv'd, 12.
Brook, R. Lord, sent with an army to the aid of the duke of Bretagne, by Hen. VII., 301, returns without doing anything, 301. Broughton, sir Thos., joyns Lambert

Simnell's followers, 285. Kill'd at Stoke Fight, 286. Brutus, said to be descended from Æneas a Trojan prince, 12. Retiring into Greece, after having unfortunately kill'd his father, he delivers his countrymen from the bondage of Pandrasus, 13. Marries Innogen the eldest daughter of Pandrasus, 14. Lands upon a desert island call'd Leogicia, 15, consults the oracle of Diana, 15. Meets with Corineus, 16, overcomes Goffarius Pictus, arrives in this island, 16. Builds Troja Nova, 17, death, 17. Brutus, sirnam'd Greenshield, succeeds Ebranc, and gives battle to Brunchildis, 18.
Buchanan, censur'd by Milton, 121, 142. Buck loses his head at Bosworth, 273. Buckingham, duke of, sends to the duke of Glocester to offer him his service on king Edw. IV.'s death, 196. Conspires to seize the person of Edw. V., 198. Assists the duke of Glocester to arrest lord Rivers the king's uncle, and his half brother lord Rich. Gray, 199. Answer to Card. Bourchier, Abp. of Canterbury, about sanctuaries, 208. Speech on that subject made by him, 208. Engages the protector to take the crown, 217. Speech to the citizens of London, to prevail with them to choose the duke of Glocester king, 231, 233. To the duke of Glocester to accept the crown, 234. Quarrels with him when king, 238. Conference with Dr. Moreton, bp. of Ely, about dethroning Rich., and setting up Hen. earl of Richmond, 240, 248. Sends to the countess and earl of Richmond, 247. Takes arms, and is defeated by means of a great flood, 248. Buckingham, Edward Stafford his eldest son, restor'd in blood, and is styl'd duke of, 274. Burhead, holding of Ethelwolf the Mercian kingdom after Bertulfe, reduces the North Welsh to obedience, 126, marries Ethelsuida, daughter of king Ethelwolfe, 126. Driven out of his kingdom by the Danes, flies to Rome, where dying, he is bury'd in a church by the English school, 131. His kingdom let by Danes to Kelwulf, 132.

Caius Sidius Geta behaves himself valiantly against the Britains, 39. Caius Volusenus sent into Britain by Cæsar to make discovery of the country and people, 28. Caligula, a Roman Emp., 38. Camalodunum, or Maldon, chief seat of Kymbelines, 38. Roman Colony, 40. Camber, one of the sons of Brutus, has Cambria or Wales allotted him, 17. Cambridge Univ., said to be founded by Sigebert king of the East-Angles, 103. Burnt by the Danes, 160. Canute, son of Swane, chosen king after his father's death by the Danish army and fleet, 162. Driven back to his ships by Ethelred, 163, returns with a great navy from Denmark, accompanied with Lachman king of Sweden, and Olave king of Norway, 163. After several conflicts with Edmund, at length divides the kingdom with him by agreement, 167. After Edmund's death, reigns sole king, 168, endeavours the extirpation of the Saxon line, 168 settles his kingdom, and makes peace with the princes round about him, 168, causes Edric, whose treason he had made use of, to be slain, and his body to be thrown over the city wall, 168, subdues Norway, 170, takes a voyage to Rome, and offering there rich gifts, vows amendment of life; dies at Shaftesbury, bury'd at Winchester, 170, character, 170.
Capell, sir William, alderman of London, severely us'd by Hen. VII., 344. Second troubles of, 395. Capis, one of the ancient kings, 25. Capoirus an ancient British king, 25. Caractacus, youngest son of Cunobeline, succeeds in the kingdom, 39, overthrown by Aulus Plautius, 39. Heads the Silures against the Romans, 42. Betray'd by Cartismandua, to whom he fled for refuge, 42. Sent to Rome, 43, speech to the Emp., 43, by the bravery of his carriage he obtains pardon for himself and all his company, 43. Carausius, grown rich with piracy, possesses himself of this island, 60, fortifies the wall of Severus, 60. In the midst of the great preparations of Constantius Chlorus against him, is slain by his friend Alectus, 61. Carinus sent by his father the Emperor to govern the isle of Britain, and slain by Dioclesian, 60.
Cartismandua queen of the Brigantines, delivers up Caractacus bound to the Romans, deserts her husband Venutius, and gives both herself and kingdom to Villocatus, one of her esquires, 42, 44. Carvilius, king of Britain, assaults the Roman camp, 36. Cassibelaun, son of Heli, gains the kingdom by common consent, 26, generosity to his brother's sons, 26. Heads the Britains against Julius Cæsar and the Romans, 34, deserted by the Trinobantes, and why, 35. Yields to Cæsar, 35, reported to have had war with Androgeus, dies and is bury'd at York, 36. Castello, Adrian de, made bp. of Hereford by Hen. VII., 306, made cardinal, and conspires against the Pope, 306. Cataracta an ancient cityi n Yorkshire, burnt by Alured, 116. Catesby, sir Wm., a lawyer and creature of Rich. III. sounds lord Hastings, to know if he was for Richard's usurpation, 218. His treachery, 219. Catullus, an ancient British king, 25.
Cerdic, a Saxon prince, lands at Cerdicshoar, and overthrows the Britains, 81, defeats king Natanleod in a battle, 82, founds the kingdom of the West-Saxons, 82.
Chambers, John, rebels against Hen. VII., 305, hang'd at York, 305. Chancery, court of, its power and description. 302. Chandois, Mons., a Breton, made earl of Bath by Hen. VII. 274. Chapel, Hen- VII.'s founded, 404. Charles VIII. the French king, aims to annex the duchy of Bretagne to the crown of France, 290, sends an embassy to Hen. VII. to prevail with him not to assist the duke of Bretagne, 290. Dissembles with Henry, 292. Gains the battle of St. Albans against the dukes of Orleans and Bretagne, 301. Dissembles with Maximilian, whose daughter he had promis'd to marry, 310. Sends an em-

INDEX.

bassy to Hen. VII. to desire him to admit of his marrying Ann of Bretagne, to whom he pleas'd, 313, his embassadors speech to Hen. VII.'s council, 313. Marries lady Ann after she was married to Maximilian, 318. Buys peace, and pays tribute to Hen. VII., 327. Noble reception of Perkin Warbeck, 332, sends him away, 332. Expedition into Italy, 346, league against him, 346. Recommends Perkin to the Scots king, 349, Death, 373.

Charles prince of Castile (Charles V.), contracted to the princess Mary, daughter to Hen. VII., 396. Cherem, an ancient British king, 25. Christian Faith receiv'd in Britain by king Lucius, 55. Preached by Fagonus and Deruvianus, 56, by Simon Zelotes, or Joseph of Arimathea, 56. Upon what occasion preach'd to the Saxons, 92. Chrysanthus, son of Marcianus, a bp., made deputy of Britain by Theodosius, 64.

Cingetorex, a king in Britain, assaults the Roman camp, 36, taken prisoner by Cæsar, 36. Cissa succeeds Ella, founder of the South-Saxon kingdom, 82.

Claudius the emp. persuaded by Bericus, though a Britain, to invade this island, 39, sends Aulus Plautius hither with an army, 39. Comes over himself, and joyns with Plautius, 40, defeats the Britains and takes Camalodunum, 40, returns to Rome, leaving Plautius behind, 40, has excessive honours decreed him by the Senate, 40. Clergy, a law to burn 'em in the hand, 303. Clifford, Sir Rob., one of the conspirators against Hen. VII. in favour of Perkin Warbeck, 334, goes to him, discourses him, and writes to his accomplices, that he is certainly Rich. Duke of York, 334. Is brought over to Henry's interest, 336. Comes to England, and gives Hen. VII. an account of the designs form'd against him, 338. Impeaches Sir William Stanley, 339. Cligellius, an ancient British king, 25. Clodius Albinus succeeds Pertinax in the Government of Britain, 57. Clotenus, one of the ancient British kings, 25.

Coilius, an ancient British king, 25. Coilus, son of Marius, leaves the kingdom to Lucius, 56. Collingburn, Will., Esq., of Lydiard in Wiltshire, hang'd for writing a dystich upon Rich. III., 251. Columbus, Christ., sends his brother Barthol. to treat with Hen. VII. about his voyage to the West-Indies, 371. Barthol. being taken by the pyrates hinders his negotiation, 371. Comail, and two other British kings slain by Keaulin and Cuthuin, 89. Comius of Arras, sent by Cæsar to make a party among the Britains, 28. Imprison'd as a Spy, 30. Conspiracy against Rich, III., 246, 250. Hen. VII. by Sir Will. Stanley, 334. Constans, of a monk made Cæsar, reduces all Spain to Constantine's obedience, 66, displacing Gerontius, is oppos'd by him, and at last slain, 66. Constantine, son of Constantius Chlorus, saluted Emp. after his father's death, 62, his mother said to be Helena daughter of Coilus a British prince, 62. His eldest son of the same name enjoys, among other provinces of the empire, this island also, 62; A soldier of the same name, saluted emp., 65. By the valour of Oedebicus and Gerontius gains France as far as Arles, 66. By the conduct of Constans and Gerontius he reduces all Spain, 66. Gerontius displac'd by him, calls in the Vandals, 66. Beseig'd by Constantius Comes, he turns priest, is carry'd to Italy, and put to death, 66. Constantine, son of prince Cador, inveigh'd against by Gildas, 88, said to have murther'd two young princes of the blood royal, 88. Constantine king of Scotland, joyning with the Danes and Irish under Anlaf, is overthrown by Athelstan, 144. Constantius Chlorus, sent against Carausius, 60, defeats Alectus, who is slain, 61, acknowledged the Britons as their deliver, 61. Divides the empire with Galerius, 62, dies at York, 62. Constantius, son of Constantine, overcomes Magnentius, who contested with him for the empire, 62. Cordelia's answer to her father, begets this displeasure, 19, married to Aganippus, king in Gaul, 19. Receives her father, rejected by his other daughters, with most dutiful affection, 20, restores him to his crown, and reigns after him, 20, vanquish'd, depos'd and imprison'd by her two sisters sons, 20. Cordes Seigneur, his hatred to the English, 311, his vain expression to that effect, 311. Writes to Henry II. to desire a peace for his Master, 326. Corineus, a Trojan commander, joyns forces with Brutus, 16, slay Imbertus, 16, arrives with Brutus in this island; Cornwall, from him denominated falls to his lot, 16, overcomes the gyant Gogmagog, 17. Cornishmen rebel against Hen. VII., 356. March as far as Blackheath, and are routed, 357, 360. Rise again for Perkin, and march with him to the seige of Exeter, 366. Deserted by him, 368. Courts of justice, what pleas belong to every one, 302. Creation of Noblemen, 271, 274. Crida, first king of Mercia, 90.

Cuichelm the West-Saxon sends Eumerus to assassin king Edwin, 98. Baptiz'd at Dorchester, dies the same year, 102. Cunedagius, son of Regan, deposes his aunt Cordelia, 20, shares the kingdom with his cousin Marganus, invaded by him, meets and overcomes him, 20. Cuneglas, a British king, one of the five that reign'd a little before the Saxons were settled, 89. Cutha helps Keaulin against Ethelbert, 86. Assists him at Fethan Laeg, 89. Cuthred, king of the West-Saxons, joyns with Ethelbald the Mercian, and gains a great victory over the Welsh, 114, has a fierce battel with Ethelbald the Mercian, which he not long survives, 114. A king of Kent of the same name, 121. Cuthulfe, brother of Keaulin, vanquishes the Britains at Bedanford, and takes several towns, 89.

Danes first appear in the West, 117. Slay the king's collectors of his customs, 118. Land at Lindisfarn in Yorkshire, pillage that monastery, slay and capture several, both fryars and others, 118. Attempting to spoil another monastery, are cut off by the English, 119. Make very great waste in Northumberland, 122. Destroy Shepey in Kent, and engage with Ecbert near the river Carr, 124, are overthrown and put to flight by Ecbert, 124. Various success in the reign of Ethelwolf, 125. Great battles between them and the English in the reign of Ethelred, with various fortune, 130, 131. Being defeated, are brought to terms by king Alfred, 132. Vast fleets of Danes arrive with fresh supplies 132, 138. Overthrown by king Athelstan, 144. Massacre committed upon them by the English in all parts of the land in the reign of king Ethelred, 157. Danius an ancient British king, 23. Dawbeny lord, beats the French at Dixmuide, 311. The Cornish rebels at Blackheath, 359.

Devonshire, Edw. Courtney made Earl of, by Hen. VII., 271.

Dinothus Abbot of Bangor, speech to Bp. Austin, 95. Dioclesian king of Syria, and his fifty daughters, having, all but one, murther'd their husbands, are said to have been driven upon this island, 11. Dis, the first peopler of this island, as some fabulously affirm, 11, the same with Samothes, 11. Dixmuyd, battel of, 311.

Donaldus, said to have headed the Caledonians against Sept'mius Severus, 59. Donaldus, king of Scotland, brought to hard conditions by Osbert and Ella kings of Northumberland, 127. Dorset, Thos. Gray Marquess of, one of the conspirators that took arms with the Duke of Bucks against Rich., 248. Flies to the Earl of Richmond in Bretagne, 249. Would leave him, but is stopp'd, and left hostage in France, 255. Imprison'd by Hen. VII., 284. Releas'd, 283.

Druids falsely alledg'd out of Cæsar to have forbidden the Britains to write their memorable deeds, 9. Druis, fabulously written the ancientest king of this island, 11.

Dudley, one of the greatest instruments of Hen. VII.'s Exactions, chosen speaker of the House of Commons, 386. Dunstane, sent by the nobles to reprove King Edwi for his luxury, 149, banish'd by the king, and his monastery rifled, 149, recall'd by Edgar, 149. Miraculous escape, when the rest of the company were kill'd by the fall of an house, 153. Dunwallo Mulmutius, son of Cloten king of Cornwall, reduces the whole island into a monarchy, 21, establishes the Molmutin laws, 21. Durstus king of the Picts, slain by the joynt forces of the Britains and Romans, 69.

Ealbald, after the death of his father Ethelbert, falls back to Paganism, 96, runs distracted, afterwards returns to his right mind and faith, by what means it happen'd, 97, gives his sister Edelburge in marriage to Edwin, 98. Dies, and leaves his son Ercombert to succeed him, 101. Eadbert shares with his brothers in the kingdom of Kent after Victred, 112. Death, 114. Eadbright, king of Northumberland and Kelwulf, wars against the Picts, 114. Joyns with Unulf king of the Picts against the Britains in Cumberland, 115 forsakes his crown for a monk's hood, 115. Eadbright, otherwise call'd Ethelbert, usurping the kingdom of Kent, and contending with Kenulph the Mercian is taken prisoner, 119. Eadburgha by chance poysons her husband Birthric with a cup which she had prepar'd for another, 120, choice propos'd to her by Charlemagne, to whom she fled, 120, assigns her a rich monastery to dwell in as abbess ; detected of unchastity, expelled and dies in Pavia, 120.

Eandred, son of Eardulf king of Northumberland, reigns after Alfwold, 121. Submits to Ecbert, 122. Eanfrid, son of Ethelfrid, succeeds in the kingdom of Bernicia, 101. Eardulf, suppos'd to have been slain by Ethelfred, made king of the Northumbrians in York after Osvald, 117, in a war rais'd against him by his people he gets the victory, 119, driven out of his kingdom by Alfwold, 119, 121. EastAngle kingdom, by whom erected, 82. Embrace the Christian faith, apostatize, and are reclaim'd to it again, 101. East Saxon kingdom, by whom begun, 82. The people converted by Mellitus, 94. Expel their bishop, and renounce their faith, are reconverted by Oswi, 104. Relapse, and are again recover'd, 106.

Ebrane succeeds Mempricius in the kingdon of Britain, 18, builds Caer Ebrace, now York, and other places, 18. Ecbert succeeds Ercombert in the kingdom of Kent, 107, dying, leaves a suspicion of having slain his uncle's sons, Elbert and Egelbright, 107. Ecbert, of the West-Saxon lineage, flies from Birthric's suspicion to Offa, and thence into France, 120, after Birthric's decease, is recall'd, and with general applause made king, 120. Subdues the Britains of Cornwall, and beyond Severn, overthrows Bernulfe the usurper of Mercia at Ellandune or Wilton, 121, the East-Angles having slain Bernulf, yield to his sovereignty, 122, drives Baldred king of Kent out of his kingdom, and causes both Kent and other provinces to submit to his scepter, 122, Withlaf of Mercia becomes tributary to him, 122. Gives the Danes battle by the river Carr, 124, in another battle he puts to flight a great army of them, together with the Cornishmen joyning with them, 124, dies, bury'd at Winchester, 124. Ecferth, son of Offa the Mercian, within four months ends his reign, 119. Ecfrid, Oswi's eldest son succeeds him in the kingdom of Northumberland, 107, wins Lindsey from Wulfer the Mercian, 107. Wars against Ethelred the brother of Wulfer, 108. Sends Bertus with an army to subdue Ireland, 109. Marching against the Picts, is cut off with most of his army, 110. Death reveng'd by Bentfrid a Northumbrian captain, 111.

Edan, king of the Scots in Britain, put to flight by Ethelfrid, 94. Edelard, king of the West-Saxons, molested with the rebellions of his kinsman Oswald, 114, overcomes those troubles, dies in peace, 114. Edgar, brother and successor of Edwi in the English monarchy, recalls Dunstan from Banishment, 149 Peaceable and prosperous reign, his favours towards the monks, 151, strict observance of justice, and care to secure the nation with a strong fleet, 151, is homag'd and row'd down the river Dee by eight kings, 151, expostulation with Kened king of Scotland, 151, cheated of Elfrida by the treacherous duke Othelwold; he revenges himself upon him. and marries her, 152. Attempting the chastity of a young lady at Andover, he is pleasantly deceiv'd by the mother, 152, dying in the height of his glory, is bury'd at Glastonbury-abby, 152, his vast navy, 152.

Edgar, Perrin Etheling, his right to the crown of England from his grandfather Edmund Ironside, 183. Excluded by Harold, son earl Godwin, 184. Edilhere, brother and successor of Anna in the kingdom of the East-Angles, 106. Edilwalk the South-Saxon, persuaded to christianity by Wulfer, 108. Edmund crown'd king of the East-Angles at Bury, 127. His army put to flight by the Danes, is taken, bound to a stake, and shot with arrows, 127. Edmund, brother and successor of Athelstan in the English monarchy, frees Mercia, and takes several towns from the Danes, 147, drives Anlas and Suthfrid out of Northumberland and Dummail out of Cumberland, 147. Strange manner of his death, 148. Edmund, surnam'd Ironside, the son of Ethelred, set up by divers of the nobles against Canute, 165, in several battles against the Danes comes off for the most part victorious, 165. Consents to divide the kingdom with Canute, 167, his death thought to have been violent and not without Canute's consent, 167, 168. Edred, third brother and successor of Athelstan, with much ado reduces the Northumbrians, and puts an end to that kingdom, 148, dies in the flower of his age; bury'd at Winchester, 148. Edric, son of Edilwalk king of the West-Saxons, slain by Kedwalla the West-Saxon, 108. Edrice, sirnam'd Streon, advanc'd by king Ethelred, marries his daughter Elgiva, 159, secretly murders two noblemen, whom he had invited to his lodging, 163, practices against the life of prince Edmund, and revolts to the Danes, 164. Cunning devices to hinder Edmund in the persecution of his victories against Canute, 166. Thought by some to have been the contriver of king Edmund's murder, 167. Government of the Mercians conferr'd upon him, 168, put to death by Canutus, his head stuck upon a pole, and set upon the highest tower in London, 169.

Edward the elder, son and successor of king Alfred, wars with Ethelwald his kinsman, who stirs up the Danes against him, 139. Proves successful and potent, divers princes and great commanders of the Danes submitting to him, 140, 142. The king and whole nation of Scotland, with several other princes and people, do him homage as their sovereign, 142, dies at Farendon, bury'd at Winchester, 142. Edward sirnam'd the Younger, Edgar's son by his first wife Egelsleda, is advanc'd to the Throne, 153, contest in his eign between the monks and secular priests, each abetted by their several parties, 153, great mischief done by the falling of a house, where a general council for deciding the controversie was held, 153, inhumanely murther'd by the treachery of his stepmother Elfrida, 153. Edward, son of Edmund Ironside, heir apparent of the crown, dies at London, 167. Edward the Confessor, son of king Ethelred by Emma, after Hardecnute's death, is crown'd at Winchester, 176, seizes on the treasures of his mother queen Emma, 176, marries Edith Earl Godwin's daughter, 176, makes preparation against Magnus king of Norway, but next year concludes a peace with Harold Harfager, 177, advances the Normans in England, which proves of ill consequence, 178. oppos'd by earl Godwin in the cause of Eustace of Boloigne, banishes the earl, and divorces his daughter, whom he had marry'd, 178, entertains D. William of Normandy, 180. Sends Odo and Radulfe with a fleet against Godwin and his sons exercising piracy, 180, reconcil'd to the earl, restores his sons and daughter to all their former dignities, 181. Said to have design'd Wm. of Normandy his successor to the crown, 186, dies and is bury'd at Westminster, 186, character, 186, the first king that touch'd for the evil, 186.

Edward V. his succession, 193, state of affairs at his father's death, 193, account of his birth, 193. Forcibly taken from lord Rivers his uncle by the dukes of Glocester and Buckingham, 199, his saying in excuse of his half brother the lord Richard Gray, 199, 200. Brought to town, 203, solemn entry, 203. He and his brother charged with bastardy, 229. Murther'd in the tower by sir James Tyrrel, 237. Edward, son of Rich. III., created Prince of Wales, at his father's coronation, 236. Edwi, son and successor of Edmund, is crown'd at Kingston, 149, banishes bp. Dunstan, for reproving his wantonness with Algiva, and proves an enemy to all monks, 149, the Mercians and Northumbrians revolt from him, and set up his brother Edgar, 149, he dies with grief, and is bury'd at Winchester, 149. Edwen, thrown out of the kingdom of Deira by Ethelfric, 91. Flying to Kedwall the East-Angle for refuge, is defended against Ethelfric, 97, exceeds in power and extent of dominion all before him, 97, marries Edelburga the sister of Eudbald, 98, wounded by an assassin from Cuichelm, 98. Strange relation of his conversion to Christianity, 99, persuades Eorpald the son of Redwell to embrace the Christian faith, 101, slain in a battle against Kedwall, 101.

Egremont, sir J., rebels against Hen. VII., 304, defeated and flies to Flanders, 305. Elanus, Eldacus, Eldol, Eledacus, reckon'd among the number of ancient British kings, 25. Elsted, sister of king Edward the elder, takes Derby from the Danes, 140, her army of Mercians victorious against the Welsh, 140. After several martial deeds, dies at Tamworth, 141. Elfred, son of king Ethelred, betray'd by

Earl Godwin, and cruelly made away by Harold, 172. Elfwald, son of Oswulf, succeeding Ethelred in Northumberland, is rebell'd against by two of his noblemen, Osbald and Ethelheard, 116, slain by the conspiracy of Siggan, one of his nobles, 116. Elfwin, slain in a battle between his brother Ecfrid and Ethelred, 109. Elidure's noble demeanour towards his depos'd brother, 24, after Archigallo's death, resumes the government, but is driven out again, and imprison'd by his two other brethren, 24, restor'd again to the sovereignty, 25. Eliud, reckon'd in the number of ancient British kings, 25.

Elizabeth, widow of sir John Gray, marry'd to Edw. IV., her pride 193, contrivances to secure the succession to her son, 193, the ancient nobility's resentment of her actions, 194, deceived by the duke of Glocester's pernicious advice, 198. Flies to sanctuary with her children, 201. Conference with Cardinal Burchier Abp. of Canterbury, who came to her to persuade her to deliver up her son Richard duke of York to the duke of Glocester, 210, 214. Speech at the delivery of her son, 215. Her marriage with king Edward said to be unlawful, and her children illegitimate, 229. Enters into a treaty with the countess of Richmond to marry the princess Elizabeth to Henry earl of Richmond, 247. Persuaded by Richard to leave sanctuary, and deliver up her daughters to him, 252. Writes to her son the marquis of Dorset to quit the earl of Richmond's party, 255. Her goods and estate seiz'd, and herself confin'd, and why, 278, 281. Her various fortunes, 281, founds Queen's College in Cambridge, 281. Elizabeth princess, is sent for by Hen. VII. immediately after his victory at Bosworth, 269. Has some fears that he will not marry her, 270. Marry'd, 275, the king not fond of her, and why, 275, delivered of her eldest son in the eighth month, 276. Crown'd, after staying two years for it, 288. Death, 383. Ella the Saxon lands with his three brothers, and beats the Britains in two battles, 82, he and his son Cissa take Andreschester in Kent by force, 82, begins his kingdom of the South-Saxons, 82. Elwold, nephew of Ethelwald, reigns king of the East-Angles after Aldulf, 122.

Emeric succeeds Otha in the kingdom of Kent, 86. Emma, daughter of Richard duke of Normandy, marry'd first to king Ethelred, 157. Afterwards to Canute, 169. Banish'd by her son in law Harold, she retires to Flanders, and is entertain'd by earl Baldwin, 172. Her treasures seiz'd on by her son king Edward; dies and is bury'd at Winchester, 180, a tradition concerning her question'd, 180. Empson, one of Hen. VII.'s horse-leeches, his descent and character, 383.

Ennianus, reckon'd among the ancient British kings, 25, depos'd for tyranny, 25.

Eorpald, son of Redwald king of the East-Angles, persuaded to Christianity by Edwin, 101, slain by Richert a pagan, 101. Ercherwin, said by Huntington to be the founder of the kingdom of the East-Saxons, 82. Ercombert succeeds Eadbald in the kingdom of Kent, 103, the first English king that commanded idols to be destroy'd, 103. Erice a Dane, made earl of Northumberland by Canute in place of Uthric slain, 165. Said by some to have made war against Malcolm king of the Scots, 169. His greatness suspected by Canute ; he is banish'd the realm, 169. Ermenred, thought to have had more right to the kingdom than Ercombert, 103.

Esca, the son of Hengist, succeeds him in the kingdom of Kent, 86. Esewin and Kentwin, the nephew and son of Kinegil, said to have succeeded Kenwalk in the government of the West-Saxons, 107, Esewin joyns battle with Wulfer at Bedanhafer, and not long after dies, 107. Estrildis belov'd by Locrine, 17, is with her daughter Sabra thrown into a river, 17.

Ethelbald, king of Mercia after Kelred, commands all the provinces on this side Humber, 112, takes the town of Somerton, 112, fraudulently assaults part of Northumberland in Eadbert's absence, 114. Encounter at Beorford with Cuthred the West-Saxon, 114, in another bloody fight at Secandune he is slain, 114. — and Ethelbert share the English Saxon kingdom between them after their father Ethelwolfe, Ethelbald marries Judith his father's widow, 128. bury'd at Shireburn, 128. Ethelbert succeeds Emeric in the kingdom of Kent, 86, defeated at Wibbandun by Keaulin and his son Cutha, 86. Enlarges his dominions from Kent to Humber, 90. Civilly receives St. Austin and his fellow preachers of the gospel, 92, is himself baptiz'd, 92. Mov'd by St. Austin, he builds St. Peter's church at Canterbury and endows it, 93, builds and endows St. Paul's church in London, and the cathedral at Rochester, 94, death and character, 96. —, Eadbert and Alric succeed their father Victred in the kingdom of Kent, 116. — the son of Ethelwolfe, after the death of Ethelbald, enjoys the whole kingdom to himself, 128, during his reign the Danes waste Kent, 128, bury'd with his brother at Sherburn, 128. Ethelbrite king of the East-Angles, slain by Offa, 122. Etheldrite refusing for twelve years her husband Ecfrid's bed, veils herself a nun, and is made able s of Ely, 109. Ethelfred now succeeds E.helrice in the kingdom of Northumberlan l, 90. He wastes the Britains, 94, overthrows Edan king of Scots, 94. In a battle at Westchester against the British forces he slays above twelve hundred monks, 95. Slain by Redwald the East-Saxon, 119. Ethelmund and Weolstan, the opposite leaders of each party in a fight between the Worcestershire-men and Wiltshire-men slain, 120. Ethelred succeeding his brother Wulfer in the kingdom of Mercia, recovers Lindsey and other parts, 109, invades the kingdom of Kent, 109, a sore battle between him and Ecfrid the Northumbrian, 110. After the violent death of his queen exchanges his crown for a monk's cowl,

INDEX.   413

110. — the son of Mollo, the usurper Alcled being forsaken by the Northumbrians and depos'd, is crown'd in his stead, 116, having caus'd three of his noblemen to be treacherously slain, is driven into banishment, 116. After ten years banishment restor'd again, 118, cruelly and treacherously puts to death Oelf and Oelwin, the sons of Elfwald, formerly king, 118, and Osred, who tho' shaven a monk, attempted again upon the kingdom, 118, marries Elfled daughter of Offa, 118, miserably slain by his people, 11C. —, son of Eandred, driven out in his fo· r::1 year, 125, re-exalted to his throne, but slain the fourth year after, 125. — king of the East-Angles, 122. —, third son of Ethelwolfe, the third monarch of the English Saxons, infested with fresh invasions of the Danes, 129. Fights several great battles with the Danes with various success, 129. Dies in the fifth year of his reign, bury'd at Winburn, 131. —, son of Edgar by Elfrida, crown'd at Kingston, 154, Dunstan at his baptism presages ill of his future slothful reign, 154. New invasions of the Danes, and great spoils committed by them in his reign, 154, 157, 160. Reduc'd to streights by the Danes, retires into Normandy, 162. Recall'd by his people, and joyfully received, 163, drives Canute the Dane back to his ships, 163. Dies at London, 165.

Ethelrice, Ida's son, expels Edwin the son of Alla out of the kingdom of Deira, 90. Ethelwald, son of Oswald king of Deira, taking part with the Mercians, withdraws his forces, 105. —, brother of Edelhere, succeeds him in the kingdom of the East-Angles, 105. Ethelward, surnam'd Mollo, set up king of the Northumbrians in the room of Oswulfe, 115, slays in battle Oswin, a lord that rebell'd against him, 116, set upon by Alcled, who assumes his place, 116. Ethelwolfe, the second monarch of the English Saxons, of a mild nature, not warlike or ambitious, 124. With his son Ethelbald gives the Danes a total defeat at Aklea or Oak-lea, 126, dedicates the tenth of his whole kingdom towards the maintenance of masses and psalms, for the prospering of him and his captains against the Danes, 126, takes a journey to Rome with his son A.fred, and marries Judith, the daughter of Charles the Bald of France, 126, driven by a conspiracy to consign half his kingdom to his son Ethelbald, 127, dies, bury'd at Winchester, 127. Ethelwolfe, Earl of Berkshire, obtains a great victory over the Danes at Englefield, 130, in another battle is slain himself, 130.

Eustace Count of Boloigne, father of the famous Geofrey, revenging the death of one of his servants, is set upon by the citizens of Canterbury, 178, complains to King Edward, who takes his part against the Cantorburians and commands earl Godwin to chastize them, but in vain, 178.

Exeter besieg'd by Perkin and the Cornish rebels, 367, makes a brave defence, 367. Hen. VII. gives his own sword to the mayor to be carry'd before him, as a reward for the bravery of the citizens, 369.

Faganus and Deruvianus, said to have preach'd the Gospel here, and to have converted almost the whole island, 56. Faustus born of Vortimer and his daughter, lives a devout life in Glamorganshire, 78.
Ferdinand, king of Spain, conquers Granada from the Moors, 324. Fergus king of Scots, said to be slain by the joynt forces of the Britains and Romans, 69. Ferrex, son of Gorbogudo, slays in fight his brother Porrex, tho' assisted with forces out of France, 21, and in revenge is slain himself by his mother Videna, 21.
Fitz-Gerauld, lord Thos., bro. to the earl of Kildare, receives Lambert Simnel as king, proclaims and crowns him in Dublin, 279, 285. Kill'd at Stoke fight, 286. Fitz-Walter lord, one of the conspirators in favour of Perkin Warbeck against Hen. VII., 334. Beheaded, 339.
Flammock, Thos. a lawyer, heads the Cornish rebels against Hen. VII., 356. His plausible pretences to stir the rabble to a rebellion, 357. Hang'd at Tyburn, 361. Flattery, odious and contemptible to a generous spirit, 171. Flemings banish'd by Hen. VII. on Perkin's account, 338.
Fox Rich., made bp. of Exeter, and Lord Privy Seal by Hen. VII., 275. Bp. of Durham, 362. is provident against the Scots, 362, employ'd in the negotiation that was the rise of the union between England and Scotland, 362. Goes to the Scots king, 372 Begins the treaty of his marriage with the princess Margaret, 373. A great master of ceremonies and court state, 380.
Francus, nam'd among the four sons of Histion, from him the Franks said to be deriv'd, 12. French manners and language first affected by the English nobility, 178. Fryon Steph., Hen. VII.'s, secretary for the French tongue, revolts to Chas. VIII., and joyns with Perkin, 332.
Fulgenius, reckon'd among the ancient British kings, 25. The commander in chief of the Caledonians against Septimius Severus, so call'd by Geoffry of Monmouth, 59.

Gabot Sebastian, a Venetian dwelling in Bristol, his voyage for discoveries in the West Indies in the reign of Hen. VII., 370. Brings three Indians to England, 403. Gaguien, Rob., French Ambassador to Hen. VII., writes a satyr against him, 318, the king orders an answer to be written to it, 319. Galgacus heads the Britains against Agricola, 52. Gaunt, citizens of, seize the person of Maximilian king of the Romans their sovereign, 310.
Germanus, in a public disputation at Verulam, puts to silence the chief of the Pelagians, 70, entreated by the Britains to head them against the Picts and Saxons, 70. Gains the victory by a religious stratagem, death, 71, death, 74. Gerontius, a Britain, by his valour advances the success of Constantine the usurper in France and Spain, 66, displac'd by him, he calls in the Vandals against him, 66, deserted by his soldiers, defends himself valiantly with the slaughter of three hundred of his enemies, 66. Kills his wife Nennichia, refusing to outlive him,

66. Geruntius, the son of Elidure, not his immediate successor, 25.
Gildas, is more credible than most of the Saxon writers, 83.
Gloucester, Richard Plantagenet duke of, hastens his brother the duke of Clarence's death, 194. Zealous for the French war, 198, charg'd but unjustly, with poysoning his brother king Edward, 198. Engages the duke of Buckingham and other lords in a conspiracy to seize the person of Edw. V., 196, speech to them, 196, pernicious advice to the queen dowager, 198. Arrests the lord Rivers, and seizes the king, 199. Affected loyalty when he brought the king to town, 204. Chosen protector, 204. Devices to get the duke of York out of sanctuary, 207. Orders preparations to be made for the coronation of Edw. V., 216, 217. Contrives the lord Hastings's death, and accuses the queen of witchcraft, 220. Speech to those that came to offer him the crown, 234, accepts of it, 234.
Godwin earl of Kent and the West Saxons stand for Hardecnute, 172, betrays prince Elfrid to Harold, 172. Call'd to account by Hardecnute, he appeases him with a very rich present, 174, earnestly exhorts Edward to take upon him the crown of England, 175. Marries his daughter to king Edward, 176. Raises forces in opposition of the French, whom the king favour'd, 178, banish'd, 179, he and his sons uniting in a great fleet, grow formidable, 181. Coming up to London with his ships, and preparing for battle, a reconciliation is made between him and the king, 181, sitting at table with the king, he suddenly sinks down dead in his seat, 182.
Gomer, the eldest son of Japhet, believ'd the first that peopled these western and northern climes, 10. Gonorill gains upon the affection of her father king Leir by her dissimulation, 19. Marry'd to Maglaunus duke of Albania, 19, ingratitude to her father after she had got what she could from him, 20. Gorbodugo, succeeds Kinmarcus in the kingdom, 21. Gorbonian succeeds Morindus in the kingdom, 24, his justice and piety, 25. Gordon, Kath., daughter to Alex. earl of Huntley, marry'd to Perkin Warbeck, 351. Sent to court by Hen. VII., 368, a pension allowed her, 623.
Granada conquer'd by Ferd. and Isabella from the Moors, 324. Gratianus Funarius, father of Valentinian, commander in chief of the Roman arms in Britain, 63. Gray, Rich. lord, half brother to Edw. V. arrested in his presence by the dukes of Glocester and Buckingham, 199. Gregory Ad. of Rome, and afterwards Pope, procures the sending over the abbot Austin and others to preach the gospel to the Saxons, 92. Griffin, prince of South-Wales, joyning with Algar, and committing great spoil in Hereford, is pursu'd by Harold earl of Kent, 182. After a peace concluded he breaks faith, and returns to hostility, 183, again reduc'd, 184, Harold sent against him, brings the Welsh to submission, 184. Lurking about the country, is taken and slain by Griffin prince of North Wales, 184.

Guendolen, daughter of Corineus, marry'd to Locrine, son of Brutus, 17, being divorc'd by him, gives him battle; wherein he is slain, 17, causes Estrildis, whom Locrine had marry'd, to be thrown into a river with her daughter Sabra, 17, governs fifteen years in behalf of her son Madan, 17. Gueniver, wife of king Arthur, kept from him by Melvas a British king in the town of Glaston, 84. Guiderius, said to have been the son of Cunobeline, and slain in a battle against Claudius, 40. Guietheline succeeds his father Gurgurtius Barbirus in the kingdom, 23. Gunhildis, sister of Swane, with her husband earl Palingus, cruelly murther'd, 157. Guorangonus, a king of Kent before it was given to the Saxons, 77. Guortimur, son of Vortiger, bends his endeavours to drive out the Saxons, 77, success against them in several battles, 78. Dying, commands his bones to be bury'd in the port of Stonar, 79. Gurguntius Barbirus succeeds Belinus in the kingdom, overcomes the Danes, and gives incouragement to Bartholmus a Spaniard to settle a plantation in Ireland, 23. Another ancient British king nam'd Gurguntius, succeeds Rivallo, 25.
Gyrtha, son of earl Godwin, accompanies his father into Flanders, together with his brothers Tosti and Swane, 179, noble advice to his brother Harold, as he was ready to give battle to duke William of Normandy, 190. Slain in the battle with his brothers Harold and Leofwin, 191. Gyrthro, or Gothrum, a Danish king, baptiz'd and receiv'd out of the font by king Alfred, 133, kingdom of the East Angles said to be bestow'd on him to hold of Alfred, 133.

Hardecnute, son of Canute by Emma, call'd over from Bruges, and receiv'd king with general acclamation, 174, calls Godwin and others to account about the death of Elfrid, 174, enrag'd at the citizens of Worcester for killing his tax-gatherers, sends an army against them, and burns the city, 174, kindly receives and entertains his half brother Edward, 175, eating and drinking hard at a great feast, falls down speechless, and soon after expiring, is bury'd at Winchester, 175. Harold, sirnam'd Harefoot, son of Canute, elected king by duke Leofric and the Mercians, 172, banishes his mother-in-law Emma, 172, perfidiousness and cruelty towards Elfrid the son of Ethelred, 172, dies, bury'd at Winchester, 173. Harold, son of Godwin, made earl of Kent, sent against Griffin prince of Wales, 183, reduces him at last to utmost extremity, 183, being cast upon the coast of Normandy and brought to duke William, he promises his endeavours to make him king of England, 185. Takes the crown himself, 186. Puts off duke William, demanding it with a slighting answer, invaded by his brother Tosti, 188, by Harold Harfager king of Norway, whom he utterly overthrows and slays, together with Tosti, 189, by duke William of Normandy, 189. Overthrown at the

INDEX. 415

battle of Hastings, and slain with his two brothers Leofwin and Gyrtha, 190.
Hastings lord, loyalty of, to Ed. V., endeavours to comfort the queen dowager, 201. appeases several tumults, 203. Satisfies those that distrusted the duke of Glocester's fidelity to the king, 218. Is caress'd, 219, sounded by Catesby the lawyer his confident, 219. Death contriv'd, 220, arrested, 220. Kept Jane Shore, 221. Order'd to prepare for death, 222, omens of it, 222. Beheaded, the people murmur at it, 224.
Hawis, alderman, persecuted by Empson and Dudley, dies of grief, 395.
Heli, reckon'd among the ancient British kings, 25. Helvias, Pertinax succeeds Ulpius Marcellus in the government of Britain, 57. Hengist and Horsa, with an army of Saxons, Jutes, and Angles, land in the isle of Thanet, 76. Hengist invites over more of his countrymen, 76, gains advantages of Vortiger by marrying his daughter to him, 77. Takes on him the title of king, 79, his several battles against the Britains, 80, treacherous slaughter of three hundred British lords, under pretence of treaty, 80. Henninus duke of Cornwall, hath Regan daughter of king Lear given him in marriage, 19.
Henry VII. succeeds Rich. III. by three titles to the crown, 266, 268. Marches to London, everywhere well receiv'd, 269. Entrance, 270, why he put off marrying the princess Elizabeth till after his coronation, and first session of parliament, 270. Crown'd, 271, institutes yeomen of the guard, 271, wisdom in procuring the settlement of the crown on himself, 272. Why he employ'd bishops, 275. Marries the princess Elizabeth, but is not very fond of her, 275, his progress to the north, 275. Hated, and why, 277. Concern at the news of Lambert Symnell's being proclaim'd in Ireland, 280. Beats the earl of Lincoln and Symnell at Stokefield, 286, punishes the rebels, 286, 288. Sanctuaries a grievance to him redress'd by the Pope, 289, concludes a truce with Jas. III. of Scotland, 289. Prudent answer to the French ambassadors about Chas. VIII.'s war with the duke of Bretagne his friend, 292. Negotiations to prevent that war, 293. Asks his second parliament's advice about it, 297. Severity in levying a tax, occasions a rebellion, 304. His saying on the news of it, 305. An excellent legislator, 306. Encourages trade, 309. Assists Maximilian king of the Romans against the Flemings his subjects, and the French, 311. Demands the crown of France of the French ambassadors, 317. The French ambassadors answer, 318. Speech at the opening his third parliament, 319. Pretends war only to raise money, 320. Gets a law for barons to alienate their lands without fines, 322, succours Maximilian effectually, 323. Preparations for the French war, 326, policy, 326, passes over to Calais, as if he meant a war, 326. Besieges Boloigne, yet treats of peace, 327, sells the French a peace, 327, arts to amuse his people about it, 327. Writes bragging letters to the Lord Mayor, 328. Perkin Warbeck set up against him, 329, 333. Subjects murmur, 334. His proceeding on news of Perkin's being own'd abroad as duke of York, 336. His spies and agents to discover the counterfeit, 336. Sends an ambassador to the arch-duke sovereign of the Netherlands, to demand him, 337. Banishes the Flemings on his denial, 338. Puts sir W. Stanly who crown'd him to death, 340, council rail'd at, 342. Forfeitures on penal laws, a blot in his reign, 343. Enters into a league with the Italian princes for the preservation of Italy against Chas. VII., 346. Favourable to lawyers, 347, makes laws to raise money, as well as to correct manners, 347. Concludes the treaty, call'd *Intercussus Magnus*, with the arch-duke, 355, gains by his wars, 355. Conduct with respect to the Cornish rebellion, 357. Hangs but the three leaders of it when it was suppress'd, 361. Brings about a treaty with Scotland, 362. Receives a consecrated sword from the Pope with great solemnity, 364. Not cruel in his executions, 369. How he lost the discovery of the West Indies, 371. Another counterfeit earl of Warwick set up against him, 374. Puts the true earl to death, and is hated for it, 375. Reasons for it, 376, passes over to Calais, has an interview with the arch-duke Philip, and is highly honour'd there, 376. Gives the Lord Mayor an account of all, 377. Answer to the Pope's invitation to accompany him in a war against the Turk, 378. chosen protector of the knights of Rhodes, 378. Converts a heretic by a dispute, 379. Prevails with his son prince Henry to be contracted to his brother's widow, 382. Answer about the union of England and Scotland, 383. Diligence to get money, 384. Remarkable memorandum of his, 385. Retainers suppress'd by him and the power of the barons lessen'd, 387. His reflections on the death of Isabella queen of Castile, 388. Would marry the queen dowager of Naples and Sicily, 389. Instructions to his ambassadors about that and other matters relating to Ferdinand and his son-in-law Philip, 389. Conference with Philip when he was driven ashore in England, about the earl of Suffolk, 392. Treats of a marriage with the lady Margaret duchess of Savoy, and sister to Philip, 394. Taken ill of a defluxion in his breast, 395, would have Hen. VI. canoniz'd, 395. Last sickness and death, 396. Lord Verulam's large character of Hen. VII., and summary of his reign, 397, 400. His wisdom, piety, peaceful virtues, victories, prerogative, council table, avarice, magnificence in building, ambition, ministers, queen and mother, treaties, politicks, intelligence, fame, the respect paid him, love to his children, industry, officers civil and military, humour, learning, 400. General character, 401. Compar'd with other princes, 402, his person and prognosticks of his reign, 402. Remarkable occurrences in his reign, 403.

Herebert, a Saxon earl, slain with most part of his army by the Danes at a place call'd Mereswat, 125.

Hialas, ambassador from Ferdinand to Hen. VIII. to conclude a marriage between the princess Katherine, and prince Arthur, 362, goes to Scotland to mediate a peace between king Henry and Jas. IV., 363, that embassy the rise of the union of Scotland with England, 363. Hinguar and Hubba, two Danish brethren, get footing by degrees in England, 129, 130. Histion, said to be descended of Japhet, and to have had four sons, who peopled the greatest part of Europe, 12.

Honorius the Emp. sends aid twice to the Britains, 64. Horsa, brother of Hengist, slain in the Saxons war against the Britains, 79, his buryal place gave name to Horsted, a town in Kent, 79.

Humbeanna and Albert, said by some to have shar'd the kingdom of East-Angles after one Elfwald, 122. Humber, king of the Hunns, invading this island, defeats and slays Albanact king of Albania, and son of Brutus, 17, defeated and drown'd, 17.

Icenians, and by their example the Trinobantes rise up in arms against the Romans, 46.

Ida the Saxon begins the kingdom of Bernicia in Northumberland, 86. Idwallo, learns by his brother's ill success to rule well, 25.

Immanuentius, slain by Cassibelan, 34. Immin, Eaba and Eadbert, nobles of Mercia, throw off Oswi, and set up Wulfer, 106.

Ina succeeds Kedwalla in the kingdom of the West-Saxons, 110, marches into Kent to demand satisfaction for the burning of Mollo, 110, pacify'd by Victred with a sum of money, and the delivering up of the accessaries, 110, vanquishes Gerent king of Wales, slays Kenwulf and Albright, and vanquishes the East-Angles, ends his days at Rome, 112. Inclosures of land, the inconveniency of 'em remedy'd, 307.

Ireland favours the title of the House of York, 279, receive Lambert Simnell as king, 279. He is crown'd there, 280. Commissioners sent there by Hen. VII. to settle matters after it, 343. Poyning's act past there in Parliament, 343.

Jago, succeeds his uncle Gurgustius, 21. James III. king of Scots concludes a seven years truce with Hen. VII., 289. Kill'd by his subjects, 306. James IV. succeeds his father Jas. III., 306. Receives Perkin Warbeck favourably, and marries him to his kinswoman, 351. Invades England for him, 354, destroys the country and returns, 354. Stands on hard terms for a peace with Hen. VII., 363. Dismisses Perkin honourably, 364. By what accident his marriage with the princess Margaret came first to be treated of, 371. Marry'd to her, 382.

Joseph of Arimathea, said to have first preach'd the christian faith in this island, 56. Joseph Michael, the blacksmith of Bodmin, one of the leaders of the Cornish rebels against Hen. VII., 356. Hang'd at Tyburn, 361, ridiculous pleasure at his death, 361. Jovinus, sent deputy into this island by the emp. Valentinian, 64.

Judges, their wise opinion about the attainder of Hen. VII.'s followers chosen members of parliament, 272. Julius Agricola, the emperor's lieutenant in Britain, almost extirpates the Ordovices, 50, finishes the conquest of the isle of Mona, 50, justice and prudence in his government, 50, brings the Britains to civility, arts, and an imitation of the Roman fashions, 50, receives triumphal honours from Titus, 51, extends his conquests to Scotland, subdues the Orcades and other Scots islands, 51. Hard put to it in conflicts, but victorious, 53, 54. Commanded home by Domitian, 54.

Julius Cæsar has intelligence that the Britains aid the Gauls, revenged on his enemies, 28. Sends Caius Volusenus to make discovery of the nature of the people, and strength of the country, 28, after him Comius of Arras is sent to make a party among the Britains, 28, the stout resistance he meets with from them at his landing, 29. Receives terms of peace from them, 30. Loses a great part of his fleet, 33, defeats the Britains, and brings them anew to terms of peace, and then sails for Belgia, 34, the year following he lands his army again, 34, has a very sharp dispute with the Britains, near the Stowr in Kent, 34. Receives terms of peace from the Trinobantes, 35, brings Cassibelan to terms, 35. Offers to Venus, the patroness of his family, a corslet of British pearl, 36. Julius Frontinus the emperor's lieutenant in Britain, tames the Silures a warlike people, 49. Julius Severus governs Britain under Adrian the emperor, 55.

Katherine, princess of Spain, married to prince Arthur, eldest son to Hen. VII., 380. Kearl surrenders the kingdom of Mercia to his kinsman Penda, 100. Keaulin succeeds his father Kenric in the kingdom of the West-Saxons, 86. He and his son Cuthin slays three British kings at Deorham, 89, gives the Britains a great rout at Fethanleage, 90. Totally routed by the Britains at Wodensbeorth, and chas'd out of his kingdom, dies in poverty, 90. Kedwalla, a West-Saxon prince, return'd from banishment, slays in fight Edelwalk the South-Saxon, and after that, Edric his successor, 108, going to the isle of Wight, he devotes the fourth part thereof to holy uses, 108, the sons of Arwald, king of that isle, slain by his order, 109, harrasses the country of the South-Saxons, 109, repell'd by the Kentish men, 109, yet revenges the death of his brother Mollo, 109. Going to Rome to be baptiz'd, dies there about five weeks after his baptism, 110. Kelred, son of Ethelred, succeeds Kenred in the Mercian kingdom, 111, possess'd with an evil spirit, he dies in despair, 111. Kelwulfe reigns king of the West-Saxons after Keola, 93.

INDEX. 417

Makes war upon the South-Saxons, 94. Dying, leaves the kingdom to his brother's sons, 95. Kelwulfe, adopted by Osric the Northumbrian to be his successor, 112, becomes a monk in Landisfarn, 113.
Kenwalla or Cadwallon, a British king joyning with Penda the Mercian, slays Edwin in battle, 101. Kened, king of the Scots, does high honour to king Edgar, 150, receives great favours from him, 150, challeng'd by him upon some words let fall, but soon pacifies him, 151.
Kenelm, a child, succeeding in the kingdom of Mercia after Kenulf, is murder'd by order of his sister Quenrid, 121, Kenred, son of Wulfer, succeeds Ethelred in the Mercian kingdom, 111, having reign'd a while, he goes to Rome, and is there shorn a monk, 111, another Kenred succeeds in the kingdom of Northumberland, and revenges the murder of his predecessor Osred, 111. Kenric, son of Kerdic, overthrows the Britains that oppose him, 85. Kills and puts to flight many of the Britains at Scaresbirig, now Salisbury, 86, afterwards at Biránvirig, now Banbury, 86. Kentish gentlemen loyal to Hen. VII., 344, 357. Kentwin, a West-Saxon king, chases the Welsh Britains to the sea-shore, 108. Kenulf has the kingdom of Mercia bequeath'd him by Ecferth, 119, leaves behind him the praise of a virtuous king, 120. Kenwalk succeeds his father Kinegils in the kingdom of the West-Saxons, 103, his successes variously delivered, 103, said to have discomfited the Britains at Pen in Somersetshire, 106, and giving battle to Wulfer, to have taken him prisoner, 106, dying, leaves the government to Sexburga his wife, 107. Kenwulfe, sirnam'd Clito, slain by Ina the West-Saxon, 112.
Keola, son of Cuthulfe, succeeds his uncle Keaulin in the West-Saxon kingdom, 90. Keolwulfe, brother of Kenulf the Mercian, after two years reign, driven out by Bernulf an usurper, 121. Keorle with the forces of Devonshire overthrows the Danes at Wigganbeorch, 125. Kerdic, a Saxon prince, lands at Kerdicshore, and overthrows the Britains, 82, defeats their king Natanleod in a battle, 82, founds the kingdom of the West-Saxons, 83, overthrows the Britains again at Kerdic'sford, and at Kerdic's leage, 83.
Kildare, earl of, assists at Lambert Simnell's coronation, 284. Writes to Hen. VII. to petition for a pardon, and is pardon'd, 287. Arrested by Poynings, and sent prisoner to England, 343. Kimarus reckon'd among the ancient British kings, 25. Kinegils and Cuichelm, succeeds Kelwulfe in the kingdom of the West-Saxons, 96. Make truce with Penda the Mercian, 101. Are converted to the christian faith, 102. Kinegils dying, leaves his son Kenwalk to succeed, 103. Kinmarcus succeeds Sisillius in the kingdom, 21. Kinwulfe, or Kenwulfe (Sigebert being thrown out and the slain by a swinekerd), is saluted king of West-Saxons, 115, behaves himself bravely in several battles against the Welsh, 115,

put to the worst at Basington by Offa the Mercian, 116, routed and slain in battle by Kineard, whom he had commanded into banishment, 116.
Knesworth, alderman, prosecuted by Empson and Dudley in Hen. VII.'s reign, 395.
Kymbeline, or Cunobeline, the successor of Tenuantius, said to be brought up in the court of Augustus, 38, chief seat in Camalodunum, or Maldon, 39.

Lancaster, the title of that house generally condemn'd, 268. Laws enacted in the reign of Hen. VII., 273. Several laws made, 302. Others, 306, 310. Others, 321, 322, 347, 349. Others, 387.
Learning and arts, when began to flourish among the Britains, 50. Among the Saxons, 107. Men famous for them in the reign of Edw. IV., 206. Of Edw. V. and Rich. III., 265. Of Hen. VII. 404.
Legend, foolish, of St. Peter's Cope, being to be seen in Westminster Abby, 207. Leil succeeds Brute Greenshield, and builds Caerleil, 18. Leofric duke of Mercia, and Siward of Northumberland, sent by Hardecnute against the people of Worcester, 174, by their counsel king Edward seizes on the treasures of his mother queen Emma, 176. They raise forces for the king against earl Godwin, 177. Leofwin, son of earl Godwin, after his father's banishment goes over with his brother Harold into Ireland, 180, he and Harold assist their father with a fleet against king Edward, 180, slain with his brother Harold, and Gyrtha another of his brothers, in the battle against William duke of Normandy, 191. Lewis XII. conquers Milan, 377. Lewis, Dr., a Welshman, carries on the correspondence between the queen dowager and the countess of Richmond, for the marriage of the princess Elizabeth to the earl of Richmond, 246.
Libels and false reports spread about against Rich. III., 252. Linceus, deliver'd in fabulous story to be the husband of one of the feign'd fifty daughters of Dioclesian king of Syria, 12, the only man sav'd by his wife, when all the rest of the fifty slew their husbands, 12. Lincoln, John de Pool, earl of, proclaim'd heir apparent of Rich. III., 282. joyns with the impostor Lambert Simnell against Hen. VII., 282. At Simnell's coronation, 284, lands in England, 284. Kill'd at Stoke-fight, 286.
Locrine, the eldest son of Brutus, has the middle part of this island, call'd Loegria, for his share in the kingdom, 17, defeats Humber, king of the Hums, 17. Lollius Urbicus draws a wall of turf between the frith of Dunbritton and Edenburgh, 55. London, with a great multitude of the inhabitants, consum'd by a sudden fire, 121. Lothair succeeds his brother Ecbert in the kingdom of Kent, 107. Lovel, lord, a great stickler for Rich. III. attainted by Hen. VII.'s parliament, 275, rebels against him, 275, flies out of England, 275. Joyns with Simnell, 283. Assists at his coronation, 284. Kill'd at Stoke, 286.
Lucius, a king in some part of Britain,

thought the first of any king in Europe who received the christian faith, 56, made the second by descent from Marius, 56, after a long reign bury'd at Gloucester, 56. Lud walls about Troynovant, and calls it Caer-Lud, or Lud's town, 25. Ludiken, the Mercian, going to revenge Bernulfe, is surpriz'd by the East-Angles, and put to the sword, 122. Lupicinus sent deputy into this island, by Julian the emperor, soon recall'd, 65. Lupus, of Troyes, assistant to Germanus of Auxerre, in reformation of British church, 70.

Madan succeeds his father Locrine in the kingdom, 17, rules well, 18. Maglaunus, duke of Albania, marries Gonorill eldest daughter of king Lear, 19. Maglocuno, sirnam'd the Island Dragon, one of the five that reign'd toward the beginning of the Saxon Heptarchy, 89. Magus, son and successor of Samothes, whom some fable to have been the first peoplers of this island, 11. Malcolm, son of Kened king of Scots, falling into Northumberland with his whole power, is entirely overthrown by Uthred, 165. —, son of the Cumbrian king, made king of Scotland by Siward, in the room of Macbeth, 182. —, king of Scotland, coming to visit king Edward, swears brotherhood with Tosti the Northumbrian, 183, afterwards in his absence harasses Northumberland, 184. Mandubratius, son of Immanuentius, favour'd by the Trinobantes against Cassibelan, 35.
Marganus, the son of Gonorill, deposes Cordelia, 21, shares the kingdom with his cousin Cunedagius, invades him, but is met and overcome by him, 21. Marganus, son of Archigallo, a good king, 20. Margaret, lady, hatred to Hen. VII., 283. Sends 2000 men to assist Lambert Simnel, 283. Palace a sanctuary for traytors against Hen. VII., 306. Contrivances to disturb that king, 329. Sets up Perkin Warbeck, 329. Instructions to him, 330. Owns him publickly to be duke of York, 331, Commends him to the Scots king, 349. —, princess, daughter to Hen. VII. marry'd to Ja. IV. the Scots king, 382. Marius, son of Aviragus, said to have overcome the Picts, and slain their king Roderick, 56. Martia, wife of king Guitheline, said to have instituted the law called Marchen Leage, 23. Martinus made deputy of the British province, failing to kill Plautus, kills himself, 63.
Mary, princess, second daughter to Henry VII., contracted to Chas', prince of Castile, afterwards Chas. V., 396. Maximianus Herculeus, forc'd to conclude a peace with Carausius, and yield him Britain, 60. Maximilian, arch duke of Austria, makes a peace with Lewis XI., contracts his daughter Margaret to Chas. the Dauphin, before contracted to king Edward's daughter Elizabeth, 283. Is Charles the VIIIth of France's rival for Anne Heiress of Bretagne, 292. His person seiz'd by the citizens of Gaunt, 310. Lord Ravenstein rebels against him, 310. Marries lady Anne by proxy, 311, his

negligence, 312. Rage upon the French king's marrying her, 326. Effectually assisted by Hen. VII. against the Flemmings, 322. Cannot assist king Henry in his French war, 326, 327. Recommends Perkins to the Scots king, 349, 351.
Maximus a Spaniard, usurping part of the Empire, is overcome at length, and kill'd by Theodosius, 65. —, a friend of Gerontius, is by him set up in Spain against Constantine the usurper, 65.
Mellitus, Justus and others, sent with Austin, the conversion of the Saxons, 93. Mellitus converts the East-Saxons, 94. St. Paul's church in London built for his cathedral by Ethelred, as that of Rochester for Justus, 94. Mempricius, one of Brutus's council, persuades him to hasten out of Greece, 14. — and Malim succeed their father Madan in the kingdom, 18, —treacherously slaying his brother, gets sole possession of the kingdom, reigns tyrannically, and is at last devour'd by wolves, 18. Merianus, reckon'd among the ancient British kings, 25.
Mollo, brother of Cedwalla, pursu'd, beset and burnt in a house whither he had fled for shelter, 109. Death reveng'd by his brother, 109. Montfort, Sir Sim., one of the conspirators against Hen. VII. in favour of Perkin Warbeck, 314. Beheaded, 339. More, Sir Thos., his history of Edw. V. and Rich. III., from 193 to 241. Morcar, son of Algar, made earl of Northumberland, in the room of Tosti, 185. He and Edwin brother of the Mercians put Tosti to flight, 188, give battel to Harold Harfager, king of Norway, but are worsted, 188. Mordred, Arthur's nephew, who is said to have given him in a battle his death's wound, 88.
Moreton, Dr. John, bishop of Ely, suspects the duke of Glocester's fidelity to Edw. V., 218. Committed to the custody of the duke of Buckingham, by Rich. III., 239. Long conference with the duke, whom he persuades to dethrone Rich. and set up Hen. earl of Richmond, 240, 242, 245. Made Abp. of Canterbury by Hen. VII., 275. Lord Chancellor, 296. Speech to Hen. VII.'s parliament, 296, 313. Hated, and gets a law for his own security, 302. Answer to the French ambassador's speech about Bretagne and Naples, 325. Death, 377. Character, 378. Morley, lord, slain at the battle of Dixmuyde, 311. Morindus, the son of Elanius by Tonguestela a valiant man, but infinitely cruel, 23.

Natanleod, chief king of Britain, routed by Kerdic the Saxon, 15 Navigation of England advanc'd by Hen. VII., 308.
Nevil, sir George, goes to Perkin Warbeck in France, 332.
Norfolk, John Howard, duke of, attainted by Hen. VIIth's first parliament, 273. Northumberland, Hen., earl of, kill'd in a mutiny against tax-gatherers, in Hen. VII.'s reign, 304.

Octa and Ebissa call'd over by Hengist their uncle, 77, possess themselves of that part of the isle which is now Northumberland, 77.

Oeneus, one in the catalogue of ancient British kings, 25. Oeric or Oisc, succeeds his father Hengist in the kingdom of Kent, and from him the Kentish kings call'd Oiscings, 82.

Offa, son of Siger, quits his kingdom of the East-Saxons, to go to Rome, and turn monk with Kenred, 111. Offa, defeating and slaying Beornred, the usurper, becomes king of Mercia after Ethelbald, 116, subdues a neighbouring people call'd Hestings, 116, gets the victory of Alric king of Kent at Ostanford, 116. Inviting Ethelbright king of the East-Angles to his palace, he treacherously causes him to be beheaded, and seizes his kingdom, 118, is at first at enmity, afterwards in league with Charles the great, 118, grants a perpetual tribute to the pope out of every house in his kingdom, 118, draws a trench of wondrous length between Mercia and the British confines, death, 118.

Orange prince, sides with the duke of Orleans against Chas. VII., taken prisoner at the battle of St. Albans in Bretagne, 301. Orleans, Lewis, duke of, retires to the duke of Bretagne, and prevents his hearkening to a peace with Chas. VIII. 291, 293. Fights the battle of St. Albans, and is taken prisoner by the French king's troops, 301. Succeeds Chas. VIII., 576.

Osbald, a nobleman, exalted to the throne of the Northumbrians after Ethelred, 119. Osbert reigns in Northumberland after the last of the Ethelreds in the time of the Danish invasion, 125. Osbert and Ella helping the Picts against Donald king of Scotland, put the Scots to flight at Sterling-bridge with great slaughter, and take the king prisoner, 127. Osfrid and Eanfrid, sons of Edwin, converted and baptiz'd, 100. Osfrid slain, together with his father in a battle against Kedwalla, 101. Oslace and Cnebban, two Saxon earls, slain by Keaulin at Wibbandun, 86. Osmund, king of the South-Saxons, 116. Osred, a child, succeeds Aldfrid in the Northumbrian kingdom, 111, slain by his kindred for his vicious life, 112. Osred, son of Alcled, advanc'd to the kingdom of Northumberland after Elfwald, is soon driven out again, 117, taken and forcibly shaven a monk at York, 117. Osric, son of Elfric, baptiz'd by Paulinus, succeeds in the kingdom of Deira, 101, turns apostate, and is slain by an irruption of Kedwalla out of a besieg'd town, 102. Osric succeeds Kenred king of Northumberland, 111.

Osric earl of Southampton, and Ethelwolfe of Berkshire, beat the Danes back to their ships, 128. Ostorius, sent vice-prætor, 41, into Britain in the room of Plautius the prætor, 41, routs the Britains, and improves his victory to the best advantage, 41, gives the government of several cities to Cogidunus a British king, his ally, 42. Defeats the Silures under the leadership of Caractacus, 42, so distress'd by them that he dies of grief, 43. Ostrid, wife of Ethelred, kill'd by her own nobles, 111.

Oswald, brother of Eanfrid, living exil'd in Scotland, is there baptiz'd, 101, with a small army entirely overthrows Kedwalla, 102, settles religion, and very much enlarges his dominions, 107, overcome and slain in battle by Penda at Maserfield, now Oswester, 103. Oswi succeeds his brother Oswald in his kingdom, 103. Persuades Sigebert to receive the christian faith, 205. Discomfits Penda's vast army, 105. Subdues all Mercia, and the greatest part of the Pictish nation, 106, shaken off by the Mercian nobles, and Wulfer set up in his stead, 106, his death, 106. Oswin, nephew of Edwin, shares with Oswi in the kingdom of Northumberland, 103. Coming to arms with him, is overmatch'd and slain by his command, 104. Oswulf has the crown of Northumberland relinquish'd to him by Eadbert, 115, slain by his own servants, 115.

Otha succeeds Esca in the kingdom of Kent, 86. Otter and Roald, two Danish leaders, landing in Devonshire, their whole forces are scatter'd, and Roald slain, 140.

Oxford University said to be founded by Alfred, 138. Burnt by the Danes, 162. —, John earl of, escapes from the castle of Hammes and joyns the earl of Richmond in France, 252. Commands the van of his army at the battle of Bosworth, 258. Commands the army against Simnel's adherents, 284. In the French expedition, 326. And against the Cornish rebels, 359. Severely and ungratefully us'd by Hen. VII. 384.

Pacatianus left governor of Britain by Constantine the Great, 62. Pandrasus a Grecian king, keeps the Trojans in servitude, 13. Set upon, and beaten by Brutus, 14. Parker, sir J., kill'd in a just in Hen. VII.'s reign, 325. Parliament, one held by Rich. III. 251. —, the first held by Hen. VII., 271, their acts, 271. About settling the crown on king Hen. singly, 272. His second, 296. Several good laws made by them, 301, 302, 303, 307. His third, 319, speech to them, 319, 320. Pass the famous statute to sell lands without fines, and open a way for the barons to alienate their estates, 322. Other acts, 323. His fourth, and their acts, 346, 348. His fifth parliament, their acts, 386. They suppress retainers, 387. Patriarck Fryar, sets up a counterfeit earl of Warwick against Hen. VII., 374.

Paulinus, sent spiritual guardian with Edelburga, to convert Northumberland to christianity, 98. Manner of his winning king Edwin to embrace the christian religion, 99. Converts the province of Lindsey, and Blecca governor of Lincoln, and builds a church in that city, 100. Payne, Dr. bp. of Meath, preaches Lambert Simnel's coronation sermon, 284.

Peada, son of Penda, and prince of the Middle Angles, is baptiz'd with all his followers, 104. South-Mercia conferr'd on him by Oswi, 105, slain by the treachery of his wife on Easter-day, 105. Pelagius, a Britain, brings new opinions into the church, 65. The Pelagian doctrine refuted by Germanus, 70. The Pelagians judg'd to banishment by Germanus, 73. Pembroke,

Jasper earl of, created duke of Bedford, 271. Penda, son of Wibba king of Mercia, has the kingdom surrender'd him by Keorle, 100 Joyns with Kadwalla against Edwyn, 101. Slays Oswald in battle, 102. In another battle Sigebert, 103. In another Anna king of the East-Angles, 104. Slain in a battle against Oswi, 105. Penissell, reckon'd in the number of the ancient British kings, 25. Peredure and Vigenius expel their brother Elidure, and share the kingdom between them, 24.

People, how they came to decay in Hen. VII.'s reign, 308. Percival, sir John, lord mayor of London, his rise, 403. Perkin Warbeck, his story as in the lord Verulam, his rise, 329, person and cunning, 329, Edw. IV. his godfather, 329. Parents and education, 330. Why call'd Perkin, 330. Presented to the duchess of Burgundy, and by her sent to Portugal, 330. Lands at Cork, and pretends to be Richard duke of York, Edward IV.'s second son, 331. The French king sends agents to him, 332. Goes to France, and is treated like a king, 332. Dismiss'd thence, he goes to the duchess of Burgundy, who owns him as duke of York, 332. Several persons of quality in England for him, 334. Beheaded on his account, 339. Attempts to land in Kent, but is afraid, 344. Several of his followers hang'd, 345. Returns to Flanders, 348. Goes to Scotland, recommended by several princes, 349. Declaration to James IV. king of Scots, 349. Favour'd by him, and has lady Katherine Gordon bestow'd on him in marriage, 359. Enters Northumberland, and puts out a proclamation against Hen. VII., 351, 352. Success of it, 354. Weeps at the Scots destroying the country when they came into England with him, 354. Dismiss'd from Scotland, 364. Lands at Cork in Ireland, 364. His counsellors, 365. Invited to Cornwall by the rebels there, 365. Lands there, joyn'd by them, and besieges Exeter, 367. Raises the siege, and flies to Sanctuary, 368. Submits on promise of life, carry'd to king Henry's court, 369. His confession not satisfactory, 370. Runs away, is taken, set in the stocks, and reads his confession, 373. Endeavours to corrupt the lieutenant of the Tower's servants, 374. Draws earl Warwick into a conspiracy, 374. Try'd, condemn'd, and hang'd at Tyburn, 375. Confession, 375.

Perjury, an example of the Divine Vengeance in Alfred, who conspir'd against king Athelstane, 143. Petilius Cerealis, utterly defeated by the Britains, 46. Commands the Roman army in Britain, 49. Petronius Turpilianus commands in chief in Britain, after Sueton Paulinus, 49.

Philip archduke of Austria, and sovereign of the Netherlands, his interview with Hen. VII., 376. Succeeds his mother-in-law queen Isabella of Spain, as king of Castile, 388. Thrown on the coast of England by a storm, 391. Entertainment and conference with Hen. VII., 391.

Picts and Scots harass the south coasts of Britain, 63. Picts and Saxons beaten by the Britains through the pious conduct of Germanus, 71. Pir, one of the ancientest race of British kings, 25.

Pons Jasper, his negotiations in England with Hen. VII. for Pope Alexander VI., 378. Pope, the, redresses the grievances of sanctuaries for Hen. VII., 289. Porrex, son of Gorgobudo, tho' assisted from France, is slain by his brother Ferrex, 21. His death reveng'd by his mother Videna, 21. Another of that name reckon'd in the list of British kings, 25. Portsmouth denominated from the larding of Porta a Saxon prince with his sons, Bida and Melga, 82.

Poynings, Sir Edward, sent to besiege Sluice, held against Maximilian by his subjects, 23. Sent into Ireland, 343. Holds a parliament, and gets the famous statute past and known by his name, 343. Arrests the earl of Kildare, and sends him prisoner to England, 343.

Prasutagus, king of the Iceni, leaving Cæsar coheir with his daughters, causes the Britains to revolt, 44. Priscus Licinius, lieutenant of this isle under Adrian, 55. Probus subdues the usurper Bonosus, who falls in the battle, 59.

Rakehells, king of, Perkin so call'd by Hen. VII., 367. Rame, Thomas, esq., his swift passage over to the earl of Richmond in Bretagne, 247. Executed at Exeter on bare suspicion, 251. Ratcliffe, sir Rich., employ'd to execute the lord Rivers and others, 228. Kill'd at the battle of Bosworth, 261. Ravenstein, lord, rebels against Maximilian king of the Romans, and sovereign of the Netherlands, 310. His piratical war, 322. Reduc'd to great streights by the English succours, 323. Readwulfe succeeding Ethelred in Northumberland, soon after his coronation is cut off with his whole army by the Danes at Alvetheli, 125. Rebellion against Hen. VII. the lord Lovel's, 275. Lambert Simnel's, 277, 288. Sir John Egremond's and John a Chambers, 305. The Cornish men's, 356. Rederchus, reckon'd among the ancient British kings, 25. Redion, one of the ancient British kings, 25. Redwald, king of the East-Angles, wars against Ethelred in defence of Edwyn, and slays him in battle, 97. Regin, son of Gorbonian, a good king, 25.

Remarkable occurrences in the reign of Edward V. and Richard III., 249, 264. Of Henry VII., 270, 403. Retainers suppresst by act of parliament, 387.

Richard III., his dissimulation on his accession to the throne, crown'd with his queen, 253. Contrives the destruction of the two young princes, 237, orders them to be murder'd, and is terrify'd in conscience, 237. Progress to Glocester 238, quarrels with the duke of Bucks, 238. Crown'd a second time at York, 239, letter to the master of his wardrobe for things for that coronation, 239. A conspiracy form'd against him by Bucks and the bishop of Ely, 241, 246. Summons the duke of Bucks to court, 249, prepares for his defence, 249. His cruelty, 251. Enters into an alliance with Scotland, and proclaims John, earl of Lincoln, heir apparent, 252, persuades the queen to leave sanctuary, 252, gets her daughter into his hands, 252, resolv'd to marry the eldest, and rid himself of his wife, 252. She dies soon after, 253. Designs to marry the princess Elizabeth, 256, how prevented, 256. His proceedings on the earl of Richmond's landing, 257. Marches against him, and encamps at Bosworth, 259, speech to his soldiers, 259. Fights the earl, and is slain, 262, wears his crown in the battle, 262. Character, 263. His body abus'd, 266, lord St. Albans calls him a tyrant, 266, says his end was just, 266, that he murder'd his two nephews, 266, his vices over-balance his virtues, 266. Was jealous of his honour, and made good laws, 261. Attainted by Hen. VIIs.' first parliament, 273.

Richmond, Hen Earl of, brought to Hen. VI. and his saying of him, 402. Receives messengers out of England with an account of the conspiracy in his favour, 247, engages to marry the princess Elizabeth, 247. Sails to England, but dares not land, 250, returns to France, 250. Is attainted, 251. In great danger in Bretagne 252, reception in France, 252. Stops the marquess Dorset going to leave him, 255. Embarks for England, lands in Wales, 256. Loses his way in his march, 257. Speech before he gave king Richard battle, 259. Crown'd in the field with king Richard's crown, by sir Will. Stanley, 263. Richmond, countess of, holds up queen Anne's train at king Richard's coronation, 236. Correspondence with the queen dowager, to advance her son the earl of Richmond, 246. Richmond palace built by Her.. VII. 370. Rivalo succeeds his father Cunedagius, 21. Rivers, Rich. Woodville earl, arrested by the duke of Glocester, 199. Beheaded at Pomfret, 228.

Romans land in Britain under the conduct of Julius Cæsar, 29. Sharp conflict with the Britains near the Stoure in Kent, 33. Are cruelly massacred by the Britains, 46. Leave the island to succour their declining affairs in other parts, 66. Come and aid the Britains against the Scots and Picts, 68. Help them to build a new wall, 69, instruct them in war, and take their last farewell, 69. Romanus, nam'd among the four sons of Histion, sprung of Japhet, and from him the Romans fabled to be deriv'd, 12. Rotherdam, Dr. Abp. of York, speech to the queen, mother of Edw. V. 201. Leaves the Great Seals with her, being lord Chancellor, 202, sends for them again, 202. The seal taken from him, 203. Imprison'd, 221 Rowena, daughter of Hengist, sent for over by her Father, 77, presents king Vortigern with a bowl of wine by her father's command, 77, is upon the king's demand given him in marriage, 77.

Rudaucus king of Cambria, subdu'd in fight, and slain by Dunwallo Mulmutius, 21. Rud-Hudibras succeeds his father Leil, and founds Caerkeint, or Canterbury, with other places, 18. Runno, the son of Peredure, not his immediate successor, 25.

Sabra thrown into the river Severn, (thence call'd Sabrina) with her mother Estrildis by Guendolen, 17. St. Albans in Bretagne, battle of, 301. Samothes, the first king that history or fable mentions to have peopled this island, 11. Samulius recorded among the ancient British kings, 25. Sanctuaries, the use and abuse of them, deliver'd by the duke of Buckingham before the lords of the council in the reign of Edw. V., 209. Grievance of 'em redressed by the Pope for Hen. VII., 289. Saron, the second king nam'd among the successors of Samothes, 11. Saxons harass the southcoasts of Britain, slay Noctaradius and Balcobaudes, 64. — invited into Britain by Vortigern and the Britains against the Scots and Picts, 74. Their original, 74. Arrive under the leading of Hengist and Horsa, 76. Beat the Scots and Picts near Stamford, 76. Fresh forces sent to them, and their bounds enlarg'd, 76. Making league with the Scots and Picts, waste the land without resistance, 77. Beaten by Guortimer in four battles, and driven into Thanet, 78. Return most of them into their own country, 78. The rest notably defeated by Ambrosius Aurelianus and the Britains, 79.

Scots, Picts and Attacots, harass the southcoast of Britain, 64. Overcome by Maximus, 65. Beaten by the Romans sent to succour the Britains, 69. They make spoil and havoc with little or no opposition, 69. Scots possess'd Ireland, and first nam'd it Scotia, 65. — king does homage to king Edward the elder, 142. To William the Norman, 170. — the rise of the union between the two nations, 362.

Sebbi, having reign'd over the East-Saxons thirty years, takes on him the habit of a monk, 107. Sebert, the son of Sleda, reigns over the East-Saxons by permission of Ethelbert, 76. Segonax, one of the four petty kings in Britain that assaulted Cæsar's camp, 36. Seius Saturninus commands the Roman fleet in Britain, 55. Selred, son of Sigebert the good, succeeds Offa in the East-Saxon kingdom, and comes to a violent end, 114. Septimius Severus, the Roman emperor, arrives in person with an army in this island, 57. His ill success against the Caledonians, 57. Nevertheless he goes on, and brings them to terms of peace, 57. Builds a wall across the island from sea to sea, 58. They taking arms again, he sends his son Antonius against them, 59. Dies at York, 'tis thought of grief, 59. Serjeants at law, a call of, 345, 388. Severus, sent over deputy into this island by the emperor Valentinian, 64. Sexburga, wife of Kenwalk, driv'n out by the nobles, disdaining her government, 107. Sexted and Siward, re-establish paganism in the East-Saxon kingdom after the death of their father Sebert, 96. In a fight against the Britains, they perish with their whole army, 97.

Shaw, Dr. John, preaches a seditious sermon to prove king Edw. IV.'s marriage with his queen was not lawful, and that her children were illegitimate, 229. Dies of shame and grief, 230. —, Sir Edmund

Lord Mayor of London, one of the conspirators to advance the duke of Glocester to the throne, 230. Discourse with the duke of Buckingham, 234. —, Sir John, the first Lord Mayor of London that went to Westminster by water to be sworn, 403. Removes the mayor's feast to Guild-Hall, 403. Shore, Jane, kept by the lord Hastings after Edward's death, 221. Is prosecuted by the lord protector, the duke of Glocester, 226. Character, 227.

Sigeard and Senfred succeed their father Sebbi in the East-Saxon kingdom, 114. Sigebert succeeds his brother Eorpwald in the kingdom of the East-Angles, 102. Founds a school or college, and betakes himself to monastical life, 103. Is forc'd into the field against Penda, 103. Slain with his kinsman Esric, 103. Sigebert, sirnam'd the Small, succeeds his father Seward king of the East-Saxons, 105. His successor Sigebert the second persuaded by Oswi to embrace christianity, 105. Murder'd by the conspiracy of two brethren, 105. His death denounc'd by the bishop for eating with an excommunicated person, 105. Sigebert, kinsman of Cuthred, succeeds him in the West-Saxon kingdom, 114. Siger, son of Sigebert the Small, and Sebbi the son of Seward, succeed in the government of the East-Saxons after Swithelm's decease, 107. Silures, a people of Britain choose Caractacus for their leader against the Romans, 42. continue the war after Caractacus is taken, against Ostolius and others, 42. Tam'd, 51.

Simnell Lambert, an impostor set up by Richard Simon, an Oxford priest, against Hen. VII., 277. Pretends to be Edward Plantagenet earl of Warwick, 277. Carry'd over to Ireland by Simon, 279. Well receiv'd there, 279. Proclaim'd king, 280. Gets a party in England, 282. Crown'd at Dublin, 284. Lands in England with an army, 285. Defeated, taken, pardon'd, and made a turn-broach, 287. Advanc'd to be king Henry's falconer, 287. Simon Zelotes, by some said to have preach'd the christian faith in this island, 56. Simon, Rich., an Oxford priest, sets up the impostor Lambert Simnell, 277. Thought to be instigated to it by some great persons, 277. Taken, imprison'd, and never heard of more, 287. Simony first practis'd in England, 107. Sisillius succeeds Jago, 21. Another of that name succeeds his father Guitheline, 23. Another British king of that name, 25. Siward, king of the East-Saxons, father of Sigebert, little said of him, 105. Siward, earl of Northumberland, sent by Hardecnute, together with Leofric, against the people of Worcester, 174. He and Leofric raise forces for king Edward against earl Godwin, 179. Makes an expedition into Scotland, vanquishes Macbeth, and places in his stead Malcolm son of the Cumbrian king, 182. Dies at York in an arm'd posture, 182. His son Waltheof taken into favour by William the Norman, and marry'd to his niece, 182.

Sleda first erects the kingdom of the East-Saxons, 82.

South-Saxon kingdom, by whom erected, 81.

South-Saxons, upon what occasion converted to christianity, 108.

Stafford, Humphrey and Thomas, rebel against Hen. VII., Humphrey taken and executed, 275. Thomas is pardon'd, 276. Stanley, Thos., lord, one of the chief councellors to Richard duke of Glocester, 216 Imprison'd, 222. Advises the lord Hastings to fly, from a dream, 222. Set at liberty, and made lord steward, 236. King Richard retains him at court, 236. Obliges him to confine his wife, the countess of Richmond, mother to Hen. VII., 251. Brave answer to king Richard threatning him to put his son to death, 261. Made earl of Derby, 271. Stanley, sir Will., crowns Hen. VII. in the field, 263. Conspires against him in favour of Perkin Warbeck, 334. Imprison'd, beheaded, 340. Reflections on his death, 340. Riches and ambition, 341. Star-chamber court describ'd, 302. Staterius, king of Albany, is defeated and slain in fight by Dunwallo Mulmutius, 21. Stepholm, an island at the mouth of the Severn, besieg'd by the Danes, 140, Stilicho represses the invading Scots and Picts, 64. Stoke, fight of, 286. Stuff and Withgar, the nephews of Kedric, bring him new levies, 82. Inherit what he won in the isle of Wight. 85.

Suebard reigns with Victred in the kingdom of Kent, 112. Suetonius Paulinus, lieutenant in Britain, attacks the isle of Mona or Anglesey, 45. Suffolk, Edmond de la Pool, earl of, kills a man, forc'd to plead his pardon, and flyes to the duchess of Burgundy, 379. Persuaded to return by Hen. VII., 380. Flyes again, is betray'd and his accomplices seiz'd, 385. Deliver'd up by the archduke, 393. Suidhelm succeeds Sigebert in the kingdom of the East-Saxons, 105, baptiz'd by Kedda. 106. Surry, Thos. Howard, earl of, attainted by Hen. VII.'s first parliament, 273. Taken into favour by Hen. VII. 304. Routs the rebel sir John Egremond, 305. Enters Scotland with an army, 362.

Swaine, in revenge of his sister's death, makes great devastations in the west of England, 158. Carries all before him as far as London, 161. Swaine, the son of earl Godwin, treacherously murders his kinsman Beorn, 176, his peace wrought with the king by Aldred bishop of Worcester, 178, touched in conscience for the slaughter of Beorn, goes barefoot to Jerusalem, and returning home dyes in Lycia, 178. Swartz Martyn, sent by the duchess of Burgundy with 2,000 men to assist Lambert Simnell the impostor against Hen. VII, 283. Sweating Sickness, the first in England, 270, its cure, 271. Returns, 404. Switherd, last king of the East-Saxons, 114. Submits to Ecbert, 122.

Taximagulus, a petty king anciently n Britain, one of the four kings that assaulted Cæsar's camp. 36. Taylor, sir J., goes to P. Warbeck in France, 33.

Tenuantius, one of the sons of Lud, has Cornwall allotted him, 26. Made king after the death of Cassibelan, 38. Teudric,

INDEX. 423

a warlike king of Britain, exchanges his crown for a hermitage, 91, said to have taken up arms in aid of his son Mouric, 91.
Theobald, brother of king Ethelfred, slain at Degsastan, 94. Theodore, a monk of Tarsus, ordain'd bp. of Canterbury by Pope Vitalian, 107, by his means the liberal arts and the Greek and Latin tongues flourish among the Saxons, 107. Theodosius sent over by the emperor Valentinian, enters London victoriously, 64, sends for Civilis and Dulcitius, 64, punishes Valentinus a Pannonian, conspiring against him, 64, returns with applause to Valentinian, 65. Theodosius, son of the former preferr'd to the empire, 65, overcomes and slays Maximus, usurping the empire, 65. Thurfert, and divers other Danish lords submit to king Edward the Elder, 141.
Titalus, succeeds his father Uffa in the kingdom of the East-Angles, 82.
Togodumnus, second son of Cunobeline, succeeds in the kingdom, 39. Overthrown by Aulus Plautius, 39. Slain in battle, 39.
Tosti, son of Godwin, made earl of Northumberland in the room of Siward, 182. Swears brotherhood with Malcolm king of Scotland, 184. Goes to Rome with Aldred bishop of York, 184. The Northumbrians rise against and expel him, 184. A story of great courage and cruelty committed by him at Hereford, 185. Making war against his brother Harold, is driv'n out of the country by Edwin and Morcar, 188. Joyning with Harold Harfager of Norway against his brother, is slain, together with Harfager in battle, 189.
Trade, consideration of it very much recommended to the parliament by the lord chancellor Morton, in Henry VII.'s time, 299, 300. Incourag'd by Hen. VII., 309. Treaty between Hen. VII. and Chas. VIII., 327. Between Hen. VII. and the princes of Italy against Chas. VIII., 346. Intercursus Magnus, the treaty so call'd, between Hen. VII. and Philip sovereign of the Netherlands, 355. Hen. VII.'s treaty of peace, and the marriage of his daughter Margaret with Jas. IV. of Scotland, 373. Trebellius Maximus sent into Britain in the room of Petronius Turpilianus, 49. Trinobantes fall off from Cassibelan, submit to Cæsar, recommend Mandubratius to his protection, 35.
Turketill, a Danish leader, submitting to king Edward, obtains leave of him to go and try his fortune in France, 140. Turkil, a Danish earl, assaults Canterbury, but is bought off, 159. Swears allegiance to king Ethelred, that he might stay and give intelligence to Swaine, 161. Leaves the English again, and joyns with Canute, 163. His greatness suspected by Canute, is banished the realm, 169.
Tyrrel, sir Jas., murders Edw. V. and his brother Richard duke of York in the Tower, 237. Confesses it in Hen. VII.'s reign, 315. Executed for a conspiracy against Hen. VII., 386.

Uffa erects the kingdom of the East-Angles, &c. His successors call'd Uffings, 82.

Ulfketel, duke of the East-Angles set upon the Danes with great valour, 158. His army defeated through the subtilty of a Danish servant, 160. Slain with several other dukes at Assandune, 167. Ulpius Marcellus, sent lieutenant to Britain by Commodus, ends the war by his valour, 56.
Urianus reckon'd in the number of ancient British kings, 25.
Uther Pendragon, thought to be the same with Natanleod, 82. Uthred submits himself with the Northumbrians to Swaine, 162. To Canute, 164. His victory over Malcolm king of the Scots, 165. He is slain by Turebrand, a Danish lord, at Canute's either command or connivance, 165.

Valentinian the emperor, sends over several deputies to this island, 64. Vaughan, sir Thos., arrested by the duke of Glocester, 199. Beheaded at Pomfret, 228. Bold speech at his death, 228.
Vectius Bolanus, sent into Britain in the room of Trebellius Maximus, 49. Venutius, king of the Brigantes, deserted by his wife Cartismandua, who marries his esquire Vellocatus, 44. Rights himself against her by arms, 44. Makes war successfully against those who took part with his wife, 44. Remains unconquer'd, 49. Veraunius succeeds A. Didius in the British war, 45. Vertue ever highly rewarded by the ancient Romans, 40. Verulam, lord, his history of Hen. VII., 266. Vespasian, fighting under Plautius, is rescu'd from danger by his son Titus, 41. For his eminent services here, receives triumphal ornaments at Rome, 41.
Victorinus, a moor, appeases a commotion in Britain by slaying a governour of his own recommending, 59. Victorinus of Tolosa, made Præfect of this island, 65. Victred, son of Ecbert, obtaining the kingdom of Kent, settles all things in peace, 109. After thirty four years reign he dies, 112. Videna slays her son Perrex, in revenge of her other son Porrex, 21.
Vigenius and Peredure, expelling their brother Elidure, share the kingdom between them, 24. Virius Lupus has the north part of the government assign'd him by Severus the emperor, 57.
Vortigern's character, 74. Advised by his council to invite in the Saxons against the Scots and Picts, 75. Bestows upon Hengist and the Saxons the isle of Thanet, 76. Then all Kent, upon a marriage with Rowena Hengist's daughter, 77. Condemn'd in a synod for incest with his daughter; he retires to a castle in Radnorshire, built for that purpose, 78. His son Guortimer dead, he resumes the government, 79. Drawn into a snare by Hengist, 79. Retiring again, is burnt in his tower, 80. Vortipor reigns in Demetia, or South-Wales, 89.

Warham, sir Will., his speech to the Archduke governor of Flanders, demanding to have Perkin Warbeck deliver'd up, 337. Warriours famous in the reign of Edw. V. and Rich. III., 265. Of Hen. VII. 403. Wars civil, between the houses of Lancashire and York, of Bosworth, 262. Of

Stoke-field, 266. Warwick, Edward Plantagenet earl of, son of George duke of Clarence, confin'd to sheriff Hutton in Yorkshire, by Rich. III. imprison'd by Hen. VII. in the Tower, 269. A counterfeit one, 278. The earl shewn to the people, to discover the imposture, 281. Another counterfeit one, 374. Drawn into a conspiracy by Perkin Warbeck, 374. Try'd and found guilty of raising a sedition, 375. Beheaded, 375. The last of the male-line of the Plantagenets, 375. Water, John, mayor of Cork, hang'd with Perkin, 375. Waterford, citizens of, their loyalty to Hen. VII., 287, 364.

West-Saxon kingdom, by whom erected, 82. West-Saxons and their king converted to the christian faith by Berinus, 102.

Wibba, succeeds Crida in the Mercian kingdom, 90. Wilford, Ralph, the counterfeit earl of Warwick, hang'd, 375. Wilfrid, bp. of the Northumbrians, depriv'd by Ecfric of his bishopric, wanders as far as Rome, 108. Returning, plants the gospel in the isle of Wight, and other places assign'd him, 108. Has the fourth part of that island given him by Kedalla, 108. Bestows it on Bertwin, a priest, his sister's son, 108. Wilibrod, a priest, goes over with twelve others to preach the gospel in Germany, 110. Entertain'd by Pepin chief regent of the Franks, and made first bishop of that nation, 110. Will. of Malmsbury, our best historian, 113.

William duke of Normandy, most honourably entertained by king Edward, and richly dismiss'd, 180. Betroths his daughter to Harold, and receives his oath to assist him to get the crown of England, 185. Sending after king Edward's death, to demand performance of his promise, is put off with a slight answer, 188. Lands with an army at Hastings, 190. Harold, who with his two brothers is slain in battle, 191. Crown'd at Westminster by Aldred, Abp. of York, 191. Wipped, a Saxon earl, slain at a place call'd Wippeds fleet, which thence took denomination, 79. Withgarburgh in the isle of Wight, so call'd from being the burial-place of Withgar, 85. Withlaff, successor of Ludiken, vanquish'd by Ecbert, Mercia becomes tributary to him, 122.

Wolsey, Thos., Hen. VII.'s chaplain, his first negotiation abroad, 394. Woodville lord, carries forces over to the assistance of the duke of Bretagne, without Hen. VII.'s leave, 294. Kill'd at the battle of St. Albans, 301. Woollen manufacture encourag'd by Hen. VII., 309.

Wulfer, son of Penda, set up by the Mercian nobles in the room of Oswi, 106. Said to have been taken prisoner by Kenwalk the West-Saxon, 106. Takes and wastes the isle of Wight, but causes the inhabitants to be baptiz'd, and gives the island to Ethelwald, king of the South-Saxons, 107. Sends Jarumannus to recover the East-Saxons, fallen off the second time from christianity, 107. Lindsey taken from him by Ecfrid of Northumberland, 108. His death accompany'd with the stain of simony, 108. Wulfheard, king Ethelwolfe's chief captain, drives back the Danes at Southampton with great slaughter, 125. Dies the same year as it is thought of age, 125. Wulktul, earl of Ely, put to flight with his whole army by the Danes, 130.

Yeomen of the guard, first instituted by Hen. VII. 271. Y'mner, king of Leogria, with others, slain in battle by Mulmutius, 21. York, Richard Plantagenet duke of, brother to Edw. V., deliver'd up by his mother to the duke of Glocester, 215. Bastardy laid to his brother and his charge, 229. Murder'd in the tower by sir J. Tyrell, 237. His body lately discover'd, 237. —, title of that house most approv'd of, 267.

Zouch, lord, attainted in parliament, for siding with Rich. III., 273.

www.ingramcontent.com/pod-product-compliance
Lightning Source LLC
Chambersburg PA
CBHW022107290426
44112CB00008B/583